Introduction to Simulink®
with Engineering Applications

Steven T. Karris

Orchard Publications
www.orchardpublications.com

Introduction to Simulink ® with Engineering Applications

Copyright © 2006 Orchard Publications. All rights reserved. Printed in the United States of America. No part of this publication may be reproduced or distributed in any form or by any means, or stored in a data base or retrieval system, without the prior written permission of the publisher.

Direct all inquiries to Orchard Publications, info@orchardpublications.com

Product and corporate names are trademarks or registered trademarks of The MathWorks™, Inc. They are used only for identification and explanation, without intent to infringe.

Library of Congress Cataloging-in-Publication Data

Library of Congress Control Number (LCCN) 2006926850

ISBN-10: 0-9744239-7-1

ISBN-13: 978-0-9744239-7-5

TXu 1–303-668

Disclaimer

The author has made every effort to make this text as complete and accurate as possible, but no warranty is implied. The author and publisher shall have neither liability nor responsibility to any person or entity with respect to any loss or damages arising from the information contained in this text.

Preface

This text is an introduction to Simulink ®, a companion application to MATLAB ®. It is written for students at the undergraduate and graduate programs, as well as for the working professional.

Although some previous knowledge of MATLAB would be helpful, it is not absolutely necessary; Appendix A of this text is an introduction to MATLAB to enable the reader to begin learning both MATLAB and Simulink simultaneously, and to perform graphical computations and programming.

Chapters 2 through 18 describe the blocks of all Simulink libraries. Their application is illustrated with practical examples through Simulink models, some of which are supplemented with MATLAB functions, commands, and statements. Some background information is provided for lesser known definitions and topics. Chapters 1 and 19 contain several Simulink models to illustrate various applied math and engineering applications. Appendix B is an introduction to difference equations as they apply to discrete-time systems, and Appendix C introduces the reader to random generation procedures.

This text supplements our *Numerical Analysis with MATLAB and Spreadsheet Applications*, ISBN 0-9709511-1-6. It is self-contained; the blocks of each library are described in an orderly fashion that is consistent with Simulink's documentation. This arrangement provides insight into how a model is used and how its parts interact with each another.

Like MATLAB, Simulink can be used with both linear and nonlinear systems, which can be modeled in continuous time, sample time, or a hybrid of these. Examples are provided in this text.

Most of the examples presented in this book can be implemented with the Student Versions of MATLAB and Simulink. A few may require the full versions of these outstanding packages, and these examples may be skipped. Some add-ons, known as Toolboxes and Blocksets can be obtained from The MathWorks,™ Inc., 3 Apple Hill Drive, Natick, MA, 01760-2098, USA, www.mathworks.com.

To get the most out of this outstanding application, it is highly recommended that this text is used in conjunction with the MATLAB and Simulink User's Guides. Other references are provided in the reference section of this text.

This is the first edition of this title, and although every effort was made to correct possible typographical errors and erroneous references to figures and tables, some may have been overlooked. Accordingly, the author will appreciate it very much if any such errors are brought to his attention so that corrections can be made for the next edition.

The author wishes to express his gratitude to the staff of The MathWorks™, the developers of MATLAB® and Simulink®, especially to Ms. Courtney Esposito, for the encouragement and unlimited support they have provided me with during the production of this text.

Our heartfelt thanks also to Mr. Howard R. Hansen, and Dr. Niel Ransom, former CTO of Alcatel, for bringing some errors on the first print to our attention.

Orchard Publications
www.orchardpublications.com
info@orchardpublications.com

Table of Contents

1 Introduction to Simulink — 1–1

1.1 Simulink and its Relation to MATLAB 1–1
1.2 Simulink Demos 1–20
1.3 Summary 1–28
1.4 Exercises 1–29
1.5 Solutions to End–of–Chapter Exercises 1–30

2 The Commonly Used Blocks Library — 2–1

2.1 The Inport, Outport, and Subsystem Blocks 2–2
2.2 The Ground Block 2–4
2.3 The Terminator Block 2–5
2.4 The Constant and Product Blocks 2–6
2.5 The Scope Block 2–7
2.6 The Bus Creator and Bus Selector Blocks 2–7
2.7 The Mux and Demux Blocks 2–11
2.8 The Switch Block 2–14
2.9 The Sum Block 2–15
2.10 The Gain Block 2–16
2.11 The Relational Operator Block 2–17
2.12 The Logical Operator Block 2–18
2.13 The Saturation Block 2–19
2.14 The Integrator Block 2–20
2.15 The Unit Delay Block 2–24
2.16 The Discrete–Time Integrator Block 2–26
2.17 Data Types and The Data Type Conversion Block 2–29
2.18 Summary 2–35
2.19 Exercises 2–39
2.20 Solutions to End–of–Chapter Exercises 2–41

3 The Continuous Blocks Library — 3–1

3.1 The Continuous–Time Linear Systems Sub–Library...3–2
    3.1.1 The Integrator Block...3–2
    3.1.2 The Derivative Block...3–2
    3.1.3 The State–Space Block..3–6
    3.1.4 The Transfer Fcn Block..3–6
    3.1.5 The Zero–Pole Block..3–8
3.2 The Continuous–Time Delays Sub–Library..3–10

Introduction to Simulink with Engineering Applications
Copyright © Orchard Publications

      3.2.1 The Transport Delay Block .... 3−10
      3.2.2 The Variable Time Delay Block .... 3−11
      3.2.3 The Variable Transport Delay Block .... 3−12
3.3 Summary .... 3−14
3.4 Exercises .... 3−16
3.5 Solutions to End−of−Chapter Exercises .... 3−17

4 The Discontinuities Blocks Library   4−1

4.1   The Saturation Block .... 4−2
4.2   The Saturation Dynamic Block .... 4−3
4.3   The Dead Zone Block .... 4−4
4.4   The Dead Zone Dynamic Block .... 4−5
4.5   The Rate Limiter Block .... 4−6
4.6   The Rate Limiter Dynamic Block .... 4−8
4.7   The Backlash Block .... 4−9
4.8   The Relay Block .... 4−11
4.9   The Quantizer Block .... 4−12
4.10 The Hit Crossing Block .... 4−13
4.11 The Coulomb and Viscous Friction Block .... 4−14
4.12 The Wrap to Zero Block .... 4−16
4.13 Summary .... 4−17
4.14 Exercises .... 4−19
4.15 Solutions to End−of−Chapter Exercises .... 4−20

5 The Discrete Blocks Library   5−1

5.1 The Discrete−Time Linear Systems Sub−Library .... 5−2
    5.1.1   The Unit Delay Block .... 5−2
    5.1.2   The Integer Delay Block .... 5−2
    5.1.3   The Tapped Delay Block .... 5−3
    5.1.4   The Discrete−Time Integrator Block .... 5−4
    5.1.5   The Discrete Transfer Fcn Block .... 5−4
    5.1.6   The Discrete Filter Block .... 5−5
    5.1.7   The Discrete Zero−Pole Block .... 5−8
    5.1.8   The Difference Block .... 5−9
    5.1.9   The Discrete Derivative Block .... 5−10
    5.1.10 The Discrete State−Space Block .... 5−11
    5.1.11 The Transfer Fcn First Order Block .... 5−14
    5.1.12 The Transfer Fcn Lead or Lag Block .... 5−15
    5.1.13 The Transfer Fcn Real Zero Block .... 5−18
    5.1.14 The Weighted Moving Average Block .... 5−19

  5.2 The Sample & Hold Delays Sub–Library 5-21
    5.2.1 The Memory Block 5-21
    5.2.2 The First–Order Hold Block 5-22
    5.2.3 The Zero–Order Hold Block 5-23
  5.3 Summary 5-25
  5.4 Exercises 5-27
  5.5 Solutions to End–of–Chapter Exercises 5-29

6 *The Logic and Bit Operations Library*   6-1

  6.1 The Logic Operations Group Sub–Library 6-2
    6.1.1 The Logical Operator Block 6-2
    6.1.2 The Relational Operator Block 6-2
    6.1.3 The Interval Test Block 6-2
    6.1.4 The Interval Test Dynamic Block 6-3
    6.1.5 The Combinational Logic Block 6-4
    6.1.6 The Compare to Zero Block 6-9
    6.1.7 The Compare to Constant Block 6-10
  6.2 The Bit Operations Group Sub–Library 6-11
    6.2.1 The Bit Set Block 6-12
    6.2.2 The Bit Clear Block 6-13
    6.2.3 The Bitwise Operator Block 6-14
    6.2.4 The Shift Arithmetic Block 6-16
    6.2.5 The Extract Bits Block 6-17
  6.3 The Edge Detection Group Sub–Library 6-18
    6.3.1 The Detect Increase Block 6-18
    6.3.2 The Detect Decrease Block 6-20
    6.3.3 The Detect Change Block 6-21
    6.3.4 The Detect Rise Positive Block 6-22
    6.3.5 The Detect Rise Nonnegative Block 6-23
    6.3.6 The Detect Fall Negative Block 6-24
    6.3.7 The Detect Fall Nonpositive Block 6-25
  6.4 Summary 6-27
  6.5 Exercises 6-31
  6.6 Solutions to End–of–Chapter Exercises 6-32

7 *The Lookup Tables Library*   7-1

  7.1 The Lookup Table Block 7-2
  7.2 The Lookup Table (2–D) Block 7-3
  7.3 The Lookup Table (n–D) Block 7-5
  7.4 The PreLookup Index Search Block 7-7

7.5 The Interpolation (n–D) Using PreLookup Block 7-8
7.6 The Direct Lookup Table (n–D) Block.. 7-9
7.7 The Lookup Table Dynamic Block 7-15
7.8 The Sine and Cosine Blocks 7-16
7.9 Summary 7-20
7.10 Exercises.. 7-22
7.11 Solutions to End–of–Chapter Exercises 7-23

8   *The Math Operations Library*   8-1

8.1 The Math Operations Group Sub-Library.. 8-2
    8.1.1   The Sum Block 8-2
    8.1.2   The Add Block.. 8-2
    8.1.3   The Subtract Block 8-3
    8.1.4   The Sum of Elements Block.. 8-4
    8.1.5   The Bias Block 8-4
    8.1.6   The Weighted Sample Time Math Block... 8-5
    8.1.7   The Gain Block 8-6
    8.1.8   The Slider Gain Block 8-6
    8.1.9   The Product Block 8-7
    8.1.10 The Divide Block 8-7
    8.1.11 The Product of Elements Block 8-7
    8.1.12 The Dot Product Block.. 8-8
    8.1.13 The Sign Block 8-9
    8.1.14 The Abs Block 8-10
    8.1.15 The Unary Minus Block... 8-10
    8.1.16 The Math Function Block 8-11
    8.1.17 The Rounding Function Block 8-13
    8.1.18 The Polynomial Block 8-14
    8.1.19 The MinMax Block.. 8-14
    8.1.20 The MinMax Running Resettable Block 8-15
    8.1.21 The Trigonometric Function Block.. 8-16
    8.1.22 The Sine Wave Function Block 8-17
    8.1.23 The Algebraic Constraint Block.. 8-18
8.2 The Vector / Matrix Operations Group Sub-Library 8-19
    8.2.1   The Assignment Block.. 8-19
    8.2.2   The Reshape Block 8-20
    8.2.3   The Matrix Concatenate Block 8-21
    8.2.4   The Vector Concatenate Block 8-23
8.3 The Complex Vector Conversions Group Sub-Library.. 8-24
    8.3.1   The Complex to Magnitude–Angle Block 8-24
    8.3.2   The Magnitude–Angle to Complex Block 8-24

	8.3.3	The Complex to Real–Imag Block	8-25
	8.3.4	The Real–Imag to Complex Block	8-26
8.4	Summary	8-28
8.5	Exercises	8-32
8.6	Solutions to End–of–Chapter Exercises	8-34

9 The Model Verification Library 9-1

- 9.1 The Check Static Lower Bound Block 9-2
- 9.2 The Check Static Upper Bound Block 9-3
- 9.3 The Check Static Range Block 9-4
- 9.4 The Check Static Gap Block 9-5
- 9.5 The Check Dynamic Lower Bound Block 9-6
- 9.6 The Check Dynamic Upper Bound Block 9-8
- 9.7 The Check Dynamic Range Block 9-9
- 9.8 The Check Dynamic Gap Block 9-10
- 9.9 The Assertion Block 9-12
- 9.10 The Check Discrete Gradient Block 9-13
- 9.11 The Check Input Resolution Block 9-14
- 9.12 Summary 9-16
- 9.13 Exercises 9-18
- 9.14 Solutions to End–of–Chapter Exercises 9-19

10 The Model-Wide Utilities Library 10-1

- 10.1 The Linearization of Running Models Sub–Library 10-2
  - 10.1.1 The Trigger–Based Linearization Block 10-2
  - 10.1.2 The Time–Based Linearization Block 10-4
- 10.2 The Documentation Sub–Library 10-6
  - 10.2.1 The Model Info Block 10-6
  - 10.2.2 The Doc Text Block 10-8
- 10.3 The Modeling Guides Sub–Library 10-9
- 10.4 Summary 10-11

11 The Ports & Subsystems Library 11-1

- 11.1 The Inport, Outport, and Subsystem Blocks 11-2
- 11.2 The Trigger Block 11-2
- 11.3 The Enable Block 11-2
- 11.4 The Function–Call Generator Block 11-3
- 11.5 The Atomic Subsystem Block 11-4
- 11.6 The Code Reuse Subsystem Block 11-9
- 11.7 The Model Block 11-17

11.8 The Configurable Subsystem Block 11-19
11.9 The Triggered Subsystem Block 11-25
11.10 The Enabled Subsystem Block 11-27
11.11 The Enabled and Triggered Subsystem Block 11-30
11.12 The Function–Call Subsystem Block 11-34
11.13 The For Iterator Subsystem Block 11-36
11.14 The While Iterator Subsystem Block 11-38
11.15 The If and If Action Subsystem Blocks 11-40
11.16 The Switch Case and The Switch Case Action Subsystem Blocks 11-41
11.17 The Subsystem Examples Block 11-41
11.18 S–Functions in Simulink 11-43
11.19 Summary 11-50

12 *The Signal Attributes Library* 12-1

12.1 The Signal Attribute Manipulation Sub–Library 12-2
    12.1.1 The Data Type Conversion Block 12-2
    12.1.2 The Data Type Duplicate Block 12-2
    12.1.3 The Data Type Propagation Block 12-4
    12.1.4 The Data Type Scaling Strip Block 12-5
    12.1.5 The Data Conversion Inherited Block 12-5
    12.1.6 The IC (Initial Condition) Block 12-6
    12.1.7 The Signal Conversion Block 12-7
    12.1.8 The Rate Transition Block 12-8
    12.1.9 The Signal Specification Block 12-11
    12.1.10 The Data Type Propagation Examples Block 12-12
12.2 The Signal Attribute Detection Sub–Library 12-13
    12.2.1 The Probe Block 12-14
    12.2.2 The Weighted Sample Time Block 12-15
    12.2.3 The Width Block 12-16
12.3 Summary 12-17

13 *The Signal Routing Library* 13-1

13.1 Signal Routing Group Sub–Library 13-2
    13.1.1 The Bus Creator Block 13-2
    13.1.2 The Bus Selector Block 13-2
    13.1.3 The Bus Assignment Block 13-2
    13.1.4 The Mux Block 13-5
    13.1.5 The Demux Block 13-5
    13.1.6 The Selector Block 13-6
    13.1.7 The Index Vector Block 13-7

  13.1.9 The Merge Block 13-8
  13.1.10 The Environmental Controller Block 13-9
  13.1.11 The Manual Switch Block.. 13-9
  13.1.12 The Multiport Switch Block 13-10
  13.1.13 The Switch Block 13-11
  13.1.14 The From Block... 13-11
  13.1.14 The Goto Tag Visibility Block 13-12
  13.1.15 The Goto Block 13-13
 13.2 The Signal Storage and Access Group Sub–Library................................. 13-14
  13.2.1 The Data Store Read Block 13-14
  13.2.2 The Data Store Memory Block 13-15
  13.2.3 The Data Store Write Block 13-15
 13.3 Summary.. 13-18

14 *The Sinks Library*   14-1

 14.1 Models and Subsystems Outputs Sub–Library.. 14-2
  14.1.1 The Outport Block 14-2
  14.1.2 The Terminator Block 14-2
  14.1.3 The To File Block 14-2
  14.1.4 The To Workspace Block 14-4
 14.2 The Data Viewers Sub–Library 14-5
  14.2.1 The Scope Block 14-6
  14.2.2 The Floating Scope Block.. 14-8
  14.2.3 The XY Graph Block 14-12
  14.2.4 The Display Block... 14-13
 14.3 The Simulation Control Sub–Library... 14-14
 14.4 Summary... 14-16

15 *The Sources Library*   15-1

 15.1 Models and Subsystems Inputs Sub–Library 15-2
  15.1.1 The Inport Block... 15-2
  15.1.2 The Ground Block 15-2
  15.1.3 The From File Block 15-2
  15.1.4 The From Workspace Block 15-2
 15.2 The Signal Generators Sub–Library.. 15-3
  15.2.1 The Constant Block.. 15-3
  15.2.2 The Signal Generator Block 15-4
  15.2.3 The Pulse Generator Block 15-5
  15.2.4 The Signal Builder Block... 15-6
  15.2.5 The Ramp Block 15-9

     15.2.6 The Sine Wave Block 15-9
     15.2.7 The Step Block 15-11
     15.2.8 The Repeating Sequence Block... 15-13
     15.2.9 The Chirp Signal Block 15-14
     15.2.10 The Random Number Block 15-14
     15.2.11 The Uniform Random Number Block.. 15-15
     15.2.12 The Band Limited White Noise Block 15-17
     15.2.13 The Repeating Sequence Stair Block 15-21
     15.2.14 The Repeating Sequence Interpolated Block.. 15-21
     15.2.15 The Counter Free-Running Block.. 15-23
     15.2.16 The Counter Limited Block 15-24
     15.2.17 The Clock Block.. 15-25
     15.2.18 The Digital Clock Block 15-26
  15.3 Summary.. 15-28

16   *The User-Defined Functions Library*   16-1

  16.1 The Fcn Block 16-2
  16.2 The MATLAB Fcn Block 16-2
  16.3 The Embedded MATLAB Function Block... 16-3
  16.4 The S-Function Block 16-7
  16.5 The Level-2 M-file S-Function Block 16-7
  16.6 The S-Function Builder Block 16-12
  16.7 The S-Function Examples Block 16-13
  16.8 Summary.. 16-14

17   *The Additional Discrete Library*   17-1

  17.1 The Transfer Fcn Direct Form II Block 17-2
  17.2 The Transfer Fcn Direct Form II Time Varying Block 17-3
  17.3 The Fixed-Point State-Space Block 17-4
  17.4 The Unit Delay External IC Block 17-6
  17.5 The Unit Delay Resettable Block.. 17-7
  17.6 The Unit Delay Resettable External IC Block 17-8
  17.7 The Unit Delay Enabled Block 17-9
  17.8 The Unit Delay Enabled Resettable Block... 17-11
  17.9 The Unit Delay Enabled External IC Block.. 17-12
  17.10 The Unit Delay Enabled Resettable External IC Block.................................... 17-13
  17.11 The Unit Delay With Preview Resettable Block 17-15
  17.12 The Unit Delay With Preview Resettable External RV Block 17-16
  17.13 The Unit Delay With Preview Enabled Block 17-17

17.14 The Unit Delay With Preview Enabled Resettable Block 17–19
17.15 The Unit Delay With Preview Enabled Resettable External RV Block 17–20
17.16 Summary 17–22

18 *The Additional Math Increment / Decrement Library*   18-1

18.1 The Increment Real World Block 18–2
18.2 The Decrement Real World Block 18–3
18.3 The Increment Stored Integer Block 18–4
18.4 The Decrement Stored Integer Block 18–5
18.5 The Decrement to Zero Block 18–6
18.6 The Decrement Time To Zero Block 18–7
18.7 Summary 18–8

19 *Engineering Applications*   19-1

19.1   Analog–to–Digital Conversion 19–1
19.2   The Zero–Order Hold and First–Order Hold as Reconstructors 19–2
19.3   Digital Filter Realization Forms 19–4
    19.3.1 The Direct Form I Realization of a Digital Filter 19–4
    19.3.2 The Direct Form II Realization of a Digital Filter 19–5
    19.3.3 The Series Form Realization of a Digital Filter 19–7
    19.3.4 The Parallel Form Realization of a Digital Filter 19–9
19.4   Models for Binary Counters 19–13
    19.4.1 Model for a 3–bit Up / Down Counter 19–13
    19.4.2 Model for a 4–bit Ring Counter 19–14
19.5   Models for Mechanical Systems 19–15
    19.5.1 Model for a Mass–Spring–Dashpot 19–15
    19.5.2 Model for a Cascaded Mass–Spring System 19–17
    19.5.3 Model for a Mechanical Accelerometer 19–19
19.6   Feedback Control Systems 19–20
19.7   Models for Electrical Systems 19–23
    19.7.1 Model for an Electric Circuit in Phasor Form 19–23
    19.7.2 Model for the Application of the Superposition Principle 19–25
19.8   Transformations 19–27
19.9   Another S–Function Example 19–28
19.10 Concluding Remarks 19–31
19.11 Summary 19–32

A Introduction to MATLAB — A-1

- A.1 MATLAB® and Simulink® A-1
- A.2 Command Window A-1
- A.3 Roots of Polynomials A-3
- A.4 Polynomial Construction from Known Roots A-4
- A.5 Evaluation of a Polynomial at Specified Values A-6
- A.6 Rational Polynomials A-8
- A.7 Using MATLAB to Make Plots A-10
- A.8 Subplots A-18
- A.9 Multiplication, Division, and Exponentiation A-18
- A.10 Script and Function Files A-26
- A.11 Display Formats A-31

B Difference Equations — B-1

- B.1 Recursive Method for Solving Difference Equations B-1
- B.2 Method of Undetermined Coefficients B-1

C Random Number Generation — C-1

- C.1 Random Numbers C-1
- C.2 An Example C-1

References — R-1

Index — IN-1

Chapter 1

Introduction to Simulink

This chapter is an introduction to Simulink. This author feels that it is best to introduce Simulink with a few examples. Tools for simulation and model–based designs are presented in the subsequent chapters. Some familiarity with MATLAB is essential in understanding Simulink, and for this purpose, Appendix A is included as an introduction to MATLAB.

1.1 Simulink and its Relation to MATLAB

The MATLAB® and Simulink® environments are integrated into one entity, and thus we can analyze, simulate, and revise our models in either environment at any point. We invoke Simulink from within MATLAB. We begin with a few examples and we will discuss generalities in subsequent chapters. Throughout this text, a left justified horizontal bar will denote the beginning of an example, and a right justified horizontal bar will denote the end of the example. These bars will not be shown whenever an example begins at the top of a page or at the bottom of a page. Also, when one example follows immediately after a previous example, the right justified bar will be omitted.

Example 1.1

For the circuit of Figure 1.1, the initial conditions are $i_L(0^-) = 0$, and $v_c(0^-) = 0.5 \text{ V}$. We will compute $v_c(t)$.

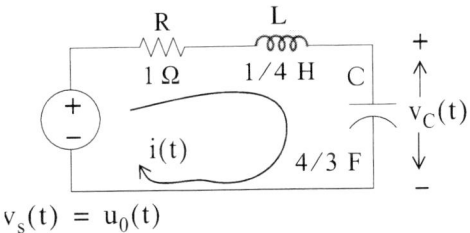

Figure 1.1. Circuit for Example 1.1

For this example,

$$i = i_L = i_C = C\frac{dv_C}{dt} \qquad (1.1)$$

and by Kirchoff's voltage law (KVL),

Chapter 1 Introduction to Simulink

$$Ri_L + L\frac{di_L}{dt} + v_C = u_0(t) \tag{1.2}$$

Substitution of (1.1) into (1.2) yields

$$RC\frac{dv_C}{dt} + LC\frac{d^2v_C}{dt^2} + v_C = u_0(t) \tag{1.3}$$

Substituting the values of the circuit constants and rearranging we get:

$$\frac{1}{3}\frac{d^2v_C}{dt^2} + \frac{4}{3}\frac{dv_C}{dt} + v_C = u_0(t)$$

$$\frac{d^2v_C}{dt^2} + 4\frac{dv_C}{dt} + 3v_C = 3u_0(t) \tag{1.4}$$

$$\frac{d^2v_C}{dt^2} + 4\frac{dv_C}{dt} + 3v_C = 3 \qquad t > 0 \tag{1.5}$$

To appreciate Simulink's capabilities, for comparison, three different methods of obtaining the solution are presented, and the solution using Simulink follows.

First Method – Assumed Solution

Equation (1.5) is a second-order, non-homogeneous differential equation with constant coefficients, and thus the complete solution will consist of the sum of the forced response and the natural response. It is obvious that the solution of this equation cannot be a constant since the derivatives of a constant are zero and thus the equation is not satisfied. Also, the solution cannot contain sinusoidal functions (sine and cosine) since the derivatives of these are also sinusoids.

However, decaying exponentials of the form ke^{-at} where k and a are constants, are possible candidates since their derivatives have the same form but alternate in sign.

It can be shown[*] that if $k_1 e^{-s_1 t}$ and $k_2 e^{-s_2 t}$ where k_1 and k_2 are constants and s_1 and s_2 are the roots of the characteristic equation of the homogeneous part of the given differential equation, the natural response is the sum of the terms $k_1 e^{-s_1 t}$ and $k_2 e^{-s_2 t}$. Therefore, the total solution will be

$$v_c(t) = \text{natural response} + \text{forced response} = v_{cn}(t) + v_{cf}(t) = k_1 e^{-s_1 t} + k_2 e^{-s_2 t} + v_{cf}(t) \tag{1.6}$$

---

[*] *For a thorough discussion, please refer to Circuit Analysis II with MATLAB Applications, ISBN 0-9709511-5-9, Appendix B.*

Simulink and its Relation to MATLAB

The values of s_1 and s_2 are the roots of the characteristic equation

$$s^2 + 4s + 3 = 0 \tag{1.7}$$

Solution of (1.7) yields of $s_1 = -1$ and $s_2 = -3$ and with these values (1.6) is written as

$$v_c(t) = k_1 e^{-t} + k_2 e^{-3t} + v_{cf}(t) \tag{1.8}$$

The forced component $v_{cf}(t)$ is found from (1.5), i.e.,

$$\frac{d^2 v_C}{dt^2} + 4\frac{dv_C}{dt} + 3v_C = 3 \qquad t > 0 \tag{1.9}$$

Since the right side of (1.9) is a constant, the forced response will also be a constant and we denote it as $v_{Cf} = k_3$. By substitution into (1.9) we get

$$0 + 0 + 3k_3 = 3$$

or

$$v_{Cf} = k_3 = 1 \tag{1.10}$$

Substitution of this value into (1.8), yields the total solution as

$$v_C(t) = v_{Cn}(t) + v_{Cf} = k_1 e^{-t} + k_2 e^{-3t} + 1 \tag{1.11}$$

The constants k_1 and k_2 will be evaluated from the initial conditions. First, using $v_C(0) = 0.5$ V and evaluating (1.11) at $t = 0$, we get

$$v_C(0) = k_1 e^0 + k_2 e^0 + 1 = 0.5$$

$$k_1 + k_2 = -0.5 \tag{1.12}$$

Also,

$$i_L = i_C = C\frac{dv_C}{dt}, \quad \frac{dv_C}{dt} = \frac{i_L}{C}$$

and

$$\left.\frac{dv_C}{dt}\right|_{t=0} = \frac{i_L(0)}{C} = \frac{0}{C} = 0 \tag{1.13}$$

Next, we differentiate (1.11), we evaluate it at $t = 0$, and equate it with (1.13). Thus,

$$\left.\frac{dv_C}{dt}\right|_{t=0} = -k_1 - 3k_2 \tag{1.14}$$

Chapter 1 Introduction to Simulink

By equating the right sides of (1.13) and (1.14) we get

$$-k_1 - 3k_2 = 0 \tag{1.15}$$

Simultaneous solution of (1.12) and (1.15), gives $k_1 = -0.75$ and $k_2 = 0.25$. By substitution into (1.8), we obtain the total solution as

$$v_C(t) = (-0.75e^{-t} + 0.25e^{-3t} + 1)u_0(t) \tag{1.16}$$

Check with MATLAB:

```
syms t                              % Define symbolic variable t
y0=-0.75*exp(-t)+0.25*exp(-3*t)+1;  % The total solution y(t), for our example, vc(t)
y1=diff(y0)                         % The first derivative of y(t)

y1 =
3/4*exp(-t)-3/4*exp(-3*t)

y2=diff(y0,2)                       % The second derivative of y(t)

y2 =
-3/4*exp(-t)+9/4*exp(-3*t)

y=y2+4*y1+3*y0                      % Summation of y and its derivatives

y =
3
```

Thus, the solution has been verified by MATLAB. Using the expression for $v_C(t)$ in (1.16), we find the expression for the current as

$$i = i_L = i_C = C\frac{dv_C}{dt} = \frac{4}{3}\left(\frac{3}{4}e^{-t} - \frac{3}{4}e^{-3t}\right) = e^{-t} - e^{-3t} \text{ A} \tag{1.17}$$

Second Method – Using the Laplace Transformation

The transformed circuit is shown in Figure 1.2.

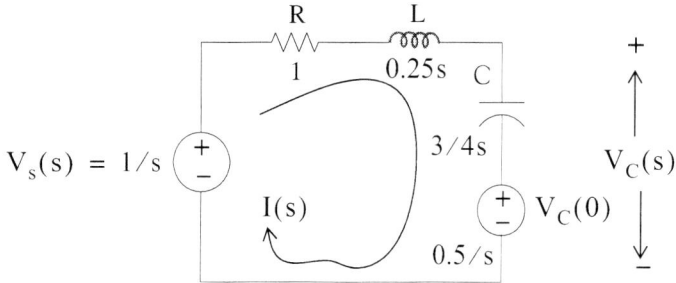

Figure 1.2. Transformed Circuit for Example 1.1

Simulink and its Relation to MATLAB

By the voltage division[*] expression,

$$V_C(s) = \frac{3/4s}{(1 + 0.25s + 3/4s)} \cdot \left(\frac{1}{s} - \frac{0.5}{s}\right) + \frac{0.5}{s} = \frac{1.5}{s(s^2 + 4s + 3)} + \frac{0.5}{s} = \frac{0.5s^2 + 2s + 3}{s(s+1)(s+3)}$$

Using partial fraction expansion,[†] we let

$$\frac{0.5s^2 + 2s + 3}{s(s+1)(s+3)} = \frac{r_1}{s} + \frac{r_2}{(s+1)} + \frac{r_3}{(s+3)} \tag{1.18}$$

$$r_1 = \left.\frac{0.5s^2 + 2s + 3}{(s+1)(s+3)}\right|_{s=0} = 1$$

$$r_2 = \left.\frac{0.5s^2 + 2s + 3}{s(s+3)}\right|_{s=-1} = -0.75$$

$$r_3 = \left.\frac{0.5s^2 + 2s + 3}{s(s+1)}\right|_{s=-3} = 0.25$$

and by substitution into (1.18)

$$V_C(s) = \frac{0.5s^2 + 2s + 3}{s(s+1)(s+3)} = \frac{1}{s} + \frac{-0.75}{(s+1)} + \frac{0.25}{(s+3)}$$

Taking the Inverse Laplace transform[‡] we find that

$$v_C(t) = 1 - 0.75e^{-t} + 0.25e^{-3t}$$

Third Method – Using State Variables

$$Ri_L + L\frac{di_L}{dt} + v_C = u_0(t) \quad [**]$$

---

[*] For derivation of the voltage division and current division expressions, please refer to *Circuit Analysis I with MATLAB Applications*, ISBN 0-9709511-2-4.

[†] A thorough discussion of partial fraction expansion with MATLAB Applications is presented in *Numerical Analysis with MATLAB and Spreadsheet Applications*, ISBN 0-9709511-1-6.

[‡] For an introduction to Laplace Transform and Inverse Laplace Transform, please refer to *Circuit Analysis II with MATLAB Applications*, ISBN 0-9709511-5-9.

[**] Usually, in State–Space and State Variables Analysis, $u(t)$ denotes any input. For distinction, we will denote the Unit Step Function as $u_0(t)$. For a detailed discussion on State–Space and State Variables Analysis, please refer to *Signals and Systems with MATLAB Computing and Simulink Modeling*, ISBN 0-9744239-9-8.

Introduction to Simulink with Engineering Applications
Copyright © Orchard Publications

Chapter 1 Introduction to Simulink

By substitution of given values and rearranging, we obtain

$$\frac{1}{4}\frac{di_L}{dt} = (-1)i_L - v_C + 1$$

or

$$\frac{di_L}{dt} = -4i_L - 4v_C + 4 \qquad (1.19)$$

Next, we define the state variables $x_1 = i_L$ and $x_2 = v_C$. Then,

$$\dot{x}_1 = \frac{di_L}{dt}* \qquad (1.20)$$

and

$$\dot{x}_2 = \frac{dv_C}{dt} \qquad (1.21)$$

Also,

$$i_L = C\frac{dv_C}{dt}$$

and thus,

$$x_1 = i_L = C\frac{dv_C}{dt} = C\dot{x}_2 = \frac{4}{3}\dot{x}_2$$

or

$$\dot{x}_2 = \frac{3}{4}x_1 \qquad (1.22)$$

Therefore, from (1.19), (1.20), and (1.22), we get the state equations

$$\dot{x}_1 = -4x_1 - 4x_2 + 4$$

$$\dot{x}_2 = \frac{3}{4}x_1$$

and in matrix form,

$$\begin{bmatrix} \dot{x}_1 \\ \dot{x}_2 \end{bmatrix} = \begin{bmatrix} -4 & -4 \\ 3/4 & 0 \end{bmatrix} \begin{bmatrix} x_1 \\ x_2 \end{bmatrix} + \begin{bmatrix} 4 \\ 0 \end{bmatrix} u_0(t) \qquad (1.23)$$

Solution[†] of (1.23) yields

---

* The notation $\dot{x}$ (x dot) is often used to denote the first derivative of the function x, that is, $\dot{x} = dx/dt$.

† The detailed solution of (1.23) is given in Signals and Systems with MATLAB Applications, ISBN 0-9744239-9-8, Chapter 5.

Simulink and its Relation to MATLAB

$$\begin{bmatrix} x_1 \\ x_2 \end{bmatrix} = \begin{bmatrix} e^{-t} - e^{-3t} \\ 1 - 0.75e^{-t} + 0.25e^{-3t} \end{bmatrix}$$

Then,

$$x_1 = i_L = e^{-t} - e^{-3t} \quad (1.24)$$

and

$$x_2 = v_C = 1 - 0.75e^{-t} + 0.25e^{-3t} \quad (1.25)$$

Modeling the Differential Equation of Example 1.1 with Simulink

To run Simulink, we must first invoke MATLAB. Make sure that Simulink is installed in your system. In the Command Window, we type:

simulink

Alternately, we can click on the Simulink icon shown in Figure 1.3. It appears on the top bar on MATLAB's Command Window.

Figure 1.3. The Simulink icon

Upon execution of the Simulink command, the **Commonly Used Blocks are** shown in Figure 1.4.

In Figure 1.4, the left side is referred to as the **Tree Pane** and displays all Simulink libraries installed. The right side is referred to as the **Contents Pane** and displays the blocks that reside in the library currently selected in the Tree Pane.

Let us express the differential equation of Example 1.1 as

$$\frac{d^2 v_C}{dt^2} = -4\frac{dv_C}{dt} - 3v_C + 3u_0(t) \quad (1.26)$$

A block diagram representing (1.26) is shown in Figure 1.5. Now, we will use Simulink to draw a similar block diagram.

Chapter 1 Introduction to Simulink

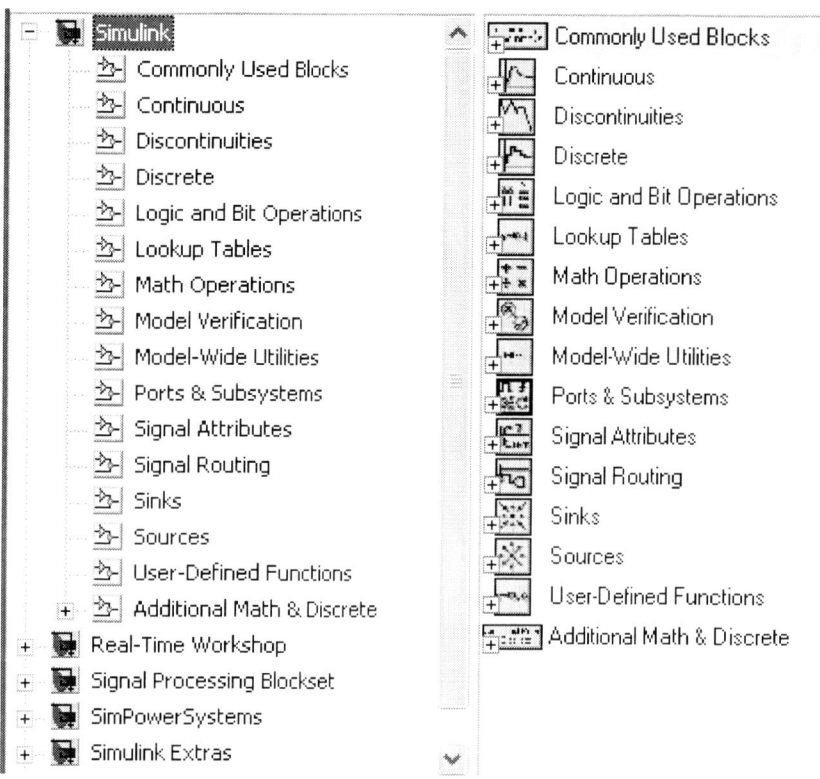

Figure 1.4. The Simulink Library Browser

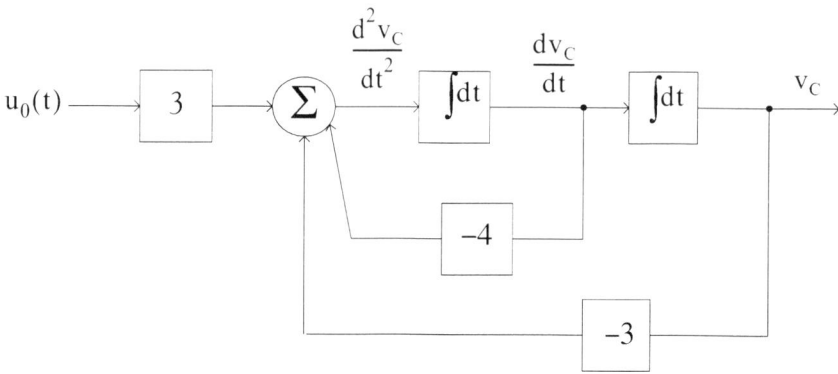

Figure 1.5. Block diagram for equation (1.26)

To model the differential equation (1.26) using Simulink, we perform the following steps:

1. On the **Simulink Library Browser**, we click on the leftmost icon shown as a blank page on the top title bar. A new model window named **untitled** will appear as shown in Figure 1.6.

Simulink and its Relation to MATLAB

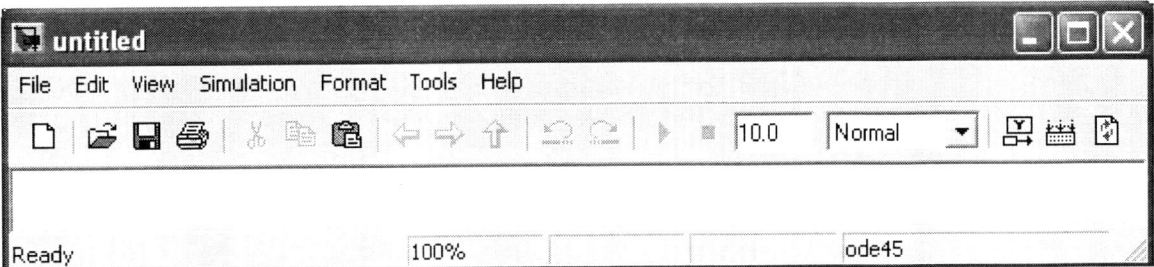

Figure 1.6. The Untitled model window in Simulink.

The window of Figure 1.6 is the model window where we enter our blocks to form a block diagram. We save this as model file name **Equation_1_26**. This is done from the File drop menu of Figure 1.6 where we choose **Save as** and name the file as **Equation_1_26**. Simulink will add the extension **.mdl**. The new model window will now be shown as **Equation_1_26**, and all saved files will have this appearance. See Figure 1.7.

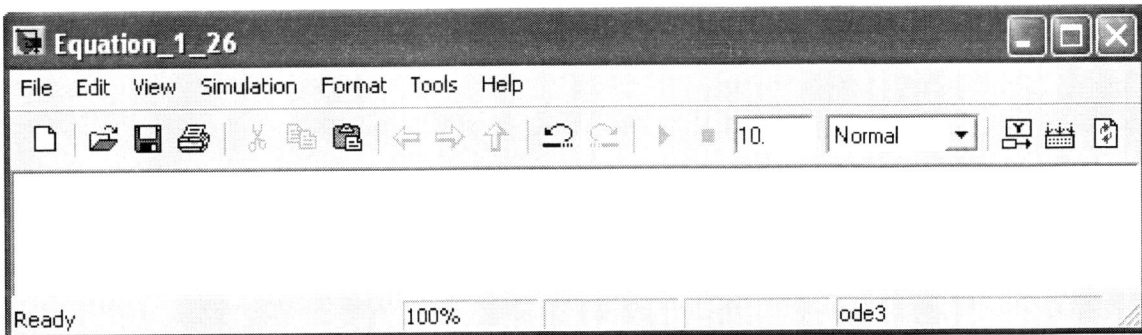

Figure 1.7. Model window for Equation_1_26.mdl file

2. With the **Equation_1_26** model window and the **Simulink Library Browser** both visible, we click on the **Sources** appearing on the left side list, and on the right side we scroll down until we see the unit step function block shown as **Step** block. See Figure 1.8. We select it, and we drag it into the **Equation_1_26** model window which now appears as shown in Figure 1.8. We save file Equation_1_26 using the File drop menu on the **Equation_1_26** model window (right side of Figure 1.8).

3. With reference to block diagram of Figure 1.5, we observe that we need to connect an amplifier with Gain 3 to the unit step function block. The Gain block in Simulink is under **Commonly Used Blocks** (first item under Simulink on the **Simulink Library Browser**). See Figure 1.8. If the **Equation_1_26** model window is no longer visible, it can be recalled by clicking on the white page icon on the top bar of the **Simulink Library Browser**.

4. We choose the Gain block and we drag it to the right of the Step block (unit step function) as shown in Figure 1.9. The triangle on the right side of the unit step function block and the > symbols on the left and right sides of the gain block are connection points. We point the mouse close to the connection point of the unit step function until is shows as a cross hair, and

Introduction to Simulink with Engineering Applications
Copyright © Orchard Publications

Chapter 1 Introduction to Simulink

draw a straight line to connect the two blocks. We double-click on the gain block and on the **Function Block Parameters**, we change the gain from 1 to 3. See Figure 1.9.

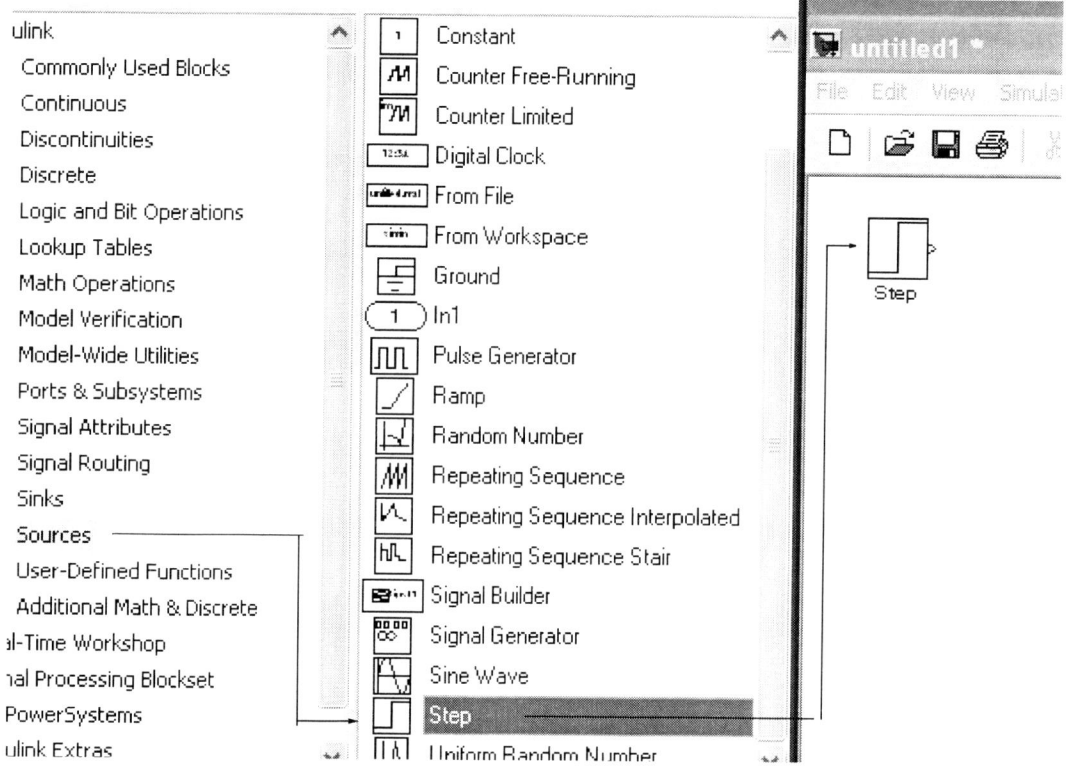

Figure 1.8. Dragging the unit step function into File Equation_1_26

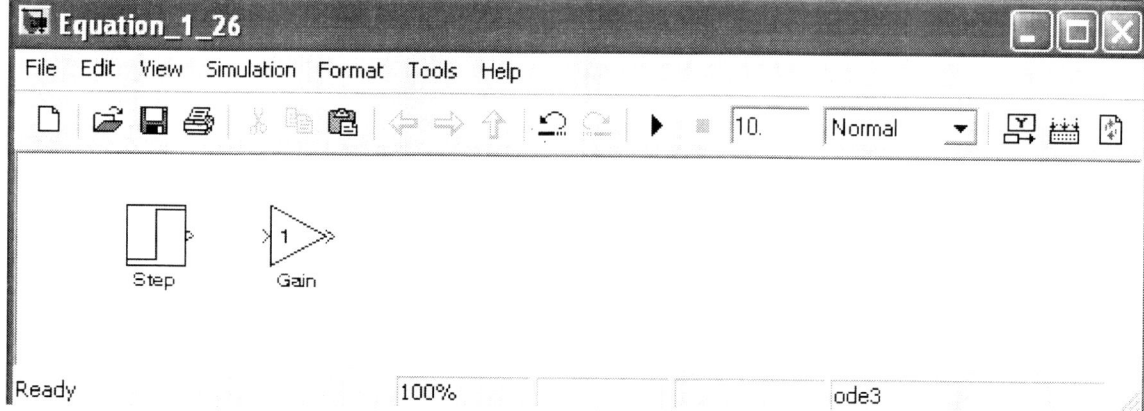

Figure 1.9. File Equation_1_26 with added Step and Gain blocks

5. Next, we need to add a thee-input adder. The adder block appears on the right side of the **Simulink Library Browser** under **Math Operations**. We select it, and we drag it into the Equation_1_26 model window. We double click it, and on the **Function Block Parameters**

1-10 Introduction to Simulink with Engineering Applications
Copyright © Orchard Publications

window which appears, we specify 3 inputs. We then connect the output of the of the gain block to the first input of the adder block as shown in Figure 1.10.

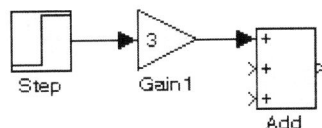

Figure 1.10. File Equation_1_26 with added gain block

6. From the **Commonly Used Blocks** of the **Simulink Library Browser**, we choose the **Integrator** block, we drag it into the Equation_1_26 model window, and we connect it to the output of the **Add** block. We repeat this step and to add a second **Integrator** block. We click on the text "Integrator" under the first integrator block, and we change it to Integrator 1. Then, we change the text "Integrator 1" under the second Integrator to "Integrator 2" as shown in Figure 1.11.

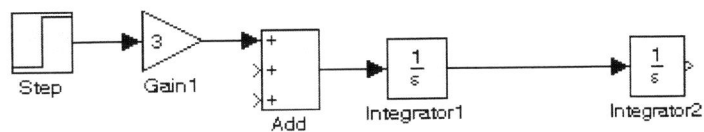

Figure 1.11. File Equation_1_26 with the addition of two integrators

7. To complete the block diagram, we add the **Scope** block which is found in the **Commonly Used Blocks** on the **Simulink Library Browser**, we click on the Gain block, and we copy and paste it twice. We flip the pasted Gain blocks by using the **Flip Block** command from the Format drop menu, and we label these as Gain 2 and Gain 3. Finally, we double-click on these gain blocks and on the **Function Block Parameters** window, we change the gains from to -4 and -3 as shown in Figure 1.12.

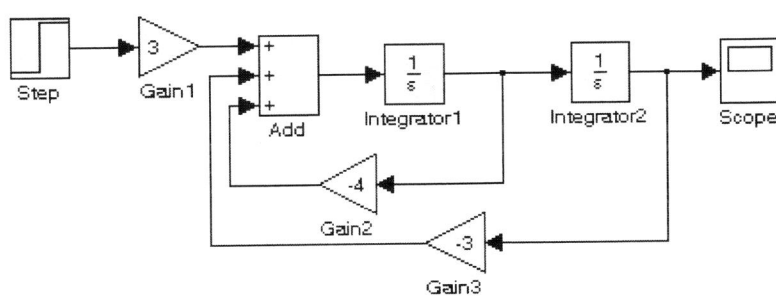

Figure 1.12. File Equation_1_26 complete block diagram

8. The initial conditions $i_L(0^-) = C\frac{dv_C}{dt}\bigg|_{t=0} = 0$, and $v_c(0^-) = 0.5$ V are entered by double clicking the Integrator blocks and entering the values 0 for the first integrator, and 0.5 for the second integrator. To obtain a true picture of the output (voltage across the capacitor), we

Chapter 1 Introduction to Simulink

double–click on the **Unit** block and in the **Source Block Parameters** window we change the Step time value from 1 to 0. We leave all other parameters in their default state. We also need to specify the simulation time. This is done by specifying the simulation time to be 10 seconds on the **Configuration Parameters** from the **Simulation** drop menu. We can start the simulation on **Start** from the **Simulation** drop menu or by clicking on the ▶ icon.

9. To see the output waveform, we double click on the **Scope** block, and then clicking on the Autoscale icon, then we right–click near the vertical axis, we click on **Axes properties**, we specify **Y–min** =0, **Y–max** = 1.5, we click on **OK**, and we obtain the waveform shown in Figure 1.13. Henceforth, we will use this procedure to scale the vertical axis in our subsequent **Scope** block displays.

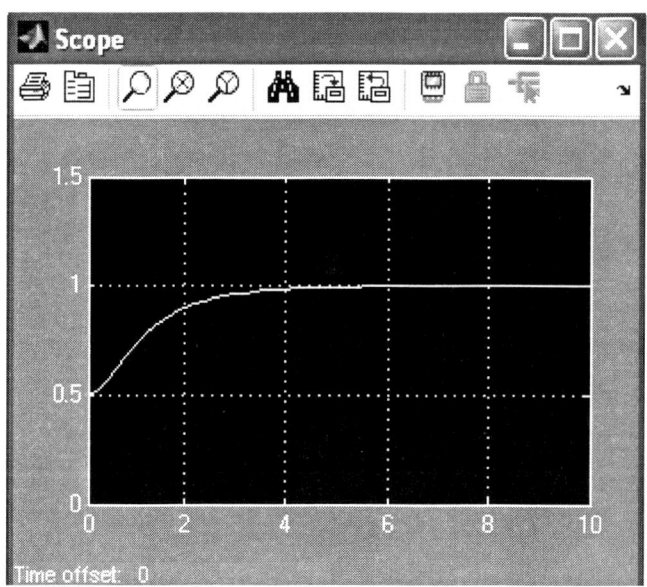

Figure 1.13. The waveform for the function $v_C(t)$ for Example 1.1

Another easier method to obtain and display the output $v_C(t)$ for Example 1.1, is to use **State–Space** block from **Continuous** in the Simulink Library Browser, as shown in Figure 1.14.

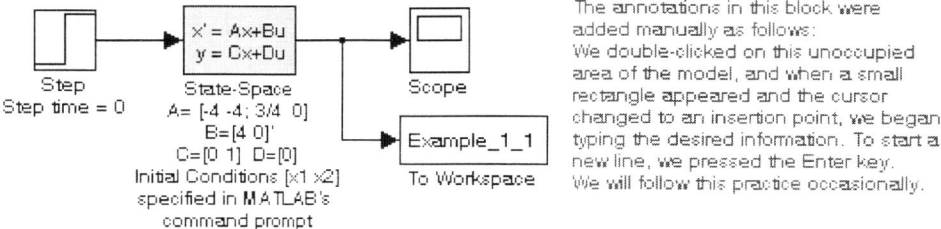

Figure 1.14. Obtaining the function $v_C(t)$ for Example 1.1 with the **State–Space** block.

The **simout To Workspace** block shown in Figure 1.14 writes its input to the workspace. In this example, we have assigned the name **Example_1_1** to it and Simulink appends it with the **.mat** extension. As we know from our MATLAB studies, the data and variables created in the MATLAB Command window, reside in the MATLAB Workspace. This block writes its output to an array or structure that has the name specified by the block's Variable name parameter. It is highly recommended that this block is included in the saved model. This gives us the ability to delete or modify selected variables at a later time. To see what variables reside in the MATLAB Workspace, we issue the command **who** or **whos**.*

From Equation 1.23,

$$\begin{bmatrix} \dot{x}_1 \\ \dot{x}_2 \end{bmatrix} = \begin{bmatrix} -4 & -4 \\ 3/4 & 0 \end{bmatrix} \begin{bmatrix} x_1 \\ x_2 \end{bmatrix} + \begin{bmatrix} 4 \\ 0 \end{bmatrix} u_0(t)$$

The output equation is

$$y = Cx + du$$

or

$$y = \begin{bmatrix} 0 & 1 \end{bmatrix} \begin{bmatrix} x_1 \\ x_2 \end{bmatrix} + [0]u$$

We double–click on the **State–Space** block, and in the **Functions Block Parameters** window we enter the constants shown in Figure 1.15.

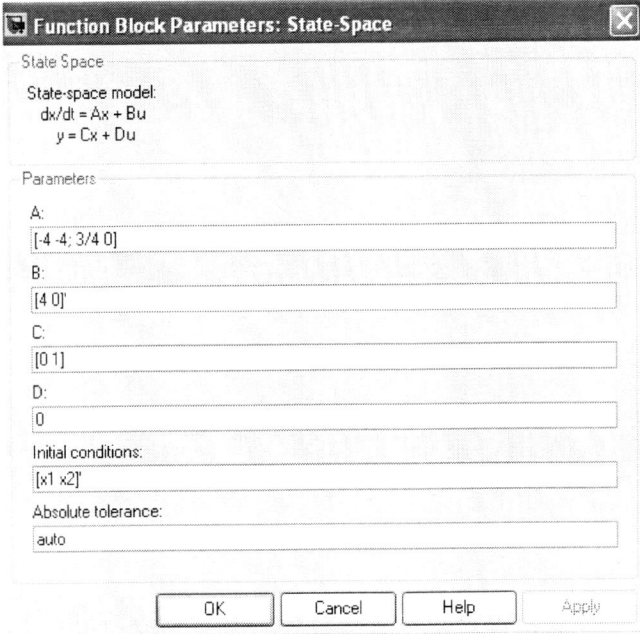

Figure 1.15. The Function block parameters for the State–Space block.

---

* **who** displays only the variables names, not the function to which each variable belongs. **whos** lists more information about each variable.

Chapter 1 Introduction to Simulink

The initials conditions [x1 x2]' are specified in MATLAB's command prompt as

x1=0; x2=0.5;

As before, to start the simulation we click on the ▶ icon, and to see the output waveform, we double click on the **Scope** block, and then clicking on the Autoscale 🔍 icon, and we scale the vertical axis as we did with the waveform of Figure 1.13. The waveform shown in Figure 1.16.

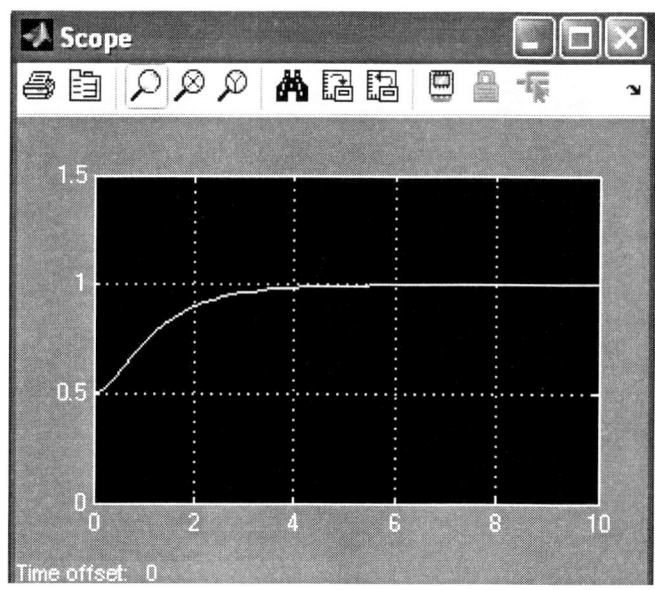

Figure 1.16. The waveform for the function $v_C(t)$ for Example 1.1 with the State–Space block.

The state–space block is the best choice when we need to display the output waveform of three or more variables as illustrated by the following example.

Example 1.2

A fourth–order network is described by the differential equation

$$\frac{d^4y}{dt^4} + a_3\frac{d^3y}{dt^3} + a_2\frac{d^2y}{dt^2} + a_1\frac{dy}{dt} + a_0 y(t) = u(t) \qquad (1.27)$$

where y(t) is the output representing the voltage or current of the network, and u(t) is any input, and the initial conditions are $y(0) = y'(0) = y''(0) = y'''(0) = 0$.

a. We will express (1.27) as a set of state equations

b. It is known that the solution of the differential equation

$$\frac{d^4 y}{dt^4} + 2\frac{d^2 y}{dt^2} + y(t) = \sin t \qquad (1.28)$$

subject to the initial conditions $y(0) = y'(0) = y''(0) = y'''(0) = 0$, has the solution

$$y(t) = 0.125[(3-t^2) - 3t\cos t] \qquad (1.29)$$

In our set of state equations, we will select appropriate values for the coefficients $a_3, a_2, a_1,$ and a_0 so that the new set of the state equations will represent the differential equation of (1.28) and using Simulink, we will display the waveform of the output $y(t)$.

1. The differential equation of (1.28) is of fourth–order; therefore, we must define four state variables that will be used with the four first–order state equations.

We denote the state variables as $x_1, x_2, x_3,$ and x_4, and we relate them to the terms of the given differential equation as

$$x_1 = y(t) \qquad x_2 = \frac{dy}{dt} \qquad x_3 = \frac{d^2 y}{dt^2} \qquad x_4 = \frac{d^3 y}{dt^3} \qquad (1.30)$$

We observe that
$$\begin{aligned} \dot{x}_1 &= x_2 \\ \dot{x}_2 &= x_3 \\ \dot{x}_3 &= x_4 \\ \frac{d^4 y}{dt^4} &= \dot{x}_4 = -a_0 x_1 - a_1 x_2 - a_2 x_3 - a_3 x_4 + u(t) \end{aligned} \qquad (1.31)$$

and in matrix form

$$\begin{bmatrix} \dot{x}_1 \\ \dot{x}_2 \\ \dot{x}_3 \\ \dot{x}_4 \end{bmatrix} = \begin{bmatrix} 0 & 1 & 0 & 0 \\ 0 & 0 & 1 & 0 \\ 0 & 0 & 0 & 1 \\ -a_0 & -a_1 & -a_2 & -a_3 \end{bmatrix} \begin{bmatrix} x_1 \\ x_2 \\ x_3 \\ x_4 \end{bmatrix} + \begin{bmatrix} 0 \\ 0 \\ 0 \\ 1 \end{bmatrix} u(t) \qquad (1.32)$$

In compact form, (1.32) is written as

$$\dot{x} = Ax + bu \qquad (1.33)$$

Also, the output is

$$y = Cx + du \qquad (1.34)$$

where

Chapter 1 Introduction to Simulink

$$\dot{x} = \begin{bmatrix} \dot{x}_1 \\ \dot{x}_2 \\ \dot{x}_3 \\ \dot{x}_4 \end{bmatrix}, \quad A = \begin{bmatrix} 0 & 1 & 0 & 0 \\ 0 & 0 & 1 & 0 \\ 0 & 0 & 0 & 1 \\ -a_0 & -a_1 & -a_2 & -a_3 \end{bmatrix}, \quad x = \begin{bmatrix} x_1 \\ x_2 \\ x_3 \\ x_4 \end{bmatrix}, \quad b = \begin{bmatrix} 0 \\ 0 \\ 0 \\ 1 \end{bmatrix}, \quad \text{and } u = u(t) \quad (1.35)$$

and since the output is defined as

$$y(t) = x_1$$

relation (1.34) is expressed as

$$y = \begin{bmatrix} 1 & 0 & 0 & 0 \end{bmatrix} \cdot \begin{bmatrix} x_1 \\ x_2 \\ x_3 \\ x_4 \end{bmatrix} + [0]u(t) \quad (1.36)$$

2. By inspection the differential equation of (1.27) will be reduced to the differential equation of (1.28) if we let

$$a_3 = 0 \qquad a_2 = 2 \qquad a_1 = 0 \qquad a_0 = 1 \qquad u(t) = \sin t$$

and thus the differential equation of (1.28) can be expressed in state–space form as

$$\begin{bmatrix} \dot{x}_1 \\ \dot{x}_2 \\ \dot{x}_3 \\ \dot{x}_4 \end{bmatrix} = \begin{bmatrix} 0 & 1 & 0 & 0 \\ 0 & 0 & 1 & 0 \\ 0 & 0 & 0 & 1 \\ -a_0 & 0 & -2 & 0 \end{bmatrix} \begin{bmatrix} x_1 \\ x_2 \\ x_3 \\ x_4 \end{bmatrix} + \begin{bmatrix} 0 \\ 0 \\ 0 \\ 1 \end{bmatrix} \sin t \quad (1.37)$$

where

$$\dot{x} = \begin{bmatrix} \dot{x}_1 \\ \dot{x}_2 \\ \dot{x}_3 \\ \dot{x}_4 \end{bmatrix}, \quad A = \begin{bmatrix} 0 & 1 & 0 & 0 \\ 0 & 0 & 1 & 0 \\ 0 & 0 & 0 & 1 \\ -a_0 & 0 & -2 & 0 \end{bmatrix}, \quad x = \begin{bmatrix} x_1 \\ x_2 \\ x_3 \\ x_4 \end{bmatrix}, \quad b = \begin{bmatrix} 0 \\ 0 \\ 0 \\ 1 \end{bmatrix}, \quad \text{and } u = \sin t \quad (1.38)$$

Since the output is defined as

$$y(t) = x_1$$

in matrix form it is expressed as

Simulink and its Relation to MATLAB

$$y = [1 \ 0 \ 0 \ 0] \cdot \begin{bmatrix} x_1 \\ x_2 \\ x_3 \\ x_4 \end{bmatrix} + [0]\sin t \quad (1.39)$$

We invoke MATLAB, we start Simulink by clicking on the Simulink icon, on the **Simulink Library Browser**, we click on the **Create a new model** (blank page icon on the left of the top bar), and we save this model as Example_1_2. On the **Simulink Library Browser** we select **Sources**, we drag the **Signal Generator** block on the Example_1_2 model window, we click and drag the **State–Space** block from the **Continuous** on Simulink Library Browser, and we click and drag the **Scope** block from the **Commonly Used Blocks** on the **Simulink Library Browser**. We also add the **Display** block found under **Sinks** on the **Simulink Library Browser**. We connect these four blocks and the complete block diagram is as shown in Figure 1.17.

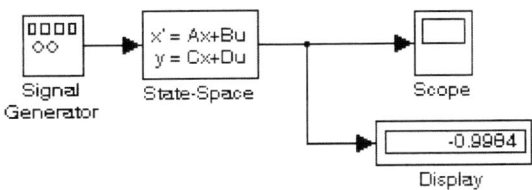

Figure 1.17. Block diagram for Example 1.2

We now double-click on the **Signal Generator** block and we enter the following in the **Function Block Parameters:**

Wave form: **sine**

Time (t): **Use simulation time**

Amplitude: **1**

Frequency: **2**

Units: **Hertz**

Next, we double-click on the **state–space** block and we enter the following parameter values in the **Function Block Parameters:**

A: [0 1 0 0; 0 0 1 0; 0 0 0 1; −a0 −a1 −a2 −a3]

B: [0 0 0 1]'

C: [1 0 0 0]

D: [0]

Chapter 1 Introduction to Simulink

Initial conditions: **x0**

Absolute tolerance: auto

Now, we switch to the MATLAB Command Window and we type the following:

>> a0=1; a1=0; a2=2; a3=0; x0=[0 0 0 0]';

We change the **Simulation Stop time** to 25, and we start the simulation by clicking on the ▶ icon. To see the output waveform, we double click on the **Scope** block, then clicking on the Autoscale icon, we obtain the waveform shown in Figure 1.18.

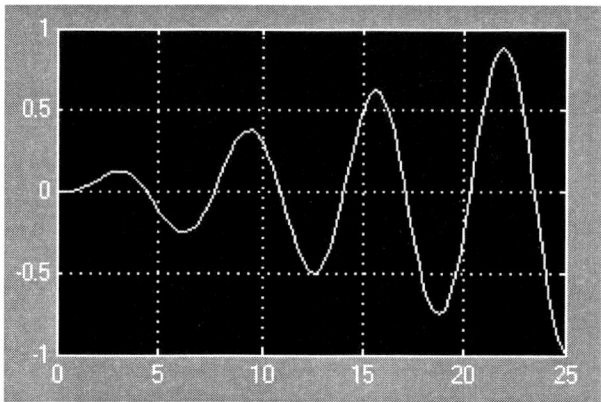

Figure 1.18. Waveform for Example 1.2

The **Display** block in Figure 1.17 shows the value at the end of the simulation stop time.

Examples 1.1 and 1.2 have clearly illustrated that the State–Space is indeed a powerful block. We could have obtained the solution of Example 1.2 using four Integrator blocks by this approach would have been more time consuming.

Example 1.3

Using **Algebraic Constraint** blocks found in the **Math Operations** library, **Display** blocks found in the **Sinks** library, and **Gain** blocks found in the **Commonly Used Blocks** library, we will create a model that will produce the simultaneous solution of three equations with three unknowns.

The model will display the values for the unknowns z_1, z_2, and z_3 in the system of the equations

Simulink and its Relation to MATLAB

$$a_1 z_1 + a_2 z_2 + a_3 z_3 + k_1 = 0$$
$$a_4 z_1 + a_5 z_2 + a_6 z_3 + k_2 = 0 \quad (1.40)$$
$$a_7 z_1 + a_8 z_2 + a_9 z_3 + k_3 = 0$$

The model is shown in Figure 1.19.

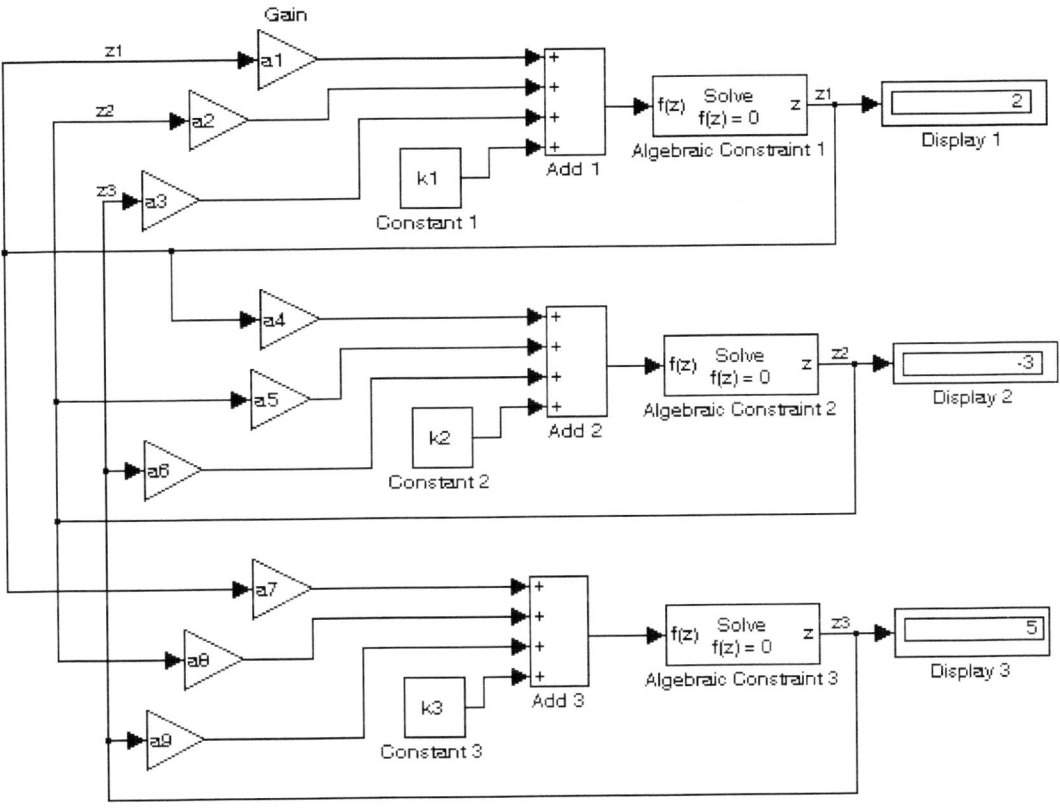

Figure 1.19. Model for Example 1.3

Next, we go to MATLAB's Command Window and we enter the following values:

a1=2; a2=−3; a3=−1; a4=1; a5=5; a6=4; a7=−6; a8=1; a9=2;...
k1=−8; k2=−7; k3=5;

After clicking on the simulation icon, we observe the values of the unknowns as $z_1 = 2$, $z_2 = -3$, and $z_3 = 5$. These values are shown in the Display blocks of Figure 1.19.

The **Algebraic Constraint** block constrains the input signal f(z) to zero and outputs an algebraic state z. The block outputs the value necessary to produce a zero at the input. The output must affect the input through some feedback path. This enables us to specify algebraic equations for index 1 differential/algebraic systems (DAEs). By default, the Initial guess parameter is zero. We

Chapter 1 Introduction to Simulink

can improve the efficiency of the algebraic loop solver by providing an Initial guess for the algebraic state z that is close to the solution value.

An outstanding feature in Simulink is the representation of a large model consisting of many blocks and lines, to be shown as a single Subsystem block. For instance, we can group all blocks and lines in the model of Figure 1.19 except the display blocks, we choose **Create Subsystem** from the **Edit** menu, and this model will be shown as in Figure 1.20[*] where in MATLAB's Command Window we have entered:

a1=5; a2=−1; a3=4; a4=11; a5=6; a6=9; a7=−8; a8=4; a9=15;...
k1=14; k2=−6; k3=9;

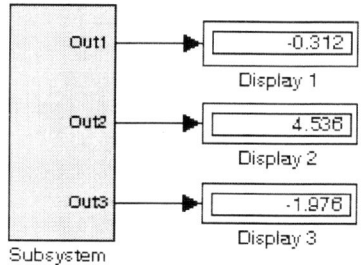

Figure 1.20. The model of Figure 1.19 represented as a subsystem

The Display blocks in Figure 1.20 show the values of z_1, z_2, and z_3 for the values specified in MATLAB's Command Window.

The Subsystem block is described in detail in Chapter 2, Section 2.1, Page 2−2.

1.2 Simulink Demos

At this time, the reader with no prior knowledge of Simulink, should be ready to learn Simulink's additional capabilities. We will explore other features in the subsequent chapters. However, it is highly recommended that the reader becomes familiar with the block libraries found in the Simulink Library Browser. Then, the reader can follow the steps delineated in The MathWorks Simulink User's Manual to run the Demo Models beginning with the **thermo** model. This model can be started by typing **thermo** in the MATLAB Command Window.

In the subsequent chapters, we will study each of the blocks under each of libraries in the Tree Pane. They are listed in Table 1.1 below in alphabetical order, library, chapter, section/subsection, and page number in which they are described.

---

[*] *The contents of the Subsystem block are not lost. We can double−click on the Subsystem block to see its contents. The Subsystem block replaces the inputs and outputs of the model with Inport and Outport blocks. These blocks are described in Section 2.1, Chapter 2, Page 2−2.*

TABLE 1.1 Simulink blocks

Block Name	Library	Chapter	Section/Subsection	Page
Abs	Math Operations Group	8	8.1.14	8–10
Add	Math Operations Group	8	8.1.2	8–2
Algebraic Constraint	Math Operations Group	8	8.1.23	8–18
Assertion	Model Verification	9	9.9	9–12
Assignment	Vector / Matrix Operations	8	8.2.1	8–19
Atomic Subsystem	Ports & Subsystems	11	11.5	11–4
Backlash	Discontinuities	4	4.7	4–9
Band-Limited White Noise	Signal Generators	15	15.2.12	15–17
Bias	Math Operations Group	8	8.1.5	8–4
Bit Clear	Bit Operations Group	6	6.2.2	6–13
Bit Set	Bit Operations Group	6	6.2.1	6–12
Bitwise Operator	Bit Operations Group	6	6.2.3	6–14
Block Support Table	Modeling Guides	10	10.3	10–9
Bus Assignment	Signal Routing Group	13	13.1.3	13–2
Bus Creator	Commonly Used blocks	2	2.6	2–7
Bus Selector	Commonly Used blocks	2	2.6	2–7
Check Discrete Gradient	Model Verification	9	9.10	9–13
Check Dynamic Gap	Model Verification	9	9.8	9–10
Check Dynamic Lower Bound	Model Verification	9	9.5	9–6
Check Dynamic Range	Model Verification	9	9.7	9–9
Check Dynamic Upper Bound	Model Verification	9	9.6	9–8
Check Input Resolution	Model Verification	9	9.11	9–14
Check Static Gap	Model Verification	9	9.4	9–5
Check Static Lower Bound	Model Verification	9	9.1	9–2
Check Static Range	Model Verification	9	9.3	9–4
Check Static Upper Bound	Model Verification	9	9.2	9–3
Chirp Signal	Signal Generators	15	15.2.9	15–14
Clock	Signal Generators	15	15.2.17	15–26
CodeReuse Subsystem	Ports & Subsystems	11	11.6	11–9
Combinational Logic	Logic Operations Group	6	6.1.5	6–4
Compare To Constant	Logic Operations Group	6	6.1.7	6–10
Compare To Zero	Logic Operations Group	6	6.1.6	6–9
Complex to Magnitude-Angle	Complex Vector Conversions Group	8	8.3.1	8–24
Complex to Real–Imag	Complex Vector Conversions Group	8	8.3.3	8–25
Configurable Subsystem	Ports & Subsystems	11	11.8	11–19
Constant	Commonly Used blocks	2	2.4	2–6
Cosine	Lookup Tables	7	7.8	7–16
Coulomb and Viscous Friction	Discontinuities	4	4.11	4–14

TABLE 1.1 Simulink blocks
(con't)

Block Name	Library	Chapter	Section/Subsection	Page
Counter Free-Running	Signal Generators	15	15.2.16	15–25
Counter Limited	Signal Generators	15	15.2.15	15–24
Data Store Memory	Signal Storage and Access Group	13	13.2.2	13–15
Data Store Read	Signal Storage and Access Group	13	13.2.1	13–14
Data Store Write	Signal Storage and Access Group	13	13.2.3	13–15
Data Type Conversion	Commonly Used blocks	2	2.17	2–29
Data Type Conversion Inherited	Signal Attribute Manipulation	12	12.1.5	12–5
Data Type Duplicate	Signal Attribute Manipulation	12	12.1.2	12–2
Data Type Propagation	Signal Attribute Manipulation	12	12.1.3	12–4
Data Type Propagation Examples	Signal Attribute Manipulation	12	12.1.10	12–12
Data Type Scaling Strip	Signal Attribute Manipulation	12	12.1.4	12–5
Dead Zone	Discontinuities	4	4.3	4–4
Dead Zone Dynamic	Discontinuities	4	4.4	4–5
Decrement Real World	Increment / Decrement	18	18.2	18–3
Decrement Stored Integer	Increment / Decrement	18	18.4	18–5
Decrement Time To Zero	Increment / Decrement	18	18.6	18–7
Decrement To Zero	Increment / Decrement	18	18.5	18–6
Demux	Commonly Used blocks	2	2.7	2–11
Derivative	Continuous-Time Linear Systems	3	3.1.2	3–2
Detect Change	Edge Detection Group	6	6.3.3	6–21
Detect Decrease	Edge Detection Group	6	6.3.2	6–20
Detect Fall Negative	Edge Detection Group	6	6.3.6	6–24
Detect Fall Nonpositive	Edge Detection Group	6	6.3.7	6–25
Detect Increase	Edge Detection Group	6	6.3.1	6–18
Detect Rise Nonnegative	Edge Detection Group	6	6.3.5	6–23
Detect Rise Positive	Edge Detection Group	6	6.3.4	6–22
Difference	Discrete–Time Linear Systems	5	5.1.8	5–9
Digital Clock	Signal Generators	15	15.2.18	15–27
Direct Lookup Table (n-D)	Lookup Tables	7	7.6	7–9
Discrete Derivative	Discrete–Time Linear Systems	5	5.1.9	5–10
Discrete Filter	Discrete–Time Linear Systems	5	5.1.6	5–5
Discrete State-Space	Discrete–Time Linear Systems	5	5.1.10	5–11
Discrete Transfer Fcn	Discrete–Time Linear Systems	5	5.1.5	5–4
Discrete Zero-Pole	Discrete–Time Linear Systems	5	5.1.7	5–8
Discrete-Time Integrator	Commonly Used blocks	2	2.16	2–26
Display	Data Viewers	14	14.2.4	14–13

Simulink Demos

TABLE 1.1 Simulink blocks

(con't)

Block Name	Library	Chapter	Section/Subsection	Page
Divide	Math Operations Group	8	8.1.10	8–7
Doc Text (DocBlock)	Documentation	10	10.2.2	10–8
Dot Product	Math Operations Group	8	8.1.12	8–8
Embedded MATLAB Function	User–Defined Functions	16	16.3	16–3
Enable	Ports & Subsystems	11	11.3	11–2
Enabled and Triggered Subsystem	Ports & Subsystems	11	11.11	11–30
Enabled Subsystem	Ports & Subsystems	11	11.10	11–27
Environment Controller	Signal Routing Group	13	13.1.9	13–9
Extract Bits	Bit Operations Group	6	6.2.5	6–17
Fcn	User–Defined Functions	16	16.1	16–2
First-Order Hold	Sample & Hold Delays	5	5.2.2	5–22
Fixed-Point State-Space	Additional Discrete	17	17.3	17–4
Floating Scope	Data Viewers	14	14.2.2	14–8
For Iterator Subsystem	Ports & Subsystems	11	11.13	11–36
From	Signal Routing Group	13	13.1.13	13–11
From File	Models and Subsystems Inputs	15	15.1.3	15–2
From Workspace	Models and Subsystems Inputs	15	15.1.4	15–2
Function-Call Generator	Ports & Subsystems	11	11.4	11–3
Function-Call Subsystem	Ports & Subsystems	11	11.12	11–34
Gain	Commonly Used blocks	2	2.10	2–16
Goto	Signal Routing Group	13	13.1.15	13–13
Goto Tag Visibility	Signal Routing Group	13	13.1.14	13–12
Ground	Commonly Used blocks	2	2.2	2–4
Hit Crossing	Discontinuities	4	4.10	4–13
IC (Initial Condition)	Signal Attribute Manipulation	12	12.1.6	12–6
If	Ports & Subsystems	11	11.15	11–40
If Action Subsystem	Ports & Subsystems	11	11.15	11–40
Increment Real World	Increment / Decrement	18	18.1	18–2
Increment Stored Integer	Increment / Decrement	18	18.3	18–4
Index Vector	Signal Routing Group	13	13.1.7	13–7
Inport	Commonly Used blocks	2	2.1	2–2
Integer Delay	Discrete-Time Linear Systems	5	5.1.2	5–2
Integrator	Commonly Used blocks	2	2.14	2–20
Interpolation (n-D) Using PreLookup	Lookup Tables	7	7.5	7–8
Interval Test	Logic Operations Group	6	6.1.3	6–2
Interval Test Dynamic	Logic Operations Group	6	6.1.4	6–3

Chapter 1 Introduction to Simulink

TABLE 1.1 Simulink blocks
(con't)

Block Name	Library	Chapter	Section/Subsection	Page
Level-2 M-File S-Function	User–Defined Functions	16	16.5	16–7
Logical Operator	Commonly Used blocks	2	2.12	2–18
Lookup Table	Lookup Tables	7	7.1	7–2
Lookup Table (2-D)	Lookup Tables	7	7.2	7–3
Lookup Table (n-D)	Lookup Tables	7	7.3	7–5
Lookup Table Dynamic	Lookup Tables	7	7.7	7–15
Magnitude–Angle to Complex	Complex Vector Conversions Group	8	8.3.2	8–24
Manual Switch	Signal Routing Group	13	13.1.10	13–9
Math Function	Math Operations Group	8	8.1.16	8–11
MATLAB Fcn	User–Defined Functions	16	16.2	16–2
Matrix Concatenate	Vector / Matrix Operations	8	8.2.3	8–21
Memory	Sample & Hold Delays	5	5.2.1	5–21
Merge	Signal Routing Group	13	13.1.8	13–8
MinMax	Math Operations Group	8	8.1.19	8–14
MinMax Running Resettable	Math Operations Group	8	8.1.20	8–15
Model	Ports & Subsystems	11	11.7	11–17
Model Info	Documentation	10	10.2.1	10–6
Multiport Switch	Signal Routing Group	13	13.1.11	13–10
Mux	Commonly Used blocks	2	2.7	2–11
Outport	Commonly Used blocks	2	2.1	2–2
Polynomial	Math Operations Group	8	8.1.18	8–14
Prelookup Index Search	Lookup Tables	7	7.4	7–7
Probe	Signal Attribute Detection	12	12.2.1	12–14
Product	Commonly Used blocks	2	2.4	2–6
Product of Elements	Math Operations Group	8	8.1.11	8–7
Pulse Generator	Signal Generators	15	15.2.3	15–5
Quantizer	Discontinuities	4	4.9	4–12
Ramp	Signal Generators	15	15.2.5	15–9
Random Number	Signal Generators	15	15.2.10	15–14
Rate Limiter	Discontinuities	4	4.5	4–6
Rate Limiter Dynamic	Discontinuities	4	4.6	4–8
Rate Transition	Signal Attribute Manipulation	12	12.1.8	12–8
Real–Imag to Complex	Complex Vector Conversions Group	8	8.3.4	8–26
Relational Operator	Commonly Used blocks	2	2.11	2–17
Relay	Discontinuities	4	4.8	4–11
Repeating Sequence	Signal Generators	15	15.2.8	15–13

TABLE 1.1 Simulink blocks
(con't)

Block Name	Library	Chapter	Section/Subsection	Page
Repeating Sequence Interpolated	Signal Generators	15	15.2.14	15–22
Repeating Sequence Stair	Signal Generators	15	15.2.13	15–21
Reshape	Vector / Matrix Operations	8	8.2.2	8–20
Rounding Function	Math Operations Group	8	8.1.17	8–13
S-Function	Ports & Subsystems User-Defined Functions	11 16	11.18 16.4	11–43 16–7
S–Function Builder	User–Defined Functions	16	16.6	16–13
S–Function Examples	User–Defined Functions	16	16.7	16–13
Saturation	Commonly Used blocks Discontinuities	2 4	2.13 4.1	2–19 4–2
Saturation Dynamic	Discontinuities	4	4.2	4–3
Scope	Data Viewers	14	14.2.1	14–6
Selector	Signal Routing Group	13	13.1.6	13–6
Shift Arithmetic	Bit Operations Group	6	6.2.4	6–16
Sign	Math Operations Group	8	8.1.13	8–9
Signal Builder	Signal Generators	15	15.2.4	15–6
Signal Conversion	Signal Attribute Manipulation	12	12.1.7	12–7
Signal Generator	Signal Generators	15	15.2.2	15–4
Signal Specification	Signal Attribute Manipulation	12	12.1.9	12–11
Sine	Lookup Tables	7	7.8	7–16
Sine Wave	Signal Generators	15	15.2.6	15–9
Sine Wave Function	Math Operations Group	8	8.1.22	8–17
Slider Gain	Math Operations Group	8	8.1.8	8–6
State-Space	Continuous-Time Linear Systems	3	3.1.3	3–6
Step	Signal Generators	15	15.2.7	15–11
Stop Simulation	Simulation Control	14	14.3	14–14
Subsystem	Commonly Used blocks	2	2.1	2–2
Subsystem Examples	Ports & Subsystems	11	11.17	11–41
Subtract	Math Operations Group	8	8.1.3	8–3
Sum	Commonly Used blocks	2	2.9	2–15
Sum of Elements	Math Operations Group	8	8.1.4	8–4
Switch	Commonly Used blocks	2	2.8	2–14
Switch Case	Ports & Subsystems	11	11.16	11–41
Switch Case Action Subsystem	Ports & Subsystems	11	11.16	11–41
Tapped Delay	Discrete–Time Linear Systems	5	5.1.3	5–3

Chapter 1 Introduction to Simulink

TABLE 1.1 Simulink blocks
(con't)

Block Name	Library	Chapter	Section/Subsection	Page
Terminator	Commonly Used blocks	2	2.3	2–5
Time-Based Linearization	Linearization of Running Models	10	10.1.2	10–4
To File	Model and Subsystem Outputs	14	14.1.3	14–2
To Workspace	Model and Subsystem Outputs	14	14.1.4	14–4
Transfer Fcn	Continuous-Time Linear Systems	3	3.1.4	3–6
Transfer Fcn Direct Form II	Additional Discrete	17	17.1	17–2
Transfer Fcn Direct Form II Time Varying	Additional Discrete	17	17.2	17–3
Transfer Fcn First Order	Discrete-Time Linear Systems	5	5.1.11	5–14
Transfer Fcn Lead or Lag	Discrete-Time Linear Systems	5	5.1.12	5–15
Transfer Fcn Real Zero	Discrete-Time Linear Systems	5	5.1.13	5–18
Transport Delay	Continuous-Time Delay	3	3.2.1	3–10
Trigger	Ports & Subsystems	11	11.2	11–2
Trigger-Based Linearization	Linearization of Running Models	10	10.1.1	10–2
Triggered Subsystem	Ports & Subsystems	11	11.9	11–25
Trigonometric Function	Math Operations Group	8	8.1.21	8–16
Unary Minus	Math Operations Group	8	8.1.15	8–10
Uniform Random Number	Signal Generators	15	15.2.11	15–16
Unit Delay	Commonly Used blocks	2	2.15	2–24
Unit Delay Enabled	Additional Discrete	17	17.7	17–9
Unit Delay Enabled External IC	Additional Discrete	17	17.9	17–12
Unit Delay Enabled Resettable	Additional Discrete	17	17.8	17–11
Unit Delay Enabled Resettable External IC	Additional Discrete	17	17.10	17–13
Unit Delay External IC	Additional Discrete	17	17.4	17–6
Unit Delay Resettable	Additional Discrete	17	17.5	17–7
Unit Delay Resettable External IC	Additional Discrete	17	17.6	17–8
Unit Delay With Preview Enabled	Additional Discrete	17	17.13	17–17
Unit Delay With Preview Enabled Resettable	Additional Discrete	17	17.14	17–19
Unit Delay With Preview Enabled Resettable External RV	Additional Discrete	17	17.15	17–20
Unit Delay With Preview Resettable	Additional Discrete	17	17.11	17–15

TABLE 1.1 Simulink blocks
(con't)

Block Name	Library	Chapter	Section/Subsection	Page
Unit Delay With Preview Resettable External RV	Additional Discrete	17	17.12	17–16
Variable Time Delay	Continuous-Time Delay	3	3.2.2	3–11
Variable Transport Delay	Continuous-Time Delay	3	3.2.3	3–12
Vector Concatenate	Vector / Matrix Operations	8	8.2.4	8–23
Weighted Moving Average	Discrete–Time Linear Systems	5	5.1.14	5–19
Weighted Sample Time	Signal Attribute Detection	12	12.2.2	12–15
Weighted Sample Time Math	Math Operations Group	8	8.1.6	8–5
While Iterator Subsystem	Ports & Subsystems	11	11.14	11–38
Width	Signal Attribute Detection	12	12.2.3	12–16
Wrap To Zero	Discontinuities	4	4.12	4–16
XY Graph	Data Viewers	14	14.2.3	14–12
Zero-Order Hold	Sample & Hold Delays	5	5.2.3	5–23
Zero-Pole	Continuous-Time Linear Systems	3	3.1.5	3–8

Introduction to Simulink with Engineering Applications
Copyright © Orchard Publications

Chapter 1 Introduction to Simulink

1.3 Summary

- MATLAB and Simulink are integrated and thus we can analyze, simulate, and revise our models in either environment at any point. We invoke Simulink from within MATLAB.

- When Simulink is invoked, the Simulink Library Browser appears. The left side is referred to as the Tree Pane and displays all libraries installed. The right side is referred to as the Contents Pane and displays the blocks that reside in the library currently selected in the Tree Pane.

- We open a new model window by clicking on the blank page icon that appears on the leftmost position of the top title bar. On the Simulink Library Browser, we highlight the desired library in the Tree Pane, and on the Contents Pane we click and drag the desired block into the new model. Once saved, the model window assumes the name of the file saved. Simulink adds the extension .mdl.

- The > and < symbols on the left and right sides of a block are connection points.

- We can change the parameters of any block by double-clicking it, and making changes in the Function Block Parameters window.

- We can specify the simulation time on the **Configuration Parameters** from the **Simulation** drop menu. We can start the simulation on **Start** from the **Simulation** drop menu or by clicking on the ▶ icon. To see the output waveform, we double click on the **Scope** block, and then clicking on the **Autoscale** 🔍 icon.

- It is highly recommended that the **simout To Workspace** block be added to the model so all data and variables are saved in the MATLAB workspace. This gives us the ability to delete or modify selected variables at a later time. To see what variables reside in the MATLAB Workspace, we issue the command **who** or **whos**.

- The state-space block is the best choice when we need to display the output waveform of three or more variables.

- We can use Algebraic Constrain blocks found in the Math Operations library, Display blocks found in the Sinks library, and Gain blocks found in the Commonly Used Blocks library, to draw a model that will produce the simultaneous solution of two or more equations with two or more unknowns.

- The Algebraic Constraint block constrains the input signal f(z) to zero and outputs an algebraic state z. The block outputs the value necessary to produce a zero at the input. The output must affect the input through some feedback path. This enables us to specify algebraic equations for index 1 differential/algebraic systems (DAEs). By default, the Initial guess parameter is zero. We can improve the efficiency of the algebraic loop solver by providing an Initial guess for the algebraic state z that is close to the solution value.

1.4 Exercises

1. Use Simulink with the Step function block, the Continuous–Time Transfer Fcn block, and the Scope block shown, to simulate and display the output waveform v_C of the RLC circuit shown below where $u_0(t)$ is the unit step function, and the initial conditions are $i_L(0) = 0$, and $v_C(0)$.

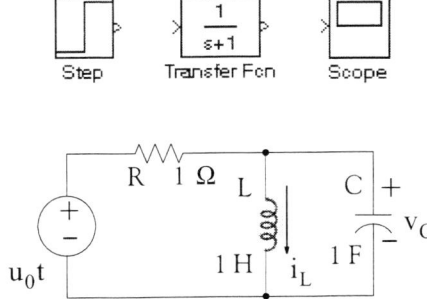

2. Repeat Exercise 1 using integrator blocks in lieu of the transfer function block.

3. Repeat Exercise 1 using the State Space block in lieu of the transfer function block.

4. Using the State–Space block, model the differential equation shown below.

$$\frac{d^2 v_C}{dt^2} + \frac{dv_C}{dt} + v_C = 2\sin(t + 30°) - 5\cos(t + 60°)$$

subject to the initial conditions $v_c(0^-) = 0$, and $v'_c(0^-) = 0.5 \text{ V}$

Chapter 1 Introduction to Simulink

1.5 Solutions to End–of–Chapter Exercises

Dear Reader:

The remaining pages on this chapter contain solutions to all end–of–chapter exercises.

You must, for your benefit, make an honest effort to solve these exercises without first looking at the solutions that follow. It is recommended that first you go through and solve those you feel that you know. For your solutions that you are uncertain, look over your procedures for inconsistencies and computational errors, review the chapter, and try again. Refer to the solutions as a last resort and rework those problems at a later date.

You should follow this practice with all end–of–chapter exercises in this book.

Solutions to End–of–Chapter Exercises

1. The s–domain equivalent circuit is shown below.

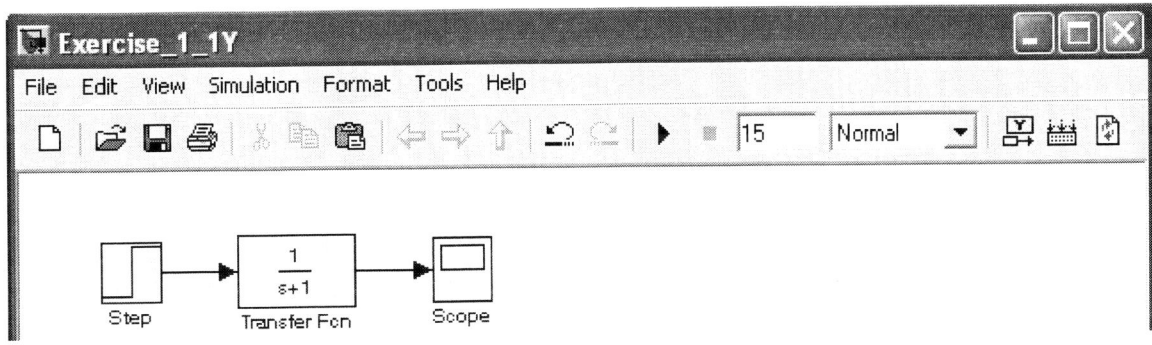

and by substitution of the given circuit constants,

By the voltage division expression,

$$V_{OUT}(s) = \frac{(s \cdot 1/s)/(s+1/s)}{(s \cdot 1/s)/(s+1/s) + 1} \cdot V_{IN}(s) = \frac{s}{s^2 + s + 1} \cdot V_{IN}(s)$$

from which

$$\text{Transfer function} = G(s) = \frac{V_{OUT}(s)}{V_{IN}(s)} = \frac{s}{s^2 + s + 1}$$

We invoke Simulink from the MATLAB environment, we open a new file by clicking on the blank page icon at the upper left on the task bar, we name this file Exercise_1_1, and from the **Sources, Continuous,** and **Commonly Used Blocks** in the **Simulink Library Browser**, we select and interconnect the desired blocks as shown below.

As we know, the unit step function is undefined at $t = 0$. Therefore, we double click on the Step block, and in the **Source Block Parameters** window we enter the values shown in the window below.

Chapter 1 Introduction to Simulink

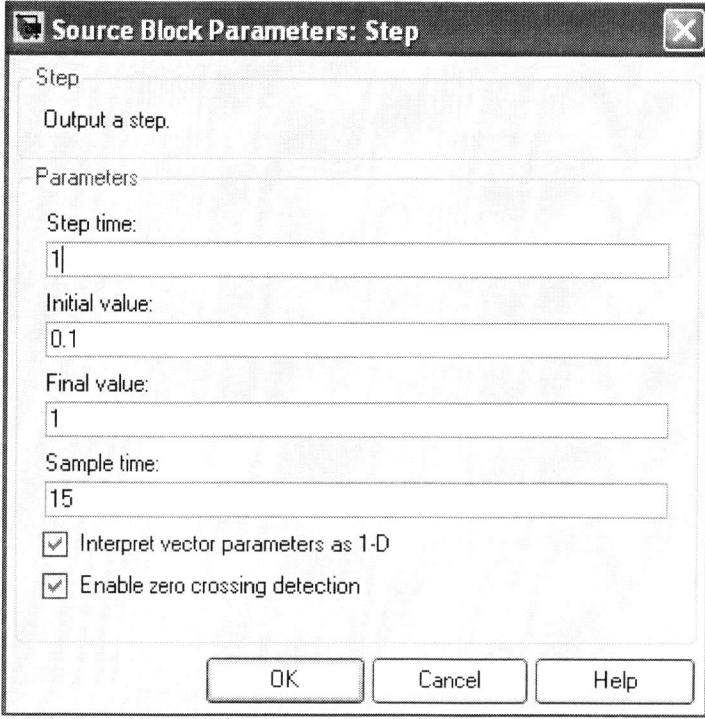

Next, we double click on the **Transfer Fcn** block and on the and in the **Source Block Parameters** window we enter the values shown in the window below.

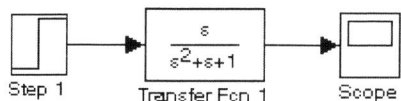

On the Exercise_1_1 window, we click on the Start Simulation ▸ icon, and by double-clicking on the **Scope** block, we obtain the Scope window shown below.

Solutions to End-of-Chapter Exercises

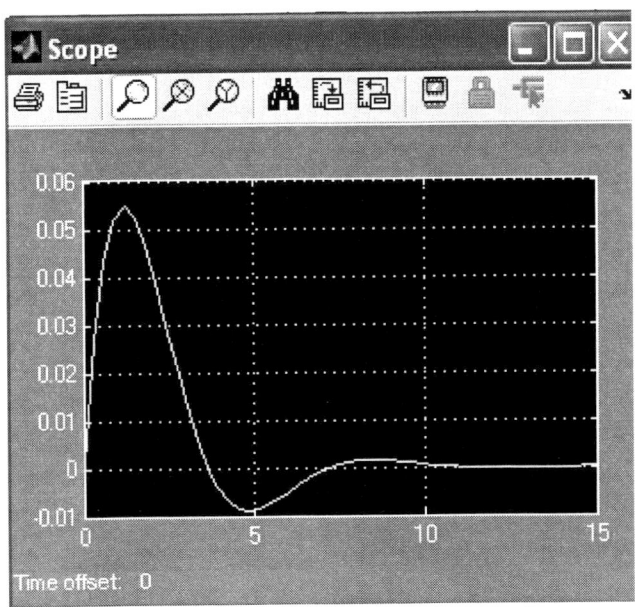

It would be interesting to compare the above waveform with that obtained with MATLAB using the **plot** command. We want the output of the given circuit which we have defined as $v_{out}(t) = v_C(t)$. The input is the unit step function whose Laplace transform is $1/s$. Thus, in the complex frequency domain,

$$V_{OUT}(s) = G(s) \cdot V_{IN}(s) = \frac{s}{s^2 + s + 1} \cdot \frac{1}{s} = \frac{1}{s^2 + s + 1}$$

We obtain the Inverse Laplace transform of $1/(s^2 + s + 1)$ with the following MATLAB script:

```
syms s
fd=ilaplace(1/(s^2+s+1))

fd = 2/3*3^(1/2)*exp(-1/2*t)*sin(1/2*3^(1/2)*t)
t=0.1:0.01:15;...
td=2./3.*3.^(1./2).*exp(-1./2.*t).*sin(1./2.*3.^(1./2).*t);...
plot(t,td); grid
```

The plot shown below is identical to that shown above which was obtained with Simulink.

Chapter 1 Introduction to Simulink

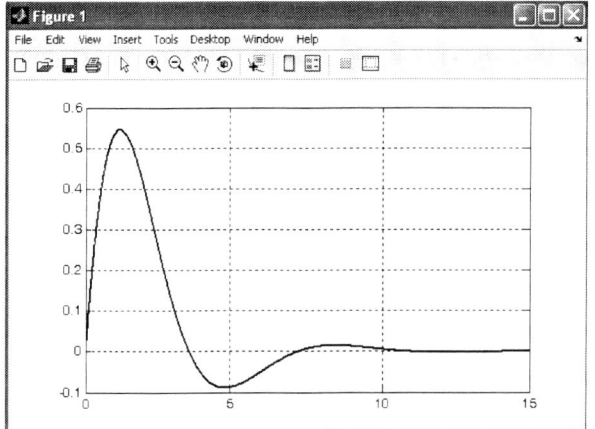

2.

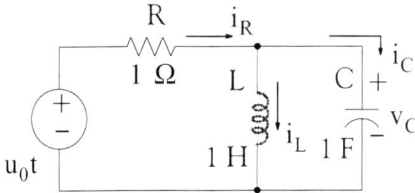

By Kirchoff's Current Law (KCL),

$$i_L + i_C = i_R$$

$$\frac{1}{L}\int_0^t v_L \, dt + C\frac{dv_C}{dt} = \frac{1 - v_C}{R}$$

By substitution of the circuit constants, observing that $v_L = v_C$, and differentiating the above integro–differential equation, we get

$$\frac{d^2 v_C}{dt^2} + \frac{dv_C}{dt} + v_C = 0$$

Invoking MATLAB, starting Simulink, and following the procedures of the examples and Exercise 1, we create the new model Exercise_1_2, shown below.

Solutions to End–of–Chapter Exercises

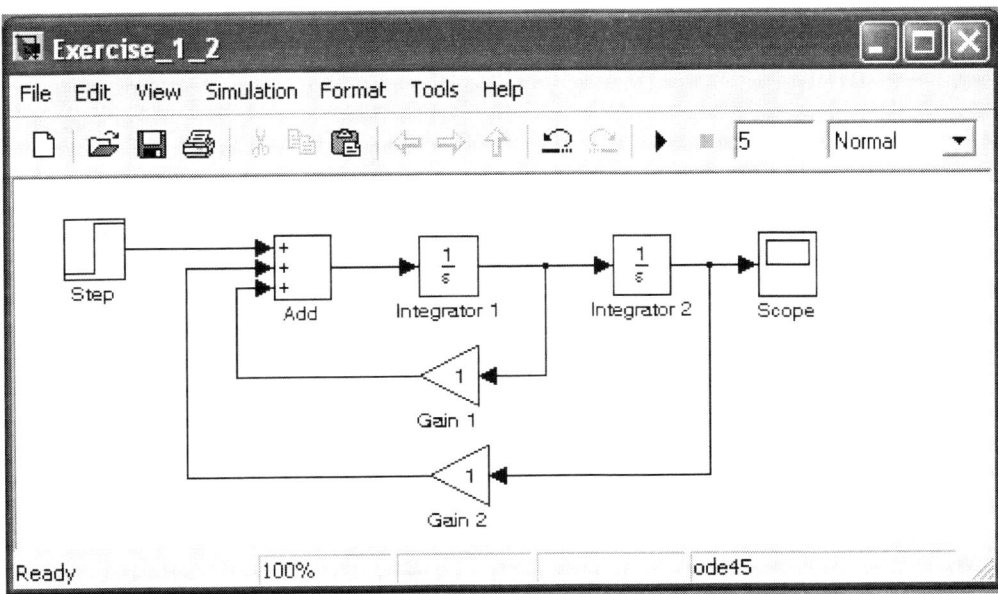

Next, we double–click on **Integrator 1** and in the **Function Block Parameters** window we set the initial value to 0. We repeat this step for **Integrator 2** and we also set the initial value to 0. We start the simulation, and double-clicking on the Scope we obtain the graph shown below.

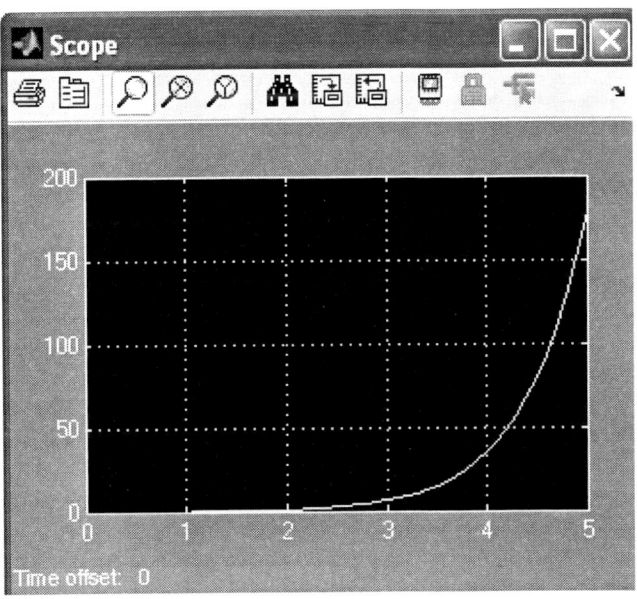

The plot above looks like the curve of a quadratic function. This is reasonable since the first integration of the unit step function yields a ramp function, and the second integration yields a quadratic function.

Chapter 1 Introduction to Simulink

3.

We assign state variables x_1 and x_2 as shown below where $x_1 = i_L$ and $x_2 = v_C$.

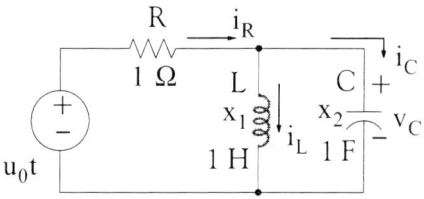

Then,

$$\dot{x}_1 = x_2$$

$$\frac{x_2 - u_0 t}{1} + x_1 + \dot{x}_2 = 0$$

$$\dot{x}_1 = x_2$$
$$\dot{x}_2 = -x_1 - x_2 + u_0 t$$

$$\dot{x}_1 = Ax + Bu \rightarrow \begin{bmatrix} \dot{x}_1 \\ \dot{x}_2 \end{bmatrix} = \begin{bmatrix} 0 & 1 \\ -1 & -1 \end{bmatrix} \begin{bmatrix} x_1 \\ x_2 \end{bmatrix} + \begin{bmatrix} 0 \\ 1 \end{bmatrix} u_0 t$$

$$y = Cx + Du \rightarrow \begin{bmatrix} 0 & 1 \end{bmatrix} \begin{bmatrix} x_1 \\ x_2 \end{bmatrix} + \begin{bmatrix} 0 \end{bmatrix} u_0 t$$

and the initial conditions are

$$x0 = \begin{bmatrix} x_{10} \\ x_{20} \end{bmatrix} = \begin{bmatrix} 0 \\ 0 \end{bmatrix}$$

We form the block diagram below and we name it Exercise_1_3.

We double-click on the State-Space block and we enter the following parameters:

A=[0 1; −1 −1]

B=[0 1]'

C=[0 1]'

D=[0]

Initial conditions: x0

The initial conditions are entered in MATLAB's Command Window as follows:

x0=[0 0]';

Solutions to End-of-Chapter Exercises

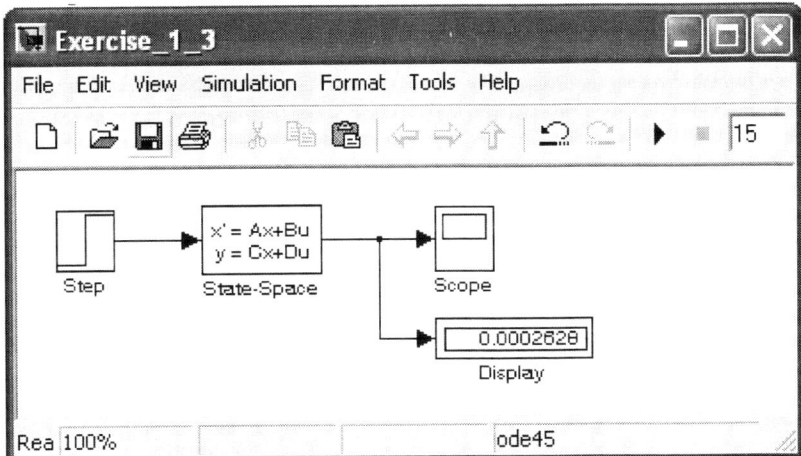

To avoid the unit step function discontinuity at $t = 0$, we double-click the Step block, and in the Source Block Parameters window, we change the Initial value from 0 to 1.

The Display block shows the output value at the end of the simulation time, in this case 15. We click on the Simulation start icon, we double-click on the Scope block, and the output waveform is as shown below. We observe that the waveform is the same as in Exercises 1 and 2.

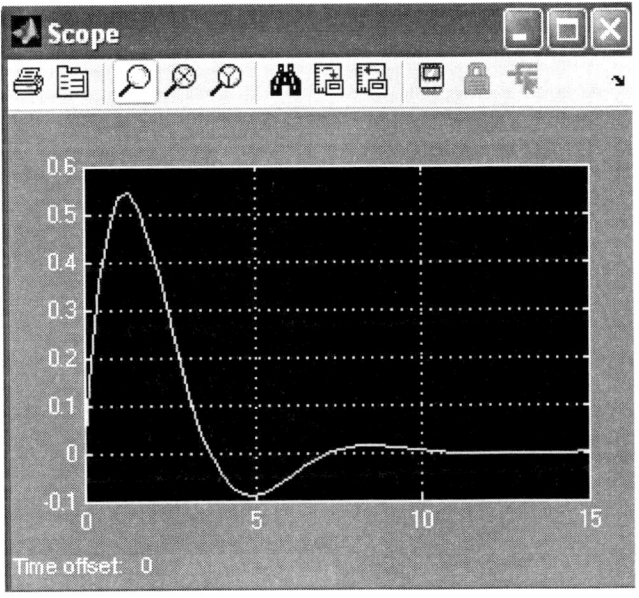

4.

$$\frac{d^2 v_C}{dt^2} + \frac{dv_C}{dt} + v_C = 2\sin(t + 30°) - 5\cos(t + 60°)$$

subject to the initial conditions $v_C(0^-) = 0$, and $v'_C(0^-) = 0.5$ V

Chapter 1 Introduction to Simulink

We let $x_1 = v_C$ and $x_2 = \dfrac{dv_C}{dt}$. Then, $\dot{x}_1 = \dfrac{dv_C}{dt} = x_2$, and $\dot{x}_2 = \dfrac{d^2 v_C}{dt^2}$. Expressing the given equation as

$$\frac{d^2 v_C}{dt^2} = -\frac{dv_C}{dt} - v_C + 2\sin(t+30°) - 5\cos(t+60°) = -x_2 - x_1 + 2\sin(t+30°) - 5\cos(t+60°)$$

we obtain the state–space equations

$$\dot{x}_1 = x_2$$
$$\dot{x}_2 = -x_2 - x_1 + 2\sin(t+30°) - 5\cos(t+60°)$$

In matrix form,

$$\dot{x} = Ax + Bu \Rightarrow \begin{bmatrix} \dot{x}_1 \\ \dot{x}_2 \end{bmatrix} = \begin{bmatrix} 0 & 1 \\ -1 & -1 \end{bmatrix} \begin{bmatrix} x_1 \\ x_2 \end{bmatrix} + \begin{bmatrix} 1 \\ 0 \end{bmatrix} (2\sin(t+30°) - 5\cos(t+60°))$$

$$y = Cx + Du \Rightarrow \begin{bmatrix} 0 & 1 \end{bmatrix} \begin{bmatrix} x_1 \\ x_2 \end{bmatrix} + \begin{bmatrix} 0 \end{bmatrix} (2\sin(t+30°) - 5\cos(t+60°))$$

subject to the initial conditions

$$x0 = \begin{bmatrix} x_{10} \\ x_{20} \end{bmatrix} = \begin{bmatrix} 0 \\ 0 \end{bmatrix}$$

Our simulation model is as shown below.

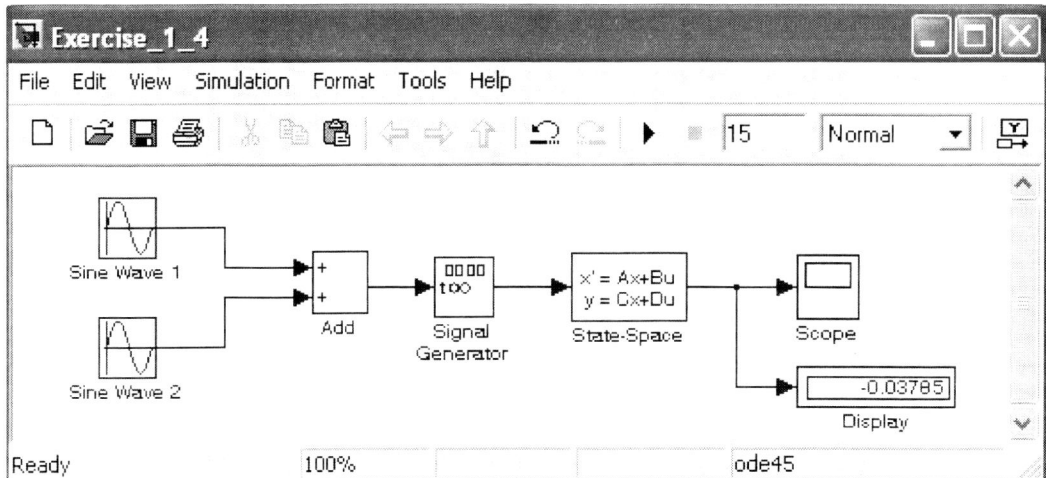

1. We double-click on the Sine Wave 1 block and in the Source Block Parameters, we make the following entries:

Solutions to End–of–Chapter Exercises

   Sine type: Time based

   Time (t): Use simulation time

   Amplitude: 2

   Bias: 0

   Frequency: 2

   Phase: pi/6

   and we click on OK

2. We double–click on the Sine Wave 2 block and in the Source Block Parameters, we make the following entries:

   Sine type: Time based

   Time (t): Use simulation time

   Amplitude: −5

   Bias: 0

   Frequency: 2

   Phase: 5*pi/6

   and we click on OK

3. We double–click on the Signal Generator block and in the Source Block Parameters, we make the following entries:

   Waveform: Sine

   Time (t): Use external signal

   Amplitude: 1

   Frequency: 2

   and we click on OK

4. We double–click on the State–Space block and in the Source Block Parameters, we make the following entries:

   A: [0 1;−1 −1], B=[1 0]', C=[0 1], D=[0], Initial conditions [x10 x20]

   and we click on OK

5. On MATLAB's Command Window we enter the initial conditions as

   x10=0; x20=0;

Chapter 1 Introduction to Simulink

6. We click on the Start Simulation icon, and double-clicking on the scope we see the waveform below after clicking on the Autoscale icon.

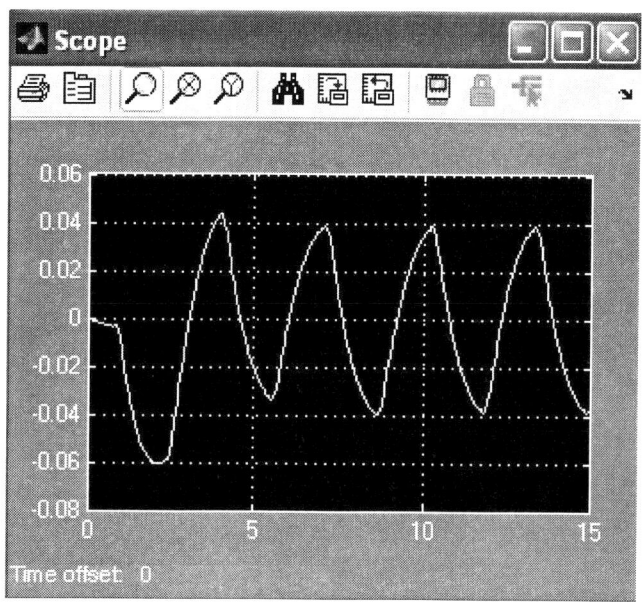

Chapter 2

The Commonly Used Blocks Library

This chapter is an introduction to the **Commonly Used Blocks** Library. This is the first library in the Simulink group of libraries and contains the blocks shown below. In this chapter, we will describe the function of each block included in this library and we will perform simulation examples to illustrate their application.

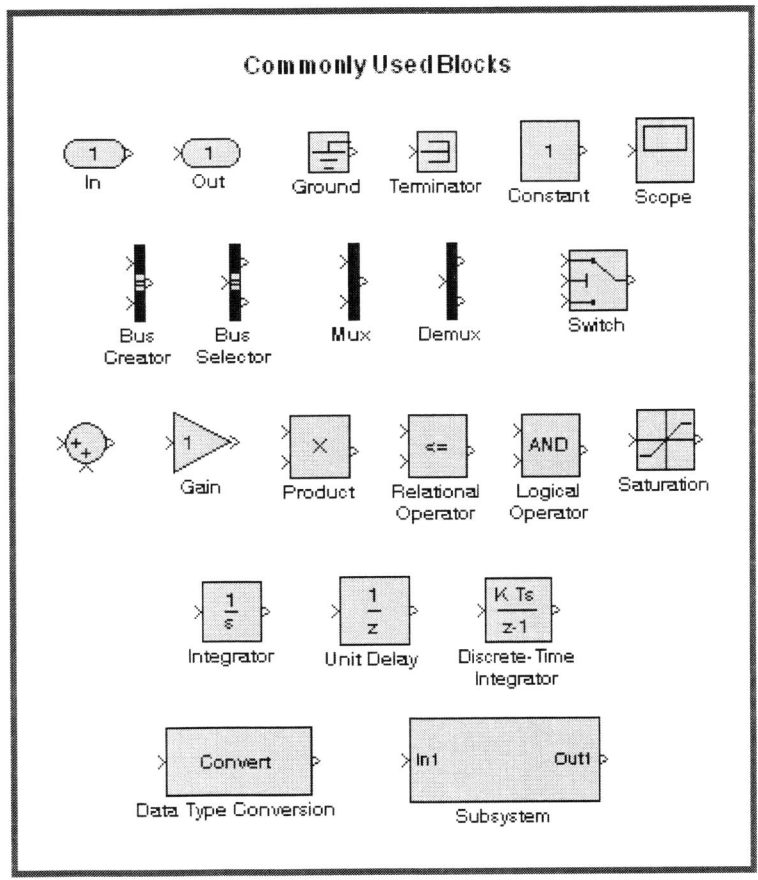

Introduction to Simulink with Engineering Applications
Copyright © Orchard Publications

Chapter 2 The Commonly Used Blocks Library

2.1 The Inport, Outport, and Subsystem Blocks

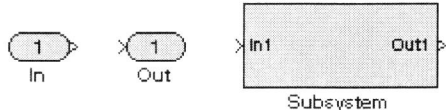

Inport blocks are ports that serve as links from outside a system into the system. **Outport blocks** are output ports for a subsystem. A **Subsystem block** represents a subsystem of the system that contains it. As our model increases in size and complexity, we can simplify it by grouping blocks into subsystems. As we can see from Example 1.3 in Chapter 1, if we increase the number of the simultaneous equations, this model increases in size and complexity.

To create a subsystem before adding the blocks it will contain, we add a **Subsystem block** to the model, then we add the blocks that make up the subsystem. If the model already contains the blocks we want to convert to a subsystem, we create the subsystem by grouping the appropriate blocks.

Example 2.1

Figure 2.1 shows the model of Example 1.1, Figure 1.12 in Chapter 1. We will create a subsystem by grouping all blocks except the **Step** and the **Scope** blocks.

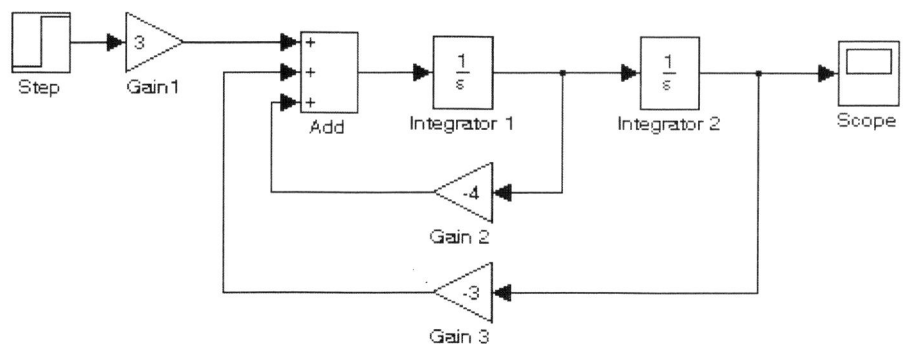

Figure 2.1. Model for Example 2.1

As a first step, we enclose the blocks and connecting lines that we want to include in the subsystem within a bounding box. This is done by forming a rectangle around the blocks and the connecting lines to select them. Then, we choose **Create Subsystem** from the **Edit** menu, and Simulink replaces the selected blocks and connecting lines with a Subsystem block as shown in Figure 2.2.

The Inport, Outport, and Subsystem Blocks

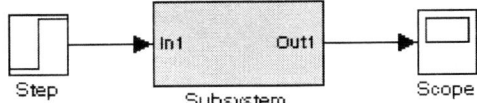

Figure 2.2. Model for Example 2.1 with Subsystem block

Next, we double-click on the Subsystem block in Figure 2.2, and we observe that Simulink displays all blocks and interconnecting lines as shown in Figure 2.3 where the Step and Scope blocks in Figure 2.2, have been replaced by In1 and Out1 blocks respectively.

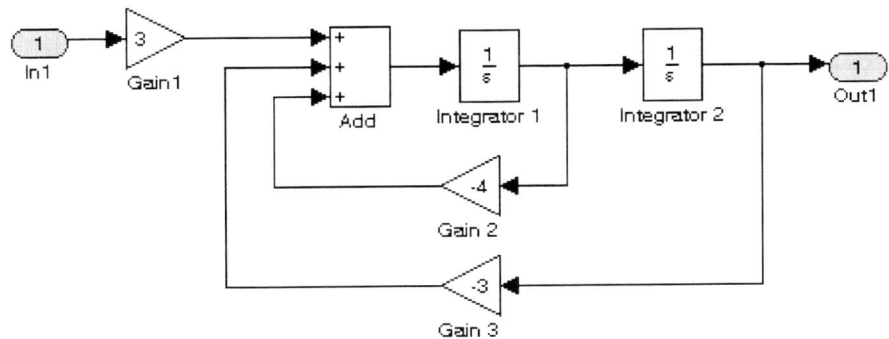

Figure 2.3. Model for Example 2.1 with Inport and Outport blocks

The Inport (In1) and Outport (Out1) blocks represent the input to the subsystem and the output from the subsystem respectively. The Inport block name appears in the Subsystem icon as a port label. To suppress display of the label In1, we select the **Inport** block, we choose **Hide Name** from the **Format** menu, then choose **Update Diagram** from the **Edit** menu.

We can create any number of duplicates of an **Inport block**. The duplicates are graphical representations of the original intended to simplify block diagrams by eliminating unnecessary lines. The duplicate has the same port number, properties, and output as the original. Changing a duplicate's properties changes the original's properties and vice versa.

To create a duplicate of an **Inport block**, we select the block, we select **Copy** from the Simulink **Edit** menu or from the block's context menu, we position the mouse cursor in the model's block diagram where we want to create the duplicate. and we select **Paste Duplicate Inport** from the Simulink **Edit** menu or the block diagram's context menu.

For the rules by which Simulink assigns port numbers, please refer to the Simulink's Help menu for this block.

Chapter 2 The Commonly Used Blocks Library

2.2 The Ground Block

The **Ground** block can be used to connect blocks whose input ports are not connected to other blocks. If we run a simulation with blocks having unconnected input ports, Simulink issues warning messages. We can avoid the warning messages by using Ground blocks. Thus, the Ground block outputs a signal with zero value. The data type of the signal is the same as that of the port to which it is connected.

Example 2.2

Let us consider the model shown in Figure 2.4 where $K1 = 3 + j1$ and $K2 = 4 + j3$ and these values have been specified in MATLAB's Command Window. Upon execution of the Simulation start command, the sum of these two complex numbers is shown in the Display block.

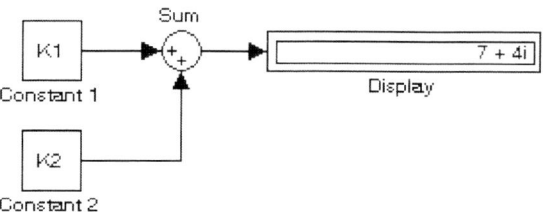

Figure 2.4. Display of the sum of two complex numbers for Example 2.2

Next, let us delete the block with the K2 value and execute the Simulation start command. The model is now shown as in Figure 2.5.

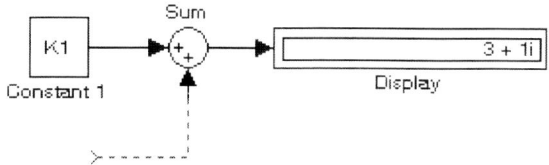

Figure 2.5. Model for Example 2.2 with Block K2 deleted.

Now, let us add the Ground block at the unconnected input of the Sum block and execute the Simulation start command. The model is now shown as in Figure 2.6.

The Terminator Block

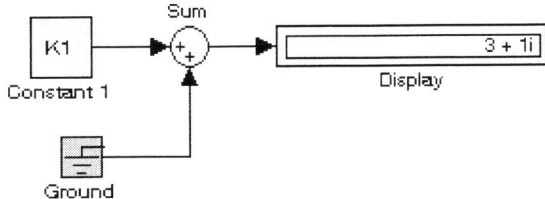

Figure 2.6. Model of Figure 2.5 with a Ground block connected to the Sum block

2.3 The Terminator Block

The **Terminator** block can be used to cap blocks whose output ports are not connected to other blocks. If we run a simulation with blocks having unconnected output ports, Simulink issues warning messages. We can avoid the warning messages by using Terminator blocks.

Example 2.3

Let us consider the unconnected output of the Sum block in Figure 2.7.

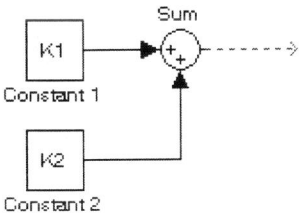

Figure 2.7. Sum block with unconnected output for Example 2.3

Figure 2.8 shows the Sum block output connected to a Terminator block.

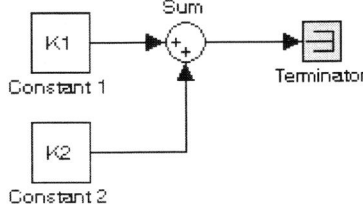

Figure 2.8. Sum block of Figure 2.7 with output connected to a Terminator block

2.4 The Constant and Product Blocks

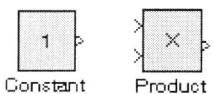

The **Constant block** is used to define a real or complex constant value. This block accepts scalar (1x1 2–D array), vector (1–D array), or matrix (2–D array) output, depending on the dimensionality of the Constant value parameter that we specify, and the setting of the Interpret vector parameters as 1–D parameter. The output of the block has the same dimensions and elements as the Constant value parameter. If we specify a vector for this parameter, and we want the block to interpret it as a vector (i.e., a 1–D array), we select the Interpret vector parameters as 1–D parameter; otherwise, the block treats the Constant value parameter as a matrix (i.e., a 2–D array).

By default, the Constant block outputs a signal whose data type and complexity are the same as that of the block's Constant value parameter. However, we can specify the output to be any supported data type supported by Simulink, including fixed-point data types. For a discussion on the data types supported by Simulink, please refer to Data Types Supported by Simulink in the Using Simulink documentation.

The **Product block** performs multiplication or division of its inputs. This block produces outputs using either element–wise or matrix multiplication, depending on the value of the **Multiplication parameter**. We specify the operations with the Number of inputs parameter. Multiply(*) and divide(/) characters indicate the operations to be performed on the inputs.

Example 2.4

The model is shown in Figure 2.9 performs the multiplication $(3 + j4) \times (4 + j3) \times (5 - j8)$. After the Start simulation command is executed, it may be necessary to stretch the Display block horizontally to read the result.

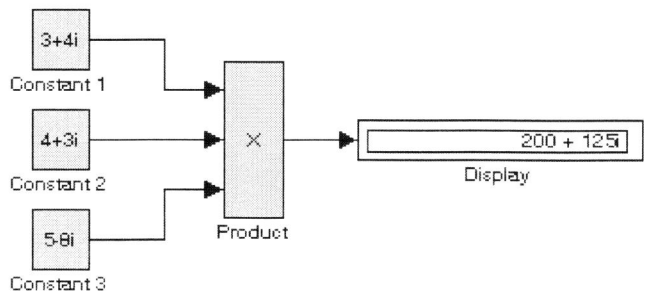

Figure 2.9. Model for Example 2.4

The Scope Block

The **Divide block** is an implementation of the Product block. It can be used to multiply or divide inputs.

Example 2.5

The model is shown in Figure 2.10 performs the division $(3 + j4)/(4 + j3)$.

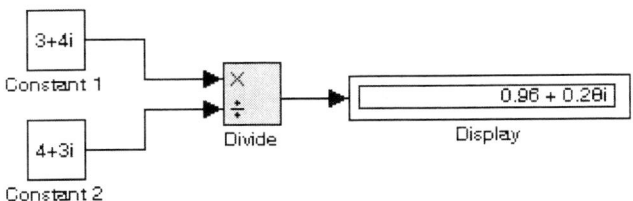

Figure 2.10. Model for Example 2.5

2.5 The Scope Block

The **Scope** block displays waveforms as functions of simulation time. The Scope block can have multiple y–axes with a common time range. We can adjust the amount of time and the range of input values displayed, we can move and resize the Scope window, and we can modify the Scope's parameter values during the simulation. The Scope block does not automatically display the waveforms, but it does write data to connected Scopes. The Scope's input signal or signals will be displayed if after a simulation is terminated, we double–click on the Scope block and the signal(s) will then be displayed. The Scope assigns colors to each signal element in this order: **yellow**, **magenta**, **cyan**, **red**, **green**, and **dark blue**. When more than six signals are displayed, the Scope cycles through the colors in the order listed. The Scope block is described in detail in Subsection 14.2.1, Chapter 14, Page 14–6.

2.6 The Bus Creator and Bus Selector Blocks

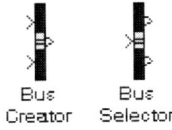

To understand the uses of the Bus Creator and Bus Selector blocks, let us review the concept of a signal bus which can be thought of as a bundle of several wires held together by tie wraps. Graph-

Introduction to Simulink with Engineering Applications
Copyright © Orchard Publications

Chapter 2 The Commonly Used Blocks Library

ically, we can represent a bus as a composite signal comprised of a set of individual signals with a group of lines, each line representing an individual signal. We use **Bus Creator** blocks to create signal buses and **Bus Selector** blocks to access the components of a bus. Simulink hides the name of a Bus Creator and Bus Selector blocks when we copy them from the Simulink library to a model. However, we can make the names visible by clicking **Show Name** on the **Format** menu. Making the names visible is a good idea since the Bus Creator, Bus Selector, Mux, and Demux blocks are all represented by a heavy vertical line. The Mux and Demux blocks are described in the next section.

The **Bus Creator** block is normally shown as a heavy vertical line. We use this block to combine a set of signals into a bus, i.e., a group of signals represented by a single line. The Bus Creator block, when used in conjunction with the **Bus Selector block**, described later also in this section, allows us to reduce the number of lines required to route signals from one part of a diagram to another. This makes our diagram easier to understand.

Example 2.6

The model of Figure 2.11 simulates the combined functions $\sin 2t$, $\frac{d}{dt}\sin 2t$, and $\int \sin 2t\, dt$ into a bus and displays all three on a single Scope block.

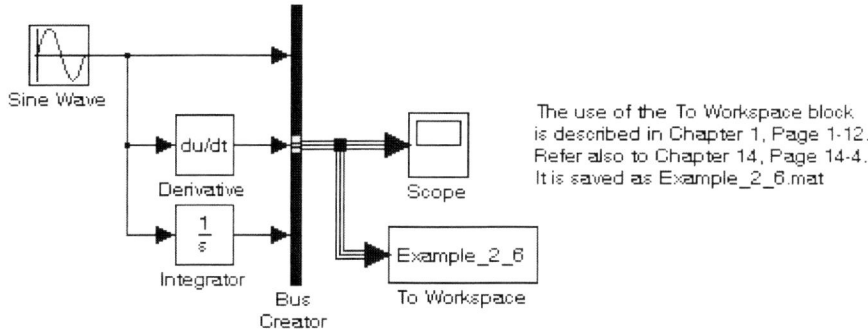

Figure 2.11. Model for Example 2.6

We begin by entering the following in the MATLAB Command Window:

syms t; y=sin(2*t), der_y=diff(y), int_y=int(y) % Requires the Symbolic Math Toolbox–see Pg A–10

and MATLAB displays

```
y =
sin(2*t)

der_y =
2*cos(2*t)

int_y =
```

The Bus Creator and Bus Selector Blocks

```
-1/2*cos(2*t)
```

From the **Sources Library**[*] browser, we select the **Sine Wave** block and we drag it into a new model window which we name **Figure_2_11**. From the **Continuous Library**[†] Browser we select the **Derivative** block and we drag it into the model window. Also, from the **Continuous Library** Browser, we select the **Integrator** block and we drag it into our model. From the **Commonly Used Blocks** Library Browser we select the **Bus Creator** block and we drag it into the model window. Then, we select the **Scope** and **Simout** to **Workspace** blocks from the **Sinks Library**[‡] and we drag them into the model window. On the model window we click on the **Integrator** block and on the **Function Block Parameters** dialog box we set the initial condition to zero. Also, on the model window we click on the **Bus Creator** block and on the **Function Block Parameters** dialog box we change the number of inputs from 2 to 3. We connect the blocks as shown in Figure 2.11.

Now, we configure Simulink to run the simulation for 10 seconds (the default value). We choose the parameters shown in Figure 2.12 from the **Simulation** menu of the model.

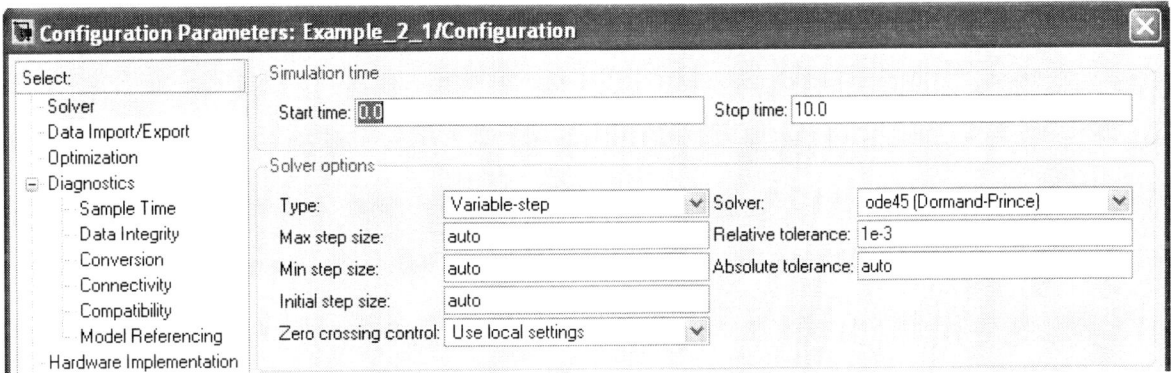

Figure 2.12. Specifying the configuration parameters for Example 2.6

We close the **Configuration Parameters** dialog box by clicking the OK button, and Simulink applies the parameters. Finally, we double click the **Scope** block and the output is as shown in Figure 2.13. To scale the vertical axis as shown in Figure 2.13, we move the cursor close to the vertical axis, we right–click, and we enter the lower and upper limits shown in Figure 2.13.

The **Bus Creator** block assigns a name to each signal on the bus that it creates. This allows us to refer to signals by name when searching for their sources (see Browsing Bus Signals) or selecting signals for connection to other blocks. The block offers two bus signal naming options. We can specify that each signal on the bus inherit the name of the signal connected to the bus (the default) or that each input signal must have a specific name. To specify that bus signals inherit

---

[*] *The Sources Blocks Library is described in Chapter 15.*
[†] *The Continuous Blocks Library is described in Chapter 3.*
[‡] *The Sinks Blocks Library is described in Chapter 14.*

their names from input ports, we select **Inherit bus signal names from input ports** from the list box on the block's parameter dialog box. The names of the inherited bus signals appear in the Signals in bus list box shown in Figure 2.14.

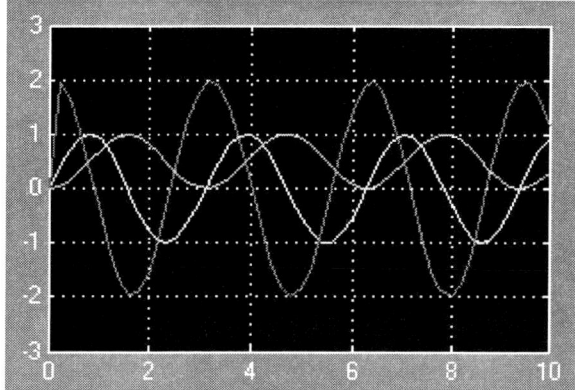

The integral of the sine wave appears with a DC component of value 0.5 being added to it. We recall that the evaluation of an indefinite integral requires the addition of a constant of integration, and for this example

$$\int \sin 2t \, dt = -\frac{1}{2}\cos 2t + C$$

but the Symbolic ToolBox ignores C whereas for t=0, C=1/2, and Simulink displays

$$-\frac{1}{2}\cos 2t + \frac{1}{2} = \frac{1}{2}(1 - \cos 2t)$$

Figure 2.13. Output waveforms for Example 2.6

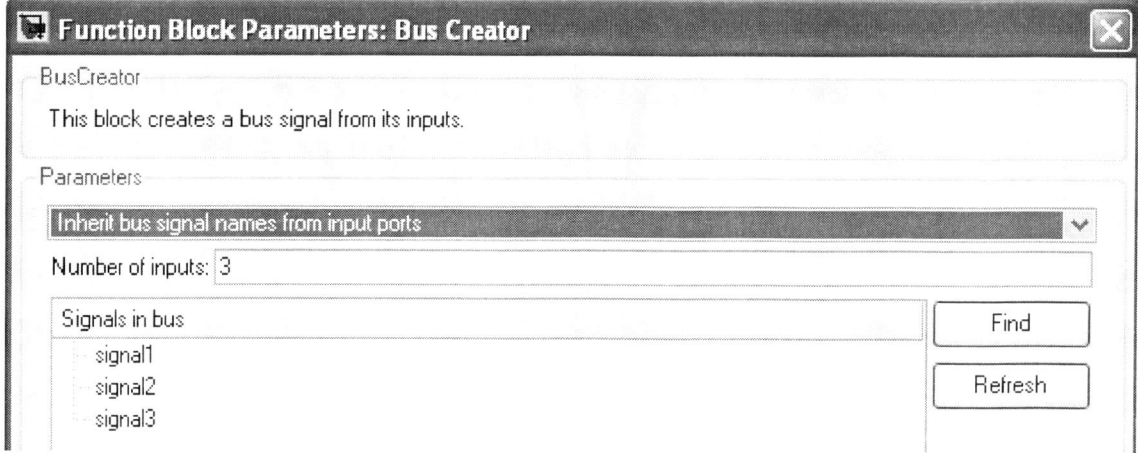

Figure 2.14. Bus Creator function block parameters dialog box

The **Bus Editor** allows us to change the properties of the bus types objects. We select the Bus Editor from the model's Tools menu. For details, please refer to the Simulink Owner's Manual or Simulink's Help menu.

Often, it is desirable to annotate our models. These annotations provide textual information about a model. We can add an annotation to any unoccupied area of our model. To insert an annotation, we double–click in an unoccupied section of the model, then a small rectangle appears, and the cursor changes to an insertion point. We start typing the annotation text and we observe that each line is centered within the rectangle. We can also left– or right–justify the annotation by first highlighting it, and making the desired selection using the Text Alignment from the **Format** drop menu. Then we can move it to the desired location by dragging it. We can

The Mux and Demux Blocks

choose another Font from the Format menu. We can delete an annotation by first selecting it, holding down the Shift key and pressing the Delete or Backspace key.

2.7 The Mux and Demux Blocks

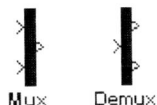

Before describing the **Mux** and **Demux** blocks, let us review the functions of a *multiplexer* (mux) and *demultiplexer* (demux).

Multiplexing is a method of sending multiple signal streams of information on a carrier at the same time in the form of a single, complex signal and then recovering the separate signals at the receiving end. Analog signals are commonly multiplexed using *Frequency Division Multiplexing* (FDM), in which the carrier bandwidth is divided into subchannels of different frequency widths, each carrying a signal at the same time in parallel. Cable television is an example of FDM. Digital signals are commonly multiplexed using *Time Division Multiplexing* (TDM), in which the multiple signals are carried over the same channel in alternating time slots. If the inputs take turns to use the output channel (time division multiplexing) then the output bandwidth need be no greater than the maximum bandwidth of any input. If many inputs may be active simultaneously then the output bandwidth must be at least as great as the total bandwidth of all simultaneously active inputs. In this case the multiplexer is also known as a *concentrator*.

A demultiplexer performs the reverse operation of a multiplexer. Figure 2.15 shows a functional block diagram of a typical 4–line time–division digital multiplexer / demultiplexer pair.

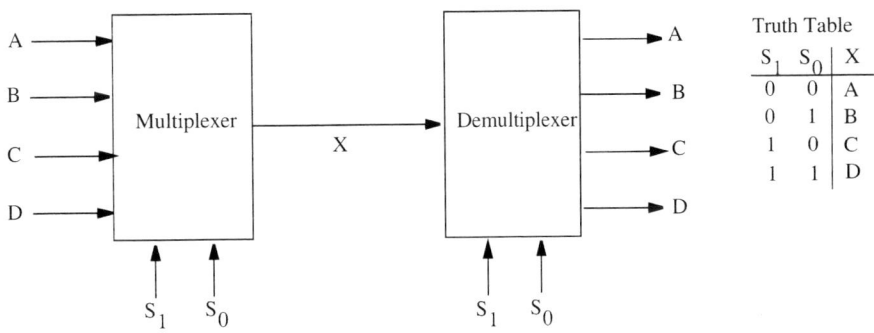

Figure 2.15. Digital Mux–Demux pair

In Figure 2.15, A, B, C, and D represent input data to be multiplexed and appear on a single transmission path denoted as X. This path will carry the data of input A, B, C, or D depending on the settings of the selection switches S_0 and S_1. These setting must be the same on both the

Chapter 2 The Commonly Used Blocks Library

multiplexer and demultiplexer. For instance, if the setting are $S_0 = 0$ and $S_1 = 1$, the output line X of the multiplexer will carry the data of signal C and it will appear at the output line C on the demultiplexer. The other combinations are shown in the truth table of Figure 2.15. A model for a digital multiplexer is presented in Chapter 11, Example 11.2, Page 11–4.

The Simulink **Mux block** combines its inputs into a single output. An input can be a scalar, vector, or matrix signal. For details, please refer to the Simulink Owner's Manual or Simulink's Help menu. The Mux block's Number of Inputs parameter allows us to specify input signal names and dimensionality as well as the number of inputs. A value of −1 means that the corresponding port can accept signals of any dimensionality. Simulink hides the name of a **Mux block** when we drag it from the Simulink block library to a model. However, we can make the name visible by clicking **Show Name** on the **Format** menu.

The Simulink **Demux block** extracts the components of an input signal and outputs the components as separate signals. The block accepts either vector (1–D array) signals or bus signals (see **Signal Buses** in the Using Simulink documentation for more information). The Number of outputs parameter allows us to specify the number and the dimensionality of each output port. If we do not specify the dimensionality of the outputs, the block determines the dimensionality of the outputs for us.

Simulink hides the name of a Demux block when we drag it from the Simulink library to a model. However, we can make the name visible by clicking **Show Name** on the **Format** menu.

Let n represent an n–element input vector, and p represent the block output scalar signals where p cannot be greater than n.

Case I: $p = n$

If we specify p outputs for a n–element input vector, the Demux block will output the same number of outputs as the number of elements in the input vector. For instance, if the input to the Demux block is a four–element vector, and we specify four outputs, the Demux block will output four scalar signals. However, if we specify the number of outputs as fewer than the number of input elements, the Demux block will distribute the elements as evenly as possible over the outputs.

Case II: $p < n$

a. $n \bmod p = 0$: The Demux block outputs p vector signals each having n/p elements. For instance, if the input to the Demux block is an eight–element vector, and we specify four outputs, the Demux block will output four two-element vectors.

b. $n \bmod p = m$: The Demux block outputs m vector signals each having $n/p + 1$ elements and $p - m$ signals having n/p elements. For instance, if the input to the Demux block is a five–ele-

The Mux and Demux Blocks

ment vector, and we specify three outputs, the Demux block will output two 2–element vector signals and one scalar signal.

For other cases please refer to the Simulink Owner's Manual or Simulink's Help menu.

We use –1 in a vector expression to indicate that the block should dynamically size the corresponding port. If a vector expression comprises positive values and –1 values, the Demux block assigns as many elements as needed to the ports with positive values and distributes the remain elements as evenly as possible over the ports with –1 values.

Example 2.7

The input to a **Demux block** is a [1 × 9] row vector (digits 1 through 9) and the block output has three ports. We want to specify that there will be four elements on the second port, and the first and third ports will be dynamically sized. We will create a model that will meet these specifications.

The model is shown in Figure 2.16. We first drag the **Constant block** from the **Sources** of the Simulink Library Browser into a new model window, we drag the **Demux block** from the **Commonly Used Blocks** Library Browser, we drag the **Display blocks** from the **Sinks** Library Browser, and we make the connections as indicated.

We double–click on the **Constant Block** and we enter the row vector [1 2 3 4 5 6 7 8 9]. We uncheck the Interpret vector parameter as 1–D. We double click on the **Demux block** and for the **Number of outputs** we enter [–1, 4 –1]. The numbers displayed appear after we start the simulation. We observe that there are three elements on the first output port, four on the second, and two on the third. The elements on the second port are as specified, and those on the first and third rows are dynamically sized.

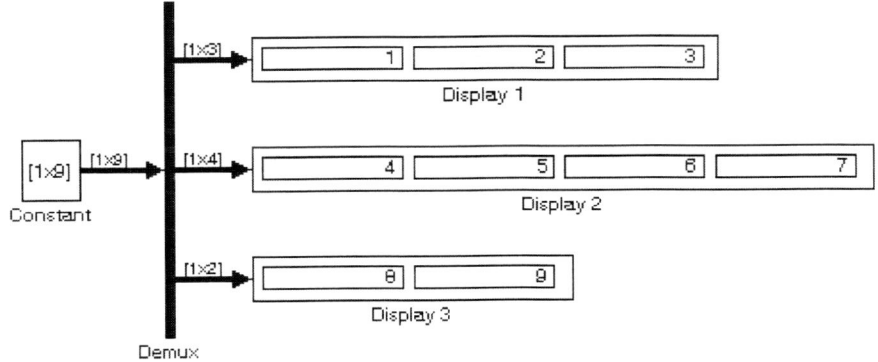

Figure 2.16. Model for Example 2.7

Chapter 2 The Commonly Used Blocks Library

For additional examples please refer to Simulink's Help menu. Some of these examples have replaced the Display blocks with Terminator blocks. As we've learned earlier, a Terminator block prevents warnings about unconnected output ports.

2.8 The Switch Block

The **Switch block** will output the first input or the third input depending on the value of the second input. The first and third inputs are called **data inputs**. The second input is called the **control input** and it is specified on the **Function Block Parameters** for the **Switch block**. The following options are available:

u2>=Threshold

u2>Threshold

u2~=0

where u2~=0 indicates a non–zero condition.

Example 2.8

In Figure 2.17, the Function Block Parameters for the Switch block has been set for u2>=Threshold, Threshold =75, in the Source Block Parameters for the $y = 75 + \sin x$ block we have entered Amplitude=1, Bias=75, Frequency =1, for the $y = 75 - \sin x$ block we have entered Amplitude=1, Bias=75, Frequency =1, Phase = $-\pi$, and in MATLAB's Command Window we have entered the statement T=75;

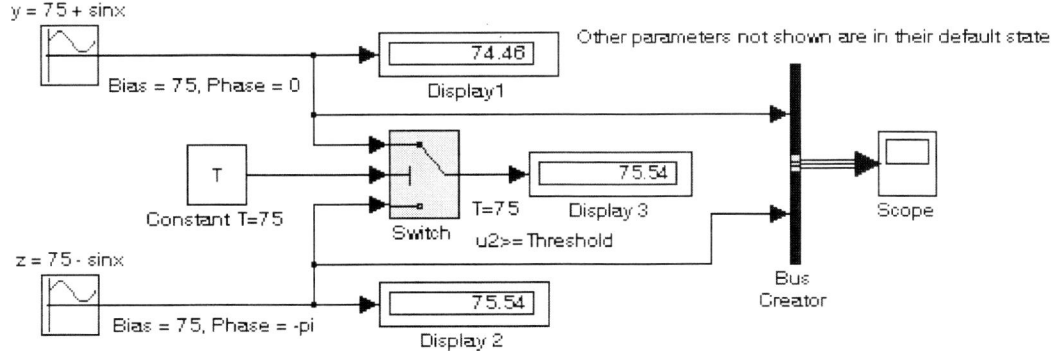

Figure 2.17. Switch block set for u2>=Threshold, Threshold T=75

The Sum Block

The model of Figure 2.17, shows that at the end of the simulation time Input 2 does not satisfy the selected criterion u2>=Threshold where Threshold =75, and thus the Switch block outputs the third input, i.e., $y = 75 - \sin x$. This can also be observed on the Scope block of Figure 2.18.

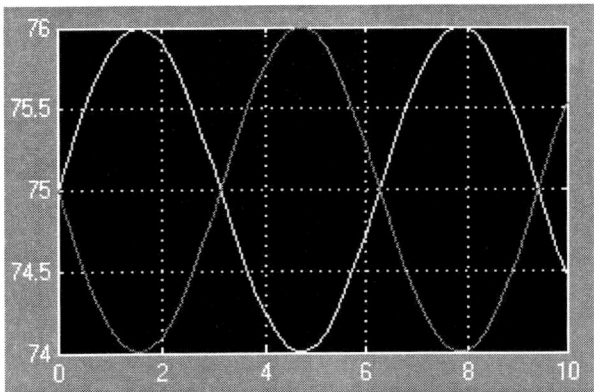

Figure 2.18. Input waveforms for the model of Figure 2.17

2.9 The Sum Block

The **Sum** block is an implementation of the Add block which is described in Subsection 8.1.2, Chapter 8, Page 8–2. This block performs addition or subtraction on its inputs. This block can add or subtract scalar, vector, or matrix inputs. From the Block Parameters dialog box we can choose the icon shape of the block, rectangular or round. We specify the operations of the block with the List of Signs parameter. Plus (+), minus (−), and spacer (|) characters indicate the operations to be performed on the inputs. If there are two or more inputs, then the number of characters must equal the number of inputs. For example, "+−+" requires three inputs and configures the block to subtract the second (middle) input from the first (top) input, and then add the third (bottom) input.

Example 2.9

Let us consider the matrices A, B, and C defined in MATLAB's Command Window as:

A=[3+4j 1+0j 5−2j; 2−3j 4+j 7−4j; 1+6j 8−5j 4+7j];
B=[4+3j 0+2j −2+5j; −3+2j 6+7j −3−4j; 1+8j −5−3j 2−7j];
C=[−2+3j 7+2j −5−2j; 3−2j 4−7j −4+3j; −3+8j 7−4j −6+9j];

The model in Figure 2.19 performs the operation $A + B - C$.

Chapter 2 The Commonly Used Blocks Library

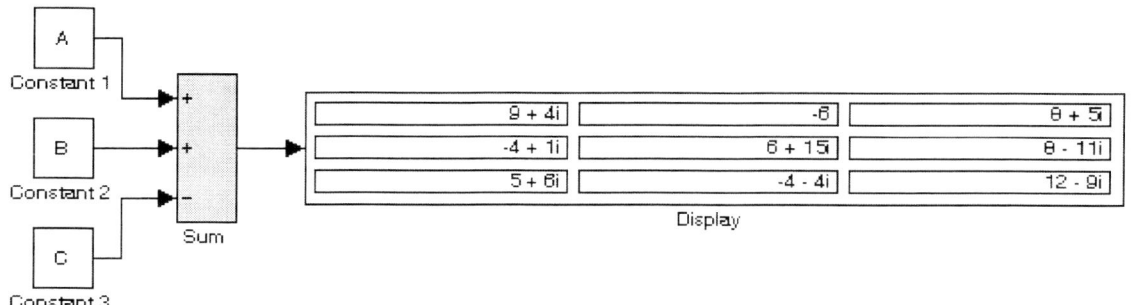

Figure 2.19. Model for Example 2.9

2.10 The Gain Block

The **Gain block** multiplies the input by a constant value (gain). The input and the gain can each be a scalar, vector, or matrix. We specify the value of the gain in the Gain parameter. The Multiplication parameter lets us specify element–wise or matrix multiplication. For matrix multiplication, this parameter also lets us indicate the order of the multiplicands.

Example 2.10

The model shown in Figure 2.20 performs the matrix multiplication $A \cdot B$ where $A = \begin{bmatrix} 1 & -1 & 2 \end{bmatrix}'$ and $B = \begin{bmatrix} 2 & 3 & 4 \end{bmatrix}$.

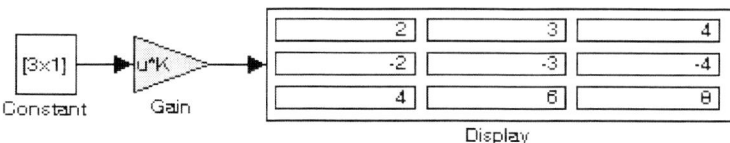

Figure 2.20. Model for Example 2.10

We double–click on the **Constant block** and we enter $\begin{bmatrix} 1 & -1 & 2 \end{bmatrix}'$. The apostrophe is required to indicate that this is a column vector. Next, we double click on the **Gain block,** we enter the row vector $\begin{bmatrix} 2 & 3 & 4 \end{bmatrix}$, and for Multiplication we choose **Matrix (u*K)**. Initially, the Display block may show just one value with two small black triangles at the lower right corner. This tells us that we must resize the Display block in both directions to see all the elements of the resultant 3×3 matrix.

2.11 The Relational Operator Block

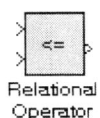

The **Relational Operator block** performs the specified comparison of its two inputs. We select the relational operator connecting the two inputs with the Relational Operator parameter. The block updates to display the selected operator. The supported operations are given below.

Operation Description:

== TRUE if the first input is equal to the second input

~= TRUE if the first input is not equal to the second input

<   TRUE if the first input is less than the second input

<= TRUE if the first input is less than or equal to the second input

>= TRUE if the first input is greater than or equal to the second input

>   TRUE if the first input is greater than the second input

Example 2.11

The model shown in Figure 2.21 determines whether the determinants of the matrices A and B defined below are equal or unequal.

$$A = \begin{bmatrix} 2 & -3 & 5 \\ 1 & 0 & -1 \\ -2 & 1 & 0 \end{bmatrix} \quad B = \begin{bmatrix} 2 & 1 & -2 \\ -3 & 0 & 1 \\ 5 & -1 & 0 \end{bmatrix}$$

In MATLAB's Command Window, we enter A and B as follows:

A=[2 -3 5; 1 0 -1; -2 1 0]; B=[2 1 -2; -3 0 1; 5 -1 0];

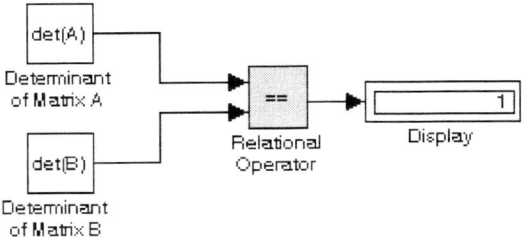

Figure 2.21. Model for Example 2.11

Chapter 2 The Commonly Used Blocks Library

In the Source Block Parameters dialog box of the Constant blocks we enter det(A) and det(B). The Display block in Figure 2.21 indicates that the determinants of Matrices A and B are equal.

2.12 The Logical Operator Block

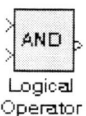

The **Logical Operator block** performs the specified logical operation on its inputs. An input value is TRUE (1) if it is nonzero and FALSE (0) if it is zero. The Boolean operation connecting the inputs is selected with the Operator parameter list in the Function Block Parameters dialog box. The block updates to display the selected operator. The logical operations are given below.

Operation Description:

    AND – TRUE if all inputs are TRUE

    OR – TRUE if at least one input is TRUE

    NAND – TRUE if at least one input is FALSE

    NOR – TRUE when no inputs are TRUE

    XOR – TRUE if an odd number of inputs are TRUE

    NOT – TRUE if the input is FALSE and vice-versa

The number of input ports is specified with the Number of input ports parameter. The output type is specified with the Output data type mode and/or the Output data type parameters. An output value is 1 if TRUE and 0 if FALSE.

Example 2.12

The model shown in Figure 2.22 simulates the Boolean expression $D = A \cdot B + C$[*] where the dot denotes the ANDing of the variables A, B, and the plus (+) sign denotes the ORing of $A \cdot B$ with C. The blocks indicated as Variable A, Variable B, and Variable C are Constant blocks. We specify the values $A = 1$, $B = 0$, and $C = 1$ in MATLAB's Command Window, and after exe-

---

[*] *The ANDing operation has precedence over the ORing operation. For instance, the Boolean expression $A \cdot B + C$ implies that A must first be ANDed with B and the result must be ORed with C as shown in Figure 2.22. The dot symbol between A and B is often omitted. For a detailed discussion on Boolean expressions, please refer to Digital Circuit Analysis and Design with an Introduction to CPLDs and FPGAs, ISBN 0-9744239-6-3.*

cution of the Simulation start command we observe the values 0 and 1 in Display 1 and Display 2 blocks respectively.

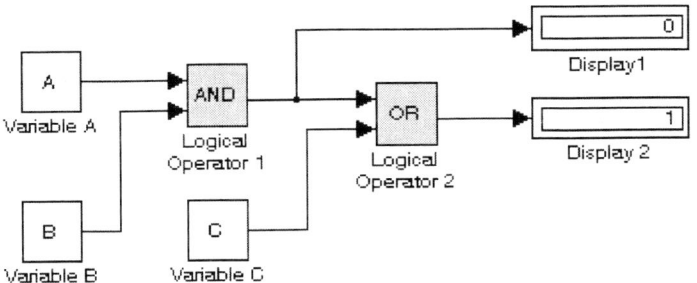

Figure 2.22. Model for Example 2.12

2.13 The Saturation Block

The **Saturation block** establishes upper and lower bounds for an input signal. When the input signal is within the range specified by the Lower limit and Upper limit parameters, the input signal passes through unchanged. When the input signal is outside these bounds, the signal is clipped to the upper or lower bound. When the Lower limit and Upper limit parameters are set to the same value, the block outputs that value.

Example 2.13

For the model shown in Figure 2.23 the Constant block performs the function $y = 3x^2$ where x and y are specified in MATLAB's Command Window as

x=0: 1: 6; y=3.*x.^2;

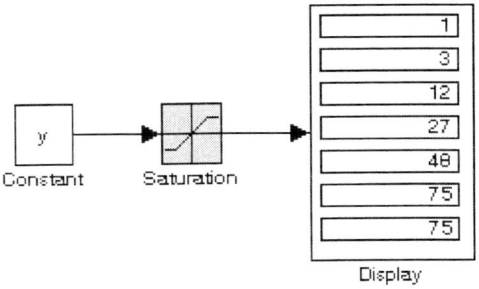

Figure 2.23. Model for Example 2.13

Chapter 2 The Commonly Used Blocks Library

and on the Function Block Parameters dialog box for the Saturation block we have specified the Upper limit at 75 and the Lower limit at 1. The MATLAB statement above specifies 7 (0 through 6) values of x and these are shown in the Display block of Figure 2.23. The last is also 75 because we specified the Upper limit to be that value.

2.14 The Integrator Block

The **Integrator block** integrates its input and it is used with continuous–time signals. As shown in the **Configuration Parameters** dialog box which is displayed after selecting the Integrator block and clicking on **Simulation** in the model window, we can use different numerical integration methods to compute the **Integrator** block's output. The **Configuration Parameters** window that appears when we double–click on the Integrator block and then on Simulation shown in Figure 2.24.

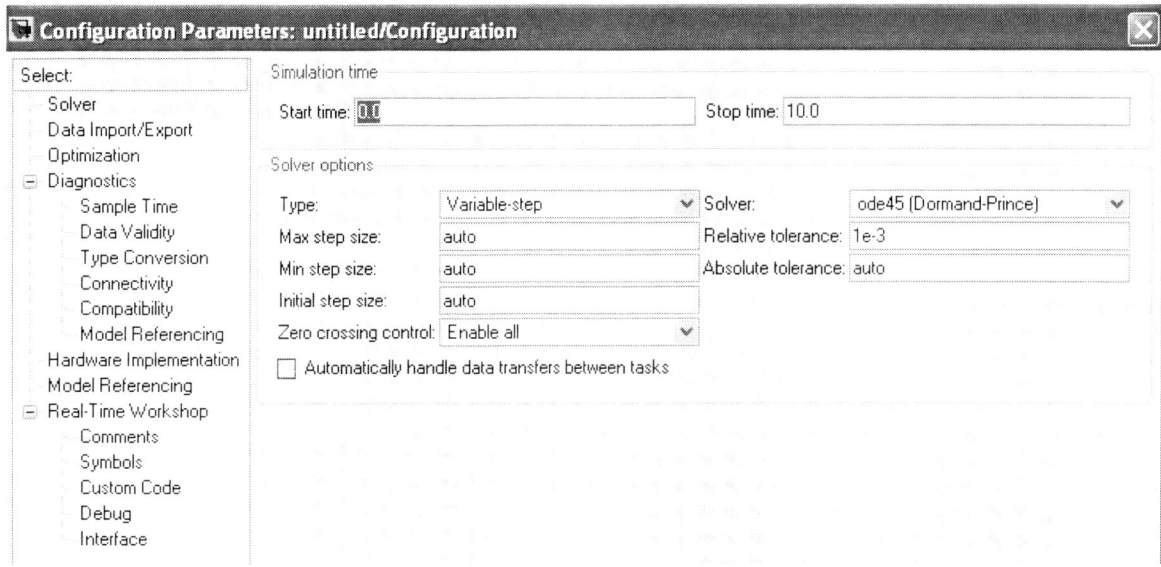

Figure 2.24. The configuration parameters window for the Integrator block

Simulink treats the Integrator block as a dynamic system with one state, its output. The Integrator block's input is the state's time derivative. The selected solver computes the output of the Integrator block at the current time step, using the current input value and the value of the state at the previous time step. The block also provides the solver with an initial condition for use in computing the block's initial state at the beginning of a simulation run. The default value of the initial condition is 0.

The Integrator Block

The **Function Block Parameter** dialog box shown in Figure 2.25 allows us to specify another value for the initial condition or create an initial value input port on the block. It also allows us to specify the upper and lower limits of integration, create an input that resets the block's output (state) to its initial value, depending on how the input changes, and create an optional state output that allows us to use the value of the block's output to trigger a block reset. Depending on the options selected, the Integrator block appears in any of the nine forms shown in Figure 2.26.

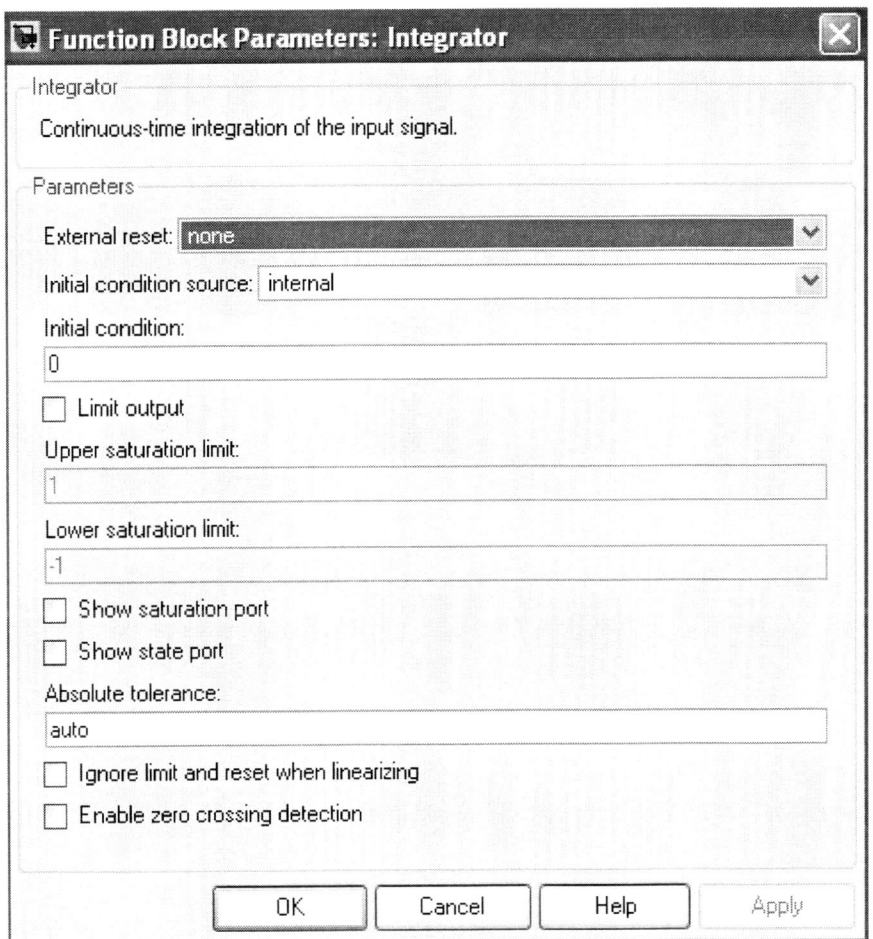

Figure 2.25. Function Block Parameters for the Continuous Integrator block

The Integrator 1 block in Figure 2.26 is the default block. This block appears when the Function Block Parameters in the dialog box are in their default states. The appearance of the Integrator 2 through Integrator 9 blocks depends on the settings in the block's parameter dialog box. Thus,

Integrator 2 block – Initial condition source: **external**. All other parameters in their default states.

Integrator 3 block – Limit output: **check mark**. All other parameters in their default states.

Integrator 4 block – External reset: **rising**. All other parameters in their default states.

Introduction to Simulink with Engineering Applications
Copyright © Orchard Publications

Chapter 2 The Commonly Used Blocks Library

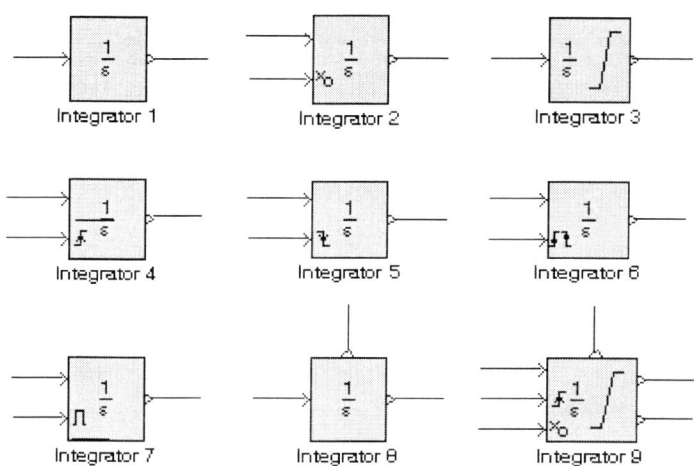

Figure 2.26. Different configurations for the Integrator block

Integrator 5 block – External reset: **falling**. All other parameters in their default states.

Integrator 6 block – External reset: **either**. All other parameters in their default states.

Integrator 7 block – External reset: **level**. All other parameters in their default states.

Integrator 8 block – Show state port: **check mark**. All other parameters in their default states.

Integrator 9 block – External reset: **rising**.

> Initial condition source: **external**.
>
> Limit output: **check mark**
>
> Show saturation port: **check mark**
>
> Show state port: **check mark**

The **Integrator** block's state port allows us to avoid creating algebraic loops when creating an integrator that resets itself based on the value of its output. An algebraic loop is formed when two or more blocks with direct feedthrough (the output of the block at time t, is a function of the input at time t) form a feedback loop. The basic problem with algebraic loops is that the output, y, at time, t, is a function of itself. An **algebraic loop** generally occurs when an input port with direct feedthrough is driven by the output of the same block, either directly, or by a feedback path through other blocks with direct feedthrough. An example of an algebraic loop is the simple loop shown in Figure 2.27.

For the model of Figure 2.27, $y = 10 - y$ or $y = 5$.

Another example of a model with algebraic loops is the model of Figure 1.19, Solution of 3 equations with 3 unknowns, Chapter 1, Page 1–19.

The Integrator Block

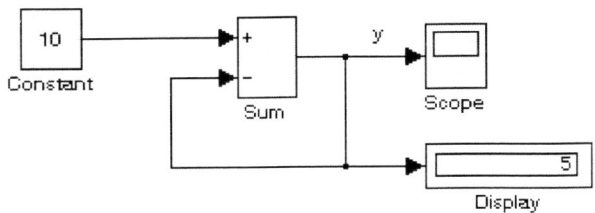

Figure 2.27. An example of an algebraic loop

For further discussion on algebraic loops, please refer to Simulink's User Manual, Help menu for the Integrator block, and MATLAB Technical Report 7.1 – Algebraic Loops and S–Functions, http://www.utexas.edu/math/Matlab/Manual/tec7.1.html. S–Functions are described in Chapter 15.

The **Integrator** block's state port makes it possible to avoid creating algebraic loops when creating an integrator that resets itself based on the value of its output. The state port shown in Integrators 8 and 9 in Figure 2.26 is intended to be used specifically for self-resetting integrators (see Creating Self-Resetting Integrators), and Handing off a state from one enabled subsystem to another (see Handing Off States Between Enabled Subsystems) in Simulink's Help menu. The state port should only be used in these two scenarios. When updating a model, Simulink checks to ensure that the state port is being used in one of these two scenarios. If not, Simulink signals an error.

Example 2.14

The model of Figure 2.28 simulates the differential equation

$$\frac{d^2 v_C}{dt^2} + 4\frac{dv_C}{dt} + 3v_C = 3u_0(t)$$

subject to the initial conditions $v_C(0) = 0.5$ and $v'_C(0) = 0$.

The Constant 1 and Constant 2 blocks represent the initial conditions.

Chapter 2 The Commonly Used Blocks Library

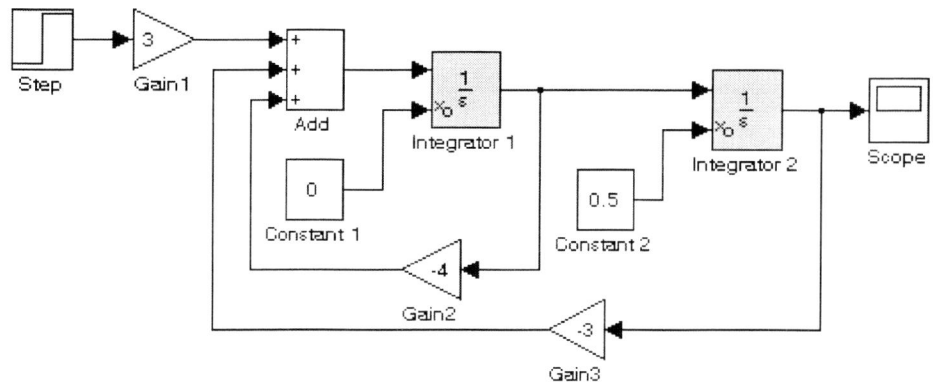

Figure 2.28. Model for Example 2.14

2.15 The Unit Delay Block

The **Unit Delay** block delays its input by the specified sample period. That is, the output equals the input delayed by one sample. If the model contains multirate transitions, we must add Unit Delay blocks between the slow–to–fast transitions. For fast–to–slow transitions we use Zero–Order Hold blocks. The Zero–Order Hold block is described in Subsection 5.2.3, Chapter 5, Page 5–23. For multirate transitions it is preferable to use the Rate Transition block since it is easier to use and offers a wider range of options. Multirate transitions and the Rate Transition block are described in Subsection 12.1.8, Chapter 12, Page 12–8.

This Unit Delay block is equivalent to the z^{-1} discrete–time operator shown in Figure 2.29. It is one of the basic blocks for designing digital filters as shown in Figure 2.30.

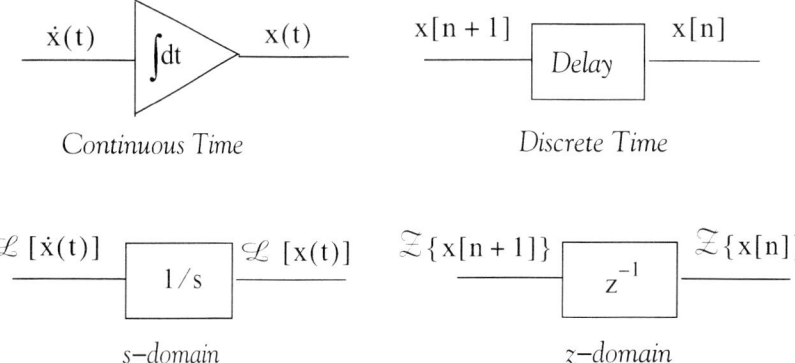

Figure 2.29. Analogy between integration and delay devices

The Unit Delay Block

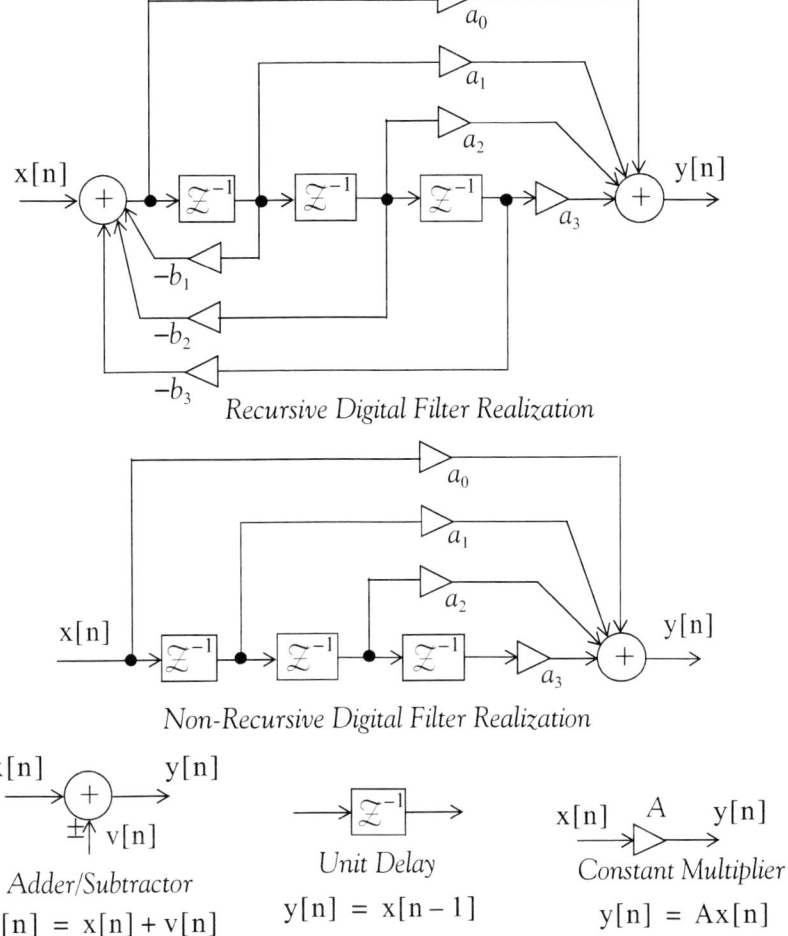

Figure 2.30. Recursive and non-recursive digital filters

The unit delay appears also in the definition of the discrete time system transfer function H(z) shown in relation (2.1) below.

$$H(z) = \frac{N(z)}{D(z)} = \frac{a_0 + a_1 z^{-1} + a_2 z^{-2} + \ldots + a_k z^{-k}}{1 + b_1 z^{-1} + b_2 z^{-2} + \ldots + b_k z^{-k}} \qquad (2.1)$$

With the Unit Delay block, the first sampling period and initial conditions are specified in the **Function Block Parameters** dialog box. The time between samples is specified with the Sample time parameter. A setting of −1 means the sample time is inherited.

The Unit Delay block also allows for discretization of one or more signals in time, or for resampling the signal at a different rate. If our model contains multirate transitions, then we must add Unit Delay blocks between the slow–to–fast transitions. The sample rate of this block must be set to that of the slower block. An example is presented in the next section of this chapter.

Chapter 2 The Commonly Used Blocks Library

2.16 The Discrete–Time Integrator Block

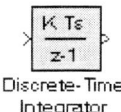
Discrete-Time Integrator

The **Discrete–Time Integrator** block performs discrete–time integration or accumulation of a signal. We use this block in discrete–time systems instead of the Continuous Integrator block in continuous–time systems. This block can integrate or accumulate using the Forward Euler, Backward Euler, and Trapezoidal methods. For a given step n, Simulink updates $y(n)$ and $x(n+1)$. The block's sample time in integration mode is T and in triggered sample time is ΔT. In accumulation mode, $T = 1$ and the block's sample time determines when the block's output is computed but not the output's value. The constant K is the gain value. Values are clipped according to upper or lower limits. Purely discrete systems can be simulated using any of the solvers. For additional information, please refer to the Simulink Owner's Manual or Simulink's Help menu.

The Discrete–Time Integrator block allows us to:

1. Define initial conditions on the block dialog box or as input to the block.
2. Define an input gain (K) value.
3. Output the block state.
4. Define upper and lower limits on the integral.
5. Reset the state depending on an additional reset input.

With continuous time systems, the **Forward Euler** method, also known as **Forward Rectangular**, or **left–hand approximation**, truncates the Taylor series[*] after two terms. Thus,

$$y(t+h) = y(t) + hy'(t) \qquad (2.2)$$

and assuming that the value at point t is correct, the Forward Euler method computes the value at point $t+h$. With Simulink, the continuous time integrator $1/s$ in discrete time integration with the Forward Euler method is approximated by $T/(z-1)$. As mentioned earlier, T is the block's sample time. The Forward Euler method is the default. With this method, input port 1 does not have direct feedthrough. The resulting expression for the output of the block at step n is

$$y(n) = y(n-1) + K \cdot T \cdot u(n-1) \qquad (2.3)$$

The steps to compute the output are listed in the Help menu for this block.

---

[*] *For a detailed discussion on Taylor series, please refer to Numerical Analysis Using MATLAB and Spreadsheets, ISBN 0-9709511-1-6*

The Discrete–Time Integrator Block

The **Backward Euler method**, also known as **Backward Rectangular** or **right-hand approximation**, also truncates the Taylor series after two terms. The difference is that the derivative is evaluated at point $t + h$ instead of at point t. Thus,

$$y(t + h) = y(t) + hy'(t + h) \qquad (2.4)$$

With Simulink, the continuous time integrator $1/s$ in discrete time integration with the Backward Euler method is approximated by $Tz/(z-1)$. With this method, input port 1 has direct feedthrough. The resulting expression for the output of the block at step n is

$$y(n) = y(n-1) + K \cdot T \cdot u(n) \qquad (2.5)$$

The steps to compute the output are listed in the Help menu.

In numerical analysis, relation (2.6) below is known as the first–order trapezoidal integration rule.

$$y(n) = \frac{1}{2}[x(n) + x(n-1)] + y(n-1) \qquad n \geq 0 \qquad (2.6)$$

With Simulink, the continuous time integrator $1/s$ in discrete time integration with the **Trapezoidal method** is approximated by $(T/2)(z+1)/(z-1)$. With this method, input port 1 has direct feedthrough. For any T, the resulting expression for the output of the block at step n is

$$y(n) = y(n-1) + K \cdot (T/2) \cdot [u(n) + u(n-1)] \qquad (2.7)$$

It is left as an end–of–chapter exercise for the reader to prove that for very small fixed T, relation (2.7) above can be approximated by

$$y(n) \approx y(n-1) + K \cdot (T/2) \cdot u(n-1)$$

If T is variable (i.e. obtained from the triggering times), the block uses another algorithm to compute its outputs. The steps to compute the output are listed in the Help menu.

A **discrete–time accumulator** is characterized by the difference equation

$$y(n) = \sum_{\ell = -\infty}^{n} x[\ell] = \sum_{\ell = -\infty}^{n-1} x[\ell] + x[n] = y[n-1] + x[n] \qquad (2.8)$$

The output $y[n]$ at time instant n is the sum of the input sample $x[n]$ at time instant n and the previous output $y[n-1]$ at time instant $n-1$, which is the sum of all previous input sample values from $-\infty$ to $n-1$. In other words, the accumulator cumulative adds, i.e., it accumulates all input sample values.

A discrete–time integrator may be represented by any of the blocks shown in Figure 2.31. Any of these blocks can be selected from the Integrator method menu in the **Function Blocks Parameters** dialog box.

Chapter 2 The Commonly Used Blocks Library

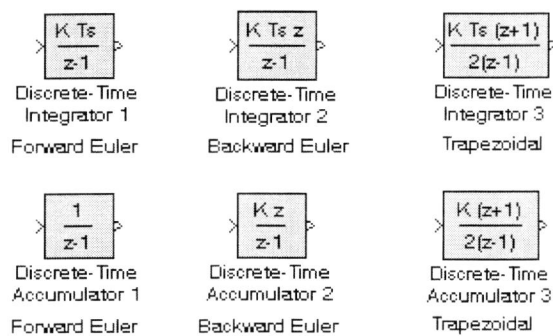

Figure 2.31. Discrete-time integrator blocks

Example 2.15

For the model of Figure 2.32, the parameters of a **Pulse Generator Block** found under the Sources Simulink Library are set as follows:

Pulse type: **Time based**

Time (t): **Use simulation time**
Amplitude: **0.25**

Period (secs): **2**

Pulse width (% of period): **50**

Phase delay (secs): **0**

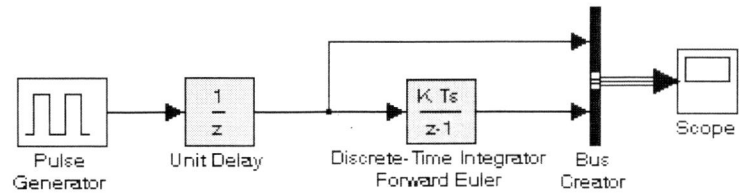

Figure 2.32. Model for Example 2.15

After the Simulation start command is issued, the Scope in Figure 2.33 displays the pulse waveform which is the output of the Unit Delay block and the output of the Discrete–Time Integrator which is the accumulation (integration) of the input waveform. To center the waveform on the scope, we right-click on the y–axis, we left–click on the Axes properties, and in the Scope properties window we enter Y–min: –1.5, and Y–max: 1.5.

Data Types and The Data Type Conversion Block

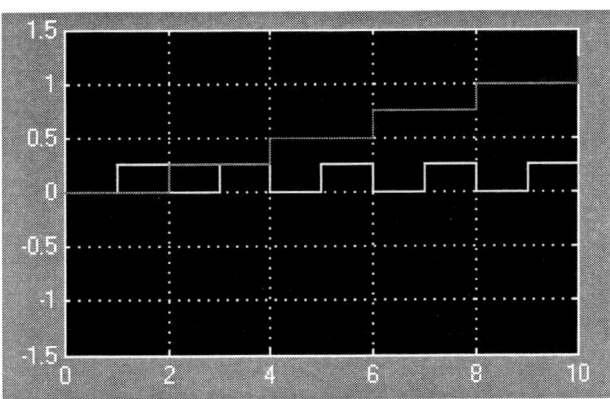

Figure 2.33. Waveforms for the model of Figure 2.32

2.17 Data Types and The Data Type Conversion Block

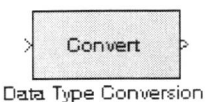

There are two classes of data types: those defined by MATLAB and Simulink users, and those strictly defined by MATLAB. The latter type is referred to as MATLAB built–in data types. Simulink supports all built–in MATLAB data types except **int64** and **uint64**. Table 2.1 lists the built-in data types supported by Simulink.

TABLE 2.1 Built-in data types supported by Simulink

Type Name	Description
single	Single-precision floating point
double	Double-precision floating point
int8	Signed 8-bit integer
uint8	Unsigned 8-bit integer
int16	Signed 16-bit integer
uint16	Unsigned 16-bit integer
int32	Signed 32-bit integer
uint32	Unsigned 32-bit integer

In addition to the above, Simulink defines the boolean (1 or 0) type and these are represented internally by the **uint8** values.

Introduction to Simulink with Engineering Applications
Copyright © Orchard Publications

Chapter 2 The Commonly Used Blocks Library

The **Data Type Conversion** block converts an input signal of any Simulink data type to the data type and scaling specified by the block's Output data type mode, Output data type, and/or Output scaling parameters. The input can be any real- or complex-valued signal. Thus, if the input is real, the output is real, and if the input is complex, the output is complex. We must specify the data type and/or scaling for the conversion. The **Data Type Conversion** block handles any data type supported by Simulink, including fixed-point data types.

The **Input and output to have equal** parameter is used to select the method by which the input is processed. The possible values are **Real World Value (RWV)** and **Stored Integer (SI)**:

We select **Real World Value (RWV)** to treat the input as $V = SQ + B^*$ where S is the slope and B is the bias. V is used to produce $Q = (V - B)/S$, which is stored in the output. This is the default value. Select **Stored Integer (SI)** to treat the input as a stored integer, Q. The value of Q is directly used to produce the output. In this mode, the input and output are identical except that the input is a raw integer lacking proper scaling information. Selecting **Stored Integer** may be useful if we are generating code for a fixed-point processor so that the resulting code only uses integers and does not use floating-point operations. We also can use **Stored Integer** if we want to partition our model based on hardware characteristics. For example, part of our model may involve simulating hardware that produces integers as output.

Example 2.16

The model is shown in Figure 2.34 uses three Data Type Conversion blocks. In the Data Type Conversion 1 block the input is processed as Stored Integer (SI) and scales the value 63 to be shown as 7.875. In the Data Type Conversion 2 block the input is processed as Real World Value (RWV) so that the input and output will be equal. We use the third block to treat the input as a Stored Integer with no scaling so that the Display 3 block will show the true value 63.

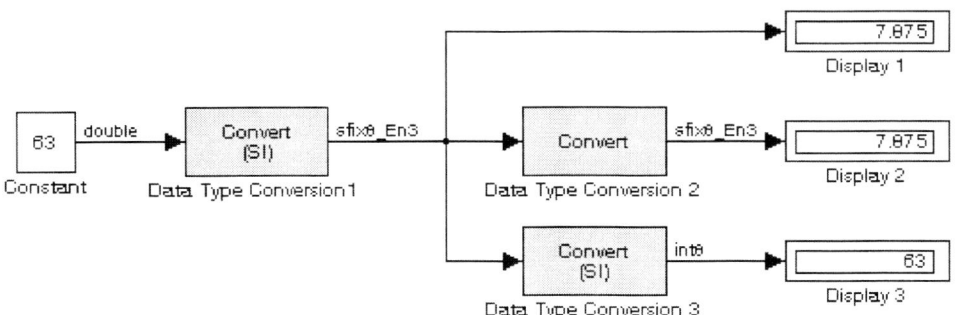

Figure 2.34. Model for Example 2.16

---

* We observe that this is the equation of a straight line with non-zero y-intercept, that is, $y = mx + b$

Data Types and The Data Type Conversion Block

We double-click the **Data Type Conversion 1** block in Figure 2.34 and on the **Function Block Parameters** dialog box shown in Figure 2.35, we change the **Output data type mode** from **Inherit via back propagation** to **Specify via dialog**. On the new **Function Block Parameters** dialog box shown in Figure 2.36, we enter the following:

Output data type: **sfix(8)**

Output scaling value: **2^−3**

Input and output to have equal: **Stored Integer (SI)**

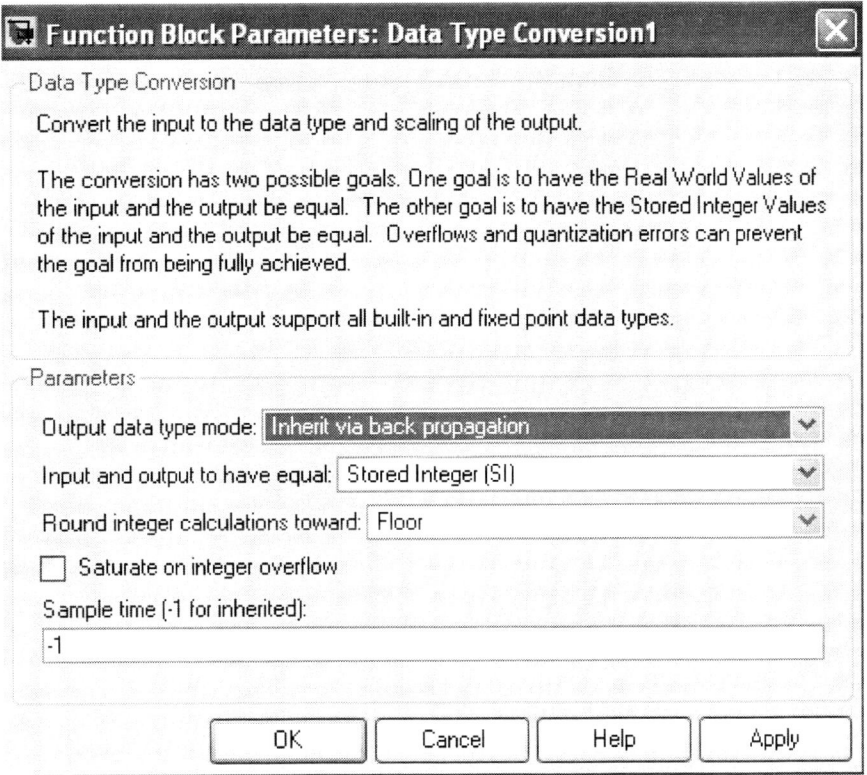

Figure 2.35. Function Block Parameters Dialog Box 1 for Example 2.16

The labels in Figure 2.34 are displayed by choosing **Format > Port/Signal Displays > Port Data Types**. Display 1 block shows the value 7.875. This is because the binary presentation of 63 with 8 bits is 00111111 and since we specified the Output scaling value as **2^−3**, the binary point is shifted 3 places to the left of the least significant bit, and becomes 00111.111 whose value in decimal is 7.875. Display 2 block shows the same value for reasons explained below. Display 3 block shows the true value 63. This is because we specified the Output scaling value as **2^0**, and thus the binary number is 00111111 whose value in decimal is 63.

Chapter 2 The Commonly Used Blocks Library

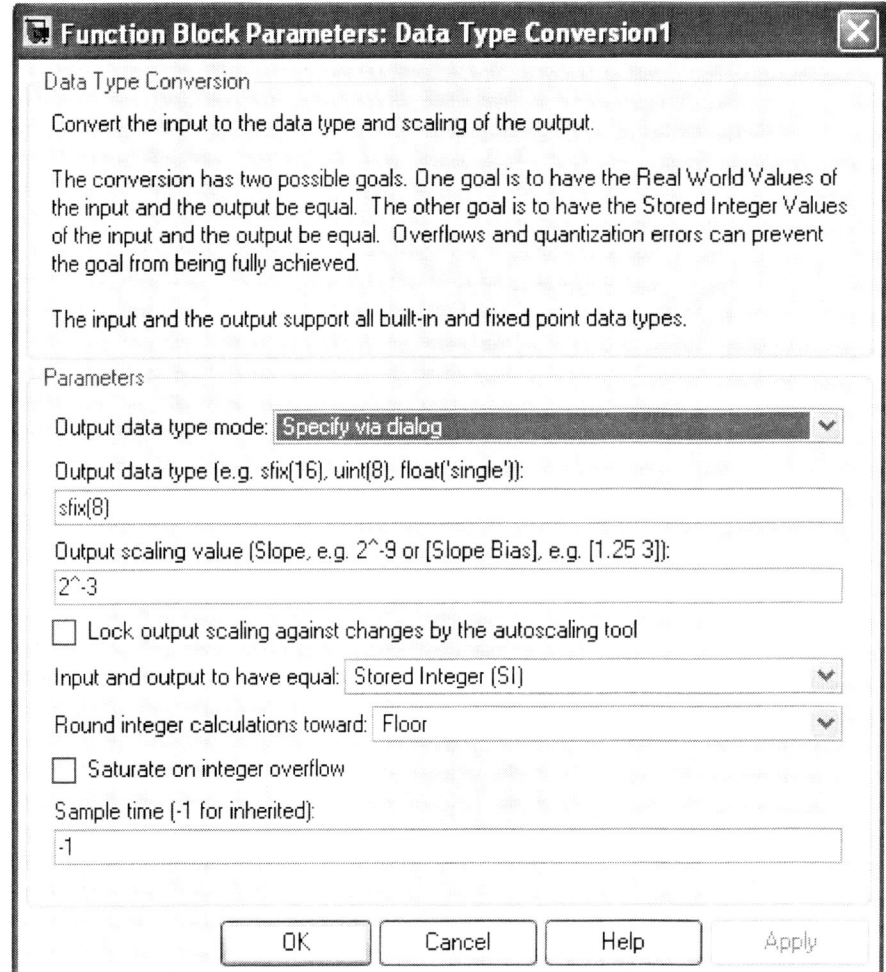

Figure 2.36. Function Block Parameters Dialog Box for the Data Type Conversion 1 block, Example 2.16

Next, we double-click the **Data Type Conversion 2** block and we enter the following information:

Output data type mode: Specify via dialog

Output data type: sfix(8)

Output scaling value: 2^–3

Input and output to have equal: Real World Value (RWV)

The Function Block Parameters dialog box for the Data Type Conversion 2 block are as shown in Figure 2.37.

Data Types and The Data Type Conversion Block

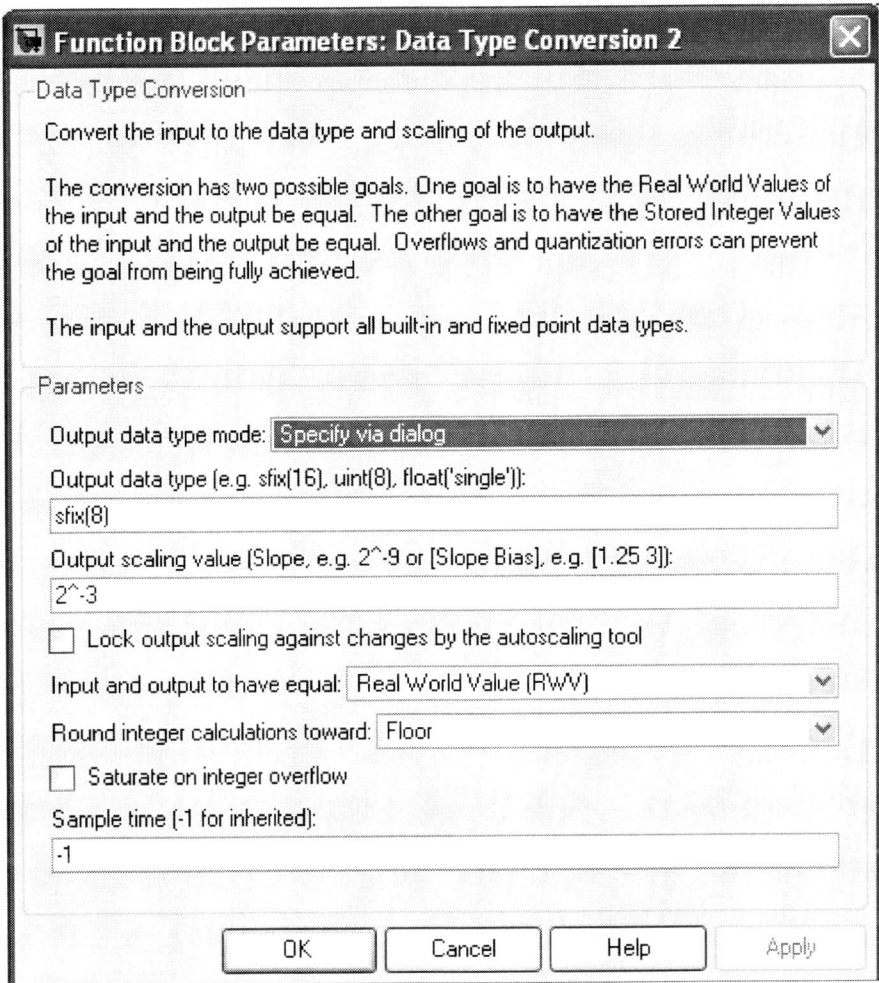

Figure 2.37. Function Block Parameters Dialog Box for the Data Type Conversion 2 block, Example 2.16

Finally, we double-click the **Data Type Conversion 3** block and we enter the following:

Output data type mode: **Specify via dialog**

Output data type: **sfix(8)**

Output scaling value: **2^0**

Input and output to have equal: **Stored Integer (SI)**

The Function Block Parameters dialog box for the Data Type Conversion 3 block are as shown in Figure 2.38.

Chapter 2 The Commonly Used Blocks Library

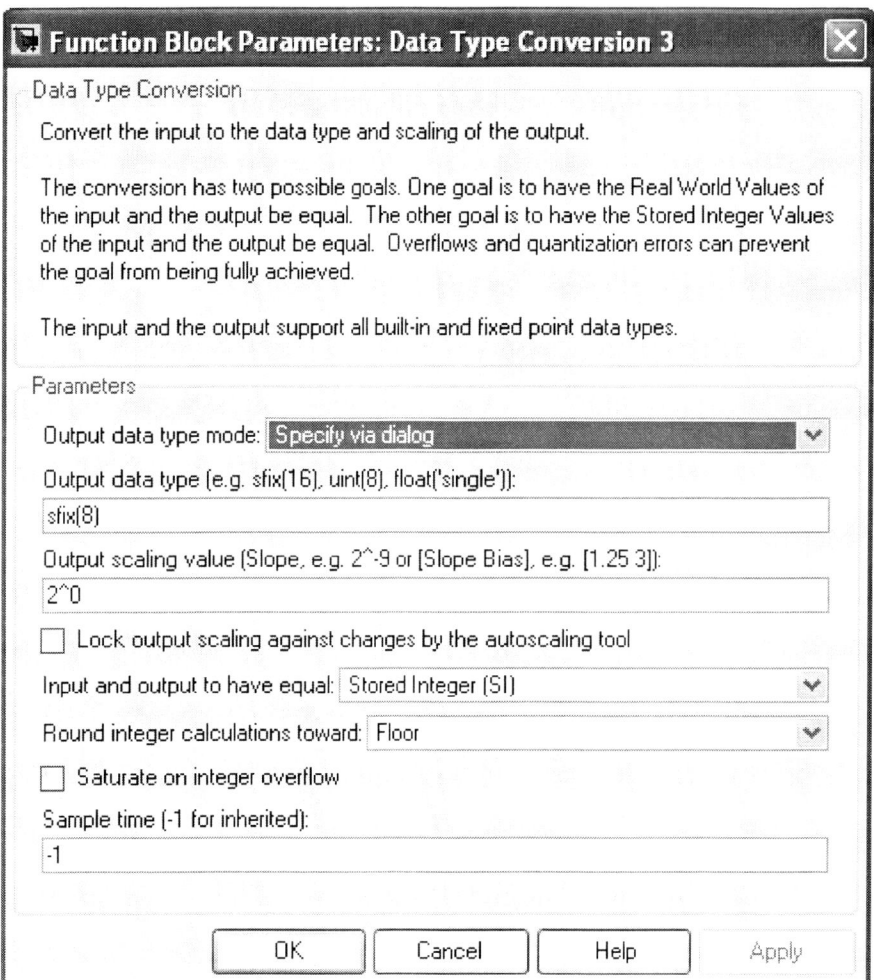

Figure 2.38. Function Block Parameters Dialog Box for the Data Type Conversion 3 block, Example 2.16

2.18 Summary

- A **Subsystem** block represents a subsystem of the system that contains it.

- **Inport** blocks are ports that serve as links from outside a system into the system.

- **Outport** blocks are output ports for a subsystem.

- The **Ground** block can be used to connect blocks whose input ports are not connected to other blocks. If we run a simulation with blocks having unconnected input ports, Simulink issues warning messages. Using Ground blocks to ground those blocks avoids warning messages. The **Ground** block outputs a signal with zero value. The data type of the signal is the same as that of the port to which it is connected.

- The **Terminator** block can be used to cap blocks whose output ports are not connected to other blocks. If we run a simulation with blocks having unconnected output ports, Simulink issues warning messages. Using Terminator blocks to cap those blocks avoids warning messages.

- The **Constant** block generates a real or complex constant value. The block generates scalar (1x1 2–D array), vector (1–D array), or matrix (2–D array) output, depending on the dimensionality of the Constant value parameter and the setting of the Interpret vector parameters as 1–D parameter. By default, the **Constant block** outputs a signal whose data type and complexity are the same as that of the block's Constant value parameter. However, we can specify the output to be any supported data type supported by Simulink, including fixed-point data types.

- The **Product** block performs multiplication or division of its inputs. This block produces outputs using either element-wise or matrix multiplication, depending on the value of the **Multiplication parameter**. We specify the operations with the Number of inputs parameter. Multiply(*) and divide(/) characters indicate the operations to be performed on the inputs.

- The **Scope** block displays waveforms as functions of simulation time. The Scope block can have multiple y-axes with a common time range.

- We use **Bus Creator** blocks to create signal buses and **Bus Selector** blocks to access the components of a bus. Simulink hides the name of a Bus Creator and Bus Selector blocks when we copy them from the Simulink library to a model. However, we can make the names visible by clicking **Show Name** on the **Format** menu.

- The **Bus Editor** allows us to change the properties of the bus types objects. We select the Bus Editor from the model's Tools menu.

- We can add an annotation to any unoccupied area of our model. To insert an annotation, we double-click in an unoccupied section of the model, a small rectangle appears, and the cursor changes to an insertion point. We start typing the annotation text and we observe that each line is centered within the rectangle. Then we can move it to the desired location by dragging it. We can choose another Font and Text Alignment from the Format menu. We can delete an

Chapter 2 The Commonly Used Blocks Library

annotation by first selecting it, holding down the Shift key and pressing the Delete or Backspace key.

- The **Mux** block combines its inputs into a single output. An input can be a scalar, vector, or matrix signal. Simulink hides the name of a **Mux block** when we drag it from the Simulink block library to a model. However, we can make the name visible by clicking **Show Name** on the **Format** menu.

- The **Demux** block extracts the components of an input signal and outputs the components as separate signals. The Number of outputs parameter allows us to specify the number and, optionally, the dimensionality of each output port. If we do not specify the dimensionality of the outputs, the block determines the dimensionality of the outputs for us. Simulink hides the name of a Demux block when we drag it from the Simulink library to a model. However, we can make the name visible by clicking **Show Name** on the **Format** menu.

- The **Switch** block outputs the first input or the third input depending on the value of the second input. The first and third inputs are called **data inputs**. The second input is called the **control input** and it is specified on the **Function Block Parameters** for the **Switch block**. The following options are available:

    u2>=Threshold

    u2>Threshold

    u2~=0

    where u2~=0 indicates a non-zero condition.

- The **Divide** block is an implementation of the Product block. It can be used to multiply or divide inputs.

- The **Gain** block multiplies the input by a constant value (gain). The input and the gain can each be a scalar, vector, or matrix. We specify the value of the gain in the Gain parameter. The Multiplication parameter lets us specify element–wise or matrix multiplication. For matrix multiplication, this parameter also lets us indicate the order of the multiplicands.

- The **Relational Operator** block performs the specified comparison of its two inputs. We select the relational operator connecting the two inputs with the Relational Operator parameter. The block updates to display the selected operator. The supported operations are given below.

    Operation Description:

    == TRUE if the first input is equal to the second input

    ~= TRUE if the first input is not equal to the second input

    < TRUE if the first input is less than the second input

    <= TRUE if the first input is less than or equal to the second input

Summary

>= TRUE if the first input is greater than or equal to the second input

> TRUE if the first input is greater than the second input

- The **Logical Operator** block performs the specified logical operation on its inputs. An input value is TRUE (1) if it is nonzero and FALSE (0) if it is zero. The Boolean operation connecting the inputs is selected with the Operator parameter list in the Function Block Parameters window. The block updates to display the selected operator. The supported operations are given below.

Operation Description:

AND – TRUE if all inputs are TRUE

OR – TRUE if at least one input is TRUE

NAND – TRUE if at least one input is FALSE

NOR – TRUE when no inputs are TRUE

XOR – TRUE if an odd number of inputs are TRUE

NOT – TRUE if the input is FALSE and vice-versa

The number of input ports is specified with the Number of input ports parameter. The output type is specified with the Output data type mode and/or the Output data type parameters. An output value is 1 if TRUE and 0 if FALSE.

- The **Saturation** block sets upper and lower bounds on a signal. When the input signal is within the range specified by the Lower limit and Upper limit parameters, the input signal passes through unchanged. When the input signal is outside these bounds, the signal is clipped to the upper or lower bound. When the Lower limit and Upper limit parameters are set to the same value, the block outputs that value.

- The **Integrator** block outputs the integral of its input. We can use different numerical integration methods to compute the **Integrator** block's output. The **Integrator** block's state port allows us to avoid creating algebraic loops when creating an integrator that resets itself based on the value of its output. An algebraic loop is formed when two or more blocks with direct feedthrough (the output of the block at time t, is a function of the input at time t) form a feedback loop. The basic problem with algebraic loops is that the output, y, at time, t, is a function of itself.

- The **Unit Delay** block delays its input by the specified sample period. That is, the output equals the input delayed by one sample. This block is equivalent to the z^{-1} discrete–time operator. This block allows for discretization of one or more signals in time, or for resampling the signal at a different rate. If our model contains multirate transitions, then we must add **Unit Delay** blocks between the slow–to–fast transitions. The sample rate of the **Unit Delay** block must be set to that of the slower block.

Chapter 2 The Commonly Used Blocks Library

- The **Discrete−Time Integrator block** performs discrete-time integration or accumulation of a signal. This block appears also in the **Discrete Library** Browser. We use this block in discrete-time systems instead of the Continuous Integrator block in continuous−time systems. The block can integrate or accumulate using the Forward Euler, Backward Euler, and Trapezoidal methods.

- There are two classes of data types: those defined by MATLAB and Simulink users, and those strictly defined by MATLAB. The latter type is referred to as MATLAB built-in data types. Simulink supports all built-in MATLAB data types except **int64** and **uint64**. Table 2.1 lists the built-in data types supported by Simulink.

- The **Data Type Conversion block** converts an input signal of any Simulink data type to the data type and scaling specified by the block's Output data type mode, Output data type, and/or Output scaling parameters. The input can be any real− or complex−valued signal. If the input is real, the output is real. If the input is complex, the output is complex. This block requires that we specify the data type and/or scaling for the conversion. Also, the Data Type Conversion block handles any data type supported by Simulink, including fixed−point data types. The **Input and output to have equal** parameter is used to select the method by which the input is processed. The possible values are **Real World Value (RWV)** and **Stored Integer (SI)**.

2.19 Exercises

1. Repeat Example 2.6 using the Mux block instead of the Bus Creator block.

2. It is desired to convert a DC signal from 2.5 volts to 5.0 volts, another DC signal from 12 volts to 15 volts, and a third from +15 volts to −15 volts. The conversions are to be performed at a distant location. Create a model that includes a Bus Creator block, a Signal bus, and a Bus Selector block to accomplish these conversions.

3. Using Constant blocks, a Product block, and the Display block, perform the operation $(3+j4)/(4+j3) \times (5-j8)$.

4. Using a Constant block, a Gain block, and a Display block, perform the matrix multiplication $A \cdot A^*$ where

$$A = \begin{bmatrix} 1+j2 & j \\ 3 & 2-j3 \end{bmatrix} \qquad A^* = \begin{bmatrix} 1-j2 & -j \\ 3 & 2+j3 \end{bmatrix}$$

5. Create a model similar to that of Example 2.5 with the constant 255 as input that will display the true value in one Display block and will scale this number by a factor of eight to be shown in another Display block.

6. Explain why when the Start simulation command is issued for the model shown below, an error message is displayed.

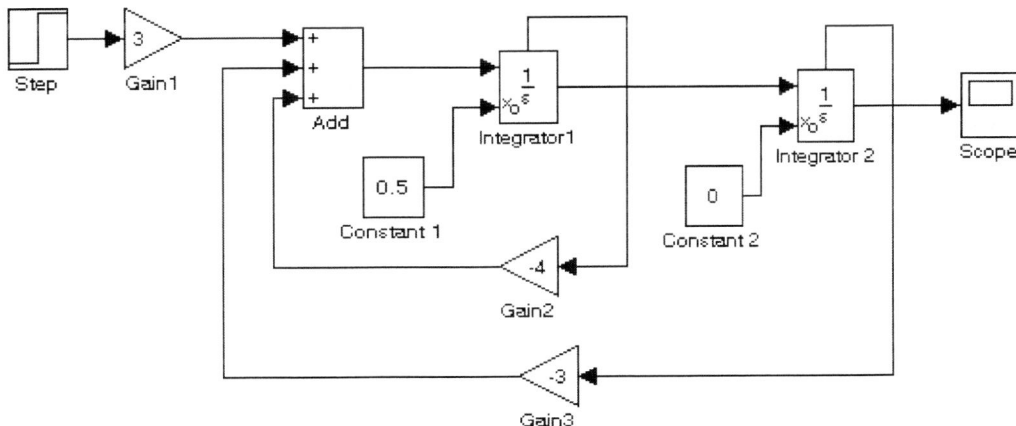

7. The parameters of a Pulse Generator Block found under the Sources Simulink Library are set as follows:

Pulse type: Time based

Time (t): Use simulation time
Amplitude: 0.25

Chapter 2 The Commonly Used Blocks Library

Period (secs): **2**

Pulse width (% of period): **50**

Phase delay (secs): **0**

Integrate this pulse using a Unit Delay block and the Backward Euler integration method. Compare the output with the Forward Euler Integration block in Example 2.9.

8. Create a model to simulate the Boolean expression $D = A(\bar{B} + C) + \bar{A}B$.[*] Display the value of the output variable D for all combinations of the variables A, B, and C.[†]

9. Using a model with a Relational Operator block, prove or disprove that the beta function $B(5, 4)$ is equal to the gamma function $\Gamma(5) \cdot \Gamma(4)/\Gamma(5 + 4)$.

10. Create a model to display a three–phase power system on a single Scope block where the waveforms of three phases are three sine waves 120° degrees apart.

11. Create a model to display a sine wave with unity amplitude clipped at points $+0.5$ and -0.5.

12. Prove that relation (2.7), Page 2-27, i.e.,

$$y(n) = y(n-1) + K \cdot (T/2) \cdot [u(n) + u(n-1)]$$

for very small fixed T, the above relation can be approximated by the relation

$$y(n) \approx y(n-1) + K \cdot (T/2) \cdot u(n-1)$$

Hint: Assume that the input has the form

$$x(n) = e^{-naT}$$

---

[*] *Variables in parentheses have precedence over other operations.*
[†] *In other words, form the truth table for this Boolean expression. For a detailed discussion on truth tables, please refer to Digital Circuit Analysis and Design with an Introduction to CPLDs & FPGAs, ISBN 0-9744239-6-3.*

2.20 Solutions to End–of–Chapter Exercises

1.
We substitute the Bus Creator block with the Mux block, we double click on the Mux block and in the Function Block Parameters window, we change the number of inputs to 3, we assign a name to the simout block, and we save it by that name with the .mat extension

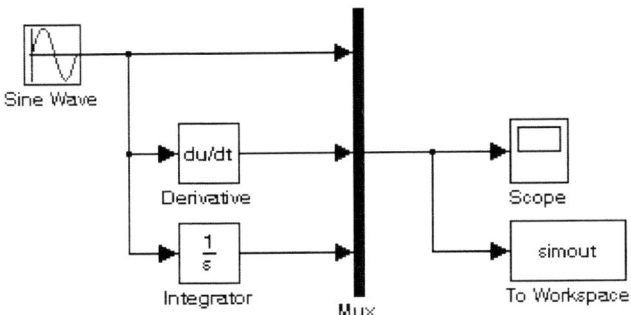

2.

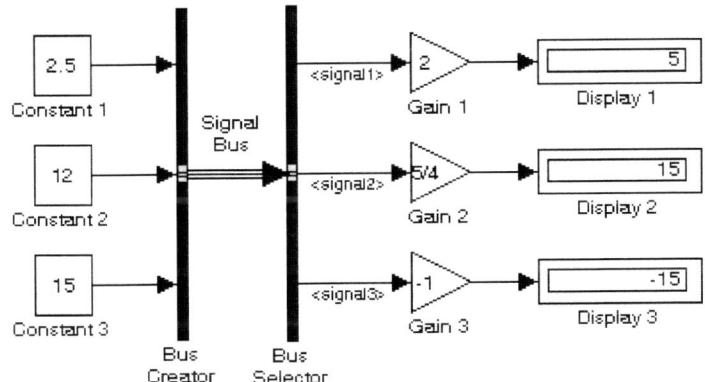

The Constant blocks are selected and dragged from the Sources Simulink Library Browser, the Bus Creator (left bus), Bus Selector (right bus), and Gain blocks from the Commonly Used Simulink Library Browser, and the Display blocks from the Sinks Simulink Library Browser. The Signal bus is normally shown as a single line arrow. It will change to a three line arrow when we click on the Start simulation icon.

The "Signal bus" annotation was created by double-clicking in a blank space of the model block, and in the small rectangle we entered this annotation. We moved it to location shown by dragging it.

3.
We connect the blocks as shown in the figure below. We double-click on the Constant blocks and we enter the complex numbers shown. Then, we double click on the Product block, and

on the Function Blocks Parameters, in Number of inputs, we type */*. This sequence defines 3 inputs, a multiplication, a division, and another multiplication. After executing the Start simulation command, it may be necessary to stretch the Display block to see the result.

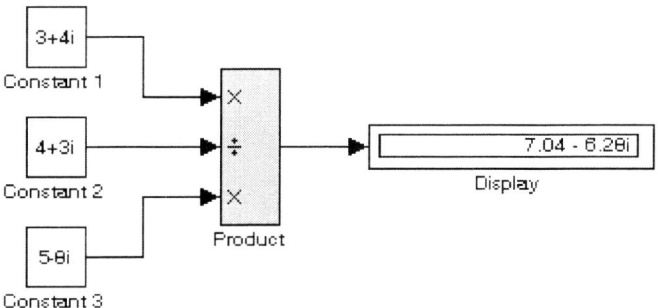

4.

$$A = \begin{bmatrix} 1+j2 & j \\ 3 & 2-j3 \end{bmatrix} \qquad A^* = \begin{bmatrix} 1-j2 & -j \\ 3 & 2+j3 \end{bmatrix}$$

We enter the elements of matrix A in the Constant block, and the elements of matrix A* in the Gain block. After the Simulate start command is executed, the product appears on the Display block.

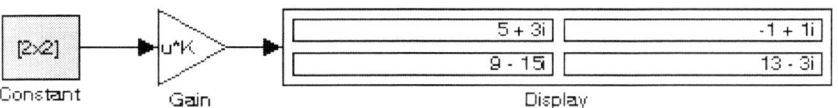

5.

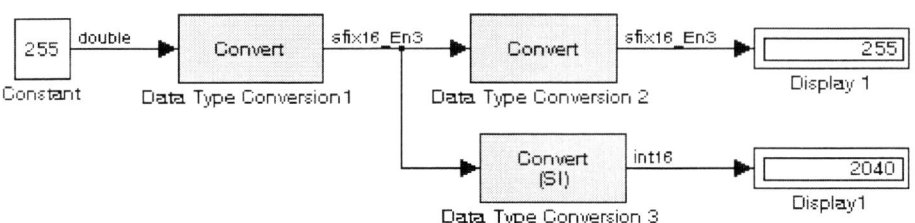

The **Data Type Conversion 1** block treats the input as a real-world value, and maps that value to an 16-bit signed generalized fixed-point data type with a scaling of 2^-3. When the value is then output from the **Data Type Conversion 2** block as a real-world value, the scaling and data type information is retained and the output value is 000011111111.000, or 255. When the value is output from the **Data Type Conversion 3** block as a stored integer, the scaling and data type information is not retained and the stored integer is interpreted as 000011111111000, or 2040. For all three Data Type Conversion blocks after double-clicking,

Solutions to End–of–Chapter Exercises

we change the **Output data type mode** from **Inherit via back propagation** to **Specify via dialog**. On the new **Function Block Parameters** window we enter the following:
Output data type – all three blocks: sfix(16)

Output scaling value – block 1: 2^–3, blocks 2 and 3: 2^0

Input and output to have equal – blocks 1 and 2: Real World Value (RWV), block 3: Stored Integer (SI)

Next, we double-click the **Data Type Conversion 2** block and we enter the following information:

Output data type mode: Specify via dialog

Output data type: sfix(8)

Output scaling value: 2^–3

Input and output to have equal: Real World Value (RWV)

Finally, we double-click the **Data Type Conversion 3** block and we enter the following:

Output data type mode: Specify via dialog

Output data type: sfix(8)

Output scaling value: 2^0

Input and output to have equal: Stored Integer (SI)

The Inport and Outport labels are displayed by choosing **Format>Port/Signal Displays>Port Data Types**.

6. The state ports are intended to be used specifically for self-resetting integrators (see Creating Self-Resetting Integrators), and Handing off a state from one enabled subsystem to another (see Handing Off States Between Enabled Subsystems) in Simulink's Help menu for the Integrator block. The state port should only be used in these two scenarios. When updating a model, Simulink checks to ensure that the state port is being used in one of these two scenarios. If not, Simulink signals an error.

7.
The simulation model and the output of the Discrete–Time Backward Euler Integrator are shown below.

Chapter 2 The Commonly Used Blocks Library

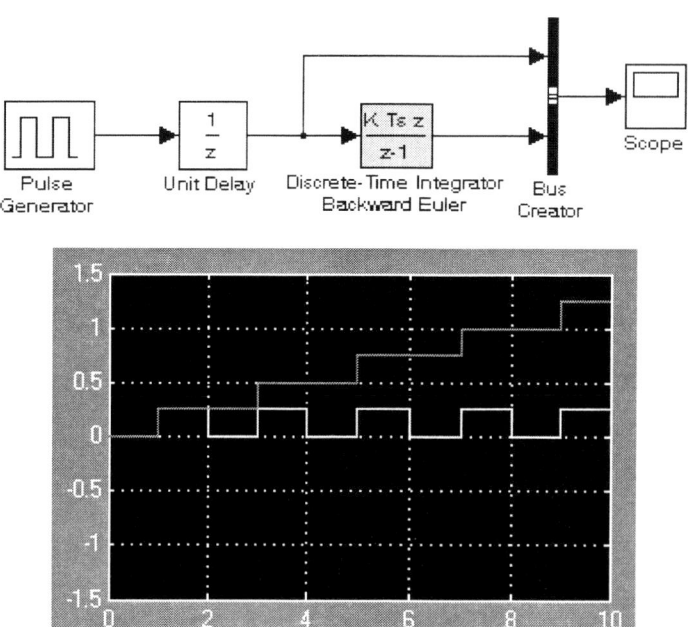

A comparison of the waveform above and that of Figure 2.33 in Example 2.15 shows that the accumulation (integration) begins one step n earlier. We recall that for the Forward Euler Discrete–Time Integrator,

$$y(n) = y(n-1) + K \cdot T \cdot u(n-1)$$

and for the Backward Euler Discrete–Time Integrator,

$$y(n) = y(n-1) + K \cdot T \cdot u(n)$$

8.
The model is shown below where the blocks indicated as Variable A, Variable B, and Variable C are Constant blocks. We begin by specifying the values for the combination $A = 0$, $B = 0$, and $C = 0$ in MATLAB's Command Window, and after execution of the Simulation start command we observe the value 0 in Display Output D block.

Solutions to End–of–Chapter Exercises

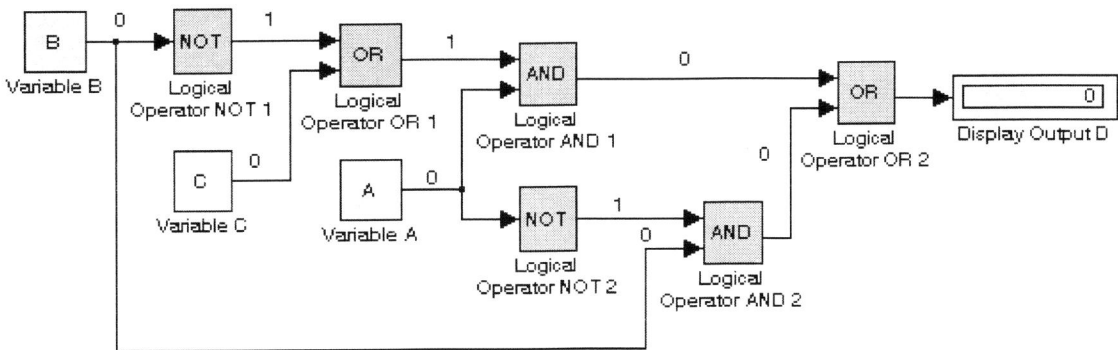

The remaining combinations for the variables A, B, and C and the corresponding value of the output D are shown in the truth table below.

Inputs			Output
A	B	C	D
0	0	0	0
0	0	1	0
0	1	0	1
0	1	1	1
1	0	0	1
1	0	1	1
1	1	0	0
1	1	1	1

9. The model below indicates that $B(5, 4) = \Gamma(5) \cdot \Gamma(4)/\Gamma(5 + 4)$.

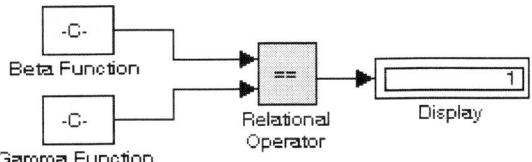

In the Source Block Parameters for the Beta Function block we enter **beta(5,4)**, and in the Source Block Parameters for the Gamma function we enter **gamma(5)*gamma(4)/gamma(9)**. For both functions, on the Signal data types we select **int8**.

10.

The model is shown below where in The Source Block Parameters for the Sine Wave 1 block the phase is specified as 0 radians, for the Sine Wave 2 block the phase is specified as $2\pi/3$ radians, and for the Sine Wave 3 block the phase is specified as $4\pi/3$ radians.

Chapter 2 The Commonly Used Blocks Library

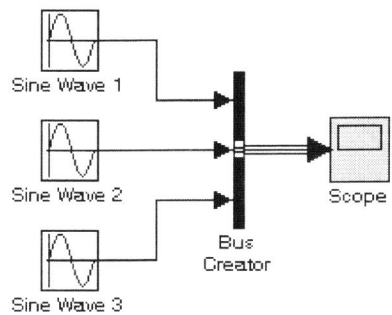

The three-phase waveforms are shown below.

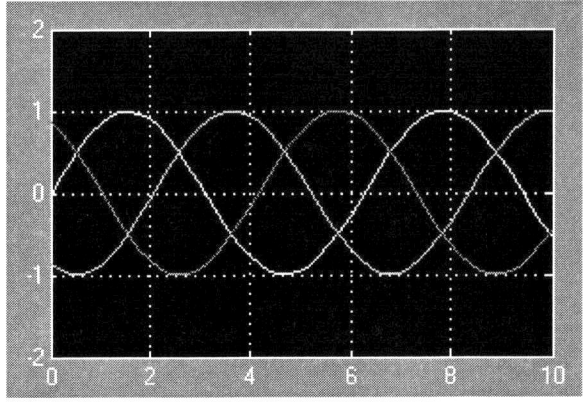

11.

The model is shown below where in the Saturation block's parameters dialog box we have specified Upper and Lower limits at points +0.5 and –0.5 respectively.

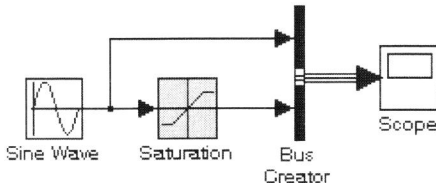

The input and output waveforms are shown below.

Solutions to End–of–Chapter Exercises

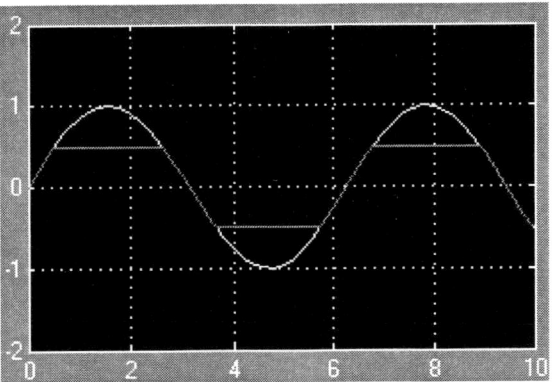

12.

Case 1: Forward Euler Discrete-Time Integrator

Discrete-Time Integrator
Forward Euler, K=1, Ts=T

This integrator, with $K = 1$, $T_s = T$, and zero initial conditions (ICs), is described as

$$y(n) = y(n-1) + Tx(n-1) \quad (1)$$

Suppose we want to find the response when the input is the decaying exponential

$$x(n) = e^{-naT} \quad (2)$$

The ZT of (1) is

$$H(z) = \frac{T}{z-1} \quad (3)$$

and the ZT of (2) is

$$X(z) = \frac{z}{z - e^{-aT}} \quad (4)$$

Then,

$$Y(z) = H(z) \cdot X(z) = \frac{Tz}{(z-1)(z-e^{-aT})} = \frac{T/(1-e^{-aT})}{z-1} - \frac{T/(1-e^{-aT})}{z-e^{-aT}} \quad (5)$$

from which

$$y(n) = \frac{T}{1-e^{-aT}}(1 - e^{-naT}) \quad (6)$$

Introduction to Simulink with Engineering Applications
Copyright © Orchard Publications

Chapter 2 The Commonly Used Blocks Library

For the continuous–time case, where

$$x(t) = e^{-at} \quad (7)$$

we obtain

$$\int_0^t e^{-at}dt = \frac{1}{a}(1 - e^{-at}) \quad (8)$$

Recalling that

$$e^{-x} = 1 - x + \frac{x^2}{2!} - \ldots + \ldots$$

for $aT \ll 1$, (6) above reduces to

$$y(n) \approx \frac{T}{1 - 1 + aT}(1 - e^{-naT}) \approx \frac{1}{a}(1 - e^{-naT}) \quad (9)$$

and thus (8) and (9) are almost identical.

Case 2: Trapezoidal Discrete-Time Integrator

Discrete-Time Integrator
Trapezoidal, K=1, Ts=T

This integrator, with $K = 1$, $T_s = T$, and zero initial conditions (ICs), is described as

$$y(n) = y(n-1) + \frac{T}{2}[x(n) + x(n-1)] \quad (10)$$

Suppose we want to find the response when the input is the decaying exponential

$$x(n) = e^{-naT} \quad (11)$$

The ZT of (10) is

$$H(z) = \frac{T}{2} \cdot \frac{z+1}{z-1} \quad (12)$$

and the ZT of (11) is

$$X(z) = \frac{z}{z - e^{-aT}} \quad (13)$$

Then,

$$Y(z) = H(z) \cdot X(z) = \frac{Tz(z+1)}{2(z-1)(z-e^{-aT})} = \frac{T/(1-e^{-aT})}{z-1} - \frac{Te^{-aT}(1+e^{-aT})/2(1-e^{-aT})}{z-e^{-aT}} \quad (14)$$

from which

$$y(n) = \frac{T}{(1-e^{-aT})}\left[1 - \frac{e^{-aT}}{2}(1+e^{-aT})e^{-naT}\right] \quad (15)$$

For $aT \ll 1$, (15) reduces to

$$y(n) \approx \frac{T}{1-1+aT}\left[1 - \frac{1-aT}{2}\cancelto{0}{}(1+1-aT)\cancelto{0}{}e^{-naT}\right] \approx \frac{1}{a}[1-e^{-naT}] \quad (16)$$

and (16) is almost identical to (9).

In both cases, we have assumed that the input is an exponential function. What about if the input is the discrete unit step function u(n) or a sinusoid? It is reasonable to assume that the same results will be obtained considering that for $aT \approx 0$, $e^{-naT} \approx 1$, and for the discrete sinusoids using Euler's identity.

Let's try using the Forward Euler Discrete–Time Integrator and the Trapezoidal Discrete–Time Integrator with a pulse signal as the input shown below.

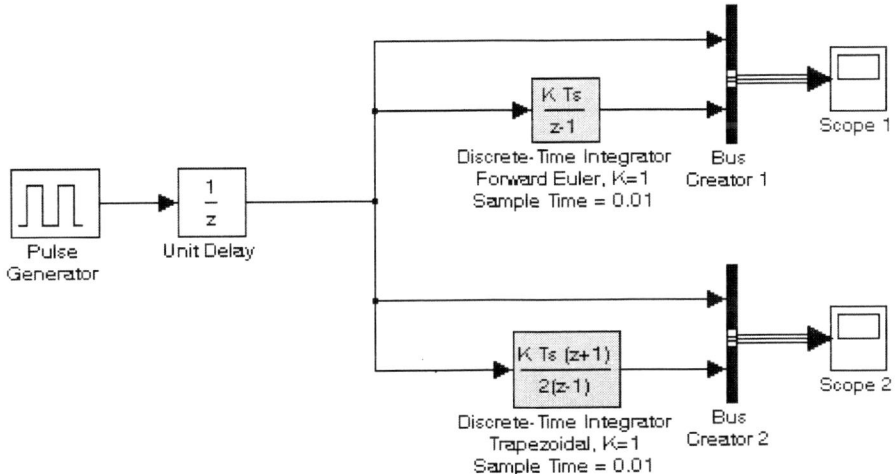

Scope 1 and Scope 2 blocks display the same outputs as shown below.

Chapter 2 The Commonly Used Blocks Library

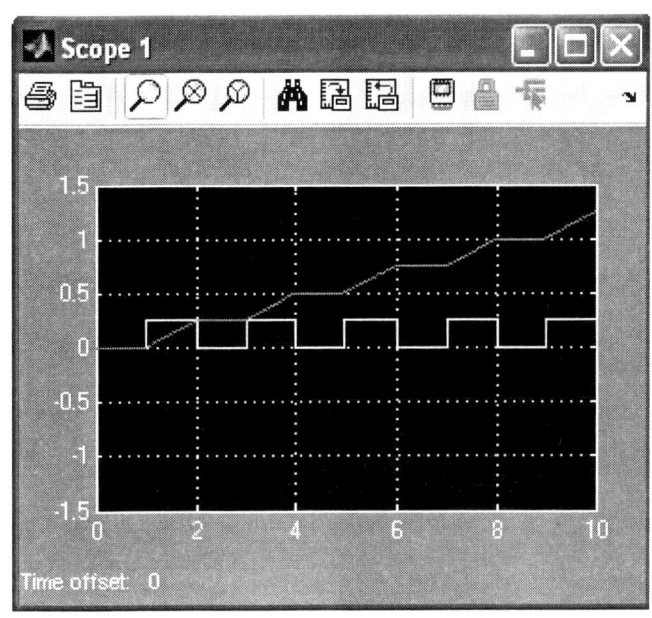

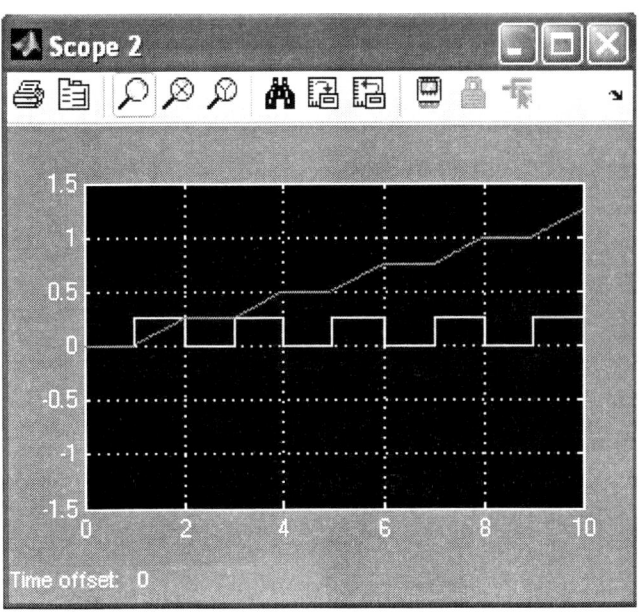

2-50 *Introduction to Simulink with Engineering Applications*
Copyright © Orchard Publications

Chapter 3

The Continuous Blocks Library

This chapter is an introduction to the **Continuous Blocks** library. This is the second library in the Simulink group of libraries and contains the **Continuous–Time Linear Systems Sub–Library**, and the **Continuous–Time Delays Sub–Library** blocks shown below. We will describe the function of each block included in this library and we will perform simulation examples to illustrate their application.

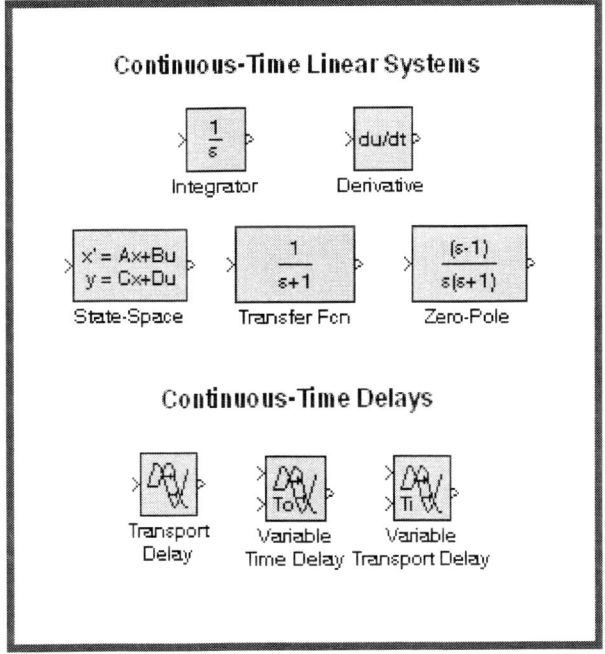

Chapter 3 The Continuous Blocks Library

3.1 The Continuous-Time Linear Systems Sub-Library

The **Continuous-Time Linear Systems Sub-Library** contains the blocks described in Subsections 3.1.1 through 3.1.5 below.

3.1.1 The Integrator Block

The **Integrator** block is described in Section 2.14, Chapter 2, Page 2–20.

3.1.2 The Derivative Block

The **Derivative block** approximates the derivative of its input. The initial output for the block is zero. The accuracy of the results depends on the size of the time steps taken in the simulation. Smaller steps allow a smoother and more accurate output curve from this block. Unlike blocks that have continuous states, the solver does not take smaller steps when the input changes rapidly. Let us consider the following simple example.

Example 3.1

We will create a model that will compute and display the waveform of the derivative of the function $y = \cos x$.

The model is shown in Figure 3.1, and the input and output waveforms are shown in Figure 3.2.

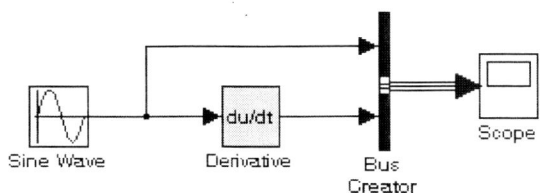

Figure 3.1. Model for Example 3.1

To convert the sine function in the Sine Wave block to a cosine function, in the Source Block Parameters dialog box we specify Phase = $\pi/2$. As we know, the derivative of the cosine function is the negative of the sine function and this is shown in Figure 3.2.

To scale the vertical axis in Figure 3.2, we move the cursor near that axis, we right–click, and we set the values as indicated. We will follow this practice in subsequent illustrations.

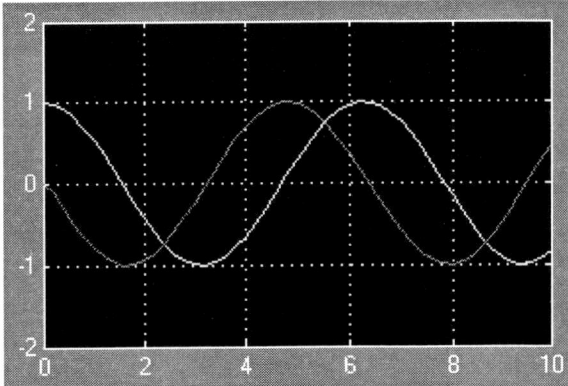

Figure 3.2. Input and output waveforms for the model of Figure 3.1

The Simulink Help for the derivative block states that using the MATLAB function **linmod** to linearize a model that contains a Derivative block can be troublesome. Let us elaborate on linearization.

We prefer to work with linear functions since the slope is constant and thus we can find the output for any input. Unfortunately, the equations that describe the behavior of most physical phenomena are non–linear. If we are interested in values of the function close to some point (a,b), we can replace the given function by its first Taylor polynomial, which is a linear function.[*] We recall that the Taylor series are defined as in relation (3.1) below.

$$f(x) = f(x_0) + f'(x_0)(x - x_0) + \frac{f''(x_0)}{2!}(x - x_0)^2 + \ldots + \frac{f^{(n)}(x_0)}{n!}(x - x_0)^n \qquad (3.1)$$

In (3.1), the first two terms on the right side define an equation of a straight line, i.e., $y = mx + b$, a linear function. For example, if $y = f(x) = x^2$, the first two terms on the right side of (3.1) at point x=3 are represented by $9 + 6(x - 3) = 6x - 9$. The same is true for a function f of two variables, say x and y, i.e., $f(x, y)$, where if we let L denote the local linearization at the point (a, b), we get

$$L(x, y) = f(a, b) + \frac{\partial f}{\partial x}(a, b)(x - a) + \frac{\partial f}{\partial y}(a, b)(y - b) \qquad (3.2)$$

---

[*] The first Taylor polynomial is often called the local linearization.

Chapter 3 The Continuous Blocks Library

Relation (3.2) yields the three numbers required to define the local linearization. The first number is the value of f at point (a, b), the second is the value of the partial derivative with respect to x at point (a, b), and the third is the value of the partial derivative with respect to y at point (a, b). Taking the partial derivative of $z = f(x, y) = x^2 + y^2$ and evaluating it at the point $(1, 2)$ we find that the local linearization is $w = L(1, 2) = 5 + 2(x-1) + 4(y-2)$. We observe that this local linearization contains x and y terms of first degree. We can plot these functions with the following MATLAB script. The plot is shown in Figure 3.3.

```
x=-3:0.01:3; y=x; z=x.^2+y.^2;...
w=5+2.*(x–1)+4.*(y–2);...
plot(x,z,x,w); grid
```

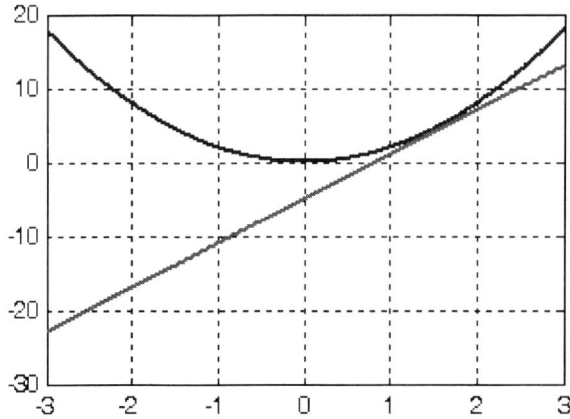

Figure 3.3. An example of linearization at a specified point

MATLAB provides three functions to extract linear functions in the form of state–space matrices A, B, C, and D. We recall that the input–output relationship in terms of these matrices is

$$\dot{x} = Ax + Bu$$
$$y = Cx + Du \tag{3.3}$$

where x represents the state(s), u the input, and y the output, and the inputs and outputs must be Inport and Outport blocks. Other blocks cannot be used as inputs and outputs.

Example 3.2

We will use the MATLAB **linmod('x')** function to extract the linear model for the model shown in Figure 3.4.

We save the given model as Figure_3_4, and in MATLAB's Command Window we execute the command [A,B,C,D]=linmod('Figure_3_4'). MATLAB displays the four matrices as

The Continuous–Time Linear Systems Sub–Library

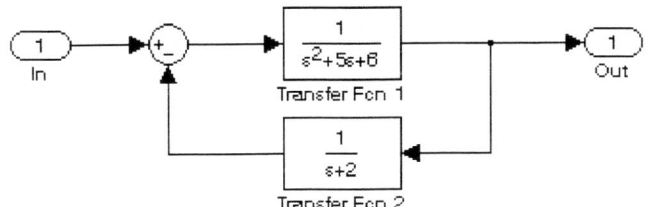

Figure 3.4. Model for Example 3.2

A =
   -5   -6   -1
    1   0   0
    0   1   -2

B =
    1
    0
    0

C =
    0   1   0

D =
    0

and thus the model of Figure 3.4 can be represented as

$$\dot{x} = \begin{bmatrix} -5 & -6 & -1 \\ 1 & 0 & 0 \\ 0 & 1 & -2 \end{bmatrix} x + \begin{bmatrix} 1 \\ 0 \\ 0 \end{bmatrix} u$$

$$y = \begin{bmatrix} 0 & 1 & 0 \end{bmatrix} x + \begin{bmatrix} 0 \end{bmatrix} u$$

The **Simulink Extras** library contains the **Switched derivative for linearization** block and the **Switched transport delay for linearization** block. The former should be used in place of the derivative when we are linearizing the model. It approximates the derivative with a proper transfer function. The latter delays the input by a specified amount of time. It can be used to simulate a time delay.

To avoid possible problems with derivatives we can incorporate the derivative block in other blocks.

Example 3.3

Let us consider the model of Figure 3.5.

Chapter 3 The Continuous Blocks Library

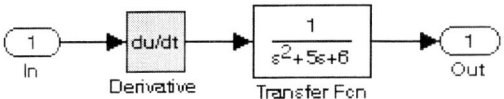

Figure 3.5. Model with derivative block

Recalling that differentiation in the time domain corresponds to multiplication by s in the complex frequency domain minus the initial value of f(t) at $t = 0^-$, that is,

$$f'(t) = \frac{d}{dt} f(t) \Leftrightarrow sF(s) - f(0^-)$$

and assuming that the initial value is zero, we can replace the model of Figure 3.5 with that of Figure 3.6.

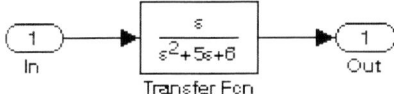

Figure 3.6. Model equivalent to the model of Figure 3.5

3.1.3 The State-Space Block

The **State-Space** block implements a system defined by the state-space equations

$$\begin{aligned} \dot{x} &= Ax + Bu \\ y &= Cx + Du \end{aligned} \quad (3.4)$$

where x and u are column vectors, matrix A must be an $n \times n$ square matrix where n represents the number of the states, matrix B must have dimension $n \times m$ where m represents the number of inputs, matrix C must have dimension $r \times n$ where r represents the number of outputs, and matrix D must have dimension $r \times m$.

For examples with the state-space block please refer to Chapter 1, Examples 1.1 and 1.2.

3.1.4 The Transfer Fcn Block

The Continuous–Time Linear Systems Sub–Library

The **Transfer Fcn** block implements a transfer function where the input $V_{in}(s)$ and output $V_{out}(s)$ can be expressed in transfer function form as the following equation

$$G(s) = \frac{V_{out}(s)}{V_{in}(s)} \tag{3.5}$$

Example 3.4

Let us consider the op amp circuit of Figure 3.7.

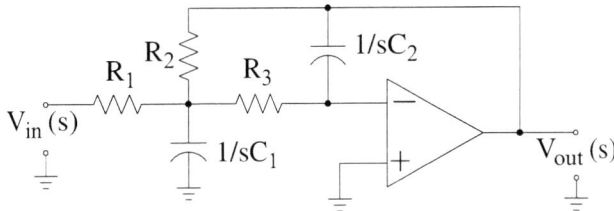

Figure 3.7. Circuit for Example 3.3 to be simulated.

It can be shown[*] that the transfer function of the op amp circuit of Figure 3.7 is given by

$$G(s) = \frac{V_{out}(s)}{V_{in}(s)} = \frac{-1}{R_1 [(1/R_1 + 1/R_2 + 1/R_3 + sC_1)(sR_3C_2) + 1/R_2]} \tag{3.6}$$

and this transfer function describes a second order lowpass filter. For simplicity, we let

$$R_1 = R_2 = R_3 = 1\ \Omega$$

$$C_1 = C_2 = 1\ F$$

and by substitution of these values into (3.6) we obtain

$$G(s) = \frac{V_{out}(s)}{V_{in}(s)} = \frac{-1}{[s^2 + 3s + 1]} \tag{3.7}$$

Assuming that the input $V_{in}(s)$ is the unit step function, we will create a model using the Transfer Fcn block to simulate the output $V_{out}(s)$.

The model is shown in Figure 3.8 where in the Function Block Parameters dialog box for the Transfer Fcn block we have entered −1 for the numerator and [1 3 1] for the denominator.

---

[*] The derivation of this transfer function is shown in Chapter 4, Signals and Systems with MATLAB Computing and Simulink modeling, ISBN 0–9744239–9–8.

Chapter 3 The Continuous Blocks Library

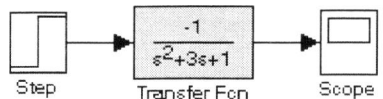

Figure 3.8. Model for Example 3.4

Upon execution of the Simulation start command, the Scope displays the waveform shown in Figure 3.9.

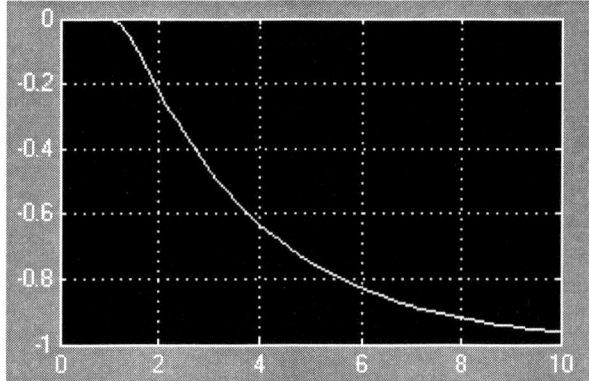

Figure 3.9. Output waveform for the model of Figure 3.8

3.1.5 The Zero-Pole Block

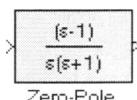

The **Zero-Pole** block implements a system with the specified zeros, poles, and gain in the s–domain. This block displays the transfer function depending on how the parameters are specified:

1. If each is specified as an expression or a vector, the icon shows the transfer function with the specified zeros, poles, and gain. If we specify a variable in parentheses, the variable is evaluated. For example, if in the Function Block Parameters dialog box we specify Zeros as [2 4 6 8], Poles as [1 3 5 7 9], and Gain as 25, the block looks like as shown in Figure 3.10.[*]

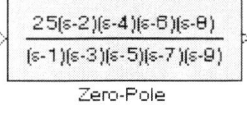

Figure 3.10. The Zero-Pole block specified in vector form

---

[*] *We may need to stretch the block to see the entire block shown above.*

The Continuous–Time Linear Systems Sub–Library

2. If each is specified as a variable, e.g., **zeros**, **poles**, **Gain**, in MATLAB's Command Window we enter

   zeros=[2 4 6 8]; poles=[1 3 5 7 9]; Gain=25;

   the block shows the variable name followed by (s) if appropriate. For this example the block appearance will be as shown in Figure 3.11.

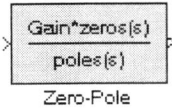

Figure 3.11. The Zero–Pole block specified as variables

Example 3.5

The system transfer function of a system has a gain factor of 1.5, zeros at $-2 \pm j$, and poles at -3 and at $-1 \pm j$. We will create a model to display the step response of this system.

The model and the input and output waveforms are shown in Figures 3.12 and 3.13 respectively.

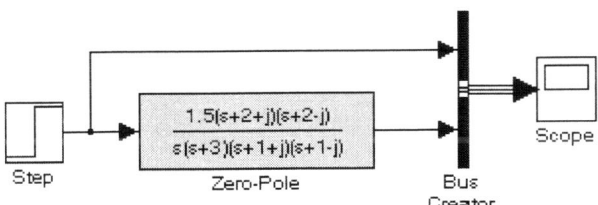

Figure 3.12. Model for Example 3.5

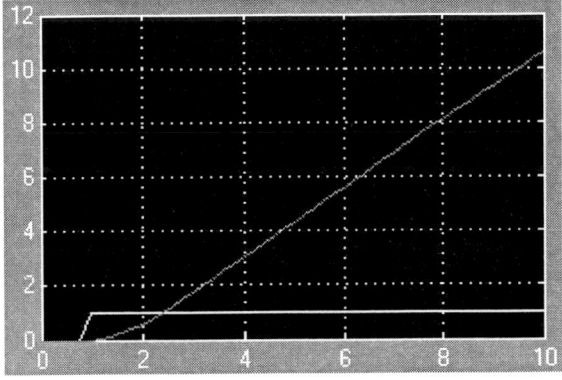

Figure 3.13. Input and output waveforms for the model of Figure 3.12

Chapter 3 The Continuous Blocks Library

3.2 The Continuous-Time Delays Sub-Library

The **Continuous-Time Delays Sub-Library** contains the blocks described in Subsections 3.2.1 through 3.2.3 below.

3.2.1 The Transport Delay Block

The **Transport Delay** block delays the input by a specified amount of time. It can be used to simulate a time delay. At the start of the simulation, the block outputs the Initial input parameter until the simulation time exceeds the Time delay parameter. The Time delay parameter must be nonnegative. Best accuracy is achieved when the delay is larger than the simulation step size.

Example 3.6

For the model shown in Figure 3.14, the Time delay in the Function Block Parameters dialog box is specified as 2, and this delay is shown in Figure 3.15.

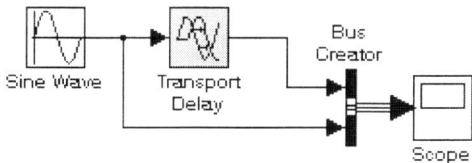

Figure 3.14. Model to illustrate the use of the Transport Delay block

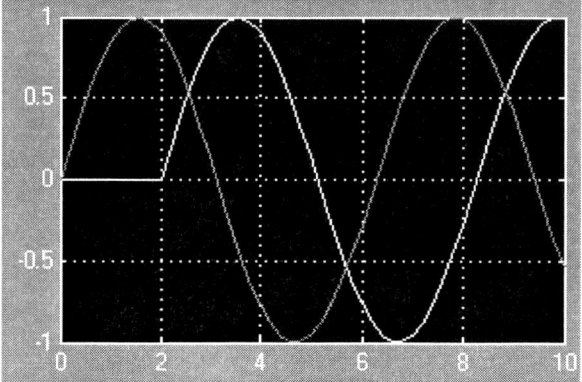

Figure 3.15. Input and output waveforms for the model of Figure 3.14

The Continuous–Time Delays Sub–Library

When an output is required at a time that does not correspond to the times of the stored input values, the Transport Delay block interpolates linearly between points. For a more detailed discussion please refer to the Help menu for this block.

The Transport Delay block does not interpolate discrete signals. Instead, it returns the discrete value at the required time.

3.2.2 The Variable Time Delay Block

The **Variable Time Delay** block and the **Variable Transport Delay** block appear as two blocks in the Simulink block library. However, they are actually the same built–in Simulink block with different settings of a Select delay type parameter. In the Variable Time Delay mode, the block has a data input, a time delay input, and a data output. The block's output at the current time step equals the value of its data input at a previous time which is equal to the current simulation time minus a delay time specified by the block's time delay input.

Example 3.7

The model in Figure 3.16 shows a Variable Time Delay block where the Signal Generator block output is a square wave and the Constant block is set to the value 0.5 to introduce a delay of 0.5 second. The input and output of the Variable Time Delay block are shown in Figure 3.17.

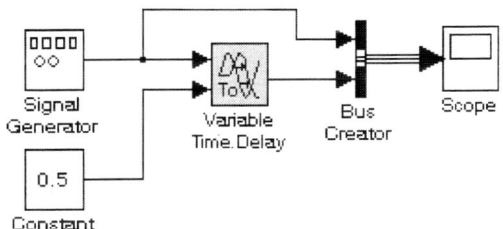

Figure 3.16. Model with Variable Time Delay

Chapter 3 The Continuous Blocks Library

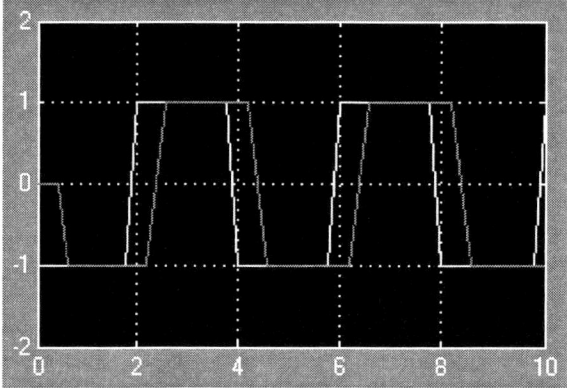

Figure 3.17. Signal Generator block and Variable Time Delay block for the model of Figure 3.16

3.2.3 The Variable Transport Delay Block

In the **Variable Transport Delay** block the output is equal to the value of its data input at an earlier time which is equal to the current time minus a transportation delay. If we let $u(t)$ be the input, $t_d(t)$ the transportation delay, and $y(t)$ the output, then

$$y = u(t - t_d(t)) \tag{3.8}$$

Example 3.8

From electric circuit theory, we know that an alternating current i_C through a capacitor C leads the voltage v_C by $90°$. Using a Variable Transport Delay block, we will create a model that will display the current and voltage waveforms.

The model and the input and output waveforms are shown in Figures 3.18 and 3.19 respectively.

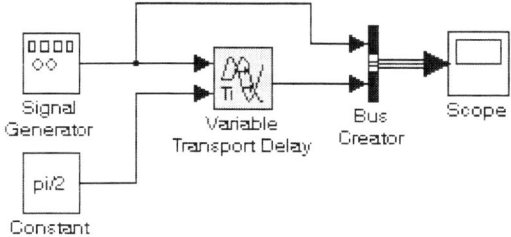

Figure 3.18. Model for Example 3.8

The Continuous–Time Delays Sub–Library

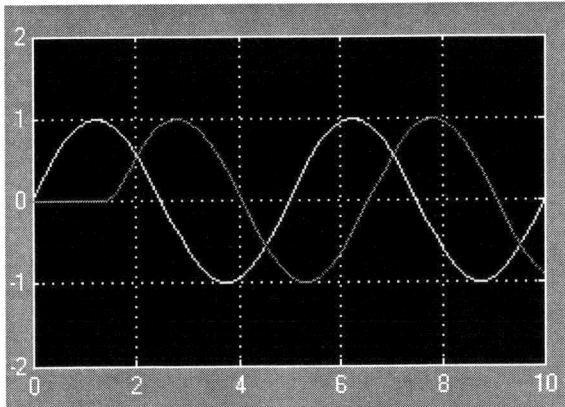

Figure 3.19. Input and output waveforms for the model of Figure 3.18

3.3 Summary

- The **Integrator** block outputs the integral of its input at the current time step.

- The **Derivative** block approximates the derivative of its input. The block accepts one input and generates one output. The initial output for the block is zero. For nonlinear models, we can use the MATLAB function **linmod** to linearize a model that contains a Derivative block. To avoid problems, it is recommended that before linearizing we replace troublesome blocks with blocks found in the Simulink Extras library in the Linearization sublibrary. To avoid possible problems with derivatives we can incorporate the derivative block in other blocks.

- MATLAB provides three functions to extract linear functions in the form of state-space matrices A, B, C, and D. The input-output relationship in terms of these matrices is

$$\dot{x} = Ax + Bu$$
$$y = Cx + Du$$

where x represents the state(s), u the input, and y the output, and the inputs and outputs must be Inport and Outport blocks. Source and Sink blocks cannot be used as inputs and outputs.

- The Simulink Extras library contains the Derivative for linearization block and the Transport Delay block. The former should be used in place of the derivative when we are linearizing the model. It approximates the derivative with a proper transfer function. The latter delays the input by a specified amount of time. It can be used to simulate a time delay.

- The **State–Space** block implements a system defined by the state–space equations

$$\dot{x} = Ax + Bu$$
$$y = Cx + Du$$

where x and u are column vectors, A and C must be matrices conformable for multiplication with x, and B and D must be matrices conformable for multiplication with u.

- The **Transfer Fcn** block implements a transfer function where the input $V_{in}(s)$ and output (y) can be expressed in transfer function form as the following equation

$$G(s) = \frac{V_{out}(s)}{V_{in}(s)}$$

- The **Zero–Pole** block implements a system with the specified zeros, poles, and gain in the s-domain. The Zero-Pole block displays the transfer function depending on how the parameters are specified. If each is specified as an expression or a vector, the icon shows the transfer function with the specified zeros, poles, and gain. If we specify a variable in parentheses, the variable is evaluated.

Summary

- The **Transport Delay** block delays the input by a specified amount of time. It can be used to simulate a time delay. At the start of the simulation, the block outputs the Initial input parameter until the simulation time exceeds the Time delay parameter, when the block begins generating the delayed input. The Time delay parameter must be nonnegative. Best accuracy is achieved when the delay is larger than the simulation step size.

- The **Variable Time Delay** block and the Variable Transport Delay block appear as two blocks in the Simulink block library. However, they are actually the same built-in Simulink block with different settings of a Select delay type parameter. In the Variable Time Delay mode, the block has a data input, a time delay input, and a data output. The block's output at the current time step equals the value of its data input at a previous time equal to the current simulation time minus a delay time specified by the block's time delay input.

- In the **Variable Transport Delay** block the output at the current time step is equal to the value of its data input at an earlier time equal to the current time minus a transportation delay. If we let $u(t)$ be the input, $t_d(t)$ the transportation delay, and $y(t)$ the output, then

$$y = u(t - t_d(t))$$

3.4 Exercises

1. Using MATLAB's **linmod('x')** function, express the model below in state–space form.

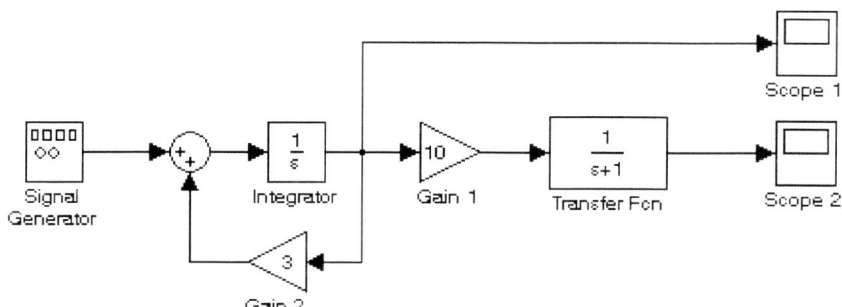

2. Create a model that includes a Transfer Fcn block to simulate the output v_{out} of the circuit below where R_g represents the internal resistance of the applied (source) voltage v_g, and R_L represents the resistance of the load that consists of R_L, L, and C. The values of the circuit constants are $R_g = 100\ \Omega$, $R_L = 1\ K\Omega$, $L = 10\ mH$, and $C = 500\ \mu F$.

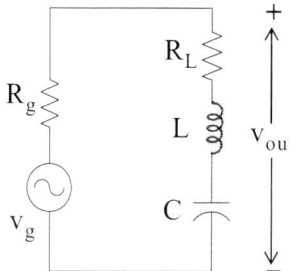

3. From electric circuit theory, it is known that charging a capacitor with a constant current produces a linear voltage across it, that is,

$$V_C = \frac{I}{C}t$$

where C is the capacitance in farads, I is the constant current through the capacitor in amperes, and V_C is the linear voltage across the capacitor in volts. Using a **Variable Transport Delay** block create a model to display the output if $I = 2\ mA$, $C = 1000\ \mu F$, and the voltage across the capacitor at some time t_0 is $V_0 = 2\ v$.

Solutions to End–of–Chapter Exercises

3.5 Solutions to End–of–Chapter Exercises

1. The first step is to replace the source and sink blocks with Inport and Outport blocks as shown below. This model is saved as **Exercise_3_1A**.

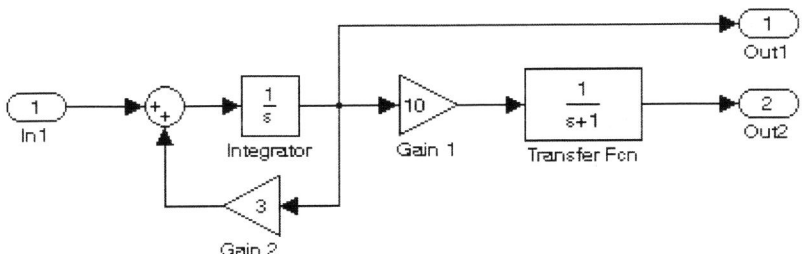

From MATLAB's Command Window we execute the statement

[A,B,C,D]=linmod('Exercise_3_1A')

and MATLAB displays

```
A =
     3      0
    10     -1
B =
     1
     0
C =
     1      0
     0      1
D =
     0
     0
```

Therefore, the linear model of the given model in state-space form is expressed as

$$\dot{x} = \begin{bmatrix} 3 & 0 \\ 10 & -1 \end{bmatrix} x + \begin{bmatrix} 1 \\ 0 \end{bmatrix} u$$

$$y = \begin{bmatrix} 1 & 0 \\ 0 & 1 \end{bmatrix} x + \begin{bmatrix} 0 \\ 0 \end{bmatrix} u$$

2.

The s–domain equivalent circuit is shown below.

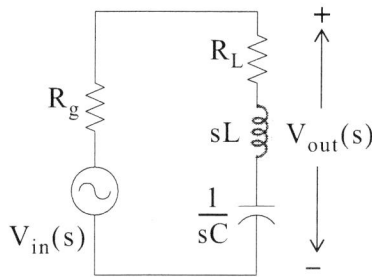

The transfer function G(s) is readily found by application of the voltage division expression

$$V_{out}(s) = \frac{R_L + sL + 1/sC}{R_g + R_L + sL + 1/sC} V_{in}(s)$$

Then,

$$G(s) = \frac{V_{out}(s)}{V_{in}(s)} = \frac{R_L + Ls + 1/sC}{R_g + R_L + Ls + 1/sC}$$

$$G(s) = \frac{V_{out}(s)}{V_{in}(s)} = \frac{LCs^2 + R_L Cs + 1}{LCs^2 + (R_g + R_L)Cs + 1}$$

With $R_g = 100\ \Omega$, $R_L = 1\ K\Omega$, $L = 10\ mH$, and $C = 500\ \mu F$, the transfer function becomes

$$G(s) = \frac{V_{out}(s)}{V_{in}(s)} = \frac{5 \times 10^{-6} s^2 + 5 \times 10^{-4} s + 1}{5 \times 10^{-6} s^2 + 5.5 \times 10^{-4} s + 1}$$

$$G(s) = \frac{V_{out}(s)}{V_{in}(s)} = \frac{s^2 + 500s + 2 \times 10^5}{s^2 + 550s + 2 \times 10^5}$$

This transfer function is very nearly unity for all values of the variable *s* and thus we expect the output to be the same as the input. In the model shown below, the Signal Generator's waveform was chosen as sawtooth with amplitude 2 and frequency 0.25 Hz.

Solutions to End–of–Chapter Exercises

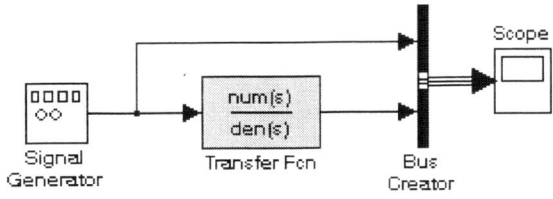

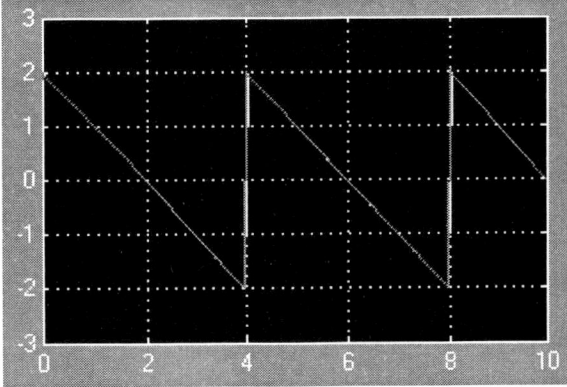

3.

$$V_C = \frac{I}{C}t = 2 \times 10^3 t$$

Slope = m = I/C. Then

$$m = \frac{I}{C} = \frac{2 \times 10^{-3}}{10^{-3}} = 2$$

$$V_C = \frac{I}{C}t = 2t$$

For $V_C = V_0 = 2$ v

$$t = t_0 = \frac{2}{2} = 1 \text{ s}$$

The model and the input and output are shown below where the slope for the Ramp block is set to 2 and the time delay of 1 second is specified by the Constant block.

Chapter 3 The Continuous Blocks Library

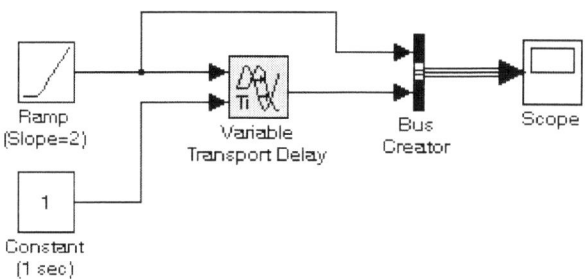

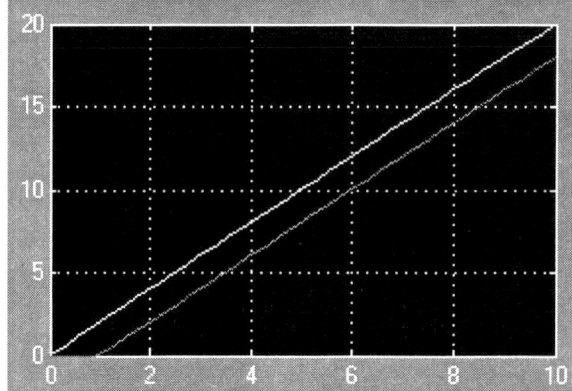

Chapter 4

The Discontinuities Blocks Library

This chapter is an introduction to the **Discontinuities Blocks** library. This is the third library in the Simulink group of libraries and contains the blocks shown below. We will describe the function of each block included in this library and we will perform simulation examples to illustrate their application.

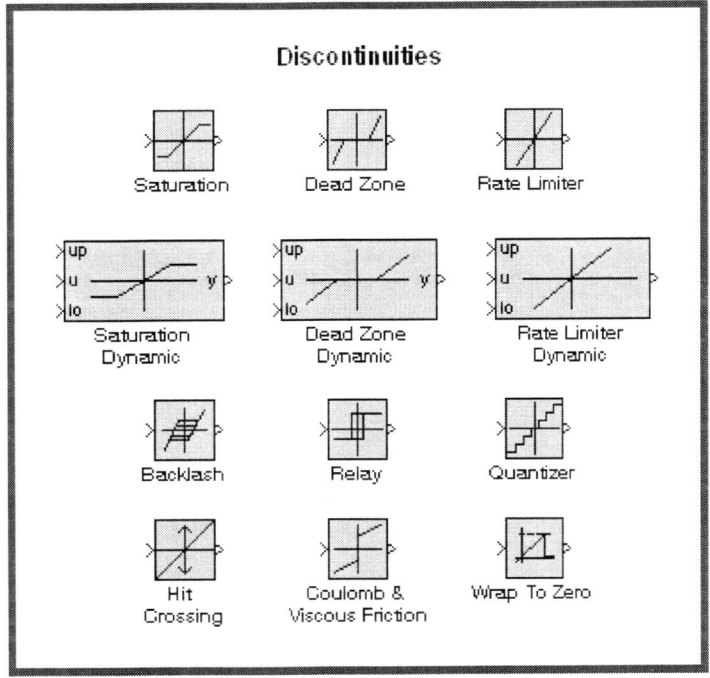

Chapter 4 The Discontinuities Blocks Library

4.1 The Saturation Block

The **Saturation** block sets upper and lower bounds on a signal. When the input signal is within the range specified by the Lower limit and Upper limit parameters, the input signal passes through unchanged. When the input signal is outside these bounds, the signal is clipped to the upper or lower bound. When the Lower limit and Upper limit parameters are set to the same value, the block outputs that value. This block is also described in Section 2.13, Chapter 2, Page 2–19.

Example 4.1 *

We will create a model with a Saturation block where the upper limit is clipped at $+0.5$ and the lower limit is clipped at -0.5. The input will be a sine function with amplitude 1 and frequency 0.25 Hz.

The model is shown in Figure 4.1 and the input and output waveforms are shown in Figure 4.2.

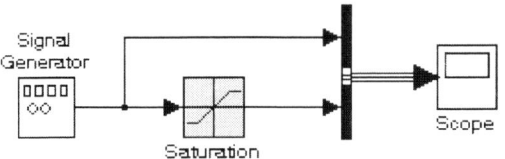

Figure 4.1. Model for Example 4.1

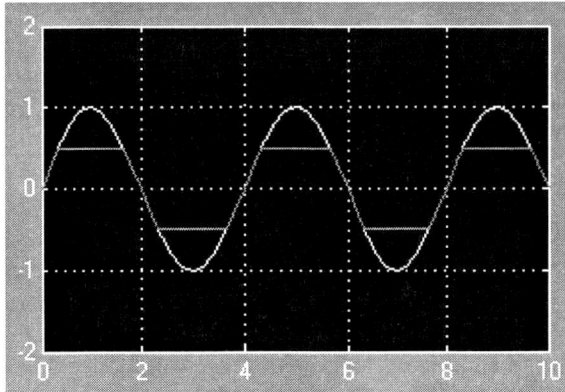

Figure 4.2. Input and output waveforms for the model of Example 4.10

---

* *Another example with the Saturation block was given as Example 2.13, Chapter 2, Page 2.19.*

4.2 The Saturation Dynamic Block

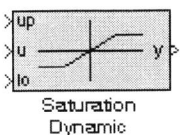

The **Saturation Dynamic** block bounds the range of the input signal to upper and lower saturation values. The input signal outside of these limits saturates to one of the bounds where the input below the lower limit is set to the lower limit, the input above the upper limit is set to the upper limit. The input for the upper limit is the **up** port, and the input for the lower limit is the **lo** port.

Example 4.2

We will create a model with a Saturation block where the upper limit is clipped at $+1$ and the lower limit is clipped at 0. The Signal Generator block is specified in the Block Parameters dialog box as a sine function with amplitude 1 and frequency $0.25\ Hz$.

The values of the Constant blocks are entered in the MATLAB Command Window as:

a=1; b=0;

The model is shown in Figure 4.3 and the input and output waveforms are shown in Figure 4.4.

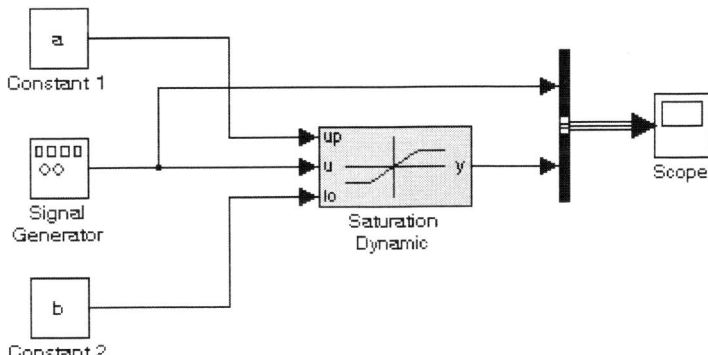

Figure 4.3. Model for Example 4.2

Chapter 4 The Discontinuities Blocks Library

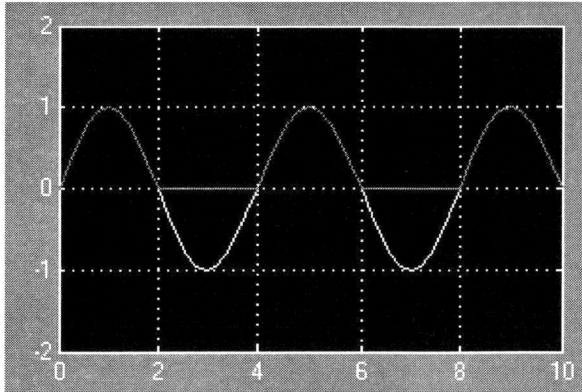

Figure 4.4. Input and output waveforms for the model of Figure 4.3

4.3 The Dead Zone Block

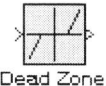

The **Dead Zone** block generates zero output within a specified region, called its **dead zone**. The lower and upper limits of the dead zone are specified as the Start of dead zone and End of dead zone parameters. The block output depends on the input and dead zone:

1. If the input is within the dead zone (greater than the lower limit and less than the upper limit), the output is zero.

2. If the input is greater than or equal to the upper limit, the output is the input minus the upper limit.

3. If the input is less than or equal to the lower limit, the output is the input minus the lower limit.

Example 4.3

We will create a model with the Dead Zone block where the Function Block Parameters dialog box for this block the start of the dead zone is −0.25, and the end of the dead zone is +0.25. The input will be a sine waveform with amplitude 1 and frequency 0.2 Hz.

The model is shown in Figure 4.5 and the input and output waveforms are shown in Figure 4.6. This model uses lower and upper limits of −0.25 and +0.25 with the Signal Generator block specified in the Block Parameters dialog box as a sine wave of unity amplitude. Since the input is greater than he upper limit, the output is the input minus the upper limit, i.e., $1.00 - 0.25 = 0.75$. Likewise, for the negative half–cycle the output is $-1.00 - (-0.25) = -0.75$.

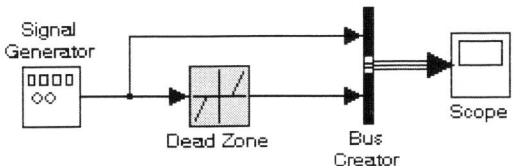

Figure 4.5. Model for Example 4.3

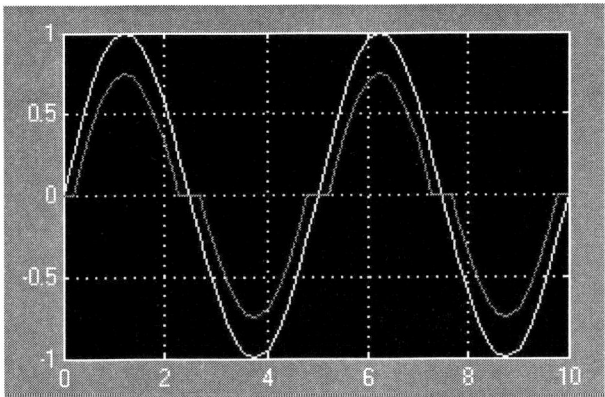

Figure 4.6. Input and output waveforms for the model of Figure 4.5

4.4 The Dead Zone Dynamic Block

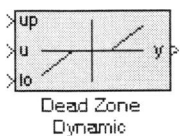

The **Dead Zone Dynamic** block dynamically bounds the range of the input signal, providing a region of zero output. The bounds change according to the upper and lower limit input signals where:

1. The input within the bounds is set to zero.

2. The input below the lower limit is shifted down by the lower limit.

3. The input above the upper limit is shifted down by the upper limit.

The input for the upper limit is the **up** port, and the input for the lower limit is the **lo** port.

Chapter 4 The Discontinuities Blocks Library

Example 4.4

We will create a model with the Dead Zone Dynamic block where the input for the upper limit is $+1.0$, and the input for the lower limit is -1.5. The input will be a sine waveform with amplitude 2 and frequency $0.2\ Hz$.

The model is shown in Figure 4.7 and the input and output waveforms are shown in Figure 4.8.

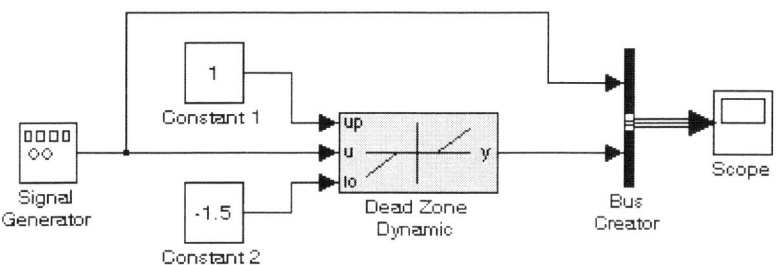

Figure 4.7. Model for Example 4.4

In Figure 4.8, the positive half–cycle of the output has a maximum value of $2.0 - 1.0 = 1.0$; that is, the input above the upper limit at the **up** port is shifted down by the upper limit whose value is $+1.0$. The input for the lower limit at the **lo** port is -1.5. The negative half–cycle of the output has a minimum value of $-2.0 - (-1.5) = -0.5$; that is, the input below the lower limit is shifted down by the lower limit.

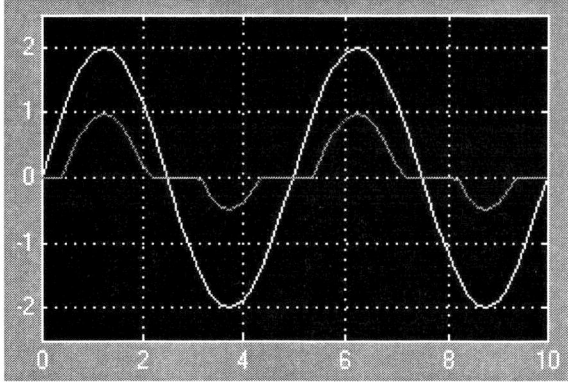

Figure 4.8. Input and output waveforms for the model of Figure 4.7

4.5 The Rate Limiter Block

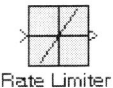

The Rate Limiter Block

The **Rate Limiter** block limits the first derivative of the signal passing through it. The equation and parameters used with this block are described in the Help menu for this block. The Function Block Parameters window for the Rate Limiter indicates that we can specify rising and falling slew rates where the default values are +1 and –1 respectively.

To understand the meaning of the slew rate, let us consider a typical operational amplifier,[*] or op amp for short. There is a limit to the rate at which the output voltage of an op amp can change. Therefore, manufacturers specify a new parameter referred to as the *slew rate*. By definition, the slew rate (SR) is the maximum rate of change of an output voltage produced in response to a large input step function and it is normally expressed in volts per microsecond, that is,

$$\text{Slew Rate} = SR = \frac{dv_{out}}{dt_{max}} \tag{4.1}$$

Of course, relation (4.1) is the slope of the output voltage under maximum rate of change conditions. Typical slew rates range from $0.1 \text{ V}/\mu s$ to $100 \text{ V}/\mu s$, and most internally compensated op amps have slew rates in the order of $1 \text{ V}/\mu s$. Figure 4.9 shows a step function of amplitude 10 V applied to the input of a unity gain op amp, and the waveform at the output of this op amp.

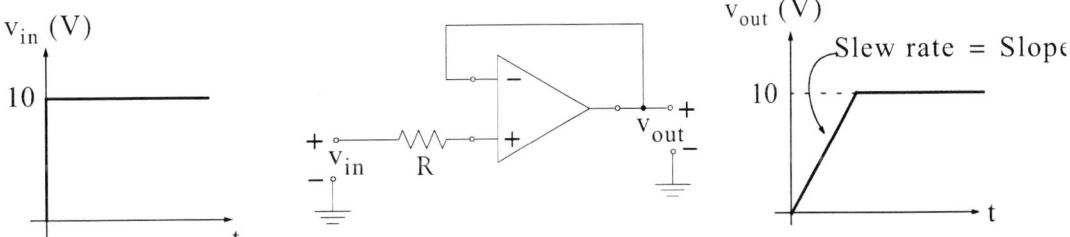

Figure 4.9. The resultant slew rate when a step function is applied to a unity gain op amp

The linearly rising slew rate shown in Figure 4.9 will not be produced if the input voltage is smaller than that specified by the manufacturer. In this case, the slew rate will be a rising exponential such as the rising voltage across a capacitor. In most op amps the slew rate is set by the charging rate of the frequency compensating capacitor and the output voltage is

$$v_{out} = V_f(1 - e^{-\omega_{ug}t}) \tag{4.2}$$

Example 4.5

We will create a model with a Rate Limiter block where the rising and falling slew rates will be the default values and the input will be the unit step function.

---

[*] *For a detailed discussion on operational amplifiers, or op amps for short, please refer to Chapter 5, Electronic Devices and Amplifier Circuits with MATLAB Applications, ISBN 0-9709511-7-5.*

Chapter 4 The Discontinuities Blocks Library

The model is shown in Figure 4.10 and the input and output waveforms are shown in Figure 4.11.

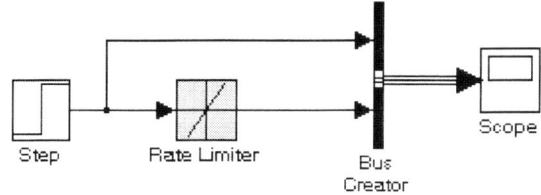

Figure 4.10. Model for Example 4.5

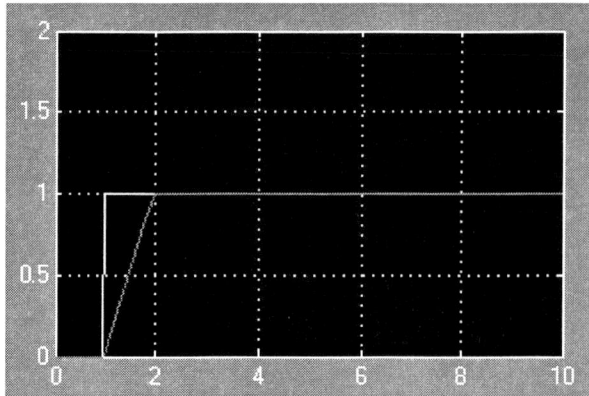

Figure 4.11. Input and output waveforms for the model of Example 4.7

4.6 The Rate Limiter Dynamic Block

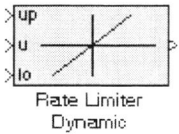

The **Rate Limiter Dynamic** block limits the rising and falling rates of the signal. The external signal **up** sets the upper limit on the rising rate of the signal. The external signal **lo** sets the lower limit on the falling rate of the signal.

Example 4.6

We will create a model with a Rate Limiter Dynamic block where the upper limit on the rising rate of the signal will be $+1$ and the lower limit on the falling rate of the signal will be -1. The input will be a sine function with amplitude 2 and frequency 2 Hz.

The model is shown in Figure 4.12 and the input and output waveforms are shown in Figure 4.13.

The Backlash Block

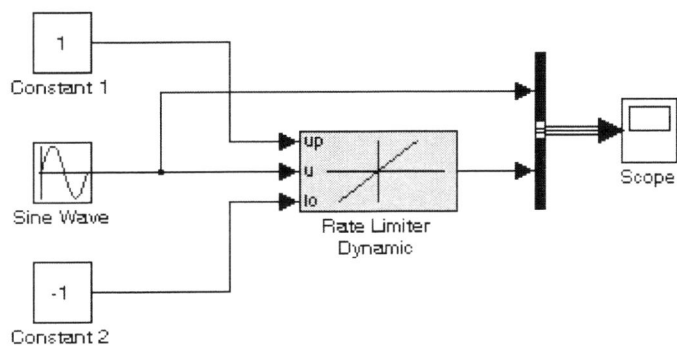

Figure 4.12. Model for Example 4.6

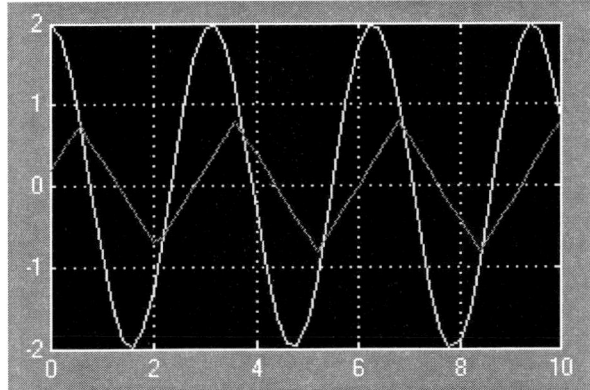

Figure 4.13. Input and output waveforms for the model of Figure 4.12

For this example, the input is specified as a sine wave, and since the rate of change (slope or derivative) of the sine is the cosine, for the Sine Wave block we specified Amplitude 2, Frequency 2 Hz, and Phase $\pi/2$. The values +1 and −1 assigned to the Constant blocks represent the rising and falling rates, that is, the slopes defined as the upper and lower limits respectively.

4.7 The Backlash[*] Block

---

[*] *In engineering, backlash is the amount of clearance between mated **gear** teeth in a **gear pair**. Some backlash is required to allow for lubrication, manufacturing errors, **deflection** under load and differential expansion between the gears and the housing. Backlash is created when the **tooth thickness** of either gear is less than the tooth thickness of an ideal gear, or the zero backlash tooth thickness. Additional backlash is created when the operating center distance of the gear pair is less than that for two ideal gears. Standard practice is to make allowance for half the backlash in the tooth thickness of each gear.*

Introduction to Simulink with Engineering Applications
Copyright © Orchard Publications

Chapter 4 The Discontinuities Blocks Library

The **Backlash** block implements a system in which a change in input causes an equal change in output. However, when the input changes direction, an initial change in input has no effect on the output. The amount of side–to–side play in the system is referred to as the **deadband**. The deadband is centered about the output. A system can be in one of three modes:

- Disengaged – In this mode, the input does not drive the output and the output remains constant.

- Engaged in a positive direction – In this mode, the input is increasing (has a positive slope) and the output is equal to the input minus half the deadband width.

- Engaged in a negative direction – In this mode, the input is decreasing (has a negative slope) and the output is equal to the input plus half the deadband width.

For illustrations and examples please refer to the Help menu for this block.

Example 4.7

We will create a model with a Backlash block with deadband width of unity and initial output zero whose input will be a square waveform with amplitude 1 and frequency 0.25 Hz.

The model is shown in Figure 4.14, and the input and output are shown in Figure 4.15.

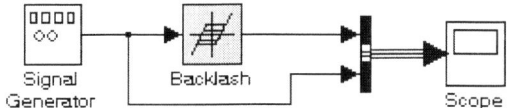

Figure 4.14. Model for Example 4.7

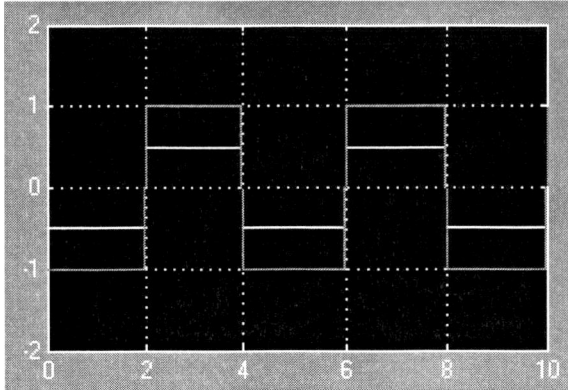

Figure 4.15. Input and output for the model of Figure 4.14

In the Function Block Parameters window for the Signal Generator block in the Block Parameters dialog box we have specified a square waveform with amplitude 1 and frequency at 0.25 Hz. In the

The Relay Block

Function Block Parameters dialog box for the Backlash block we have specified the deadband width at 1 and initial output at 0. In Figure 4.15, we observe that the deadband extends from −0.5 to +0.5.

4.8 The Relay Block

The **Relay** block output can switch between two specified values. When the relay is on, it remains on until the input drops below the value of the Switch off point parameter. When the relay is off, it remains off until the input exceeds the value of the Switch on point parameter. The block accepts one input and generates one output. The Switch on point value must be greater than or equal to the Switch off point. Specifying a Switch on point value greater than the Switch off point value models hysteresis, whereas specifying equal values models a switch with a threshold at that value.

Example 4.8

The Function Block Parameters dialog box for the Relay block in Figure 4.16 are specified as:

a. Switch on point: 10

b. Switch off point: 0

c. Output when on: 1

d. Output when off: 0

We will choose appropriate values for blocks a and b so that the Relay block output will be on.

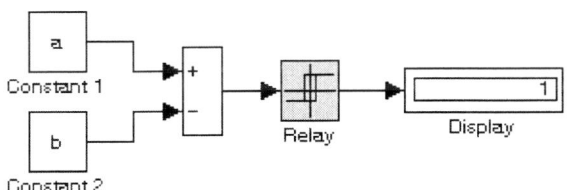

Figure 4.16. Model for Example 4.8

Two appropriate values would be a = 11 and b = 1. Thus in the MATLAB Command Window we have entered:

a=11; b=1;

Chapter 4 The Discontinuities Blocks Library

4.9 The Quantizer Block

The **Quantizer** block passes its input signal through a stair–step function so that many neighboring points on the input axis are mapped to one point on the output axis. The effect is to quantize a smooth signal into a stair–step output. The output is computed using the round–to–nearest method, which produces an output that is symmetric about zero. That is,

$$y = q \times \text{round}(u/q) \qquad (4.3)$$

where y is the output, u is the input, and q is the quantization interval.

Example 4.9

We will create a model with a Quantizer block with Quantization Interval 0.25. The input will be a sine waveform with amplitude 1 and frequency 0.25 Hz.

The model is shown in Figure 4.17 and the input and output waveforms are shown in Figure 4.18.

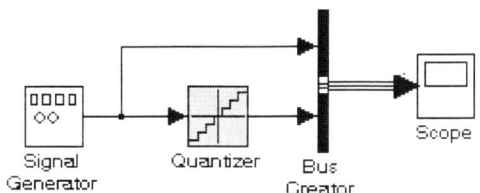

Figure 4.17. Model for Example 4.9

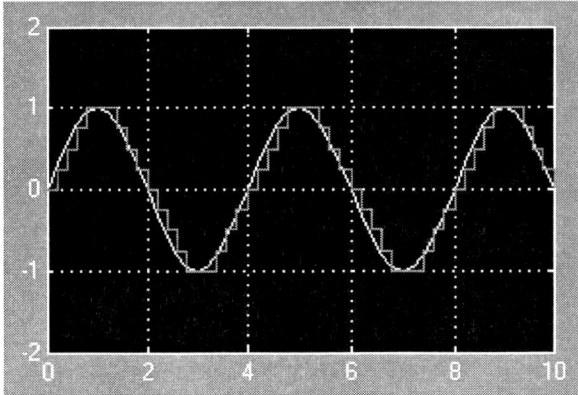

Figure 4.18. Input and output waveforms for the model of Figure 4.17

4.10 The Hit Crossing Block

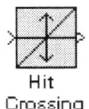

The **Hit Crossing** block detects when the input reaches the Hit crossing offset parameter value in the direction specified by the Hit crossing direction (rising, falling, or either) parameter. To see where the crossing occurs, we click on the Show output port check box. If the Show output port check box is not selected, the block ensures that the simulation finds the crossing point but does not generate an output.

Example 4.10

We will create a model with the Hit Crossing block where the Hit crossing offset is set at -1. The input is a sine waveform with amplitude 1 and frequency 0.25 Hz.

The model is shown in Figure 4.19, and the input and output waveform in Figure 4.20. The Data Type Conversion block converts the output of the Hit Crossing block which is Boolean, i.e., logical 0 or logical 1, to double so that both inputs to the Bus Creator block are of the same type.

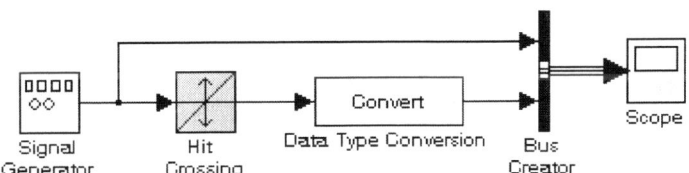

Figure 4.19. Model for Example 4.10

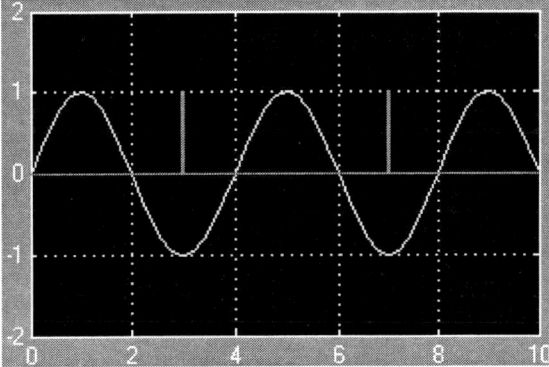

Figure 4.20. Input and output waveforms for the model of Figure 4.19

Chapter 4 The Discontinuities Blocks Library

As stated in the Help menu, the use of the Hit Crossing block is illustrated in the **hardstop** and **clutch** demos. In the **hardstop** demo, the Hit Crossing block is in the Friction Model subsystem. In the **clutch** demo, the Hit Crossing block is in the Lockup Detection subsystem.

4.11 The Coulomb and Viscous Friction Block

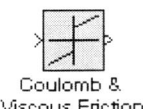

The **Coulomb and Viscous Friction** block models Coulomb (static) and Viscous (dynamic) friction. The block produces an offset at zero and a linear gain elsewhere. The offset corresponds to the Coulombic friction; the gain corresponds to the viscous friction.

As we know from physics, friction is a force that resists the relative motion or tendency to such motion of two bodies in contact. Friction is undesirable in some parts of rotating machinery such as bearings and cylinders, but very beneficial in the automotive industry such as the design of brakes and tires. Theoretically, there should be no friction in a motor with zero velocity, but in reality, a small amount of "static" (no velocity) friction known as Coulomb friction, is always present even in roller or ball type anti-friction bearings. Viscous friction, on the other hand, is friction force caused by the viscosity of lubricants.

The Coulomb friction function, the Viscous friction function, and the combined Coulomb plus Viscous friction functions are illustrated in Figure 4.21.

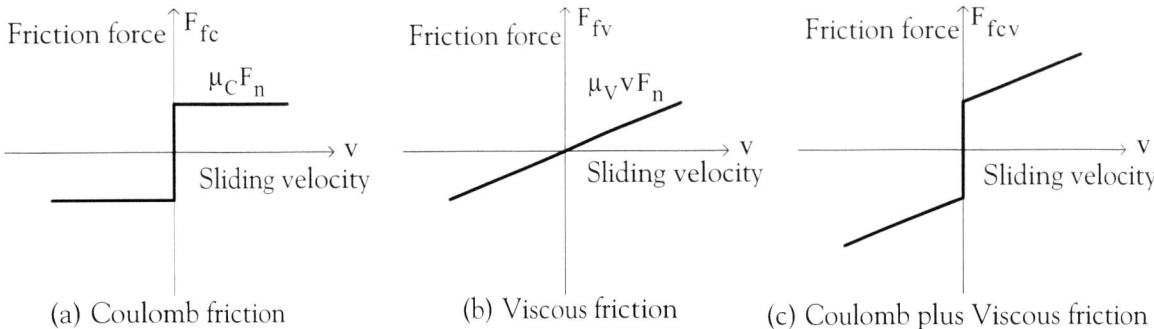

Figure 4.21. Coulomb friction and Viscous friction functions

The Coulomb friction function is defined as

$$F_{fc} = \pm\mu_C F_n \qquad (4.4)$$

where μ_C is the Coulomb friction coefficient.

The Viscous friction function is defined as

The Coulomb and Viscous Friction Block

$$F_{fv} = \mu_v v F_n \qquad (4.5)$$

and the Coulomb plus Viscous friction is defined as

$$F_{fc+fv} = \mu_v v F_n \pm \mu_C F_n \qquad (4.6)$$

Coulomb friction force can be represented by at least four different continuous functions. Each of these functions involves one constant that controls the level of accuracy of that function's representation of the friction force. Simulink uses the default values [1 3 2 0] for the offset (Coulomb friction value). For the signal gain (coefficient of viscous friction) at nonzero input points the default is 1.

Example 4.11

We will create a model with the Coulomb and Viscous Friction block where the Function Block Parameters for this block the offset are the default values, the gain is 2, and the input is the Step function.

The model is shown in Figure 4.22 and the input and output waveforms are shown in Figure 4.23.

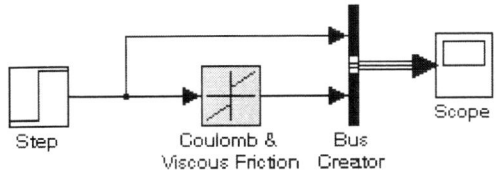

Figure 4.22. Model for Example 4.11

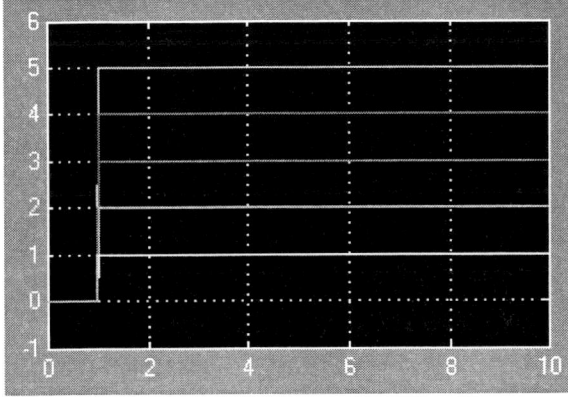

Figure 4.23. Input and output waveforms for the model of Figure 4.22

Chapter 4 The Discontinuities Blocks Library

4.12 The Wrap to Zero Block

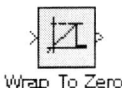

The **Wrap To Zero** block sets the output to zero if the input is above the value set by the Threshold parameter, and outputs the input if the input is less than or equal to the Threshold.

Example 4.12

We will create a model with a Wrap to Zero block where the Threshold in the Function Block Parameters is specified as 75. We will choose an appropriate value for the input to this block so that the output will display the input value.

The model is shown in Figure 4.24. Any input value equal of less than 75 will cause the Wrap to Zero block to display the input value.

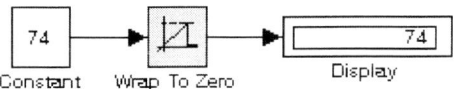

Figure 4.24. Model for Example 4.12

Summary

4.13 Summary

- The **Saturation** block sets upper and lower bounds on a signal. When the input signal is within the range specified by the Lower limit and Upper limit parameters, the input signal passes through unchanged. When the input signal is outside these bounds, the signal is clipped to the upper or lower bound. When the Lower limit and Upper limit parameters are set to the same value, the block outputs that value.

- The **Saturation Dynamic** block bounds the range of the input signal to upper and lower saturation values. The input signal outside of these limits saturates to one of the bounds where the input below the lower limit is set to the lower limit, the input above the upper limit is set to the upper limit. The input for the upper limit is the up port, and the input for the lower limit is the lo port.

- The **Dead Zone** block generates zero output within a specified region, called its dead zone. The lower and upper limits of the dead zone are specified as the Start of dead zone and End of dead zone parameters. The block output depends on the input and dead zone.

- The **Dead Zone Dynamic** block dynamically bounds the range of the input signal, providing a region of zero output. The bounds change according to the upper and lower limit input signals.

- The **Rate Limiter** block limits the first derivative of the signal passing through it. We can specify rising and falling slew rates.

- The **Rate Limiter Dynamic** block limits the rising and falling rates of the signal. The external signal up sets the upper limit on the rising rate of the signal. The external signal lo sets the lower limit on the falling rate of the signal.

- The **Backlash** block implements a system in which a change in input causes an equal change in output. However, when the input changes direction, an initial change in input has no effect on the output. The amount of side-to-side play in the system is referred to as the deadband. The deadband is centered about the output.

- The **Relay** block allows its output to switch between two specified values. When the relay is on, it remains on until the input drops below the value of the Switch off point parameter. When the relay is off, it remains off until the input exceeds the value of the Switch on point parameter. The block accepts one input and generates one output. The Switch on point value must be greater than or equal to the Switch off point. Specifying a Switch on point value greater than the Switch off point value models hysteresis, whereas specifying equal values models a switch with a threshold at that value.

- The **Quantizer** block passes its input signal through a stair-step function so that many neighboring points on the input axis are mapped to one point on the output axis. The effect is to quantize a smooth signal into a stair-step output. The output is computed using the round-to-nearest method, which produces an output that is symmetric about zero.

Chapter 4 The Discontinuities Blocks Library

- The **Hit Crossing** block detects when the input reaches the Hit crossing offset parameter value in the direction specified by the Hit crossing direction (rising, falling, or either) parameter. To see where the crossing occurs, we click on the Show output port check box. If the Show output port check box is not selected, the block ensures that the simulation finds the crossing point but does not generate output.

- The **Coulomb and Viscous Friction** block models Coulomb (static) and viscous (dynamic) friction. The block models a discontinuity at zero and a linear gain otherwise. The offset corresponds to the Coulombic friction; the gain corresponds to the viscous friction.

- The **Wrap To Zero** block sets the output to zero if the input is above the value set by the Threshold parameter, and outputs the input if the input is less than or equal to the Threshold.

4.14 Exercises

1. Create a model with a Backlash block whose input is the Step block and the Function Block Parameters for both blocks are the default values.

2. Create a model with the Coulomb and Viscous Friction block where the Function Block Parameters for this block the offset are the default values, the gain is 0.5, and the input is the Ramp function with unity slope.

3. Using the Dead Zone block, create a model that will display the following input (yellow) and output (magenta) waveforms.

4. Using the Hit Crossing block, create a model with the Hit crossing offset set at 1 and the input is a square waveform with amplitude 1 and frequency 0.25 Hz.

5. Create a model with a Quantizer block with Quantization Interval 0.2. The input is a straight line passing through the origin with slope 0.25.

6. Create a model with a Relay block and choose appropriate values so that the relay will be in the off condition.

Chapter 4 The Discontinuities Blocks Library

4.15 Solutions to End-of-Chapter Exercises

1.

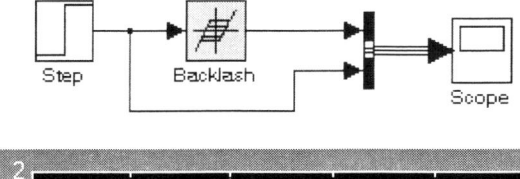

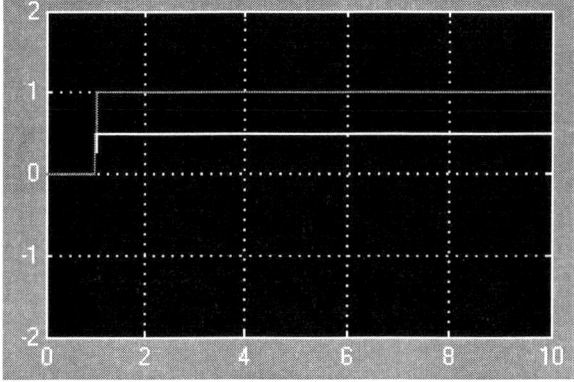

2.

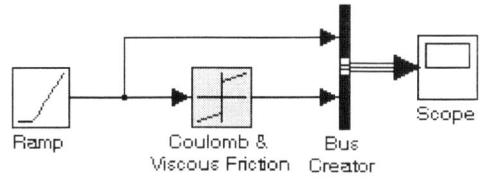

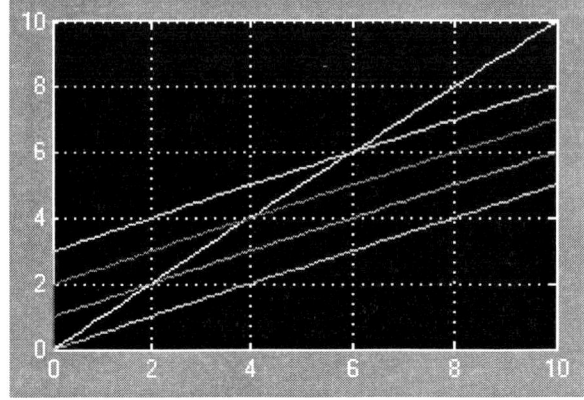

3.

The model is shown below where the waveform for the Signal Generator block is chosen as Saw Tooth, unity amplitude, and 0.2 Hz frequency. The Dead Zone block parameters are set for lower limit of −0.5 and upper limit +0.5

Solutions to End-of-Chapter Exercises

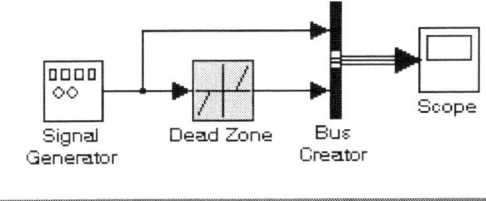

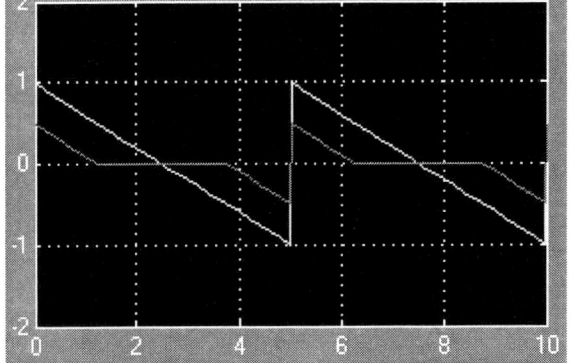

4.

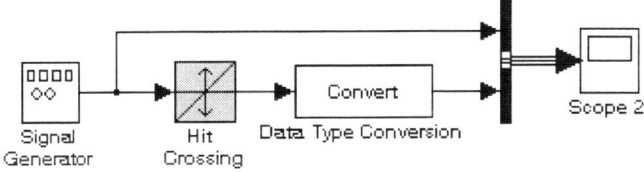

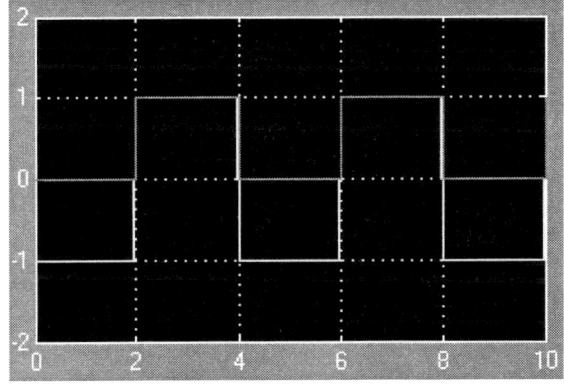

The output of the Hit Crossing block is shown as a pulse with 50% duty cycle. Since the input signal reaches the offset value and remains at this value, the block outputs 1 from the hit time till the time when the input signal leaves the offset value.

Chapter 4 The Discontinuities Blocks Library

5.

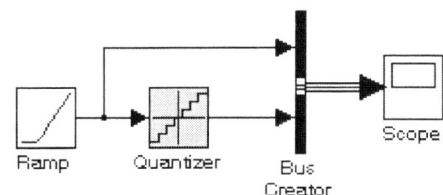

The Ramp block slope is set at 0.25. The Quantizer block is set for Quantization Interval 0.2.

6.

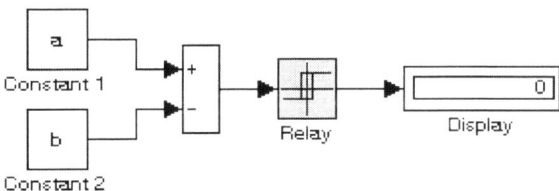

The Function Block Parameters for the Relay block in the above model are specified as:

a. Switch on point: 4

b. Switch off point: 0

c. Output when on: 1

d. Output when off: 0

Two appropriate values would be a = 5 and b = 4. Thus, in the MATLAB Command Window we enter:

a=5; b=4;

Chapter 5

The Discrete Blocks Library

This chapter is an introduction to the **Discrete Blocks** library. This is the fourth library in the Simulink group of libraries and contains the **Discrete-Time Linear Systems Sub-Library**, and the **Sample & Hold Delays Sub-Library** blocks shown below. We will describe the function of each block included in this library and we will perform simulation examples to illustrate their application.

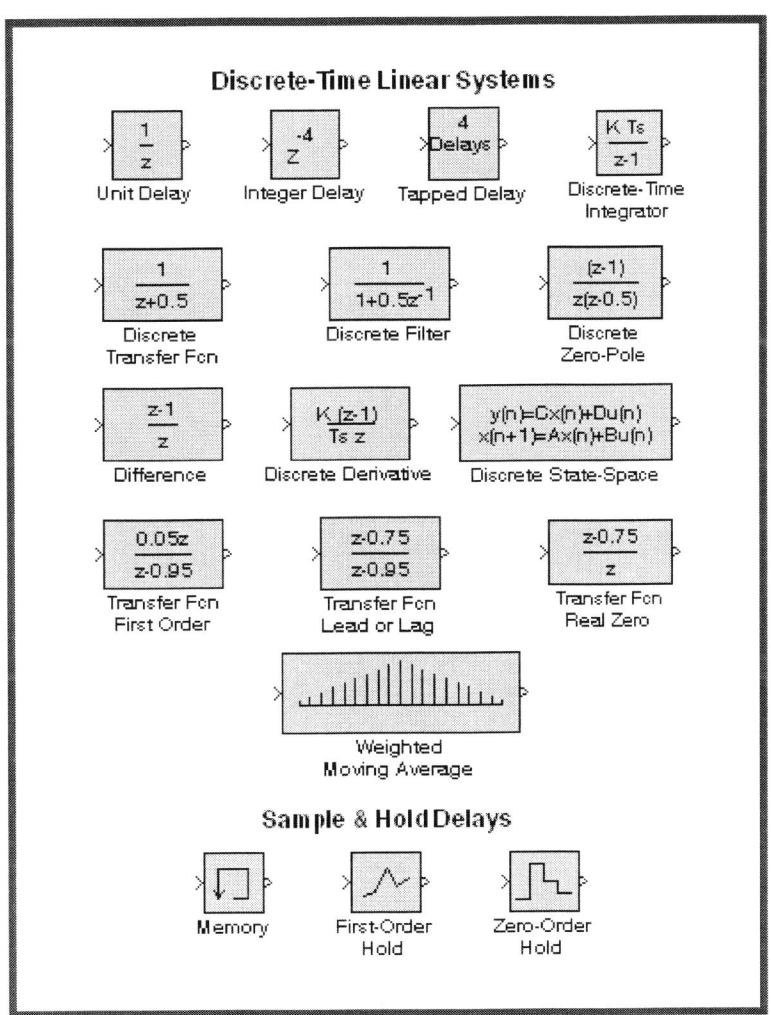

Chapter 5 The Discrete Blocks Library

5.1 The Discrete-Time Linear Systems Sub-Library

The **Discrete-Time Linear Systems Sub-Library** contains the blocks described in Subsections 5.1.1 through 5.1.14 below.

5.1.1 The Unit Delay Block

The **Unit Delay** block is described in Chapter 2, Section 2.15, Chapter 2, Page 2-24.

5.1.2 The Integer Delay Block

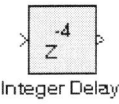

The **Integer Delay** block delays its input by N sample periods. Both the input and the output can be scalar or vector.

Example 5.1

We will create a model using an Integer Delay block with five delays (N = 5) where the input will be a discrete sine wave with amplitude 1, frequency 1 Hz, and sample time 0.1 s.

The model is shown in Figure 5.1 and the input and output waveforms are shown in Figure 5.2.

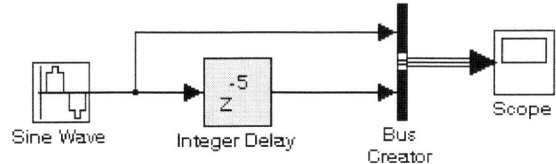

Figure 5.1. Model for Example 5.1

For the Sine Wave block, in the Block Parameters dialog box we specified:

Sine type: **Time based**

Sample time: **0.1**

For the Integer Delay block, in the Block Parameters dialog box we specified:

Initial condition: **0.0**

Number of delays: **5**

The Discrete–Time Linear Systems Sub–Library

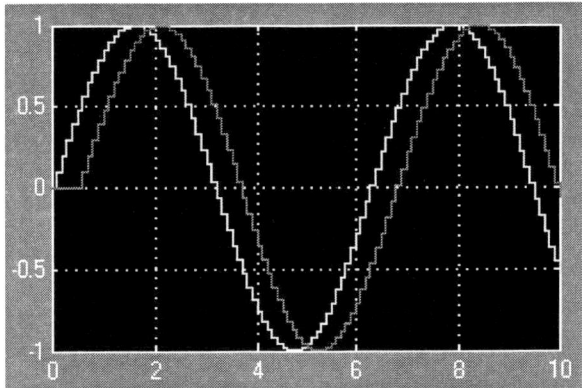

Figure 5.2. Input and output waveforms for the model of Figure 5.1

5.1.3 The Tapped Delay Block

The **Tapped Delay** block delays its input by the specified number of sample periods, and outputs all the delayed versions. Each delay is equivalent to the z^{-1} discrete–time operator, which is represented by the Unit Delay block.

Example 5.2

We will create a model using a Tapped Delay block with five delays ($N = 5$) where the input is a a discrete sine wave with amplitude 1, frequency 0.5 Hz, and sample time 0.25 s.

The model is shown in Figure 5.3 and the input and output waveforms are shown in Figure 5.4. We observe that unlike the Integer Delay block in Subsection 5.1.2, the Tapped Delay block outputs all the delayed versions.

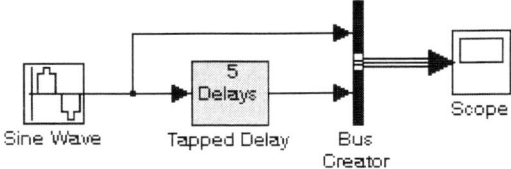

Figure 5.3. Model for Example 5.2

For the Sine Wave block, in the Block Parameters dialog box we specified Sine type: **Time based**, Frequency: **0.5**, Sample time: **0.25**. For the Tapped Delay block, in the Block Parameters dialog box we specified Initial condition: **0.0**, Number of delays: **5**

Introduction to Simulink with Engineering Applications
Copyright © Orchard Publications

Chapter 5 The Discrete Blocks Library

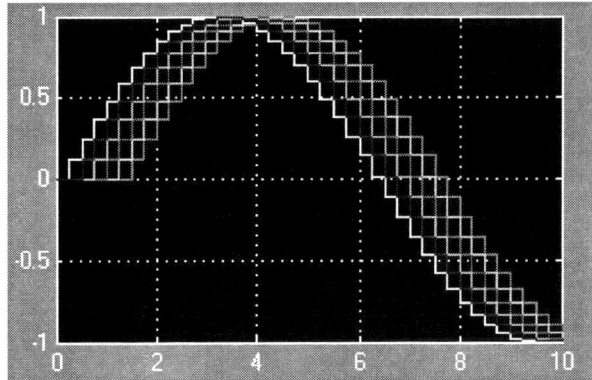

Figure 5.4. Input and output waveforms for the model of Figure 5.3

5.1.4 The Discrete-Time Integrator Block

The **Discrete-Time Integrator** block is described in Section 2.16, Chapter 2, Page 2–26.

5.1.5 The Discrete Transfer Fcn Block

The **Discrete Transfer Fcn** block implements the $\mathcal{Z}$-transform transfer function described by the following equation:

$$G(z) = \frac{N(z)}{D(z)} = \frac{a_0 z^n + a_1 z^{n-1} + \ldots + a_m z^{n-m}}{b_0 z^n + b_1 z^{n-1} + \ldots + b_m z^{n-m}} \quad (5.1)$$

The order of the denominator must be greater than or equal to the order of the numerator.

Example 5.3

It is known that the discrete transfer function of a system is

$$G(z) = \frac{0.951 z}{z^2 + 0.618 z + 1}$$

The Discrete–Time Linear Systems Sub–Library

We will create a model to display the input and output waveforms when the input is the discrete sine wave with amplitude 1, frequency 1 r/s, and sample time 0.1 s.

The model is shown in Figure 5.5 and the input and output waveforms are shown in Figure 5.6 where in the Function Block Parameters for the Discrete Transfer Fcn block we have entered:

Numerator coefficient: [0.951 0]

Denominator coefficient: [1 0.618 1]

Sample time: 0.1

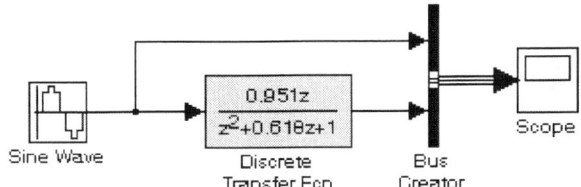

Figure 5.5. Model for Example 5.3

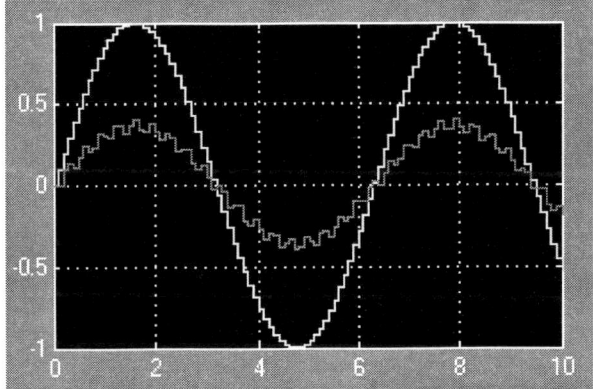

Figure 5.6. Input and Output waveforms for the model of Figure 5.5

5.1.6 The Discrete Filter Block

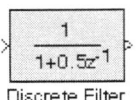

The **Discrete Filter** block implements Infinite Impulse Response (IIR) and Finite Impulse Response (FIR) filters. We must specify the filter as a ratio of polynomials in z^{-1}. We can specify that the block will have a single output or multiple outputs where the outputs correspond to a set of filters that have the same denominator polynomial but different numerator polynomials.

Chapter 5 The Discrete Blocks Library

Digital filters are classified in terms of the duration of the impulse response, and in forms of realization.

1. Impulse Response Duration

a. An *Infinite Impulse Response* (IIR) digital filter has infinite number of samples in its impulse response h[n]

b. A *Finite Impulse Response* (FIR) digital filter has a finite number of samples in its impulse response h[n]

2. Realization

a. In a *Recursive Realization* digital filter the output is dependent on the input and the *previous* values of the output. In a recursive digital filter, both the coefficients a_i and b_i are present.

b. In a *Non-Recursive Realization* digital filter the output depends on present and past values of the input only. In a non-recursive digital filter, only the coefficients a_i are present, that is, $b_i = 0$.

For block diagrams of third–order (3–delay element) recursive and non–recursive realizations please refer to Figure 2.30, Chapter 2, Page 2–25. Generally, IIR filters are implemented by recursive realization, whereas FIR filters are implemented by non–recursive realization.

Example 5.4

The step response indicates how a system will respond when the input is the unit step function. For this example, it is known that the transfer function of a system is

$$G(s) = \frac{5(s+3)}{s^2 + 3s + 15}$$

We will use the bilinear transformation to convert the transfer function to the Z-transform equivalent and create a model showing the waveforms of both the step response in the s–domain and in the z–domain. The bilinear transformation is

$$G(z) = G(s)\big|_{s = 2 \times Fs \times (z-1)/(z+1)}$$

and the MATLAB function for this conversion is **[numd,dend]=bilinear(num,den,fs)** where **num** and **den** are row vectors containing numerator and denominator transfer function coefficients in descending powers of s, **fs** is the sample frequency in Hz, and **numd** and **dend** are the z–transform coefficients for the discrete transfer function. Thus, for this example in MATLAB's Command Window we type the following:

The Discrete–Time Linear Systems Sub–Library

num=[1 3]; den=[1 3 15]; fs=0.25; [numd,dend] = bilinear(num,den,fs)

and MATLAB displays

```
numd =
    0.2090    0.3582    0.1493
dend =
    1.0000    1.7612    0.8209
```

Therefore,

$$G(z) = \frac{0.2090 + 0.3582z^{-1} + 0.1493z^{-2}}{1 + 1.7612z^{-1} + 0.8209z^{-2}}$$

and with this information we create the model shown in Figure 5.7.

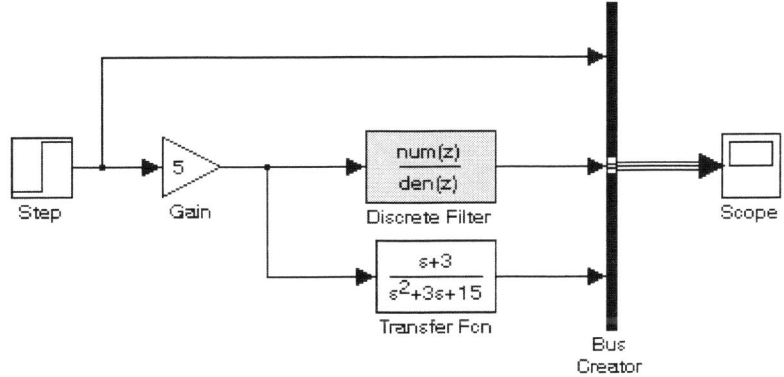

Figure 5.7. Model for Example 5.4

The output waveforms for the continuous and discrete transfer functions are shown in Figure 5.8.

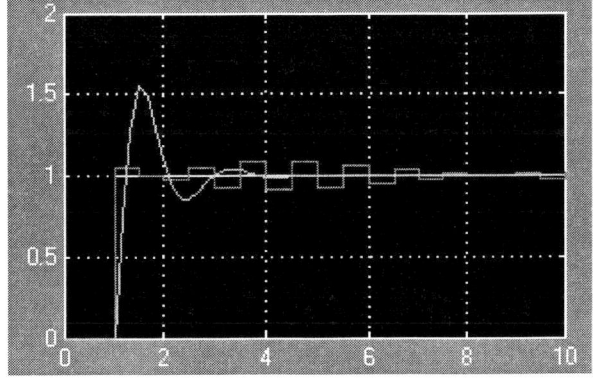

Figure 5.8. Waveforms for the model of Figure 5.7

Chapter 5 The Discrete Blocks Library

5.1.7 The Discrete Zero–Pole Block

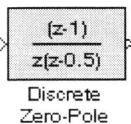

The **Discrete Zero–Pole** block implements a discrete system with the specified zeros, poles, and gain in terms of the delay operator $\mathcal{Z}$. A transfer function can be expressed in factored or zero-pole–gain form, which, for a single-input, single-output system in MATLAB, is

$$H(z) = K\frac{N(z)}{D(z)} = K\frac{(z-z_1)(z-z_2)\ldots(z-z_n)}{(z-p_1)(z-p_2)\ldots(z-p_n)} \tag{5.2}$$

where z_i represents the zeros, p_i the poles, and K is the gain. The number of poles must be greater than or equal to the number of zeros. If the poles and zeros are complex, they must be complex conjugate pairs.

Example 5.5

It is known that the discrete transfer function of a system is

$$H(z) = \frac{(z-0.5)}{(z-0.25)(z-0.75)}$$

We will create a model to display the input and output waveforms when the input is the discrete sine wave with amplitude 1, frequency 1 r/s, and sample time 0.1 s.

The model is shown in Figure 5.9 and the input and output waveforms are shown in Figure 5.10 where in the Function Block Parameters for the Discrete Pole-Zero block we have entered:

Numerator coefficient: [0.5]

Denominator coefficient: [0.25 0.75]

Sample time: 0.1

We also specified sample time 0.1 for the discrete sine wave block.

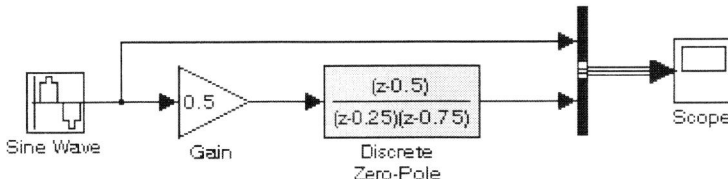

Figure 5.9. Model for Example 5.5

The Discrete–Time Linear Systems Sub–Library

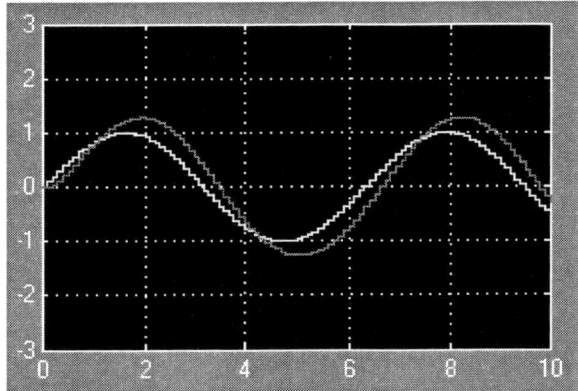

Figure 5.10. Input and output waveforms for the model of Figure 5.9

5.1.8 The Difference Block

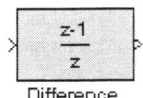

The **Difference** block outputs the current input value minus the previous input value.

Example 5.6

Using the Difference block, we will create a model that will output the current input value minus the previous input value.

The model is shown in Figure 5.11 and the input and output waveforms in Figure 5.12. The Display blocks show the input and output values at the end of the simulation time, that is, at the end of $10\ s$.

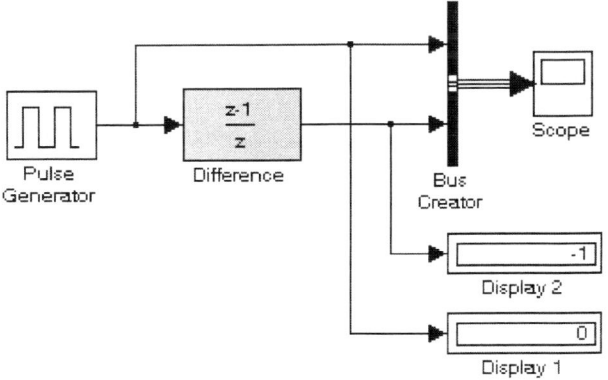

Figure 5.11. Model for Example 5.6

Chapter 5 The Discrete Blocks Library

For this example, the amplitude for the Pulse Generator block is specified as 1, the period as 4, and the pulse width as 50%. The initial condition for the previous input in the Difference block was set to 0.

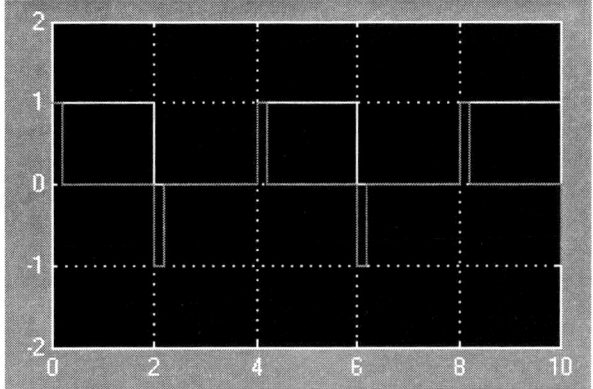

Figure 5.12. Input and output waveforms for the model of Example 5.11

5.1.9 The Discrete Derivative Block

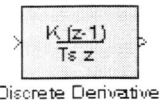

The **Discrete Derivative** block computes a discrete time derivative by subtracting the input value at the previous time step from the current value, and dividing by the sample time. We observe that this block is the same as the Difference block except that the numerator in this case is multiplied by the Gain K, and it is divided by the sample time Ts.

Example 5.7

We will create a model using the Discrete Derivative block with gain K = 1 whose input is a Sine Wave in the Discrete mode with amplitude 1 and frequency 1 Hz.

The model is shown in Figure 5.13 and the input and output waveforms in Figure 5.14. The Discrete Sine Wave is obtained from the Continuous Sine Wave block where in the Block Parameters dialog box for this block the Sample time is specified as 1.

The Discrete–Time Linear Systems Sub–Library

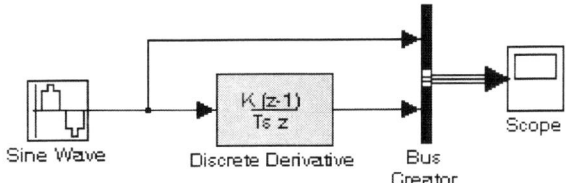

Figure 5.13. Model for Example 5.7

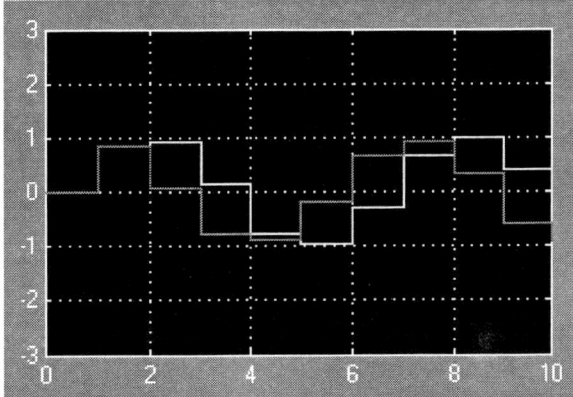

Figure 5.14. Input and output waveforms for the model of Figure 5.13

5.1.10 The Discrete State–Space Block

The **Discrete State-Space** block implements the system described by the equations

$$\begin{aligned} x[n+1] &= Ax[n] + Bu[n] \\ y[n] &= Cx[n] + Du[n] \end{aligned} \quad (5.3)$$

where n represents the current sample, $n + 1$ represents the next sample, u is the input, x is the state, and y is the output. Matrix A must be an $n \times n$ square matrix where n represents the number of the states, matrix B must have dimension $n \times m$ where m represents the number of inputs, matrix C must have dimension $r \times n$ where r represents the number of outputs, and matrix D must have dimension $r \times m$.

Example 5.8

In Example 1.1, Chapter 1, Page 1–6, we derived the continuous–time state–space equations

Chapter 5 The Discrete Blocks Library

or
$$\dot{x} = Ax + bu \tag{5.4}$$

$$\begin{bmatrix} \dot{x}_1 \\ \dot{x}_2 \end{bmatrix} = \begin{bmatrix} -4 & -4 \\ 3/4 & 0 \end{bmatrix} \begin{bmatrix} x_1 \\ x_2 \end{bmatrix} + \begin{bmatrix} 4 \\ 0 \end{bmatrix} u_0(t) \tag{5.5}$$

and
$$y = Cx + du \tag{5.6}$$

or
$$y = \begin{bmatrix} 0 & 1 \end{bmatrix} \begin{bmatrix} x_1 \\ x_2 \end{bmatrix} + [0]u \tag{5.7}$$

Using the MATLAB **c2d** function we will convert (5.5) and (5.7) to their equivalent discrete-time state space equations shown in relation (5.3), with a sampling period of 0.1. Then, using the Discrete State–Space block, we will create a model to display the output waveform and the value of the output at the end of the simulation time.

To convert the given matrices to their discrete–time state–space, we use the MATLAB statement

[Ad,Bd]=c2d(A,B,Ts)

where **Ad** and **Bd** are the discrete–time state–space matrices which are equivalent to the continuous–time state–space matrices **A** and **B**, and **Ts** is the sampling period specified as *0.1 s*. Thus, for this example, we use the MATLAB script

Ac=[-4 -4; 3/4 0]; Bc=[4 0]'; Ts=0.1; [Ad,Bd]=c2d(Ac,Bc,Ts)

and MATLAB displays

```
Ad =
    0.6588   -0.3280
    0.0615    0.9868
Bd =
    0.3280
    0.0132
```

Thus, the relation
$$x[n+1] = Ax[n] + Bu[n]$$
becomes

$$\begin{bmatrix} x_1[n+1] \\ x_2[n+1] \end{bmatrix} = \begin{bmatrix} 0.6588 & -0.3280 \\ 0.0615 & 0.9868 \end{bmatrix} \begin{bmatrix} x_1[n] \\ x_2[n] \end{bmatrix} + \begin{bmatrix} 0.3280 \\ 0.0132 \end{bmatrix} u[n] \tag{5.8}$$

The discrete–time state–space equation for the output is

The Discrete–Time Linear Systems Sub–Library

or

$$y[n] = Cx[n] + Du[n]$$

$$y[n] = \begin{bmatrix} 0 & 1 \end{bmatrix} \begin{bmatrix} x_1[n] \\ x_2[n] \end{bmatrix} + Du[n] \qquad (5.9)$$

The model is shown in Figure 5.15 where we have included the continuous state–space block for comparison. We can make the **simout To Workspace** block active by assigning a name to it.

In the Function Block Parameters for the continuous–time state-space we have entered the values shown in (5.5), and in the Function Block Parameters for the discrete-time state-space we have entered the values shown in (5.8) and (5.9) with $D = 0$ and Sample time $= 0.1$.

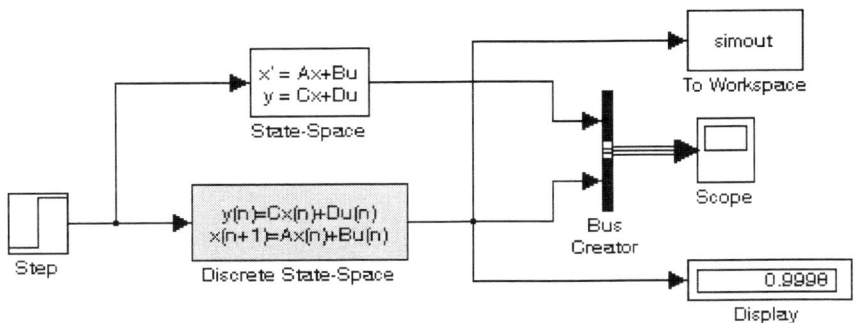

Figure 5.15. Model for Example 5.8

Figure 5.16 shows the output waveforms for both the continuous state–space block and the discrete state-space block.

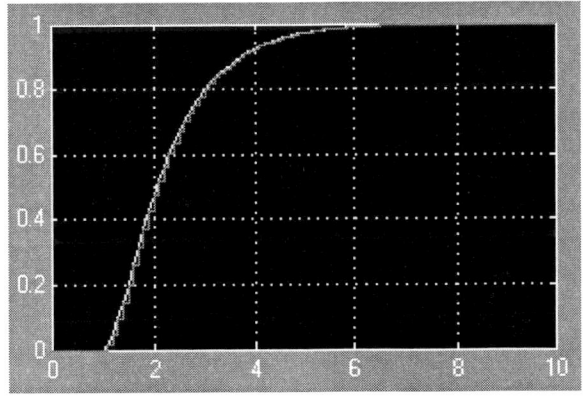

Figure 5.16. Waveforms for the model of Figure 5.15

Chapter 5 The Discrete Blocks Library

5.1.11 The Transfer Fcn First Order Block

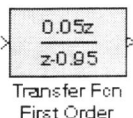

The **Transfer Fcn First Order** block implements a discrete–time first order transfer function of the input. The transfer function has a unity DC gain.

Example 5.9

It is known that the discrete transfer function of a first order system is

$$G(z) = \frac{0.3z}{z - 0.7}$$

We will create a model to display the input and output waveforms when the input is the discrete sine wave with amplitude 1, frequency 1 r/s, and sample time 0.1 s.

The model is shown in Figure 5.17 and the input and output waveforms are shown in Figure 5.18. The sample rate for the discrete Sine Wave block is specified as 0.1 s.

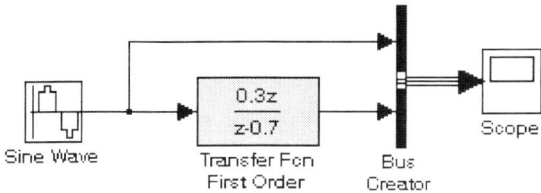

Figure 5.17. Model for Example 5.9

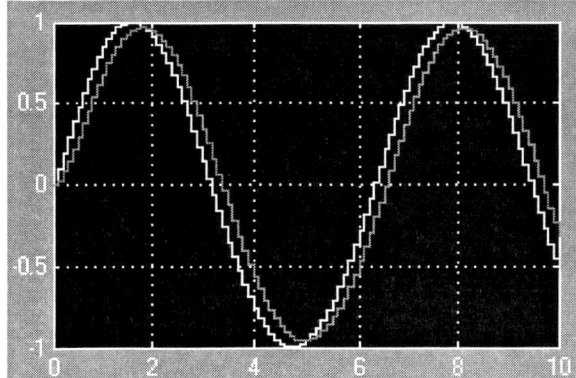

Figure 5.18. Input and output waveforms for the model of Figure 5.17

5.1.12 The Transfer Fcn Lead or Lag Block

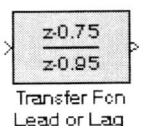
Transfer Fcn Lead or Lag

The **Transfer Fcn Lead or Lag** block implements a discrete-time lead or lag compensator of the input. The instantaneous gain of the compensator is one, and the DC gain is equal to $(1-z)/(1-p)$, where z is the zero and p is the pole of the compensator. The block implements a lead compensator when $0 < z < p < 1$, and implements a lag compensator when $0 < p < z < 1$.

Lead and lag compensators are used quite extensively in control systems. A lead compensator can increase the stability or speed of response of a system; a lag compensator can reduce (but not eliminate) the steady state error. Depending on the effect desired, one or more lead and lag compensators may be used in various combinations. Lead, lag, and lead/lag compensators are usually designed for a system in transfer function form.

In general, the transfer function of a **lead compensator** is defined as

$$G(s)_{lead} = \frac{s+a}{s+b} \qquad (5.10)$$

where $b > a$, both a and b are real, and the lead compensator has a positive phase angle.

The transfer function of a **lag compensator** is defined as

$$G(s)_{lag} = \frac{a(s+b)}{b(s+a)} \qquad (5.11)$$

where $b > a$. We observe that in (5.11) the zero is at $s = -b$ and the pole is at $s = -a$. Both a and b are real, and the lag compensator has a negative phase angle. The ratio a/b is the gain factor.

The transfer function of a **lead-lag compensator** is defined as

$$G(s)_{lead-lag} = \frac{(s+a_1)(s+b_2)}{(s+b_1)(s+a_2)} \qquad (5.12)$$

Example 5.10

An R–C network implementation of a lead compensator is shown in Figure 5.19 where $C = 1 \text{ F}$, $R_1 = R_2 = 1 \text{ }\Omega$, and $v_C(0) = 0$.

a. We will derive its transfer function

Chapter 5 The Discrete Blocks Library

b. Using the bilinear transformation we will convert the continuous–time transfer function to its equivalent discrete–time transfer function. We will use the sample rate of $0.25\ s$.

c. We will create a model that includes the Transfer Fcn Lead of Lag block.

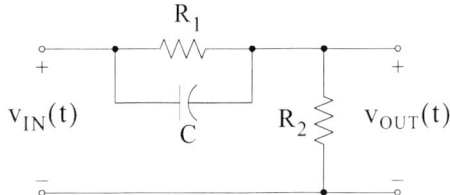

Figure 5.19. R-C lead compensator for Example 5.10

1. The s–domain equivalent circuit is shown in Figure 5.20.

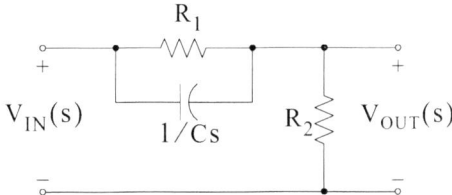

Figure 5.20. The s-domain equivalent circuit of Figure 5.19

By KCL,

$$\frac{V_{OUT}(s) - V_{IN}(s)}{R_1} + \frac{V_{OUT}(s) - V_{IN}(s)}{1/Cs} + \frac{V_{OUT}(s)}{R_2} = 0$$

$$\frac{V_{OUT}(s)}{R_1} + \frac{V_{OUT}(s)}{R_2} + CsV_{OUT}(s) = \frac{V_{IN}(s)}{R_1} + CsV_{IN}(s)$$

$$\left(\frac{1}{R_1} + \frac{1}{R_2} + Cs\right)V_{OUT}(s) = \left(\frac{1}{R_1} + Cs\right)V_{IN}(s)$$

Thus,

$$G(s) = \frac{V_{OUT}(s)}{V_{IN}(s)} = \frac{1/R_1 + Cs}{1/R_1 + 1/R_2 + Cs} \tag{5.13}$$

and by substitution of the given values,

$$G(s) = \frac{s+1}{s+2} \tag{5.14}$$

2. Using MATLAB's bilinear transformation function, we obtain

num=[1 1]; den=[1 2]; fs=0.25; [numd,dend] = bilinear(num,den,fs)

numd =

```
    0.6000    0.2000
dend =
    1.0000    0.6000
```

Therefore, the discrete transfer function is

$$G(z) = \frac{0.6 + 0.2z^{-1}}{1 + 0.6z^{-1}}$$

or

$$G(z) = \frac{z + 1/3}{z + 0.6}$$

3. The model is shown in Figure 5.21. The input and output waveforms are shown in Figure 5.22. The sample rate for the discrete Sine Wave block is specified as 0.1 s.

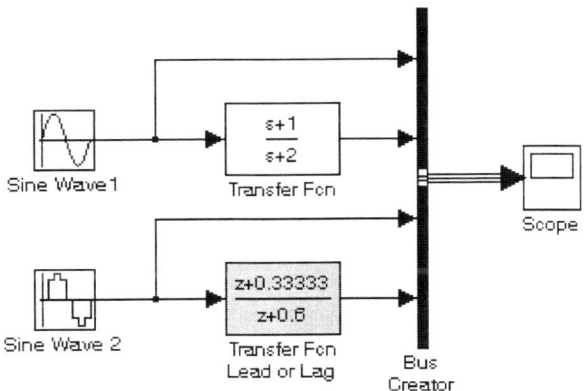

Figure 5.21. Model for Example 5.10

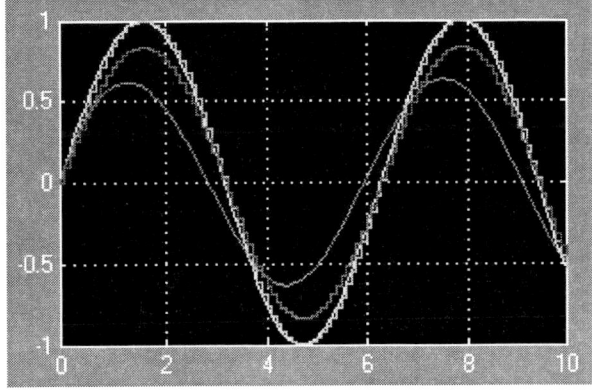

Figure 5.22. Input and output waveforms for the model of Figure 5.21

Chapter 5 The Discrete Blocks Library

5.1.13 The Transfer Fcn Real Zero Block

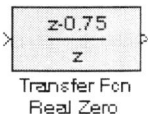

The **Transfer Fcn Real Zero** block implements a discrete–time transfer function that has a real zero and no pole.

Example 5.11

We will create a model with a Transfer Fcn Real Zero block that has a real zero with value 0.5.

The model is shown in Figure 5.23 and the input and output waveforms are shown in Figure 5.24. The sample rate for the discrete Sine Wave block has been set to 0.1 s.

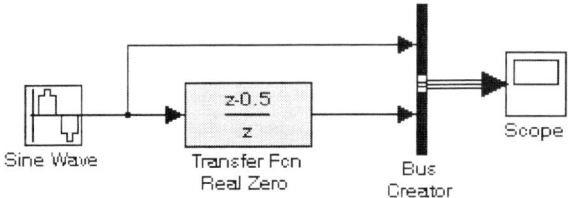

Figure 5.23. Model for Example 5.11

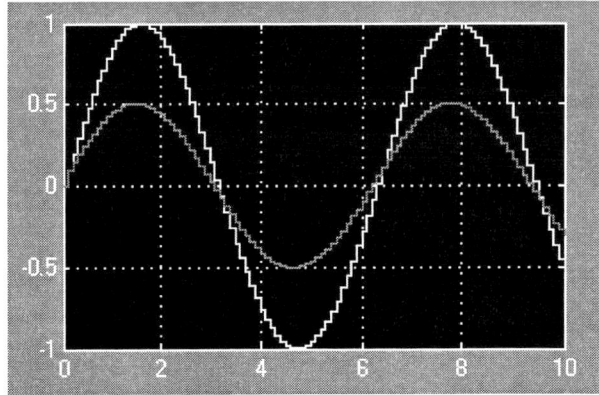

Figure 5.24. Input and output waveforms for the model of Figure 5.23

The Discrete–Time Linear Systems Sub–Library

5.1.14 The Weighted Moving Average Block

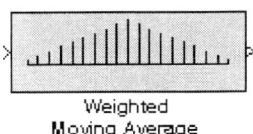

The **Weighted Moving Average** block samples and holds the N most recent inputs, multiplies each input by a specified value (given by the Weights parameter), and stacks them in a vector. This block supports both single–input / single–output (SISO) and single–input / multi–output (SIMO) modes. For a detailed discussion please refer to the Help menu for this block.

The following discussion will help us understand the meaning of a weighted moving average.

Suppose that the voltages displayed by an electronic instrument in a 5-day period, Monday through Friday, were 23.5, 24.2, 24.0, 23.9 and 24.1 volts respectively. The average of those five readings is

$$\frac{23.5 + 24.2 + 24.0 + 23.9 + 24.1}{5} = 23.94$$

Now, suppose that on the following Monday the reading was found to be 24.2 volts. Then, the new 5–day average based on the last five days, Tuesday through Monday is

$$\frac{24.2 + 24.0 + 23.9 + 24.1 + 24.2}{5} = 24.08$$

We observe that the 5–day average has changed from 23.94 to 24.08 volts. In other words, the average has "moved" from 23.94 to 24.08 volts. Hence, the name **moving average**.

However, a more meaningful moving average can be obtained if we assign weights to each reading where the most recent reading carries the most weight. Thus, using a 5–day moving average we could take the reading obtained on the 5th day and multiply it by 5, the 4th day by 4, the 3rd day by 3, the 2nd day by 2, and the 1st day by 1. We could now add these numbers and divide the sum by the sum of the multipliers, i.e., 5+4+3+2+1=15. Thus, the 5–day weighted moving average would be

$$\frac{1 \times 24.2 + 2 \times 24.0 + 3 \times 23.9 + 4 \times 24.1 + 5 \times 24.2}{15} = 24.09$$

and the value 24.09 is referred to as the **Weighted Moving Average (WMA)**.

An **Exponential Moving Average (EMA)** takes a percentage of the most recent value and adds in the previous value's exponential moving average times 1 minus that percentage. For instance, suppose we wanted a 10% EMA. We would take the most recent value and multiply it by 10% then add that figure to the previous value's EMA multiplied by the remaining percent, that is,

Chapter 5 The Discrete Blocks Library

$$\text{Most Recent Value} \times 0.1 + \text{Previous Value's EMA} \times (1 - 0.1) \qquad (5.15)$$

Alternately, we can use the following formula to determine the percentage to be used in the calculation:

$$\text{Exponential Percentage} = \frac{2}{\text{Time Periods} + 1} \qquad (5.16)$$

For example, if we wanted a 20 period EMA, we would use

$$\frac{2}{20+1} = 9.52\ \% \qquad (5.17)$$

Example 5.12

The price of a particular security (stock) over a 5–day period is as follows:

$$77\ \ 80\ \ 82\ \ 85\ \ 90$$

where the last value is the most recent. We will create single-input / single output (SISO) model with a Weighted Moving Average block to simulate the weighted moving average over this 5–day period.

For this example, we will represent the SISO output as follows:

$$y_1(k) = a_1 u(k) + b_1 u(k-1) + c_1 u(k-2) + d_1 u(k-3) + e_1 u(k-4) \qquad (5.18)$$

where

$$u(k) = 5/15\ \ u(k-1) = 4/15\ \ u(k-2) = 3/15\ \ u(k-3) = 2/15\ \ u(k-4) = 1/15 \qquad (5.19)$$

The model is shown in Figure 5.25 where in the Function Block Parameters dialog box for the Weighted Moving Average block we have entered:

Weights:

$$[5/15\ \ 4/15\ \ 3/15\ \ 2/15\ \ 1/15]$$

Initial conditions:

$$[85\ \ 82\ \ 80\ \ 77]$$

Constant block – Output scaling value: [1.25 3]

Weighted Moving Average block – Parameter data types: sfix(16), Parameter scaling: 2^{-4}

Signal data types: sfix(16), Parameter scaling: 2^{-6}

The Sample & Hold Delays Sub–Library

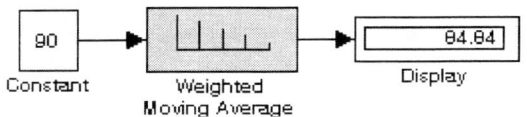

Figure 5.25. Model for Example 5.12

5.2 The Sample & Hold Delays Sub-Library

The **Sample & Hold Delays Sub–Library** contains the blocks described in Subsections 5.2.1 through 5.2.3 below.

5.2.1 The Memory Block

The **Memory** block outputs its input from the previous time step, applying a one integration step sample–and–hold to its input signal.

Example 5.13

We will create a model using a Memory block whose output is subtracted from its input where the input is a pulse generator with amplitude 1, period 5 s, pulse width 50%, and Phase delay 1 sec. For the Memory block, the Initial condition is specified as 0 and the Inherit sample time is checked.

The model is shown in Figure 5.26 and the input and output waveforms are shown in Figure 5.27.

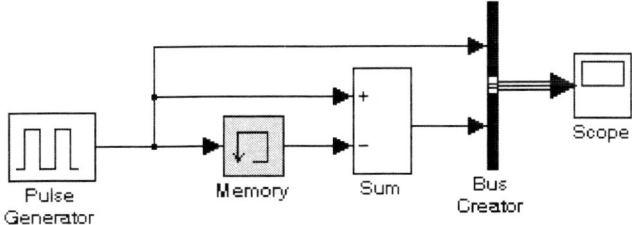

Figure 5.26. Model for Example 5.13

Chapter 5 The Discrete Blocks Library

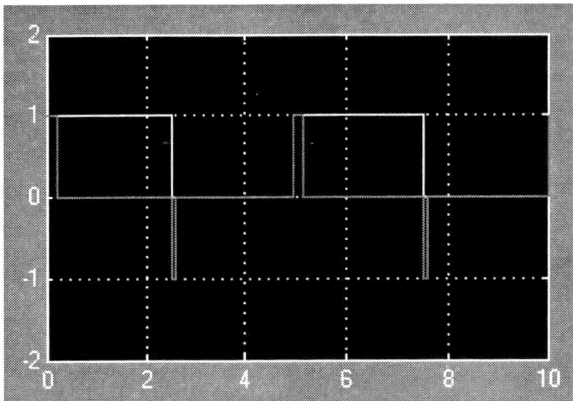

Figure 5.27. Input and output waveforms for the model of Figure 5.26

5.2.2 The First–Order Hold Block

The **First-Order Hold** block implements a first–order sample–and–hold that operates at the specified sampling interval. In some signal processing applications it is necessary to retain (hold) the value that a signal has at a specified instant of time. A circuit used to perform this function is referred to as **sample-and-hold circuit**. For example, a sample–and–hold circuit can be used to provide a steady voltage into a device that cannot process a continuously varying signal. An analog–to–digital converter is such a device.

Example 5.14

We will create a model using a First–Order Hold block with sample time 0.5 s where the input is a sine wave with amplitude 1, and frequency 1 Hz.

The model is shown in Figure 5.28 and the input and output waveforms are shown in Figure 5.29.

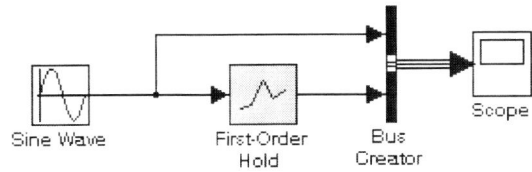

Figure 5.28. Model for Example 5.14

The Sample & Hold Delays Sub–Library

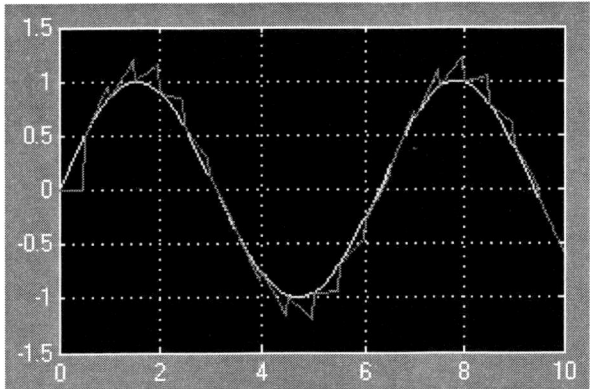

Figure 5.29. Input and output waveforms for the model of Figure 5.28

5.2.3 The Zero–Order Hold Block

The **Zero–Order Hold** block samples and holds its input for the specified sample period. The block accepts one input and generates one output, both of which can be scalar or vector. If the input is a vector, all elements of the vector are held for the same sample period. If the model contains multirate transitions, we must add Zero–Order Hold blocks between the fast–to–slow transitions. The sample rate of the Zero–Order Hold must be set to that of the slower block. For slow–to–fast transitions, we use the Unit Delay block which was described in Section 2.15, Chapter 2, Page 2–24.

For multirate transitions it is preferable to use the Rate Transition block since it is easier to use and offers a wider range of options. The Rate Transition block and multirate transitions are described in Subsection 12.1.8, Chapter 12, Page 12–8.

Example 5.15

We will create a model using a Zero–Order Hold block with sample time 1 and input a random waveform with amplitude 1 and frequency 1 Hz.

The model is shown in Figure 5.30 and the input and output waveforms are shown in Figure 5.31.

Chapter 5 The Discrete Blocks Library

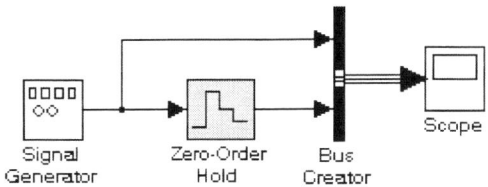

Figure 5.30. Model for Example 5.15

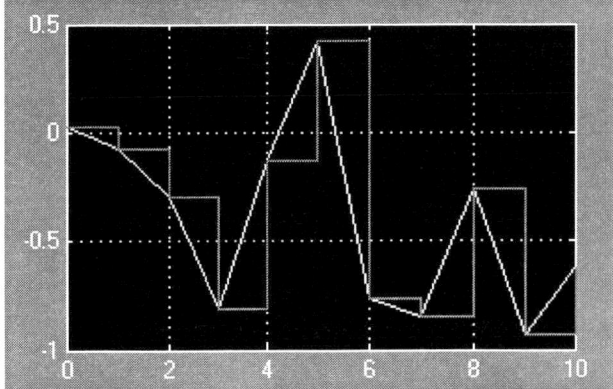

Figure 5.31. Input and output waveforms for the model of Figure 5.30

Summary

5.3 Summary

- The **Unit Delay** block delays its input by the specified sample period. That is, the output equals the input delayed by one sample. This block is equivalent to the z^{-1} discrete–time operator. This block allows for discretization of one or more signals in time, or for resampling the signal at a different rate. If our model contains multirate transitions, then we must add **Unit Delay** blocks between the slow–to–fast transitions. The sample rate of the **Unit Delay** block must be set to that of the slower block.

- The **Integer Delay** block delays its input by N sample periods. This block accepts one input and generates one output, both of which can be scalar or vector.

- The **Tapped Delay** block delays its input by the specified number of sample periods, and outputs all the delayed versions. Each delay is equivalent to the z^{-1} discrete-time operator, which is represented by the Unit Delay block.

- The **Discrete–Time Integrator block** performs discrete-time integration or accumulation of a signal. This block appears also in the **Discrete Library** Browser. We use this block in discrete–time systems instead of the Continuous Integrator block in continuous–time systems. The block can integrate or accumulate using the Forward Euler, Backward Euler, and Trapezoidal methods.

- The **Discrete Transfer Fcn** block implements the z–transform transfer function described by the following equation:

$$G(z) = \frac{N(z)}{D(z)} = \frac{a_0 z^n + a_1 z^{n-1} + \ldots + a_m z^{n-m}}{b_0 z^n + b_1 z^{n-1} + \ldots + b_m z^{n-m}}$$

The order of the denominator must be greater than or equal to the order of the numerator.

- The **Discrete Filter** block implements Infinite Impulse Response (IIR) and Finite Impulse Response (FIR) filters. We must specify the filter as a ratio of polynomials in z^{-1}. We can specify that the block have a single output or multiple outputs where the outputs correspond to a set of filters that have the same denominator polynomial but different numerator polynomials.

- The **Discrete Zero-Pole** block implements a discrete system with the specified zeros, poles, and gain in terms of the delay operator $\mathcal{Z}$. A transfer function can be expressed in factored or zero-pole-gain form, which, for a single-input, single-output system in MATLAB, is

$$G(z) = K\frac{N(z)}{D(z)} = K\frac{(z-z_1)(z-z_2)\ldots(z-z_n)}{(z-p_1)(z-p_2)\ldots(z-p_n)}$$

where z_i represents the zeros, p_i the poles, and K the gain. The number of poles must be greater than or equal to the number of zeros.

Chapter 5 The Discrete Blocks Library

- The **Difference** block outputs the current input value minus the previous input value.

- The **Discrete Derivative** block computes a discrete time derivative by subtracting the input value at the previous time step from the current value, and dividing by the sample time. This block is the same as the Difference block except that the numerator is multiplied by the Gain K and it is divided by the sample time Ts.

- The **Discrete State-Space** block implements the system described by the equations

$$x[n+1] = Ax[n] + Bu[n]$$
$$y[n] = Cx[n] + Du[n]$$

where n represents the current sample, $n+1$ represents the next sample, u is the input, x is the state, and y is the output. Matrix A must be an $n \times n$ square matrix where n represents the number of the states, matrix B must have dimension $n \times m$ where m represents the number of inputs, matrix C must have dimension $r \times n$ where r represents the number of outputs, and matrix D must have dimension $r \times m$.

- The **Transfer Fcn First Order** block implements a discrete-time first order transfer function of the input. The transfer function has a unity DC gain.

- The **Transfer Fcn Lead or Lag** block implements a discrete-time lead or lag compensator of the input. The instantaneous gain of the compensator is one, and the DC gain is equal to $(1-z)/(1-p)$, where z is the zero and p is the pole of the compensator. The block implements a lead compensator when $0 < z < p < 1$, and implements a lag compensator when $0 < p < z < 1$.

- The **Transfer Fcn Real Zero** block implements a discrete-time transfer function that has a real zero and no pole.

- The **Weighted Moving Average** block samples and holds the N most recent inputs, multiplies each input by a specified value (given by the Weights parameter), and stacks them in a vector. This block supports both single–input/single–output (SISO) and single–input/multi–output (SIMO) modes.

- The **Memory** block outputs its input from the previous time step, applying a one integration step sample-and-hold to its input signal.

- The **First–Order Hold** block implements a first–order sample–and–hold that operates at the specified sampling interval. In some signal processing applications it is necessary to retain (hold) the value that a signal has at a specified instant of time.

- The **Zero–Order Hold** block samples and holds its input for the specified sample period. The block accepts one input and generates one output, both of which can be scalar or vector. If the input is a vector, all elements of the vector are held for the same sample period.

5.4 Exercises

1. It is known that the transfer function of a system is

$$G(s) = \frac{0.5279}{s^2 + 1.0275s + 0.5279}$$

   Use the bilinear transformation to convert this transfer function to the $\mathcal{Z}$-transform equivalent, and create a model showing the waveforms of both the step response in the s–domain and in the z–domain.

2. It is known that the discrete transfer function of a system is

$$G(z) = \frac{0.8394z^2 - 1.5511z + 0.8394}{z^2 - 1.5511z + 0.6791}$$

   Create a model to display the input and output waveforms when the input is the unit step function and the sample time is specified as 0.1 s.

3. It is known that the discrete transfer function of a system is

$$G(z) = \frac{0.2(z^2 - 1.1z + 0.3)}{z^3 - 2.4z^2 + 1.91z - 0.504}$$

   Create a model to display the input and output waveforms when the input is the discrete sine function and the sample time is specified as 0.1 s.

4. An R–C network implementation of a lag compensator is shown below where $C = 1\ F$, $R_1 = R_2 = 1\ \Omega$, and $v_C(0) = 0$.

   a. Derive its transfer function

   b. Use the bilinear transformation, convert the continuous–time transfer function to its equivalent discrete–time transfer function. Use the sample rate of 0.25 s.

   c. Create a model that includes the Transfer Fcn Lead or Lag block to implement the discrete–time transfer function.

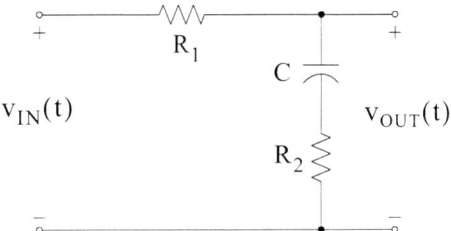

Chapter 5 The Discrete Blocks Library

5. The price of a particular security (stock) over a 5-day period is as follows:

$$77 \quad 80 \quad 82 \quad 85 \quad 90$$

where the last value is the most recent. Create a a single-input / multi-output (SIMO) model with a Weighted Moving Average block to simulate the weighted moving average over this 5-day period.

5.5 Solutions to End-of-Chapter Exercises

1.

Using the bilinear transformation we enter the following in MATLAB's Command window:

num=[0.5279]; den=[1 1.0275 0.5279]; fs=0.25; [numd,dend] = bilinear(num,den,fs)

MATLAB outputs the following z–domain coefficients:

```
numd =
    0.4087    0.8174    0.4087
dend =
    1.0000    0.4303    0.2045
```

The model and the waveforms are shown below.

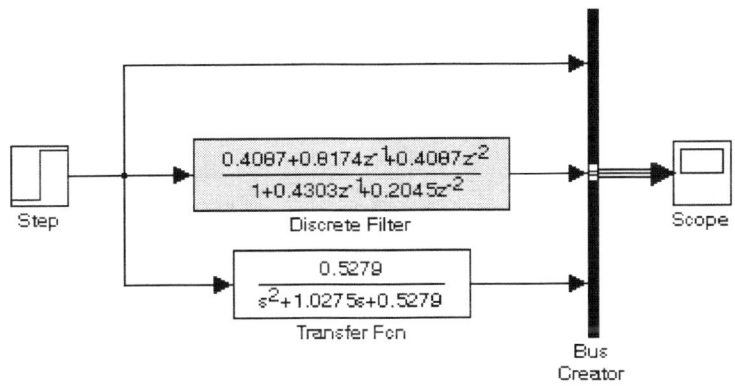

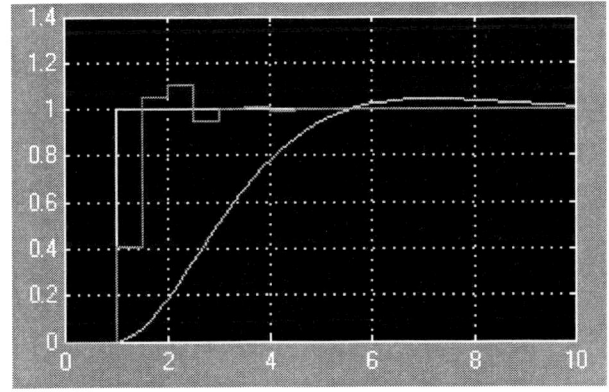

Chapter 5 The Discrete Blocks Library

2.

The model and the input and output waveforms are shown below where in the Function Block Parameters for the Discrete Transfer Fcn block we have entered:

Numerator coefficient: [0.8394 -1.5511 0.8394]

Denominator coefficient: [1 -1.5511 0.6791]

Sample time: 0.1

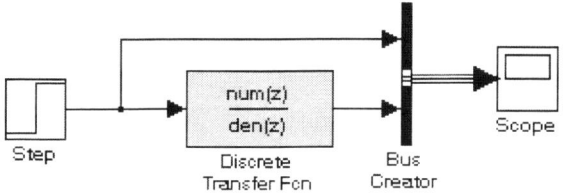

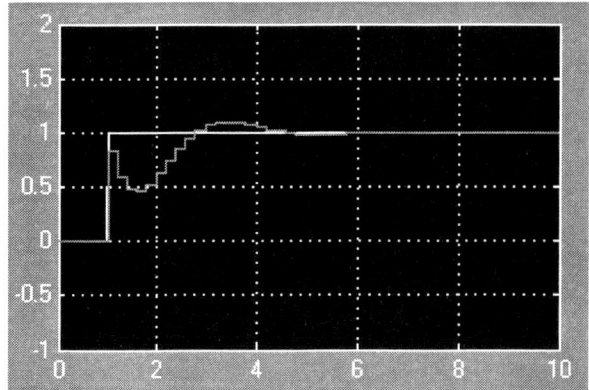

3.

The model and the input and output waveforms are shown below where in the Function Block Parameters for the Discrete Transfer Fcn block we have entered:

Numerator coefficient: [1 −1.1 0.3]

Denominator coefficient: [1 -2.4 1.91 -0.504]

Sample time: 0.1

We also specify sample time 0.1 for the discrete sine wave block.

Solutions to End–of–Chapter Exercises

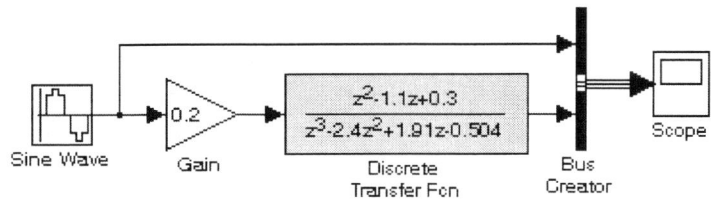

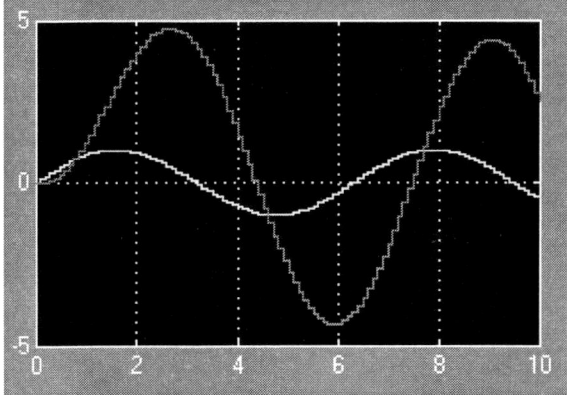

4.

a.

The s–domain equivalent circuit is shown below.

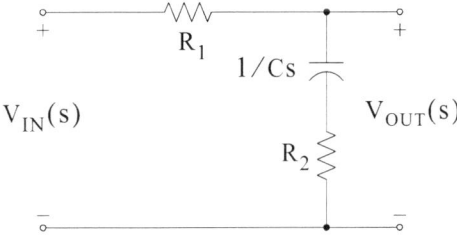

Application of the voltage division expression yields,

$$V_{OUT}(s) = \frac{1/Cs + R_2}{R_1 + 1/Cs + R_2} \cdot V_{IN}(s)$$

$$G(s) = \frac{V_{OUT}(s)}{V_{IN}(s)} = \frac{1/Cs + R_2}{R_1 + 1/Cs + R_2} = \frac{R_2 Cs + 1}{(R_1 + R_2)Cs + 1}$$

and by substitution of the given values,

$$G(s) = \frac{s+1}{2s+1} = \frac{2(s+1)}{(s+0.5)} \tag{5.20}$$

b.

Using MATLAB's bilinear transformation function, we obtain

num=[2 2]; den=[1 0.5]; fs=0.25; [numd,dend] = bilinear(num,den,fs)

numd =
    3   1

dend =
    1   0

Therefore, the discrete transfer function is

$$G(z) = \frac{3 + z^{-1}}{1 + 0} = \frac{3z + 1}{z + 0} = \frac{z + 1/3}{(1/3)z + 0}$$

c.

The model and the input and output waveforms are shown below. The sample rate for the discrete Sine Wave block is specified as 0.1 s.

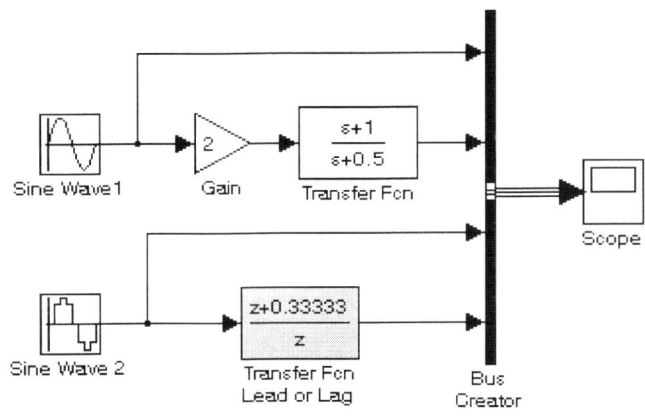

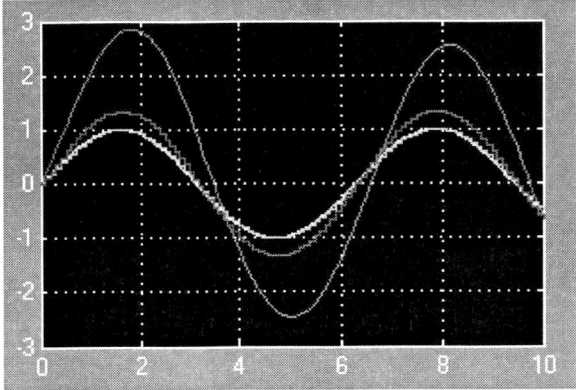

Solutions to End-of-Chapter Exercises

5.

The SIMO model is represented by the following equations:

$$y_1(k) = a_1u(k) + b_1u(k-1) + c_1u(k-2) + d_1u(k-3) + e_1u(k-4)$$
$$y_2(k) = a_2u(k) + b_2u(k-1) + c_2u(k-2) + d_2u(k-3)$$
$$y_3(k) = a_3u(k) + b_3u(k-1) + c_3u(k-2)$$
$$y_4(k) = a_4u(k) + b_4u(k-1)$$
$$y_5(k) = a_5u(k) \quad \text{(Input)}$$

where

$$u(k) = 5/15 \quad u(k-1) = 4/15 \quad u(k-2) = 3/15 \quad u(k-3) = 2/15 \quad u(k-4) = 1/15$$

The model is shown below where in the Function Block Parameters dialog box we entered:

Weights:
$$[5/15 \ 4/15 \ 3/15 \ 2/15 \ 1/15; 5/15 \ 4/15 \ 3/15 \ 2/15 \ 0;$$
$$5/15 \ 4/15 \ 3/15 \ 0 \ 0; 5/15 \ 4/15 \ 0 \ 0 \ 0; 5/15 \ 0 \ 0 \ 0 \ 0]$$

Initial conditions:
$$[85 \ 82 \ 80 \ 77]$$

Constant block - Output scaling value: [1.25 3]

Weighted Moving Average block – Parameter data types: $sfix(16)$, Parameter scaling: 2^{-4}

Signal data types: $sfix(16)$, Parameter scaling: 2^{-6}

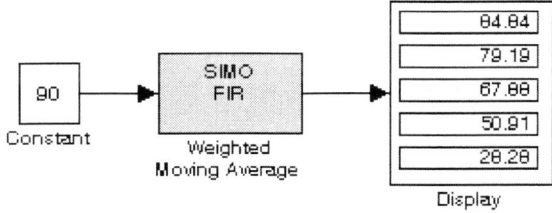

The value at the top is the sum of the 5-day WMAs, the next value is the sum of the WMAs Tuesday through Friday, the next Wednesday through Friday, and so on. Shown below is a table with the values computed in an Excel spreadsheet for comparison.

	Monday	Tuesday	Wednesday	Thursday	Friday	Sum
Price	77	80	82	85	90	
Weight	1/15	2/15	3/15	4/15	5/15	
WMA	5.133	10.667	16.400	22.667	30.000	84.867

Chapter 5 The Discrete Blocks Library

NOTES

Chapter 6

The Logic and Bit Operations Library

This chapter is an introduction to the **Logic and Bit Operations** Library. This is the fifth library in the Simulink group of libraries and contains the **Logic Operations Group Sub-Library**, the **Bit Operations Group Sub-Library**, and the **Edge Detection Group Sub-Library** blocks shown below. We will describe the function of each block included in this library and we will perform simulation examples to illustrate their application.

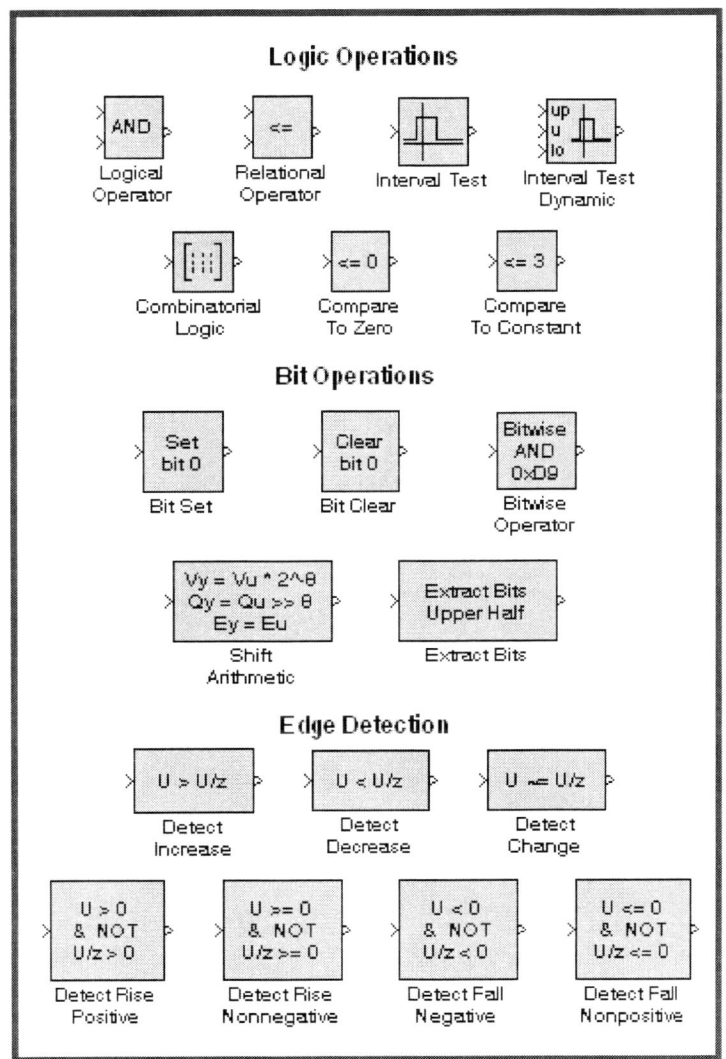

Chapter 6 The Logic and Bit Operations Library

6.1 The Logic Operations Group Sub-Library

The **Logic Operations Group Sub-Library** contains the blocks described in Subsections 6.1.1 through 6.1.7 below.

6.1.1 The Logical Operator Block

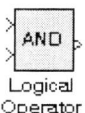

The **Logical Operator** block is described in Section 2.12, Chapter 2, Page 2–18.

6.1.2 The Relational Operator Block

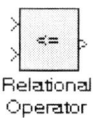

The **Relational Operator** block is described in Section 2.11, Chapter 2, Page 2–17.

6.1.3 The Interval Test Block

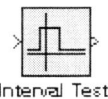

The **Interval Test** block performs a test to determine if a signal is in a specified interval. The block outputs TRUE if the input is between the values specified by the Lower limit and Upper limit parameters. The block outputs FALSE if the input is outside those values. The output of the block when the input is equal to the Lower limit or the Upper limit is determined by whether the boxes next to Interval closed on left and Interval closed on right are selected in the dialog box.

Example 6.1

We will create a model with an Interval Test block where the Upper limit parameter is set to the binary value [01111111], the Lower limit is set to the binary value [10000000], and the boxes next to Interval closed on left and Interval closed on right are selected in the dialog box. Select the largest positive value and the smallest negative value so that the Interval Test block will be TRUE.

The model is shown in Figure 6.1. We recall that in an 8–bit binary string the largest positive number is 127 (binary [01111111]) and the smallest negative number in an 8–bit binary string is

The Logic Operations Group Sub–Library

−128 (binary [10000000]). In the model of Figure 6.1, the Constant 1 and Constant 2 blocks have been specified as Output data type **sfix(8)**, the Display 1 and Display 3 blocks have been specified as **binary (Stored Integer)**, and the Display 2 block has been specified as Format **short**.

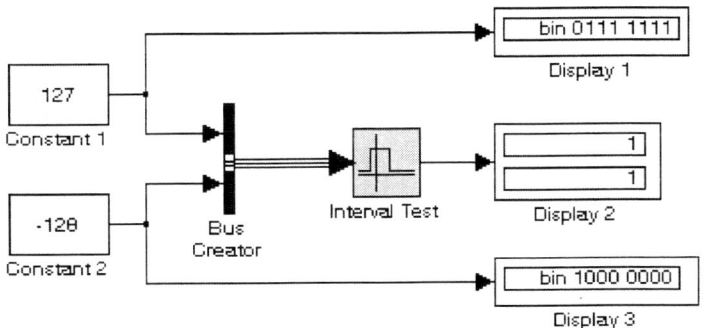

Figure 6.1. Model for Example 6.1

6.1.4 The Interval Test Dynamic Block

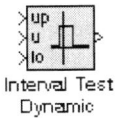

Like the Interval Test block, the **Interval Test Dynamic** block performs a test to determine if a signal is in a specified interval. This block outputs TRUE (1) if the input is between the values of the external signals **up** and **lo**. The block outputs FALSE (0) if the input is outside those values. The output of the block when the input is equal to the signal **up** or the signal **lo** is determined by whether the boxes next to Interval closed on left and Interval closed on right are selected in the Parameters dialog box.

Example 6.2

We will create a model with an Interval Test Dynamic block where the external signal **up** is specified as the decimal value [127], the external signal **lo** is specified as the decimal value [−128], and the boxes next to Interval closed on left and Interval closed on right are both checked in the Block Parameters dialog box. We will use a Display block to show the output when the input to the Interval Test Dynamic block is specified for the decimal value [129].

The model is shown in Figure 6.2. The Constant 1, Constant 2, and Constant 3 blocks have been specified as Output data type **sfix(12)**, the Display 1, Display 3, and Display 4 blocks have been specified as **binary (Stored Integer)**, and the Display 2 block has been specified as Format **short**.

Chapter 6 The Logic and Bit Operations Library

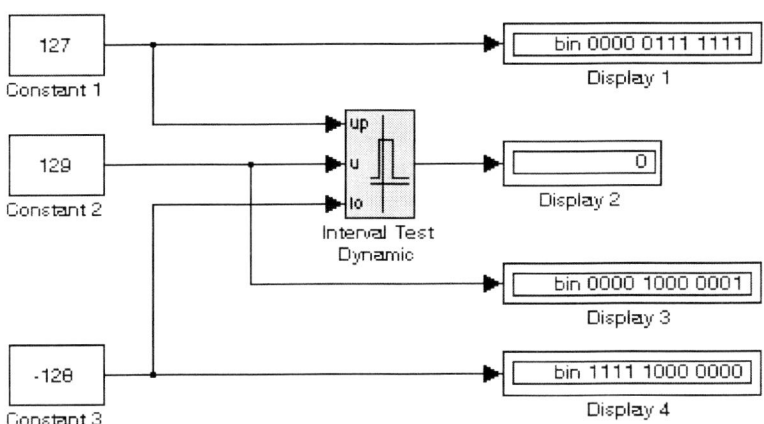

Figure 6.2. Model for Example 6.2

6.1.5 The Combinatorial Logic Block

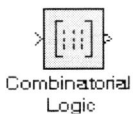

The **Combinatorial Logic** block, often referred to as combinational block, implements a standard truth table for modeling programmable logic arrays (PLAs)[*], logic circuits, decision tables, and other Boolean expressions. In a Combinatorial Logic block we specify a matrix that defines all outputs as the Truth table parameter. Each row of the matrix contains the output for a different combination of input elements. We must specify outputs for every combination of inputs. The number of columns is the number of block outputs.

Example 6.3

We will create a model with Combinatorial Logic blocks to implement a full adder[†] logic circuit.

The Truth table for a full adder digital circuit is shown in Table 6.1 where X is the augend, Y is the addend, C_{IN} is the carry from a previous addition, S is the Sum of the present addition, and C_{OUT} is the output carry, i.e., the carry generated by the present addition.

---

[*] For a detailed description of PLAs, please refer to Digital Circuit Analysis and Design with an Introduction to CPLDs and FPGAs, ISBN 0-9744239-6-3.
[†] For a detailed description of full adders, full subtractors, and other logic circuits please refer to the reference cited above.

The Logic Operations Group Sub–Library

TABLE 6.1 Truth table for a full adder

Inputs			Outputs	
X	Y	C_{IN}	S	C_{OUT}
0	0	0	0	0
0	0	1	1	0
0	1	0	1	0
0	1	1	0	1
1	0	0	1	0
1	0	1	0	1
1	1	0	0	1
1	1	1	1	1

The model is shown in Figure 6.3 where we have specified:

Constant blocks - Constant value: [0 0 0], [0 0 1], ... [1 1 1] in Constant blocks 1 through 8 respectively – Signal data types: **boolean** – Interpret vector parameters: **check mark**

Combinatorial Logic blocks (all) – Truth table: [0 0; 1 0; 1 0; 0 1; 1 0; 0 1; 0 1; 1 1] – Sample time: –1

Display blocks – Format: **short**

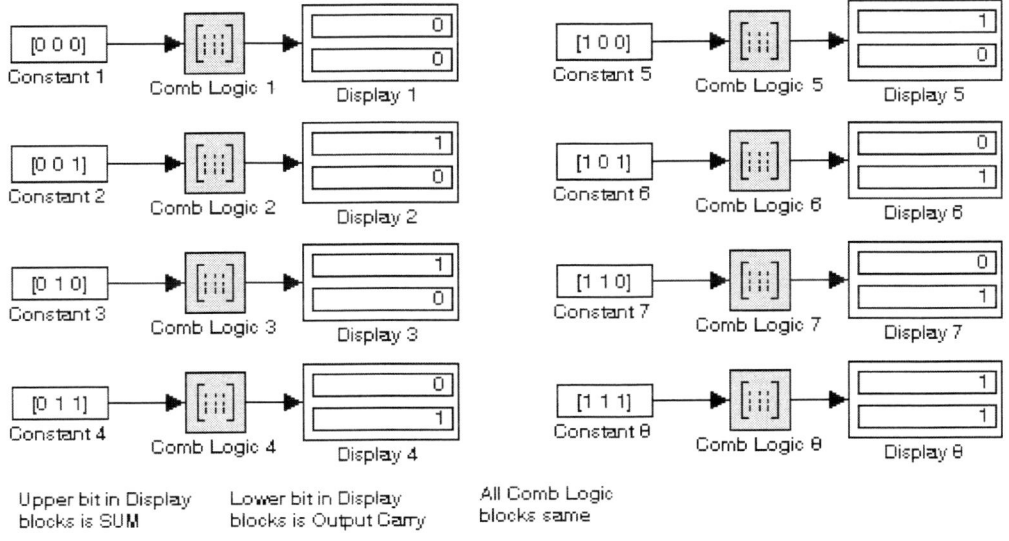

Figure 6.3. Model for Example 6.3

Chapter 6 The Logic and Bit Operations Library

The model of Figure 6.3 looks more presentable in Figure 6.4 where the individual segments were lined–up one below the other,* we selected all Combinatorial Logic blocks, and from the Edit drop menu we selected Create Subsystem.

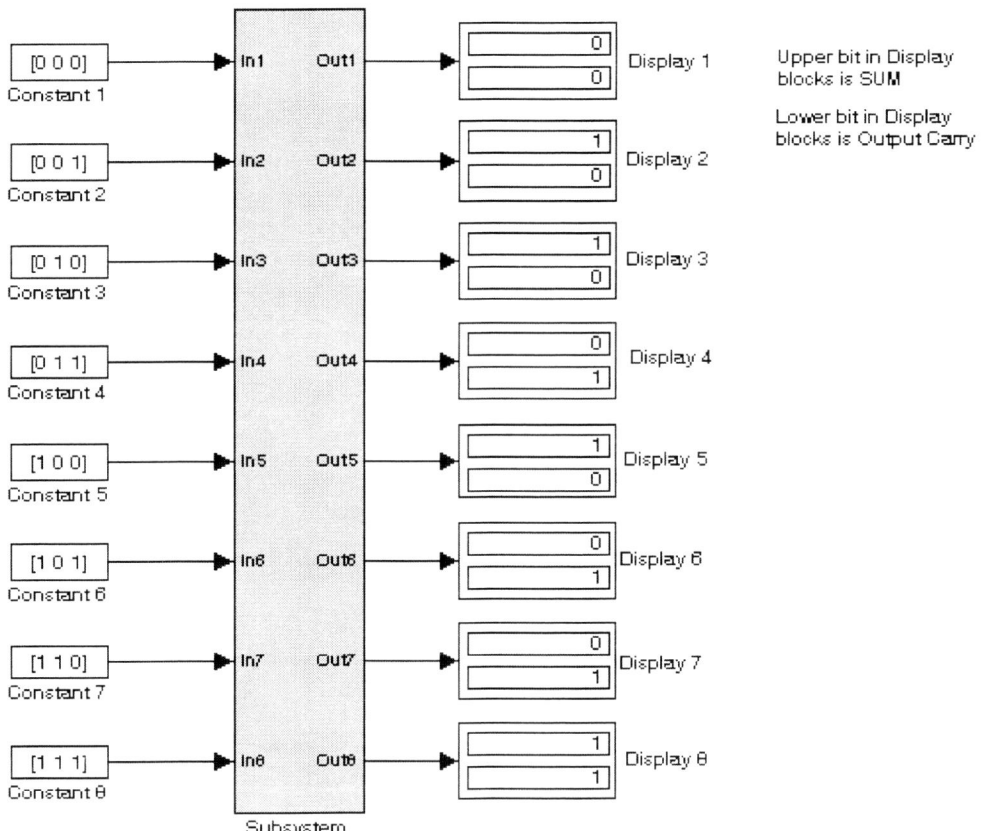

Figure 6.4. Modified model for Example 6.3

We can also implement sequential circuits (that is, circuits with states) with the Combinatorial Logic block by including an additional input for the state of the block and feeding the output of the block back into this state input.

Example 6.4

We will create a model with Combinatorial Logic blocks to simulate a Set–Reset (S–R) flip-flop constructed with NAND gates.

---

* It was necessary to edit the view (Fit Selection to View) so that we could see all segments of the model and select all Combinatorial Logic blocks at once.

Figure 6.5(a) shows a basic *Set–Reset (S–R) flip flop* constructed with two NAND gates, and Figure 6.5(b) shows the symbol for the S–R flip flop where S stands for Set and R stands for Reset.

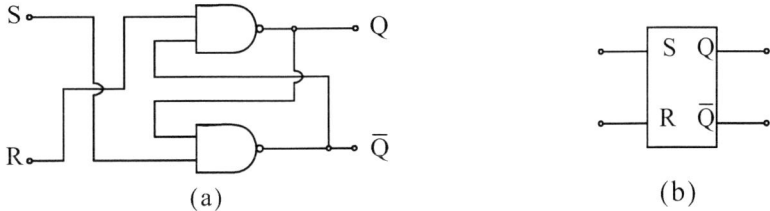

Figure 6.5. Construction and symbol for the S–R flip flop

We recall that for a 2–input NAND gate the output is logical 0 when both inputs are 1s and the output is 1 otherwise. We denote the *present state* of the flip flop as Q_n and the *next state* as Q_{n+1}, and with reference to Figure 6.5(a) we construct the *characteristic table* shown in Table 6.2.

TABLE 6.2 Characteristic table for the SR flip flop with NAND gates

Inputs		Present State	Next State		
S	R	Q_n	Q_{n+1}		
0	0	0	1	But $\overline{Q_{n+1}} = 1$ also	The condition where S = R = 0 must be avoided
0	0	1	1	But $\overline{Q_{n+1}} = 1$ also	
0	1	0	0	No Change	
0	1	1	0	Reset (or Clear)	
1	0	0	1	Set	
1	0	1	1	No Change	
1	1	0	0	No Change	
1	1	1	1	No Change	

The characteristic table of Table 6.2 shows that when both inputs S and R are logic 0 simultaneously, both outputs Q and $\overline{Q}$ are logic 1 which is an invalid condition since Q and $\overline{Q}$ are complements of each other. Therefore. the S = R = 0 condition must be avoided during flip–flop operation with NAND gates.* When R = 1 and S = 0, the next state output Q_{n+1} becomes 0 regardless of the previous state Q_n and this is known as the reset or clear condition, that is, whenever Q = 0, we say that the flip–flop is reset or clear. When R= 0 and S = 1, the next state output Q_{n+1} becomes 1 regardless of the previous state Q_n and this is known as the preset or simply

---

* *For an S–R flip-flop constructed with NOR gates, the condition S=R=1 must be avoided. For a detailed discussion please refer to Chapter 8, Section 8.2 of Digital Circuit Analysis and Design with an Introduction to CPLDs and FPGAs, ISBN 0-9744239-6-3.*

set condition, that is, whenever Q = 1, we say that the flip–flop is set. When R = 1 and S = 1, the next state output Q_{n+1} remains the same as the present state, i.e., there is no state change.

The model is shown in Figure 6.6.

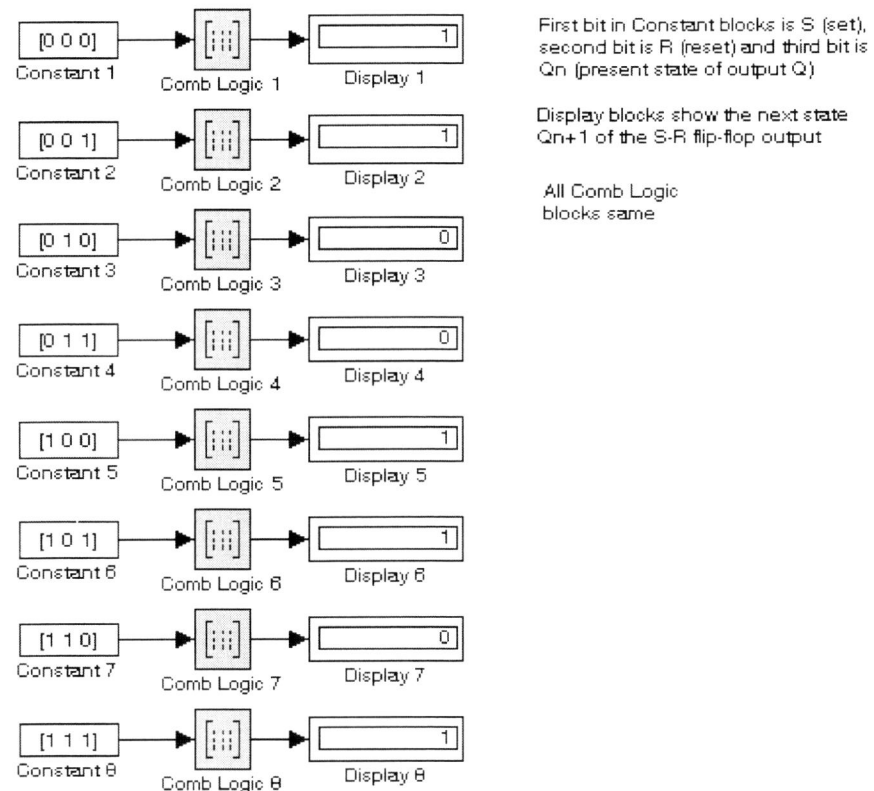

Figure 6.6. Model for Example 6.4

For the model in Figure 6.6, we have specified:

Constant blocks 1 through 8 – Constant value: [0 0 0], [0 0 1], ... [1 1 1] – Signal data types: **boolean** – Interpret vector parameters: **check mark**
Combinatorial Logic blocks (all) – Truth table: [1; 1; 0; 0; 1; 1; 0; 1] – Sample time: –1 – Display blocks – Format: **short**

The model looks more presentable in Figure 6.7 where we selected all Combinatorial Logic blocks, and from the Edit drop menu we selected Create Subsystem.

The Logic Operations Group Sub–Library

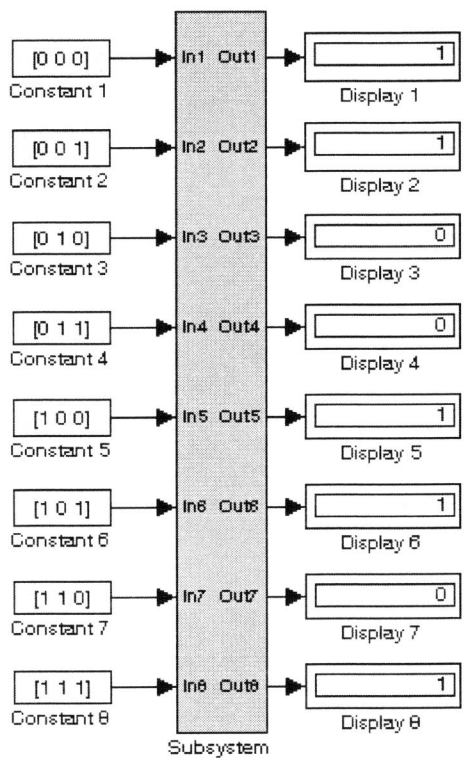

First bit in Constant blocks is S (set), second bit is R (reset) and third bit is Qn (present state of output Q)

Display blocks show the next state Qn+1 of the S-R flip-flop output

Figure 6.7. Simplified model for Example 6.4

6.1.6 The Compare to Zero Block

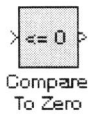

The **Compare To Zero** block compares an input signal to zero. We specify how the input is compared to zero with the Operator parameter. The Operator parameters are listed in Table 6.3.

TABLE 6.3 Operator parameters for the Compare to Zero block

Operator	Action
==	Determine whether the input is equal to the specified constant
~=	Determine whether the input is not equal to the specified constant
<	Determine whether the input is less than the specified constant
<=	Determine whether the input is less than or equal to the specified constant
>	Determine whether the input is greater than the specified constant
>=	Determine whether the input is greater than or equal to the specified constant

Introduction to Simulink with Engineering Applications
Copyright © Orchard Publications

Chapter 6 The Logic and Bit Operations Library

Example 6.5

We will create a model with the Compare To Zero block to test a matrix for singularity.

As we know, an n square matrix A is called *singular* if $detA = 0$; if $detA \neq 0$, it is called non-singular. To test for singularity, we will use the operator $==$. For this example we will use the matrix

$$A = \begin{bmatrix} 1 & 2 & 3 \\ 2 & 3 & 4 \\ 3 & 5 & 7 \end{bmatrix}$$

The model is shown in Figure 6.8 where the matrix A was defined in MATLAB's Command window as

A=[1 2 3; 2 3 4; 3 5 7];

In the model of Figure 6.8, the Display 1 block value of zero indicates that the matrix is singular and the Display 2 block indicates logical 1, a true condition.

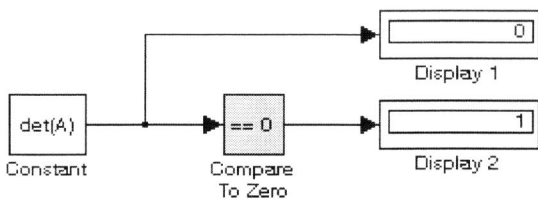

Figure 6.8. Model for Example 6.5

6.1.7 The Compare to Constant Block

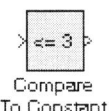

The **Compare To Constant** block compares an input signal to a constant. We must specify the constant in the Constant value parameter and how the input is compared to the constant value with the specified Operator parameter. The Operator parameters are listed in Table 6.4.

The Bit Operations Group Sub–Library

TABLE 6.4 Operator parameters for the Compare to Constant block

Operator	Action
==	Determine whether the input is equal to the specified constant
~=	Determine whether the input is not equal to the specified constant
<	Determine whether the input is less than the specified constant
<=	Determine whether the input is less than or equal to the specified constant
>	Determine whether the input is greater than the specified constant
>=	Determine whether the input is greater than or equal to the specified constant

The output is 0 if the comparison is false, and 1 if it is true.

Example 6.6

We will create a model with the Compare To Zero block to determine whether the product **A*****B** of matrices **A** and **B**, where **A** = $[a_1 \ a_2 \ ... \ a_n]$, and **B** = $[b_1 \ b_2 \ ... \ b_n]'$, results in a positive or negative value. The elements $[a_1 \ a_2 \ ... \ a_n]$ and $[b_1 \ b_2 \ ... \ b_n]'$ are assumed to be real numbers.

We observe that **A** is a row vector and **B** is a column vector and thus the product **A*****B** is conformable for multiplication. The model is shown in Figure 6.9 where in MATLAB's Command Window we have entered

A=[1 2 3 4 5]; B=[-2 6 -3 -8 -4]';

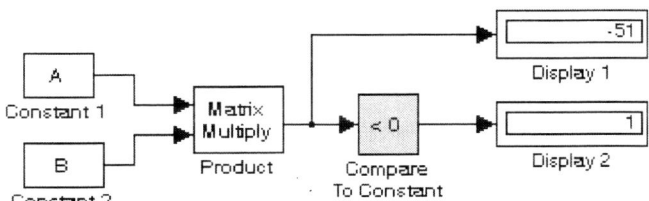

Figure 6.9. Model for Example 6.6

In the model of Figure 6.9, the Display 1 block value of –51 indicates the product **A*****B** and the Display 2 block indicates logical 1, a true condition.

6.2 The Bit Operations Group Sub–Library

The **Bit Operations Group Sub–Library** contains the blocks described in Subsections 6.2.1 through 6.2.5 below.

Chapter 6 The Logic and Bit Operations Library

6.2.1 The Bit Set Block

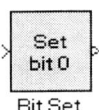

The **Bit Set** block sets the specified bit of the stored integer to one. Scaling is ignored. We specify the bit to be set to one with the Index of bit parameter. Bit zero is the least significant bit.

Example 6.7

We will express the row vector [12 8 5 7] in 8–bit binary form, and using the Bit Set block we will create a model that will convert this vector to [13 12 7 15]. The converted vector will be displayed in binary form.

The model is shown in Figure 6.10.

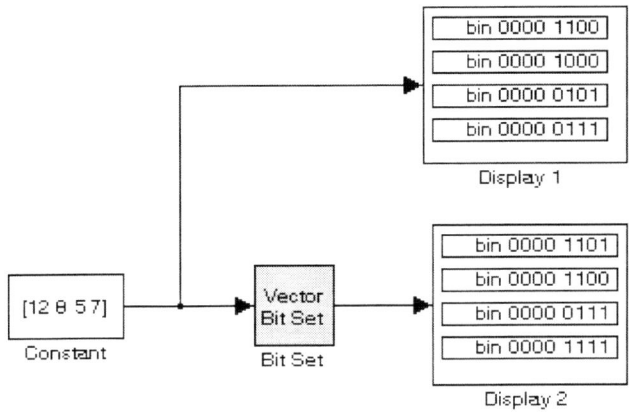

Figure 6.10. Model for Example 6.7

For this model we have configured the blocks as follows:

Constant block – Constant value: [12 8 5 7] – Signal data types: **uint(8)**

Set bit block – Function block Parameters, Index bit: [0 2 1 3]

Sink block parameters – Display 1 and Display 2 blocks, Format: **Binary (Stored Integer)**

The Bit Operations Group Sub–Library

6.2.2 The Bit Clear Block

The **Bit Clear** block sets the specified bit, given by its index, of the stored integer to zero. Scaling is ignored. We can specify the bit to be set to zero with the Index of bit parameter. Bit zero is the least significant bit.

Example 6.8

We will express the row vector [14 8 5 12] in 8–bit binary form and using the Bit Clear block we will create a model that will convert this vector to [6 0 5 4]. We will display the converted vector in binary form.

The model is shown in Figure 6.11.

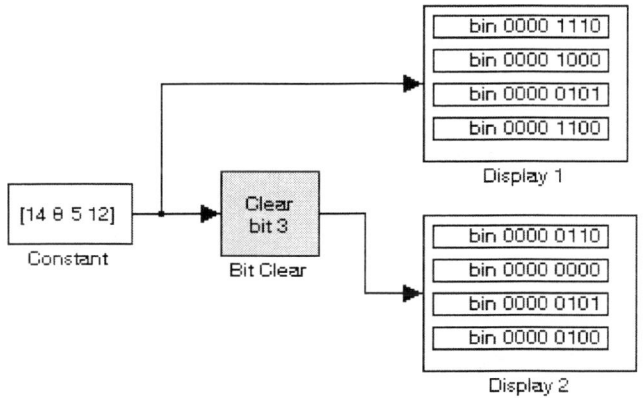

Figure 6.11. Model for Example 6.8

For this model we have configured the blocks as follows:

Constant block - Constant value: [14 8 5 12] - Signal data types: **uint(8)**

Clear bit block - Function block Parameters, Index bit: **3**

Sink block parameters - Display 1 and Display 2 blocks, Format: **Binary (Stored Integer)**

Chapter 6 The Logic and Bit Operations Library

6.2.3 The Bitwise Operator Block

The **Bitwise Operator** block performs the specified bitwise operation on its operands. Unlike the logic operations performed by the Logical Operator block described in Section 2.12, Chapter 2, Page 2–18, bitwise operations treat the operands as a vector of bits rather than a single number. The operations are listed below.

Operation Description:

   AND – TRUE if the corresponding bits are all TRUE

   OR – TRUE if at least one of the corresponding bits is TRUE

   NAND – TRUE if at least one of the corresponding bits is FALSE

   NOR – TRUE if no corresponding bits are TRUE

   XOR – TRUE if an odd number of corresponding bits are TRUE

   NOT – TRUE if the input is FALSE and vice-versa

The Bitwise Operator block cannot be used for shift operations. Shift operations are described in Subsection 6.2.4.

The size of the output of the Bitwise Operator block depends on the number of inputs, their vector size, and the selected operator. For a single vector input, the block applies the operation (except the NOT operator) to all elements of the vector. If a bit mask is not specified, then the output is a scalar. If a bit mask is specified, then the output is a vector. The NOT operator accepts only one input, which can be a scalar or a vector. If the input is a vector, the output is a vector of the same size containing the bitwise logical complements of the input vector elements.

For two or more inputs, the block performs the operation between all of the inputs. If the inputs are vectors, the operation is performed between corresponding elements of the vectors to produce a vector output. If we do not select the Use bit mask check box, the block will accept multiple inputs. We select the number of input ports from the Number of input ports parameter. The input data types must be identical. For more information on the Bitwise Operator block please refer to the Simulink Help menu for this block.

Example 6.9

We will create a model containing a 3–input Bitwise AND block, a 3–input Bitwise NOR block, and a 2–input Bitwise XOR block. The inputs to the Bitwise AND and Bitwise NOR blocks are:

The Bit Operations Group Sub−Library

$$(152)_{10} = (10011000)_2$$
$$(141)_{10} = (10001101)_2$$
$$(75)_{10} = (01001011)_2$$

The inputs to the Bitwise XOR block are:

$$(152)_{10} = (10011000)_2$$
$$(141)_{10} = (10001101)_2$$

The model is shown in Figure 6.12.

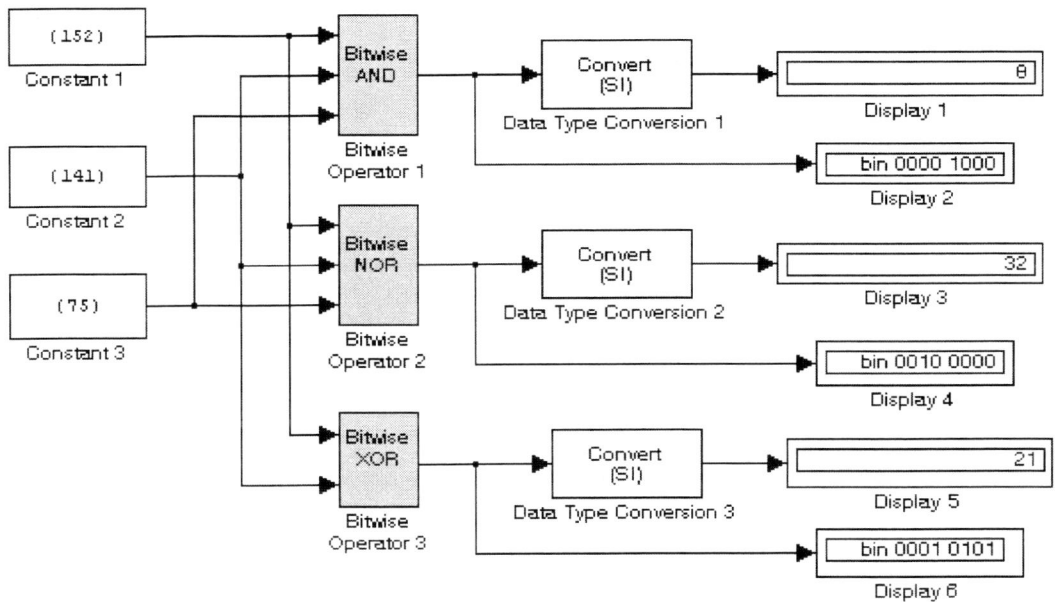

Figure 6.12. Model for Example 6.9

For the model of Figure 6.12 we have entered:

Constant blocks 1, 2, and 3 − Constant value: [152], [141], and [75] respectively − Signal data types: **uint8**

Bitwise AND block − Operator: **AND**, Number of input ports: **3**

Bitwise NOR block − Operator: **NOR**, Number of input ports: **3**

Bitwise XOR block − Operator: **XOR**, Number of input ports: **2**

Data type Conversion 1, 2, and 3 blocks - Output data type mode: **Specify via dialog** − Output data type: **'double'** - Input and output to have equal: **Stored Integer (SI)**

Display 1, 3, and 5 blocks − Format: **decimal (Stored Integer)**

Chapter 6 The Logic and Bit Operations Library

Display 2, 4, and 6 blocks – Format: **binary (Stored Integer)**

A binary value used to selectively screen out or let through certain bits in a data value. Masking is performed by using a logical operator (AND, OR, XOR, NOT) to combine the mask and the data value. For example, the mask [00111111], when used with the AND operator, removes (masks off) the two uppermost bits in a data value but does not affect the rest of the value.

If we select the Use bit mask check box, then a single input is associated with the bit mask that we have specified with the Bit Mask parameter. We can specify the bit mask using any MATLAB expression in the Command Window. For example, we can specify the bit mask [10100110] as $[2^7 + 2^5 + 2^2 + 2^1]$. For long strings, we can use hexadecimal bit masks, e.g., ['**DA87**'], and ['**E2F9B**']. If the bit mask is larger than the input signal data type, it is ignored.

We can use the bit mask to perform a bit set or a bit clear on the input. To perform a bit set, we set the Operator parameter list to OR and create a bit mask with a 1 for each corresponding input bit that we want to set to 1. To perform a bit clear, we set the Operator parameter list to AND and create a bit mask with a 0 for each corresponding input bit that we want to set to 0.

6.2.4 The Shift Arithmetic Block

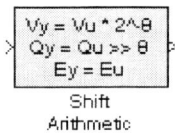

The **Shift Arithmetic** block is be used to shift the bits or the binary point of a binary word, or both. This block performs arithmetic bit shifts on signed numbers. Therefore, the most significant bit is recycled for each bit shift. If the bits and the binary point are to be shifted to the left, we specify negative values.

Example 6.10

We will create a model with a Shift Arithmetic block with inputs decimal +32.75 and decimal –48.875 to display the outputs when both of these numbers are shifted left by 3 bits and the binary point is shifted left by 2 bits.

The model is shown in Figure 6.13 where the Constant blocks have been set for Output data type **sfix(12)** and the output scaling value **2^–3**. Since it is specified that the bits and the binary point are to be shifted to the left, in the Shift Arithmetic block we enter the values –3 and –2 respectively. All three display blocks have been set for binary (Stored Integer) format. We can check the Shift Arithmetic block outputs as follows:

The Bit Operations Group Sub–Library

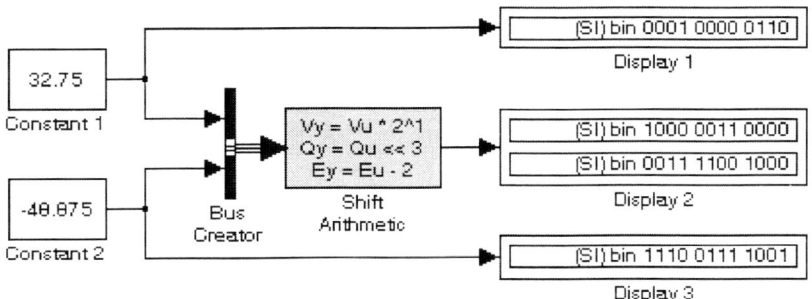

Figure 6.13. Model for Example 6.10

$$(+32.75)_{10} = (0001\ 0000\ 0.110)_2$$

and after shifting 3 bits to the left and the binary point 2 places to the left we obtain

$$1000\ .0011\ 0000$$

Likewise,

$$(-48.875)_{10} = (-0001\ 1000\ 0.111)_2 = (1110\ 0111\ 1.001)_{2s\ complement}$$

and after shifting 3 bits to the left and the binary point 2 places to the left we obtain

$$0011\ .1100\ 1000$$

6.2.5 The Extract Bits Block

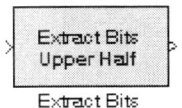

Extract Bits

The **Extract Bits** block allows us to output a contiguous selection of bits from the stored integer value of the input signal. The Bits to extract parameter defines the method by which we select the output bits. We select Upper half to output the half of the input bits that contain the most significant bit. If there is an odd number of bits in the input signal, the number of output bits is given by

$$Number\ of\ output\ bits\ =\ ceil(Number\ of\ input\ bits/2)^* \qquad (6.1)$$

We select Lower half to output the half of the input bits that contain the least significant bit. If there is an odd number of bits in the input signal, the number of output bits is given by relation (6.1).

---

* The notation Ceil( ) rounds "up", e.g., ceil(4.6) rounds to 5, and ceil(-4.6) rounds to -4. The notation Floor( ) rounds "down", e.g., floor(8.999) = 8.

Chapter 6 The Logic and Bit Operations Library

We select Range starting with most significant bit to output a certain number of the most significant bits of the input signal. We specify the number of most significant bits to output in the Number of bits parameter.

We select Range ending with least significant bit to output a certain number of the least significant bits of the input signal. We specify the number of least significant bits to output in the Number of bits parameter.

We select Range of bits to indicate a series of contiguous bits of the input to output in the Bit indices parameter. We indicate the range in [start end] format, and the indices of the input bits are labeled contiguously starting at 0 for the least significant bit.

Example 6.11

We will create a model with an Extract Bits block to accept the decimal number 65403 as the input and outputs the binary number [1111 1111].

The model is shown in Figure 6.14 where the Constant block is set for Signal data types – Output data type mode: uint16, the Display 1 block shows the given decimal number in binary form, and the Display 2 block shows the Upper Half of that binary number. Both display blocks have been set for binary (Stored Integer) format. Had we specified the display blocks for decimal (Stored Integer), Display 1 block would show the decimal number 65403 and Display 2 block would show the decimal value 255 which is equivalent to binary 1111 1111.

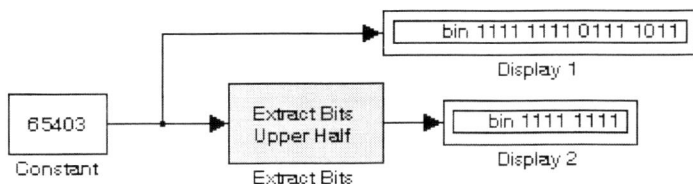

Figure 6.14. Model for Example 6.11

6.3 The Edge Detection Group Sub-Library

The **Edge Detection Group Sub-Library** contains the blocks described in Subsections 6.3.1 through 6.3.7 below.

6.3.1 The Detect Increase Block

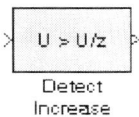

The Edge Detection Group Sub–Library

The **Detect Increase** block determines if an input is strictly greater than its previous value. The output is true (not 0), when the input signal is greater than its previous value. The output is false (equal to 0), when the input signal is less than or equal to its previous value.

Example 6.12

We will create a model with the Detect Increase block to display changes in output for changes in the input.

The model is shown in Figure 6.15 and the input and output waveforms are shown in Figure 6.16. In Figure 6.15, the Signal Generator block is specified for a square waveform of amplitude 1 and frequency 0.5, the Unit Delay is included to delay the Step block one time unit, the Detect Increase block initial value is specified as 0, and the Convert Block is used to convert the output signal of the Detect Change block from **uint(8)** to **double**. The waveforms in Figure 6.16 indicate that the output is true (not 0), when the input signal is greater than its previous value. The output is false (equal to 0), when the input signal is less than or equal to its previous value.

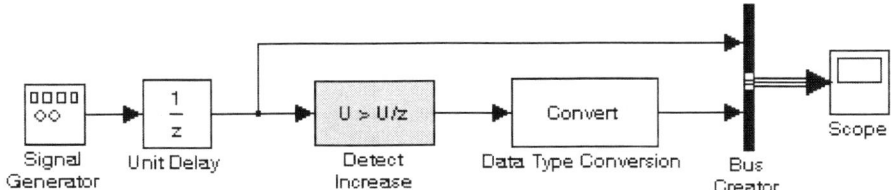

Figure 6.15. Model for Example 6.12

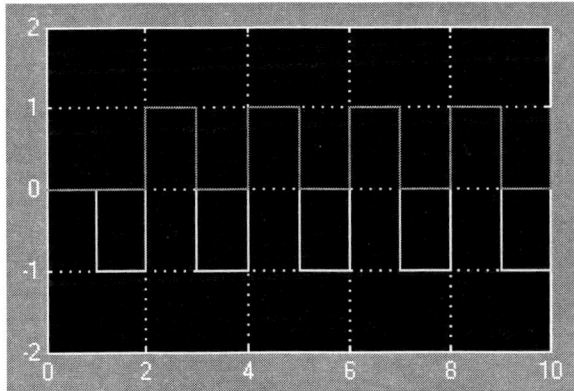

Figure 6.16. Input and output waveforms for the model of Figure 6.15

6.3.2 The Detect Decrease Block

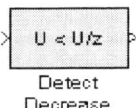
Detect Decrease

The **Detect Decrease** block determines if an input is strictly less than its previous value where the output is true (not 0), when the input signal is less than its previous value, and the output is false (equal to 0), when the input signal is greater than or equal to its previous value.

Example 6.13

We will create a model with the Detect Decrease block to display changes in output for changes in the input.

The model is shown in Figure 6.17 and the input and output waveforms are shown in Figure 6.18. In Figure 6.17, the Signal Generator block is set for a square waveform of amplitude 1 and frequency 0.5, the Unit Delay is included to delay the Step block one time unit, the Detect Decrease block initial value was set to 0, and the Convert Block is used to convert the output signal of the Detect Change block from **uint(8)** to **double**. The waveforms in Figure 6.18 indicate that the output waveform is true (not 0), when the input signal is less than its previous value, and the output is false (equal to 0), when the input signal is greater than or equal to its previous value.

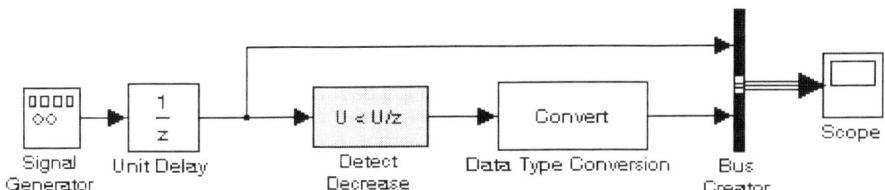

Figure 6.17. Model for Example 6.13

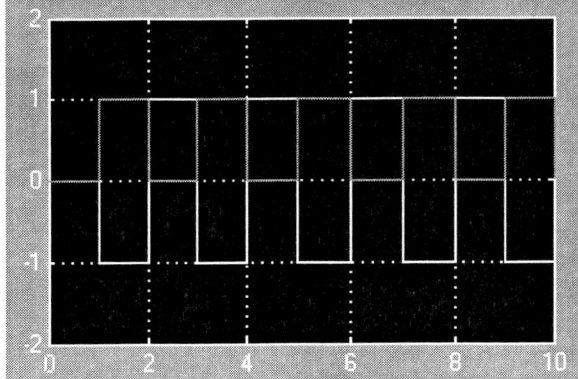

Figure 6.18. Input and output waveforms for the model of Figure 6.17

The Edge Detection Group Sub–Library

6.3.3 The Detect Change Block

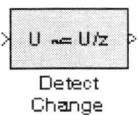
Detect Change

The **Detect Change** block determines if an input does not equal its previous value where the output is true (not 0), when the input signal does not equal its previous value, and the output is false (equal to 0), when the input signal equals its previous value.

Example 6.14

We will create a model with the Detect Change block to display changes in output for changes in the input.

The model is shown in Figure 6.19 and the input and output waveforms are shown in Figure 6.20. In Figure 6.19, the Detect Change block value was set to 0, and the Convert Block is used to convert the output signal of the Detect Change block from **uint(8)** to **double**. The waveforms in Figure 6.20 indicate that the output waveform is 0 for the interval $0 < t < 1$ because the step function is also 0 during this interval. At $t = 1$ the step function jumps to 1 and thus the output assumes a non–zero value, in this case 1. For $t > 1$, there are no further changes in the input signal and thus the output drops to 0 indicating that the input signal equals its previous value.

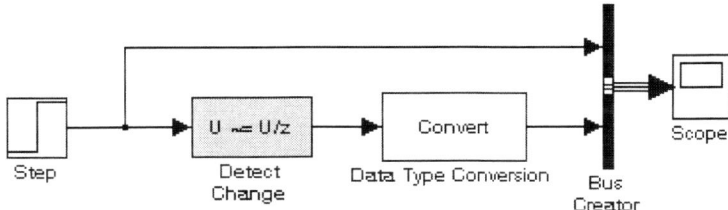

Figure 6.19. Model for Example 6.14

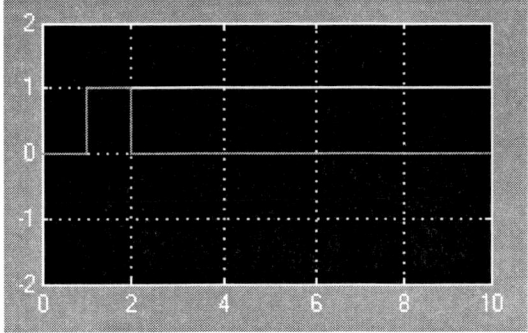

Figure 6.20. Input and output waveforms for the model of Figure 6.19

6.3.4 The Detect Rise Positive Block

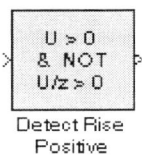

The **Detect Rise Positive** block determines if the input is strictly positive, and its previous value was nonpositive. The output is true (not 0), when the input signal is greater than zero, and its previous value was less than zero. The output is false (equal to 0), when the input is negative or zero, or if the input is positive and its previous value was also positive.

Example 6.15

We will create a model with the Detect Rise Nonnegative block to display changes in output for changes in the input.

The model is shown in Figure 6.21 and the input and output waveforms are shown in Figure 6.22.

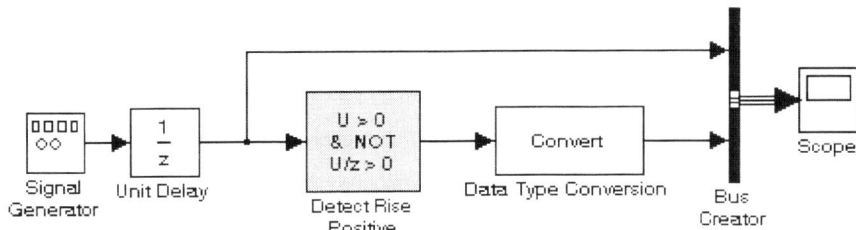

Figure 6.21. Model for Example 6.15

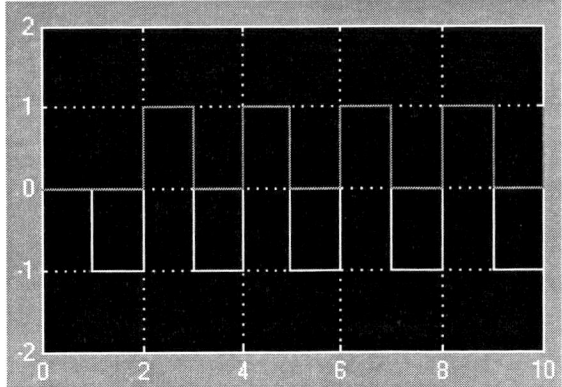

Figure 6.22. Input and output waveforms for the model of Figure 6.21

In Figure 6.21, the Signal Generator block is specified as a square waveform of amplitude 1 and frequency 0.5, the Unit Delay is included to delay the Step block one time unit, the Detect Rise

Nonnegative block initial value was set to 0, and the Convert Block is used to convert the output signal of the Detect Change block from uint(8) to double. The waveforms in Figure 6.22 indicate that the output is true (not 0), when the input signal is greater than zero, and its previous value was less than zero. The output is false (equal to 0), when the input is negative or zero, or if the input is positive and its previous value was also positive.

6.3.5 The Detect Rise Nonnegative Block

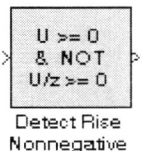

The **Detect Rise Nonnegative** block determines if the input is greater than or equal to zero, and its previous value was less than zero. The output is true (not 0), when the input signal is greater than or equal to zero, and its previous value was less than zero. The output is false (equal to 0), when the input signal is less than zero, or if nonnegative, its previous value was greater than or equal to zero.

Example 6.16

We will create a model with the Detect Rise Nonnegative block to display changes in output for changes in the input.

The model is shown in Figure 6.23 and the input and output waveforms are shown in Figure 6.24.

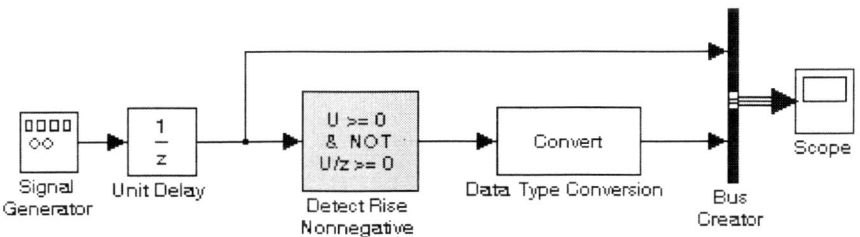

Figure 6.23. Model for Example 6.16

In Figure 6.23, the Signal Generator block is set for a square waveform of amplitude 1 and frequency 0.5, the Unit Delay is included to delay the Step block one time unit, the Detect Rise Nonnegative block initial value was set to 0, and the Convert Block is used to convert the output signal of the Detect Change block from uint(8) to double. The waveforms in Figure 6.24 indicate that the output is true (not 0), when the input signal is greater than or equal to zero, and its previous value was less than zero. The output is false (equal to 0), when the input signal is less than zero, or if nonnegative and its previous value was greater than or equal to zero.

Chapter 6 The Logic and Bit Operations Library

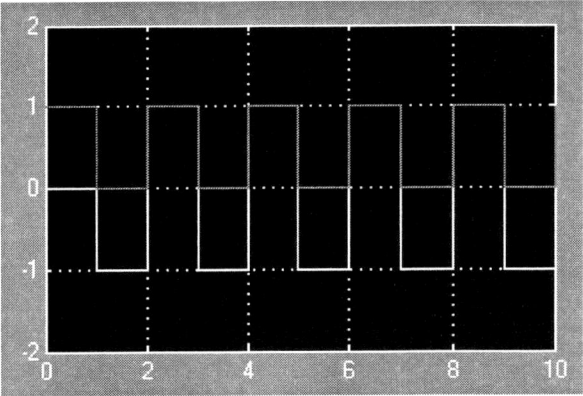

Figure 6.24. Input and output waveforms for the model of Figure 6.23

6.3.6 The Detect Fall Negative Block

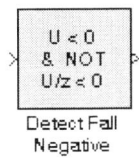

The **Detect Fall Negative** block determines if the input is less than zero, and its previous value was greater than or equal to zero. The output is true (not 0), when the input signal is less than zero, and its previous value was greater than or equal to zero. The output is false (equal to 0), when the input signal is greater than or equal to zero, or if the input signal is nonnegative and its previous value was positive or zero.

Example 6.17

We will create a model with the Detect Fall Negative block to display changes in output for changes in the input.

The model is shown in Figure 6.25 and the input and output waveforms are shown in Figure 6.26.

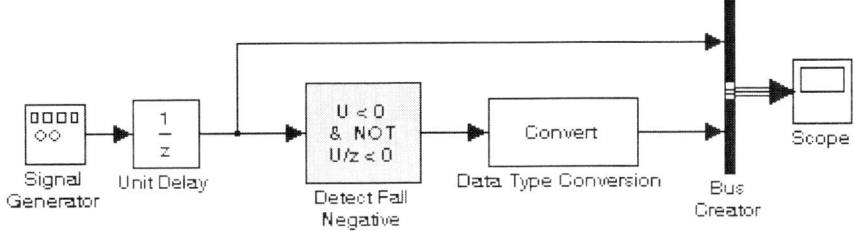

Figure 6.25. Model for Example 6.17

6-24 Introduction to Simulink with Engineering Applications
Copyright © Orchard Publications

The Edge Detection Group Sub–Library

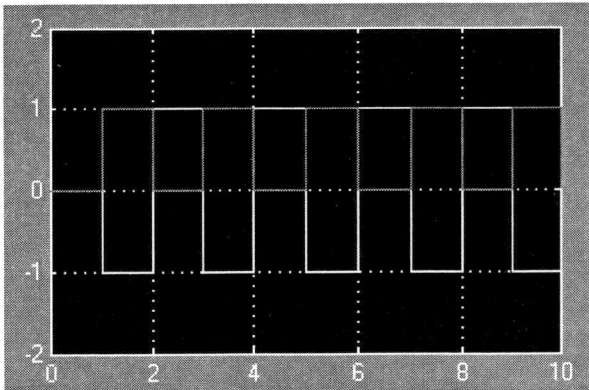

Figure 6.26. Input and output waveforms for the model of Figure 6.25

In Figure 6.25, the Signal Generator block is set for a square waveform of amplitude 1 and frequency 0.5, the Unit Delay is included to delay the Step block one time unit, the Detect Fall Negative block initial value was set to 0, and the Convert Block is used to convert the output signal of the Detect Change block from **uint(8)** to **double**. The waveforms in Figure 6.26 indicate that the output is true (not 0), when the input signal is less than zero, and its previous value was greater than or equal to zero. The output is false (equal to 0), when the input signal is greater than or equal to zero, or if the input signal is nonnegative and its previous value was positive or zero.

6.3.7 The Detect Fall Nonpositive Block

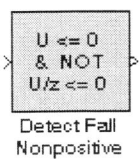

The **Detect Fall Nonpositive** block determines if the input is less than or equal to zero, and its previous value was positive. The output is true (not 0), when the input signal is less than or equal to zero, and its previous value was greater than zero. The output is false (equal to 0), when the input signal is greater than zero, or if it is nonpositive and its previous value was nonpositive.

Example 6.18

We will create a model with the Detect Fall Nonpositive block to display changes in output for changes in the input.

The model is shown in Figure 6.27 and the input and output waveforms are shown in Figure 6.28.

Chapter 6 The Logic and Bit Operations Library

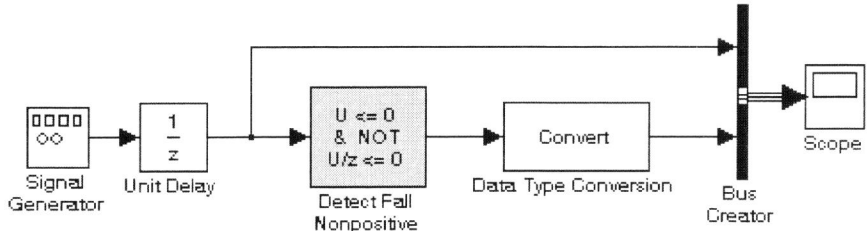

Figure 6.27. Model for Example 6.18

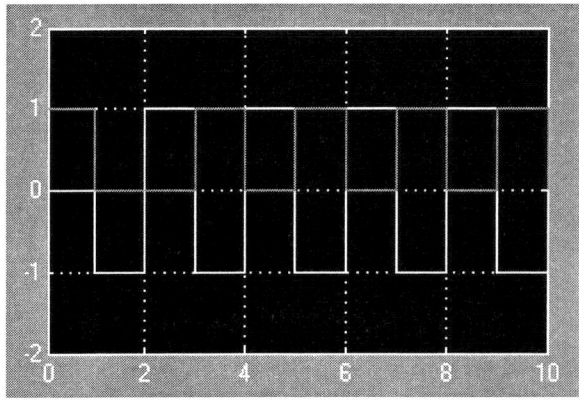

Figure 6.28. Input and output waveforms for the model of Figure 6.27

In Figure 6.27, the Signal Generator block is set for a square waveform of amplitude 1 and frequency 0.5, the Unit Delay is included to delay the Step block one time unit, the Detect Fall Nonpositive block initial value was set to 0, and the Convert Block is used to convert the output signal of the Detect Change block from **uint(8)** to **double**. The waveforms in Figure 6.28 indicate that the output is true (not 0), when the input signal is less than or equal to zero, and its previous value was greater than zero. The output is false (equal to 0), when the input signal is greater than zero, or if it is nonpositive and its previous value was nonpositive.

Summary

6.4 Summary

- The **Logical Operator block** performs the specified logical operation on its inputs. An input value is TRUE (1) if it is nonzero and FALSE (0) if it is zero. The Boolean operation connecting the inputs is selected with the Operator parameter list in the Function Block Parameters window. The block updates to display the selected operator. The supported operations are given below.

  Operation Description:

  AND – TRUE if all inputs are TRUE

  OR – TRUE if at least one input is TRUE

  NAND – TRUE if at least one input is FALSE

  NOR – TRUE when no inputs are TRUE

  XOR – TRUE if an odd number of inputs are TRUE

  NOT – TRUE if the input is FALSE and vice-versa

  The number of input ports is specified with the Number of input ports parameter. The output type is specified with the Output data type mode and/or the Output data type parameters. An output value is 1 if TRUE and 0 if FALSE.

- The **Relational Operator block** performs the specified comparison of its two inputs. We select the relational operator connecting the two inputs with the Relational Operator parameter. The block updates to display the selected operator. The supported operations are given below.

  Operation Description:

  $==$ TRUE if the first input is equal to the second input

  $\sim=$ TRUE if the first input is not equal to the second input

  $<$ TRUE if the first input is less than the second input

  $<=$ TRUE if the first input is less than or equal to the second input

  $>=$ TRUE if the first input is greater than or equal to the second input

  $>$ TRUE if the first input is greater than the second input

- The **Interval Test** block performs a test to determine if a signal is in a specified interval. The block outputs TRUE if the input is between the values specified by the Lower limit and Upper limit parameters. The block outputs FALSE if the input is outside those values. The output of the block when the input is equal to the Lower limit or the Upper limit is determined by whether the boxes next to Interval closed on left and Interval closed on right are selected in the dialog box.

Chapter 6 The Logic and Bit Operations Library

- The **Interval Test Dynamic** block performs a test to determine if a signal is in a specified interval. This block outputs TRUE if the input is between the values of the external signals **up** and **lo**. The block outputs FALSE if the input is outside those values. The output of the block when the input is equal to the signal **up** or the signal **lo** is determined by whether the boxes next to Interval closed on left and Interval closed on right are selected in the dialog box.

- The **Combinatorial Logic** block implements a standard truth table for modeling programmable logic arrays (PLAs), logic circuits, decision tables, and other Boolean expressions. In a Combinatorial Logic block we specify a matrix that defines all outputs as the Truth table parameter. Each row of the matrix contains the output for a different combination of input elements. We must specify outputs for every combination of inputs. The number of columns is the number of block outputs. We can also implement sequential circuits (that is, circuits with states) with the Combinatorial Logic block by including an additional input for the state of the block and feeding the output of the block back into this state input. We can also implement sequential circuits (that is, circuits with states) with the Combinatorial Logic block by including an additional input for the state of the block and feeding the output of the block back into this state input.

- The **Compare To Zero** block compares an input signal to zero. We specify how the input is compared to zero with the Operator parameter. The Operator parameters are listed in the table below.

Operator	Action
==	Determine whether the input is equal to the specified constant
~=	Determine whether the input is not equal to the specified constant
<	Determine whether the input is less than the specified constant
<=	Determine whether the input is less than or equal to the specified constant
>	Determine whether the input is greater than the specified constant
>=	Determine whether the input is greater than or equal to the specified constant

The output is 0 if the comparison is false, and 1 if it is true.

- The **Compare To Constant** block compares an input signal to a constant. We must specify the constant in the Constant value parameter and how the input is compared to the constant value with the Operator parameter. The Operator parameters are the same as those of the Compare to Zero block listed above.

- The **Bit Set** block sets the specified bit of the stored integer to one. Scaling is ignored. We specify the bit to be set to one with the Index of bit parameter, where bit zero is the least significant bit.

Summary

- The **Bit Clear** block sets the specified bit, given by its index, of the stored integer to zero. Scaling is ignored. We can specify the bit to be set to zero with the Index of bit parameter, where bit zero is the least significant bit.

- The **Bitwise Operator** block performs the specified bitwise operation on its operands. Unlike the logic operations performed by the Logical Operator block, bitwise operations treat the operands as a vector of bits rather than a single number. The supported operations are given below.

  Operation Description:

  AND – TRUE if the corresponding bits are all TRUE

  OR – TRUE if at least one of the corresponding bits is TRUE

  NAND – TRUE if at least one of the corresponding bits is FALSE

  NOR – TRUE if no corresponding bits are TRUE

  XOR – TRUE if an odd number of corresponding bits are TRUE

  NOT – TRUE if the input is FALSE and vice-versa

- Masking is performed by using a logical operator (AND, OR, XOR, NOT) to combine the mask and the data value.

- The **Shift Arithmetic** block is be used to shift the bits or the binary point of a binary word, or both. This block performs arithmetic bit shifts on signed numbers. Therefore, the most significant bit is recycled for each bit shift. If the bits and the binary point are to be shifted to the left, we specify negative values.

- The **Extract Bits** block allows us to output a contiguous selection of bits from the stored integer value of the input signal. The Bits to extract parameter defines the method by which we select the output bits. We select Upper half to output the half of the input bits that contain the most significant bit. If there is an odd number of bits in the input signal, the number of output bits is given by

$$Number\ of\ output\ bits\ =\ ceil(Number\ of\ input\ bits/2)$$

We select Lower half to output the half of the input bits that contain the least significant bit. If there is an odd number of bits in the input signal, the number of output bits is given by the relation above.

- The **Detect Increase** block determines if an input is strictly greater than its previous value. The output is true (not 0), when the input signal is greater than its previous value. The output is false (equal to 0), when the input signal is less than or equal to its previous value.

Chapter 6 The Logic and Bit Operations Library

- The **Detect Decrease** block determines if an input is strictly less than its previous value where the output is true (not 0), when the input signal is less than its previous value, and the output is false (equal to 0), when the input signal is greater than or equal to its previous value.

- The **Detect Change** block determines if an input does not equal its previous value where the output is true (not 0), when the input signal does not equal its previous value, and the output is false (equal to 0), when the input signal equals its previous value.

- The **Detect Rise Positive** block determines if the input is strictly positive, and its previous value was nonpositive. The output is true (not 0), when the input signal is greater than zero, and its previous value was less than zero. The output is false (equal to 0), when the input is negative or zero, or if the input is positive and its previous value was also positive.

- The **Detect Rise Nonnegative** block determines if the input is greater than or equal to zero, and its previous value was less than zero. The output is true (not 0), when the input signal is greater than or equal to zero, and its previous value was less than zero. The output is false (equal to 0), when the input signal is less than zero, or if nonnegative, its previous value was greater than or equal to zero.

- The **Detect Fall Negative** block determines if the input is less than zero, and its previous value was greater than or equal to zero. The output is true (not 0), when the input signal is less than zero, and its previous value was greater than or equal to zero. The output is false (equal to 0), when the input signal is greater than or equal to zero, or if the input signal is nonnegative and its previous value was positive or zero.

- The **Detect Fall Nonpositive** block determines if the input is less than or equal to zero, and its previous value was positive. The output is true (not 0), when the input signal is less than or equal to zero, and its previous value was greater than zero. The output is false (equal to 0), when the input signal is greater than zero, or if it is nonpositive and its previous value was nonpositive.

6.5 Exercises

1. Convert the row vector [8125 5963 2473 8690] to [8117 5961 2472 8690] by creating a model using the Bit Clear block. Display the converted vector in decimal form.

2. Create a model with the Bitwise Operator block to convert the binary number [01111111] to the binary number [01100010] using the bit mask check box to specify the appropriate bits.

3. Create a model with Combinatorial Logic blocks to implement a full subtractor[*] logic circuit.

4. Create a model with the Detect Change block to display changes in output when the input is a square waveform.

5. Create a model with an Extract Bits block that accepts the decimal number 65403 as the input and outputs the binary number [0111 1011].

6. Create a model with an Extract Bits block that accepts the decimal number 65403 as the input and outputs the binary number [1111].

7. Create a model with an Extract Bits block that accepts the decimal number 65403 as the input and outputs the binary number [111011].

8. Create a model with an Extract Bits block that accepts the decimal number 65403 as the input and outputs the binary number [11110111].

9. Create a model with a Shift Arithmetic block with inputs decimal +32.75 and decimal −48.875 to display the outputs when both of these numbers are shifted right by 3 bits and the binary point is shifted right by 2 bits.

---

[*] *For a detailed description of a full subtractor and other logic circuits please refer to Digital Circuit Analysis and Design with an Introduction to CPLDs and FPGAs, ISBN 0-9744239-6-3.*

Chapter 6 The Logic and Bit Operations Library

6.6 Solutions to End–of–Chapter Exercises

1.

The given vector is shown in the Display 1 block and the converted vector in Display 2 block.

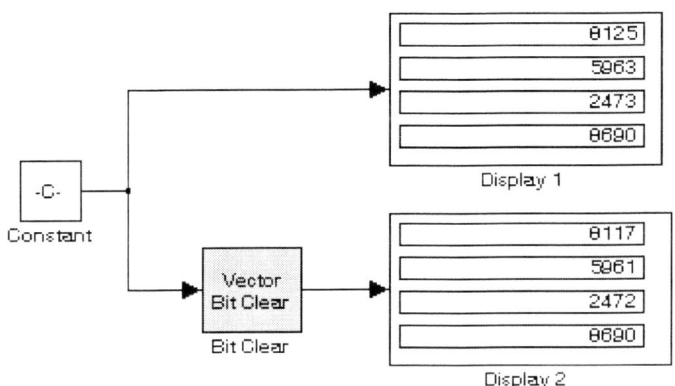

For this model we have configured the blocks as follows:

Constant block – Constant value: [8125 5963 2473 8690] – Signal data types: **int(32)**

Clear bit block – Function block Parameters, Index bit: [3 1 0 2]

Display 1 and Display 2 blocks, Format: **decimal (Stored Integer)**

2.

The model is shown below where we have configured the blocks as follows:

Constant block - Constant value: [127] – Signal data types: **uint(8)**

Bitwise Operator block – Operator: AND – Use bit mask: Check mark – Bit Mask: $2^6 + 2^5 + 2^1$

Display 1 and Display 2 blocks, Format: **binary (Stored Integer)**

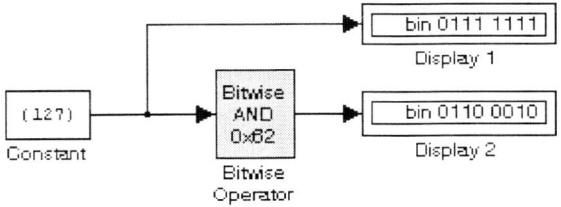

3.

The Truth table for a full subtractor digital circuit is shown below where X is the minuend, Y is the subtrahend, Z is the previous borrow, addition, D is the difference resulting from the of the present subtraction, and B is the present borrow.

Solutions to End–of–Chapter Exercises

Inputs			Outputs	
X	Y	Z	D	B
0	0	0	0	0
0	0	1	1	1
0	1	0	1	1
0	1	1	0	1
1	0	0	1	0
1	0	1	0	0
1	1	0	0	0
1	1	1	1	1

The model is shown below where we have specified:

Constant blocks - Constant value: [0 0 0], [0 0 1], ... [1 1 1] in Constant blocks 1 through 8 respectively – Signal data types: **boolean** – Interpret vector parameters: **check mark**

Combinatorial Logic blocks (all) – Truth table: [0 0; 1 1; 1 1; 0 1; 1 0; 0 0; 0 0; 1 1] – Sample time: –1

Display blocks – Format: **short**

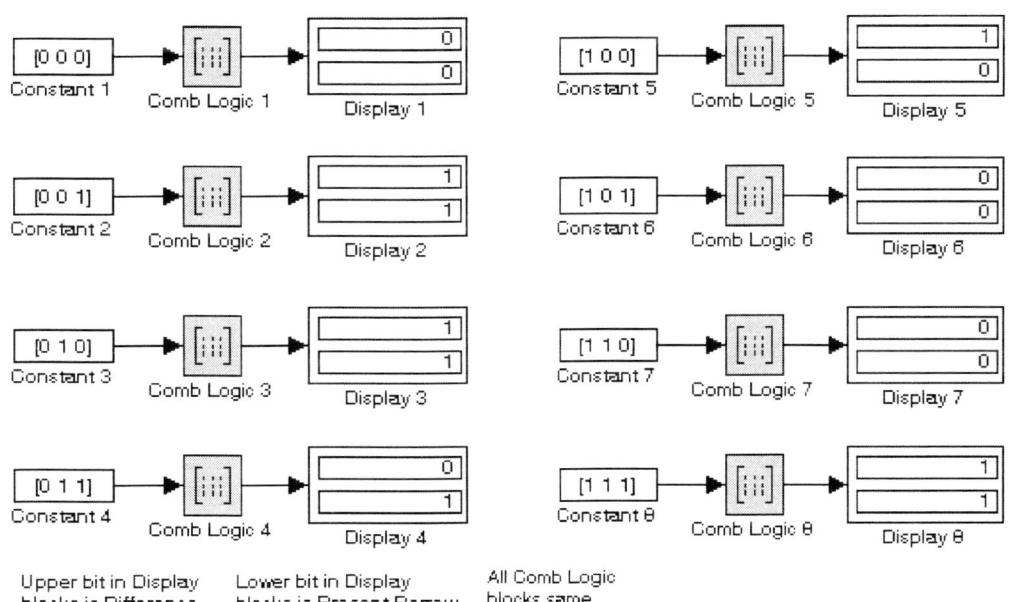

The model looks more presentable below where we lined-up the individual segments one below the other, we selected all Combinatorial Logic blocks, and from the Edit drop menu we selected Create Subsystem.

Chapter 6 The Logic and Bit Operations Library

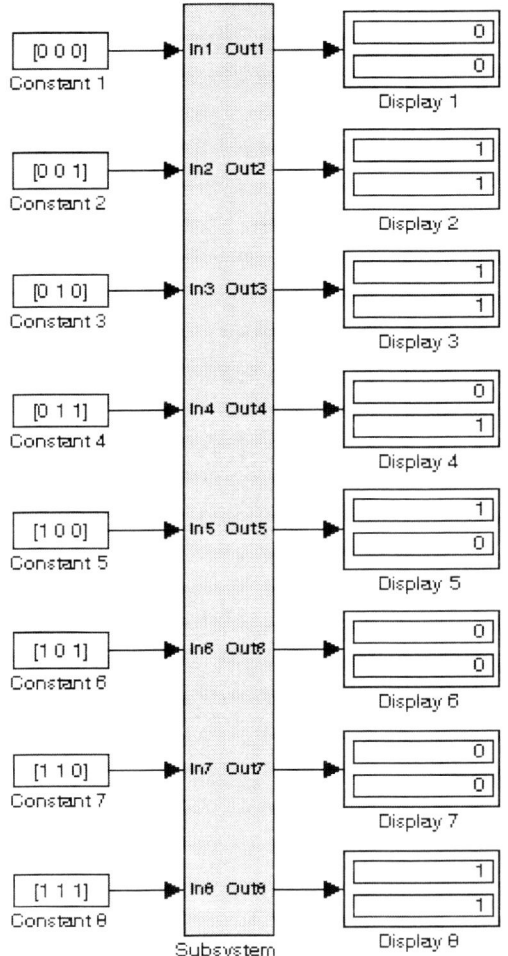

4.

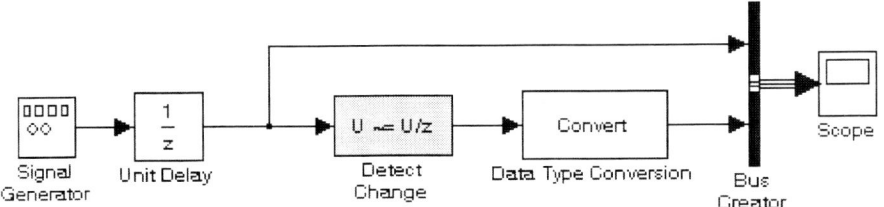

In the model above, the Signal Generator block was set to square waveform with amplitude 1 and frequency 0.5 Hz. The Unit Delay is included to delay the Step block one time unit, the Detect Change block value was set to 0, and the Convert Block is used to convert the output signal of the Detect Change block from **uint(8)** to **double**. The waveforms below indicate that the output waveform remains at a non-zero value for all t > 1 since the input changes repeatedly every time interval.

Solutions to End–of–Chapter Exercises

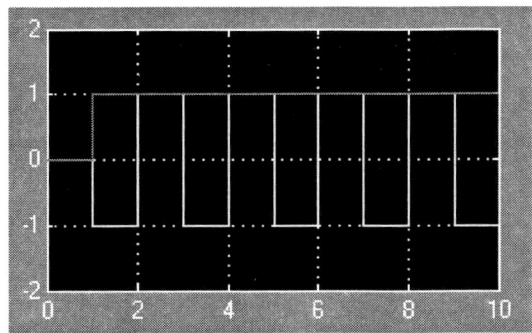

5.

The model is shown below where the Constant block is set for Signal data types – Output data type mode: **uint16**, the Display 1 block shows the given decimal number in binary form, and the Display 2 block shows the Lower Half of that binary number. Both display blocks have been set for **binary (Stored Integer)** format.

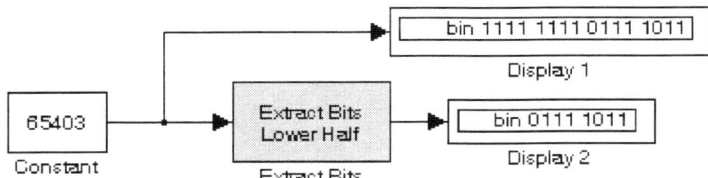

6.

The binary equivalent of the decimal number 65403 is 1111 1111 0111 1011 and since we want the output to be 1111, we select Range starting with most significant bit for the Bits to extract parameter, and specify 4 for the Number of bits parameter. The model is shown below.

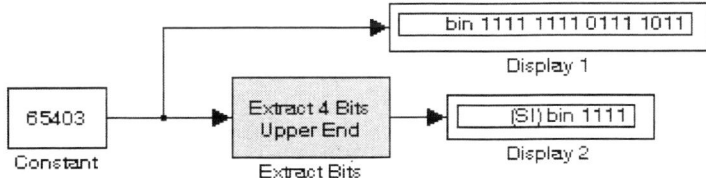

7.

The binary equivalent of the decimal number 65403 is 1111 1111 0111 1011 and since we want the output to be 111011, we select Range starting with least significant bit for the Bits to extract parameter, and specify 6 for the Number of bits parameter. The model is shown below.

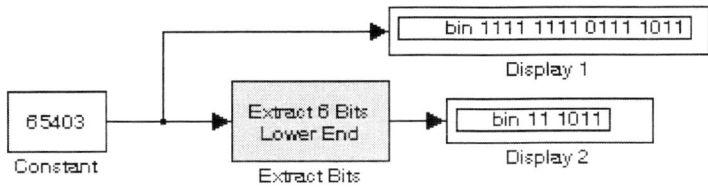

8.

The binary equivalent of the decimal number 65403 is 1111 1111 0111 1011 and since we want the output to be 11110111, we select Range of bits for the Bits to extract parameter, and we specify [5 12] for the Bit indices parameter. The model is shown below.

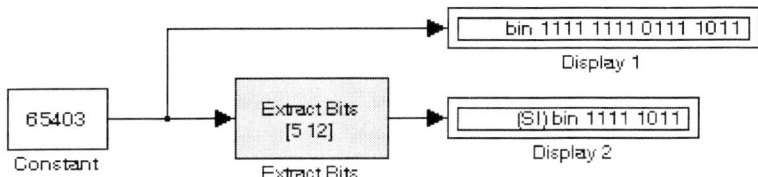

9.

The model is shown below where the Constant blocks have been set for Output data type **sfix(12)** and the output scaling value 2^−3. Since it is specified that the bits and the binary point are to be shifted to the right, in the Shift Arithmetic block we enter positive values, that is, the values 3 and 2 respectively. All three display blocks have been set for binary (Stored Integer) format. We can check the Shift Arithmetic block outputs as follows:

$$(+32.75)_{10} = (0001\ 0000.110)_2$$

and after shifting 3 bits to the right and the binary point 2 places to the right we obtain

$$0000\ 0010\ 0000$$

and the binary point is understood to be to the right of the least significant bit.

Likewise,

$$(-48.875)_{10} = (-0001\ 1000.111)_2 = (1110\ 0111.001)_{2s\ complement}$$

and after shifting 3 bits to the right and the binary point 2 places to the right we obtain

$$1111\ 1100\ 1111$$

and the binary point is understood to be 2 places to the right of the least significant bit.

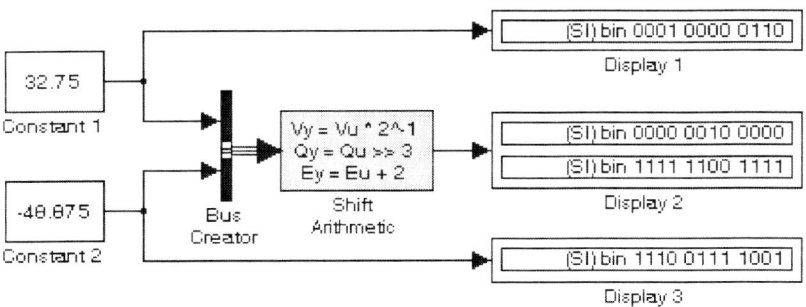

Chapter 7

The Lookup Tables Library

This chapter is an introduction to the **Lookup Tables** library. This is the sixth library in the Simulink group of libraries and contains the blocks shown below. We will describe the function of each block included in this library and we will perform simulation examples to illustrate their application. The terminology *monotonically increasing* [*] is used throughout this chapter, and it is defined in the footnote below.

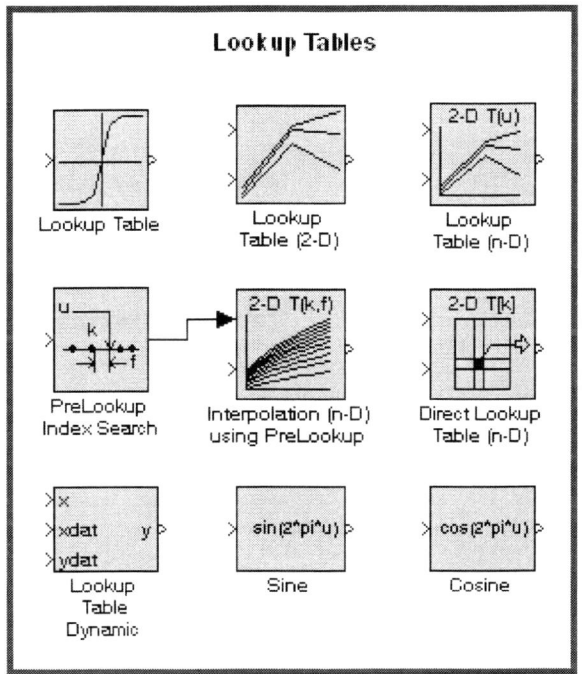

---

[*] *Monotonically increasing and monotocically decreasing sequences are sequences in which the successive values either consistently increase or decrease but do not oscillate in relative value. Each value of a monotonic increasing sequence is greater than, or equal to the preceding value; likewise, each value of a monotonic decreasing sequence is less than, or equal to the preceding value. Stated in other words, a monotonically increasing function is one resulting from a partially ordered domain to a partially ordered range such that* $x \leq y$ *implies that* $f(x) \leq f(y)$. *Likewise, a monotonically decreasing function is one resulting from a partially ordered domain to a partially ordered range such that* $x \leq y$ *implies that* $f(x) \geq f(y)$.

Chapter 7 The Lookup Tables Library

7.1 The Lookup Table Block

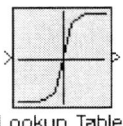

The **Lookup Table** block computes an approximation to a function $y = f(x)$ where the data vectors x and y are given, and it is required that the x data vector must be monotonically increasing. Moreover, the length of the x and y data vectors must be the same. Please refer to the Help menu for this block for additional information. The Lookup Table icon displays a graph of the input vector versus the output vector. When a parameter is changed on the Block Parameters dialog box, the graph is automatically redrawn when we click on the Apply button.

To define a table, we specify the Vector of input values parameter as a $1 \times n$ vector and the Vector of output values parameter as another $1 \times n$. The block generates output based on the input values using one of these methods selected from the Look-up method parameter list:

1. *Interpolation–Extrapolation*—This is the default method; it performs linear interpolation and extrapolation of the inputs.

    If a value matches the block's input, the output is the corresponding element in the output vector. If no value matches the block's input, then the block performs linear interpolation between the two appropriate elements of the table to determine an output value. If the block input is less than the first or greater than the last input vector element, then the block extrapolates using the first two or last two points.

2. *Interpolation–Use End Values*—This method performs linear interpolation as described above but does not extrapolate outside the end points of the input vector. Instead, the end–point values are used.

The methods 3, 4, and 5 listed below neither interpolate nor extrapolate. Also, there is no difference among these methods when the input x corresponds exactly to table breakpoints.

3. *Use Input Nearest*—With this method the element in x nearest the current input is found. The corresponding element in y is then used as the output.

4. *Use Input Below*—With this method the element in x nearest and below the current input is found. The corresponding element in y is then used as the output. If there is no element in x below the current input, the nearest element is used.

5. *Use Input Above*—With this method the element in x nearest and above the current input is found. The corresponding element in y is then used as the output. If there is no element in x above the current input, the nearest element is used.

To create a table with step transitions, we repeat an input value with different output values.

The Lookup Table (2–D) Block

Example 7.1

We will create a model with a Lookup Table block configured to use a vector of input values given by [1:5], and a vector of output values given by log([1:5]).[*]

The model is shown in Figure 7.1 where the Display 1 block shows the true values of the natural log for the range [1:5] and the Display 2 block shows the Lookup Table values for the same range of numbers. In the Constant block we have specified the range [1:5] and the Lookup Table block has been configured with Vector of input values [1:5], Vector output values log([1:5]), and Lookup method **Interpolation – Extrapolation**. The Math Function block is part of the Math Operations library, and it is described in Subsection 8.1.16, Chapter 8, Page 8.11.

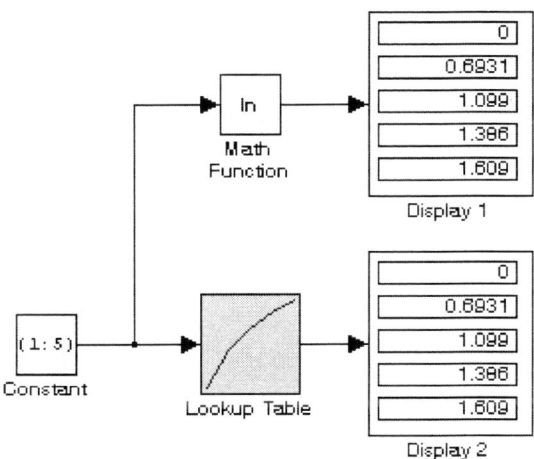

Figure 7.1. Model for Example 7.1

7.2 The Lookup Table (2–D) Block

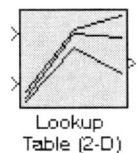

The **Lookup Table (2–D)** block computes an approximation for a function $z = f(x, y)$ when the data points x, y, and z are given. The Row index input values parameter is a $1 \times m$ vector of x data points, the Column index input values parameter is a $1 \times n$ vector of y data points, and the Matrix of output values parameter is an $m \times n$ matrix of z data points. Both the row and column

---

[*] *We recall that in MATLAB and Simulink log(x) implies the natural logarithm of x. The common (base 10) logarithm is denoted as log10(x).*

Chapter 7 The Lookup Tables Library

vectors must be monotonically increasing. The block generates output based on the input values using one of these methods selected from the Look-up method parameter list:

Interpolation–Extrapolation — This is the default method; it performs linear interpolation and extrapolation of the inputs. If the inputs match row and column parameter values, the output is the value at the intersection of the row and column. If the inputs do not match row and column parameter values, then the block generates output by linearly interpolating between the appropriate row and column values. If either or both block inputs are less than the first or greater than the last row or column values, the block extrapolates using the first two or last two points.

Interpolation–Use End Values — This method performs linear interpolation as described above but does not extrapolate outside the end points of x and y. Instead, the end-point values are used.

Use Input Nearest — This method does not interpolate or extrapolate. Instead, the elements in x and y nearest the current inputs are found. The corresponding element in z is then used as the output.

Use Input Below — This method does not interpolate or extrapolate. Instead, the elements in x and y nearest and below the current inputs are found. The corresponding element in z is then used as the output. If there are no elements in x or y below the current inputs, then the nearest elements are found.

Use Input Above — This method does not interpolate or extrapolate. Instead, the elements in x and y nearest and above the current inputs are found. The corresponding element in z is then used as the output. If there are no elements in x or y above the current inputs, then the nearest elements are found.

Example 7.2

Consider the matrix

$$A = \begin{bmatrix} 1 & 1-j & 2 \\ 1+j & 3 & j \\ 2 & -j & 0 \end{bmatrix}$$

We will create a model using the Lookup Table (2-D) block to display the second element of the third row of the Inverse matrix of A.

The model is shown in Figure 7.2 where in the Lookup Table (2-D) block we have entered:

The Lookup Table (n–D) Block

Row and Column index of input values: [1 2 3]

Vector of output values: inv(A)

Lookup method: Interpolation-Extrapolation

and in MATLAB's Command Window we entered

A=[1 1–j 2; 1+j 3 j; 2 –j 0];

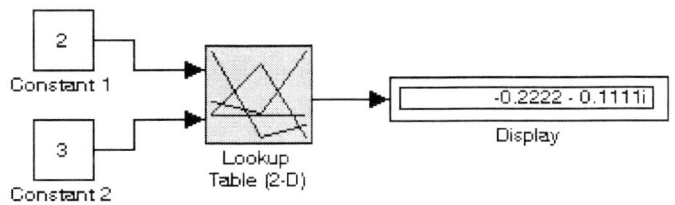

Figure 7.2. Model for Example 7.2

Check with MATLAB:

A =

```
   1.0000               1.0000 - 1.0000i   2.0000
   1.0000 + 1.0000i     3.0000             0 + 1.0000i
   2.0000               0 - 1.0000i        0
```

inv(A)

```
   0.1111 - 0.0000i    0.0000 + 0.2222i    0.5556 - 0.1111i
        0 - 0.2222i    0.4444 - 0.0000i   -0.2222 - 0.1111i
   0.5556 + 0.1111i   -0.2222 + 0.1111i   -0.1111
```

7.3 The Lookup Table (n–D) Block

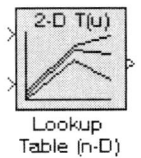

The **Lookup Table (n–D)** block n–dimensional interpolated table lookup including index searches. The table is a sample representation of a function of N variables. Breakpoint sets relate the input values to the positions in the table. The first dimension corresponds to the top (or left) input port. Thus, the block generates an output value by comparing the block inputs with the breakpoint set parameters. The first input identifies the first dimension (row) breakpoints, the second breakpoint set identifies a column, the third a page, and so on.

Chapter 7 The Lookup Tables Library

Example 7.3

We will create a model using a Lookup Table (n–D) block with the following specifications:

Number of table dimensions: 2

First input (row) breakpoint set: x=[0 1 2 3 4 5];

Second input (column) breakpoint set: y=[0 1 2 3 4 5];

Index search method: **Binary Search**

Table data:

A=[0 1 2 3 4 5; 6 7 8 9 10 11; 12 13 14 15 16 17;...
18 19 20 21 22 23; 24 25 26 27 28 29; 30 31 32 33 34 35];

Interpolation and extrapolation method: **Linear**

The model is shown in Figure 7.3 where in the Lookup Table (n–D) block we have entered the following:

Number of table dimensions: 2

First input (row) breakpoint set: **x**

Second input (column) breakpoint set: **y**

Index search method: **Binary Search**

Table data: **A**

Interpolation and extrapolation method: **Linear**

In MATLAB's Command Window we have entered:

x=[0 1 2 3 4 5]; y=[0 1 2 3 4 5];

A=[0 1 2 3 4 5; 6 7 8 9 10 11; 12 13 14 15 16 17;...
18 19 20 21 22 23; 24 25 26 27 28 29; 30 31 32 33 34 35];

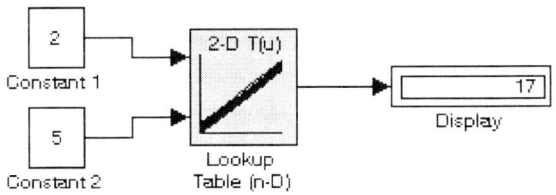

Figure 7.3. Model for Example 7.3

The Display block shows the value of the element located on Row 2 and Column 5. We can verify that with MATLAB by typing

A(3,6)
ans =
    17

The indices (2,5) in Simulink and (3,6) in MATLAB are same since Simulink uses zero–based indices whereas MATLAB uses one–based indices.

7.4 The PreLookup Index Search Block

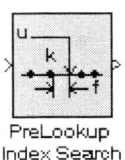

The **PreLookup Index Search** block calculates the indices and interval fractions for the input value in the **Breakpoint data** parameter. This block is intended for use with the Interpolation (n–D) Using PreLookup block which is described in the next section. To use this block, we must define a set of breakpoint values. In normal use, this breakpoint data set corresponds to one dimension of a Table data parameter in an Interpolation (n–D) using PreLookup block. The block generates a pair of outputs for each input value by calculating the index of the breakpoint set element that is less than or equal to the input value and the resulting fractional value that is a number $0 \leq f < 1$ that represents the input value's normalized position between the index and the next index value for in-range input.

Example 7.4

The breakpoint data in a PreLookup Index Search block is [0 1 2 3 4 5 6 7 8 9]. We will create a model to display the (index, fraction) pair denoted as k and f on the block when the input value u is 4.13.

The model is shown in Figure 7.4 where in the Display block the first value is the index, i.e., $k = 4$, and the second value is the fraction, i.e. $f = 0.13$

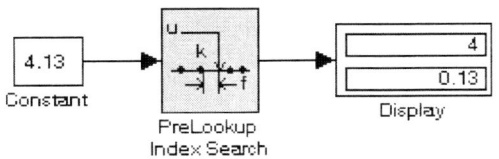

Figure 7.4. Model for Example 7.4

Chapter 7 The Lookup Tables Library

7.5 The Interpolation (n–D) Using PreLookup Block

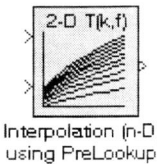

Interpolation (n-D) using PreLookup

The **Interpolation (n–D) Using PreLookup** block uses the precalculated indices and interval fractions from the PreLookup Index Search block to perform the equivalent operation that the Lookup Table (n–D) performs. This block supports two interpolation methods: flat (constant) interval lookup and linear interpolation. These operations can be applied to 1–D, 2–D, 3–D, 4–D, and higher dimensioned tables. We define a set of output values as the Table data parameter. These table values must correspond to the breakpoint data sets that are in the PreLookup Index Search block. The block generates its output by interpolating the table values based on the (index, fraction) pairs fed into the block by each PreLookup Index Search block.

The block generates output based on the input values:

1. If the inputs match breakpoint parameter values, the output is the table value at the intersection of the row, column, and higher dimensions' breakpoints.

2. If the inputs do not match row and column parameter values, the block generates output by interpolating between the appropriate table values. If either or both block inputs are less than the first or greater than the last row or column parameter values, the block extrapolates from the first two or last two points in each corresponding dimension.

Example 7.5

We will create a model with an Interpolation (n–D) Using PreLookup block with two input indices representing the rows and columns of a square matrix and the output set to display the square root of a number in the range of integer numbers 1 through 100. For this example, we want to define the two inputs such that the output displayed will be the square root of 12.

We can form a *10 × 10* array with the row vector a = [1 2 3 4 5 6 7 8 9 10] and the column vector b = [1 2 3 4 5 6 7 8 9 10]' and multiplying these. The products are as shown below.

1	2	3	4	5	6	7	8	9	10
2	4	6	8	10	12	14	16	18	20
3	6	9	12	15	18	21	24	27	30
4	8	12	16	20	24	28	32	36	40
5	10	15	20	25	30	35	40	45	50
6	12	18	24	30	36	42	48	54	60
7	14	21	28	35	42	49	56	63	70

8	16	24	32	40	48	56	64	72	80
9	18	27	36	45	54	63	72	81	90
10	20	30	40	50	60	70	80	90	100

We can address any element of this array by indexing the rows and columns. Recalling that Simulink uses zero–based indexing, we can access the number 12 by the indices (1, 5), (2, 3), (3, 2), or (5, 1). The model is shown in Figure 7.5 where the indices for the Constant blocks are as shown, the Interpolation (n–D) Using PreLookup block has been set for

Number of table dimensions: **2**

Table data: **sqrt(a*b)**

Interpolation and Extrapolation methods: **Linear**

and in MATLAB's Command Window we entered

a=[1; 2; 3; 4; 5; 6; 7; 8; 9; 10]; b=a';

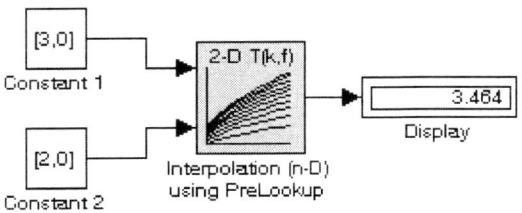

Figure 7.5. Model for Example 7.5

7.6 The Direct Lookup Table (n–D) Block

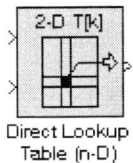

The **Direct Lookup Table (n–D)** block uses its block inputs as zero–based indices into an n–D table. The number of inputs varies with the shape of the output desired. The output can be a scalar, a vector, or a 2–D matrix. The lookup table uses zero–based indexing, thus an input of 2 returns the third element in that dimension. We recall that MATLAB uses one–based indexing and thus an input of 2 returns the second element in that dimension.

We define a set of output values as the Table data parameter, and we specify whether the output shape is an element, a column, or a 2–D matrix. The first input specifies the zero–based index to the first dimension higher than the number of dimensions in the output, the second input specifies the index to the next table dimension, and so on, as illustrated in the Help menu for this

Chapter 7 The Lookup Tables Library

block. The Help menus shows also the 15 different icons that this block displays depending on the options we choose in the block's dialog box.

To better understand the use of this block, let us review multi-dimensional arrays and illustrate with examples.

Let us consider the matrix A defined in MATLAB as

A=[1 2 3; 2 4 −5; 3 −5 6];

This is a two-dimensional array that uses two subscripts where the first references the row (1st dimension), and the second references the column (2nd dimension). Thus, A(3,3) is a two-dimensional array with 3 rows and 3 columns are displayed below.

A =
  1   2   3
  2   4 −5
  3 −5   6

A three-dimensional array adds another dimension to the two-dimensional array where the additional dimension is another page* behind the two-dimensional array. Thus for a 3×3 three-dimensional array with three pages the first page is displayed as

$$\begin{bmatrix} (1,1,1) & (1,2,1) & (1,3,1) \\ (2,1,1) & (2,2,1) & (2,3,1) \\ (3,1,1) & (3,2,1) & (3,3,1) \end{bmatrix}$$

the second page is displayed as

$$\begin{bmatrix} (1,1,2) & (1,2,2) & (1,3,2) \\ (2,1,2) & (2,2,2) & (2,3,2) \\ (3,1,2) & (3,2,2) & (3,3,2) \end{bmatrix}$$

and the third page is displayed as

$$\begin{bmatrix} (1,1,3) & (1,2,3) & (1,3,3) \\ (2,1,3) & (2,2,3) & (2,3,3) \\ (3,1,3) & (3,2,3) & (3,3,3) \end{bmatrix}$$

---

* *The term **page** used to describe the third dimension can be thought of as two or more two-dimensional arrays stacked one on top of another in the same way the pages of a closed book are stacked one on top of another. Dimensions higher than three can be created but it is not possible to visualize.*

The Direct Lookup Table (n–D) Block

It is to be noted that in a three–dimensional array the page number is indicated by the third index in each element of the array. For instance, the fourth page would contain the elements (1, 1, 4), (1, 2, 4), and so on.

Suppose that A is defined as

A=[1 2 3; –2 4 5; 3 –1 8];

and we want to add a third dimension to A by adding a second page with another matrix whose elements are [4 5 6; –1 3 2; 7 8 –2]. The second page is defined as

A(:,:,2)=[4 5 6; –1 3 2; 7 8 -2]

and thus in MATLAB's Command Window we type

A=[1 2 3; –2 4 5; 3 –1 8]; A(:,:,2)=[4 5 6; –1 3 2; 7 8 –2];

and MATLAB outputs

```
A(:,:,1)  =
      1     2     3
     -2     4     5
      3    -1     8
A(:,:,2)  =
      4     5     6
     -1     3     2
      7     8    -2
```

Now suppose that we want to add a third page whose all elements have the same value, say 2. We enter
A(:,:,3)=2;

and when we type

A(:,:,3)=2

MATLAB displays

```
      2     2     2
      2     2     2
      2     2     2
```

Next let us consider the $3 \times 3 \times 3$ three–dimensional array

A(:,:,1)=[1 2 3; –2 4 5; 3 –1 8]; A(:,:,2)=[4 5 6; –1 3 2; 7 8 –2];...
A(:,:,3)=[2 4 –6; –3 5 8; 7 9 –2]

and suppose that we want to convert it to a four–dimensional array. We enter

Chapter 7 The Lookup Tables Library

A(:,:,1)=[1 2 3; −2 4 5; 3 −1 8];
A(:,:,2)=[4 5 6; −1 3 2; 7 8 −2];
A(:,:,3)=[2 4 −6; − 3 5 8; 7 9 −2]

and MATLAB outputs

```
A(:,:,1,1) =
     0     0     0
     0     0     0
     0     0     0
A(:,:,2,1) =
     0     0     0
     0     0     0
     0     0     0
A(:,:,3,1) =
     0     0     0
     0     0     0
     0     0     0
A(:,:,1,2) =
     1     2     3
    -2     4     5
     3    -1     8
A(:,:,2,2) =
     4     5     6
    -1     3     2
     7     8    -2
A(:,:,3,2) =
     2     4    -6
    -3     5     8
     7     9    -2
```

We observe that A(:,:,1,1), A(:,:,2,1), and A(:,:,3,1) are padded with zeros to maintain the corresponding sizes of the dimensions.

The MATLAB User's Manual describes the procedure for generating arrays using MATLAB functions, and several examples are provided.

Let us suppose that we want to generate a four–dimensional array with 10 rows, 5 columns, 3 pages, with a fourth dimension and all elements are 2. The array that will satisfy this requirement is

a=ones(10,5,3,1)*2

The Direct Lookup Table (n–D) Block

and when this statement is executed, MATLAB displays

```
a(:,:,1) =
     2    2    2    2    2
     2    2    2    2    2
     2    2    2    2    2
     2    2    2    2    2
     2    2    2    2    2
     2    2    2    2    2
     2    2    2    2    2
     2    2    2    2    2
     2    2    2    2    2
     2    2    2    2    2
```

Arrays a(:,:,2) and a(:,:,3) also display the same array.

The following example is similar to that in the Help menu for this block.

Example 7.6

We will create a model with a Direct Lookup Table (n–D) block with the four–dimensional array a=ones(10,3,4,3), to display the first column of the array a(:,:,4,3).

In MATLAB's Command Window we enter

a=ones(10,3,4,3); L=prod(size(a)); a(1:L)=[1:L]';

The model is shown in Figure 7.6 where in the Direct Lookup Table (n–D) block we have entered

Number of table dimensions: 4

Input select this object from table: Column

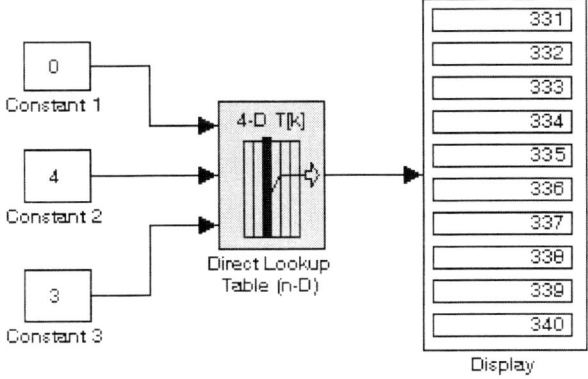

Figure 7.6. Model for Example 7.6

Chapter 7 The Lookup Tables Library

Make table an input: unchecked

Table data: a

Constant 1 block: 0 (The Lookup table uses zero–based indexing so 0 is the index for the first column.

Constant 2 block: 4 (or uint16(3) if we wish to specify unassigned integer number)

Constant 3 block: 3 (or uint8(3) if we wish to specify unassigned integer number)

To verify the Display block in Figure 7.6, in MATLAB's Command Window we enter

a(:,:,4,3)

and MATLAB displays the array below.

```
331    341    351
332    342    352
333    343    353
334    344    354
335    345    355
336    346    356
337    347    357
338    348    358
339    349    359
340    350    360
```

To display the second or third column, in the Display 1 block we replace 0 with 1 or 2 as appropriate.

Example 7.7

It is given that a=ones(5,5,3,4,2); L=prod(size(a)); a(1:L)=[1:L]'; We will create a model to display the output corresponding to this array if the **Input select this object from table** is specified as **2–D Matrix**.

The model is shown in Figure 7.7 where in MATLAB's Command Window we have entered

a=ones(5,5,3,4,2); L=prod(size(a)); a(1:L)=[1:L]';

The Lookup Table Dynamic Block

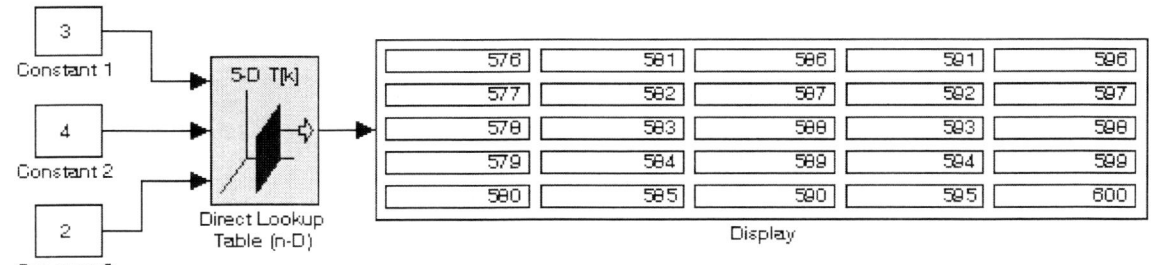

Figure 7.7. Model for Example 7.7

The values in the Display block of Figure 7.7 can be verified by typing

a(:,:,3,4,2)

in MATLAB's Command Window which displays the array below.

```
576   581   586   591   596
577   582   587   592   597
578   583   588   593   598
579   584   589   594   599
580   585   590   595   600
```

7.7 The Lookup Table Dynamic Block

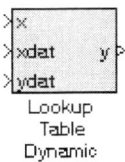

The **Lookup Table Dynamic** block computes an approximation to some function $y = f(x)$ given x and y data vectors. The lookup method can use interpolation, extrapolation, or the original values of the input. Unlike the Lookup Table block, the Lookup Table Dynamic block allows us to change the table data without stopping the simulation. For example, we may want to automatically incorporate new table data if the physical system we are simulating changes.

There are certain restrictions in using this block. Please refer to the Help menu for this block.

Example 7.8

The square root of the numbers 50 through 56 is given in the table below. We will create a model with a Lookup Table Dynamic block to compute an approximation to $f(52.6)$.

Chapter 7 The Lookup Tables Library

x	50	51	52	53	54	55	56
$y = f(x) = \sqrt{x}$	7.071	7.141	7.211	7.280	7.348	7.416	7.483

The model is shown in Figure 7.8 where in MATLAB's Command Window we have entered:

xdata=[50 51 52 53 54 55 56];...
ydata=[7.07107 7.14143 7.21110 7.28011 7.34847 7.41620 7.48331];

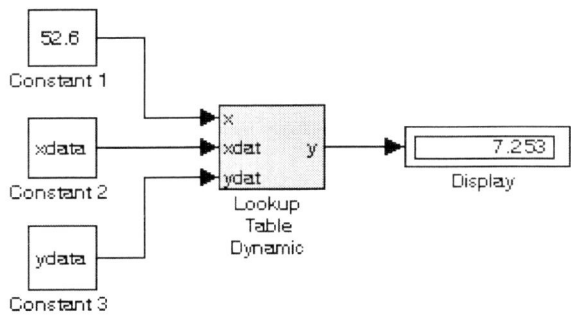

Figure 7.8. Model for Example 7.8

7.8 The Sine and Cosine Blocks

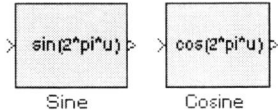

The **Sine and Cosine** blocks implement a sine and / or cosine wave in fixed point using a lookup table method that uses quarter wave symmetry. From Fourier series[*] textbooks we recall that:

1. Any waveform that repeats itself after some time, can be expressed as a series of harmonically related sinusoids, i.e., sinusoids whose frequencies are multiples of a *fundamental* frequency (or first harmonic). For example, a series of sinusoids with frequencies 1 MHz, 2 MHz, 3 MHz, and so on, contains the fundamental frequency of 1 MHz, a second harmonic of 2 MHz, a third harmonic of 3 MHz, and so on. In general, any periodic waveform f(t) can be expressed as

---

[*] *For a detailed discussion on Fourier series, please refer to Signals and Systems with MATLAB Computing and Simulink Modeling, ISBN 0-9744239-9-8.*

The Sine and Cosine Blocks

$$f(t) = \frac{1}{2}a_0 + a_1\cos\omega t + a_2\cos 2\omega t + a_3\cos 3\omega t + a_4\cos 4\omega t + \ldots \qquad (7.1)$$
$$+ b_1\sin\omega t + b_2\sin 2\omega t + b_3\sin 3\omega t + b_4\sin 4\omega t + \ldots$$

or

$$f(t) = \frac{1}{2}a_0 + \sum_{n=1}^{\infty}(a_n\cos n\omega t + b_n\sin n\omega t) \qquad (7.2)$$

where the first term $a_0/2$ is a constant, and represents the DC (average) component of $f(t)$. Thus, if $f(t)$ represents some voltage $v(t)$, or current $i(t)$, the term $a_0/2$ is the average value of $v(t)$ or $i(t)$.

The terms with the coefficients a_1 and b_1 together, represent the fundamental frequency component ω[*]. Likewise, the terms with the coefficients a_2 and b_2 together, represent the second harmonic component 2ω, and so on.

2. Odd functions have only sine terms.

3. Even functions have no sine terms.

4. If there is half–wave symmetry, only odd harmonics (sine and cosine) are present.

Quarter–wave symmetry implies that a waveform contains only sine odd harmonics and these can be formed digitally with a series of zeros and ones.[†] With quarter–wave symmetry, we begin with a single quadrant, we copy it, we reverse the copy, we shift it by 90 degrees, we add it to the first quarter to obtain half of the waveform, and finally we copy the half waveform, we reverse it, we shift it by 180 degrees, and we add it to the first half too obtain the full waveform.

In Simulink, the Sine and Cosine block can output the following functions of the input signal, depending upon what we select for the Output formula parameter:

$$\sin(2\pi x)$$
$$\cos(2\pi x)$$
$$e^{i\pi x}$$
$$\sin(2\pi x) \text{ and } \cos(2\pi x)$$

We define the number of lookup table points in the Number of data points for lookup table parameter. The block implementation is most efficient when we specify the lookup table data

---

[*] *We recall that* $k_1\cos\omega t + k_2\sin\omega t = k\cos(\omega t + \theta)$ *where* θ *is a constant.*

[†] *Sinewaves with repeating long sequences of zeros and ones are referred to as "magic sinewaves".* **They can be created with simple but extremely carefully chosen digitally switched pulses.**

Chapter 7 The Lookup Tables Library

points to be $2^n + 1$, where n is an integer. We use the Output word length parameter to specify the word length of the fixed-point output data type. The fraction length of the output is the output word length minus 2.

A function Lookup Table is a procedure by which we approximate a function by a table with a finite number of points (x,y). A tutorial on producing Lookup Tables in Simulink is presented in the Simulink Fixed Point User's Guide.

Simulink implements lookup tables that use breakpoints whose spacing is uneven, even, and power of two. For a comparison, please review the Simulink demo **fxpdemo_approx_sin**. To open the demo, type at the MATLAB prompt

fxpdemo_approx_sin

There are three fixed–point lookup tables in this model. All three lookup tables approximate the function $\sin 2\pi x$ over the first quadrant. All three achieve a worst-case error of less than 2^{-8}.

The example below illustrates the creation of a model using the Repeating Stair Sequence block described in the Sources Library, Section 15.2.13, Chapter 15, Page15–21, and the Lookup Table block described in this chapter.

Example 7.9

We will create a model using the **uneven** spacing fixed–point option of a Lookup Table block to approximate the function $\sin 2\pi x$ over the first quadrant.

The model is shown in Figure 7.9 and the input and output waveforms in Figure 7.10. For the model of Figure 7.9, the Configuration Parameters are chosen as Type: **Fixed-step**, and Solver: **Discrete (no continuous states)**. For the Repeating Stair Sequence block the Vector of output values was set as **linspace(0, 0.25, 50)**. For the Lookup Table block the Vector of input values is specified as **xuneven**, the Table data is specified as **yuneven**, and the Lookup method is specified as **Interpolation - Use End Values**.

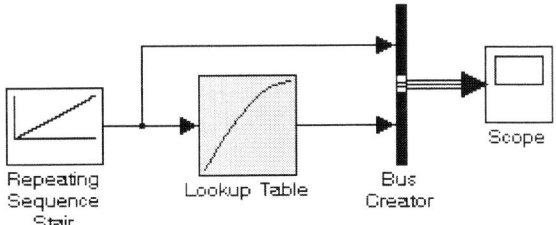

Figure 7.9. Model for Example 7.9

The Sine and Cosine Blocks

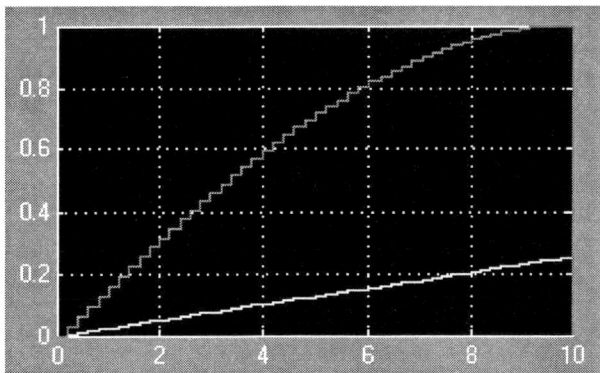

Figure 7.10. Input and output waveforms for the model of Figure 7.9

Chapter 7 The Lookup Tables Library

7.9 Summary

- A function Lookup Table is a procedure by which we approximate a function by a table with a finite number of points (x, y). Simulink implements lookup tables that use breakpoints whose spacing is uneven, even, and power of two. For a comparison, please review the Simulink demo **fxpdemo_approx_sin**. To view this demo, type at the MATLAB prompt

  fxpdemo_approx_sin

- The **Lookup Table** block computes an approximation to a function $y = f(x)$ where the data vectors x and y are given. The length of the x and y data vectors provided to this block must match. The length of the x and y data vectors provided to this block must match. It is required that the x data vector must be monotonically increasing. To create a table with step transitions, we repeat an input value with different output values.

- The **Lookup Table (2–D)** block computes an approximation for a function $z = f(x, y)$ when the data points x, y, and z are given. The Row index input values parameter is a $1 \times m$ vector of x data points, the Column index input values parameter is a $1 \times n$ vector of y data points, and the Matrix of output values parameter is an $m \times n$ matrix of z data points. Both the row and column vectors must be monotonically increasing.

- The **Lookup Table (n–D)** block evaluates a sampled representation of a function in N variables by interpolating between samples to give an approximate value for, even when the function is known only empirically. The block efficiently maps the block inputs to the output value using interpolation on a table of values defined by the block's parameters. Interpolation methods are flat (constant), linear, and cubic spline. We can apply any of these methods to 1–D, 2–D, 3–D, or higher dimensional tables.

- The **PreLookup Index Search** block calculates the indices and interval fractions for the input value in the Breakpoint data parameter. To use this block, we must define a set of breakpoint values. In normal use, this breakpoint data set corresponds to one dimension of a Table data parameter in an Interpolation (n–D) using PreLookup block. The block generates a pair of outputs for each input value by calculating the index of the breakpoint set element that is less than or equal to the input value and the resulting fractional value that is a number $0 \leq f < 1$ that represents the input value's normalized position between the index and the next index value for in-range input.

- The **Interpolation (n–D) Using PreLookup** block uses the precalculated indices and interval fractions from the PreLookup Index Search block to perform the equivalent operation that the Lookup Table (n–D) performs. This block supports two interpolation methods: flat (constant) interval lookup and linear interpolation. These operations can be applied to 1–D, 2–D, 3–D, 4–D, and higher dimensioned tables.

Summary

- The **Direct Lookup Table (n–D)** block uses its block inputs as zero-based indices into an n–D table. The number of inputs varies with the shape of the output desired. The output can be a scalar, a vector, or a 2–D matrix. The lookup table uses zero-based indexing, thus an input of 2 returns the third element in that dimension. We recall that MATLAB uses one-based indexing and thus an input of 2 returns the second element in that dimension.

- The **Lookup Table Dynamic** block computes an approximation to some function $y = f(x)$ given x and y data vectors. The lookup method can use interpolation, extrapolation, or the original values of the input. Unlike the Lookup Table block, the Lookup Table Dynamic block allows us to change the table data without stopping the simulation.

- The **Sine and Cosine** blocks implement a sine and / or cosine wave in fixed point using a lookup table method that uses quarter wave symmetry. In Simulink, the Sine and Cosine block can output the following functions of the input signal, depending upon what we select for the Output formula parameter:

$$\sin(2\pi x) \quad \sin(2\pi x) \quad \cos(2\pi x) \quad e^{i\pi x} \quad \sin(2\pi x) \text{ and } \cos(2\pi x)$$

7.10 Exercises

1. Define a lookup table that will display a square waveform in the ranges $-2 < x < 2$ and $-1 < y < 1$.

2. Bessel functions* of the first kind are denoted as $J_n(x)$ where the subscript n indicates the order for n = 0, 1, 2, 3, ... Thus, $J_0(x)$ denotes the zero order of the first kind of Bessel functions. Create a model with a Lookup Table block configured to display the values of x from 0 to 1.0 in steps of 0.1 for $J_0(x)$.

3. It is given that a=ones(5,5,3,4,2); L=prod(size(a)); a(1:L)=[1:L]'; Create a model to display the output corresponding to this array if the **Input select this object from table** is specified as **column**.

4. Create a model with an Interpolation (n−D) Using PreLookup block with two input indices representing the rows and columns of a square matrix and the output set to display the square root of a number in the range of integer numbers 1 through 100. For this example, we want to define the two inputs such that the output displayed will be the square root of 19.25.
Hint: $19.25 = 3.5 \times 5.5$.

5. Consider the matrix

$$A = \begin{bmatrix} 1 & 1-j & 2 \\ 1+j & 3 & j \\ 2 & -j & 0 \end{bmatrix}$$

Create a model using the Lookup Table (2-D) block to interpolate and display the value of the Inverse matrix of A at $(x, y) = (2.75, 5.25)$.

6. Using the data of the table below create a model with a Lookup Table Dynamic block to compute an approximation to $f(1.35)$.

x	1.1	1.2	1.5	1.7	1.8	2.0
y=f(x)	1.112	1.219	1.636	2.054	2.323	3.011

---

* *For a detailed discussion of Bessel functions, please refer to Numerical Analysis Using MATLAB and Spreadsheets, ISBN 0–9709511–1–6.*

Solutions to End-of-Chapter Exercises

7.11 Solutions to End-of-Chapter Exercises

1.

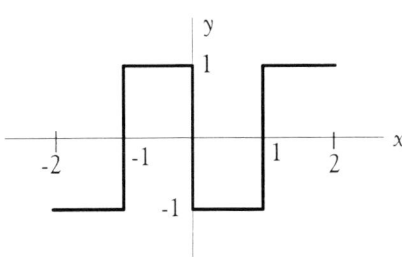

Vector x of input values: -2 -1 -1 0 0 1 1 2

Vector y of output values: -1 -1 1 1 -1 -1 1 1

We observe that this waveform has three step discontinuities: at $x = -1$, $x = 0$, and $x = 1$.

2.

The model is shown below where in the Constant block we have enter the range [0:0.1:1.0], and in the Lookup Table block we have entered Vector of input values [0:0.0:1.0], Vector output values besselj(0, [0:0.0:1.0]'), and Lookup method **Interpolation – Extrapolation**.

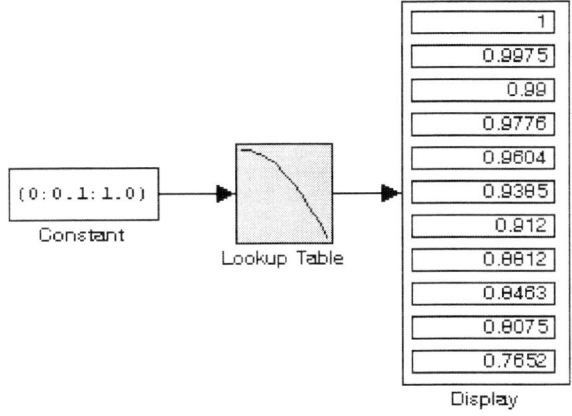

3.

The model is shown below where we have entered:

Number of table dimensions: 5

Input select this object from table: Column

Make table an input: unchecked

Table data: a

Constant blocks: The values shown

Chapter 7 The Lookup Tables Library

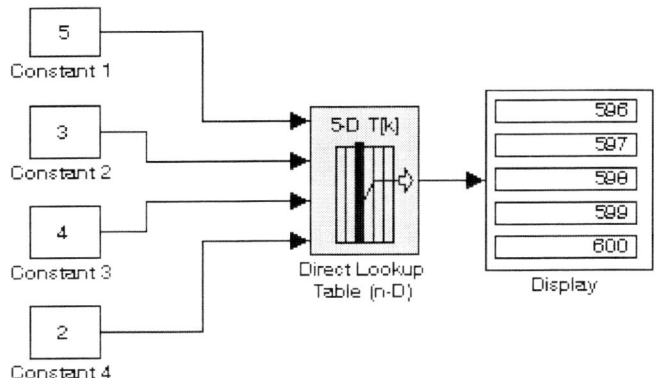

To verify the Display block values, in MATLAB's Command Window we enter

a(:,:,3,4,2)

and MATLAB displays the array below.

576	581	586	591	596
577	582	587	592	597
578	583	588	593	598
579	584	589	594	599
580	585	590	595	600

4.

The model is shown below where the PreLookup Index Search blocks 1 and 2 were set for:

Breakpoint data: [1 2 3 4 5 6 7 8 9 10]

Index search method: **Linear Search**

Process out of range input: Linear Extrapolation

We can form a 10×10 array with the row vector a = [1 2 3 4 5 6 7 8 9 10] and the column vector b = [1 2 3 4 5 6 7 8 9 10]' and multiplying these.

The Interpolation (n–D) Using PreLookup block has been set for

Number of table dimensions: **2**

Table data: **sqrt(a*b)**

Interpolation and Extrapolation methods: **Linear**

and in MATLAB's Command Window we enter

a=[1; 2; 3; 4; 5; 6; 7; 8; 9; 10]; b=a';

Solutions to End-of-Chapter Exercises

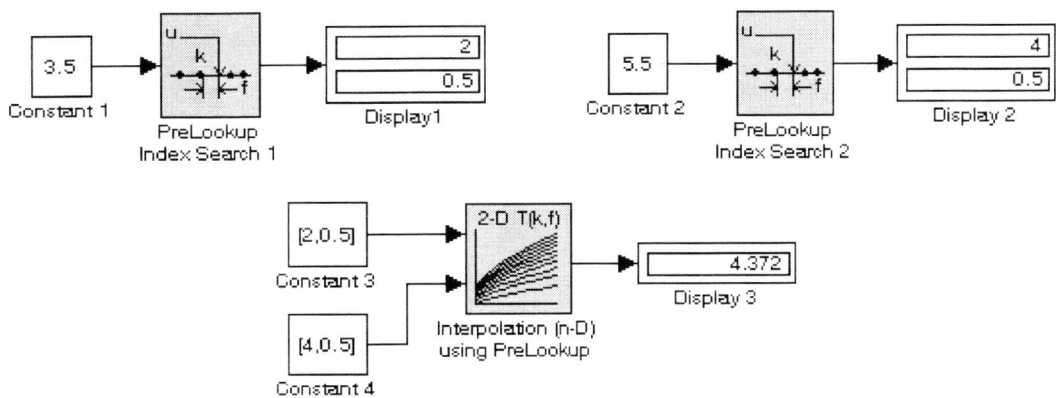

5.

The model is shown below where Row and Column index of input values have been defined as [1 2 3] and [4 5 6] respectively.

Vector of output values: **inv(A)**

Lookup method: **Interpolation-Extrapolation**

and in MATLAB's Command Window we entered

A=[1 1−j 2; 1+j 3 j; 2 −j 0];

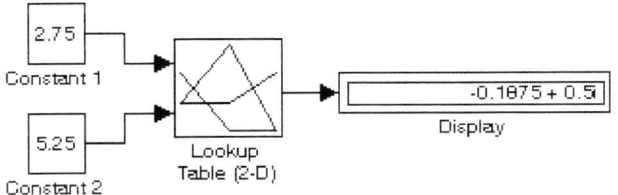

6.

The model is shown below where in MATLAB's Command Window we have entered:

xdata=[1.1 1.2 1.5 1.7 1.8 2.0]; ydata=[1.112 1.219 1.636 2.054 2.323 3.011];

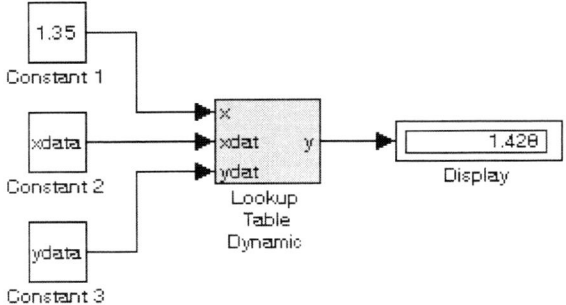

Chapter 7 The Lookup Tables Library

NOTES:

Chapter 8

The Math Operations Library

This chapter is an introduction to the **Math Operations** Library. This is the seventh library in the Simulink group of libraries and contains and contains the **Math Operations Group Sub−Library**, the **Vector / Matrix Operations Group Sub−Library**, and the **Complex Vector Conversions Group Sub−Library**. We will describe the function of each block included in this library and we will perform simulation examples to illustrate their application.

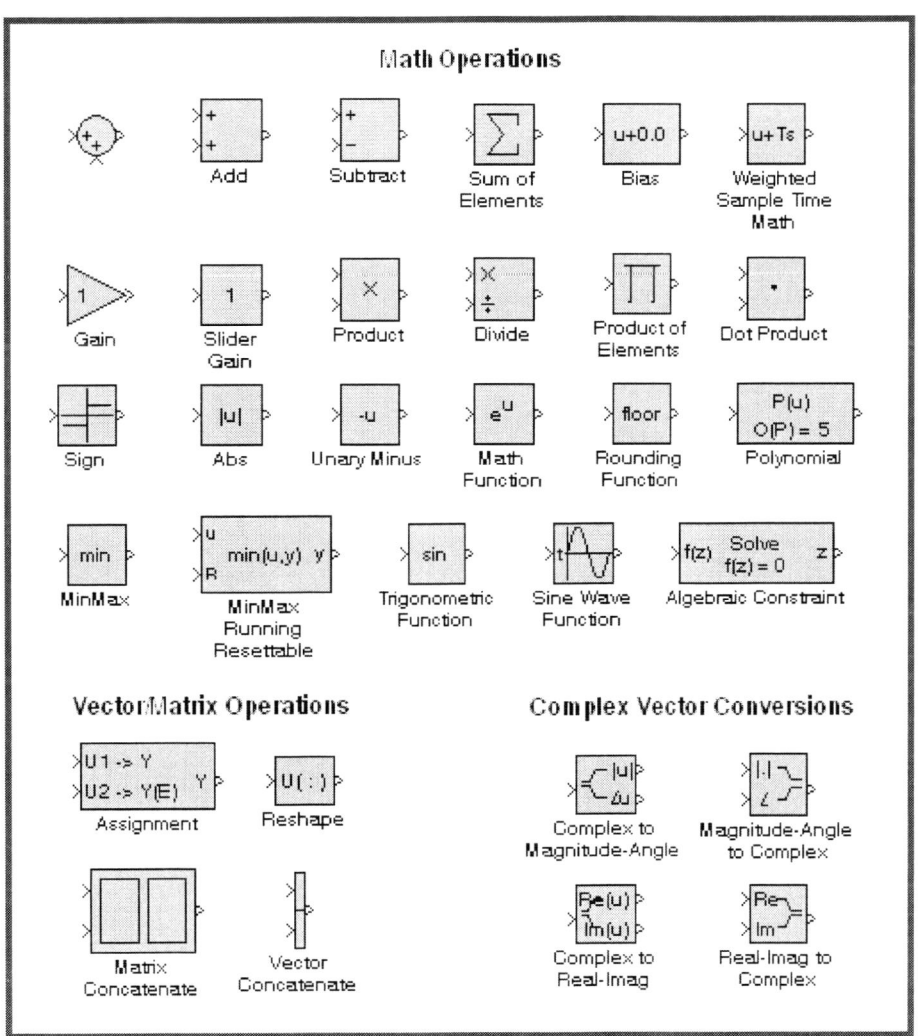

Chapter 8 The Math Operations Library

8.1 The Math Operations Group Sub-Library

The **Math Operations Group Sub-Library** contains the blocks described in Subsections 8.1.1 through 8.1.23 below.

8.1.1 The Sum Block

The **Sum** block is an implementation of the Add block which is described in Section 8.1.2 below. We can choose the icon shape (round or rectangular) of the block on the Block Parameters dialog box.

8.1.2 The Add Block

The **Add** block performs addition or subtraction on its inputs. This block can add or subtract scalar, vector, or matrix inputs. It can also collapse the elements of a single input vector. We specify the operations of the block with the List of Signs parameter. Plus (+), minus (−), and spacer (|) characters indicate the operations to be performed on the inputs. The spacer character creates extra space between ports on the block's icon.

If there are two or more inputs, then the number of characters must equal the number of inputs. For example, "+−+" requires three inputs and configures the block to subtract the second (middle) input from the first (top) input, and then add the third (bottom) input.

Example 8.1

The matrices A, B, and C are defined as shown. We will create a model using the Add block to display the result of $A + B - C$.

$$A = \begin{bmatrix} 1 & -1 & -4 \\ 5 & 7 & -2 \\ 3 & -5 & 6 \end{bmatrix} \quad B = \begin{bmatrix} 5 & 9 & -3 \\ -2 & 8 & 2 \\ 7 & -4 & 6 \end{bmatrix} \quad C = \begin{bmatrix} 4 & 6 & 1 \\ -3 & 8 & -2 \\ 5 & -2 & 3 \end{bmatrix}$$

The model is shown in Figure 8.1 where in the MATLAB's Command Window we have entered

A=[1 −1 4; 5 7 −2; 3 −5 6]; B=[5 9 −3; −2 8 2; 7 −4 6]; C=[4 6 1; −3 8 −2; 5 −2 3];

The Math Operations Group Sub–Library

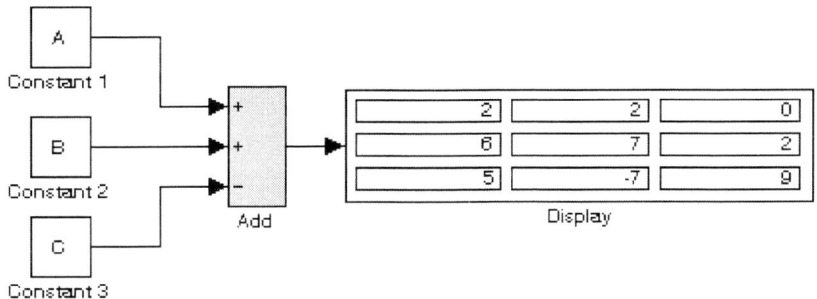

Figure 8.1. Model for Example 8.1

8.1.3 The Subtract Block

The **Subtract** block is an implementation of the Add block which is described in Subsection 8.1.2 above.

Example 8.2

Let $a = 1/(4+j3)$ and $b = 1/(2-j5)$. We will create a model using a Subtract block to perform the operation $a - b$.

The model is shown in Figure 8.27 where in MATLAB's Command Window we have entered a=1/(4+3j); b=1/(2−5j);

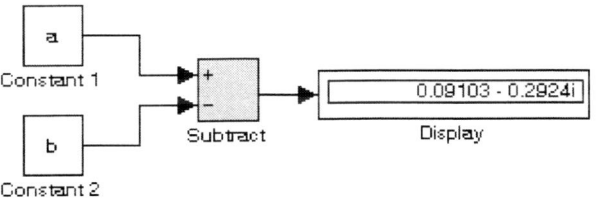

Figure 8.2. Model for Example 8.2

Chapter 8 The Math Operations Library

8.1.4 The Sum of Elements Block

The **Sum of Elements** block is an implementation of the Add block described in Subsection 8.1.2 above.

8.1.5 The Bias Block

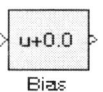

The **Bias** block adds a bias (offset) to the input signal.

Example 8.3

We will create a model using a Bias block to display the waveform $y = \sin x + 1$.

The model is shown in Figure 8.3 and the input and output waveforms are shown in Figure 8.4 where for the Bias block Block Parameters dialog box we specified Bias: **1**

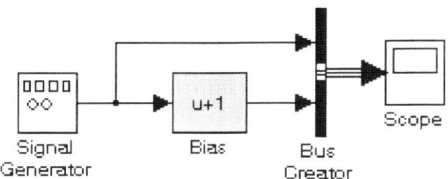

Figure 8.3. Model for Example 8.3

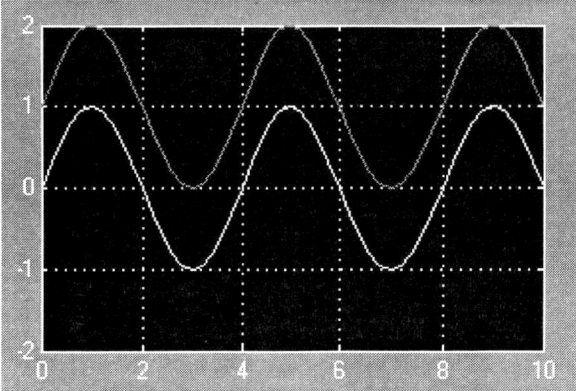

Figure 8.4. Input and output waveforms for the model of Figure 8.3

8.1.6 The Weighted Sample Time Math Block

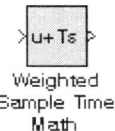

The **Weighted Sample Time Math** block adds, subtracts, multiplies, or divides the input signal, u, by a weighted sample time Ts. We use the Operation parameter to specify the math operation. This block also allows us to use only the weight with either the sample time or its inverse. We enter the weighting factor in the Weight value parameter. If the weight is 1, w is removed from the equation.

Example 8.4

We will create a model using a Weighted Sample Time Math block where the input signal is a Digital Clock block specified at Sample time 1, and the Weighted Sample Time Math block Operation parameter is specified as Divide with Weight value 2.

The model is shown in Figure 8.5 and the input and output waveforms are shown in Figure 8.6.

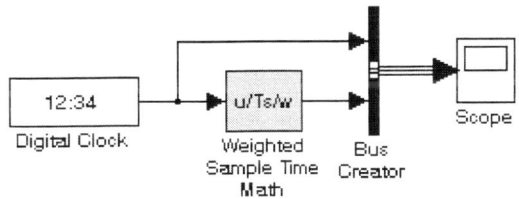

Figure 8.5. Model for Example 8.4

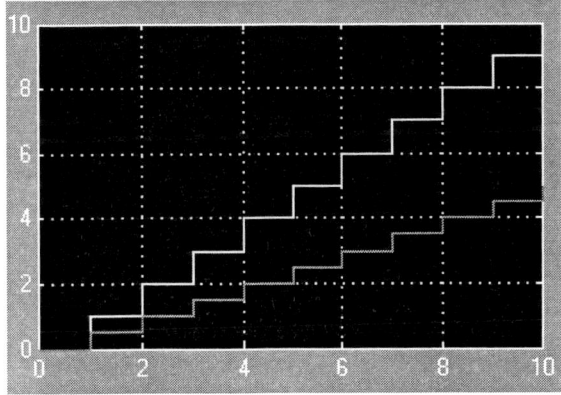

Figure 8.6. Input and output waveforms for the model of Figure 8.5

8.1.7 The Gain Block

The **Gain** block multiplies the input by a constant value (gain). The input and the gain can each be a scalar, vector, or matrix. This block was described in Section 2.10, Chapter 2, Page 2–16.

8.1.8 The Slider Gain Block

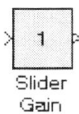

The **Slider Gain** block is used to vary a scalar gain during a simulation. The default for the lower limit is 0, and the default for the upper limit is 2.

Example 8.5

We will create a model using a Slider Gain block to display the input and output sinusoidal waveforms when the Slider Gain block has been specified as 0.5.

The model is shown in Figure 8.7 and the input and output waveforms are shown in Figure 8.8.

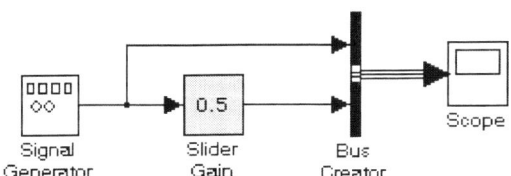

Figure 8.7. Model for Example 8.5

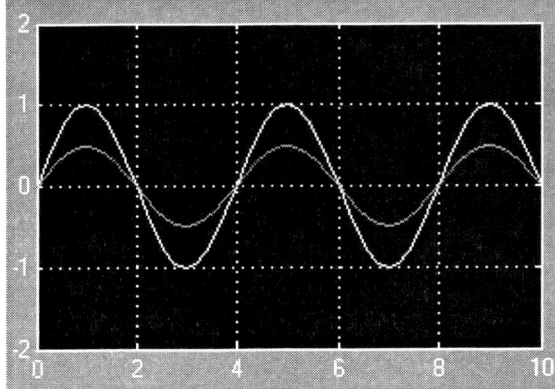

Figure 8.8. Input and output waveforms for the model of Figure 8.7

The Math Operations Group Sub-Library

8.1.9 The Product Block

The **Product** block performs multiplication or division of its inputs. This block is described in Section 2.4, Chapter 2, Page 2–6. To perform a dot product on input vectors, we use the Dot Product block described in Section 8.1.12, this chapter, Page 8–8.

Example 8.6

We will create a model using a Product block to perform element–by–element multiplication of the row vectors a = [1 2 3 4 5] and b = [–2 6 –3 8 7].

The model is shown in Figure 8.9 where in MATLAB's Command Window we have entered

a=[1 2 3 4 5]; b=[–2 6 –3 8 7];

and the Product block Multiplication has been specified as **element–wise**.

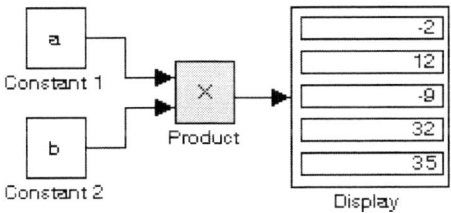

Figure 8.9. Model for Example 8.6

8.1.10 The Divide Block

The **Divide** block is an implementation of the Product block. The Product block is described in Section 2.4, Chapter 2, Page 2–6.

8.1.11 The Product of Elements Block

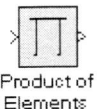

Chapter 8 The Math Operations Library

The **Product of Elements** block is used to multiply of divide inputs. It is essentially a Product block. The Product block was described in Section 2.4, Chapter 2, Page 2–6.

Example 8.7

We will create a model using the Product of Elements block to compute the product a · b where

$$a = [1 \quad 0 \quad -3 \quad 0 \quad 5 \quad 7 \quad 9]$$
$$b = [2 \quad -8 \quad 0 \quad 0 \quad 4 \quad 10 \quad 12]$$

The model is shown in Figure 8.10 where in MATLAB's Command Window we have entered
a=[1 0 −3 0 5 7 9]; b=[2 −8 0 0 4 10 12];

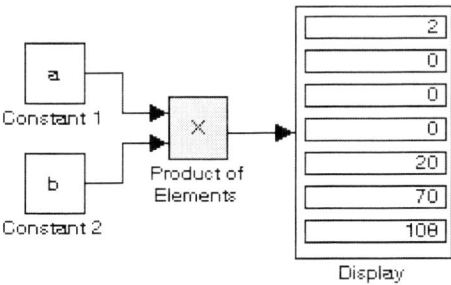

Figure 8.10. Model for Example 8.7

8.1.12 The Dot Product Block

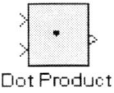

The **Dot Product** block generates the dot product of its two input vectors. The scalar output, y, is equal to the MATLAB operation y=sum(conj(A.*B)) where vectors A and B are defined as $A = [a_1 \; a_2 \; ... \; a_n]$, $B = [b_1 \; b_2 \; ... \; b_n]$, and $A*B = [a_1 b_1 + a_2 b_2 + \; ... \; + a_n b_n]$

Example 8.8

We will create a model using a Dot Product block to perform the dot (inner) product of the row vectors $A = [1 \; 2 \; 3 \; 4 \; 5]$ and $B = [-2 \; 6 \; -3 \; 8 \; 7]$.

The model is shown in Figure 8.11 where in MATLAB's Command Window we have entered
A=[1 2 3 4 5]; B=[−2 6 −3 8 7];

The Math Operations Group Sub-Library

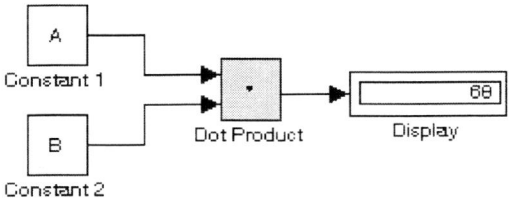

Figure 8.11. Model for Example 8.8

8.1.13 The Sign Block

The **Sign** block indicates the sign of the input. The output is 1 when the input is greater than zero, the output is 0 when the input is equal to zero, and the output is −1 when the input is less than zero.

Example 8.9

We will create a model using the Sign block to determine whether the expression

$$x = \frac{1}{(-0.224)^7} + \frac{2}{(0.294)^8} - \frac{3}{(0.484)^2}$$

is positive, zero, or negative.

Solution:

The model is shown in Figure 8.12 where in MATLAB's Command Window we have entered

x=1/(−0.224)^7+2/(0.294)^8−3/(0.484)^2;

MATLAB outputs the value x = 477.786 and thus the Sign block outputs 1 indicating a positive value.

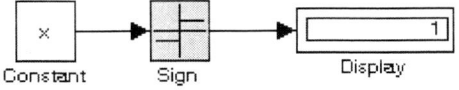

Figure 8.12. Model for Example 8.9

Chapter 8 The Math Operations Library

8.1.14 The Abs Block

The **Abs** block outputs the absolute value of the input. This block accepts real signals of any data type supported by Simulink, except Boolean, and supports real fixed–point data types. The block also accepts complex single and double inputs. Outputs are a real value of the same data type as the input.

When the **Saturate on integer overflow** is selected, the block maps signed integer input elements corresponding to the most negative value of that data type to the most positive value of that data type. Thus, if the input is x and the signal data type is specified as int8 for the interval $-127 \leq x \leq 0$, the output is the absolute value of the input, but when the input is -128, the output displayed is 127. Likewise, if the input signal data type is specified as int16, for the input -32768, the output is 32767, and if the input signal data type is specified as int32, for the input -2147483648, the output is 2147483647.

When the **Saturate on integer overflow** is not selected, the block ignores signed integer input elements and outputs the absolute value of the input.

If the input is a complex number, the signal data type must be specified either as **single** or **double**.

Example 8.10

We will create a model using the Abs block to display the absolute value of the product

$$(-3 - j4) \times (5 - j8)$$

The model is shown in Figure 8.13 where the input signal type is specified as **double**.

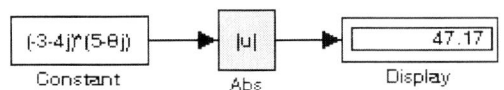

Figure 8.13. Model for Example 8.10

8.1.15 The Unary Minus Block

The Math Operations Group Sub-Library

The **Unary Minus** block negates the input. The block accepts only signed data types. For signed data types, we cannot accurately negate the most negative value since the result is not representable by the data type. In this case, the behavior of the block is controlled by the Saturate to max or min when overflows occur check box in the Block Parameters dialog box. If selected, the most negative value of the data type wraps to the most positive value. If not selected, the operation has no effect. If an overflow occurs, then a warning is returned to the MATLAB command line.

Example 8.11

We will create a model using a Unary Minus block to negate the number 101101101.

The model is shown in Figure 8.14 where the Signal data types for the Constant block is set to Inherit from constant value, and the Display block is set for Binary (Stored Integer).

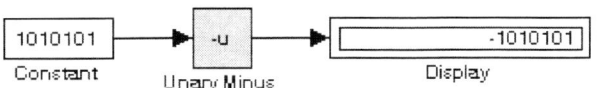

Figure 8.14. Model for Example 8.11

8.1.16 The Math Function Block

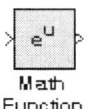

The **Math Function** block performs the following mathematical functions:

    exp

    log

    10^u

    log10

    magnitude^2

    square

    sqrt

    pow (power)

    conj (complex conjugate)

    reciprocal

    hypot (computation of the square root of the sum of squares)

Chapter 8 The Math Operations Library

rem (remainder after division)

mod (modulus after division)*

transpose (transpose of a vector or matrix)

hermitian (a square matrix such that $A^{T*} = A$)

The block output is the result of the operation of the function on the input or inputs. The name of the function appears on the block. Simulink automatically draws the appropriate number of input ports. We use the Math Function block instead of the Fcn block when we want vector or matrix output, because the Fcn block produces only scalar output. For data types supported, please refer to the Help menu for this block.

Example 8.12

We will create a model with a Hermitian block to output the output the Hermitian matrix of A defined as

$$A = \begin{bmatrix} 1 & 1-j & 2 \\ 1+j & 3 & j \\ 2 & -j & 0 \end{bmatrix}$$

The model is shown in Figure 8.15 where in MATLAB's Command Window we entered

A=[1 1-j 2; 1+j 3 j; 2 -j 0];

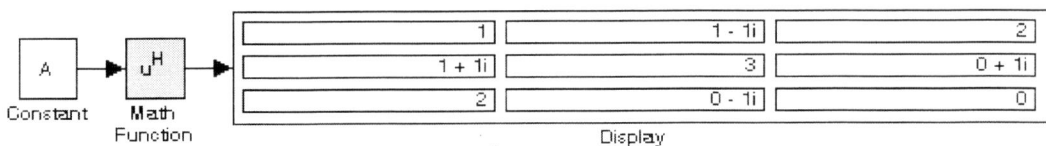

Figure 8.15. Model for Example 8.12

Check:

$$A = \begin{bmatrix} 1 & 1-j & 2 \\ 1+j & 3 & j \\ 2 & -j & 0 \end{bmatrix} \quad A^T = \begin{bmatrix} 1 & 1+j & 2 \\ 1-j & 3 & -j \\ 2 & j & 0 \end{bmatrix} \quad A^{T*} = \begin{bmatrix} 1 & 1-j & 2 \\ 1+j & 3 & j \\ 2 & -j & 0 \end{bmatrix} = A$$

---

* For differences between **rem** and **mod** type help rem and help mod in MATLAB's Command Window.

8.1.17 The Rounding Function Block

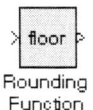
Rounding Function

The **Rounding Function** block applies a rounding function to the input signal to produce the output signal. The name of the selected function appears on the block where **floor** rounds each element of the input signal to the nearest integer value towards minus infinity, **ceil** rounds each element of the input signal to the nearest integer towards positive infinity, **round** rounds each element of the input signal to the nearest integer, and **fix** rounds each element of the input signal to the nearest integer towards zero.

Example 8.13

We will create a model using the Rounding Function block to round the number 3.495 towards minus infinity, towards positive infinity, to the nearest integer, and to the nearest integer towards zero.

The model is shown in Figure 8.16 where **floor** rounds the given number to the nearest integer value towards minus infinity, **ceil** rounds it to the nearest integer towards positive infinity, **round** rounds it to the nearest integer, and **fix** rounds it to the nearest integer towards zero.

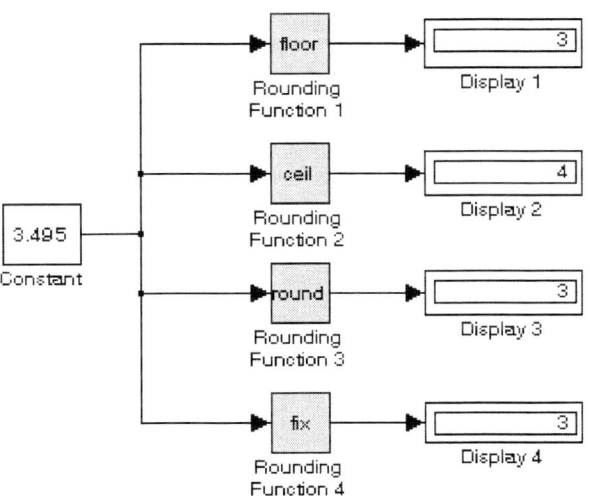

Figure 8.16. Model for Example 8.13

Chapter 8 The Math Operations Library

8.1.18 The Polynomial Block

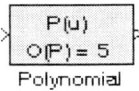

The **Polynomial** block uses a coefficients parameter to evaluate a real polynomial for the input value. We define a set of polynomial coefficients in the form accepted by the MATLAB **polyval** command. The block then calculates P(u) for the input u. Inputs and coefficients must be real.

Example 8.14

We will create a model using the Polynomial block to evaluate the polynomial

$$p(x) = x^6 - 3x^5 + 5x^3 - 4x^2 + 3x + 2$$

at $x = -3.7$.

The model is shown in Figure 8.17 where in MATLAB's Command Window we have entered the coefficients of $p(x)$, i.e.,

px=[1 -3 0 5 -4 3 2];

and in the Parameters dialog box for the Polynomial block we have typed **px**.

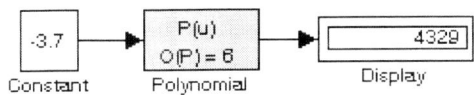

Figure 8.17. Model for Example 8.14

8.1.19 The MinMax Block

The **MinMax** block outputs either the minimum or the maximum element or elements of the inputs. We choose the function to apply by selecting one of the choices from the Function parameter list. If the block has one input port, the input must be a scalar or a vector. The block outputs a scalar equal to the minimum or maximum element of the input vector. If the block has multiple input ports, the non-scalar inputs must all have the same dimensions. The block expands any scalar inputs to have the same dimensions as the non-scalar inputs. The block outputs a signal having the same dimensions as the input. Each output element equals the minimum or maximum of the corresponding input elements.

The Math Operations Group Sub–Library

Example 8.15

We will create a model using a MinMax block to display smallest and the largest numbers in the row vector

$$a = [1\ -1\ -4\ 5\ 7\ -2\ 3\ -5\ 6\ 9\ -3\ 8\ 2\ 4\ 8\ 5]$$

The model is shown in Figure 8.18 where in MATLAB's Command Window we have entered

a=[1 -1 -4 5 7 -2 3 -5 6 9 -3 8 2 4 8 5];

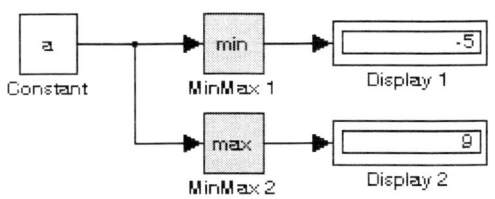

Figure 8.18. Model for Example 8.15

8.1.20 The MinMax Running Resettable Block

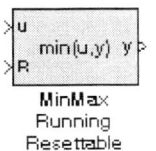

The **MinMax Running Resettable** block outputs the minimum or maximum of all past inputs **u**. We specify whether the block outputs the minimum or the maximum with the Function parameter. The block can reset its state based on an external reset signal **R**. When the reset signal **R** is TRUE, the block resets the output to the value of the Initial condition parameter.

Example 8.16

Let the input **u** in a MinMax Running Resettable block be

$$u = [1\ -1\ -4\ 5\ 7\ -2\ 3\ -5\ 6\ 9\ -3\ 8\ 2\ 4\ 8\ 5]$$

We will create a model that will display all positive values of **u** and will display all negative values of **u**.

The model is shown in Figure 8.19 where in MATLAB's Command Window we have entered

u=[1 -1 -4 5 7 -2 3 -5 6 9 -3 8 2 4 8 5];

and the initial conditions in both MinMax Running Resettable blocks is set to zero.

Chapter 8 The Math Operations Library

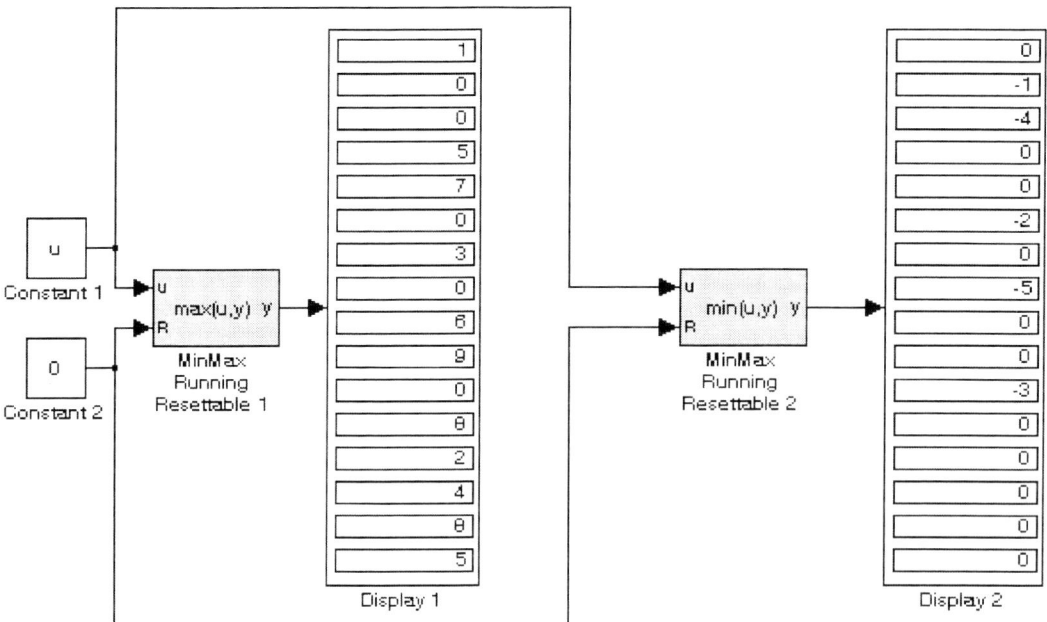

Figure 8.19. Model for Example 8.16

8.1.21 The Trigonometric Function Block

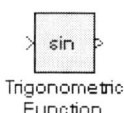

The **Trigonometric Function** block performs the principle trigonometric functions **sine**, **cosine**, and **tangent**, the Inverse trigonometric functions **asin**, **acos**, **atan**, and **atan2**[*], the hyperbolic functions **sinh**, **cosh**, and **tanh**, and the Inverse hyperbolic functions **asinh**, **acosh**, and **atanh**. The block output is the result of the operation of the function on the input or inputs. The name of the function appears on the block. If we select the **atan2** function, the block displays two inputs. The first (upper) input is the y–axis or complex part of the function argument. The second (lower) input is the x–axis or real part of the function argument.

---

[*] *The trigonometric function atan2(y,x) is referred to as the four-quadrant inverse tangent whereas atan is referred to as the two-quadrant inverse tangent. We recall that for $-\infty < x < \infty$, $-\pi/2 < \mathrm{atan}\, x < \pi/2$ and thus the two-quadrant atan(x) returns the inverse tangent in the range $[-\pi/2, \pi/2]$. The four-quadrant atan2(y,x) returns the inverse tangent in the range $[-\pi, \pi]$.*

The Math Operations Group Sub–Library

We should use the Trigonometric Function block instead of the Fcn block when we want dimensionalized output, because the Fcn block can produce only scalar output.

Example 8.17

We will create a model to display the values of the hyperbolic functions *sinhx* and *coshx* for $x = 9.5$.

The model is shown in Figure 8.20.

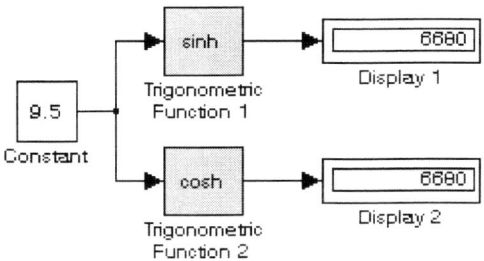

Figure 8.20. Model for Example 8.17

We recall that

$$\sinh x = \frac{e^x - e^{-x}}{2} \qquad \cosh x = \frac{e^x + e^{-x}}{2}$$

and thus for $x \gg 0$, $\sinh x \approx \cosh x \approx \frac{1}{2}e^x$

8.1.22 The Sine Wave Function Block

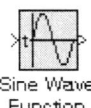

The **Sine Wave Function** block generates a sinusoid. The block can operate in either time-based or sample-based mode. The time-based mode has two submodes: continuous mode or discrete mode. The value of the Sample time parameter determines whether the block operates in continuous mode or discrete mode. Thus, zero (the default) causes the block to operate in continuous mode and a value greater than zero causes the block to operate in discrete mode.

Example 8.18

We will create a model using two Sine Wave Function blocks, one to display the waveform operating in the continuous mode, and the other to display the waveform operating in the discrete mode.

Chapter 8 The Math Operations Library

The model is shown in Figure 8.21 and the waveforms in Figure 8.22 where the frequency of the Sinewave Function 1 block was specified as 2.5 Hz, the Digital Clock block was specified for sample time 2.5, the Sine type in the Sinewave Function 2 block was selected as **Sample based**, and the Time as **Use external signal**.

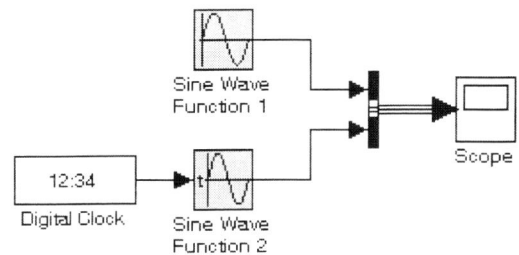

Figure 8.21. Model for Example 8.18

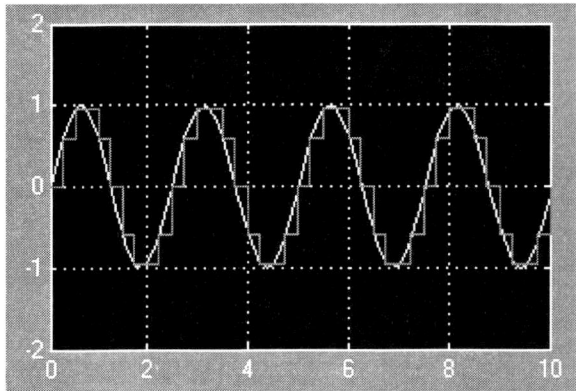

Figure 8.22. Output waveforms for the model of Figure 8.21

8.1.23 The Algebraic Constraint Block

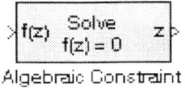

The **Algebraic Constraint** block constrains the input signal $f(z)$ to zero and outputs an algebraic state z. The block outputs the value necessary to produce a zero at the input. The output must affect the input through a feedback path. This block accepts and outputs real values of type **double**.

An example using this block was presented in Chapter 1 as Example 1.3. Another example is given below.

The Vector / Matrix Operations Group Sub–Library

Example 8.19

We will create a model using an Algebraic Constraint block to find a solution for the non-linear equation

$$F(z) = z^2 + 4z + 3 + \sin z - z\cos z$$

The model is shown in Figure 8.23 where in the Algebraic Constraint block the Initial guess value entered is -1. The z^2 term is represented by the u^2 block from the Math Function block and the sine and cosine blocks from the Trigonometric Function block both of which are blocks within the Math Operations library. We observe that all inputs are feedbacks from the output of the Algebraic Constraint block.

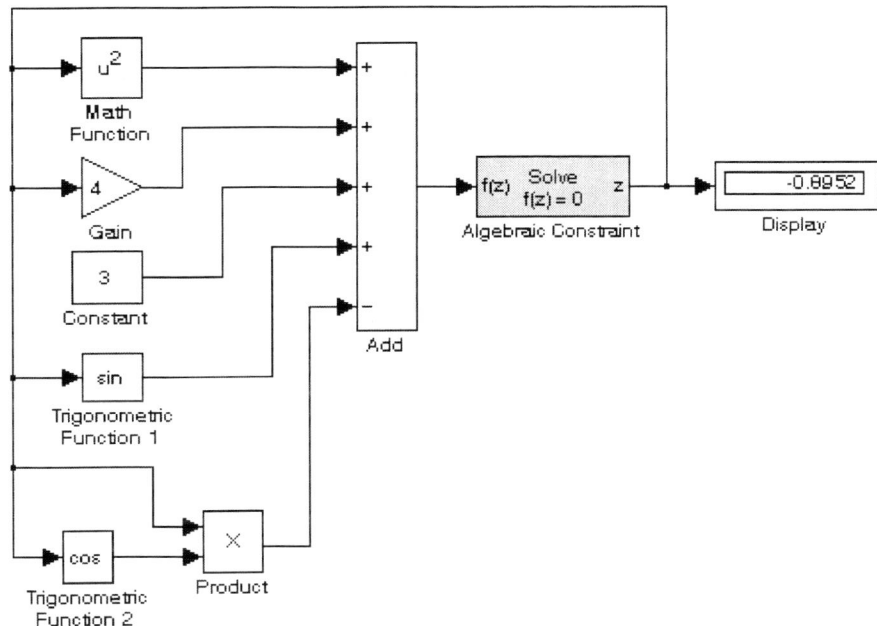

Figure 8.23. Model for Example 8.19

8.2 The Vector / Matrix Operations Group Sub–Library

The **Vector / Matrix Operations Group Sub–Library** contains the blocks described in Subsections 8.2.1 through 8.2.4 below.

8.2.1 The Assignment Block

Chapter 8 The Math Operations Library

The **Assignment** block assigns values to specified elements of the signal. We specify the indices of the elements to be assigned values either by entering the indices in the block's dialog box, or by connecting an external indices source or sources to the block. The signal at the block's data port, labeled U2 in most modes, specifies values to be assigned to Y. The block replaces the specified elements of Y with elements from the data signal, leaving unassigned elements unchanged from their initial values. If the assignment indices source is internal or is external and the Initialize using input option is selected, the Assignment block uses the signal at the block's initialization port, labeled U1, to initialize the elements of the output signal before assigning them values from U2.

Example 8.20

We will create a model using an Assignment block to assign the value 6 in the zero-based index mode A(1, 2) position of the matrix A defined as

$$A = \begin{bmatrix} 1 & 2 & 3 \\ 4 & 5 & 0 \\ 7 & 8 & 9 \end{bmatrix}$$

The model is shown in Figure 8.24 where we have made the following entries:

Constant 1 block - Constant value: [1 2 3; 4 5 0; 7 8 9]

Constant 2 block - Constant value: [6]

Assignment block - Input type: **Matrix** - Index mode: **Zero-based** - Rows: **1** - Columns: **2**

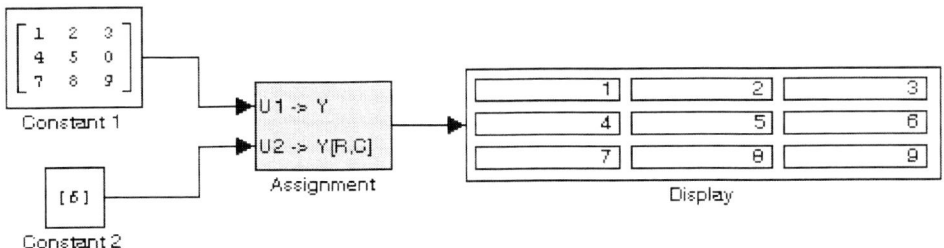

Figure 8.24. Model for Example 8.20

8.2.2 The Reshape Block

The Vector / Matrix Operations Group Sub–Library

The **Reshape** block changes the dimensionality of the input signal to another dimensionality that we specify, using the block's Output dimensionality parameter. The Output dimensionality parameter allows us to select the 1–D array, Column vector, Row vector, or Customize options. These options are described in the Help menu for this block.

Example 8.21

We will create a model using the Reshape block to convert the row vector

$$A = [1 \quad 0 \quad -3 \quad -2 \quad 5 \quad 7 \quad 9 \quad 4 \quad 6]$$

to a column vector.

The model is shown in Figure 8.25 where in MATLAB's Command Window we have entered

A=[1 0 -3 -2 5 7 9 4 6];

and for the Reshape block we have selected the Column vector Output dimensionality option.

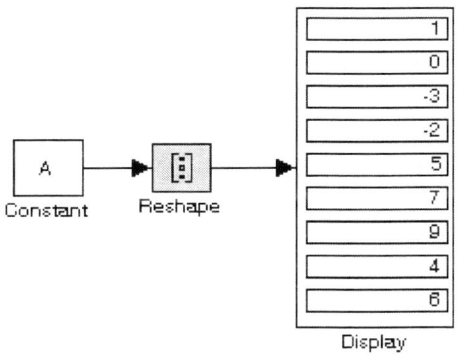

Figure 8.25. Model for Example 8.21

8.2.3 The Matrix Concatenate Block

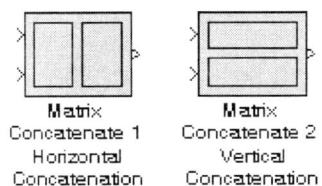

The **Matrix Concatenate** block concatenates input matrices u1 u2 u3 ... un along rows or columns, where n is specified by the Number of inputs parameter. When the Concatenate method parameter is set to Horizontal, the block concatenates the input matrices along rows.

y = [u1 u2 u3 ... un]   % Equivalent MATLAB code

Chapter 8 The Math Operations Library

For horizontal concatenation, inputs must all have the same row dimension, M, but can have different column dimensions. The output matrix has dimension M–by–Ni, where Ni is the number of columns in input ui (i =1, 2, ..., n).

When the Concatenate method parameter is set to Vertical, the block concatenates the input matrices along columns.

y = [u1;u2;u3;...;un]   % Equivalent MATLAB code

For vertical concatenation, inputs must all have the same column dimension, N, but can have different row dimensions. The output matrix has dimension Mi–by–N, where Mi is the number of rows in input ui (i = 1, 2, ..., n).

Example 8.22

We will create a model using a Matrix Concatenate block to concatenate horizontally the matrices A, B, and C defined as

$$A = \begin{bmatrix} 1 & -1 & -4 \\ 5 & 7 & -2 \\ 3 & -5 & 6 \end{bmatrix} \quad B = \begin{bmatrix} 5 & 9 & -3 \\ -2 & 8 & 2 \\ 7 & -4 & 6 \end{bmatrix} \quad C = \begin{bmatrix} 4 & 6 \\ -3 & 8 \\ 5 & -2 \end{bmatrix}$$

The model is shown in Figure 8.26 where in MATLAB's Command Window we have entered

A=[1 –1 4; 5 7 –2; 3 –5 6]; B=[5 9 –3; –2 8 2; 7 –4 6]; C=[4 6; –3 8; 5 –2];

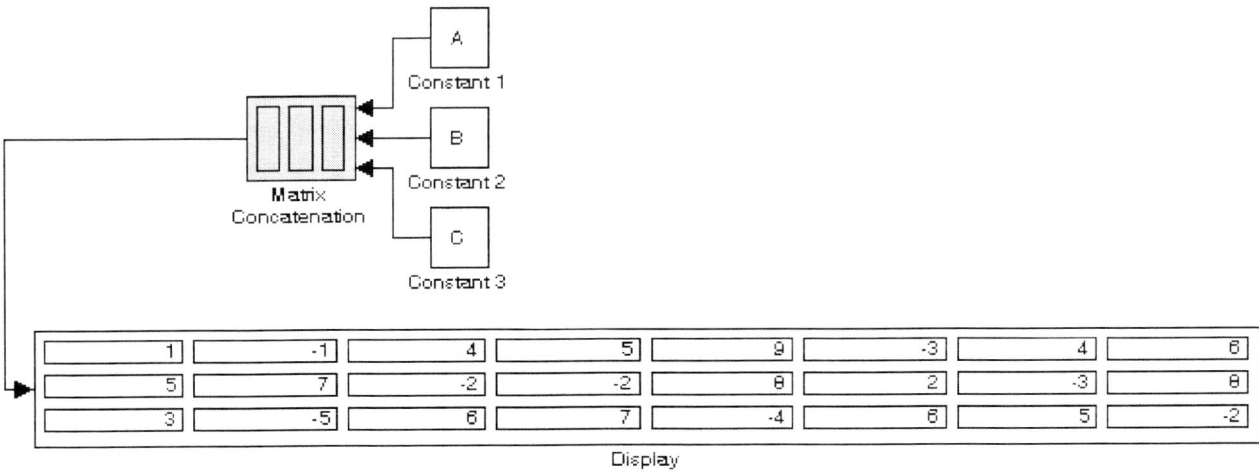

Figure 8.26. Model for Example 8.22

8.2.4 The Vector Concatenate Block

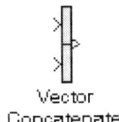

The **Vector Concatenate** block is a special case of the Matrix Concatenate block where the block operates in Vector Concatenation Mode, Horizontal Matrix Concatenation Mode, or Vertical Matrix Concatenation Mode. In Vector Concatenation Mode, all input signals must be either row vectors ($1 \times m$ matrices) or column vectors ($m \times 1$ matrices) or a combination of vectors and either row or column vectors. The output is a vector if all inputs are vectors.

The output is a row or column vector if any of the inputs are row or column vectors, respectively.

Example 8.23

We will create a model using a Vector Concatenate block to concatenate vertically the column vectors a, b, and c defined as

$$a = \begin{bmatrix} 1 \\ 5 \\ 3 \end{bmatrix} \quad b = \begin{bmatrix} 5 \\ -2 \\ 7 \end{bmatrix} \quad c = \begin{bmatrix} 4 \\ -3 \\ 5 \end{bmatrix}$$

The model is shown in Figure 8.27 where in MATLAB's Command Window we have entered the column vectors

a=[1 5 3]'; b=[5 -2 7]'; c=[4 -3 5]';

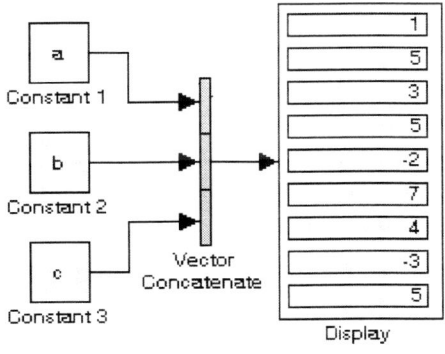

Figure 8.27. Model for Example 8.23

Chapter 8 The Math Operations Library

8.3 The Complex Vector Conversions Group Sub-Library

The **Complex Vector Conversions Group Sub-Library** contains the blocks described in Subsections 8.3.1 through 8.3.4 below.

8.3.1 The Complex to Magnitude-Angle Block

The **Complex to Magnitude–Angle** block accepts a complex–valued signal of type double in the form of $x + jy$. It outputs the magnitude, the phase angle in radians, or magnitude and phase depending on the setting of the Output parameter. The outputs are real values of type double. The input can be an array of complex signals, in which case the output signals are also arrays. The magnitude signal array contains the magnitudes of the corresponding complex input elements. The angle output similarly contains the angles of the input elements

Example 8.24

We will create a model using a Complex to Magnitude–Angle block to convert the complex number $5.43 - j4.54$ to the polar form $A\angle\theta$.

The model is shown in Figure 8.28 where the Complex to Magnitude–Angle block Output parameter has been specified as **Magnitude and angle.**

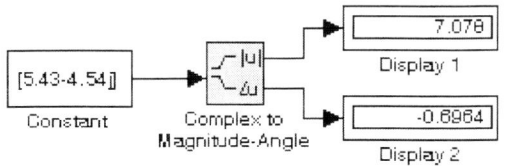

Figure 8.28. Model for Example 8.24

8.3.2 The Magnitude-Angle to Complex Block

The **Magnitude–Angle to Complex** block converts magnitude and / or phase angle inputs to a complex–valued output signal. The inputs must be real-valued signals of type double. The angle input is assumed to be in radians. The data type of the complex output signal is double.

The Complex Vector Conversions Group Sub–Library

The inputs can both be signals of equal dimensions, or one input can be an array and the other a scalar. If the block has an array input, the output is an array of complex signals. The elements of a magnitude input vector are mapped to magnitudes of the corresponding complex output elements. An angle input vector is similarly mapped to the angles of the complex output signals. If one input is a scalar, it is mapped to the corresponding component (magnitude or angle) of all the complex output signals.

Example 8.25

We will create a model using a Magnitude–Angle to Complex block to convert $120 \angle 240°$ to its equivalent real and imaginary components.

The model is shown in Figure 8.29 where the magnitude is entered in the Constant 1 block and phase angle in radians is entered in the Constant 2 block.

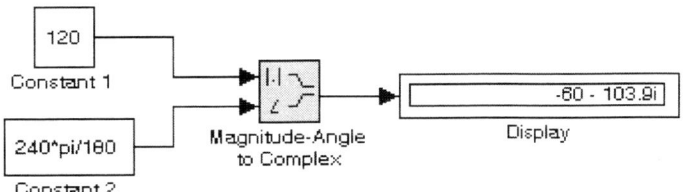

Figure 8.29. Model for Example 8.25

8.3.3 The Complex to Real–Imag Block

The **Complex to Real–Imag** block accepts a complex–valued signal of any data type supported by Simulink, including fixed-point data types. It outputs the real and / or imaginary part of the input signal, depending on the setting of the Output parameter. The real outputs are of the same data type as the complex input. The input can be an array (vector or matrix) of complex signals, in which case the output signals are arrays of the same dimensions. The real array contains the real parts of the corresponding complex input elements. The imaginary output similarly contains the imaginary parts of the input elements.

Example 8.26

Let us consider the electric network of Figure 8.30.

Chapter 8 The Math Operations Library

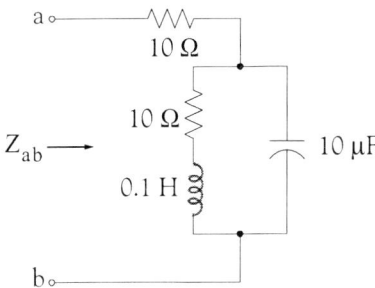

Figure 8.30. Electric network for Example 8.26

With the given values of resistance, inductance, and capacitance, the impedance Z_{ab} as a function of the radian frequency ω can be computed from the following expression.

$$Z_{ab} = Z = 10 + \frac{10^4 - j(10^6/\omega)}{10 + j(0.1\omega - 10^5/\omega)} \quad (8.1)$$

Assuming that the operating frequency is $f = 100\ Hz$, we will create a model to display the real and imaginary values of the relation (8.1).

The model is shown in Figure 8.31 where in MATLAB's Command Window we have entered

Z=10+(10^4 −j*10^6/(2*pi*60))/(10 + j*(0.1*(2*pi*60)−10^5/(2*pi*60)));

Display 1 block shows the real component and Display 2 shows the imaginary component.

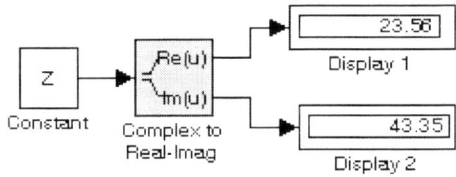

Figure 8.31. Model for Example 8.26

8.3.4 The Real–Imag to Complex Block

The **Real–Imag to Complex** block converts real and/or imaginary inputs to a complex-valued output signal. The inputs can both be arrays (vectors or matrices) of equal dimensions, or one input can be an array and the other a scalar. If the block has an array input, the output is a complex array of the same dimensions. The elements of the real input are mapped to the real parts of

The Complex Vector Conversions Group Sub–Library

the corresponding complex output elements. The imaginary input is similarly mapped to the imaginary parts of the complex output signals. If one input is a scalar, it is mapped to the corresponding component (real or imaginary) of all the complex output signals.

Example 8.27

We will create a model to convert the rectangular form of the complex number $25 + j40$ to the polar form $A\angle\theta°$ where A is the magnitude and the angle θ is in degrees (not radians).

The model is shown in Figure 8.32 where $A = 47.17$, $\theta = 57.99°$, and the Gain $K = 180/\pi$.

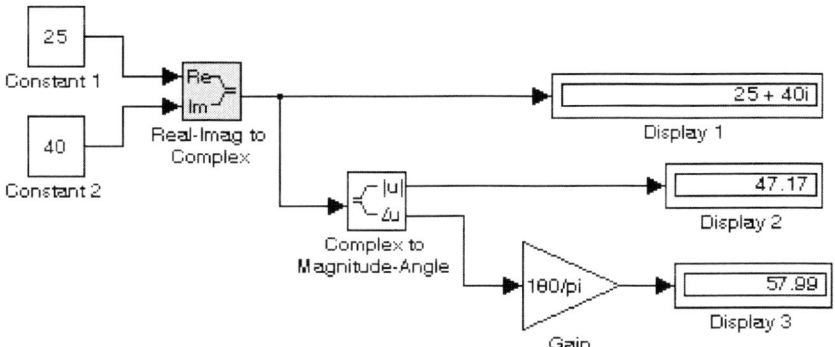

Figure 8.32. Model for Example 8.27

8.4 Summary

- The **Sum** block is an implementation of the Add block. We can choose the icon shape (round or rectangle) of the block.

- The **Add** block performs addition or subtraction on its inputs. This block can add or subtract scalar, vector, or matrix inputs. It can also collapse the elements of a single input vector. We specify the operations of the block with the List of Signs parameter. Plus (+), minus (−), and spacer (|) characters indicate the operations to be performed on the inputs.

- The **Subtract** block is an implementation of the Add block.

- The **Sum of Elements** block is an implementation of the **Add** block.

- The **Bias** block adds a bias (offset) to the input signal.

- The **Weighted Sample Time Math** block adds, subtracts, multiplies, or divides the input signal, u, by a weighted sample time **Ts**. We use the Operation parameter to specify the math operation. This block also allows us to use only the weight with either the sample time or its inverse.

- The **Gain** block multiplies the input by a constant value (gain). The input and the gain can each be a scalar, vector, or matrix.

- The **Slider Gain** block allows us to vary a scalar gain during a simulation using a slider. The block accepts one input and generates one output. In the Slider Gain dialog box Low indicates the lower limit of the slider range where the default is 0, and High indicates the upper limit of the slider range where the default is 2.

- The **Product** block performs multiplication or division of its inputs.

- The **Divide** block is an implementation of the Product block.

- The **Product of Elements** block is used to multiply of divide inputs. It is essentially a Product block.

- The **Dot Product** block generates the dot product of its two input vectors. The scalar output, y, is equal to the MATLAB operation y=sum(conj(A.*B)) where vectors A and B are defined as $A = [a_1 \; a_2 \; ... \; a_n]$, $B = [b_1 \; b_2 \; ... \; b_n]$, and $A*B = [a_1 b_1 + a_2 b_2 + \; ... \; + a_n b_n]$.

- The **Sign** block indicates the sign of the input. The output is 1 when the input is greater than zero, the output is 0 when the input is equal to zero, and the output is −1 when the input is less than zero.

- The **Abs** block outputs the absolute value of the input. This block accepts real signals of any data type supported by Simulink, except Boolean, and supports real fixed-point data types. The block also accepts complex single and double inputs.

Summary

- The **Unary Minus** block negates the input. The block accepts only signed data types. For signed data types, we cannot accurately negate the most negative value since the result is not representable by the data type.

- The **Math Function** block performs the following common mathematical functions:

  exp

  log

  10^u

  log10

  magnitude^2

  square

  sqrt

  pow (power)

  conj (complex conjugate)

  reciprocal

  hypot (computation of the square root of the sum of squares)

  rem (remainder after division)

  mod (modulus after division)

  transpose (transpose of a vector or matrix)

  hermitian (a square matrix such that $A^{T*} = A$)

  The name of the function appears on the block. Simulink automatically draws the appropriate number of input ports.

- The **Rounding Function** block applies a rounding function to the input signal to produce the output signal. The name of the selected function appears on the block where **floor** rounds each element of the input signal to the nearest integer value towards minus infinity, **ceil** rounds each element of the input signal to the nearest integer towards positive infinity, **round** rounds each element of the input signal to the nearest integer, and **fix** rounds each element of the input signal to the nearest integer towards zero.

- The **Polynomial** block uses a coefficients parameter to evaluate a real polynomial for the input value. We define a set of polynomial coefficients in the form accepted by the MATLAB **polyval** command. The block then calculates P(u) at each time step for the input u. Inputs and coefficients must be real.

Chapter 8 The Math Operations Library

- The **MinMax** block outputs either the minimum or the maximum element or elements of the inputs. We choose the function to apply by selecting one of the choices from the Function parameter list.

- The **MinMax Running Resettable** block outputs the minimum or maximum of all past inputs u. We specify whether the block outputs the minimum or the maximum with the Function parameter. The block can reset its state based on an external reset signal R. When the reset signal R is TRUE, the block resets the output to the value of the Initial condition parameter.

- The **Trigonometric Function** block performs the principle trigonometric functions sine, cosine, and tangent, the Inverse trigonometric functions asin, acos, atan, and atan2, the hyperbolic functions sinh, cosh, and tanh, and the Inverse hyperbolic functions asinh, acosh, and atanh. The block output is the result of the operation of the function on the input or inputs. The name of the function appears on the block. If we select the atan2 function, the block displays two inputs. The first (upper) input is the y–axis or complex part of the function argument. The second (lower) input is the x–axis or real part of the function argument.

- The **Sine Wave Function** block generates a sinusoid. The block can operate in either time-based or sample-based mode. The time-based mode has two submodes: continuous mode or discrete mode. The value of the Sample time parameter determines whether the block operates in continuous mode or discrete mode.

- The **Algebraic Constraint** block constrains the input signal $f(z)$ to zero and outputs an algebraic state z. The block outputs the value necessary to produce a zero at the input. The output must affect the input through a feedback path. This block accepts and outputs real values of type double.

- The **Assignment** block assigns values to specified elements of the signal. We specify the indices of the elements to be assigned values either by entering the indices in the block's dialog box or by connecting an external indices source or sources to the block. The signal at the block's data port, labeled U2 in most modes, specifies values to be assigned to Y. The block replaces the specified elements of Y with elements from the data signal, leaving unassigned elements unchanged from their initial values.

- The **Reshape** block changes the dimensionality of the input signal to another dimensionality that we specify, using the block's Output dimensionality parameter. The Output dimensionality parameter allows us to select the 1-D array, Column vector, Row vector, or Customize options. These options are described in the Help menu for this block.

- The **Matrix Concatenate** block concatenates input matrices u1 u2 u3 ... un along rows or columns, where n is specified by the Number of inputs parameter. When the Concatenation method parameter is set to Horizontal, the block concatenates the input matrices along rows.

    y = [u1 u2 u3 ... un]   % Equivalent MATLAB code

Summary

For horizontal concatenation, inputs must all have the same row dimension, M, but can have different column dimensions.

When the Concatenation method parameter is set to Vertical, the block concatenates the input matrices along columns.

```
y = [u1;u2;u3;...;un]     % Equivalent MATLAB code
```

For vertical concatenation, inputs must all have the same column dimension, N, but can have different row dimensions.

- The **Vector Concatenate** block is a special case of the Matrix Concatenate block where the block operates in Vector Concatenation Mode, Horizontal Matrix Concatenation Mode, or Vertical Matrix Concatenation Mode. In Vector Concatenation Mode, all input signals must be either row vectors [1xM matrices] or column vectors [Mx1 matrices] or a combination of vectors and either row or column vectors. The output is a vector if all inputs are vectors. The output is a row or column vector if any of the inputs are row or column vectors, respectively.

- The **Complex to Magnitude–Angle** block accepts a complex–valued signal of type double in the form of $x + jy$. It outputs the magnitude, the phase angle in radians, or magnitude and phase depending on the setting of the Output parameter. The outputs are real values of type double.

- The **Magnitude–Angle to Complex** block converts magnitude and/or phase angle inputs to a complex-valued output signal. The inputs must be real-valued signals of type double. The angle input is assumed to be in radians.

- The **Complex to Real–Imag** block accepts a complex-valued signal of any data type supported by Simulink, including fixed-point data types. It outputs the real and/or imaginary part of the input signal, depending on the setting of the Output parameter. The real outputs are of the same data type as the complex input.

- The **Real–Imag to Complex** block converts real and/or imaginary inputs to a complex-valued output signal. The inputs can both be arrays (vectors or matrices) of equal dimensions, or one input can be an array and the other a scalar.

Chapter 8 The Math Operations Library

8.5 Exercises

1. Create a model using an Abs block to display the magnitude of the expression

$$z = \frac{(-j1.49)(-0.8+j4.52)(-1.2-j7.4)}{(5+j1.84)(2.5-j4.8)(3.25+j5.2)}$$

2. Three phasors* are defined as $A = 3\angle 60°$, $B = -4\angle 30°$, and $C = 5\angle -45°$. Create a model using an Abs block to display the result of the operation $A - B + C$.

3. Create a model using an Algebraic Constraint block to find a solution for the non-linear equation

$$F(x) = 3x^5 - 2x^3 + 6x - 8$$

4. Create a model using an Assignment block to assign the value 7 in the zero-based index mode elements [2 5] position of the vector A defined as $A = [0\ 5\ 10\ 15\ 20\ 25]$.

5. Create a model using a Complex to Magnitude-Angle block to convert the array of complex number $7.5 - j15.4$, $28.4 + j12.2$, and $48.3 - j72.8$ to the polar form $A_1 \angle \theta_1$, $A_2 \angle \theta_2$, and $A_3 \angle \theta_3$ respectively.

6. Create a model using one Magnitude-Angle to Complex block to convert $8\angle 30°$, $20\angle 45°$, and $50\angle 60°$ to their equivalent real and imaginary components.

7. Create a model using the appropriate Math Function block from the Math Operations library to invert the elements of the matrix

$$A = \begin{bmatrix} 1 & 1-j & 2 \\ 1+j & 3 & j \\ 2 & -j & 5 \end{bmatrix}$$

8. Create a model using a Matrix Concatenation block to concatenate vertically the matrices A, B, and C defined as

$$A = \begin{bmatrix} 1 & -1 & -4 \\ 5 & 7 & -2 \\ 3 & -5 & 6 \end{bmatrix} \quad B = \begin{bmatrix} 5 & 9 & -3 \\ -2 & 8 & 2 \\ 7 & -4 & 6 \end{bmatrix} \quad C = \begin{bmatrix} 1 & -2 & 3 \\ -3 & 6 & -4 \end{bmatrix}$$

9. Create a model using a MinMax block to display the largest number in the row vector

$$a = [1\ -1\ -4\ 5\ 7\ -2\ 3\ -5\ 6\ 9\ -3\ 8\ 2\ 4\ 8\ 5]$$

---

* A phasor is a rotating vector.

Exercises

10. Create a model using the Reshape block to convert the row vector

$$A = [1 \quad 0 \quad -3 \quad -2 \quad 5 \quad 7 \quad 9 \quad 4 \quad 6]$$

    to a 3×3 matrix.

11. Create a model using the **atan2** trigonometric function block to find the phase angle of the complex number $108 + j84$ in degrees.

Chapter 8 The Math Operations Library

8.6 Solutions to End-of Chapter Exercises

1.

The model is shown below where for the Constant block we have Signal data types we have selected double and in MATLAB's Command Window we have entered

z=((−1.49j)*(−0.8+4.52j)*(−1.2−7.4j))/((5+1.84j)*(2.5−4.8j)*(3.25+5.2j));

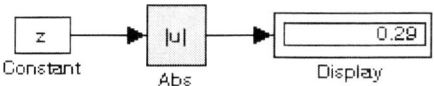

2.

The model is shown below where in MATLAB's Command Window we have entered

A=3*(cos(60*pi/180)+j*sin(60*pi/180)); B=−4*(cos(30*pi/180)+j*sin(30*pi/180));...
C=5*(cos(−45*pi/180)+j*sin(−45*pi/180));

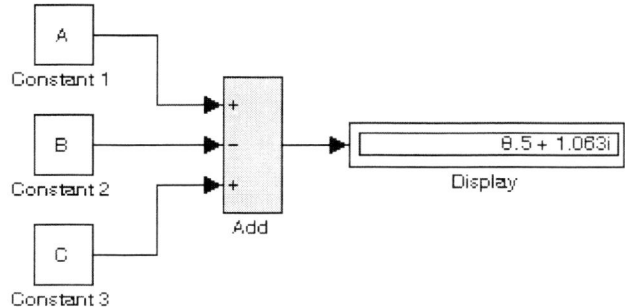

3.

We recall that the Algebraic Constraint block accepts and outputs real values of type **double**. Since the given polynomial is of fifth power and complex roots, if present occur in complex conjugate pairs, we expect at least one real root.

The model is shown below and it displays the only real root. We can use MATLAB to verify that the remaining four roots are complex and occur in conjugate pairs.

The fifth and third powers in the first and second terms of the given polynomial are represented by the u^v block from the Math Function block.

Solutions to End-of Chapter Exercises

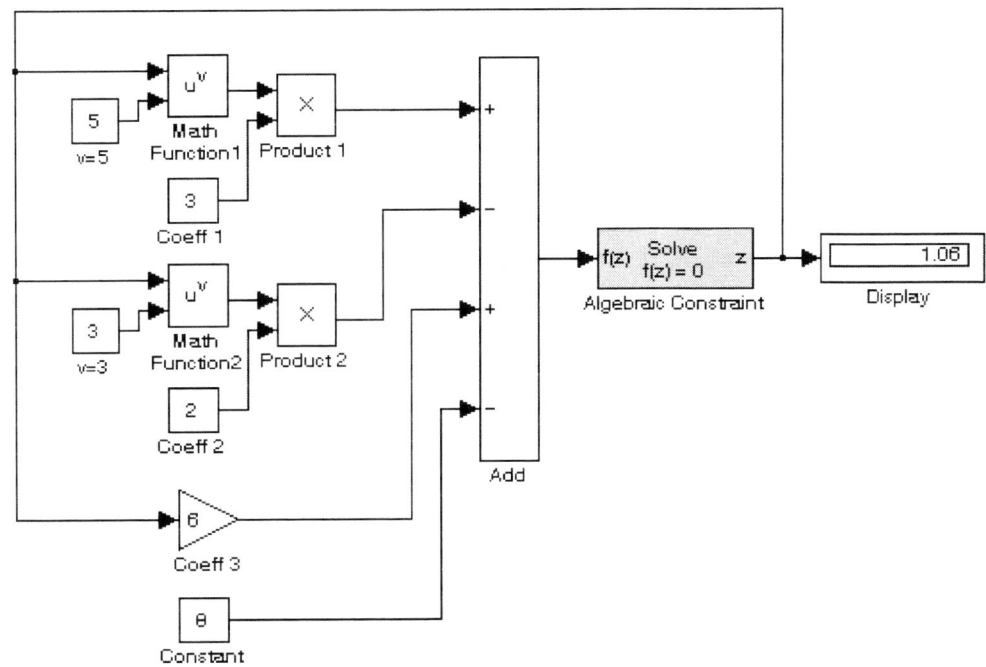

4.

The model is shown below where we have made the following entries:

Constant 1 block - Constant value: [0:5:25]

Constant 2 block - Constant value: [7]

Assignment block - Input type: **Vector** - Index mode: **Zero-based** - Elements: [2 5]

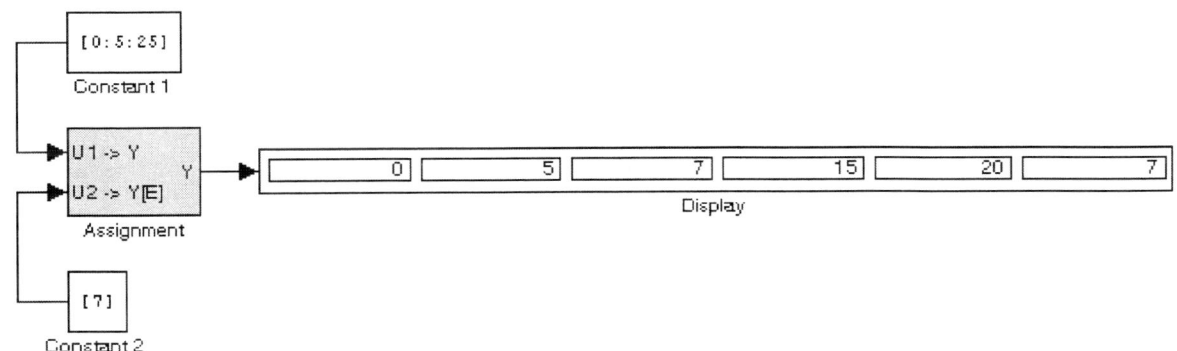

5.

The model is shown below where in MATLAB's Command Window we have entered

A=[7.5−15.4j 28.4+12.2j 48.3−72.8j];

Chapter 8 The Math Operations Library

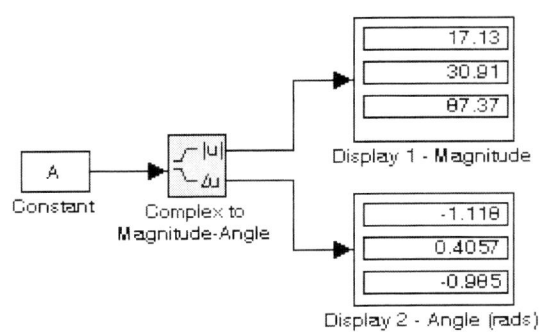

6.

The model is shown below where in the Constant 1 block we have enter the magnitudes and in the Constant 2 block we have entered in phase angles in radians.

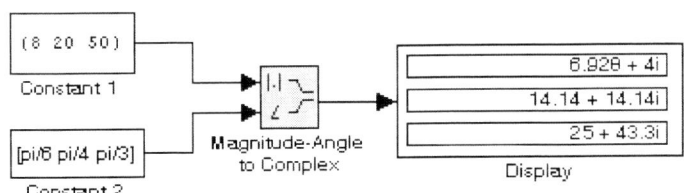

7.

The appropriate block to accomplish this task is the Reciprocal Function block which we select from the Math Function selection of blocks. The model is shown below where in MATLAB's Command Window we have entered

A=[1 1–j 2; 1+j 3 j; 2 –j 4];

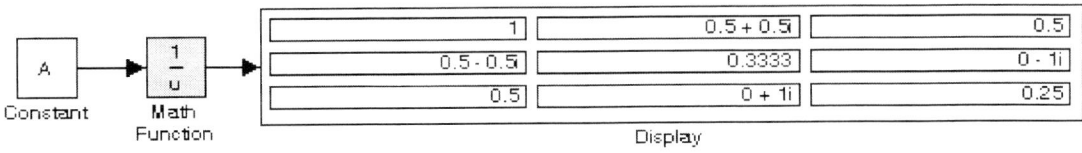

8.

The model is shown below where in MATLAB's Command Window we have entered

A=[1 –1 4; 5 7 –2; 3 –5 6]; B=[5 9 –3; –2 8 2; 7 –4 6]; C=[1 –2 3; –3 6 –4];

Solutions to End-of Chapter Exercises

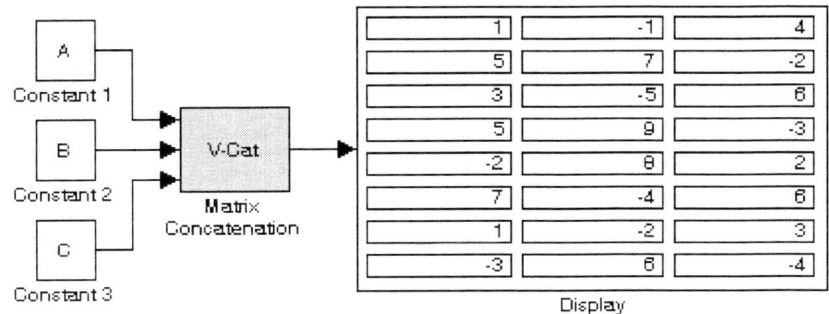

9.

The model is shown below where in MATLAB's Command Window we have entered

a=[1 −1 −4 5 7 −2 3 −5 6 9 −3 8 2 4 8 5];

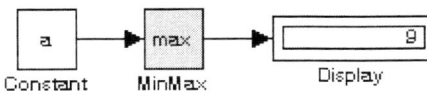

10.

The model is shown below where in MATLAB's Command Window we have entered

A=[1 0 −3 −2 5 7 9 4 6];

and for the Reshape block we have selected the Customize Output dimensionality option with Output dimensions [3, 3].

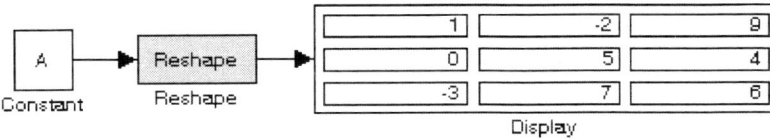

11.

The model is shown below where the Constant 1 block contains the imaginary part of the complex number, the Constant 2 block contains the real part of the complex number, and the Gain block contains the factor $180/\pi$ to convert radians to degrees.

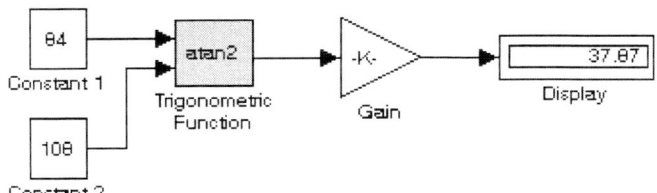

Chapter 8 The Math Operations Library

NOTES

Chapter 9

The Model Verification Library

This chapter is an introduction to the **Model Verification Library**, also referred to as the **Run–Time Model Verification Library.** This is the eighth library in the Simulink group of libraries and contains the blocks shown below. The blocks in this library are intended to facilitate creation of self–validating models. We use model verification blocks to check whether the signals exceed specified limits during simulation.

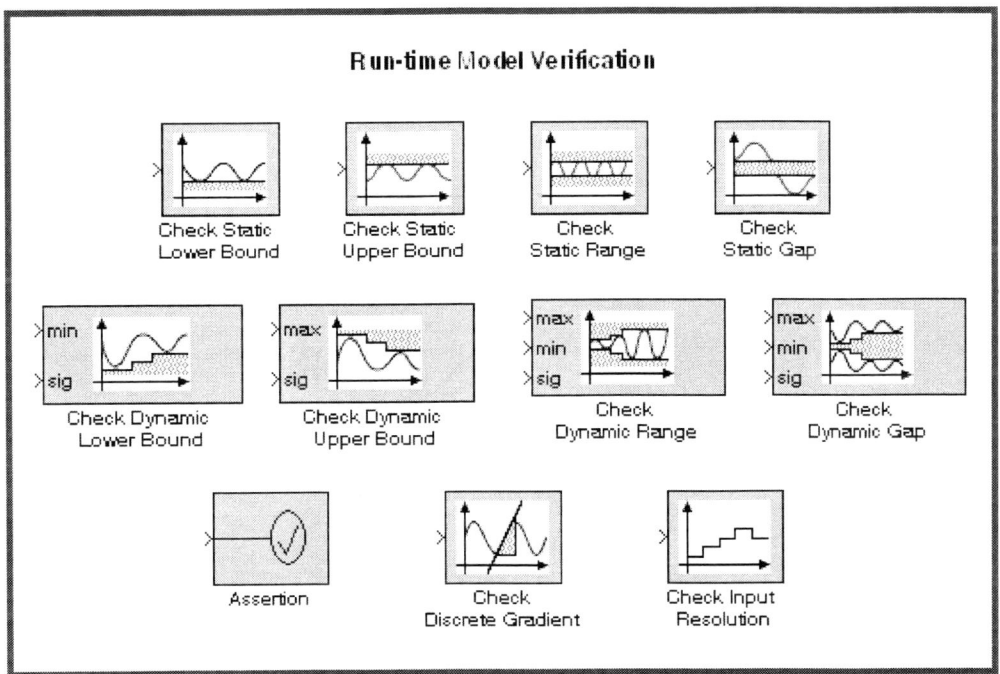

Chapter 9 The Model Verification Library

9.1 The Check Static Lower Bound Block

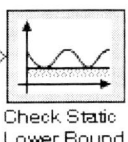

The **Check Static Lower Bound** block performs a check to verify that each element of the input signal is greater than or equal to a specified lower bound. The block's parameter dialog box allows us to specify the value of the lower bound and whether the lower bound is inclusive. If the verification condition is true, the block takes no action. If not, simulation is halted and an error message is displayed.

Example 9.1

In the model of Figure 9.1, the amplitude of a sinusoidal signal may vary ±10% from its nominal value of 1 volt. We will configure this model to display error messages when the lower inclusive boundary is specified as −1 volt.

The Signal Generator block is specified for a sine waveform with amplitude 1.1 volt, frequency 0.3 Hz, and the Check Static Lower Bound block is specified at −1 with the Inclusive boundary checked, Enable assertion checked, Output assertion signal checked, and icon type **graphic**. The Convert block was inserted to convert the **Boolean** output of the Check Dynamic Gap to **double** as required by the Bus Creator block.

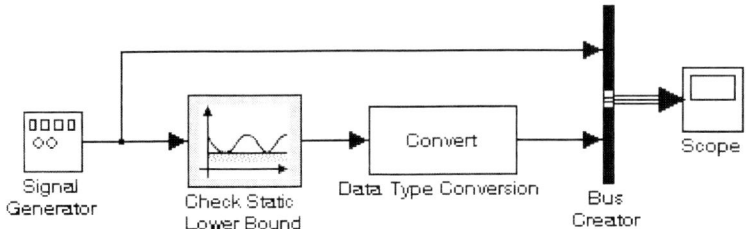

Figure 9.1. Model for Example 9.1

The input and output waveforms are shown in Figure 9.2.

The Check Static Upper Bound Block

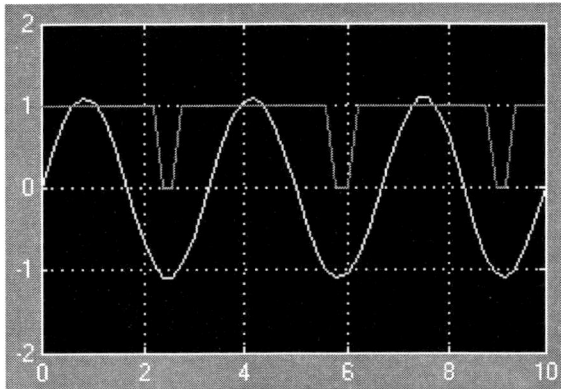

Figure 9.2. Input and output waveforms for the model of Figure 9.1

9.2 The Check Static Upper Bound Block

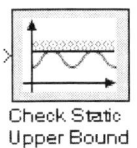

The **Check Static Upper Bound** block performs a check to verify that each element of the input signal is less than or equal to a specified lower bound. The block's parameter dialog box allows us to specify the value of the upper bound and whether the bound is inclusive. If the verification condition is true, the block takes no action. If not, simulation is halted and an error message is displayed.

Example 9.2

In the model of Figure 9.3, the amplitude of a sinusoidal signal may vary ±10% from its nominal value of 1 volt. We will configure this model to display error messages when the lower boundary inclusive boundary is specified as −1 volt.

The Signal Generator block is specified for a sine waveform with amplitude 1.1 volt, frequency 0.3 Hz, and the Check Static Upper Bound block is specified at +1 with the Inclusive boundary checked, Enable assertion checked, Output assertion signal checked, and icon type **graphic**. The Convert block was inserted to convert the **Boolean** output of the Check Dynamic Gap to **double** as required by the Bus Creator block.

The input and output waveforms are shown in Figure 9.4.

Introduction to Simulink with Engineering Applications
Copyright © Orchard Publications

Chapter 9 The Model Verification Library

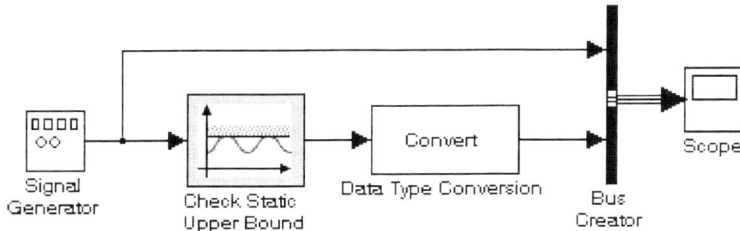

Figure 9.3. Model for Example 9.2

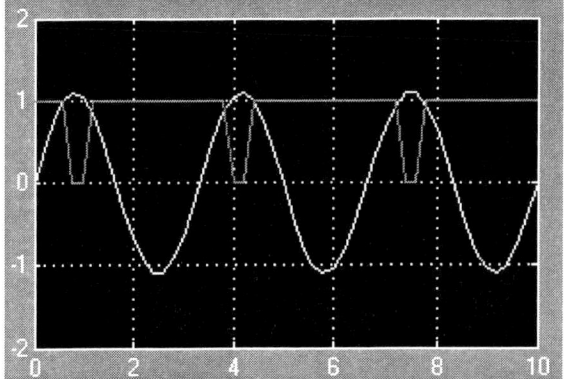

Figure 9.4. Input and output waveforms for the model of Figure 9.3

9.3 The Check Static Range Block

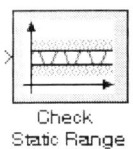

The **Check Static Range** block performs checks to verify that each element of the input signal falls inside the same range of amplitudes. The block's parameter dialog box allows us to specify the upper and lower bounds of the valid amplitude range and whether the range includes the bounds. If the verification condition is true, the block takes no action. If not, simulation is halted and an error message is displayed.

Example 9.3

In the model of Figure 9.5, the amplitude of a sinusoidal signal may vary ±10% from its nominal value of 1 volt. We will configure this model to convert a sine waveform of amplitude 1 to a pulse waveform of the same amplitude and frequency.

The Check Static Gap Block

The Signal Generator block is specified for a sine waveform with amplitude 1 volt, frequency 0.3 Hz, and the Check Static Range block is specified as 1.0 with the Inclusive upper bound checked, as 0 with the Inclusive lower bound checked, Enable assertion checked, Output assertion signal checked, and icon type **graphic**. The Convert block was inserted to convert the **Boolean** output of the Check Dynamic Gap to **double** as required by the Bus Creator block.

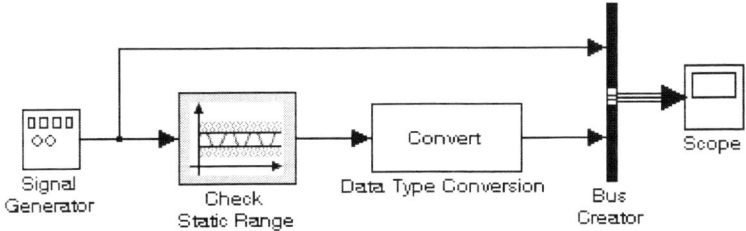

Figure 9.5. Model for Example 9.3

The input and output waveforms are shown in Figure 9.6.

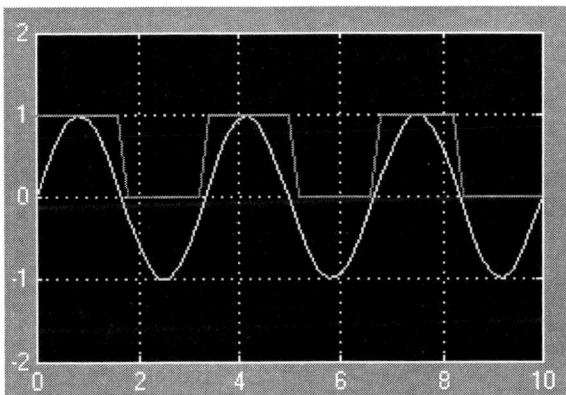

Figure 9.6. Input and output waveforms for the model of Figure 9.5

9.4 The Check Static Gap Block

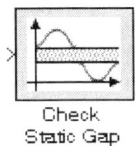

The **Check Static Gap** block performs a check to verify that each element of the input signal is less than or equal to a static lower bound, or greater than or equal to a static upper bound. If the verification condition is true, the block takes no action. If not, simulation is halted and an error message is displayed.

Chapter 9 The Model Verification Library

Example 9.4

We will configure the model of Figure 9.7 whose input is a sawtooth waveform to display error messages when the upper bound is specified at 0.5 or greater and the lower bound is specified as −0.5 or less.

The Signal Generator block is specified for a sawtooth waveform with amplitude 1 volt, frequency 0.5 Hz, and the Check Static Gap block is specified at 0.5 with the Inclusive upper bound checked, at −0.5 with the Inclusive lower bound checked, Enable assertion checked, Output assertion signal checked, and icon type **graphic**. The Convert block was inserted to convert the **Boolean** output of the Check Dynamic Gap to **double** as required by the Bus Creator block. The input and output waveforms are shown in Figure 9.8.

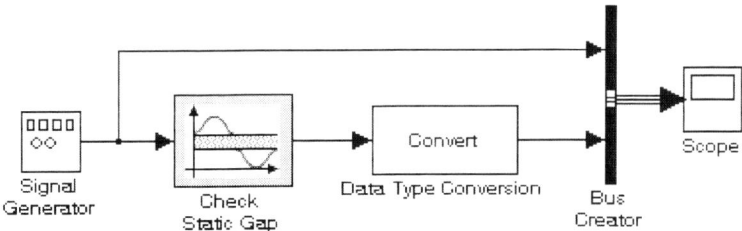

Figure 9.7. Model for Example 9.4

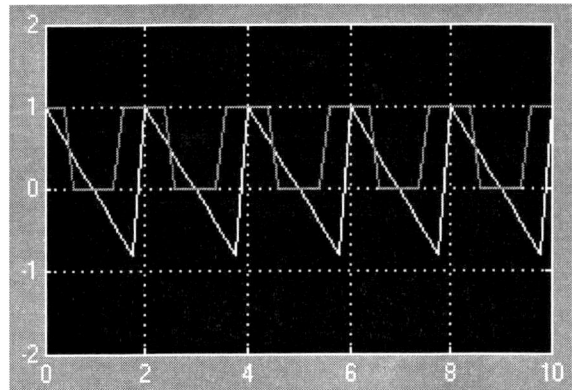

Figure 9.8. Input and output waveforms for the model of Figure 9.7

9.5 The Check Dynamic Lower Bound Block

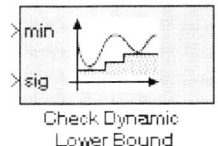

The Check Dynamic Lower Bound Block

The **Check Dynamic Lower Bound** block performs a check to verify that the amplitude of a test signal is less than the amplitude of a reference signal at the current time step. The test signal is the signal connected to the input labeled **sig**. If the verification condition is true, the block takes no action. If not, simulation is halted and an error message is displayed.

Example 9.5

For the model of Figure 9.9 the amplitude of a sinusoidal signal may vary ±10% from its nominal value of 1 volt. We will configure the model to display error messages when the amplitude exceeds −1 volt.

The Signal Generator block has been specified as a sine waveform with the amplitude set at 1.1, frequency at 0.1 Hz, Constant blocks with the values shown, in the Check Dynamic Lower Bound block the Enable assertion and Output assertion signal are checked, and the icon type is selected as **graphic**. The Convert block was inserted to convert the **Boolean** output of the Lower Bound block to **double** as required by the Bus Creator block. The input and output waveforms are shown in Figure 9.10.

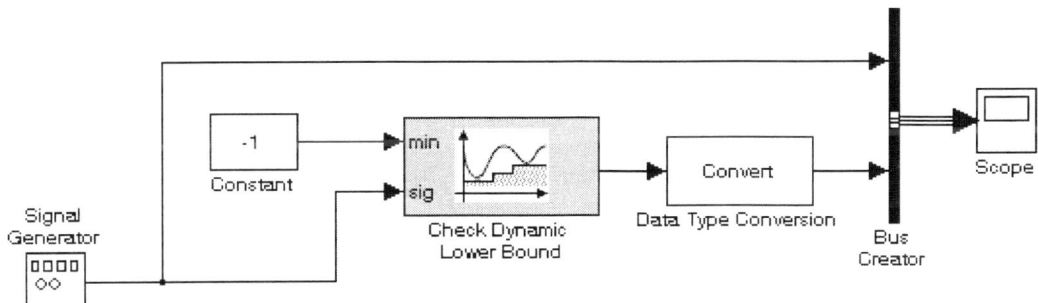

Figure 9.9. Model for Example 9.5

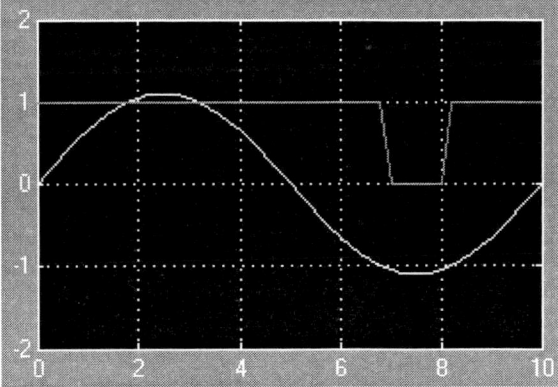

Figure 9.10. Input and output waveforms for the model of Figure 9.9

9.6 The Check Dynamic Upper Bound Block

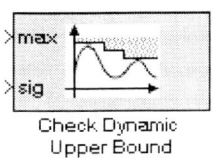

The **Check Dynamic Upper Bound** block performs checks to verify that the amplitude of a test signal is greater than the amplitude of a reference signal. The test signal is the signal connected to the input labeled **sig**. If the verification condition is true, the block takes no action. If not, simulation is halted and an error message is displayed.

Example 9.6

For the model of Figure 9.11 the amplitude of a sinusoidal signal may vary ±10% from its nominal value of 1 volt. We will configure the model to display error messages when the amplitude exceeds +1 volt.

The Signal Generator block has been selected as a sine waveform with the amplitude set at 1.1, frequency at 0.1 Hz, Constant blocks at the values shown, in the Check Dynamic Upper Bound block the Enable assertion and Output assertion signal are checked, and the icon type is selected as **graphic**. The Convert block was inserted to convert the **Boolean** output of the Check Dynamic Upper Bound block to **double** as required by the Bus Creator block. The input and output waveforms are shown in Figure 9.12.

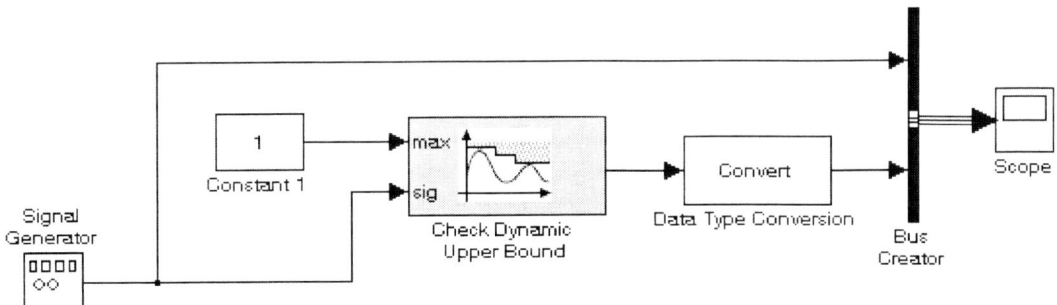

Figure 9.11. Model for Example 9.6

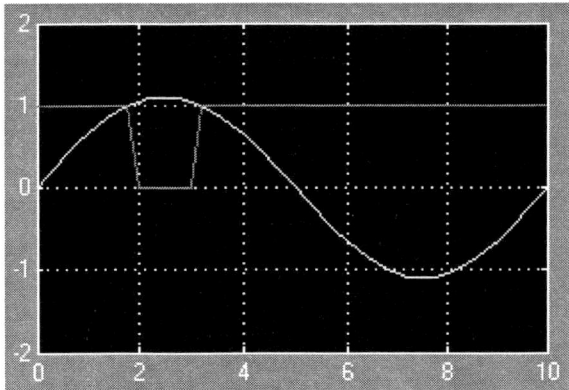

Figure 9.12. Input and output waveforms for the model of Figure 9.11

9.7 The Check Dynamic Range Block

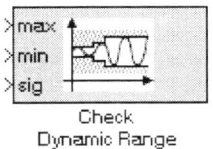

The **Check Dynamic Range** block performs a check to verify that a test signal falls within a range of amplitudes. The width of the range can vary from time step to time step. The input labeled **sig** is the test signal, and the inputs labeled **min** and **max** are the lower and upper bounds respectively of the valid range. If the verification condition is true, the block takes no action. If not, simulation is halted and an error message is displayed.

Example 9.7

The amplitude of a random waveform may vary ±20% from its nominal value of 1 volt. We will create a model using a Check Dynamic Range block to display error messages when the amplitude exceeds ±1 volt.

In Figure 9.13 the Signal Generator block has been selected as a random waveform with amplitude specified at 1.2, frequency at 1 Hz, Constant blocks with the values as indicated, in the Check Dynamic Range block the Enable assertion and Output assertion signal are checked, and the icon type is selected as **graphic**. The Convert block was inserted to convert the **Boolean** output of the Check Dynamic Range block to **double** as required by the Bus Creator block. The input and output waveforms are shown in Figure 9.14.

Chapter 9 The Model Verification Library

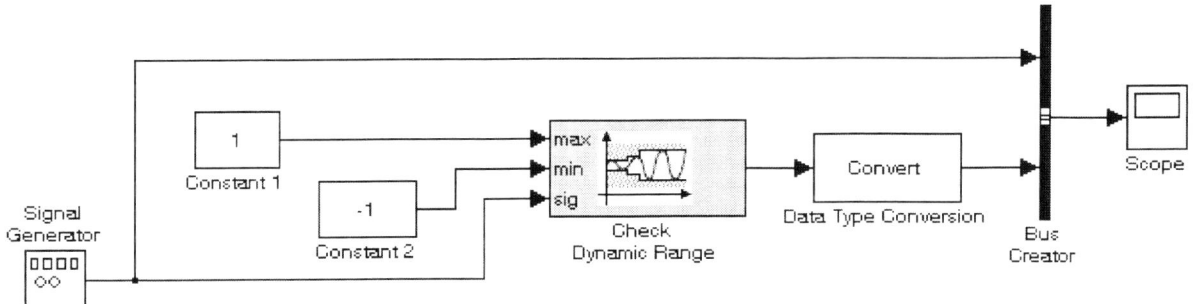

Figure 9.13. Model for Example 9.7

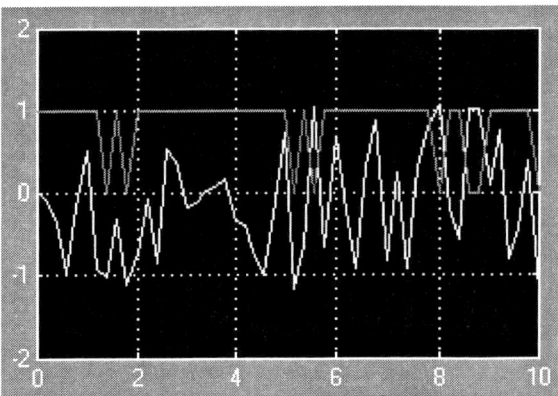

Figure 9.14. Input and output waveforms for the model of Figure 9.13

As stated above this block performs a check to verify that a signal falls inside a range of amplitudes that varies from time step to time step.

9.8 The Check Dynamic Gap Block

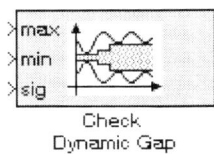

The **Check Dynamic Gap** block performs checks to determine whether a gap of possibly varying width occurs in the range of a signal's amplitudes. The test signal is the signal connected to the input labeled **sig**, and the inputs labeled **min** and **max** specify the lower and upper bounds respectively of the dynamic gap. If the verification condition is true, the block takes no action. If not, simulation is halted and an error message is displayed.

The Check Dynamic Gap Block

Example 9.8

The amplitude of a sinusoidal signal may vary ±10% from its nominal value of 1 volt. We will create a model using a Check Dynamic Gap block to display error messages when the amplitude exceeds ±1 volt.

In Figure 9.15, the Signal Generator block has been selected as a sine waveform with amplitude set at 1.1, frequency at 0.1 Hz, Constant blocks with the values shown, in the Check Dynamic Gap block the Enable assertion and Output assertion signal are checked, and the icon type is selected as **graphic**. The Convert block was inserted to convert the **Boolean** output of the Check Dynamic Gap block to **double** as required by the Bus Creator block. The input and output waveforms are shown in Figure 9.16.

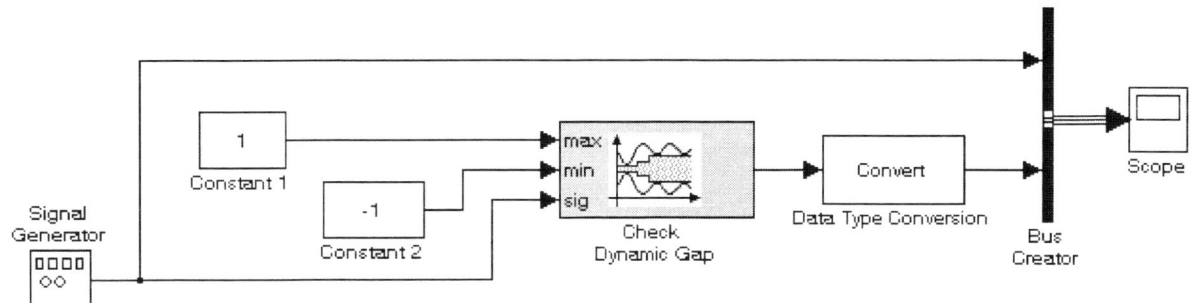

Figure 9.15. Model for Example 9.8

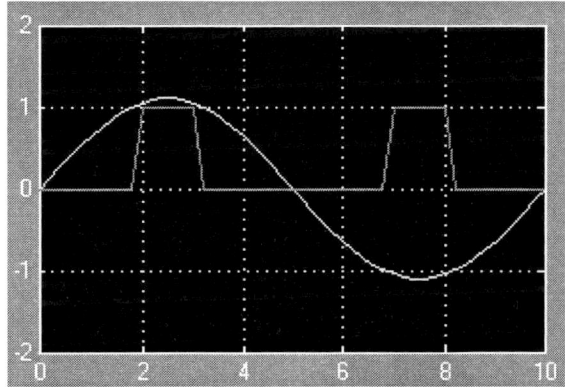

Figure 9.16. Input and output waveforms for the model of Figure 9.15

The Assertion warnings are listed in MATLAB's Command Window.

9.9 The Assertion Block

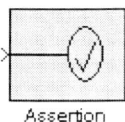

The **Assertion** block verifies that the elements of the signal at its input have a non–zero value. If all elements are non–zero, the block takes no action. If any element is zero, the block halts the simulation and displays an error message. The block's parameter dialog box allows us to specify that the block should display an error message when the assertion fails but allows the simulation to continue.

Example 9.9

In the model of Figure 9.17, the Signal Generator block was specified for a square waveform, inadvertently the amplitude was specified as 0, and thus the Scope block displayed 0 also. To this model we will add an Assertion block to display an error message.

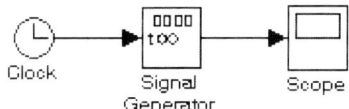

Figure 9.17. Model for Example 9.9 without Assertion block

The model with the addition of an Assertion block is shown in Figure 9.18 where after the simulation command is executed, the following message is displayed:

```
Assertion detected in 'Figure_9_18/Assertion' at time 0.000000
```

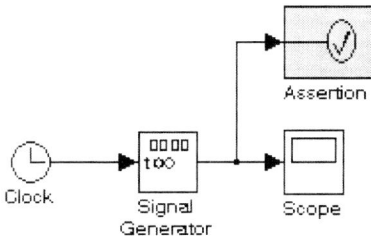

Figure 9.18. Model for Example 9.9 with Assertion block

9.10 The Check Discrete Gradient Block

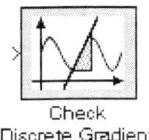

The **Check Discrete Gradient** block performs a check to determine whether the absolute value of the difference between successive samples of the element is less than an upper bound. The block's parameter dialog box allows us to specify the value of the upper bound whose default value is unity. If the verification condition is true, the block takes no action. Otherwise, the block halts the simulation and displays an error message in the Simulation Diagnostics Viewer.

Example 9.10

In Figure 9.19, the Digital Clock block has been set for Sample time 1 as shown on the Scope block and thus the difference between successive samples is 1. We will add a Check Discrete Gradient block specifying that the value of the upper bound is unity (the default) to determine whether an error message will be displayed.

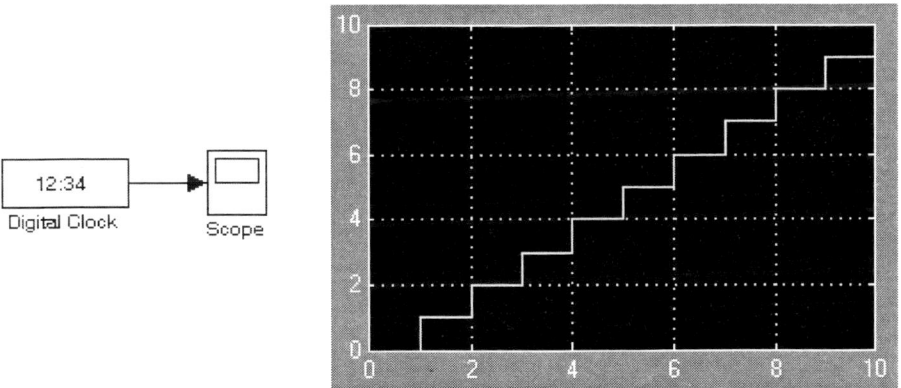

Figure 9.19. Model for Example 9.10 without a Check Discrete Gradient block

The model with the addition of a Check Discrete Gradient block where the value of the upper bound is specified as 1 (default), is shown in Figure 9.20. After the simulation command is executed, the following message is displayed:

```
Assertion detected in 'Figure_9_20/Check Discrete Gradient' at time
1.000000.
```

However, if the Digital Clock block is specified for Sample time less than 1, no error message will be displayed.

Chapter 9 The Model Verification Library

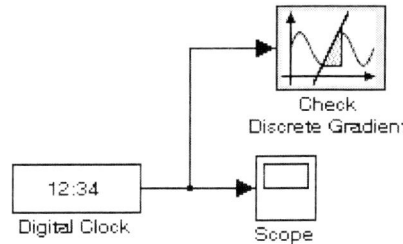

Figure 9.20. Model for Example 9.2 with a Check Discrete Gradient block

9.11 The Check Input Resolution Block

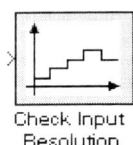

The **Check Input Resolution** block performs a check to determine whether the input signal has a specified scalar or vector resolution.[*] If the resolution is a scalar, the input signal must be a multiple of the resolution within a 10^{-3} tolerance. If the resolution is a vector, the input signal must equal an element of the resolution vector. If the verification condition is true, the block takes no action. If not, simulation is halted and an error message is displayed.

In general, the resolution of an $n-bit$ analog-to-digital (A/D) converter that spans an input voltage of X volts is given by $X/(2^n-1)$ where n is the number of bit. For instance, an A/D converter with a range of 0 to 12 volts, with $n = 8$ the range is divided to $12/255 \approx 47.1$ mV so the resolution is 47.1 mV.

Example 9.11

In the model of Figure 9.21, the resolution for both Check Input Resolution blocks is specified as the row vector

---

[*] *Accuracy and resolution have different meaning. Accuracy is the degree with which an instrument measures a variable in terms of an accepted standard value or true value; usually measured in terms of inaccuracy but expressed as accuracy; often expressed as a percentage of full-scale range. Resolution is the smallest change in the parameter being measured that causes a detectable change in the output of the instrument. For a detailed discussion on accuracy and resolution, please refer to Electronic Devices and Amplifier Circuits with MATLAB Applications, ISBN 0-9709511-7-5.*

The Check Input Resolution Block

$$12 \times \left[\frac{1}{(2^7-1)} \quad \frac{1}{(2^8-1)} \quad \frac{1}{(2^9-1)} \quad \frac{1}{(2^{10}-1)} \quad \frac{1}{(2^{11}-1)}\right]$$

and the Enable assertion and Output assertion signal is checked. The values 1 (true) and 0 (false) in the Display blocks are justified as follows:

Since the resolution specified in the Check Input Resolution blocks is a vector, the input signal must be equal to an element of the resolution vector. The resolution specified in the Constant 1 block is an element of the resolution vector and thus the output is 1 indicating a True condition. However, the resolution specified in the Constant 2 block is not an element of the resolution vector and thus the output is 0 indicating a False condition.

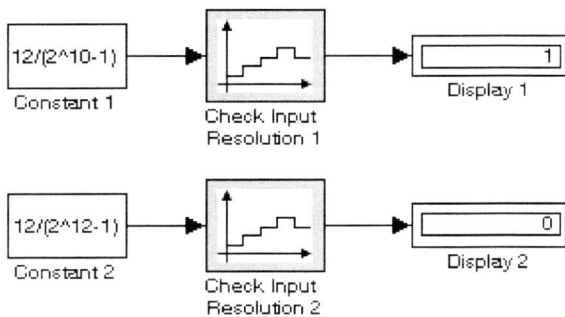

Figure 9.21. Model for Example 9.11

9.12 Summary

The blocks in the Model Verification library are intended to facilitate creation of self–validating models. For instance, we can use model verification blocks to verify that signals do not exceed specified limits during simulation. When we are satisfied that a model is correct, we can turn error checking off by disabling the verification blocks. We need not to physically remove them from the model.

- The **Check Static Lower Bound** block performs a check to verify that each element of the input signal is greater than (or optionally equal to) a specified lower bound at the current time step. The block's parameter dialog box allows us to specify the value of the lower bound and whether the lower bound is inclusive. If the verification condition is true, the block takes no action. If not, the block halts the simulation and displays an error message.

- The **Check Static Upper Bound** block performs a check to verify that each element of the input signal is less than (or optionally equal to) a specified lower bound at the current time step. The block's parameter dialog box allows us to specify the value of the upper bound and whether the bound is inclusive. If the verification condition is true, the block takes no action. If not, the block halts the simulation and displays an error message.

- The **Check Static Range** block performs a check to ascertain that each element of the input signal falls inside the same range of amplitudes at each time step. The block's parameter dialog box allows us to specify the upper and lower bounds of the valid amplitude range and whether the range includes the bounds. If the verification condition is true, the block takes no action. If not, the block halts the simulation and displays an error message.

- The **Check Static Gap** block performs a check to verify that each element of the input signal is less than (or optionally equal to) a static lower bound or greater than (or optionally equal to) a static upper bound at the current time step. If the verification condition is true, the block takes no action. If not, the block halts the simulation and displays an error message.

- The **Check Dynamic Lower Bound** block performs a check to verify that the amplitude of a test signal is less than the amplitude of a reference signal at the current time step. The test signal is the signal connected to the input labeled **sig**. If the verification condition is true, the block takes no action. If not, the block halts the simulation and displays an error message.

- The **Check Dynamic Upper Bound** block performs a check to verify that the amplitude of a test signal is greater than the amplitude of a reference signal at the current time step. The test signal is the signal connected to the input labeled **sig**. If the verification condition is true, the block takes no action. If not, the block halts the simulation and displays an error message.

- The **Check Dynamic Range** block performs a check to verify that a test signal falls inside a range of amplitudes at each time step. The width of the range can vary from time step to time step. The input labeled **sig** is the test signal. The inputs labeled **min** and **max** are the lower and

Summary

upper bounds of the valid range at the current time step. If the verification condition is true, the block takes no action. If not, the block halts the simulation and displays an error message.

- The **Check Dynamic Gap** block performs checks to determine whether a gap of possibly varying width occurs in the range of a signal's amplitudes. The test signal is the signal connected to the input labeled **sig**. The inputs labeled **min** and **max** specify the lower and upper bounds of the dynamic gap, respectively. If the verification condition is true, the block takes no action. If not, the block halts the simulation and displays an error message.

- The **Assertion** block verifies that the elements of the signal at its input have a non-zero value. If all elements are non-zero, the block takes no action. If any element is zero, the block halts the simulation, by default, and displays an error message. The block's parameter dialog box allows us to specify that the block should display an error message when the assertion fails but allows the simulation to continue.

- The **Check Discrete Gradient** block performs a check to determine whether the absolute value of the difference between successive samples of the element is less than an upper bound. The block's parameter dialog box allows us to specify the value of the upper bound (1 by default). If the verification condition is true, the block takes no action. Otherwise, the block halts the simulation and displays an error message in the Simulation Diagnostics Viewer.

- The **Check Input Resolution** block performs a check to determine whether the input signal has a specified scalar or vector resolution. If the resolution is a scalar, the input signal must be a multiple of the resolution within a 10^{-3} tolerance. If the resolution is a vector, the input signal must equal an element of the resolution vector. If the verification condition is true, the block takes no action. If not, the block halts the simulation and displays an error message.

Chapter 9 The Model Verification Library

9.13 Exercises

1. Consider the model shown below where the inputs and outputs of the Signal Generator block are also shown, and in the parameters for the Assertion block the Enable Assertion is checked and the Stop simulation when assertion fails is unchecked. The Signal Generator block has been specified for a sine waveform of amplitude 1 and frequency 0.25 Hz to accept an external signal, i.e., the Clock block. Under those conditions will the Assertion block produce a warning?

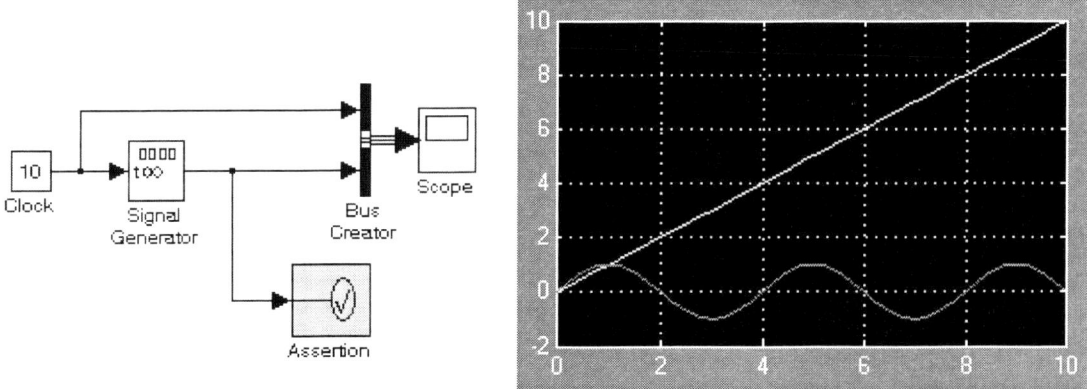

2. It is known that noise voltages generated within the circuitry of an analog–to–digital converter are 0.75 mv ± 10%. Create a model using a Check Dynamic Gap block to display error messages when the amplitude exceeds this range.

3. For the models shown below, the resolution in both Check Input Resolution blocks 1 and 2 has been specified as

$$\frac{12}{(2^n - 1)}$$

with n = 9. What is the maximum value that can be specified in Constant block 1 to cause the Display 1 block to display 0 (False), and what is the minimum value that will cause the Display 2 block to display 1 (True)?

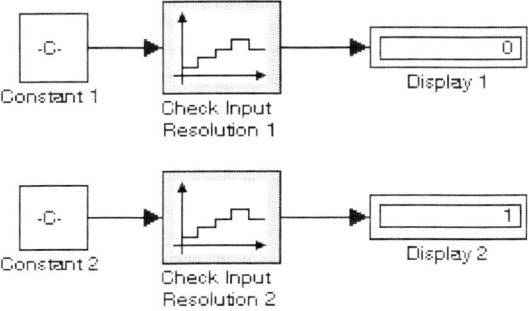

Solutions to End-of-Chapter Exercises

9.14 Solutions to End-of-Chapter Exercises

1.

The Assertion block detects a 0 value at the start of the simulation time, in this case 10 seconds as shown by the Clock block, and thus in MATLAB's Command Window it outputs the message:

`Assertion detected in 'Exercise_9_1/Assertion' at time 0.000000.`

However, the simulation continues for 10 seconds since the Stop simulation when assertion fails is unchecked.

2.

The model and input and output waveforms are shown below. Since voltage noise occurs in random, we set the Signal Generator block for Random waveform with amplitude 0.01 and frequency at 0.1 Hz. To allow for the ±10% tolerance from the nominal 0.75 mv value, we set the Constant blocks for +0.0085 and −0.0085.

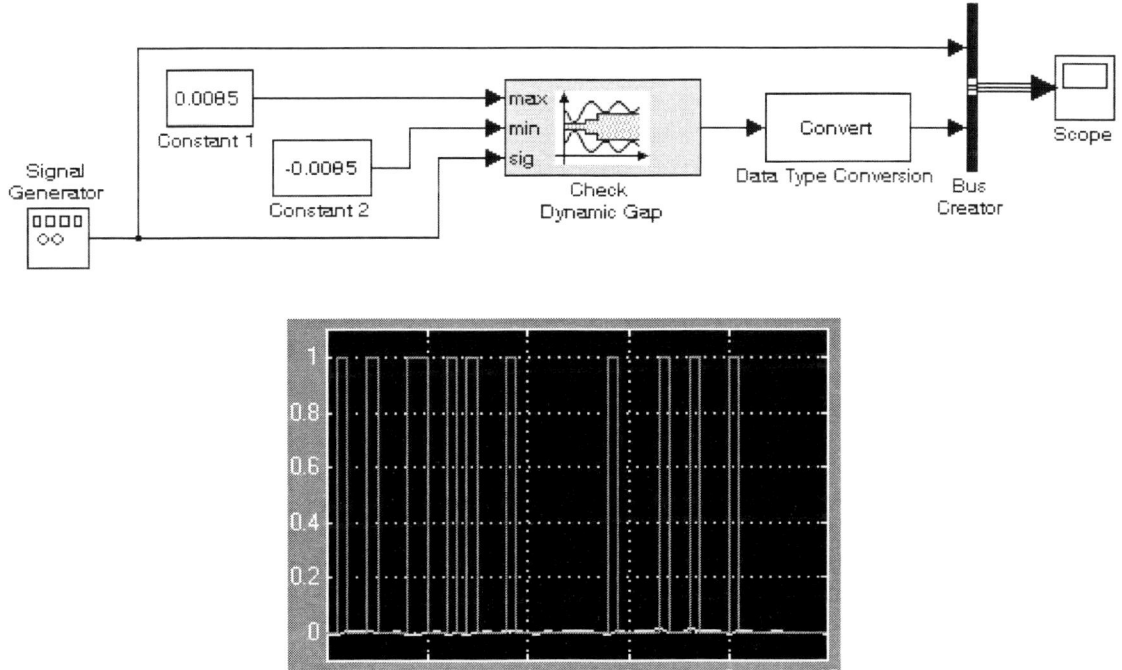

The output waveform is logic 0 (False) whenever assertions are detected, and jumps to 1 (True) when no assertions are detected. The precise times when assertions are detected are displayed in MATLAB's Command Window.

Chapter 9 The Model Verification Library

3.

Since the resolution specified in both Check Input Resolution blocks is the scalar

$$\frac{12}{(2^9-1)}$$

the input signal must be a multiple of this resolution within a 10^{-3} tolerance. Since,

$$\frac{12}{(2^9-1)} = 0.0235$$

any value equal of greater than 0.0235 will cause a display 1 (True), and any value less than 0.0235 will cause a display of 0 (False) as shown in the models below.

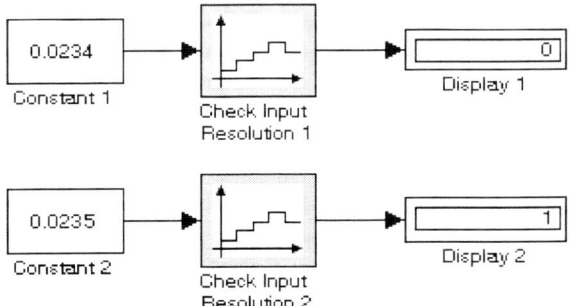

Upon execution of the Simulation command, MATLAB's Command Window displays Assertions detected in the Check Input Resolution block 1 from 0 to 10 in steps of 0.2.

Chapter 10

The Model-Wide Utilities Library

This chapter is an introduction to the **Model-Wide Utilities** library. This is the ninth library in the Simulink group of libraries and contains the **Linearization of Running Models Sub-Library**, the **Documentation Sub-Library**, and the **Modeling Guides Sub-Library**. We will describe the function of each block included in this library and we will perform simulation examples to illustrate their application.

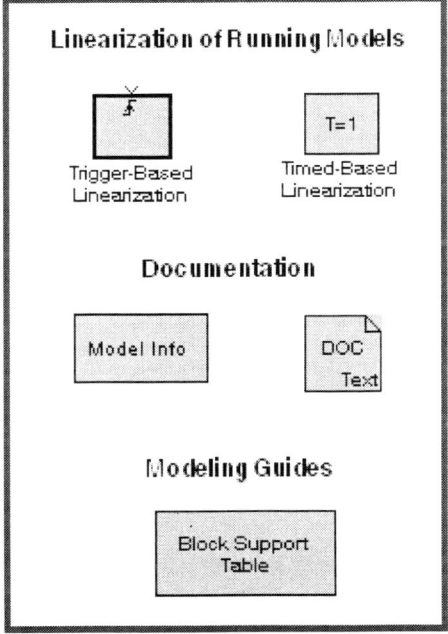

Chapter 10 The Model–Wide Utilities Library

10.1 The Linearization of Running Models Sub-Library

The **Linearization of Running Models Sub-Library** contains the blocks described in Subsections 10.1.1 and 10.1.2 below.

10.1.1 The Trigger–Based Linearization Block

The **Trigger–Based Linearization** block, when triggered, invokes the MATLAB functions **linmod** or **dlinmod** to create a linear model for the system. No trimming[*] is performed. The linear model is stored in the base workspace as a structure, along with information about the operating point at which the snapshot was taken. Multiple snapshots are appended to form an array of structures.

The name of the structure used to save the snapshots is the name of the model appended by _Trigger_Based_Linearization, for example, vdp_Trigger_Based_Linearization. The structure has the fields shown in the Help menu for this block.

Example 10.1

We will use a Trigger–Based Linearization block to extract the linear model for the model shown in Figure 10.1.

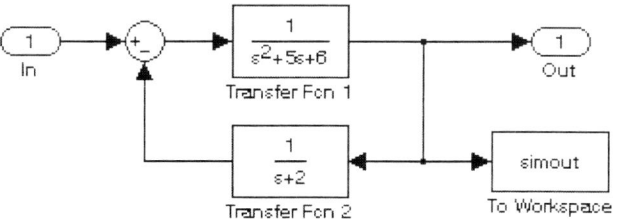

Figure 10.1. Model for Example 10.1

This is the same model as that of Figure 3.4, Example 3.2, Chapter 3, Page 3–4, where with the execution of the command [A,B,C,D]=linmod('Figure_3_4') the linear model in the form of the state–space MATLAB displayed the four matrices as

A =

---

[*] The trim *function uses a Simulink model to determine steady–state points of a dynamic system that satisfy input, output, and state conditions that we can specify. For details please type* **help trim** *in MATLAB's Command Window.*

```
        -5    -6    -1
         1     0     0
         0     1    -2
B =
         1
         0
         0
C =
         0     1     0
D =
         0
```

and thus the model of Figure 10.1 can be represented as

$$\dot{x} = \begin{bmatrix} -5 & -6 & -1 \\ 1 & 0 & 0 \\ 0 & 1 & -2 \end{bmatrix} x + \begin{bmatrix} 1 \\ 0 \\ 0 \end{bmatrix} u$$

$$y = \begin{bmatrix} 0 & 1 & 0 \end{bmatrix} x + \begin{bmatrix} 0 \end{bmatrix} u$$

Next, let us reconsider the model of Figure 10.1 shown as Figure 10.2 where we have included a Trigger-Based Linearization block triggered by a Pulse Generator block whose period is arbitrarily specified for 10 seconds.

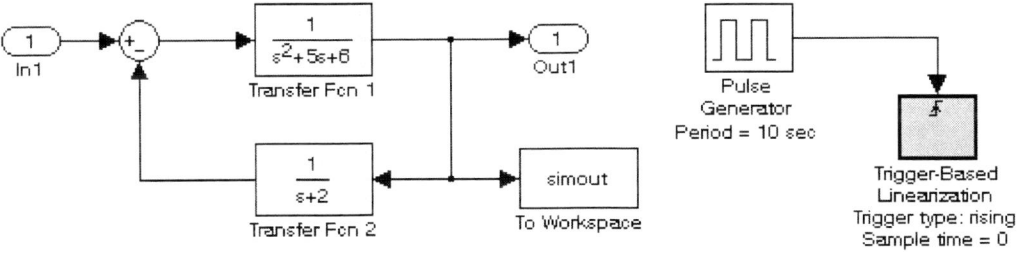

Figure 10.2. Model for Example 10.1 with Trigger-Based Linearization

For the model of Figure 10.2, we execute the simulation command, we save this model as **Figure_10_2.mdl**, and in MATLAB's Command Window we type and execute the command

Figure_10_2_Trigger_Based_Linearization

MATLAB displays the following:

```
Figure_10_2_Trigger_Based_Linearization =

        a: [3x3 double]
        b: [3x1 double]
```

Chapter 10 The Model-Wide Utilities Library

```
            c: [0 1 0]
            d: 0
    StateName: {3x1 cell}
   OutputName: {'Figure_10_2/Out1'}
    InputName: {'Figure_10_2/In1'}
     OperPoint: [1x1 struct]
           Ts: 0
```

We observe that a, b, c, and d indicate the sizes of the state–space matrices A, B, C, and D respectively.

10.1.2 The Time–Based Linearization Block

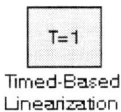

The **Time–Based Linearization** block invokes the MATLAB functions **linmod** or **dlinmod** to create a linear model for the system when the simulation clock reaches the time specified by the Linearization time parameter. No trimming is performed. The linear model is stored in the base workspace as a structure, along with information about the operating point at which the snapshot was taken. Multiple snapshots are appended to form an array of structures.

The name of the structure used to save the snapshots is the name of the model appended by _Timed_Based_Linearization, for example, **vdp_Timed_Based_Linearization**. The structure has the fields shown in the Help menu for this block.

Example 10.2

The model shown in Figure 10.3 is the same model as that of Figure 10.1, Example 10.1. We will use a Time-Based Linearization block to extract its linear model.

We begin by adding a Time-Based Linearization block with the linearization time arbitrarily set for 2 seconds, and the new model is now as shown in Figure 10.4.

The Linearization of Running Models Sub–Library

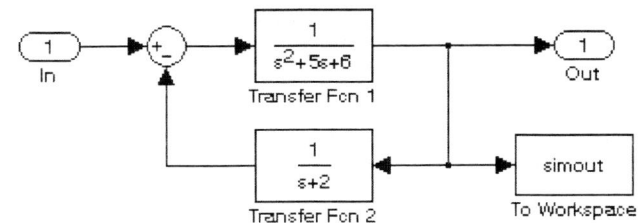

Figure 10.3. Model for Example 10.2

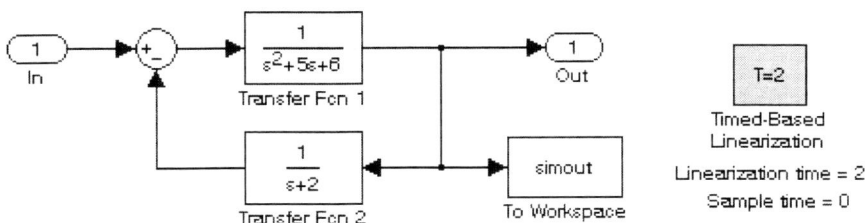

Figure 10.4. Model for Example 10.2 with Timed–Based Linearization block

For the model of Figure 10.4, we execute the simulation command, we save this model as **Figure_10_2.mdl**, and in MATLAB's Command Window we type

Figure_10_4_Timed_Based_Linearization

and when this command is executed MATLAB displays the following:

```
Figure_10_4_Timed_Based_Linearization =

             a: [3x3 double]
             b: [3x1 double]
             c: [0 1 0]
             d: 0
     StateName: {3x1 cell}
    OutputName: {'Figure_10_4/Out'}
     InputName: {'Figure_10_4/In'}
      OperPoint: [1x1 struct]
            Ts: 0
```

We observe that a, b, c, and d indicate the sizes of the state-space matrices A, B, C, and D respectively.

Chapter 10 The Model–Wide Utilities Library

We can use state and simulation time logging to extract the model states and inputs at operating points. For example, suppose that we want to get the states of the Figure_10_4 model at linearization times of 3 seconds and 7 seconds. This can be done with the following steps:

1. We open the model and drag an instance of this block from the Model–Wide Utilities library and drop the instance into the model.

2. We open the block's parameter dialog box and set the Linearization time to [3 7].

3. We open the model's Configuration Parameters dialog box from the Simulation drop menu and we select the Data Import/Export pane.

4. We check States and Time on the Save to Workspace control panel, we leave all other parameters in their default state, and we click on OK to confirm the selections and close the dialog box.

5. We start the simulation.

6. At the end of the simulation, we type and execute **whos** in MATLAB's Command Window, and the following variables appear in the MATLAB workspace:

   `Figure_10_4_Timed_Based_Linearization, tout, and xout.`

7. We obtain the indices to the operating point times by entering and executing the following in MATLAB's Command Window:

   ind1 = find(`Figure_10_4_Timed_Based_Linearization`(1).OperPoint.t==tout);
   ind2 = find(`Figure_10_4_Timed_Based_Linearization`(1).OperPoint.t==tout);

   We type and execute **whos** in MATLAB's Command Window, and the indices **ind1** and **ind2** are now included in the MATLAB workspace:

8. We obtain the state vectors at the operating points by entering and executing the following in MATLAB's Command Window:

   x1 = xout(ind1,:); x2 = xout(ind2,:);

10.2 The Documentation Sub-Library

The **Documentation Sub-Library** contains the blocks described in Subsections 10.2.1 and 10.2.2 below.

10.2.1 The Model Info Block

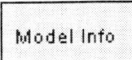

The **Model Info** block displays revision control information about a model as an annotation block in the model's block diagram.

The Documentation Sub–Library

Example 10.3

The model in Figure 10.5 solves the non-linear equation

$$f(z) = z^2 + 4z + 3 + \sin z - z\cos z$$

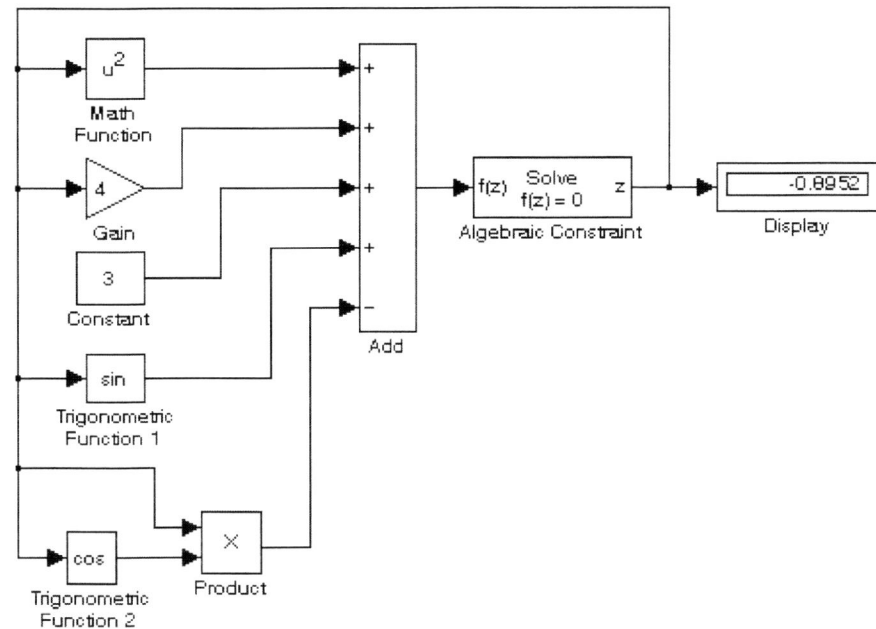

Figure 10.5. Model for Example 10.3

We would like to add a Model Info block to indicate that this model was created by John Smith on 02/16/06 and was last modified by Bill Johnson on 04/27/06.

We drag a Model Info block into the model of Figure 10.5, we double–click it, and on the Model Info dialog box shown in Figure 10.6 we enter the desired information. The model now appears as shown in Figure 10.7.

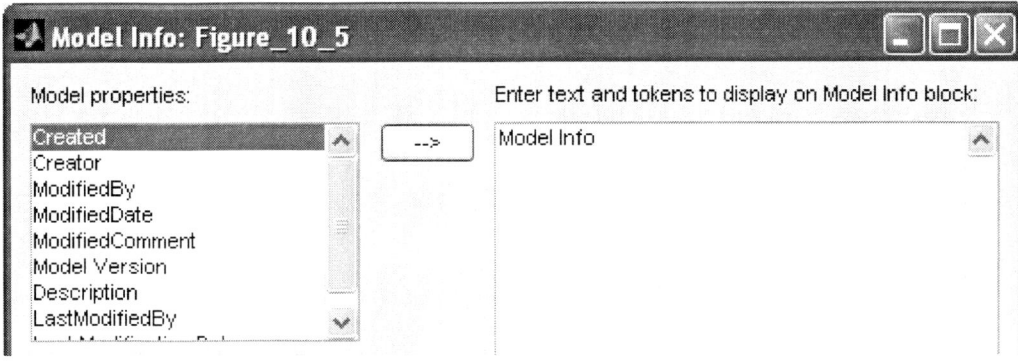

Figure 10.6. Model Properties and Text for the Model Info block

Chapter 10 The Model–Wide Utilities Library

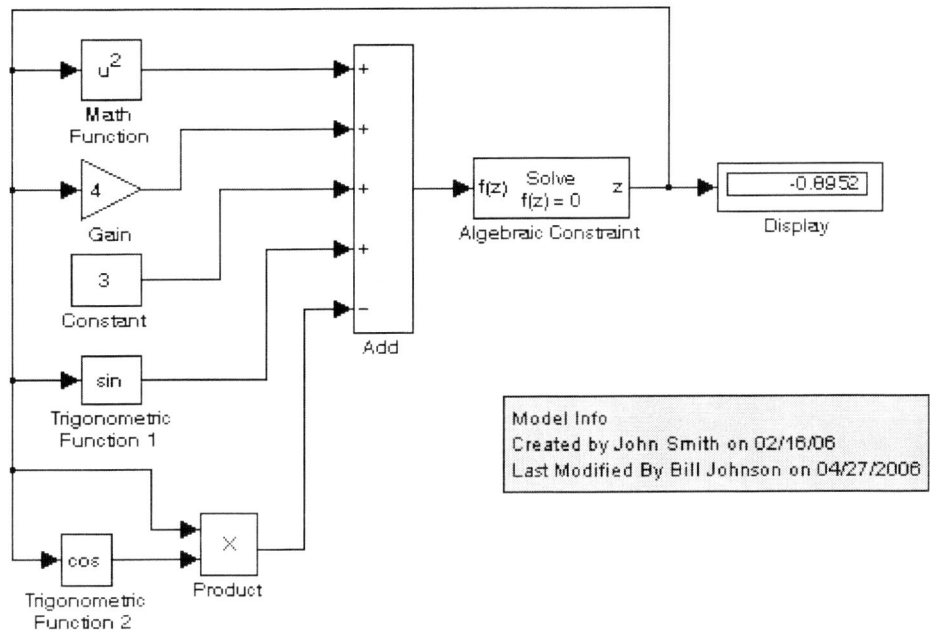

Figure 10.7. Updated model for Example 10.3

10.2.2 The Doc Text Block

The **Doc Text** block or **DocBlock** allows us to create and edit text that documents a model and save that text with the model. To create a file that contains relevant text, we double-click on this block to open the file in the text editor that we have selected in the MATLAB Preferences dialog box. We use the text editor to modify the text and save the file. Simulink stores the contents of the saved file in the model file block.

Example 10.4

In Figure 10.8 the DOC Text block is provided to justify the necessity for the Data Type Conversion block. Let us insert appropriate text for justification.

We double-click on the DOC Text block and in the Text Editor we replace the displayed message with the following text:

The Convert block was inserted to convert the Boolean output of the
Check Dynamic Gap to double as required by the Bus Creator block.

The Modeling Guides Sub–Library

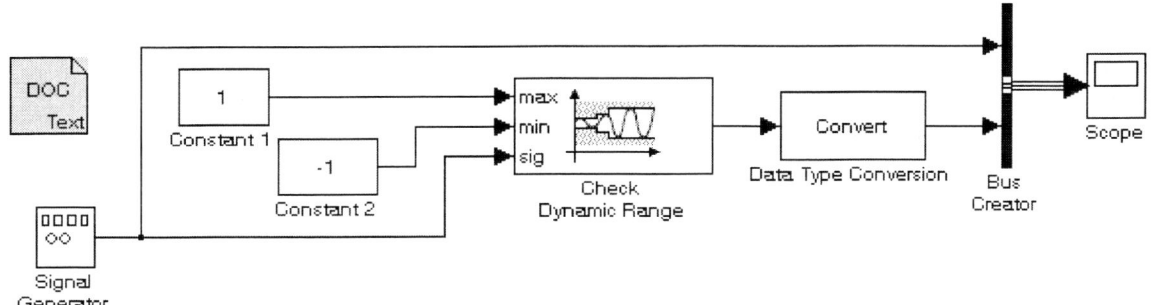

Figure 10.8. Model for Example 10.4

This message will be displayed on MATLAB's Editor whenever we double click on the Doc Text block in the model of Figure 10.8.

10.3 The Modeling Guides Sub–Library

The Modeling Guides Sub-Library contains only the Block Support Table which is described below.

The **Block Support Table** block includes a table which describes the data types that are supported by blocks in the main Simulink library. All blocks that can generate code contain an "X" in the column titled "Code Generation Support". A subset of these blocks is not recommended for production code as flagged by Note N6. Guidelines to determine when a block is recommended for production code are listed below the table. Some blocks include caveats and notes that should be taken into account when they are used. Caveats and notes are indicated in the table by "C#" and "N#", respectively, and are described below the table.

Example 10.5

For the model of Figure 10.9, we will determine the types of data the Clock, Signal Generator, and the Scope blocks will accept.

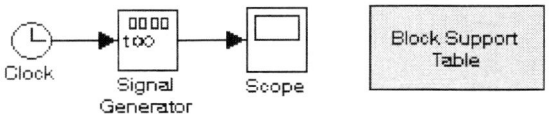

Figure 10.9. Model for Example 10.5

Chapter 10 The Model–Wide Utilities Library

We double-click on the Block Support Table block and from the table displayed we find that the Clock and Signal Generator blocks will accept the **double** data type but as noted by Note N6 neither is recommended for production code. The Scope block will accept all data types listed in the table.

10.4 Summary

- The **Trigger−Based Linearization** block, when triggered, invokes the MATLAB command **linmod** or **dlinmod** to create a linear model for the system.

- The **Time−Based Linearization** block invokes the MATLAB command **linmod** or **dlinmod** to create a linear model for the system when the simulation clock reaches the time specified by the Linearization time parameter.

- The **Model Info** block The Model Info block displays revision control information about a model as an annotation block in the model's block diagram.

- The **Doc Text** block or **DocBlock** allows us to create and edit text that documents a model and save that text with the model.

- The **Block Support Table** block describes the data types that are supported by blocks in the main Simulink library.

NOTES

Chapter 11

The Ports & Subsystems Library

This chapter is an introduction to the **Ports & Subsystems** library. This is the tenth library in the Simulink group of libraries and contains the blocks shown below. All nonvirtual subsystems, defined in Section 11.17, are shown with a bold border. We will describe the function of each block included in this library and we will perform simulation examples to illustrate their application.

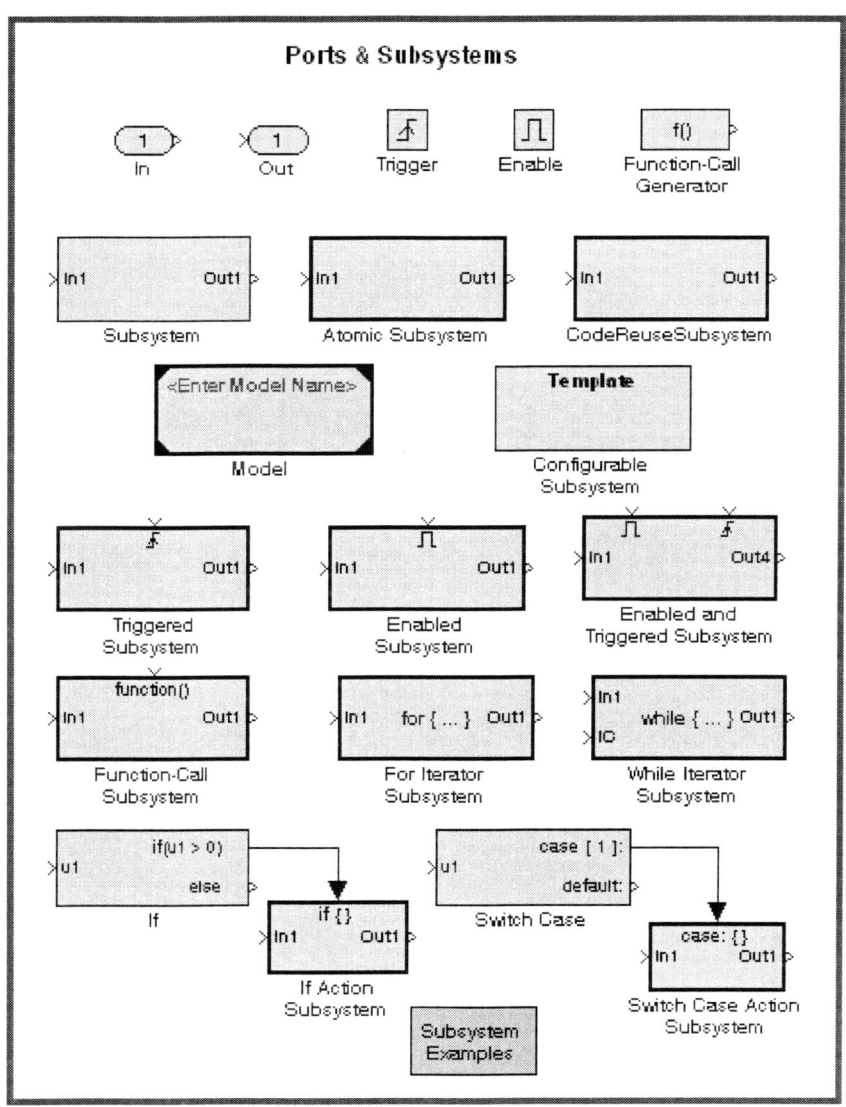

Chapter 11 The Ports & Subsystems Library

11.1 The Inport, Outport, and Subsystem Blocks

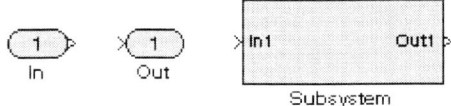

Inport blocks are ports that serve as links from outside a system into the system. **Outport** blocks are output ports for a subsystem. A **Subsystem** block represents a subsystem of the system that contains it. These blocks are described in Section 2.1, Chapter 2, Page 2−2.

11.2 The Trigger Block

The **Trigger** block is used with a subsystem or a model to allow its execution only when triggered by an external signal provided by the Trigger block. We can configure this block to enable a change in the value of the external signal to trigger execution of a subsystem once on each integration step when the value of the signal that passes through the trigger port changes in a specifiable way. We can also configure the Trigger block to accept a function−call trigger. This allows a Function−Call Generator block or S−function[*] to trigger execution of a subsystem or model multiple times during a time step. A subsystem or model can contain only one Trigger block. Examples are presented in Sections 11.9 and 11.11, this chapter, Pages 11−25 and 11−30. For additional information, please refer also to Triggered Subsystems in Simulink's documentation.

11.3 The Enable Block

The **Enable** block adds an enable block to a subsystem to make it an enabled subsystem. Enable subsystems are subsystems that execute at each simulation step where the control signal has a positive value. A **Control Signal** is a signal that determines whether a subsystem executes. An enabled subsystem has a single control input which can have a scalar or vector value. If the input is a scalar, the subsystem executes if the input is greater than zero. For instance, if the signal is a waveform (sinusoid, square, sawtooth, etc.), crosses zero, and the slope is positive, the subsystem is enabled. If the signal crosses zero and the slope becomes negative, the subsystem is disabled. If the input is a vector, the subsystem executes if any of the vector elements is greater than zero.

At the start of simulation, Simulink initializes the states of blocks inside an enabled subsystem to their initial conditions. When an enabled subsystem restarts, that is, it executes after having been

---

[*] *An introduction and an example of an S−Function is presented in Section 11.18, this Chapter, Page 11−43.*

disabled, the States parameters determine the status of the blocks contained in the enabled subsystem. Thus,

reset resets the states to their initial conditions (zero if not defined).

held holds the states at their previous values.

We can output the enabling signal by selecting the **Show output** port check box in the Block Parameters dialog box. Selecting this option allows the system to process the enabling signal.

To add an Enable block to a subsystem model, we double-click on the subsystem block, and when the subsystem appears, we drag the Enable block into it. An example is presented in Section 11.6, Figure 11.15, this chapter, Page 11-14.

11.4 The Function–Call Generator Block

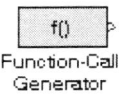

The **Function-Call Generator** block executes a function–call subsystem at the rate specified by the block's Sample time parameter. We can execute multiple function–call subsystems in a prescribed order by first connecting a Function–Call Generator block to a Demux block that has as many output ports as there are function–call subsystems to be controlled. Then, we can connect the output ports of the Demux block to the systems to be controlled. The system connected to the first demux port executes first, the system connected to the second demux port executes second, and so on. We can configure Stateflow®[*] blocks to execute function–call subsystems, thereby extending the capabilities of the blocks. For more information on their use in Stateflow, please refer to the Stateflow documentation.

Example 11.1

The model of Figure 11.1 shows how a Function–Call Generator and a Demux can be used to control four different Function–Call Subsystem blocks. The Function–Call Subsystem block is described in Section 11.12, this chapter, Page 11-34.

---

[*] *A Stateflow diagram is a graphical representation of a finite state machine where states and transitions form the basic building blocks of the system. Stateflow provides a block that we can include in a Simulink model.*

Chapter 11 The Ports & Subsystems Library

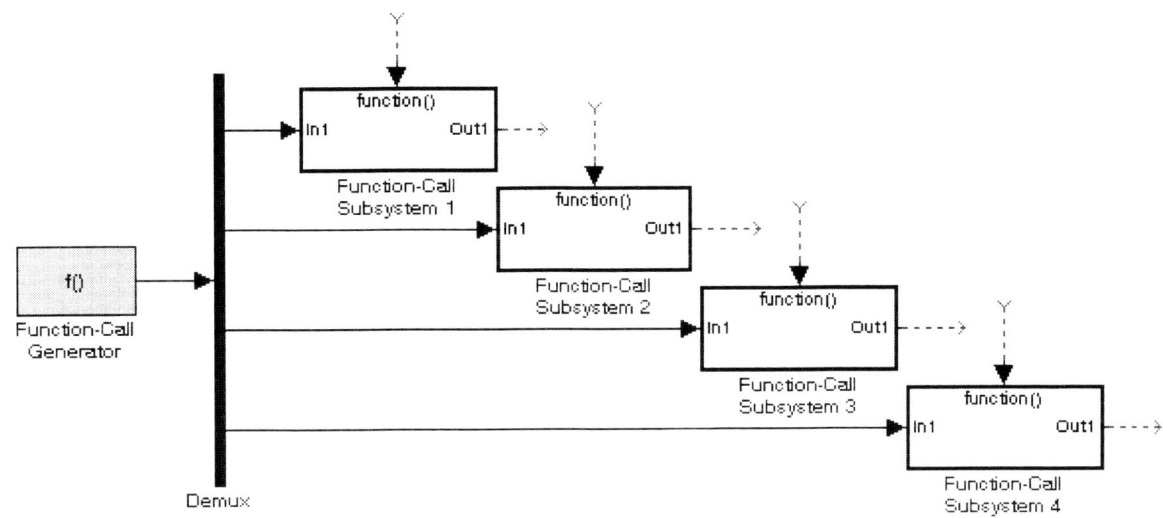

Figure 11.1. Model for Example 11.1

11.5 The Atomic Subsystem Block

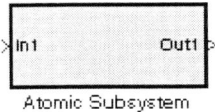

In Chapter 2, Section 2.1, Page 2-2, we described the Subsystem, Inport, and Outport blocks. As we recall, we select the blocks and lines which will become parts of the subsystem using a bounding box, then we choose Create Subsystem from the Edit menu. Simulink replaces the blocks with a Subsystem block. When we double-click the subsystem block, a model appears which displays the blocks that we have selected, and adds Inport and Outport blocks to indicate the signals entering and leaving the subsystem.

We can also create a subsystem using the **Atomic Subsystem** block. This is done by copying the Atomic Subsystem block from the Ports & Subsystems library into our model. Then we can add blocks to the subsystem by opening the Subsystem block and copying blocks into it.

Example 11.2

Figure 11.2 shows a four-line-to-one-line digital multiplexer whose truth table is shown as Table 11.1 below. This model is saved as **Figure_11_2**.

The Atomic Subsystem Block

TABLE 11.1 *Truth table for Example 11.2*

Inport 6	Inport 5	Output
0	0	D
0	1	C
1	0	B
1	1	A

We will use an Atomic Subsystem block to create a subsystem for this multiplexer. We do so by selecting all blocks in this model and copying them into new model which we name **Figure_11_2S**. From the Ports & Subsystems library, we drag the Atomic Subsystem block into model **Figure_11_2S** and we save it with the same name. It is shown as Figure 11.3, and it is annotated as **Saved as Figure_11_2S**.

Next, we double-click the Atomic Subsystem block in Figure 11.3, and we observe that it is now displayed with an Inport block and an Outport block connected by a straight line as shown in Figure 11.4. It is annotated as **Figure_11_2S/Atomic Subsystem**, and it is saved with this name.

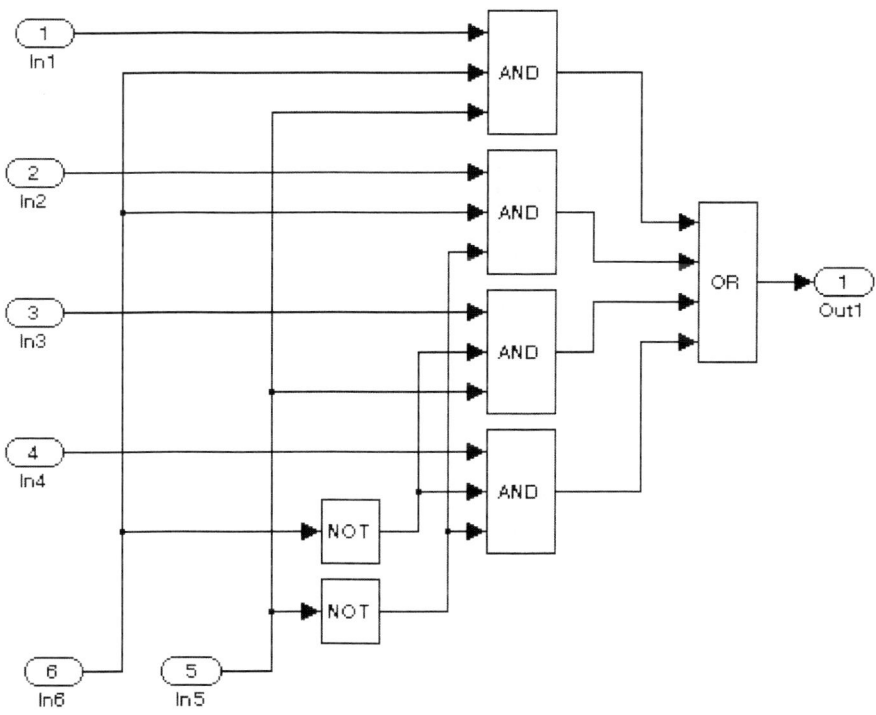

Figure 11.2. Digital multiplexer circuit for Example 11.2

Chapter 11 The Ports & Subsystems Library

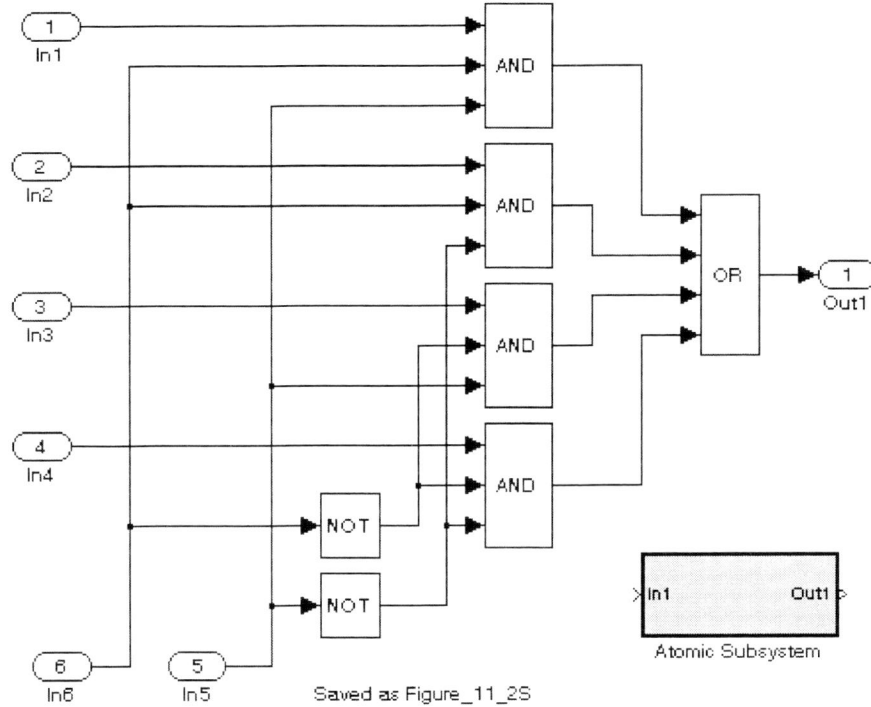

Figure 11.3. Model for Example 11.2 saved as Figure_11_2S

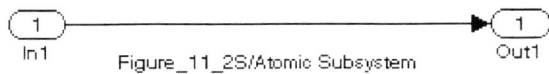

Figure 11.4. The updated appearance of the Atomic Subsystem block of Figure 11.3

We open the model of Figure 11.2, saved as **Figure_11_2**, we choose Select All from the Edit menu, and we drag it into the model of Figure 11.4 which now appears as in Figure 11.5. We save the model of Figure 11.5 with the same name as that of Figure 11.4, i.e., **Figure_11_2S/Atomic Subsystem**.

Now, we reopen the model of Figure 11.3 and we observe that the Atomic Subsystem block appears as shown in Figure 11.6. We double-click on the Atomic Subsystem block of Figure 11.6 and we observe that it has the appearance of Figure 11.5.

We no longer need the In1 and Out1 blocks on top of the model of Figure 11.5, so we delete them, and we also delete the interconnecting line. We also relabel the In and Out blocks as In 1, In 2,..., In 6, and Out, and we save this model with the same name. We return to the model with the Atomic Subsystem block, we copy it into a new model, we expand it, and we save it. It is shown as Figure 11.7.

The Atomic Subsystem Block

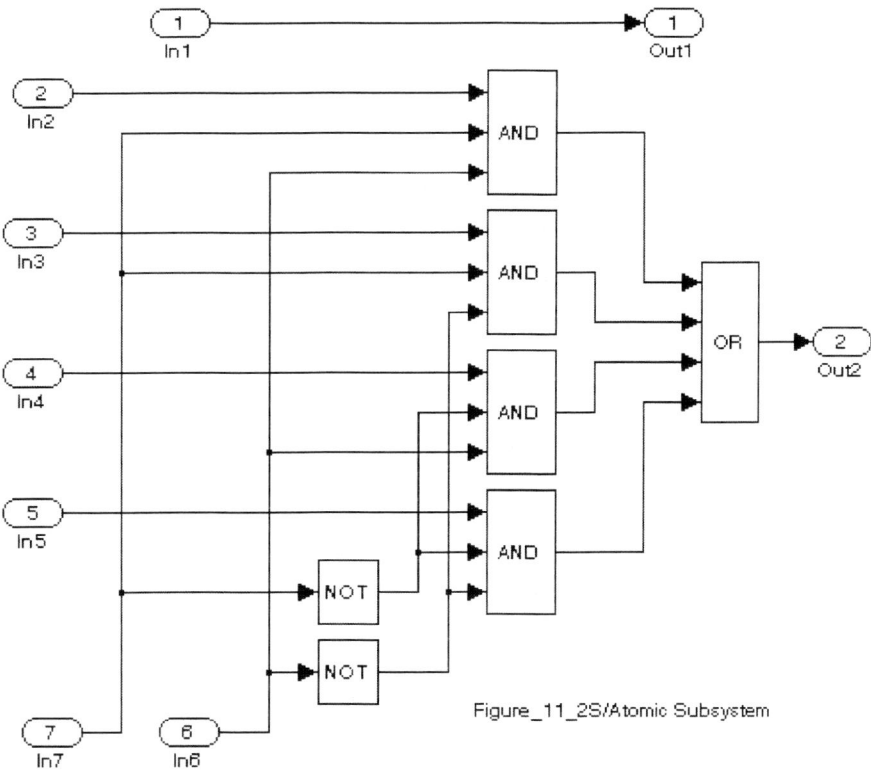

Figure 11.5. The model of Figure 11.2 copied into the model of Figure 11.4

Chapter 11 The Ports & Subsystems Library

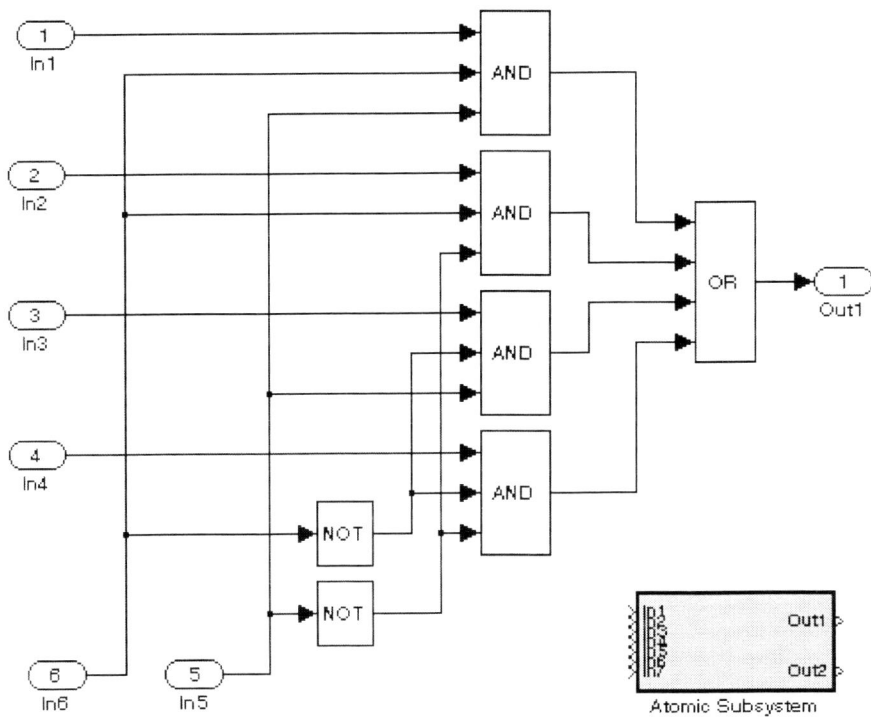

Figure 11.6. Updated appearance of the Atomic Subsystem block

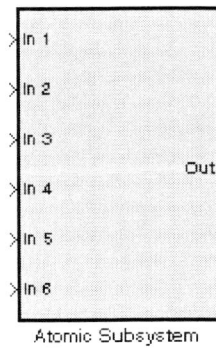

Figure 11.7. The multiplexer of Example 11.2 shown as an Atomic Subsystem.

To verify that the Atomic Subsystem of Figure 11.7 performs in accordance with the truth table, we assign the variables A, B, C, and D and control lines C0 and C1 as shown in Figure 11.8 and successively we assign the values shown below in MATLAB's Command Window. With these values, the output of the digital multiplexer is logical 1 (True).

A=1; C0=1; C1=1;
B=1; C0=0; C1=1;
C=1; C0=1; C1=0;
D=1; C0=0; C1=0;

The Code Reuse Subsystem Block

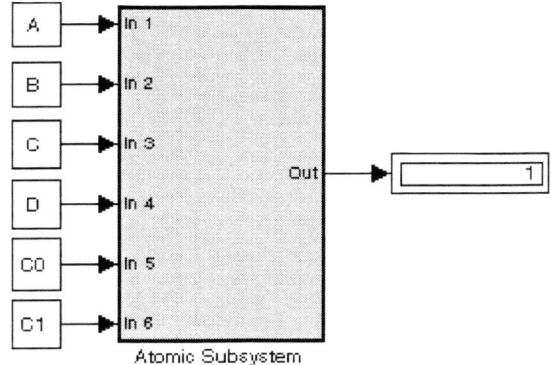

Figure 11.8. The Atomic Subsystem with inputs and output to verify the truth table of Example 11.2

11.6 The Code Reuse Subsystem Block

The **Code Reuse Subsystem** block is a Subsystem block that represents a subsystem of the system that contains it. It is very similar to the Atomic Subsystem which we discussed in the previous section. We can create a subsystem either by copying the Subsystem (or Atomic Subsystem) block from the Ports & Subsystems library into our model and add blocks to the subsystem by opening the Subsystem block and copying blocks into its window, or by selecting the blocks and lines that are to make up the subsystem using a bounding box, then choosing Create Subsystem from the Edit menu. Simulink replaces the blocks with a Subsystem block. When we double-click the block, the window displays the blocks which we selected.

Example 11.3

Figure 11.9 is a block diagram of a decimal–to–BCD encoder digital circuit. We will use the truth table of Table 11.2 to create a model for the decimal–to–BCD encoder circuit.

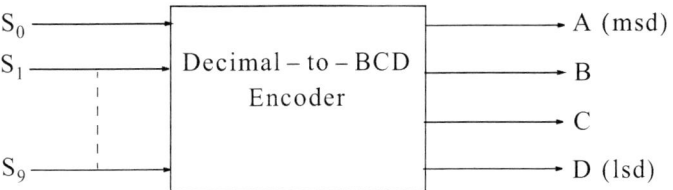

Figure 11.9. Block diagram for decimal-to-BCD encoder

Introduction to Simulink with Engineering Applications
Copyright © Orchard Publications

Chapter 11 The Ports & Subsystems Library

TABLE 11.2 Truth table for decimal-to-BCD encoder

Inputs										Outputs			
S_0	S_1	S_2	S_3	S_4	S_5	S_6	S_7	S_8	S_9	A	B	C	D
1	0	0	0	0	0	0	0	0	0	0	0	0	0
0	1	0	0	0	0	0	0	0	0	0	0	0	1
0	0	1	0	0	0	0	0	0	0	0	0	1	0
0	0	0	1	0	0	0	0	0	0	0	0	1	1
0	0	0	0	1	0	0	0	0	0	0	1	0	0
0	0	0	0	0	1	0	0	0	0	0	1	0	1
0	0	0	0	0	0	1	0	0	0	0	1	1	0
0	0	0	0	0	0	0	1	0	0	0	1	1	1
0	0	0	0	0	0	0	0	1	0	1	0	0	0
0	0	0	0	0	0	0	0	0	1	1	0	0	1

From the truth table above we derive the following relations:

$$\begin{aligned} A &= S_8 + S_9 \\ B &= S_4 + S_5 + S_6 + S_7 \\ C &= S_2 + S_3 + S_6 + S_7 \\ D &= S_1 + S_3 + S_5 + S_7 + S_9 \end{aligned} \qquad (11.1)$$

where A is the most significant bit and D is the least significant bit. We can implement the decimal-to-BCD encoder with either the circuit of Figure 11.10 or the circuit of Figure 11.11. The latter is more practical since five-input OR gates are not standard IC devices. In both circuits the input S_0 is terminated inside the circuit since it does not appear in the relations of (11.1).

The problem statement instructs us to design a logic circuit whose inputs are the decimal numbers 0 through 9 denoted as switches S_0 through S_9, and the output is the BCD code, that is, the logic circuit has ten input lines and four output lines as shown in Figures 11.10 and 11.11. Obviously, only one of the ten switches S_0 through S_9 will be closed (will be logical 1) at any time and thus the truth table is as presented.

The Code Reuse Subsystem Block

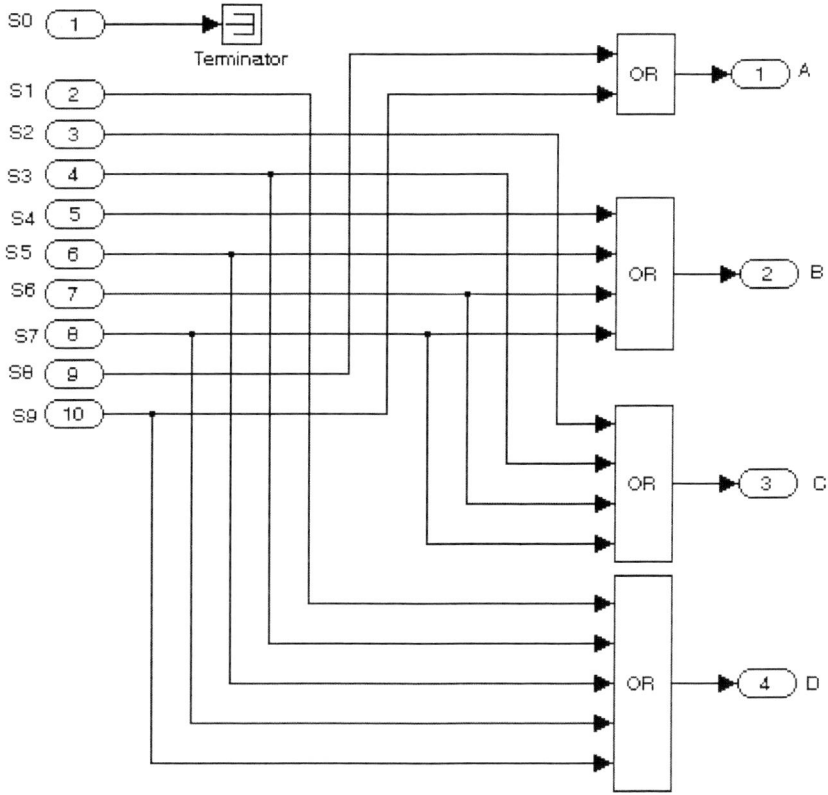

Figure 11.10. Decimal–to–BCD encoder circuit with non–standard OR gates

We save the model in Figure 11.10 as **Figure_11_10**, and we save the model in Figure 11.11 as **Figure_11_11**. Next, we open a new model and we name it **Figure_11_12**. From the Ports & Subsystems library we drag a Code Reuse Subsystem block into model **Figure_11_12** and we label it **Code Reuse Subsystem 1**. We double–click on the Code Reuse Subsystem 1 block and in the Figure_11_12/Code Reuse Subsystem 1 window we drag the model of **Figure_11_10**, and we save it. Now, we double–click on the Code Reuse Subsystem 1 block in the model **Figure_11_12** and the encoder circuit of Figure 11.10 appears.

Chapter 11 The Ports & Subsystems Library

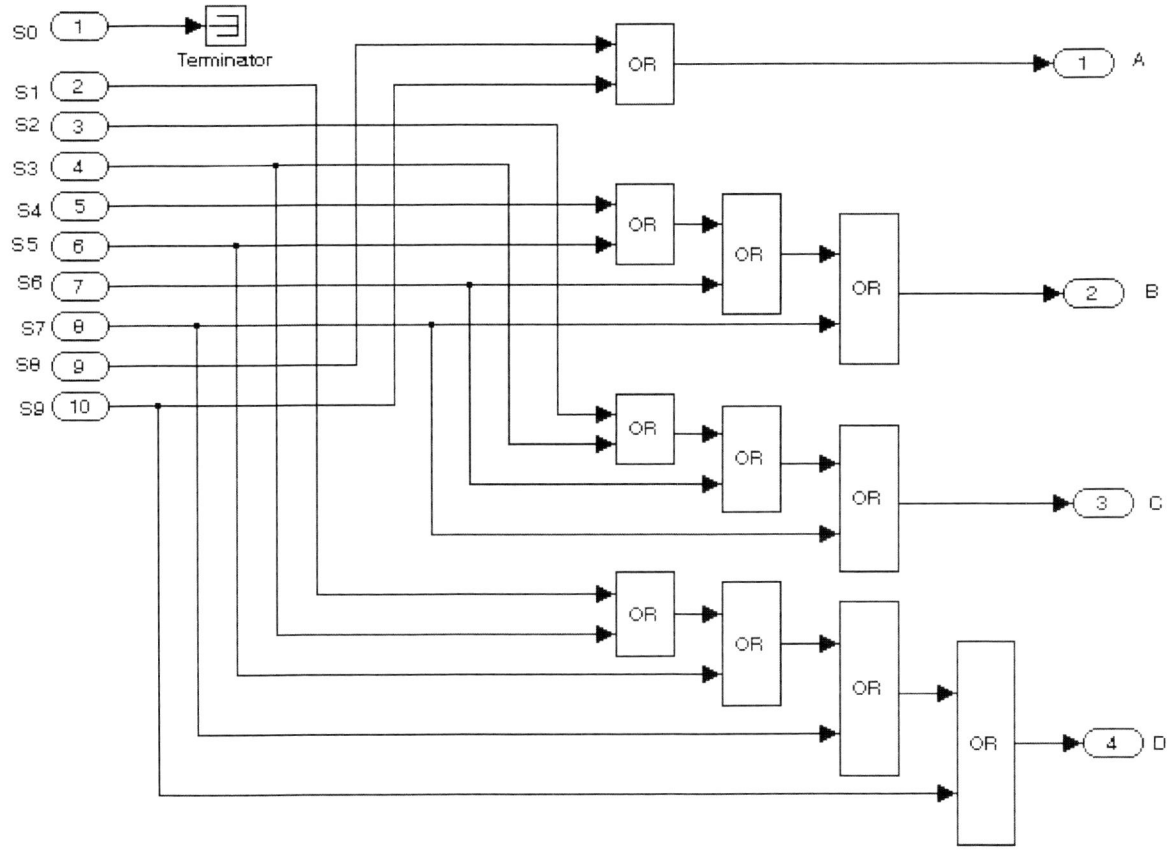

Figure 11.11. Decimal–to–BCD encoder with standard 2–input OR gates

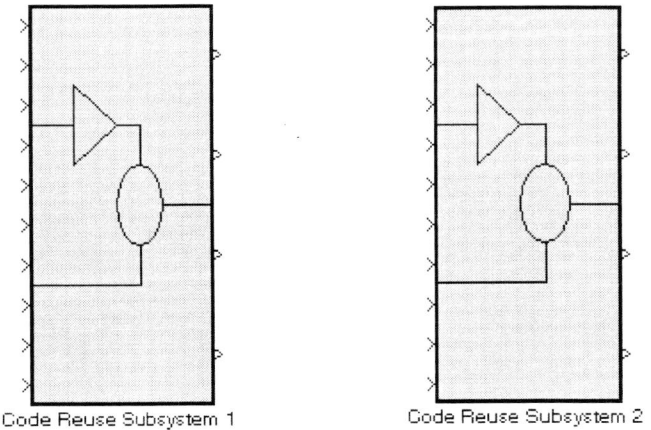

Figure 11.12. Models of Figures 11.10 and 11.11 shown as subsystems

The Code Reuse Subsystem Block

We repeat these steps for model **Figure_11_11** shown in Figure 11.11 and we label it **Code Reuse Subsystem 2** as shown in Figure 11.12.

We can verify that the outputs of both subsystems in Figure 11.12 are as specified in the given truth table. With the inputs and outputs labeled as shown in Figure 11.13, we can verify the BCD codes 0000 0001 0010 ... 1001 by entering the values of $S_1, S_2, ..., S_9$ in MATLAB's Command Window. The MATLAB script below displays the BCD value 1001 which is equivalent to decimal number 9.

S0=0; S1=0; S2=0; S3=0; S4=0; S5=0; S6=0; S7=0; S8=0; S9=0;
S0=0; S1=0; S2=1; S3=0; S4=0; S5=0; S6=0; S7=0; S8=0; S9=0;
S0=0; S1=0; S2=0; S3=1; S4=0; S5=0; S6=0; S7=0; S8=0; S9=0;
S0=0; S1=0; S2=0; S3=0; S4=0; S5=0; S6=0; S7=0; S8=0; S9=1;

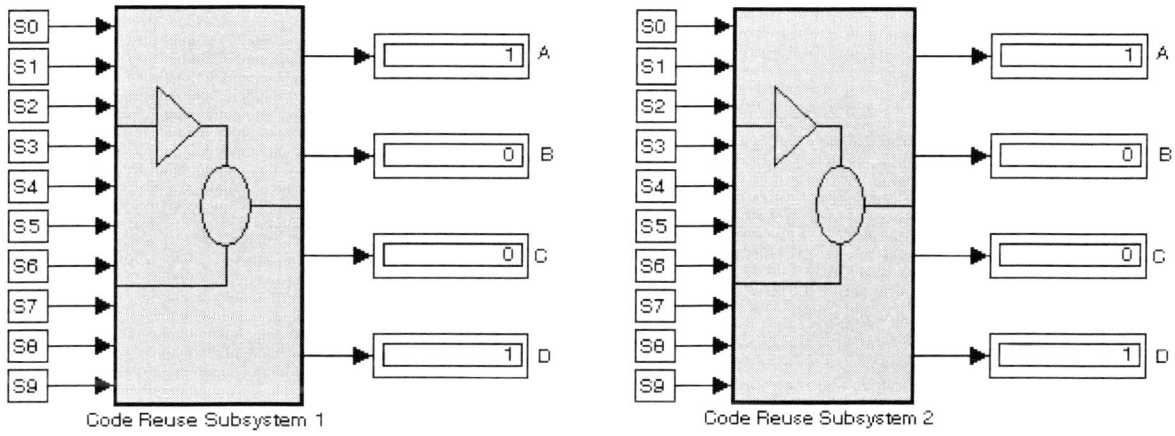

Figure 11.13. Subsystems for truth table verification of Table 11.2, Example 11.3

Example 11.4

In this example, we will add an Enable block to Code Reuse Subsystem 1 of Figure 11.13 which now is shown in Figure 11.14. We will use a Pulse Generator block to generate the enable control signal.

Chapter 11 The Ports & Subsystems Library

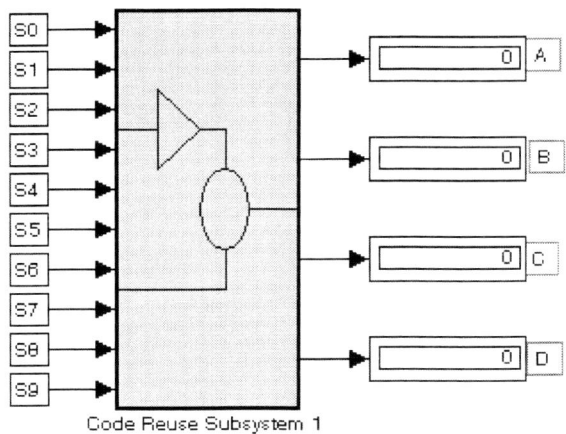

Figure 11.14. Subsystem for Example 11.4

We cannot drag the Enable block into the subsystem model of Figure 11.14; we must double-click it, and when its subsystem appears, from the Ports & Subsystems library we drag the Enable block which now appears as shown in Figure 11.15. We save it as **Figure_11_15**.

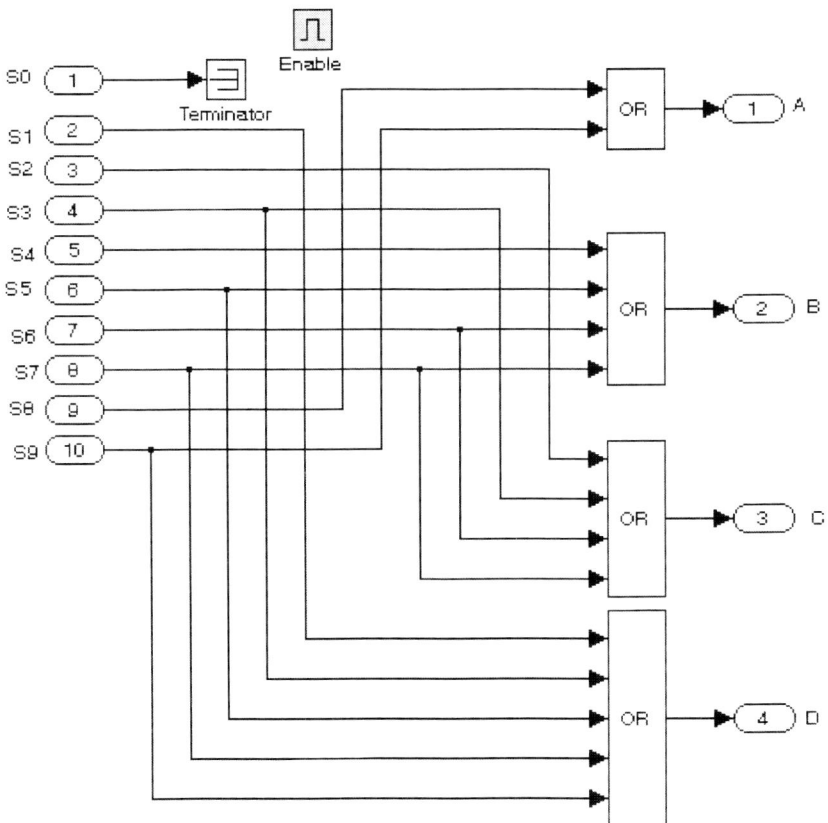

Figure 11.15. Model for Example 11.4 with Enable block

The Code Reuse Subsystem Block

The subsystem of Figure 11.14 now appears as shown in Figure 11.16 with another input on top of it for the Enable control signal. To this input we connect a Pulse Generator block as shown in Figure 11.17.

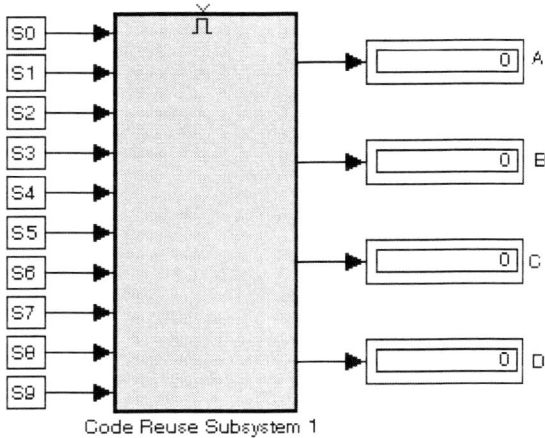

Figure 11.16. The Code Reuse Subsystem 1 block with the Enable input on top

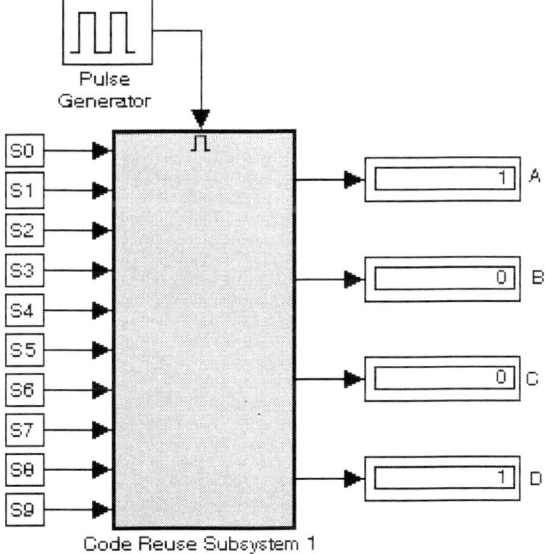

Figure 11.17. The Code Reuse Subsystem 1 block with Pulse Generator block connected to Enable port

When the Simulation command is executed, the outputs are $A = 1$, $B = 0$, $C = 0$, and $D = 1$ since the last entry into MATLAB's Command Window was as follows:

S0=0; S1=0; S2=0; S3=0; S4=0; S5=0; S6=0; S7=0; S8=0; S9=1;

Chapter 11 The Ports & Subsystems Library

Next, we remove the Pulse Generator block from the model of Figure 11.17 and reissue the Simulate command. We observe that all four outputs are now zero as shown in Figure 11.18 even though in MATLAB's Command Window we have entered

S0=0; S1=0; S2=0; S3=0; S4=0; S5=0; S6=0; S7=0; S8=0; S9=1;

This occurred because the Enable Control Signal provided by the Pulse Generator block has been removed.

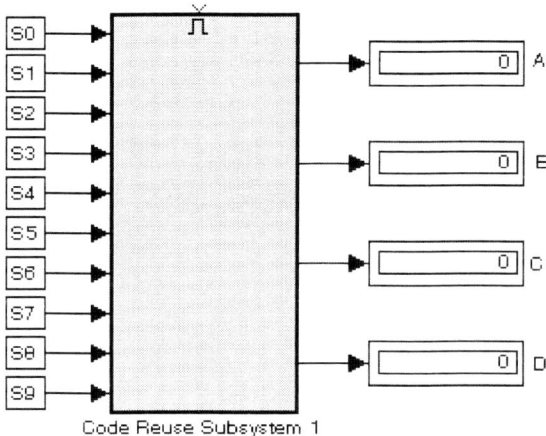

Figure 11.18. Outputs when the Pulse Generator block is removed from the subsystem of Figure 11.17

As stated earlier, we can output the enabling signal by selecting the **Show** output port check box. When we choose this option we allow the subsystem to display the status the Enable signal. The subsystem then appears as shown in Figure 11.19 assuming that the Pulse Generator block is connected as shown in Figure 11.17.

The Model Block

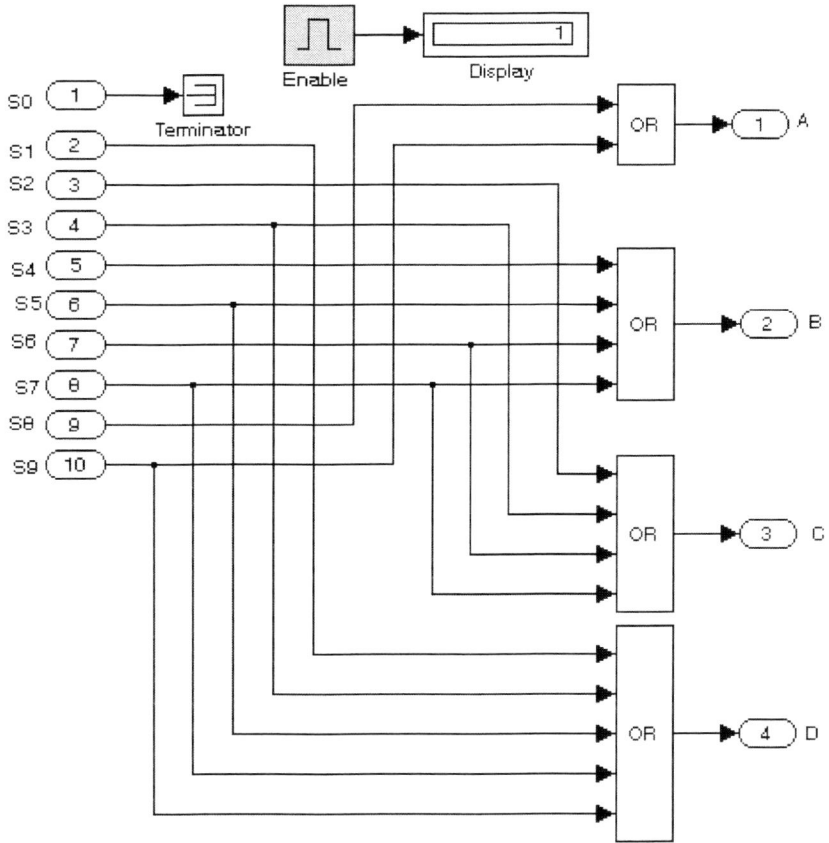

Figure 11.19. The Enable block with the Show output selected

11.7 The Model Block

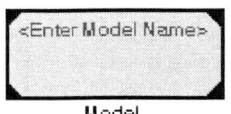

The **Model** block is used to specify the name of a Simulink model. The name must be a valid MATLAB identifier. The model must exist on the MATLAB path and the MATLAB path must contain no other model having the same name. To add the name of a saved model on the MATLAB path, we open the Command Window, we choose **Set Path** from the **File** menu, we click on the **Add Folder field**, we select the path to be added from the **Browse for Folder**, and we click on OK.

Chapter 11 The Ports & Subsystems Library

Example 11.5

We will use the Model block to specify the model **Figure_11_11** which we saved by this name in Example 11.3, Page 11-11.

We open a new model and we drag a Model block into it. The Model block appears as shown in Figure 11.20.

Figure 11.20. The first appearance of a Model block in a new model

We double click on the Model block and in the Parameters dialog box we enter the saved model name without the < and the > symbols and without the .mdl extension. The Model block now appears as shown in Figure 11.21.

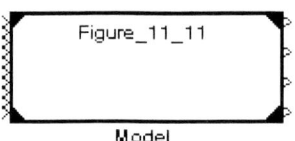

Figure 11.21. The appearance of a Model block with a saved model name

Next, we double-click on the Model block in Figure 11.21 and the model **Figure_11_11** appears as shown in Figure 11.22. This is the same model as that shown in Figure 11.11.

The Configurable Subsystem Block

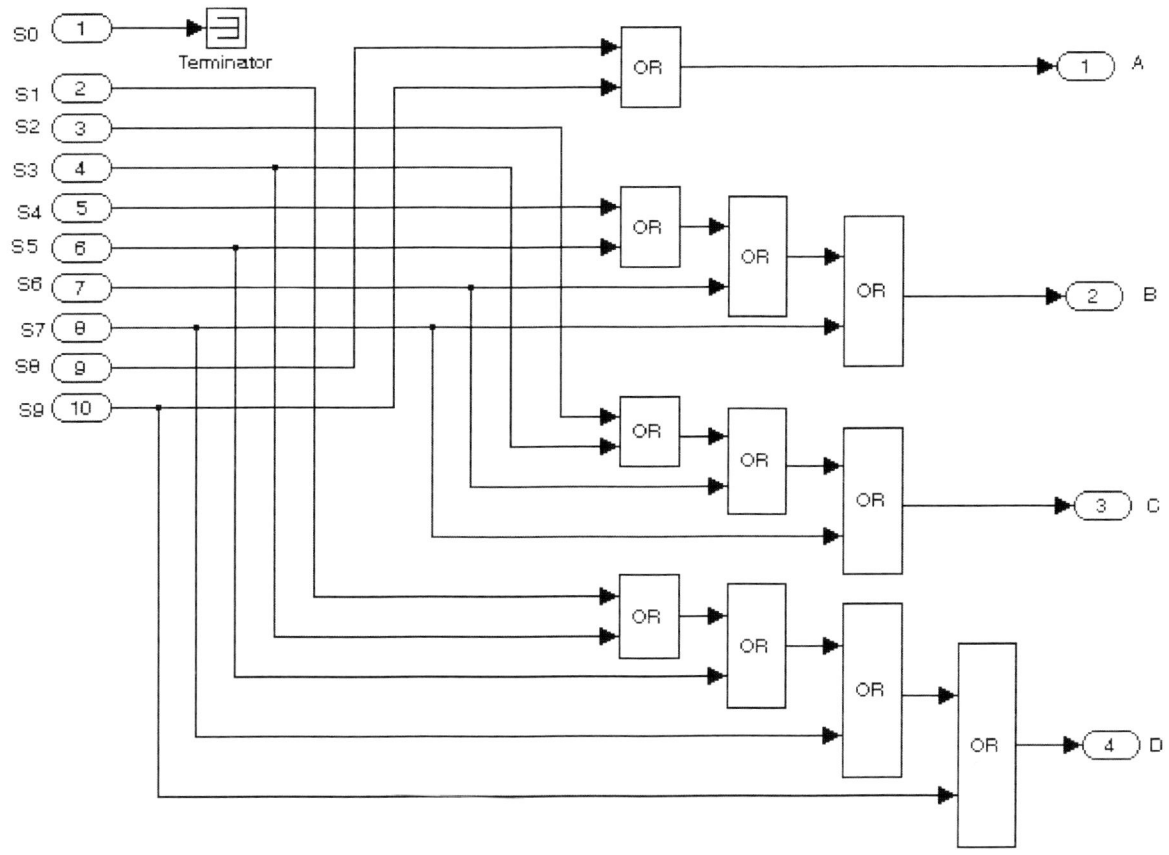

Figure 11.22. Model displayed by the Model block in Figure 11.21

11.8 The Configurable Subsystem Block

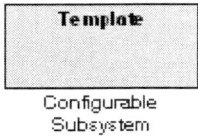

The **Configurable Subsystem** block[*] represents one of a set of blocks contained in a specified library of blocks. The block's context menu lets us choose which block the configurable subsystem represents. A configurable Subsystem block simplifies the creation of models that represent families of designs.

---

[*] We cannot insert this block to a new model window. This block must be placed in a library to be used. We create a new library by choosing **New Library** from the **File** menu.

Chapter 11 The Ports & Subsystems Library

For example, suppose that we want to model a full adder[*] digital circuit that offers a choice of logic gates, e.g., NAND, NOR, AND, OR and NOT, or by the combination of two half–adders. To model such a design, we must first create a library of models of the logic gates available. We would then use a Configurable Subsystem block in our model to represent the choice of the logic. To model a particular variant of the basic design, a user need only choose the logic gate type, using the configurable block's dialog box.

To create a configurable subsystem in a model, we must first create a library containing a master configurable subsystem and the blocks that it represents. We can then create configurable instances of the master subsystem by dragging copies of the master subsystem from the library and dropping them into models. We can add any type of block to a master configurable subsystem library. Simulink derives the port names for the configurable subsystem by making a unique list from the port names of all the choices. Simulink uses default port names for non–subsystem block choices.

Example 11.6

We will create a new library with two binary full–adder circuits. The first will be designed with a combination of AND, OR, and NOT gates as shown in Figure 11.23, and the second will be formed by cascading two half–adders as shown in Figure 11.24. We will create a subsystem for each, and these subsystems will constitute the blocks of the new library where Subsystem 1 will represent the full–adder of Figure 11.23, and Subsystem 2 will represent the full adder of Figure 11.24. Then, we will create a model for a four-bit binary adder by cascading four one–bit full adder blocks of the Subsystem 1.

In both models of Figures 11.23 and 11.24 the first output represents the Sum bit and the second output represents the Carry bit. It is not necessary to assign Outport blocks but it is necessary to assign Inport blocks as shown, otherwise the inputs would be shown as unconnected lines. Next, we create subsystems for each by enclosing all blocks except the Inport blocks, and we choose Create Subsystem from the Edit menu. The created subsystems are as shown on the left side of Figures 11.25 and 11.26. The Inport blocks are no longer required and are deleted. The subsystem blocks are thus simplified as shown on the right side of Figures 11.25 and 11.26.

We will now create a new library. This is done by clicking on File>New>Library, and we name it **Library_Example_11_6**. From the subsystem model of Figure 11.25 we drag the Subsystem 1A block into this new library. We also drag the Subsystem 2A block from the model of Figure 11.26 into this library. Our library now looks as shown in Figure 11.27 where Subsystem 1A block represents the full-adder implemented with AND, OR, and NOT gates, and Subsystem 2A block represents the full-adder implemented with two half-adders.

---

[*] *For a detailed discussion and design of a full adder digital circuit please refer to Digital Circuit Analysis and Design with an Introduction to CPLDs and FPGAs, ISBN 0-9744239-6-3.*

The Configurable Subsystem Block

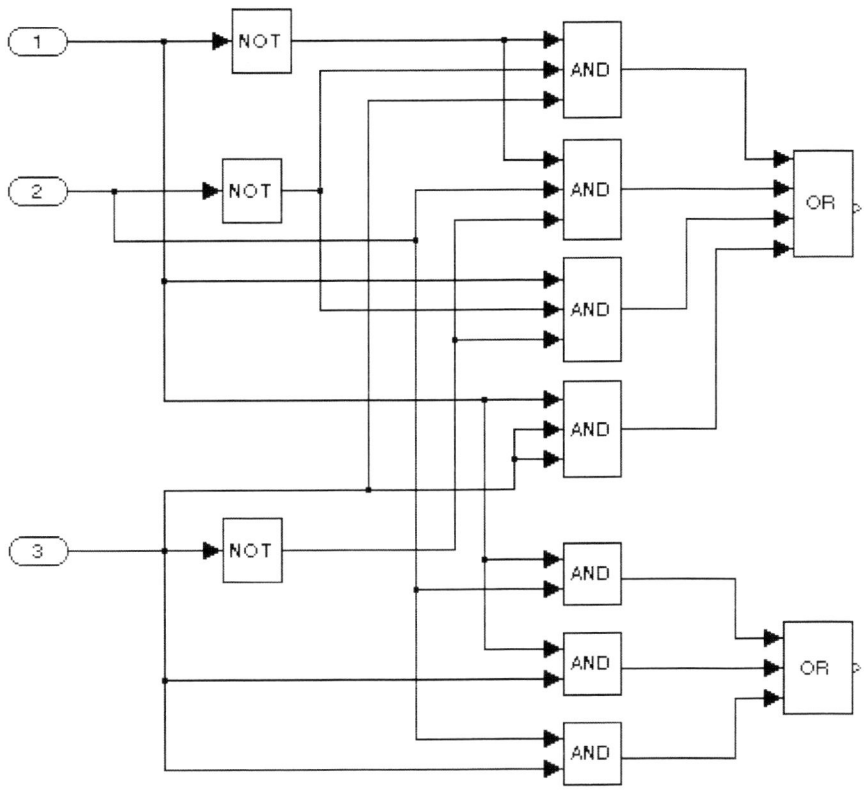

Figure 11.23. Full–Adder circuit for Subsystem 1

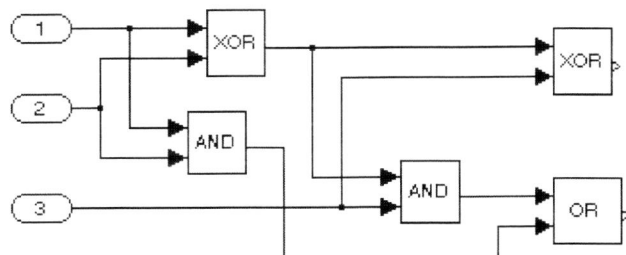

Figure 11.24. Full–Adder circuit for Subsystem 2

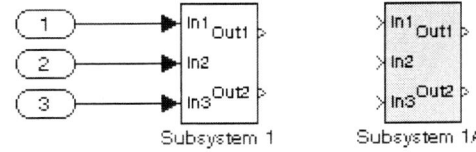

Figure 11.25. The model of Figure 11.23 shown as a subsystem

Chapter 11 The Ports & Subsystems Library

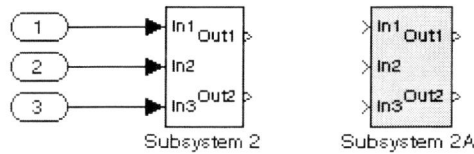

Figure 11.26. The model of Figure 11.24 shown as a subsystem

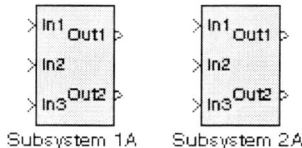

Figure 11.27. Library with Subsystems 1A and 2A blocks

We save the library, and then we drag a Configurable Subsystem block in the library. The library now looks as shown in Figure 11.28.

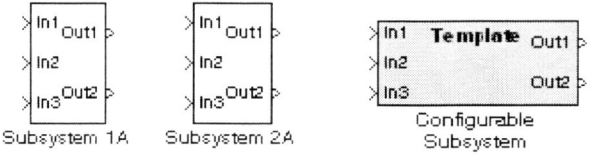

Figure 11.28. The library with the addition of the Configurable Subsystem

We double click on Configurable Subsystem block and in the Configuration dialog box we place check marks in the Member squares as shown in Figure 11.29. The Port names panel shows the inputs indicated as Inports. To see the outputs, we click on the Outports tab.

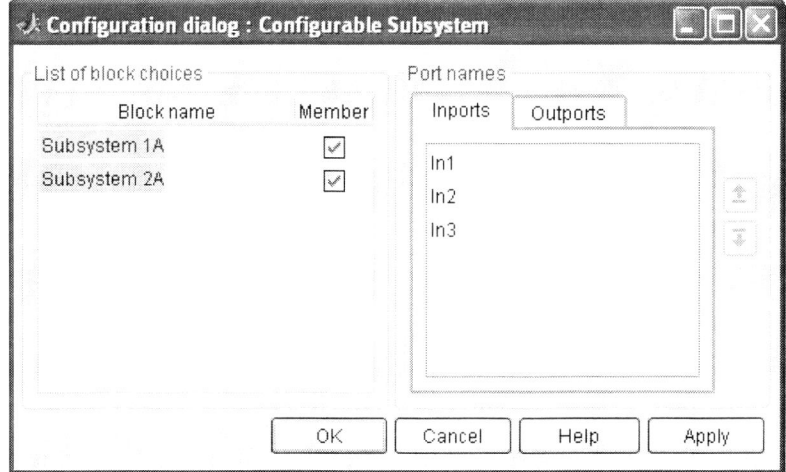

Figure 11.29. The Configuration dialog for the library of Example 11.6

The Configurable Subsystem Block

We can now select either Subsystem 1A or Subsystem 2A from the Configuration dialog to implement the 4–bit Adder by cascading four one–bit adders. For this example we choose Subsystem 1A. This is done by unselecting Subsystem 2A on the Configuration dialog box of Figure 11.29.

We create a new model by dragging the Configurable Subsystem block from this library into this model, copy and paste this block three times, and we interconnect these as shown in Figure 11.30.

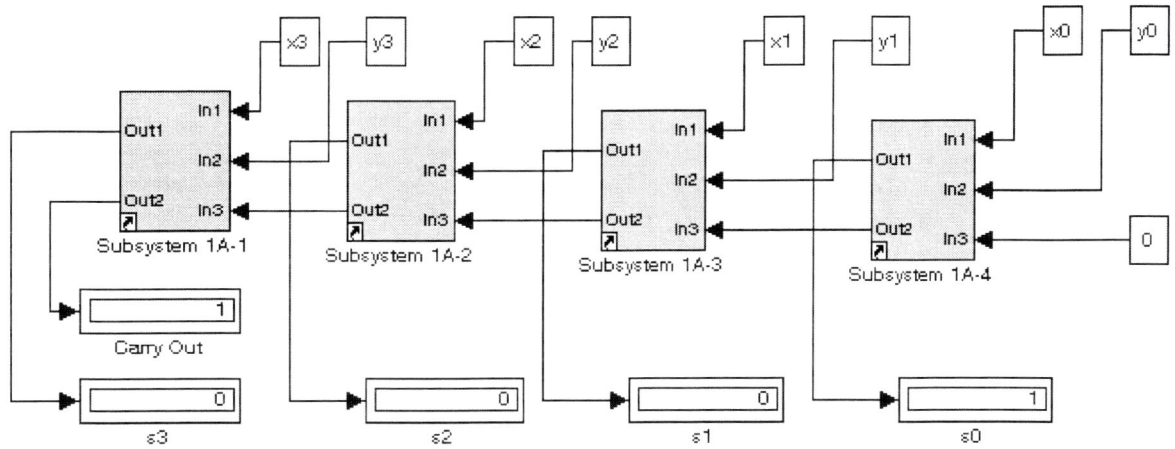

Figure 11.30. Four-bit binary adder for Example 11.6 with Subsystem 1A blocks

In the model of Figure 11.30, the carry bit of the right–most one–bit adder is set to zero since there is no previous one–bit adder. We observe that Simulink displays small arrows on the bottom left corner of each of the subsystem blocks. A small arrow indicates that each subsystem block represents a library link in the model, and it is only visible if the **Link Library Display** option of the **Format** menu is selected **All**.

To verify that the 4–bit adder of Figure 11.30 operates properly, let us perform the binary addition

$$\begin{array}{r} 1011 \\ + \; 0110 \\ \hline 10001 \end{array}$$

In MATLAB's Command Window we enter

x0=1; y0=0; x1=1; y1=1; x2=0; y2=1; x3=1; y3=0;

and the addition is verified where the most significant bit of the sum is displayed as Carry Out.

Should we, later decide to replace the Subsystem 1A blocks with Subsystem 2A blocks, we return to our library, we click on the Configurable Subsystem block, on the Configuration dialog of Figure 11.29 we unselect Subsystem 1A block and we select the Subsystem 2A block. We copy this block into our model of Figure 11.30 and we replace the Subsystem 1A blocks with Subsystem 2A blocks. The new model is now as shown in Figure 11.31.

Chapter 11 The Ports & Subsystems Library

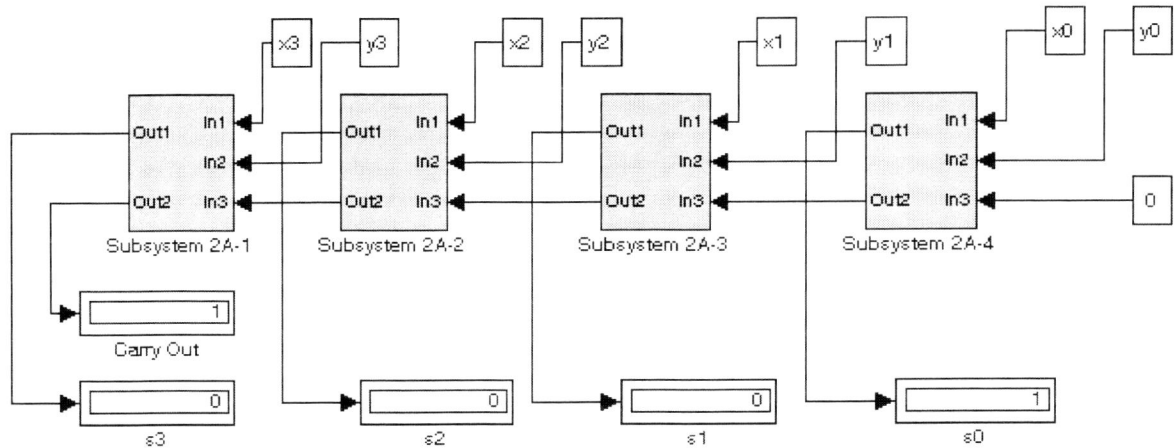

Figure 11.31. Four-bit binary adder for Example 11.1 with Subsystem 2 blocks

Using the Subsystem 1 or Subsystem 2 blocks in Figure 11.30 or Figure 11.31 we can create another library with subsystems representing a 4-bit adder block as shown in Figure 11.32. Of course, we can next combine four 4–bit adder blocks to form a 16–bit adder subsystems, and so on.

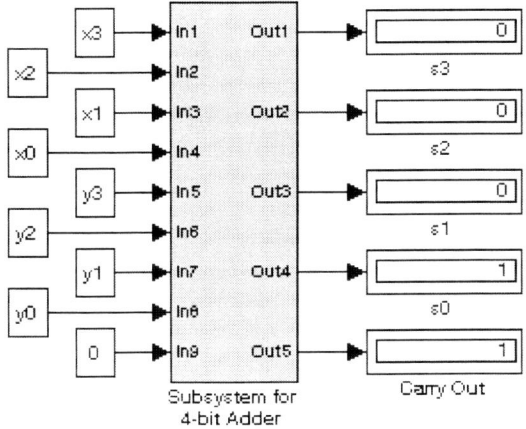

Figure 11.32. A 4–bit Adder Subsystem

For more details on Creating a Master Configurable Subsystem please refer to the Help menu for the Configurable Subsystem block.

11.9 The Triggered Subsystem Block

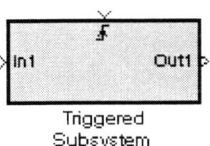

A **Triggered Subsystem** block is used to represent a subsystem whose execution is triggered by an external input.

Example 11.7

Let us reconsider the Atomic Subsystem block of Figure 11.8, Example 11.2, Section 11.5, this chapter, Page 11–9, repeated below as Figure 11.33, and add a Trigger block to it. We will use a Pulse Generator block to generate the trigger control signal. The Display block indicates the value 1, provided that in MATLAB's Command Window we have enter the following script:

A=1; C0=1; C1=1;
B=1; C0=0; C1=1;
C=1; C0=1; C1=0;
D=1; C0=0; C1=0;

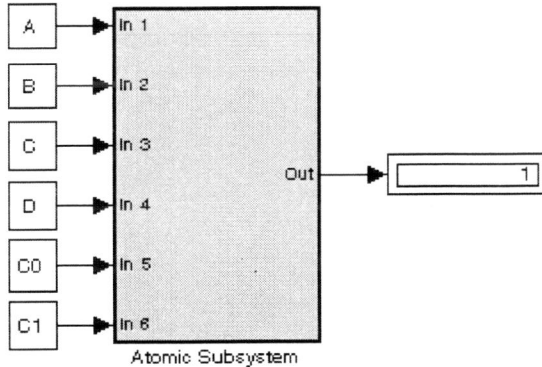

Figure 11.33. The Atomic Subsystem block for a four–line–to–one–line digital multiplexer

We cannot drag the Trigger block into the subsystem model of Figure 11.33; we must double click it, and when its subsystem appears, from the Ports & Subsystems library we drag the Trigger block which now appears as shown in Figure 11.34. We save it as **Figure_11_34**.

Chapter 11 The Ports & Subsystems Library

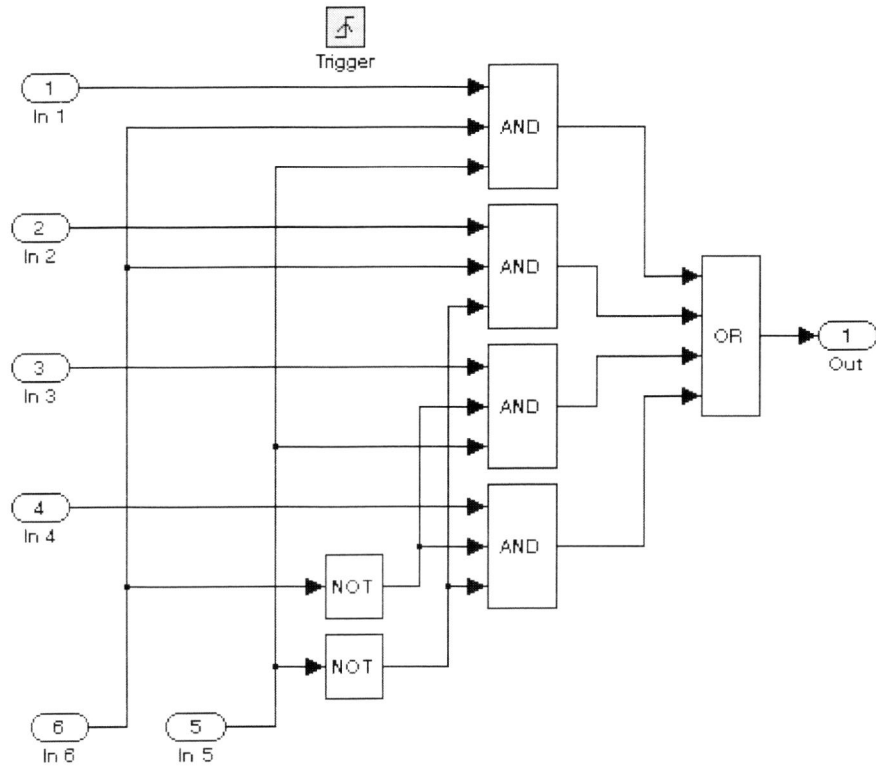

Figure 11.34. Model for Example 11.7 with Trigger block

The subsystem of Figure 11.33 now appears as shown in Figure 11.35 with another input on top of it for the Trigger control signal. We observe that the Display block now indicates the value 0; this is because with the addition of the Trigger control input without a signal, the subsystem block is disabled. To this input we connect a Pulse Generator block as shown in Figure 11.36.

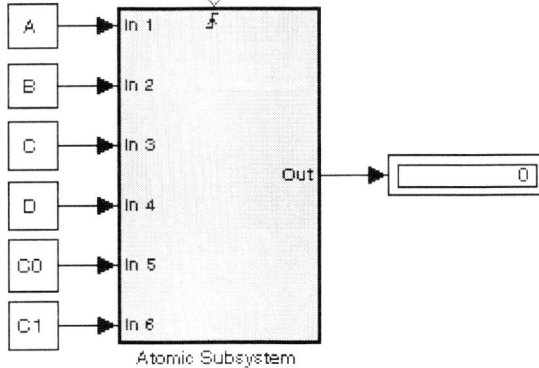

Figure 11.35. The Atomic Subsystem block with the Trigger input on top

11-26 *Introduction to Simulink with Engineering Applications*
Copyright © Orchard Publications

The Enabled Subsystem Block

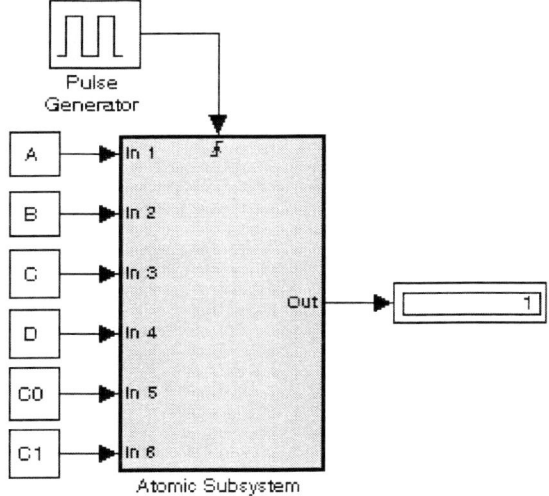

Figure 11.36. The Atomic Subsystem block with Pulse Generator connected to Trigger port

We observe that, because the subsystem is now enabled, the Display block now indicates the value 1, provided that in MATLAB's Command Window we have enter the following script:

A=1; C0=1; C1=1;
B=1; C0=0; C1=1;
C=1; C0=1; C1=0;
D=1; C0=0; C1=0;

11.10 The Enabled Subsystem Block

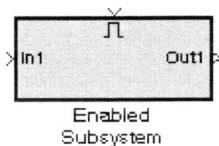

The **Enable Subsystem** block represents a subsystem whose execution is enabled by an external input which can be a scalar or a vector. If the input is a scalar, the subsystem executes if the input value is greater than zero. If the input is a vector, the subsystem executes if any of the vector elements is greater than zero. Consider the waveform of Figure 11.37 where an up arrow denotes an enable condition, and a down arrow denotes a disable condition.

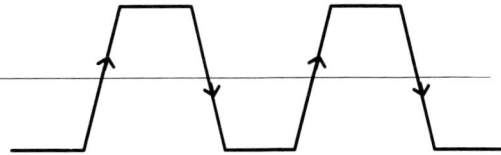

Figure 11.37. An alternating waveform that can cause alternate enable and disable conditions

Chapter 11 The Ports & Subsystems Library

Thus, when the control input signal is alternating, the subsystem will be alternately enabled and disabled. Simulink uses the zero–crossing slope method to determine whether an enable is to occur. Thus, if the signal crosses zero and the slope is positive, the subsystem is enabled, and if the slope is negative at the zero crossing, the subsystem is disabled.

We create an enabled subsystem by copying an Enable block from the Ports & Subsystems library into a subsystem. Simulink adds an enable symbol and an enable control input port to the Subsystem block, and although an enabled subsystem does not execute while it is disabled, the output signal is still available to other blocks. While an enabled subsystem is disabled, we can choose to hold the subsystem outputs at their previous values or reset them to their initial conditions. We choose **held** to cause the output to maintain its most recent value and we choose **reset** to cause the output to revert to its initial condition.

Example 11.8

The model of Figure 11.38 is the same as that of Figure 2.28, Example 2.14, Section 2.14, Chapter 2, Page 2–24. We will create a subsystem using an Enabled Subsystem block by grouping all blocks except the Step and the Scope blocks, then we add an appropriate Enable control input to the created subsystem block.

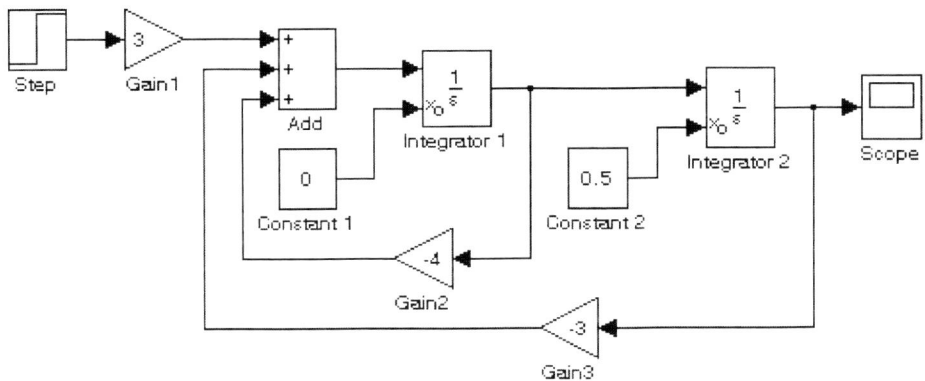

Figure 11.38. Model for Example 11.8

We open a new model, and from the Ports & Subsystems library we drag the Enabled Subsystem shown in Figure 11.39.

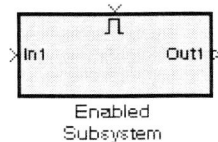

Figure 11.39. The Enable and Triggered Subsystem for replacing the model of Figure 11.38

The Enabled Subsystem Block

We double-click on the Enabled Subsystem block of Figure 11.39, we drag the entire model of Figure 11.38 into the Enable Subsystem window, we replace the Step and Scope blocks with the In and Out ports, for the Enable block we select the Show output port check box, and we connect its output to a Display block as shown in Figure 11.40.

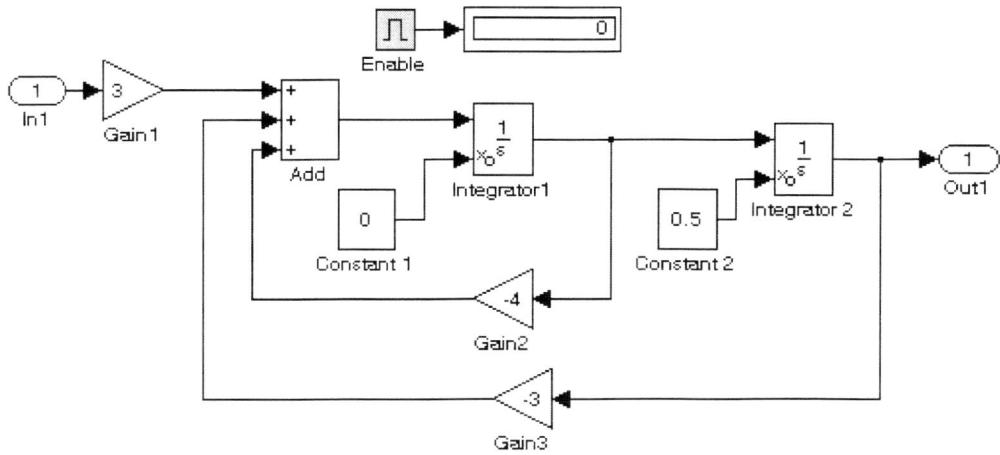

Figure 11.40. Contents of the Enable Subsystem block for the Subsystem of Figure 11.39

We return to the Enabled and Triggered Subsystem of Figure 11.39, we drag the Pulse Generator and Step blocks from the Sources library, and we connect them to the Enable and Triggered inputs of the subsystem. We also add a Bus Creator block and a Scope block by dragging them from the Commonly Used Blocks Library. The model now is as shown in Figure 11.41.

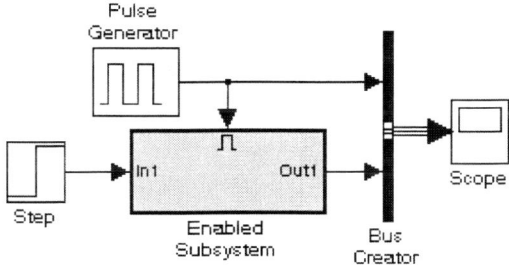

Figure 11.41. The model of Figure 11.40 replaced with an Enabled Subsystem block

After execution of the Simulation command for the model of Figure 11.41, the Enable signal and Subsystem outputs are displayed on the Scope block as shown in Figure 11.42.

Chapter 11 The Ports & Subsystems Library

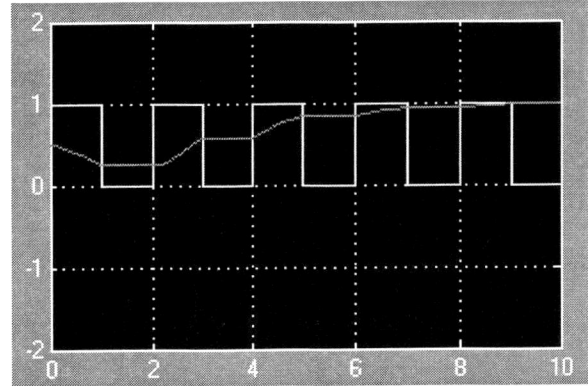

Figure 11.42. The Enable signal and Subsystem block outputs for the model of Figure 11.38

11.11 The Enabled and Triggered Subsystem Block

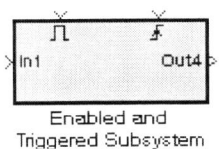

The **Enabled and Triggered Subsystem** block is a combination of the enabled subsystem and the triggered subsystem. When the trigger occurs, Simulink checks the enable input port to evaluate the enable control signal. If its value is greater than zero, Simulink executes the subsystem. If both inputs are vectors, the subsystem executes if at least one element of each vector is nonzero. The subsystem executes once at the time step at which the trigger event occurs. We create a triggered and enabled subsystem by dragging both the Enable and Trigger blocks from the Ports & Subsystems library into an existing subsystem. Simulink adds enable and trigger symbols and enable and trigger and enable control inputs to the Subsystem block.

Example 11.9

Figure 11.43 is a model for the second–order, discrete–time transfer function

$$H(z) = \frac{0.5(1+0.25z^{-2})}{1+0.1z^{-1}-0.75z^{-2}} \qquad (11.2)$$

We will create a subsystem using an Enabled and Triggered Subsystem block by grouping all blocks except the Pulse Generator and the Scope blocks, and we will add appropriate Enable and Trigger control inputs to the created subsystem block. The delay blocks 1/Z are specified for Sample time −1 (Inherited).

The Enabled and Triggered Subsystem Block

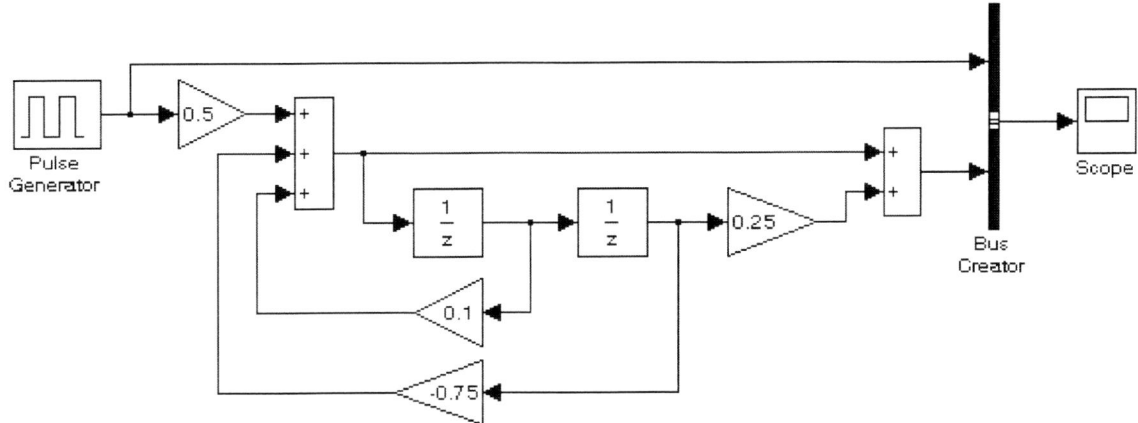

Figure 11.43. Model for Example 11.9

We open a new model, and from the Ports & Subsystems library we drag the Enabled and Triggered Subsystem shown in Figure 11.26.

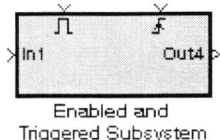

Figure 11.44. The Enable and Triggered Subsystem for replacing the model of Figure 11.43

We double-click on the Enabled and Triggered block of Figure 11.44, we drag the entire model of Figure 11.43 into the Enable and Triggered Subsystem window, we replace the Pulse Generator and Scope blocks with the In and Out ports, for the Trigger and Enable blocks we select the Show output port check box, and we connect their outputs to Display blocks as shown in Figure 11.45.

We return to the Enabled and Triggered Subsystem of Figure 11.44, we drag the Pulse Generator and Step blocks from the Sources library and we connect them to the Enable and Triggered inputs of the subsystem. We also connect a Sine Wave block to its input and a Scope block to its output as shown in Figure 11.46 where the Sine Wave block is specified for Sample time 0.2.

Chapter 11 The Ports & Subsystems Library

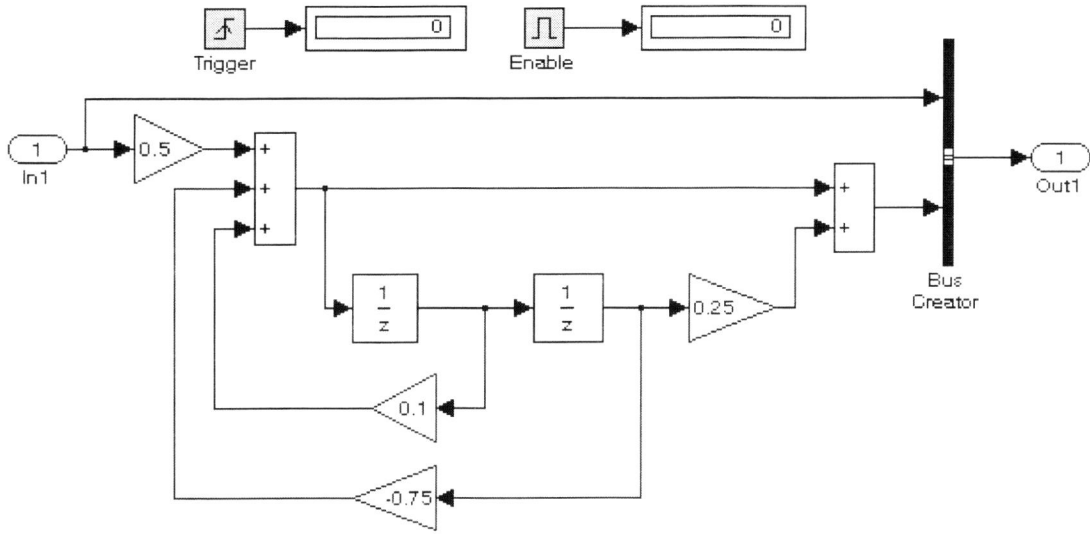

Figure 11.45. Contents for the Enable and Triggered Subsystem block for the Subsystem of Figure 11.44

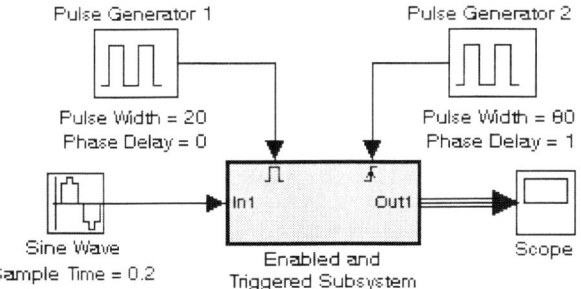

Figure 11.46. The model of Figure 11.43 replaced with an Enabled and Triggered Subsystem block

After execution of the Simulation command for the model of Figure 11.46, the Enable and Triggered Subsystem block output is as shown in Figure 11.47.

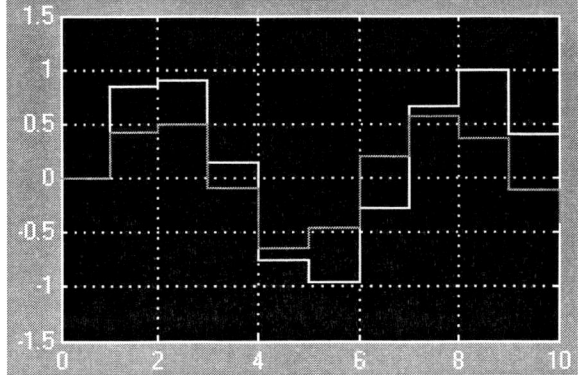

Figure 11.47. Output waveforms for the Enabled and Triggered Subsystem of Figure 11.46

The Enabled and Triggered Subsystem Block

We also observe that the outputs of Trigger and Enable blocks in Figure 11.45 are now as shown in Figure 11.48 indicating that the trigger and enable commands were issued.

Figure 11.48. The outputs of the Trigger and Enable blocks after the Simulation command is issued

The model in Figure 11.49 is the model of Figure 11.46 with execution context to which a block belongs and *execution context indicators*.* The **execution context** is the sorted order index for each block and it is shown in the upper right corner of each block. It is shown as **s:b** where is **s** denotes the subsystem and **b** denotes the block's sorted order. Thus, the execution context 0:0 shown inside the Sine Wave block indicates that this block is the first block[†] in the subsystem's execution context, and the Pulse Generator 1 block is the next. The execution context 0:2 is not shown; that would be the Enable input in the Subsystem block. The execution context 0:4 is not shown either; that would be the Trigger input in the Subsystem block. In the execution context 0:5{1} 0 indicates that the Enabled and Triggered Subsystem block resides in the model's root system, 5 indicates that the subsystem is the fifth block on the root subsystem's sorted list, and {1} indicates that the index of the enabled subsystem is 1.

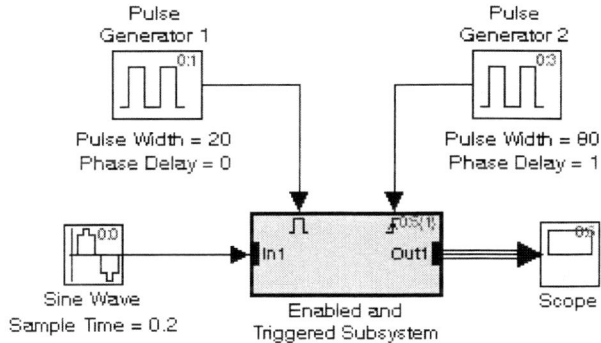

Figure 11.49. The model of Figure 11.46 with Execution Context and context indicators

The Enabled and Triggered Subsystem block in Figure 11.49 also shows two vertical bars at the input and output ports referred to as *execution context bars*.[‡] These bars indicate that at these ports execution contexts will not be propagated.

---

* To see the context indicators, we invoke Format>Block Displays>Sorted order
† We must remember that the default indexing in Simulink is the zero–based indexing.
‡ To see the execution context bars, we invoke Format>Block Displays>Execution Context Indicator

11.12 The Function–Call Subsystem Block

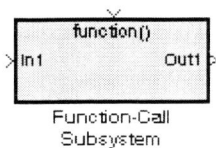

The **Function–Call Subsystem** block is used to represent a subsystem that can be invoked as a function by another block. With a Function–Call Subsystem block we can create a triggered subsystem whose execution is determined by logic internal to an S–function instead of by the value of a signal. A subsystem so configured is called a Function–Call subsystem.

To implement a Function–Call Subsystem we can use a Trigger block – as in Example 11.7, Section 11.9, Page 11-26 – in which we select **function–call** as the Trigger type parameter. Another method is to connect an S–Function block output directly to the trigger port. A third method is to use an S–Function using the **ssEnableSystemWithTid** and **ssDisableSystemWithTid** to enable or disable the triggered subsystem, and the **ssCallSystemWithTid** macro to call the triggered subsystem. These are discussed in the Simulink documentation.

All blocks in a triggered subsystem must have either inherited (–1) or constant (inf) sample time. This is to indicate that the blocks in the triggered subsystem run only when the triggered subsystem is triggered. A triggered subsystem cannot contain continuous blocks, such as an Integrator block.

Function–Call subsystems implement callable functions using Simulink blocks. They are executed by a **function–call initiator**. S–Functions, Function–Call generators, and Stateflow charts, the latter being the most common, are all function–call initiators.

Example 11.10

The model shown in Figure 11.50 is the same as in Example 11.9. The delay blocks 1/Z are specified for Sample time –1 (Inherited). We will create a subsystem using a Function–Call Subsystem block by grouping all blocks in Figure 11.50 except the Pulse Generator and the Scope blocks. We will add a Trigger control input to the created subsystem block.

We open a new model, and from the Ports & Subsystems library we drag the Function–Call Subsystem shown in Figure 11.51.

We double–click on the block of Figure 11.51, we drag the entire model of Figure 11.50 into the Function–Call Subsystem window, we replace the Pulse Generator and Scope blocks with the In and Out ports, for the Trigger block we select the Show output port check box, and we connect their outputs to Display blocks as shown in Figure 11.52.

The Function–Call Subsystem Block

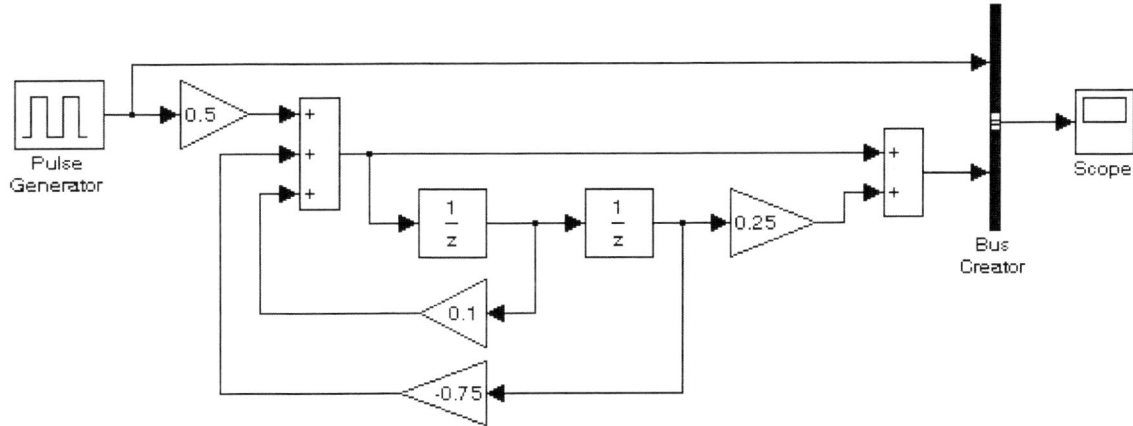

Figure 11.50. Model for Example 11.10

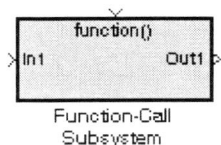

Figure 11.51. The Function–Call Subsystem for replacing the model of Figure 11.50

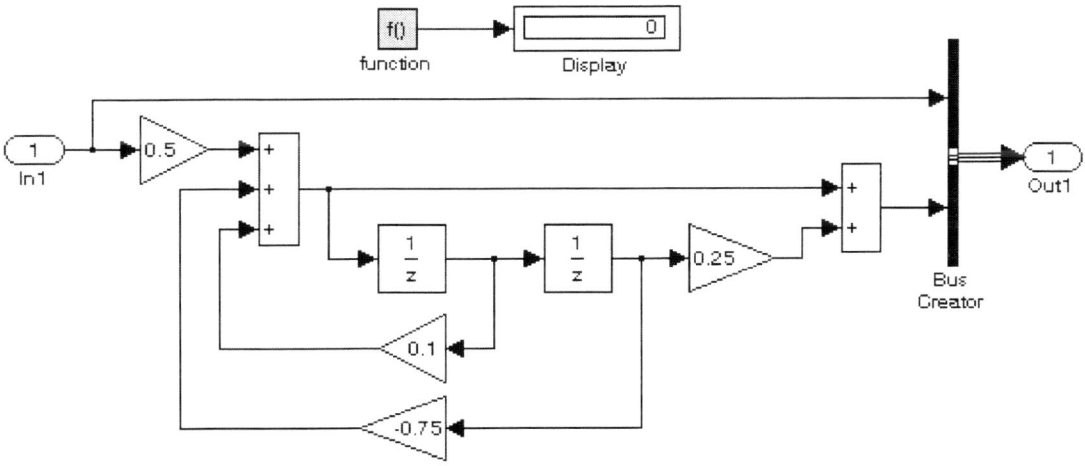

Figure 11.52. Contents for the Function–Call Subsystem block for the Subsystem of Figure 11.51

We return to the Function–Call Subsystem of Figure 11.51, to the Function input on top of the block we connect A Function–Call Generator block, to the In1 input we connect a Rate Transition[*] block, to the Out1 output we connect another Rate Transition block, and we add the In1 and Out1 ports, and the new model is now as shown in Figure 11.53.

---

[*] *The Rate Transition block is described in Subsection 12.1.8, Chapter 12, Page 12-8*

Introduction to Simulink with Engineering Applications
Copyright © Orchard Publications

Chapter 11 The Ports & Subsystems Library

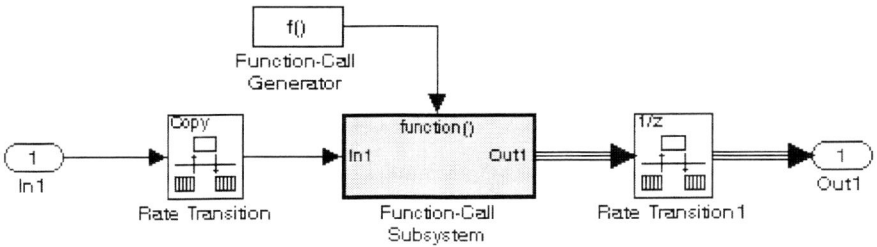

Figure 11.53. The model of Figure 11.50 replaced with a Function-Call Subsystem block

The model of Figure 11.53 does not illustrate the full power of a Function–Call Subsystem. Function–Call Subsystems are not executed directly by Simulink; the S–function determines when to execute the subsystem. When the subsystem completes execution, control returns to the S–function. For a detailed description for this block, and an illustration of the interaction between a Function–Call Subsystem and an S–function, please refer to Simulink's Help menu.

Function–Call subsystems are a powerful modeling construct. We can configure Stateflow® blocks to execute function-call subsystems, thereby extending the capabilities of the blocks. For more information on their use in Stateflow, please refer to the Stateflow documentation.

11.13 The For Iterator Subsystem Block

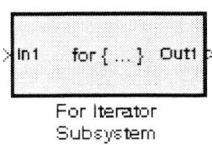

The **For Iterator Subsystem** block is a subsystem that executes repeatedly during a simulation time step until an iteration variable exceeds a specified iteration limit. We can use this block the same way as a **for** loop in MATLAB.

Example 11.11

The components of the For Iterator Subsystem in Figure 11.54 are shown in Figure 11.55 and this subsystem was created following the steps of Examples 11.2 and 11.3. The Display block in Figure 11.55 shows the constant assigned to the input of the For Iterator Subsystem in Figure 11.54. The **XY Graph** block[*] appears in Simulink's Sink library and displays an X–Y plot of its inputs in a MATLAB figure window. We will assign an appropriate value to the Memory block in Figure 11.55 so that the XY Graph block will display a linear segment for the equation $y = -x + 5$.

---

[*] *The XY Graph block is described in Subsection 14–2–3, Chapter 14, Page 14–12.*

The For Iterator Subsystem Block

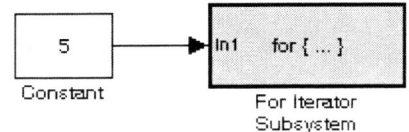

Figure 11.54. For Iterator Subsystem for Example 11.11

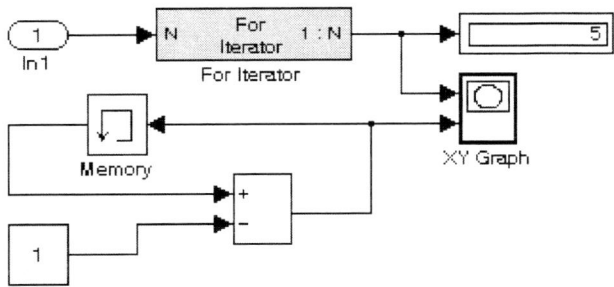

Figure 11.55. Contents of the For Iterator Subsystem block for the Subsystem of Figure 11.54

The straight line equation $y = -x + 5$ has slope $m = -1$, and y–intercept $b = 5$. Since the slope is negative, we want the y values to decrease with increasing values of x, and since the y–intercept is 5, we set the initial value in the Memory block to 5. Next, we double click on the XY Graph block, and on the Block parameters we set $x-min = 0$, $x-max = 6$, $y-min = 0$, and $y-max = 6$. After execution of the Simulation command the XY Graph block displays the straight line shown in Figure 11.56.

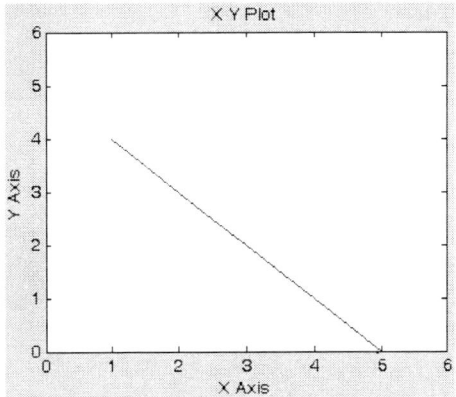

Figure 11.56. XY plot for the model of Figure 11.55

Introduction to Simulink with Engineering Applications
Copyright © Orchard Publications

Chapter 11 The Ports & Subsystems Library

11.14 The While Iterator Subsystem Block

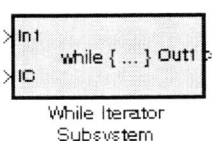

The **While Iterator Subsystem** block is a Subsystem block that is pre–configured to serve as a starting point for creating a subsystem that executes repeatedly while a condition is satisfied during a simulation time step. The While Iterator block, when placed in a subsystem, repeatedly executes the contents of the subsystem at the current time step while a specified condition is true. If a While Iterator block is placed within a subsystem, it makes it an atomic subsystem.

We can use this block to implement the block–diagram equivalent of a C program while or do-while loop. In particular, the block's While loop style parameter allows us to choose either the **do-while** mode, or the **while** mode.

In the **do-while** mode, the While Iterator block has one input, the while condition input, whose source must reside in the subsystem. At each time step, the block runs all the blocks in the subsystem once and then checks whether the while condition input is true. If the input is true, the iterator block runs the blocks in the subsystem again. This process continues as long as the while condition input is true and the number of iterations is less than or equal to the iterator block's Maximum number of iterations parameter.

In the **while** mode, the iterator block has two inputs: a while condition input and an initial condition (IC) input. The source of the initial condition signal must be external to the while subsystem. At the beginning of the time step, if the IC input is true, the iterator block executes the contents of the subsystem and then checks the while condition input. If the while condition input is true, the iterator executes the subsystem again. This process continues as long as the while condition input is true and the number of iterations is less than or equal to the iterator block's Maximum number of iterations parameter. If the IC input is false at the beginning of a time step, the iterator does not execute the contents of the subsystem during the time step.

Example 11.12

We will create a model to compute the sum of the first N integers where the sum should be equal or less than 1000.

We begin by dragging a While Iterator Subsystem block into a new model as shown in Figure 11.57. We double–click on it and the subsystem now appears as shown in Figure 11.58. We add and interconnect In1, Out1, Sum, Memory, and Relational Operator blocks, and the model of Figure 11.58 is now as shown in Figure 11.59. This example is similar to the example given in Simulink's Help menu for the While Iterator Subsystem block.

The While Iterator Subsystem Block

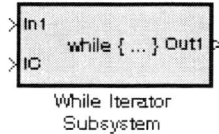

Figure 11.57. The While Iterator Subsystem block before configuration, Example 11.12

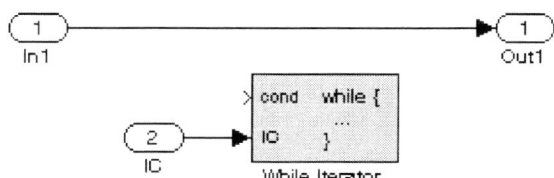

Figure 11.58. The While Iterator block for the While Iterator Subsystem block of Figure 11.57

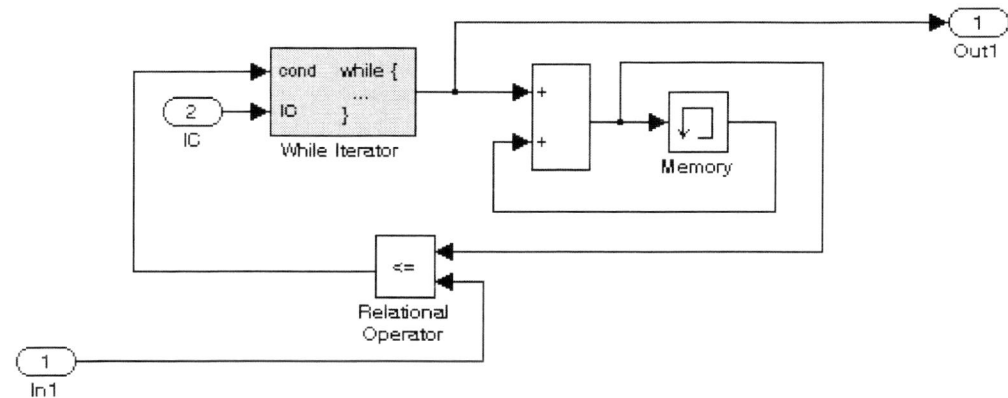

Figure 11.59. The contents of the While Iterator Subsystem of Figure 11.57

We return to the While Iterator Subsystem of Figure 11.57 and we add the Constant, Relational Operator, and Display blocks as shown in Figure 11.60. The output of the Relational Operator block is True (logical one) and this establishes the Initial Condition (IC) input to the While Iterator Subsystem block. As noted below the Display block in the model of Figure 11.60, the number of iterations is specified in the While Iterator is 5. The Display block in the model of Figure 11.61 indicates that the sum of the first N integers after 5 iterations is 765.

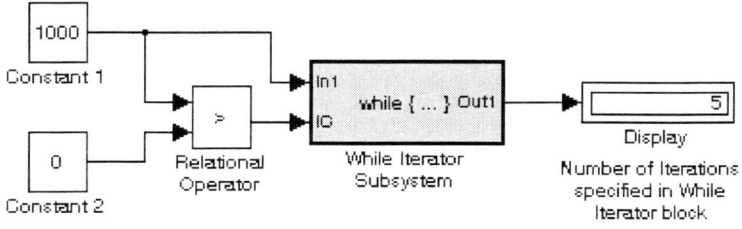

Figure 11.60. Final form for the model for Example 11.12

Chapter 11 The Ports & Subsystems Library

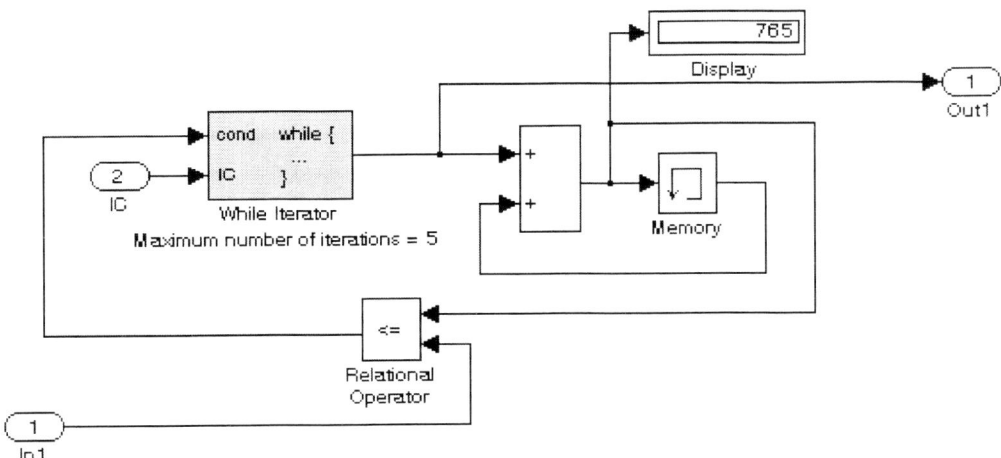

Figure 11.61. Model for Example 11.12 to indicate the sum of the first N integers

11.15 The If and If Action Subsystem Blocks

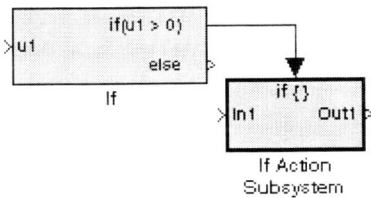

The **If** block, along with an If Action subsystem, implements standard C–like if–else logic. The **If Action Subsystem** block is a Subsystem block that is pre–configured to serve as a starting point for creating a subsystem whose execution is triggered by an If block.

For an example, please refer to the Help menu for the If block which includes also a pseudocode.[*]

---

[*] *Abbreviated p-code. A machine language for a nonexistent processor (a pseudomachine). Such code is executed by a software interpreter. The major advantage of p–code is that it is portable to all computers for which a p–code interpreter exists. The p–code approach has been tried several times in the microcomputer industry, with mixed success. The best known attempt was the UCSD p–System.*

11.16 The Switch Case and The Switch Case Action Subsystem Blocks

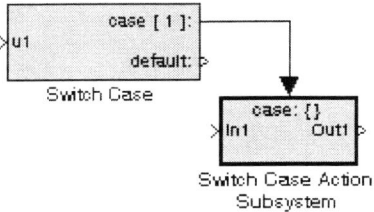

The **Switch Case** block implement a C–like switch control flow statement. The **Switch Case Action Subsystem** block is a Subsystem block that is pre–configured to serve as a starting point for creating a subsystem whose execution is triggered by a **Switch Case** block.

For an example, please refer to the Help menu for the Switch Case block that includes also a pseudocode.

11.17 The Subsystem Examples Block

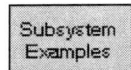

The **Subsystem Examples** block includes a library of S–functions. To run an example, in MATLAB's Command Window we type

sfundemos

and MATLAB will display the S–Function directory blocks shown in Figure 11.62. In this text we will be concerned with the M-file S–Functions only. An introduction to S–functions with an example is presented in the next section.

Next, we double-click on the M–file S–Functions block of Figure 11.62 and MATLAB displays the Level–1 and Level–2 M-file S–Functions shown in Figure 11.63.

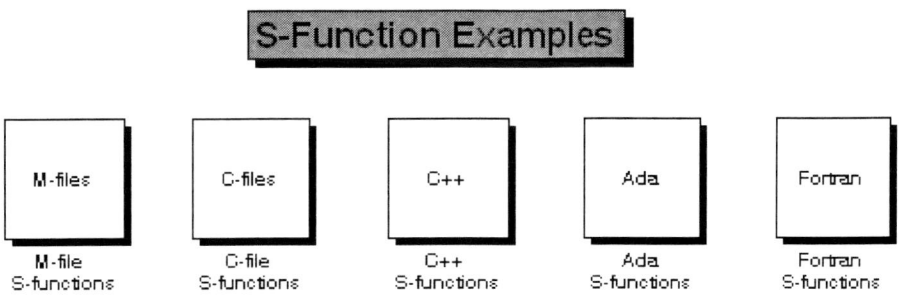

Figure 11.62. S–Function directory blocks

Chapter 11 The Ports & Subsystems Library

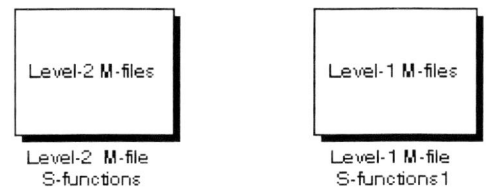

Figure 11.63. Levels of M–file S–Functions

The Level–1 M–file S–Functions are shown in Figure 11.64 and the Level–1 M–file S–Functions are shown in Figure 11.65.

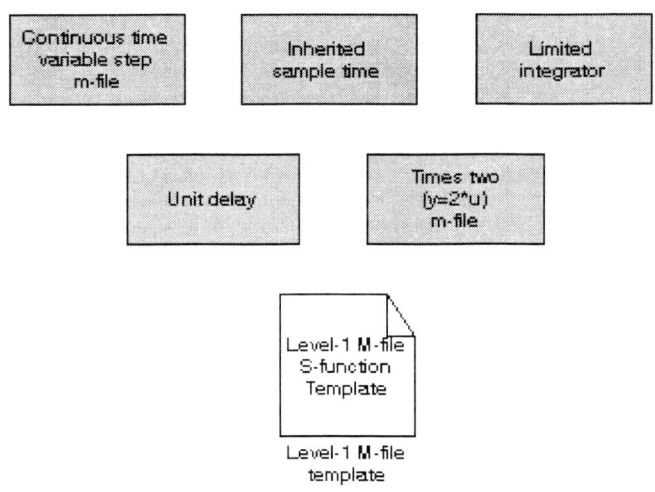

Figure 11.64. List of Level–1 M–file S–Functions

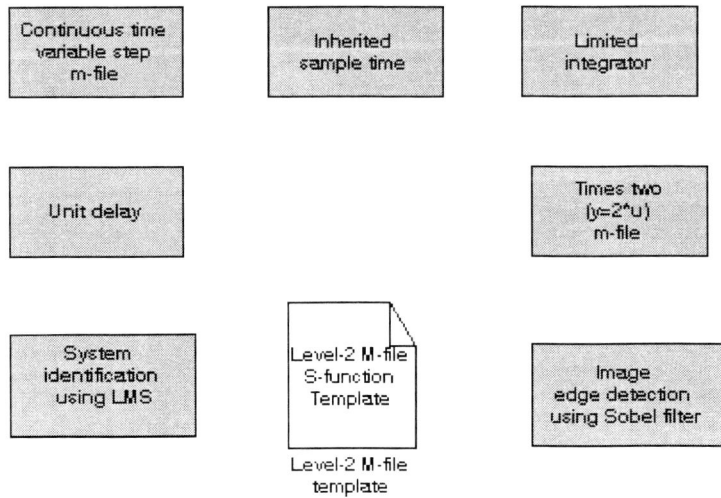

Figure 11.65. List of Level–2 M–file S–Functions

S–Functions in Simulink

Figure 11.66 shows the Subsystem Semantics (Definitions) for the Simulink family of subsystems.

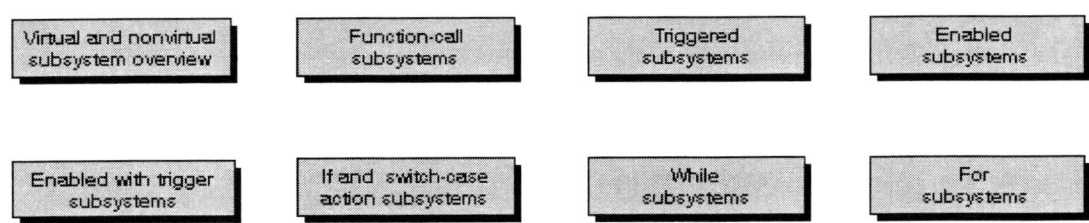

Figure 11.66. Classes and types of Simulink subsystems

Simulink consists of two classes of subsystems, Virtual subsystems and Nonvirtual subsystems. **Virtual subsystems** provide graphical hierarchy in models and do not impact execution. **Nonvirtual subsystems** are executed as a single unit (atomic execution) by Simulink. The blocks within a nonvirtual subsystem execute only when all subsystems inputs are valid. All nonvirtual subsystems are drawn with a bold border.

It is highly recommended that each of the subsystem blocks shown in Figure 11.66 be explored to become familiar with them.

11.18 S–Functions in Simulink

An **S–function** is a computer language description of a Simulink block. S–functions can be written in MATLAB, C, C++, Ada, or Fortran. Files in C, C++, Ada, and Fortran S–functions are compiled as **mex**-files using the **mex** utility.[*] S–functions use a special calling syntax that enables us to interact with Simulink's equation solvers. The form of an S–function is very general and applies to continuous, discrete, and hybrid systems.

S–functions allow us to add our own blocks to Simulink models. After we write our S–function and place its name in an S–Function block. We can also use S–functions with the **Real-Time Workshop**.[†] With m–file S–Functions we can define our own ordinary differential equations, discrete-time system equations and any type of algorithm that can be used with Simulink block diagrams.

To become familiar with S–Functions, we begin our discussion with an example.

---

[*] *For a discussion on mex–files please refer to in the online MATLAB documentation. These files are dynamically linked into MATLAB when specified. In this text we will only be concerned with m–files.*

[†] *Real-Time Workshop® is an extension of the capabilities provided by MATLAB and Simulink. It generates, and compiles source code from Simulink models to create real-time software applications on a variety of systems. Refer to Writing S–Functions for Real-Time Workshop and the Real-Time Workshop documentation for more information.*

Chapter 11 The Ports & Subsystems Library

Example 11.13

For the simple RC circuit of Figure 11.41 it can be shown[*] that the state–space equations are

$$\frac{dx}{dt} = \left(-\frac{1}{RC}\right)x + V_s \qquad (11.3)$$

$$y = x$$

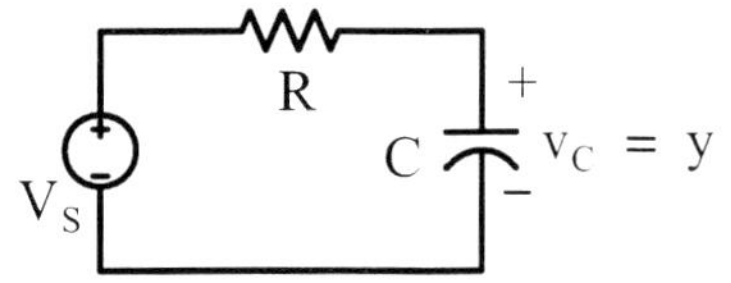

Figure 11.67. RC circuit for Example 11.13

Example 11.14

We will create an S–Function block that implements the relations of (11.3). We begin by writing the function m–file below and we save it as **RCckt.m**

```
function dx = RCckt(t,x,Vs)
%
% Model for RC series circuit, function m-file RCckt.m
%
% Define circuit constants
%
R = 10^6;              % Resistance in Ohms
C = 10^(-6);           % Capacitance in Farads

dx = -1/(R*C)*x+Vs;    % The arguments x and dx are column vectors
                       % for state and derivative respectively. The
                       % variable t on the first line above specifies
                       % the simulation time. The default is [0 10].
```

To test this function m–file for correctness, on MATLAB's Command Window we issue the command

[t,x,Vs]=ode45(@RCckt, [0 10], 0, [ ], 1)

The above command specifies a simulation time interval [0 10], an initial condition value of **0**, the null vector [ ] can be used for options, and the input value is set to **1**. Upon execution of this command MATLAB displays several values for **t**, **x**, and **Vs**.

Next, we write the S–function m–file shown below, and we save it as **RCckt_sfun.m**

An explanation for each line of this file is provided afterwards.

---

[*] *For a detailed discussion on state variables, please refer to Signals and Systems with MATLAB Applications, ISBN 0-9709511-6-7.*

S–Functions in Simulink

```
function [sys,x0,str,ts]=...
         RCckt_sfcn(t,x,u,flag,xinit)
%
% This is the m-file S-Function RCckt_sfcn.m
%
switch flag

    case 0                      % Initialize

        str = [];
        ts = [0 0];
        x0 = xinit;

% Alternately, the three lines above can be combined into a single line as
% [sys,x0,str,ts]=mdlInitializeSizes(t,x,u)

        sizes = simsizes;
            sizes.NumContStates = 1;
            sizes.NumDiscStates = 0;
            sizes.NumOutputs = 1;
            sizes.NumInputs = 1;
            sizes.DirFeedthrough = 0;
            sizes.NumSampleTimes = 1;

        sys =simsizes(sizes);
    case 1                      % Derivatives

        Vs = u;

        sys = RCckt(t,x,Vs);

    case 3                      % Output

        sys = x;

    case {2 4 9}                % 2:discrete
                                % 3:calcTimeHit
                                % 9:termination
        sys = [];

    otherwise

        error(['unhandled flag =',num2str(flag)]);

end
```

The first line of the S–function m-file **RCckt_sfun.m** is written as

```
function [sys,x0,str,ts]=...
         RCckt_sfcn(t,x,u,flag,xinit)
```

This specifies the input and output arguments.

   a. Input arguments

     t – time variable

Chapter 11 The Ports & Subsystems Library

x – column vector for the state variables

u – column vector for the input variables; will be supplied by other Simulink blocks

flag – an indication of which group of information and calculations. The table below lists the integer numbers assigned to an S–function routine.

TABLE 11.3 Flags used in S-function m-files

Flag	S-Function Routine	Simulation Stage
0	mdlInitializeSizes	Initialization - sets input and output vector sizes and specifies initial conditions for the state variables.
1	mdlDerivatives	Calculation of derivatives
2	mdlUpdate	Update of discrete states - not used for this example
3	mdlOutputs	Calculation of outputs
4	mdlGetTimeOfNextVarHit	Calculation of next sample hit - not used for this example
9	mdlTerminate	End of simulation tasks

`xinit` – additional supplied parameter; in this example the initial condition

a. Output arguments

sys – a vector of information requested by Simulink. This vector will hold different information depending on the **flag** value as shown in the table below.

TABLE 11.4 Information for vector sys for different flag values

Flag	Information requested
0	sys = [a, b, c, d, e, f, g] a = number of continuous time states b = number of discrete time states c = number of outputs d = number of inputs e = not used but must be set to 0 if requested f = applies to direct algebraic feed through of input to output, 0 for No, 1 for Yes. It is relevant if during flag=3, the output variables depend on the input variables. g = number of sample times. For continuous systems must be set to 1.
1	sys = column vector of the state variables derivatives
3	sys = column vector of output variables
2,4,9	sys = [ ] (null vector) if not applicable

x0 – a column vector of initial conditions. Applies only to **flag** = 0

S–Functions in Simulink

str – reserved for future use; for m–file S–functions it must be set to null vector. Applies only to **flag** = 0

ts – an array of two columns to specify sample time and time offsets. For continuous-time systems it is set to [0 0]. If it is desired that S–function should run at the same rate as the block to which it is connected (inherited sample time), we must set **ts** to [–1 0]. If we want to run at discrete sample time, say 0.25 seconds starting at 0.1 seconds after the start of simulation time, we must set **ts** to [0.25 0.1]. Applies only to **flag** = 0.

Let us now review the m–file S–function **RCckt_sfcn** structure.

We begin with the function **RCckt_sfcn** defined as follows:

```
function [sys,x0,str,ts]=...
        RCckt_sfcn(t,x,u,flag,xinit)
%
% This is the m-file S-Function RCckt_sfun.m
%
```

Next, we use **flag**; this specifies an integer value that indicates the task to be performed by the S–function and begins with the statement
```
switch flag
```
Initialization begins with

```
    case 0                      % Initialize
        str = [];               % Must be set to null. Reserved for future use
        ts = [0 0];             % Specify sampling time. For continuous-time
                                % systems is always set to [0 0]
        x0 = xinit;             % Column vector for initial conditions
```

Simulink will not recognize our m–file S–function unless we provide specific information about number of inputs, number of outputs, states, and other characteristics. This information is provided with the **simsizes** function. This function returns an initialized structure of the variables in which we can assign the required values. Thus, in MATLAB's Command Window we invoke this command as shown below and we manually enter the values shown.

```
        sizes = simsizes;
            sizes.NumContStates = 1;
            sizes.NumDiscStates = 0;
            sizes.NumOutputs = 1;
            sizes.NumInputs = 1;
            sizes.DirFeedthrough = 0;
            sizes.NumSampleTimes = 1;
```

Direct Feedthrough in line 5 above implies that the output is controlled by the value of the input. Generally, if an S–Function has an input port, it has direct feedthrough if the input **u** is accessed in mdlOutputs. For instance, if y = ku where **u** is the input, **k** is the gain, and **y** is the output, the system has direct feedthrough only if *flag=3*.

After we initialize the sizes structure we invoke **simsizes** again as shown below

Chapter 11 The Ports & Subsystems Library

```
        sys =simsizes(sizes);
```

and this passes the information in the sizes structure to sys which is a vector that holds the information required by Simulink.*

For **case 1** (derivatives) we assign V_S to the input u and then we apply it to the **RCckt.m** file. Thus,

```
    case 1                          % Derivatives
        Vs = u;
        sys = RCckt(t,x,Vs);
```

For **case 3** (output) we assign the output x to the input sys. Thus,

```
    case 3                          % Output
        sys = x;
```

Flags 2, 4, and 9 are not used so they output the null vector sys = [] shown below.

```
    case {2 4 9}                    % 2:discrete
                                    % 3:calcTimeHit
                                    % 9:termination
        sys = [];

    otherwise
        error(['unhandled flag =',num2str(flag)]);

end
```

Next, we open a window to create a new model, from the **User–Defined Functions** library we drag an S–Function block into it, in the Function Block Parameters dialog box we assign the S–function name **RCckt_sfcn** to it, we type the initial condition 0, and we add the other blocks shown in Figure 11.68. The parameter values can be constants, names of variables defined in the model's workspace, or MATLAB expressions. The input and output waveforms are shown in Figure 11.69.

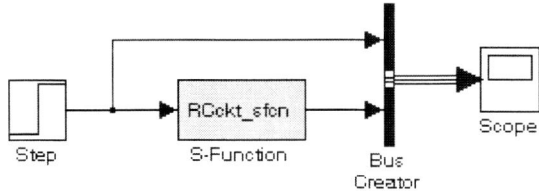

Figure 11.68. Model for Example 11.14

---

* Upon execution of the statement sys=simsizes(sizes), MATLAB displays a row vector of seven 0s, one for each of the simsizes function above. Sys(5) is reserved for root finding and for the present must be set to 0.

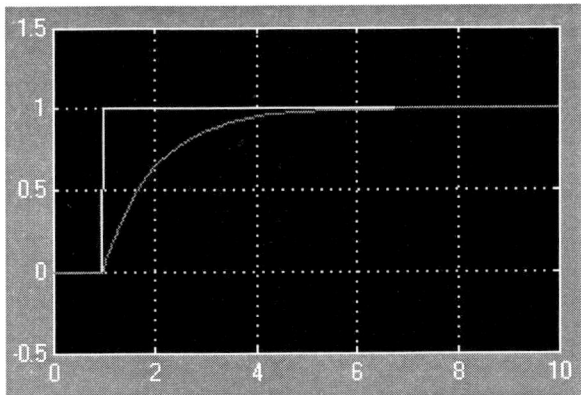

Figure 11.69. Input and output waveforms for the model of Figure 11.68

Chapter 11 The Ports & Subsystems Library

11.19 Summary

- A **Subsystem** block represents a subsystem of the system that contains it. We use subsystems to group blocks together in our model to manage model complexity.

- **Inport** blocks are ports that serve as links from outside a system into a subsystem.

- **Outport** blocks are output ports for a subsystem.

- The **Trigger** block is used with a subsystem or a model allowing its execution to be triggered by an external signal.

- The **Enable** block adds an external enable block to a subsystem to make it an enabled subsystem.

- The **Function–Call Generator** block executes a function–call subsystem at the rate specified by the block's Sample time parameter.

- The **Atomic Subsystem** block can be used as an alternate method of creating a subsystem in lieu of the method of selecting blocks and lines that are to make up the subsystem using a bounding box and choosing Create Subsystem from the Edit menu.

- The **Code Reuse Subsystem** block is a Subsystem block that represents a subsystem of the system that contains it. It is very similar to the Atomic Subsystem block.

- The **Model** block is used to specify the name of a Simulink model. The name must be a valid MATLAB identifier. The model must exist on the MATLAB path and the MATLAB path must contain no other model having the same name.

- The **Configurable Subsystem** block represents one of a set of blocks contained in a specified library of blocks. The block's context menu lets us choose which block the configurable subsystem represents. A configurable Subsystem block simplifies the creation of models that represent families of designs.

- The **Triggered Subsystem** block is used to represent a subsystem whose execution is triggered by external input.

- The **Enable Subsystem** block represents a subsystem whose execution is enabled by an external input.

- The **Enabled and Triggered Subsystem** block is a combination of the enabled subsystem and the triggered subsystem.

- The **Function–Call Subsystem** block is used to represent a subsystem that can be invoked as a function by another block.

- The **For Iterator Subsystem** block is a subsystem that executes repeatedly during a simulation time step until an iteration variable exceeds a specified iteration limit.

Summary

- The **While Iterator Subsystem** block is a Subsystem block that is pre–configured to serve as a starting point for creating a subsystem that executes repeatedly while a condition is satisfied during a simulation time step.

- The **If** block, along with an If Action subsystem, implements standard C–like if–else logic. The **If Action Subsystem** block is a Subsystem block that is pre–configured to serve as a starting point for creating a subsystem whose execution is triggered by an If block.

- The **Switch Case** block implement a C–like switch control flow statement. The **Switch Action Subsystem** block is a Subsystem block that is pre–configured to serve as a starting point for creating a subsystem whose execution is triggered by a **Switch Case** block.

- The **Subsystem Examples** block includes a library of S–functions.

- An **S–function** is a computer language description of a Simulink block. S–functions can be written in MATLAB, C, C++, Ada, or Fortran. Files in C, C++, Ada, and Fortran S–functions are compiled as **mex**-files using the **mex** utility.

Chapter 11 The Ports & Subsystems Library

NOTES

Chapter 12

The Signal Attributes Library

This chapter is an introduction to the **Signal Attributes** library. This is the eleventh library in the Simulink group of libraries and consists of two sub–libraries, the **Signal Attribute Manipulation Sub–Library**, and the **Signal Attribute Detection Sub–Library** blocks shown below. We will describe the function of each block included in this library and we will perform simulation examples to illustrate their application.

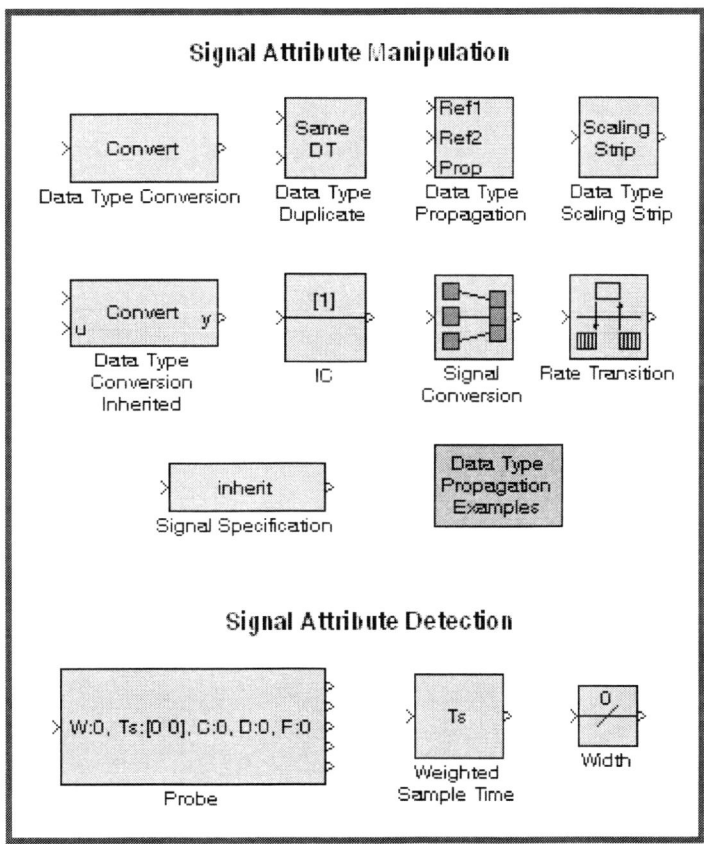

Chapter 12 The Signal Attributes Library

12.1 The Signal Attribute Manipulation Sub-Library

The **Signal Attribute Manipulation Sub-Library** contains the blocks described in Subsections 12.1.1 through 12.1.10 below.

12.1.1 The Data Type Conversion Block

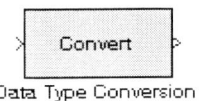

The **Data Type Conversion block** converts an input signal of any Simulink data type to the data type and scaling specified by the block's Output data type mode, Output data type, and / or Output scaling parameters. The input can be any real– or complex–valued signal. If the input is real, the output is real, and if the input is complex, the output is complex. When using this block, we must specify the data type and / or scaling for the conversion. The data types and the Data Type Conversion block are described in Section 2.17, Chapter 2, Page 2–29.

12.1.2 The Data Type Duplicate Block

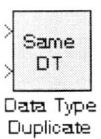

The **Data Type Duplicate** block is used to ascertain that all inputs have the same data type. We use the Data Type Duplicate block to check for consistency of data types among blocks. If all signals do not have the same data type, the block returns an error message. The Data Type Duplicate block is typically used in such a way that one signal to the block controls the data type for all other blocks. The other blocks are set to inherit their data types via back propagation. The block is also used in a user created library. These library blocks can be placed in any model, and the data type for all library blocks are configured according to the usage in the model. To create a library block with more complex data type rules than duplication, we use the Data Type Propagation block which is described in Subsection 12.1.3, this chapter, Page 12–4.

Example 12.1

Let us consider the model of Figure 12.1. For all three gain blocks the Signal data types have been specified as **Inherit via back propagation**. The gains in Gain 2 and Gain 3 blocks are very high and thus the Display 2 and Display 3 blocks output the value of 0 indicating an overflow condition. To obtain the true values in Display 2 and Display 3 blocks, we change the Signal data types from **Inherit via back propagation** to uint(16) and uint(32) respectively as shown in Figure 12.2.

The Signal Attribute Manipulation Sub−Library

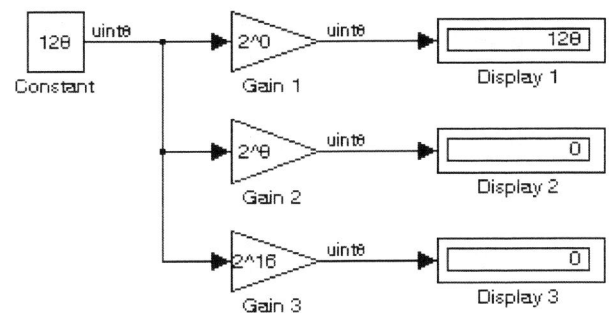

Figure 12.1. Model 1 for Example 12.1

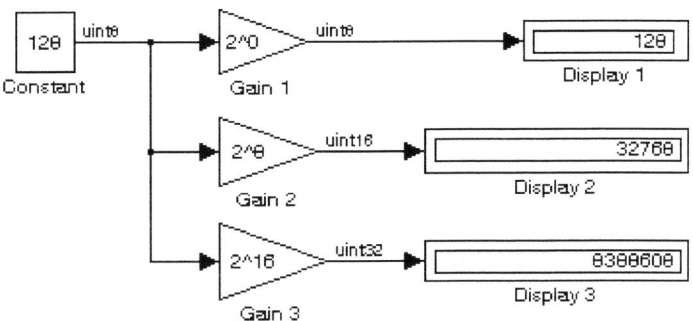

Figure 12.2. Model 2 for Example 12.1

Next, we return to the model of Figure 12.1, we add a Data Type Duplicate block, and we specify the Signal data type for the Constant block as uint(32), and now our model appears as shown in Figure 12.3. The advantage here is that we can specify any Signal data type and that will be inherited by the three gain blocks.

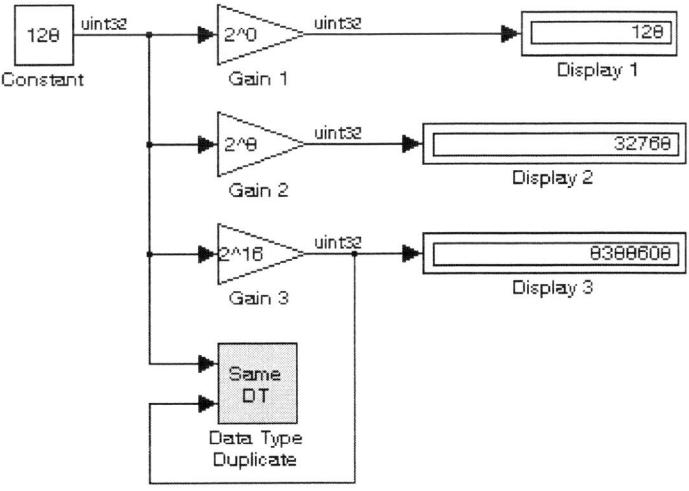

Figure 12.3. Model 3 for Example 12.1

Chapter 12 The Signal Attributes Library

12.1.3 The Data Type Propagation Block

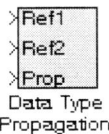

The **Data Type Propagation** block allows us to control the data type and scaling of signals in our model. We can use this block in conjunction with fixed–point blocks that have their Specify data type and scaling parameter configured to **Inherit via back propagation**. The block has three inputs: **Ref1** and **Ref2** are the reference inputs, while the **Prop** input back propagates the data type and scaling information gathered from the reference inputs. This information is subsequently passed on to other fixed–point blocks.

Example 12.2

The model of Figure 12.4 performs the arithmetic operation $2.5(5.75 + 2.375 + 1.8125)$. The **Ref1** signal represents the sum of the terms, the **Ref2** signal represents the multiplier, and the **Prop** signal is the product. For all four Constant blocks the parameter Signal data types is specified as **Inherit from "Constant value"**, and for the Sum and Product blocks the parameter Signal data types is specified as **Inherit via back propagation**. The Display block Format is specified as **decimal (Stored Integer.)**

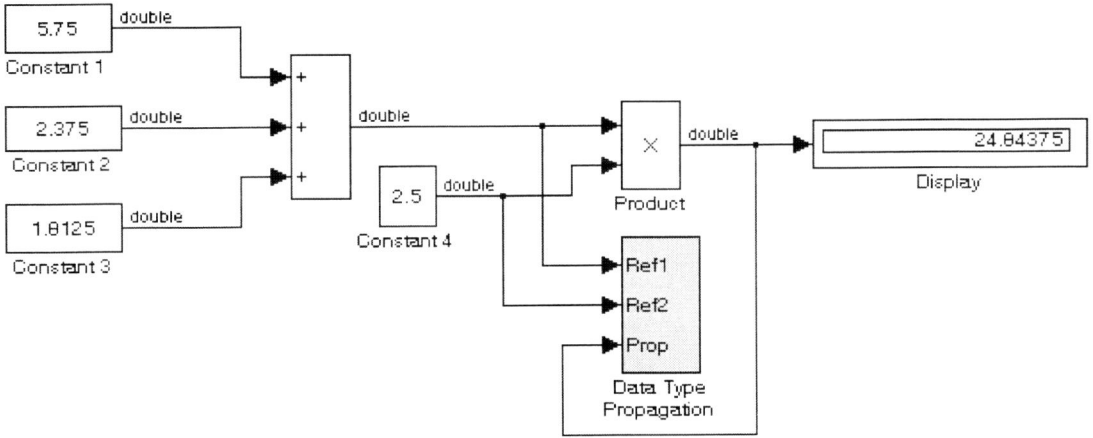

Figure 12.4. Model for Example 12.2

12.1.4 The Data Type Scaling Strip Block

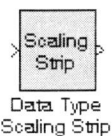
Data Type
Scaling Strip

The **Data Type Scaling Strip** block removes the scaling off a fixed–point signal. It maps the input data type to the smallest built in data type that has enough data bits to hold the input. The stored integer value of the input is the value of the output. The output always has nominal scaling (slope = 1.0 and bias = 0.0), so the output does not make a distinction between real world value and stored integer value.

Example 12.3

For the model of Figure 12.5, the parameters for the Constant block the Signal data types were specified as Output data type ufix(8) and output scaling value 2^{-3}. Accordingly, the binary presentation of the constant 5.875 is

$$(00101.111)_2 = 1 \times 2^2 + 1 \times 2^0 + 1 \times 2^{-1} + 1 \times 2^{-2} + 1 \times 2^{-3} = (5.875)_{10}$$

The Scaling Strip block removes the scaling and thus it outputs the value

$$(00101111)_2 = 1 \times 2^5 + 1 \times 2^3 + 1 \times 2^2 + 1 \times 2^1 + 1 \times 2^0 = (47)_{10}$$

Figure 12.5. Model for Example 12.3

12.1.5 The Data Conversion Inherited Block

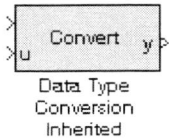
Data Type
Conversion
Inherited

The **Data Type Conversion Inherited** block converts one data type to another using inherited data types. In other words, this block dictates that different types of data be converted to be all the same. The first input is used as the reference signal and the second input is converted to the

Chapter 12 The Signal Attributes Library

reference type by inheriting the data type and scaling information. Either input is scalar expanded such that the output has the same width as the widest input.

Example 12.4

I the model of Figure 12.6, the input at u from the Constant 2 bloc appears at the output y but the signal has been converted to that specified by the first input, i.e., ufix(8) 2^{-3}.

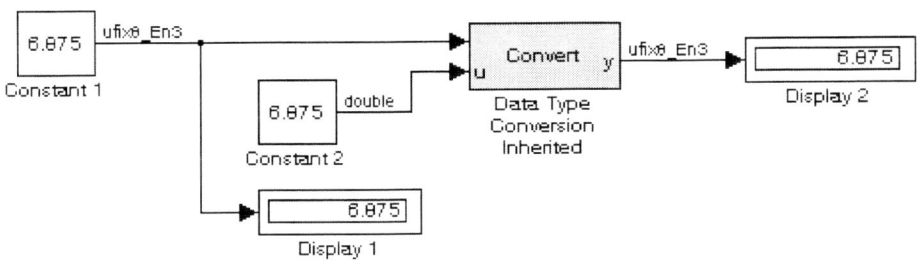

Figure 12.6. Model for Example 12.4

12.1.6 The IC (Initial Condition) Block

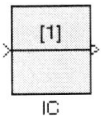

The **IC (Initial Condition)** block sets the initial condition of the signal at its input port, i.e., the value of the signal at t=0. The block does this by outputting the specified initial condition at t=0, regardless of the actual value of the input signal. Thereafter, the block outputs the actual value of the input signal. This block is useful for providing an initial guess for the algebraic state variables in the loop.

Example 12.5

In the model of Figure 12.7, the Memory block introduces a delay of 1 second while the IC block establishes an initial condition of 2. The output waveforms with and without the initial condition are shown in Figure 12.8.

The Signal Attribute Manipulation Sub-Library

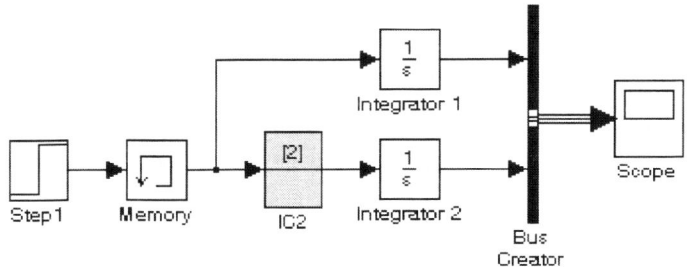

Figure 12.7. Model for Example 12.5

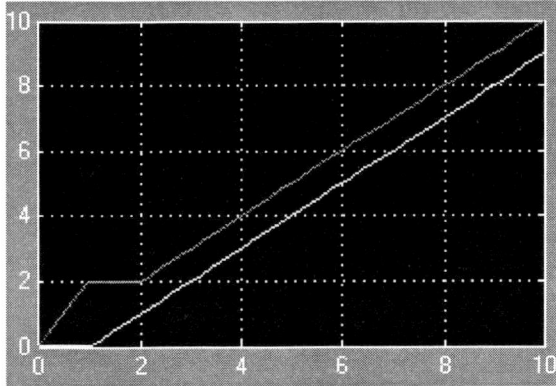

Figure 12.8. Output waveforms for the model of Figure 12.7

12.1.7 The Signal Conversion Block

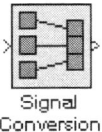

The **Signal Conversion** block converts a signal from one type to another. The block's Output parameter allows us to choose the type of conversion to be performed. We can choose one of the four types listed below:

Contiguous copy – Converts a muxed signal whose elements occupy discontiguous areas of memory to a vector signal whose elements occupy contiguous areas of memory. The block does this by allocating a contiguous area of memory for the elements of the muxed signal and copying the values from the discontiguous areas (represented by the block's input) to the contiguous areas (represented by the block's output) at each time step.

Bus copy – Outputs a copy of the bus connected to the block's input.

Chapter 12 The Signal Attributes Library

Virtual bus – Converts a nonvirtual bus to a virtual bus. This option enables us to combine an originally nonvirtual bus with a virtual bus.

Nonvirtual bus – Converts a virtual bus to a nonvirtual bus.

Example 12.6

In the model of Figure 12.9, the Signal Conversion block's output is specified as Contiguous copy. Accordingly the numbers 5.878 and 5.879 originally occupying discontiguous areas of memory, are converted to a vector signal whose elements occupy contiguous areas of memory as indicated in the Display block.

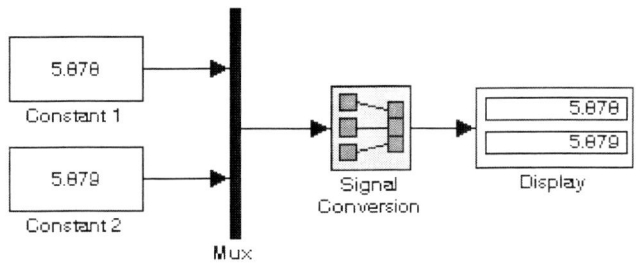

Figure 12.9. Model for Example 12.6

12.1.8 The Rate Transition Block

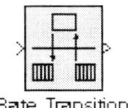

The **Rate Transition** block transfers data from the output of a block operating at one rate to the input of another block operating at a different rate. Systems containing blocks that are sampled at different rates are referred to as **multirate systems**. The Rate Transition block's parameters allows us to specify options that trade data integrity and deterministic transfer for faster response and / or lower memory requirements.

Example 12.7

In the model of Figure 12.10, the parameters for the Discrete Zero–Pole blocks 1 and 2 are specified as Zeros: −0.2, Poles: 0.5. The Sample time for the Discrete Zero–Pole block 1 is specified as [1 0.5] where 1 is the sample time, and 0.5 is the offset. Since the initial condition is zero, the offset causes no output until t = 0.5. The Sample time for the Discrete Zero–Pole block 2 is spec-

The Signal Attribute Manipulation Sub–Library

ified as 0.75 with no offset. Accordingly, the model of Figure 12.10 is a multirate system and the output waveforms are shown in Figure 12.11.

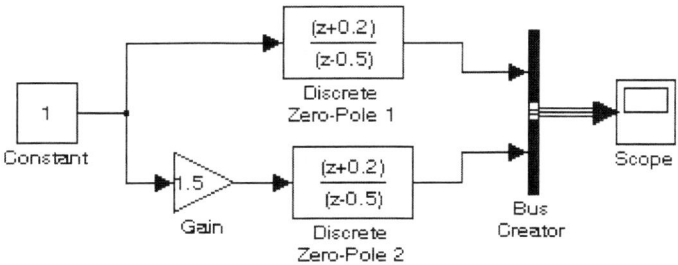

Figure 12.10. Model for Example 12.7

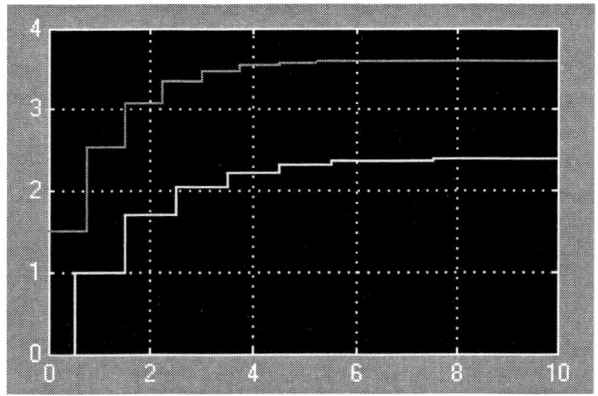

Figure 12.11. Output waveforms for the multirate model of Figure 12.10

An application of the Rate Transition block is illustrated with the next example.

Example 12.8

The model of Figure 12.12 shows three multirate systems where the sample times are as indicated. The Rate Transition 1 block behaves as a Zero–Order Hold block in a fast–to–slow transition, while the Rate Transition 2 block behaves as a Unit Delay block in a slow–to–fast transition. After the simulation command is executed, a label appears on the upper left of the block to indicate its behavior. The Rate Transition 1 block behaves as a Zero–Order Hold block and this is indicated as ZOH. Likewise, the Rate Transition 2 block behaves as a Unit Delay block and this is indicated as $1/z$. The Unit Delay block is described in Section 2.15, Chapter 2, Page 2–24, and the Zero–Order Hold block is described in Subsection 5.2.3, Chapter 5, Page 5–23. For other behaviors of the Rate Transition block, please refer to the Help menu for this block.

Chapter 12 The Signal Attributes Library

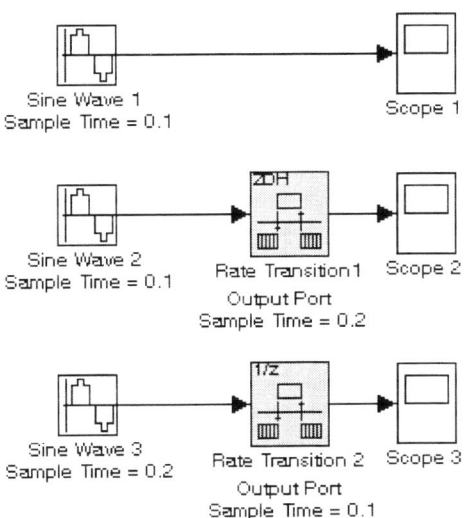

Figure 12.12. Model for Example 12.8

The waveforms displayed by the Scope blocks in Figure 12.12 are shown in Figures 12.13, 12.14, and 12.15. The amplitude for all three Sine Wave blocks is specified as 2.

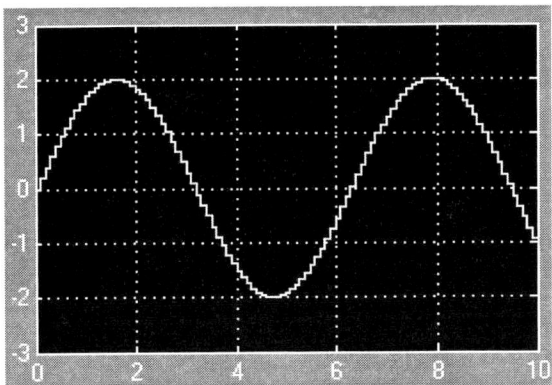

Figure 12.13. Waveform for Scope 1 in Figure 12.12

The Signal Attribute Manipulation Sub–Library

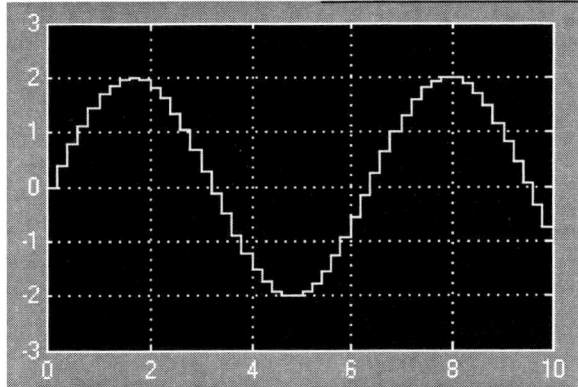

Figure 12.14. Waveform for Scope 2 in Figure 12.12

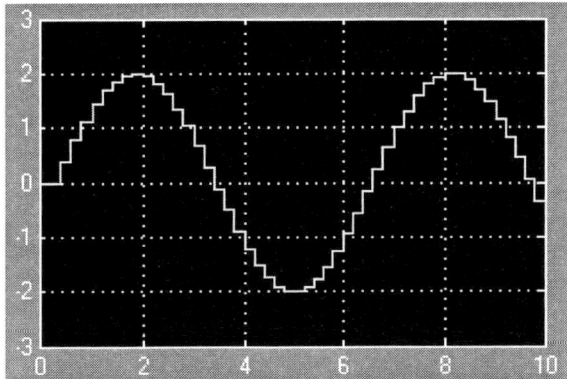

Figure 12.15. Waveform for Scope 3 in Figure 12.12

12.1.9 The Signal Specification Block

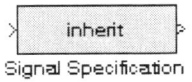

The **Signal Specification** block allows us to specify the attributes of the signal connected to its input and output ports. If the specified attributes conflict with the attributes specified by the blocks connected to its ports, Simulink displays an error. If no conflict exists, Simulink eliminates the Signal Specification block from the compiled model, that is, the Signal Specification block behaves as a virtual block.

Example 12.9

In the model of Figure 12.16, the Zero-Order Hold and the Unit Delay blocks are both specified for Inherited Sample Time and thus no conflict exists and the Signal Specification block is a virtual block. However, if the Sample Time for the Unit Delay block is changed to 0.2 as shown in

Chapter 12 The Signal Attributes Library

Figure 12.17, Simulink displays an error message that an illegal rate transition was found involving the Unit Delay block.

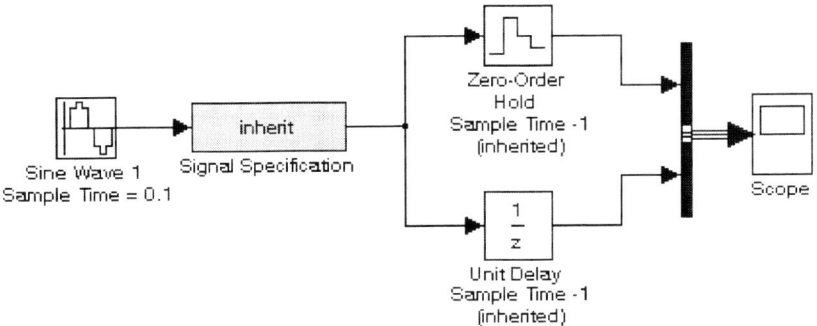

Figure 12.16. Model with the Signal Specification block acting as a virtual block

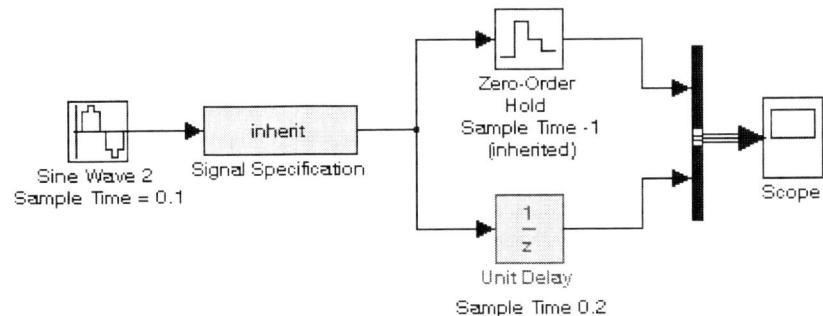

Figure 12.17. Model where the attributes (sample times) of the Signal Specification block do not agree

12.1.10 The Data Type Propagation Examples Block

The **Data Type Propagation Examples** block shown in Figure 12.18 contains example uses of Data Type Propagation blocks.

The Signal Attribute Detection Sub–Library

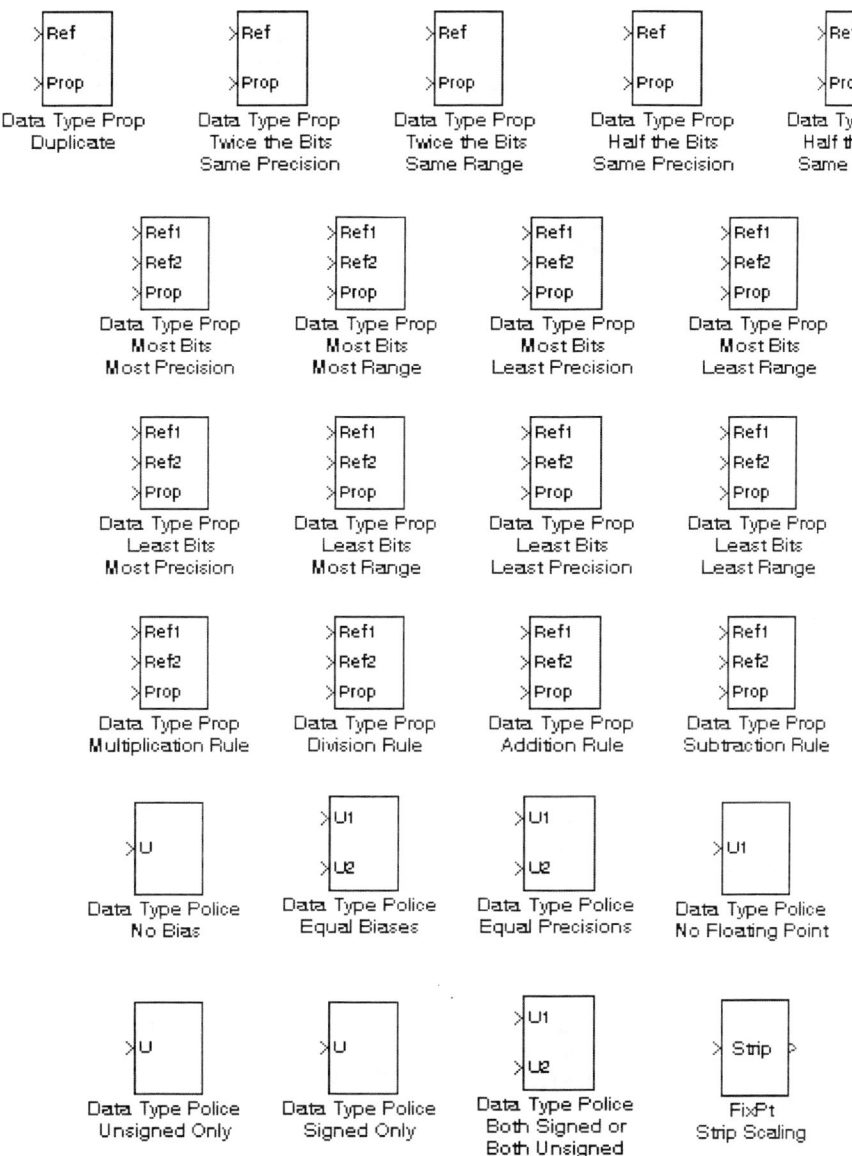

Figure 12.18. Example uses of Data Type Propagation blocks

12.2 The Signal Attribute Detection Sub-Library

The **Signal Attribute Detection Sub–Library** contains the blocks described in Subsections 12.2.1 through 12.2.3 below.

Chapter 12 The Signal Attributes Library

12.2.1 The Probe Block

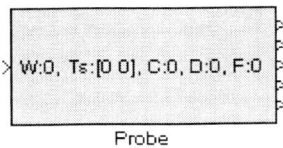

The **Probe** block provides essential information about the signal on its input. The block can output the input signal's width, dimensionality, sample time, and/or a flag indicating whether the input is a complex-valued signal. The block has one input port. The number of output ports depends on the information that we select for probing. Each probed value is output as a separate signal on a separate output port. During simulation, the block's icon displays the probed data.

Example 12.10

In the model of Figure 12.19, the Display 1 block indicates the number of the elements of the probed signal, the Display 2 block is a 2×1 vector that specifies the period and offset of the sample time, respectively, the Display 3 block shows the value 0 implying that the probed signal is not complex, the Display 4 block indicates the output the dimensions of the probed signal, and the Display 5 block shows the value 0 implying that the probed signal is not framed.[*]

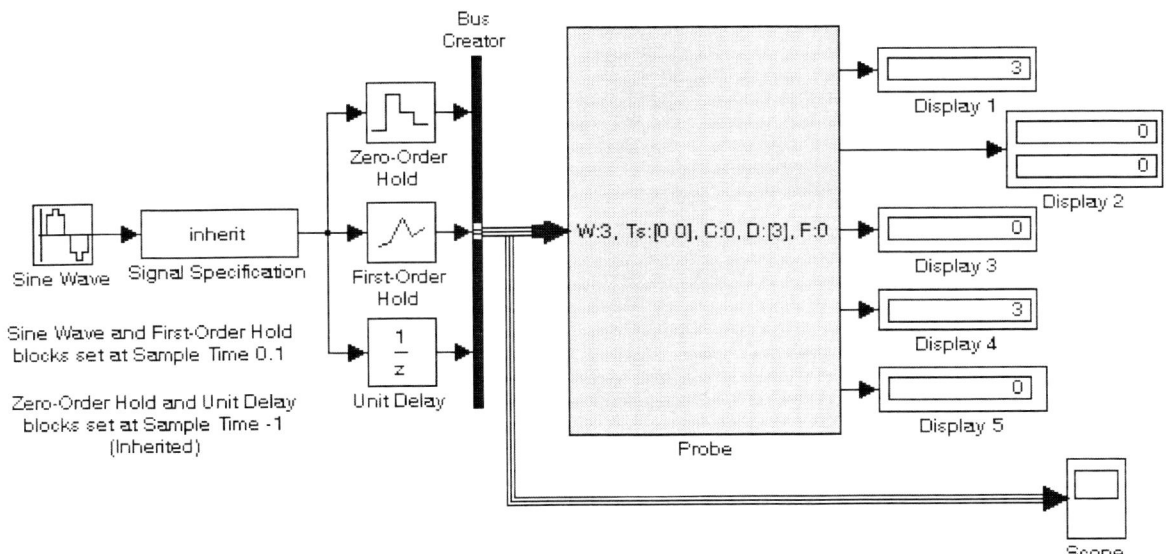

Figure 12.19. Model for Example 12.10

---

[*] *Please logon to http://festvox.org/docs/speech_tools−1.2.0/x15608.htm#SIGPR−EXAMPLE−FRAMES for a description of frame−based signals.*

12.2.2 The Weighted Sample Time Block

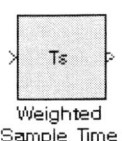

The **Weighted Sample Time** block adds, subtracts, multiplies, or divides the input signal, u, by a weighted sample time **Ts**. The math operation is specified with the Operation parameter. Also, we can specify to use only the weight with either the sample time or its inverse. We enter the weighting factor in the Weight value parameter. If the weight is 1, w is removed from the equation.

Example 12.11

In the model of Figure 12.20, the parameters for all blocks are specified as annotated. Thus, the Display 1 block shows the values of the constant blocks, the Display 2 block shows the Weighted Sample Time, the Display 3 block shows the inverse of the Weighted Sample Time, and the Display 4 block shows the results of the division $u/Ts/w$, where $w = 2$ for $u = 1, 2,$ and 3.

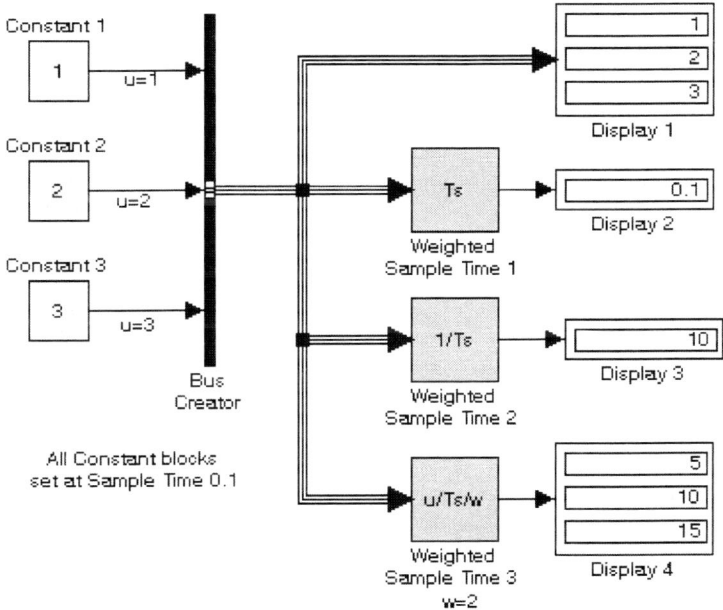

Figure 12.20. Model for Example 12.11

12.2.3 The Width Block

The **Width** block generates an output that displays the width of its input vector, or the sum of the widths of two or more vectors.

Example 12.12

In the model of Figure 12.21, the vectors A and B are specified in MATLAB's Command Window as

A=[1 3 5 7 9]; B=[2 4 6 8];

The Width block outputs the sum of the widths of the vectors A and B.

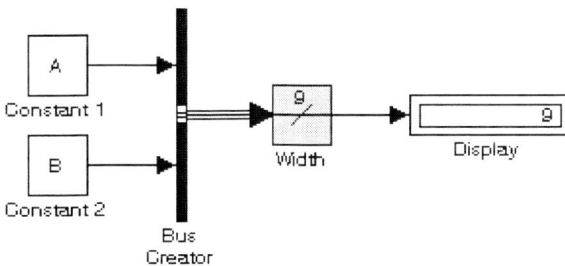

Figure 12.21. Model for Example 12.12

12.3 Summary

- The **Data Type Conversion block** converts an input signal of any Simulink data type to the data type and scaling specified by the block's Output data type mode, Output data type, and/or Output scaling parameters.

- The **Data Type Duplicate** block is used to ascertain that all inputs have the same data type. We use the Data Type Duplicate block to check for consistency of data types among blocks. If all signals do not have the same data type, the block returns an error message.

- The **Data Type Propagation** block allows us to control the data type and scaling of signals in our model. We can use this block in conjunction with fixed-point blocks that have their Specify data type and scaling parameter configured to Inherit via back propagation.

- The **Data Type Scaling Strip** block removes the scaling off a fixed point signal. It maps the input data type to the smallest built in data type that has enough data bits to hold the input. The stored integer value of the input is the value of the output.

- The **Data Type Conversion Inherited** block converts one data type to another using inherited data types. In other words, this block commands that different types of data be converted to be all the same. The first input is used as the reference signal and the second input is converted to the reference type by inheriting the data type and scaling information.

- The **IC (Initial Condition)** block sets the initial condition of the signal at its input port, i.e., the value of the signal at $t=0$. The block does this by outputting the specified initial condition at $t=0$, regardless of the actual value of the input signal. Thereafter, the block outputs the actual value of the input signal.

- The **Signal Conversion** block converts a signal from one type to another. The block's Output parameter lets us select the type of conversion to be performed. We can choose one of four types: Contiguous copy, Bus copy, Virtual bus, or Nonvirtual bus.

- The **Rate Transition** block transfers data from the output of a block operating at one rate to the input of another block operating at a different rate. Systems containing blocks that are sampled at different rates are referred to as **multirate systems**.

- The **Signal Specification** block allows us to specify the attributes of the signal connected to its input and output ports. If the specified attributes conflict with the attributes specified by the blocks connected to its ports, Simulink displays an error at the beginning of a simulation.

- The **Data Type Propagation Examples** block contains example uses of Data Type Propagation blocks.

- The **Probe** block provides essential information about the signal on its input. The block can output the input signal's width, dimensionality, sample time, and/or a flag indicating whether the input is a complex-valued signal.

Chapter 12 The Signal Attributes Library

- The **Weighted Sample Time** block adds, subtracts, multiplies, or divides the input signal, u, by a weighted sample time Ts. The math operation is specified with the Operation parameter.

- The **Width** block generates an output that displays the width of its input vector, or the sum of the widths of two or more vectors.

Chapter 13

The Signal Routing Library

This chapter is an introduction to the **Signal Routing** library. This is the twelfth library in the Simulink group of libraries and consists of two sub-libraries, the **Signal Routing Group Sub–Library,** and the **Signal Storage & Access Group Sub–Library** blocks shown below. We will describe the function of each block included in this library and we will perform simulation examples to illustrate their application.

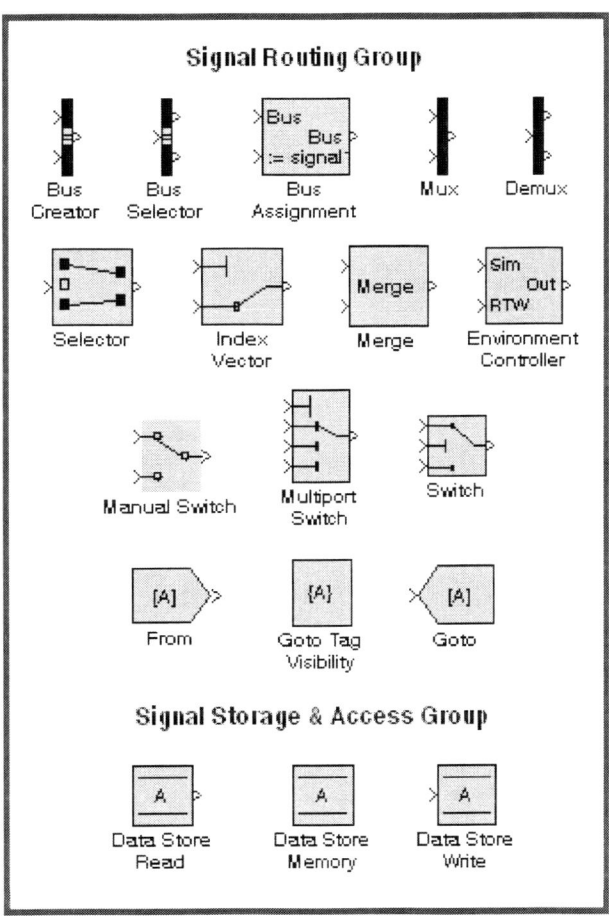

Chapter 13 The Signal Routing Library

13.1 Signal Routing Group Sub-Library

The **Signal Routing Group Sub-Library** contains the fifteen blocks described in Subsections 13.1.1 through 13.1.15 below.

13.1.1 The Bus Creator Block

The **Bus Creator** block combines a set of signals into a group of signals represented by a single line. This block is described in Section 2.6, Chapter 2, Page 2–7.

13.1.2 The Bus Selector Block

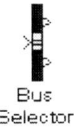

The **Bus Selector** block outputs a specified subset of the elements of the bus at its input. This block is described in Section 2.6, Chapter 2, Page 2–7.

13.1.3 The Bus Assignment Block

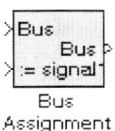

The **Bus Assignment** block assigns values, specified by signals connected to its assignment (:=) input ports, to specified elements of the bus connected to its Bus input port. We use the block's dialog box to specify the bus elements to be assigned values. The block displays an assignment input port for each bus element to be assigned a signal.

In the Function Block Parameters dialog box, the **Signals in the bus** displays the names of the signals contained by the bus at the block's Bus input port. We can click any item in the list to select it. To find the source of the selected signal, we click the adjacent Find button. Simulink opens the subsystem containing the signal source, if necessary, and highlights the source's icon. We use the **Select** button to move the currently selected signal into the adjacent list of signals to be assigned values (see Signals that are being assigned below). To refresh the display (e.g., to reflect modifications to the bus connected to the block), we click the adjacent **Refresh** button.

Signal Routing Group Sub–Library

In the Function Block Parameters dialog box, the **Signals that are being assigned** lists the names of bus elements to be assigned values. This block displays an assignment input port for each bus element in this list. The label of the corresponding input port contains the name of the element. We can re-order the signals by using the **Up**, **Down**, and **Remove** buttons. Port connectivity is maintained when the signal order is changed.

Occasionally, we may see three question marks (???) before the name of a bus element. This indicates that the input bus no longer contains an element of that name, for example, because the bus has changed since the last time we refreshed the Bus Assignment block's input and bus element assignment lists. We can fix the problem either by modifying the bus to include a signal of the specified name, or by removing the name from the list of bus elements to be assigned values.

Example 13.1

We begin with the model 13.1. Initially, the Bus Assignment 1 block appears with two inputs, one for the block's Bus input port, and the other which serves as the assignment input port for each bus element to be assigned a signal. We double–click on this block and we configure the Function Block Parameters as shown in Figure 13.2. The output waveforms are shown in Figure 13.3.

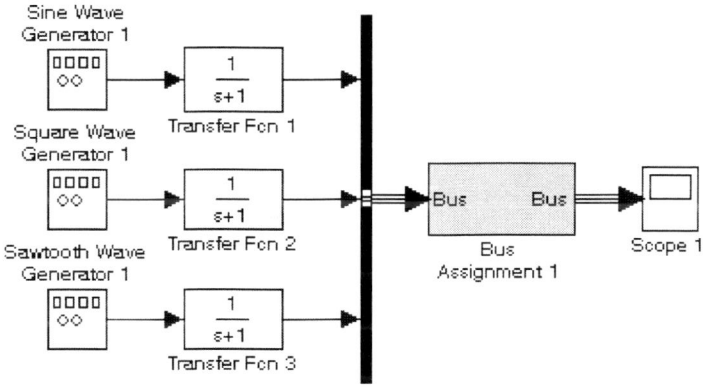

Figure 13.1. Model for Example 13.1

Next, suppose that we wish to replace the Square Wave Generator 1 block and the Sawtooth Wave Generator 1 block with a Random Wave Generator block and a Band-Limited White Noise block. Instead of replacing the blocks, we add the Random Wave Generator block and the Band-Limited White Noise block as shown in Figure 13.4, we double–click on the Bus Assignment block, and we use the **Select** button to move the currently selected signal into the adjacent list of signals to be assigned values. To refresh the display, we click the adjacent **Refresh** button, and the Function Block Parameters dialog box now appears as shown in Figure 13.5. When this is done, the output waveforms appear as shown in Figure 13.6.

Chapter 13 The Signal Routing Library

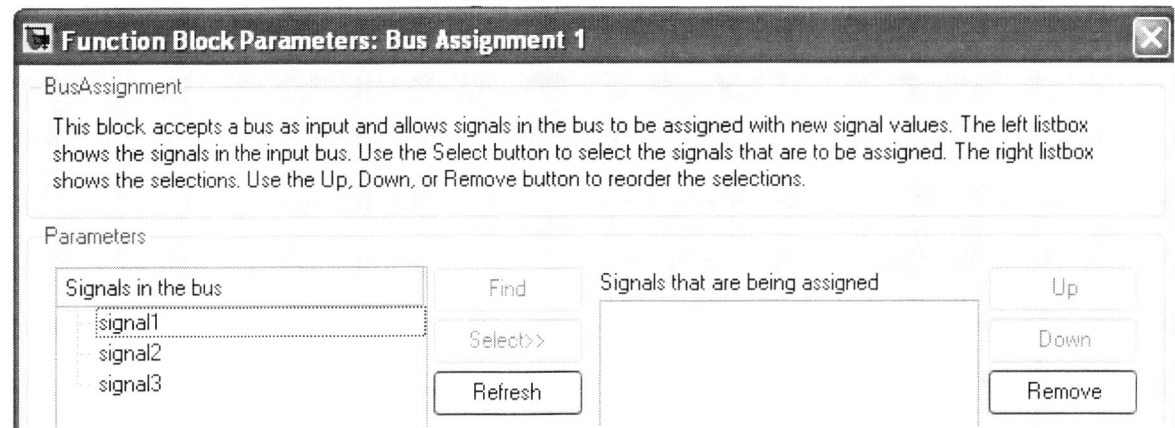

Figure 13.2. Configuration of the Function Block Parameters for the Bus Assignment Block in Figure 13.1

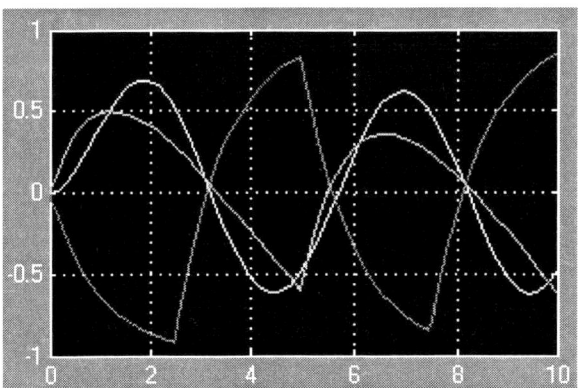

Figure 13.3. Output waveforms for the model of Figure 13.1

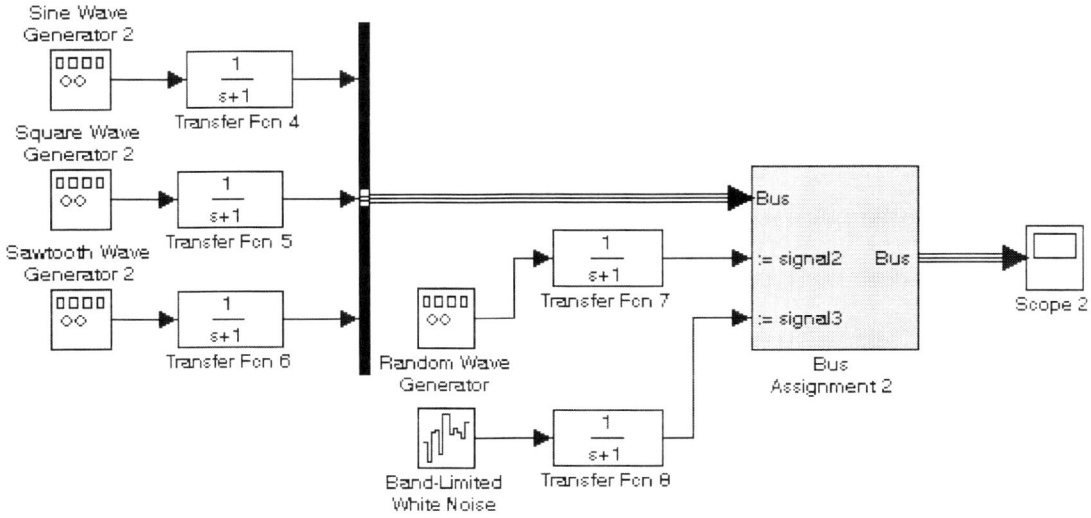

Figure 13.4. Modified model for Example 13.1

13-4   Introduction to Simulink with Engineering Applications
Copyright © Orchard Publications

Signal Routing Group Sub–Library

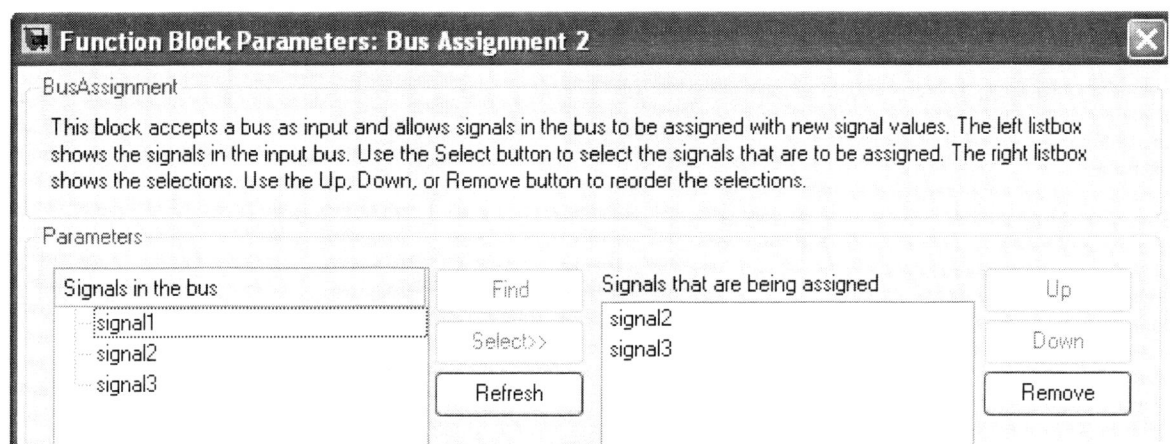

Figure 13.5. Configuration of the Function Block Parameters for the Bus Assignment Block in Figure 13.4

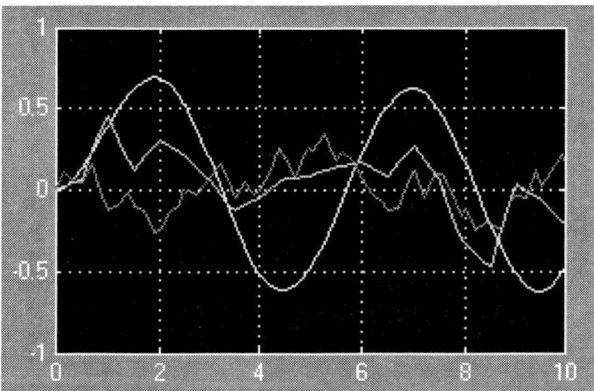

Figure 13.6. Output waveforms for the model of Figure 13.4

13.1.4 The Mux Block

The **Mux** block combines its inputs into a single output. An input can be a scalar, vector, or matrix signal. This block is described in Section 2.7, Chapter 2, Page 2–11.

13.1.5 The Demux Block

The **Demux** block extracts the components of an input signal and outputs the components as separate signals. This block is described in Section 2.7, Chapter 2, Page 2–11.

Chapter 13 The Signal Routing Library

13.1.6 The Selector Block

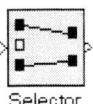

The **Selector** block generates as output selected elements of an input vector or matrix. If the input type is vector, the block outputs a vector of selected elements specified by element indices. The meaning of the indices depends on the setting of the Index mode parameter. If the setting is One–based (the default), the index of the first input element is 1, the second 2, and so on. If the setting is Zero–based, the index of the first element is 0, the second element 1, and so on.

If the input type is matrix, the Selector block outputs a matrix of elements selected from the input matrix. The block determines the row and column indices of the elements to select either from its Rows and Columns parameters or from external signals. We set the block's Source of row indices and Source of column indices to the source that we choose (internal or external). If we set either source to external, the block adds an input port for the external indices signal. If we set both sources to external, the block adds two input ports.

Example 13.2

For the model of Figure 13.7, the elements a11, a12, ...a44 of the 4×4 matrix in the Constant block are specified in MATLAB's Command Window as:

a11=2; a12=−1; a13=0; a14=−3;...
a21=−1; a22=1; a23=0; a24=−1;...
a31=4; a32=0; a33=3; a34=−2;...
a41=−3; a42=0; a43=0; a44=1;

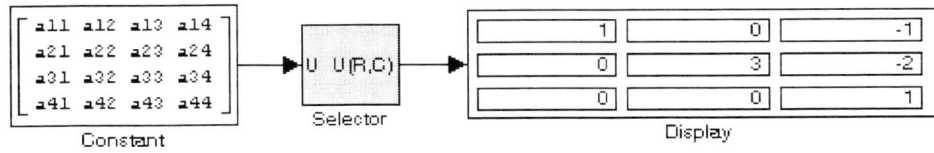

Figure 13.7. Model for Example 13.2

The Display block shows the cofactor of a_{11} defined as $(-1)^{i+j}[M_{ij}]$, where the index i denotes the ith row, the index j denotes the jth column, and M is the minor of the element a_{ij}.

In the Selector block Function Block Parameters dialog box we specified the parameters as follows:

Input type: **Matrix**

Signal Routing Group Sub–Library

Index mode: **One–based**

Source of row indices: **Internal**

Rows: [2 3 4]

Source of column indices: **Internal**

Columns: [2 3 4]

13.1.7 The Index Vector Block

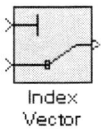

The **Index Vector** block switches the output between different inputs based on the value of the first input, referred to as the **Control Input**. This block is an implementation of the Multiport Switch block which is described in Subsection 13.1.11, this chapter, Page 13–10.

Example 13.3

For the Index Vector block in Figure 13.8, the parameters are specified as Number of inputs 2, and the Use zero–based indexing box is unchecked. All other parameters are left in their default state. Since the Control Input is specified as 2, the Index Vector block outputs the value of Data Input 2.

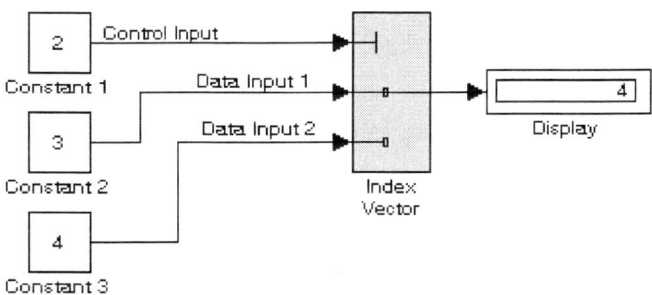

Figure 13.8. Model for Example 13.3

Introduction to Simulink with Engineering Applications
Copyright © Orchard Publications

Chapter 13 The Signal Routing Library

13.1.8 The Merge Block

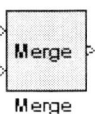

The **Merge** block combines its inputs into a single output line whose value at any time is equal to the most recently computed output of its driving blocks. We can specify any number of inputs by setting the block's Number of inputs parameter. This block is useful in creating alternately executing subsystems as illustrated by the example below.

Example 13.4

The Enable Subsystem 1 and 2 blocks in the model of Figure 13.9 are specified as shown in Figure 13.10. This model outputs the half–wave rectification* waveform shown in Figure 13.11.

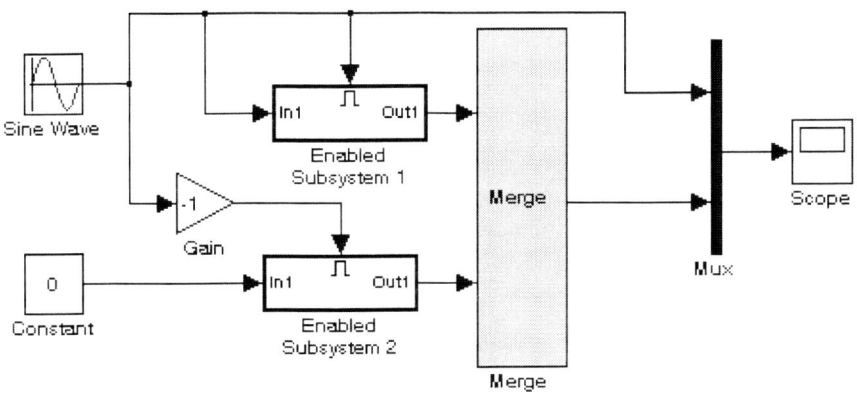

Figure 13.9. Model for Example 13.4

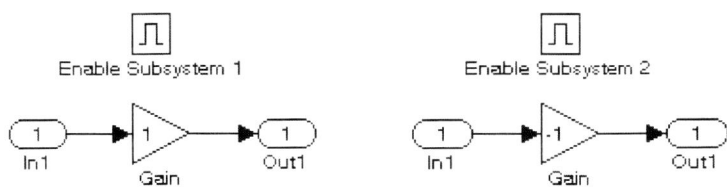

Figure 13.10. Configuration of the Enabled Subsystem 1 and 2 blocks in Figure 13.9

---

* For the creation of a full–wave rectification waveform, please refer to the Help menus for the Merge block and click on the "Creating Alternately Executing Subsystems" link. Full–wave rectifiers are used in the conversion from AC to DC signals. For a detailed discussion, please refer to Signals & Systems with MATLAB Computing and Simulink Modeling, ISBN 0-9744239-9-8.

Signal Routing Group Sub–Library

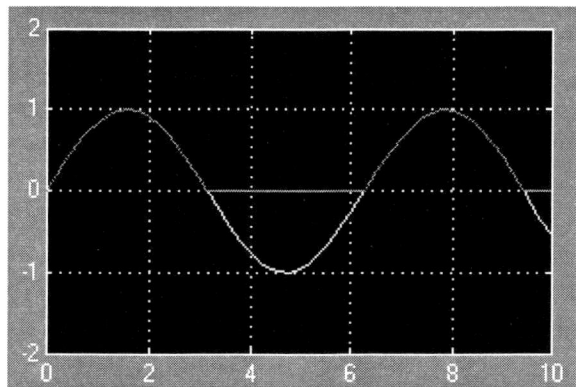

Figure 13.11. Waveforms for the model of Figure 13.9

13.1.9 The Environmental Controller Block

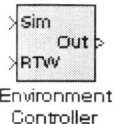

The **Environmental Controller** block outputs the signal at its Sim port only if the model that contains it is being simulated. It outputs the signal at its Real–Time Workshop[*] (RTW) port only if code is being generated from the model.

13.1.10 The Manual Switch Block

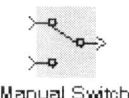

The **Manual Switch** block is a toggle switch that selects one of its two inputs to pass through to the output. There is no dialog box for this block; to toggle between inputs, we double-click the block. The block retains its current state when the model is saved.

Example 13.5

In Figure 13.12, the matrix A is defined in MATLAB's Command Window as

A=[1 2 –3; 2 –4 2; –1 2 –6];

---

[*] *Real–Time Workshop is an extension of MATLAB and Simulink capabilities that generates source code from Simulink models to create real–time software applications. We will not discuss source code generation in this text. Examples are provided in the "Real–Time Workshop For Use with Simulink" documentation.*

Chapter 13 The Signal Routing Library

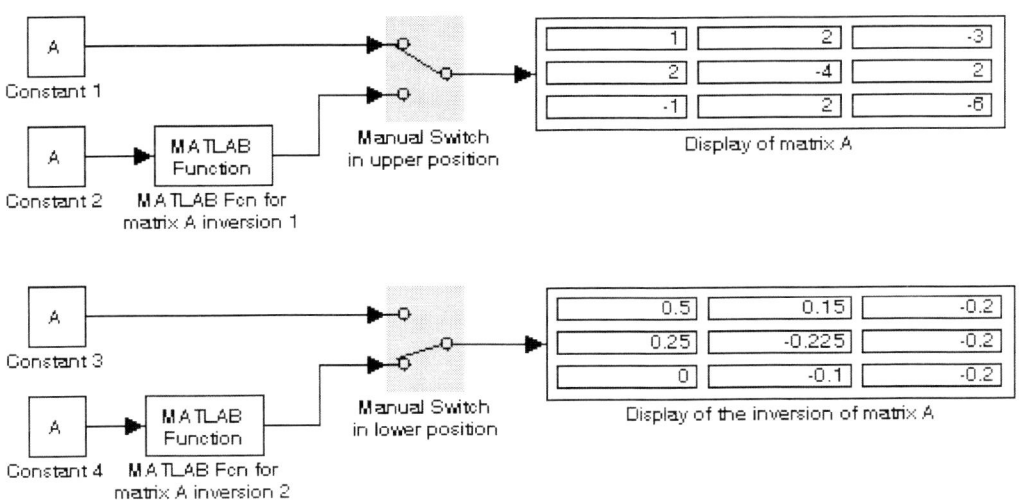

Figure 13.12. Model for Example 13.5

The MATLAB function in the block's parameters dialog box is specified as **inv** (for matrix inversion), and when the Switch block is as shown in the upper model of Figure 13.5, we execute the simulation command, Display 1 block shows the elements of the matrix. When we double-click on the Switch block, it changes to the position shown in the lower model of Figure 13.5, and when we issue the simulation command, Display 2 block shows the elements of the inverted matrix.

13.1.11 The Multiport Switch Block

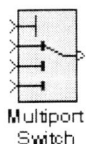

The **Multiport Switch** block chooses between a number of inputs. The first (top) input is called the **control input**, while the rest of the inputs are called **data inputs**. The value of the control input determines which data input is passed through to the output port. If the control input is an integer value, the specified data input is passed through to the output. For example, if the one-based indexing parameter is selected and the control input is 1, the first data input is passed through to the output. If the control input is 2, the second data input is passed through to the output, and so on.

Example 13.6

The model of Figure 13.3 outputs the value 64 corresponding to the control input value 4.

Signal Routing Group Sub–Library

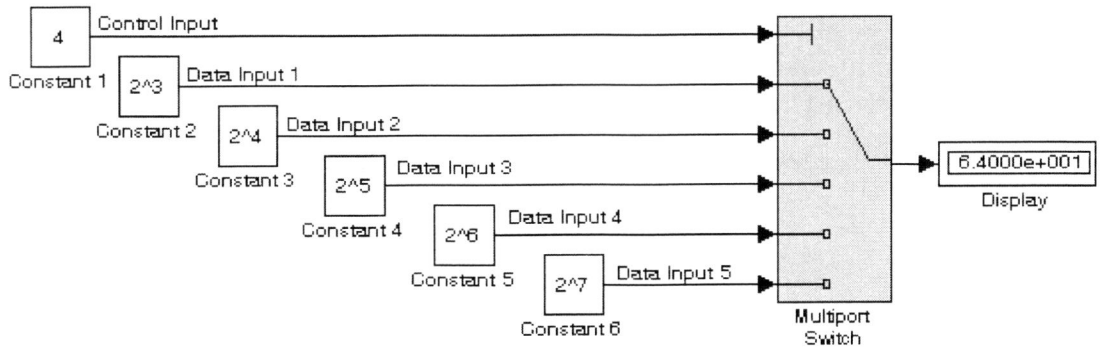

Figure 13.13. Model for Example 13.6

13.1.12 The Switch Block

The **Switch** block outputs the first (top) input or the third (bottom) input depending on the value of the second (middle) input. The first and third inputs are the **data inputs**. The second input is the **control input**. This block is described in Section 2.8, Chapter 2, Page 2–14.

13.1.13 The From Block

The **From** block accepts a signal from a corresponding Goto block which is described in Subsection 13.1.15, this chapter, Page 13–13, and passes it as output. The visibility of a Goto block tag determines the From blocks that can receive its signal.

Example 13.7

In Figure 13.14, the matrix A is defined in MATLAB's Command Window as

A=[1 2 −3; 2 −4 2; −1 2 −6];

In the upper model of Figure 13.14, the Display 1 block shows the elements of matrix A. In the lower model of Figure 13.14, the Constant 2 block sends the elements of matrix A to the Goto block, it is accepted by the From block, and outputs it to the Display 1 block.

The upper and lower models in Figure 13.14 are equivalent. As we can see, the From and Goto blocks allow us to pass a signal from one block to another without a physical connection.

Chapter 13 The Signal Routing Library

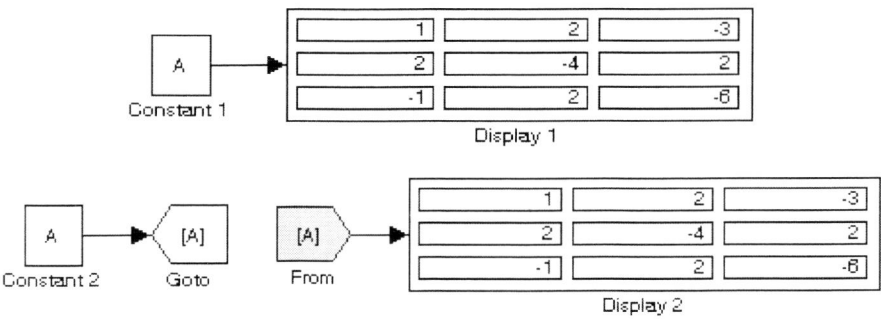

Figure 13.14. Models for Example 13.7

To associate a Goto block with a From block, we enter the Goto block's tag in the Goto Tag parameter. A From block can receive its signal from only one Goto block, although a Goto block can pass its signal to more than one From block.

13.1.14 The Goto Tag Visibility Block

The **Goto Tag Visibility** block defines the accessibility of Goto block tags that have **scoped** visibility. The tag specified as the Goto tag parameter is accessible by From blocks in the same subsystem that contains the Goto Tag Visibility block and in subsystems below it in the model hierarchy. A Goto Tag Visibility block is required for Goto blocks whose Tag visibility parameter value is specified as **scoped**. No Goto Tag Visibility block is needed if the tag visibility is either local or global. When **scoped**, the block shows the tag name enclosed in braces ({}).

Example 13.8

The model in Figure 13.15, is the same as that of in Figure 13.14, except that it includes the Goto Tag Visibility Tag block.

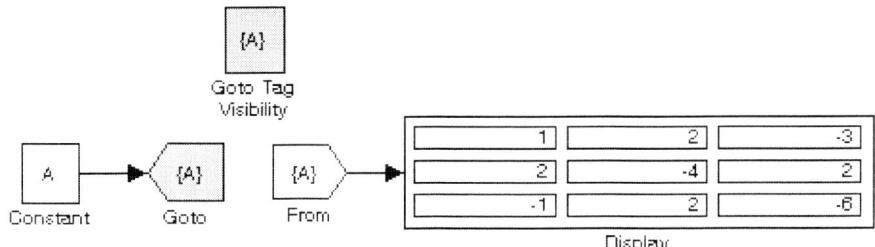

Figure 13.15. Model for Example 13.8

Signal Routing Group Sub–Library

As indicated, in Figure 13.15, the Goto Tag Visibility block has no input and no output but it must be included whenever the visibility is specified as **scoped**. Since the tag visibility is specified as **scoped**, the Goto Tag Visibility block is shown in the model with the tag name enclosed in braces ({}).

13.1.15 The Goto Block

The **Goto** block passes its input to its corresponding From blocks. From and Goto blocks allow us to pass a signal from one block to another without actually connecting them. A Goto block can pass its input signal to more than one From block, although a From block can receive a signal from only one Goto block. The input to that Goto block is passed to the From blocks associated with it as though the blocks were physically connected. Goto blocks and From blocks are matched by the use of Goto tags, defined in the Tag parameter. The Tag visibility parameter determines whether the location of From blocks that access the signal is limited. The three options are:

1. **Local**, the default, means that From and Goto blocks using the same tag must be in the same subsystem. A **local** tag name is enclosed in brackets ([]).

2. **Global** means that From and Goto blocks using the same tag can be anywhere in the model except in locations that span nonvirtual subsystem boundaries. The rule that From-Goto block connections cannot cross nonvirtual subsystem boundaries has the following exception. A Goto block connected to a state port in one conditionally executed subsystem is visible to a From block inside another conditionally executed subsystem. A **global** tag name is not enclosed.

3. **Scoped** means that From and Goto blocks using the same tag must be in the same subsystem or at any level in the model hierarchy below the Goto Tag Visibility block that does not entail crossing a nonvirtual subsystem boundary, i.e., the boundary of an atomic, conditionally executed, or function-call subsystem or a model reference. A **scoped** tag name is enclosed in braces ({}).

Example 13.9

The upper and lower models in Figure 13.16, are equivalent and thus both Scope 1 and Scope 2 blocks display the same waveform shown in Figure 13.17.

Chapter 13 The Signal Routing Library

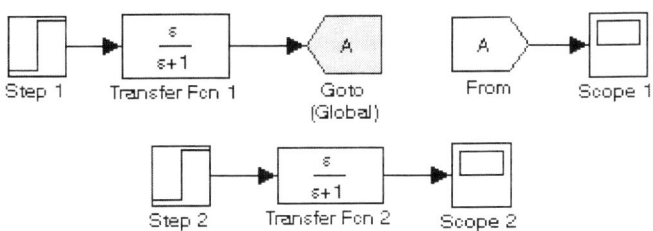

Figure 13.16. Model for Example 13.9

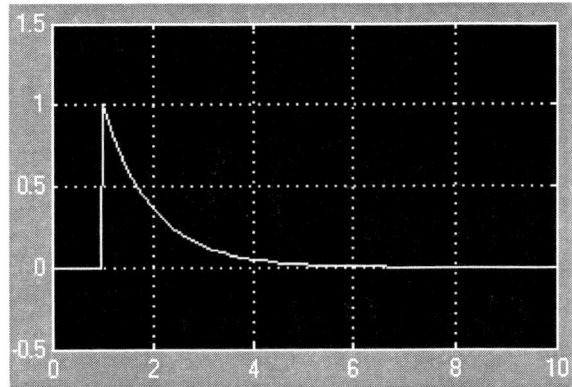

Figure 13.17. Waveform displayed in Scope 1 and Scope 2 blocks in Figure 13.16

13.2 The Signal Storage and Access Group Sub–Library

Data stores are signals that are accessible at any point in a model hierarchy at or below the level in which they are defined. Because they are accessible across model levels, data stores allow subsystems and model references to share data without having to use I/O ports to pass the data from level to level. The **Signal Storage and Access Group Sub–Library** contains the three blocks described in Subsections 13.2.1 through 13.2.3 below.

13.2.1 The Data Store Read Block

The **Data Store Read** block copies data from the named data store to its output. The data store from which the data is read is determined by the location of the Data Store Memory block or signal object that defines the data store. More than one Data Store Read block can read from the same data store. For more information, please refer to Working with Data Stores and Data Store Memory in Help menu for this block. An example is presented in Subsection 13.2.3, this chapter, Page 13–15.

The Signal Storage and Access Group Sub–Library

13.2.2 The Data Store Memory Block

The **Data Store Memory** block defines and initializes a named shared data store, which is a memory region usable by Data Store Read and Data Store Write blocks with the same data store name. The location of the Data Store Memory block that defines a data store determines the Data Store Read and Data Store Write blocks that can access the data store:

1. If the Data Store Memory block is in the top-level system, the data store can be accessed by Data Store Read and Data Store Write blocks located anywhere in the model.

2. If the Data Store Memory block is in a subsystem, the data store can be accessed by Data Store Read and Data Store Write blocks located in the same subsystem or in any subsystem below it in the model hierarchy.

An example is presented in Subsection 13.2.3 below.

13.2.3 The Data Store Write Block

The **Data Store Write** block copies the value at its input to the named data store. Each write operation performed by a Data Store Write block writes over the data store, replacing the previous contents. The data store to which this block writes is determined by the location of the Data Store Memory or signal object that defines the data store. More than one Data Store Write block can write to the same data store.

Example 13.10

In this example, we will create a model that will alternately will display the outputs of a low–pass filter and a high–pass filter whose transfer functions are $1/(s+1)$, and $s/(s+1)$ respectively, when the input is the step function.

We begin with a new model, we drag two Data Store Memory blocks into it, and for the first we define the name **lpfilter**, and for the second the name **hpfilter** as shown in Figure 13.18. Then, we drag two Step blocks, two Transfer Fcn blocks, two Gain blocks, two Data Store Write blocks, and two Scope blocks into the same model, we connect them as shown, and to the first Data Store Write block we assign the name **lpfilter**, and to the second the name **hpfilter** as shown in Figure 13.18.

Chapter 13 The Signal Routing Library

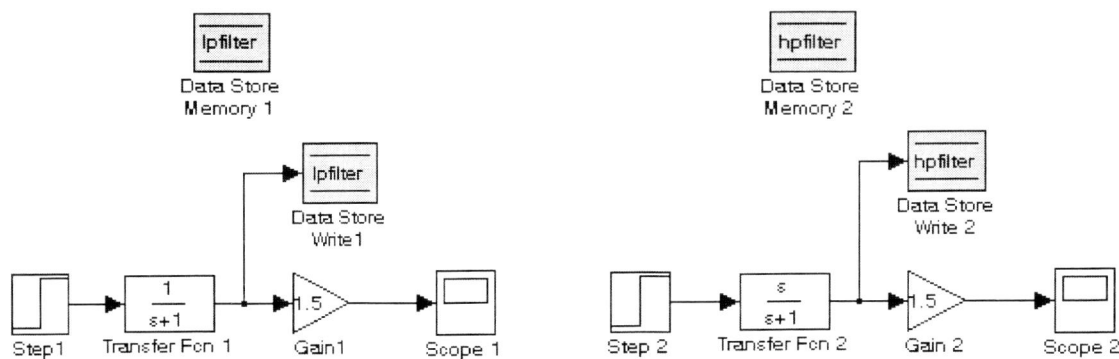

Figure 13.18. Initial model for Example 13.10

Next, we select the Transfer Fcn 1, Gain 1, and Data Store 1 blocks by enclosing them in a bounding box around them, we choose Create Subsystem from the Edit menu. We label this subsystem as Subsystem 1. We repeat for the Transfer Fcn 2, Gain 2, and Data Store 2 blocks, and we label this subsystem as Subsystem 2. The model is now as shown in Figure 13.19, after reshaping and renaming the subsystem blocks.

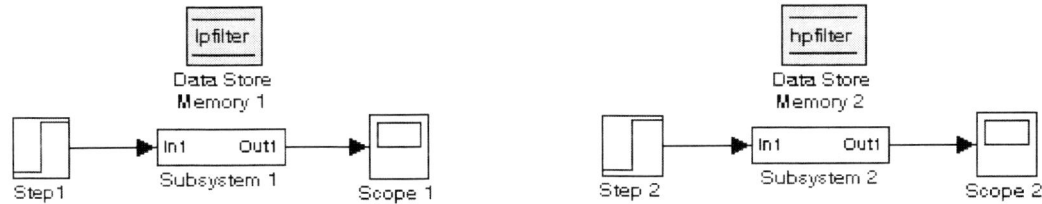

Figure 13.19. Modified model for Example 13.10

Now, we revise the model of Figure 13.19 by adding the Manual Switch block as shown in Figure 13.20 so that we can switch between Subsystem 1 for the low–pass filter, and Subsystem 2 for the high–pass filter to observe their waveforms shown in Figures 13.21 and 13.22 respectively.

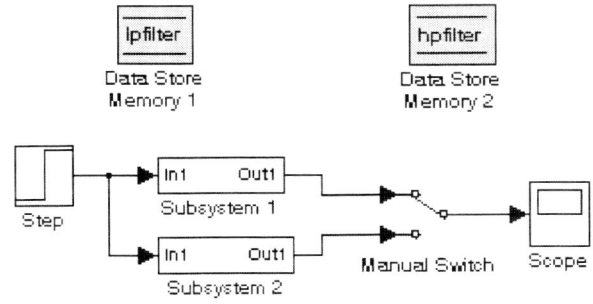

Figure 13.20. The model of Example 13.10 in its final form

13-16   Introduction to Simulink with Engineering Applications
          Copyright © Orchard Publications

The Signal Storage and Access Group Sub–Library

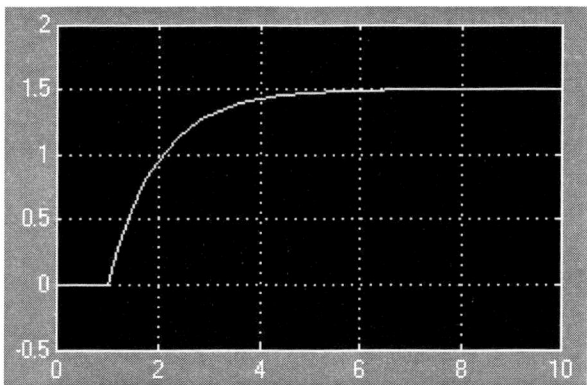

Figure 13.21. Waveform of the output of Subsystem 1 (Low-pass filter with Gain = 1.5)

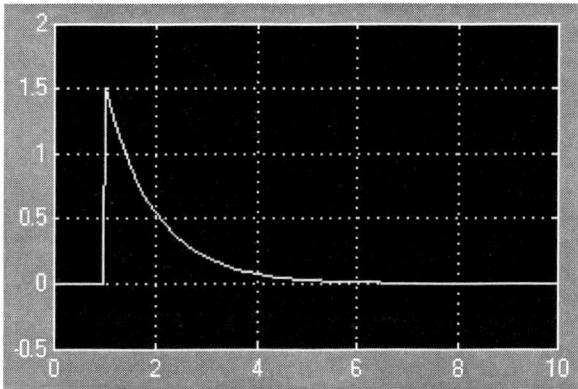

Figure 13.22. Waveform of the output of Subsystem 2 (High-pass filter with Gain = 1.5)

In Example 13.10 we illustrated the use of the Data Store Memory block and the Data Store Write block. The use of the Data Store Read block is illustrated in Figure 13.23.

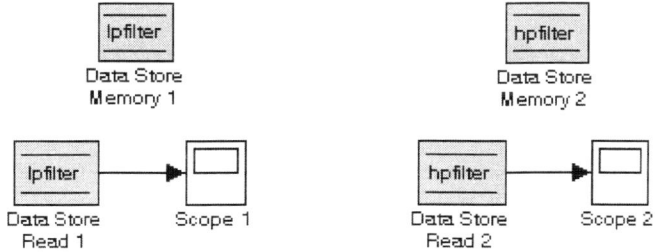

Figure 13.23. Models to illustrate the use of the Data Store Read block

The Scope 1 and Scope 2 blocks in Figure 13.23 display the same waveforms as those in Figure 13.21 and Figure 13.22.

13.3 Summary

- The **Bus Creator** block combines a set of signals into a group of signals represented by a single line.

- The **Bus Selector** block outputs a specified subset of the elements of the bus at its input.

- The **Bus Assignment** block assigns values, specified by signals connected to its assignment (:=) input ports, to specified elements of the bus connected to its Bus input port.

- The **Mux block** combines its inputs into a single output. An input can be a scalar, vector, or matrix signal.

- The **Demux block** extracts the components of an input signal and outputs the components as separate signals.

- The **Selector** block generates as output selected elements of an input vector or matrix. If the input type is vector, the block outputs a vector of selected elements specified by element indices. If the input type is matrix, the Selector block outputs a matrix of elements selected from the input matrix.

- The **Index Vector** block switches the output between different inputs based on the value of the first input, referred to as the Control Input. This block is an implementation of the Multiport Switch block.

- The **Merge** block combines its inputs into a single output line whose value at any time is equal to the most recently computed output of its driving blocks. We can specify any number of inputs by setting the block's Number of inputs parameter.

- The **Environmental Controller** block outputs the signal at its **Sim** port only if the model that contains it is being simulated. It outputs the signal at its Real–Time Workshop (**RTW**) port only if code is being generated from the model.

- The **Manual Switch** block is a toggle switch that selects one of its two inputs to pass through to the output. There is no dialog box for this block; to toggle between inputs, we double-click the block. The block retains its current state when the model is saved.

- The **Multiport Switch** block chooses between a number of inputs. The first (top) input is called the **control input**, while the rest of the inputs are called **data inputs**. The value of the control input determines which data input is passed through to the output port.

- The **Switch** block outputs the first (top) input or the third (bottom) input depending on the value of the second (middle) input. The first and third inputs are the **data inputs**. The second input is the **control input**.

- The **From** block accepts a signal from a corresponding Goto block, then passes it as output.

Summary

- The **Goto Tag Visibility** block defines the accessibility of Goto block tags that have scoped visibility.

- The **Goto** block passes its input to its corresponding From blocks.

- The **Data Store Read** block copies data from the named data store to its output. The data store from which the data is read is determined by the location of the Data Store Memory block or signal object that defines the data store.

- The **Data Store Memory** block defines and initializes a named shared data store, which is a memory region usable by Data Store Read and Data Store Write blocks with the same data store name.

- The **Data Store Write** block copies the value at its input to the named data store. Each write operation performed by a Data Store Write block writes over the data store, replacing the previous contents.

Chapter 13 The Signal Routing Library

NOTES

Chapter 14

The Sinks Library

This chapter is an introduction to the **Sinks** library. This is the thirteenth library in the Simulink group of libraries and consists of three sub–libraries, the **Model & Subsystem Outputs Sub-Library**, the **Data Viewers Sub-Library**, and the **Simulation Control Sub-Library** blocks shown below. We will describe the function of each block included in this library and we will perform simulation examples to illustrate their application.

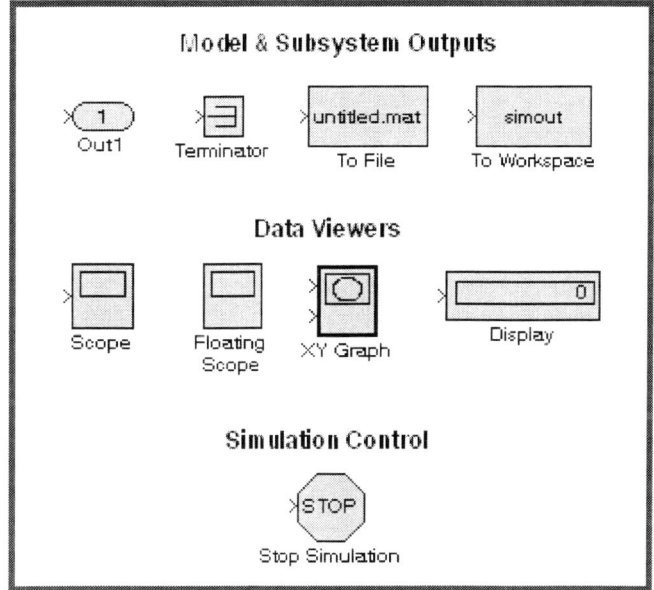

Chapter 14 The Sinks Library

14.1 Models and Subsystems Outputs Sub-Library

The **Models and Subsystems Outputs Sub-Library** contains the blocks described in Subsections 14.1.1 through 14.1.4 below.

14.1.1 The Outport Block

The **Outport** block creates an external output or an output port for a subsystem. This block is described in Section 2.1, Chapter 2, Page 2-2.

14.1.2 The Terminator Block

The **Terminator** block can be used to cap blocks whose output ports are not connected to other blocks. If we run a simulation with blocks having unconnected output ports, Simulink issues warning messages. We use Terminator blocks to cap those blocks to avoid warning messages. This block is described in Section 2.3, Chapter 2, Page 2-5.

14.1.3 The To File Block

The **To File** block writes its input to a matrix in a MAT-file. The block writes one column for each time step: the first row is the simulation time; the remainder of the column is the input data, one data point for each element in the input vector.

Example 14.1

Let us consider matrix C defined as

$$C = \begin{bmatrix} 1 & 2 & 3 & 4 \\ -1 & 1 & 0 & -1 \\ 4 & 0 & 3 & -2 \\ -3 & -1 & 2 & -4 \end{bmatrix}$$

where the elements of the first row are time points,[*] and the remaining rows contain data points that correspond to the time point in that column. Thus at time 3, the outputs are 0, 3, and 2,

---

[*] *The time points must always be monotonically increasing.*

Models and Subsystems Outputs Sub-Library

which are the data points for the third column encountered at time 3. We enter the elements of matrix C in MATLAB's Command Window as

C=[1 2 3 4; -1 1 0 -1; 4 0 3 -2; -3 -1 2 -4];

and we save it as **matrixC.mat** by selecting **Save Workspace As** from MATLAB's **File** menu.

Next, we drag the **From File** block[*] found in the Sources library and the **To File** block into a new model as shown in Figure 14.1 where to the **From File** block we have assigned the name **matrixC**, and to the **To File** block we have assigned the name **matrixCToFile.mat**.

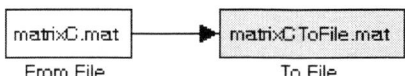

Figure 14.1. Example of copying the contents of a From File block to a To File block

Upon execution of the simulation command the contents of the **matrixC** file are copied into the **matrixCToFile.mat** file and saved by that name. We can verify this as follows:

In MATLAB's Command Window we type

open matrixCToFile.mat

```
    ans =
        ans: [4x51 double]
```

Next, in MATLAB's Command Window we type

whos

```
    Name        Size         Bytes  Class
    C           4x4            128  double array
    ans         1x1           1756  struct array
    tout        51x1           408  double array

    Grand total is 272 elements using 2292 bytes
```

From MATLAB's Command Window we select **Import Data** from the **File** menu, and we choose the file **matrixCToFile.mat**. The **Import Wizard** window displays the data shown in Figure 14.2.

---

[*] *The From File block belongs to the Model and Subsystem Input sub-library described in the Sources Library, Section 15.1.3, Chapter 15., Page 15-2.*

Introduction to Simulink with Engineering Applications
Copyright © Orchard Publications

14-3

Chapter 14 The Sinks Library

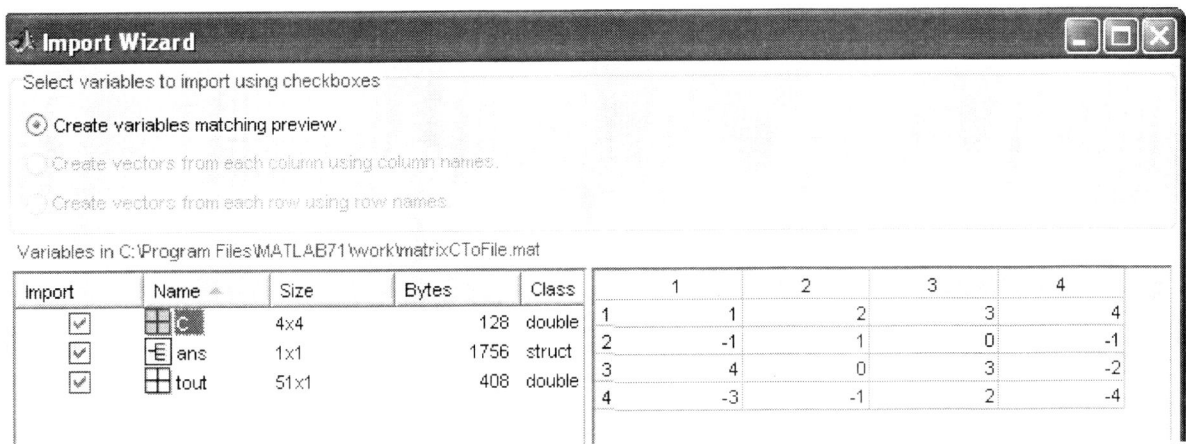

Figure 14.2. Displaying the contents of matrix C of Example 14.1 in Import Wizard

14.1.4 The To Workspace Block

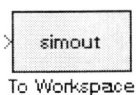

The **To Workspace** block writes its input to the workspace. This block writes its output to an array or structure that has the name specified by the block's Variable name parameter. The Save format parameter determines the output format.

The MATLAB Workspace consists of the set of variables generated by the execution of a program and these are stored in memory.

Example 14.2

Let us consider the matrix multiplication $A \cdot B$ where $A = [1\ -1\ 2]'$ and $B = [2\ 3\ 4]$, and create a model to include a To Workspace block at the output.

Matrix A is a 3×1 size and matrix B is a 1×3 size and matrix so these matrices are conformable for multiplication. The model is shown in Figure 14.3 where to the To Workspace block we assigned the name **matrixmult**.

Next, in MATLAB's Command Window we type

    who

and MATLAB lists the current workspace variables as

```
Your variables are:
matrixmult    simout    tout
```

The Data Viewers Sub-Library

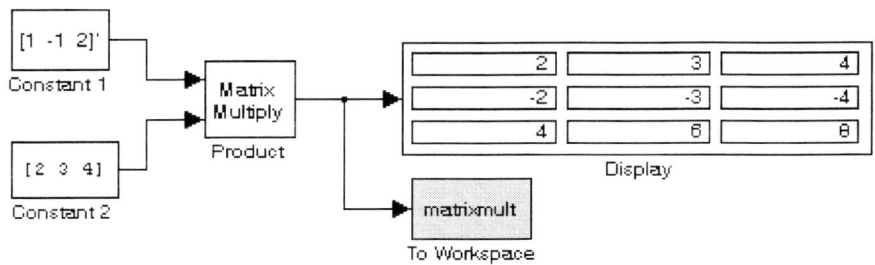

Figure 14.3. Model for Example 14.2

Also, in MATLAB's Command Window we type

    whos

and MATLAB lists the current workspace variables and information about their size and class as

```
Name              Size      Bytes    Class
matrixmult        1x1       4482     struct array
simout            1x1       4482     struct array
tout              51x1       408     double array
Grand total is 1035 elements using 9372 bytes
```

If we exit MATLAB, the workspace is cleared. But we can save any or all of the variables to a **MAT-file.**[*] MAT-files use the .mat extension. We can then invoke this MAT-file at a later time.

To save the workspace variables for this file, we select **Save Workspace As** from MATLAB's **File** menu.

14.2 The Data Viewers Sub-Library

The **Data Viewers Sub-Library** contains the four blocks described in Subsections 14.2.1 through 14.2.4 below.below.

---

[*] A MAT-file stores data in binary (not human-readable) form. We need not know the internal format of a MAT-file. This file writes the arrays currently in memory to a file as a continuous byte stream. For a detailed discussion please log on to www.csb.yale.edu/userguides/ datamanip/matlab/pdf/**matfile_format.pdf**.

Chapter 14 The Sinks Library

14.2.1 The Scope Block

The **Scope** block displays its input with respect to simulation time. The Scope block can have multiple axes (one per port), but all axes have a common time range with independent y-axes. The Scope allows us to adjust the amount of time and the range of input values displayed. We can move and resize the Scope window and we can modify the Scope's parameter values during the simulation. At the end of the simulation, Simulink transmits data to the connected Scopes but does not automatically open the Scope windows. The signal(s) will be displayed when we double-click on the Scope block after simulation termination.

If the signal is continuous, the Scope produces a point–to–point plot. If the signal is discrete, the Scope produces a stair–step plot. When displaying a vector or matrix signal, the Scope assigns colors to each signal element in this order: yellow, magenta, cyan, red, green, and dark blue. When more than six signals are displayed, the Scope cycles through the colors in the order listed. We set y–limits by right–clicking an axis and choosing Axes Properties.

When we open the Scope block we observe several toolbar icons that enable us to zoom in on displayed data, preserve axis settings from one simulation to the next, limit data displayed, and save data to the workspace. The toolbar icons are labeled in the Help menu for this block. The Help menu provides more information than what is provided in this subsection.

Example 14.3

The model shown in Figure 14.4 displays a sine waveform, a square waveform, a sawtooth waveform, and a random signal waveform on a single Scope block with one input. All four generators are Signal Generator blocks configured to produce and display the four different waveforms. Each was specified at 0.2 Hz frequency, and all other parameters were left in their default states. The waveforms are shown in Figure 14.5.

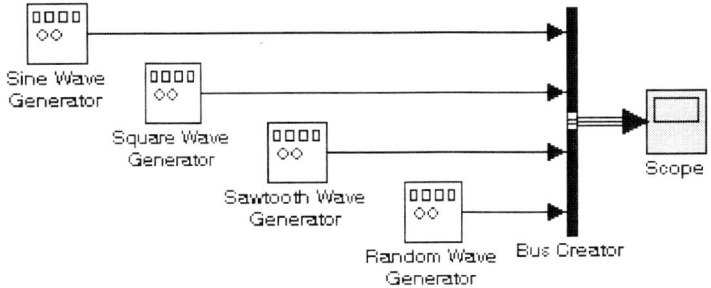

Figure 14.4. Model for Example 14.3

The Data Viewers Sub-Library

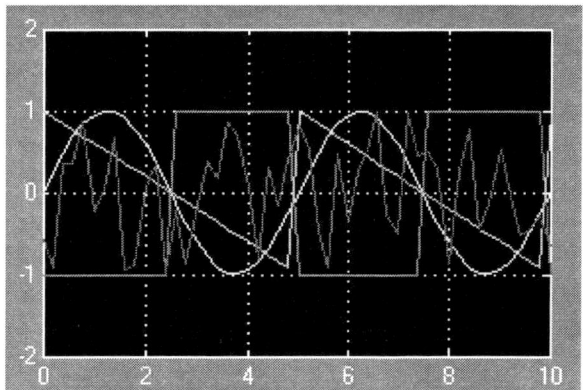

Figure 14.5. Waveforms for sine wave, square wave, sawtooth wave and random wave signal generators

In all of the previous examples we have shown the Scope block with only one input where the signals from the previous blocks have been combined via a Bus Creator block. However, we can display the Scope block with two or more inputs as illustrated with the following example.

Example 14.4

The model shown in Figure 14.6 displays a sine waveform, a square waveform, a sawtooth waveform, and a random signal waveform on a single Scope block with four inputs. All four generators are Signal Generator blocks configured to produce and display the four different waveforms. Each was specified at 0.2 Hz frequency, and all other parameters were left in their default states.

On the Scope block we click on the Parameters icon (second from left), and we specify **Number of Axes: 4**. The waveforms are shown in Figure 14.7.

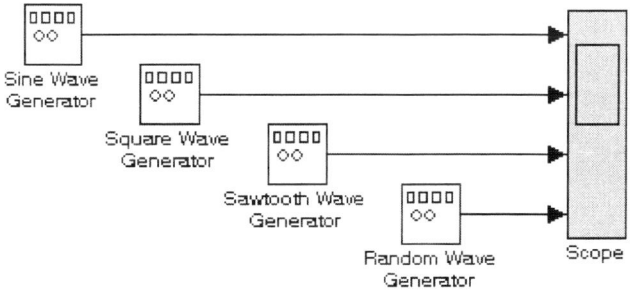

Figure 14.6. Model for Example 14.4

Chapter 14 The Sinks Library

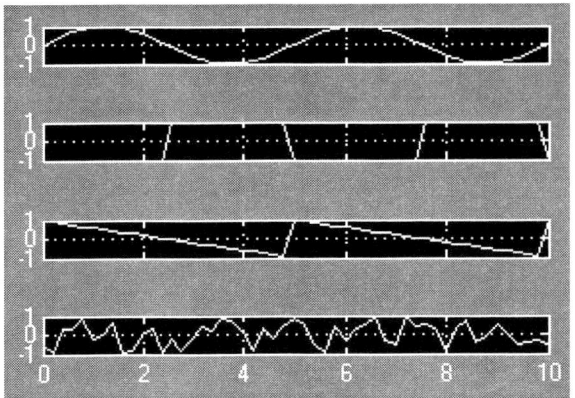

Figure 14.7. Waveforms for the model of Figure 14.6

14.2.2 The Floating Scope Block

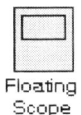

One of the options appearing on the General parameters pane for the Scope block described in the previous subsection, is the **Floating Scope**. A Floating scope is a Scope block that can display the signals carried on one or more lines. We can create a Floating Scope block in a model either by copying a Scope block from the Simulink Sinks library into a model and selecting this option or, more simply, by copying the Floating Scope block from the Sinks library into the model window. The Floating Scope block has the Floating scope parameter selected by default. The procedure for using and displaying one or more signals on a Floating Scope is illustrated with the example below.

Example 14.5

The model shown in Figure 14.8 displays a sine waveform, a square waveform, a sawtooth waveform, and a random signal waveform on a single Floating Scope block with four inputs. All four generators are Signal Generator blocks configured to produce and display the four different waveforms. Each specified set at 0.2 Hz frequency, and all other parameters were left in their default states.

Before executing the simulation command, we click on the Floating Scope whose display is as shown in Figure 14.9. On the Floating Scope block, we click on the Parameters icon (second from left – to the right of the print icon), and we specify **Number of Axes: 4**. The Floating Scope block now becomes a a multi-axis floating scope as shown in Figure 14.10.

The Data Viewers Sub-Library

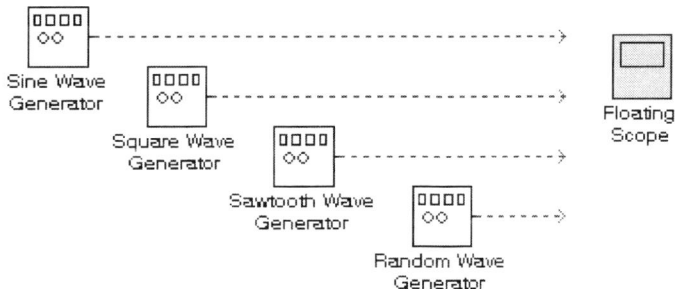

Figure 14.8. Model for Example 14.5

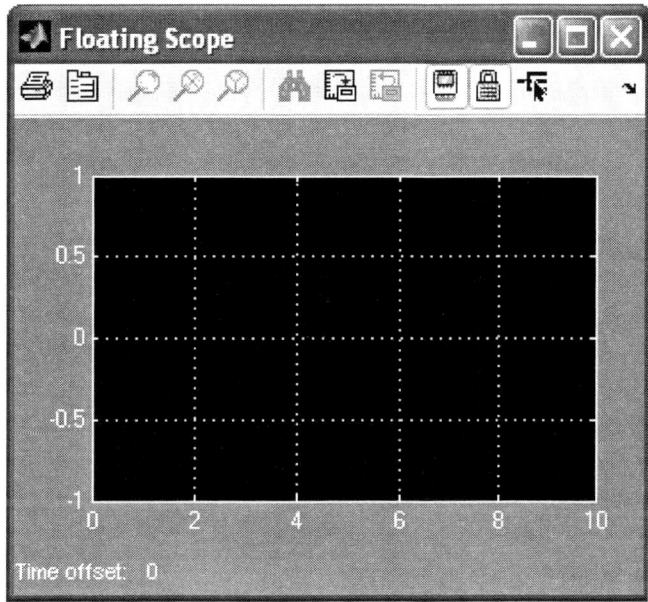

Figure 14.9. Floating Scope for the model of Figure 14.8

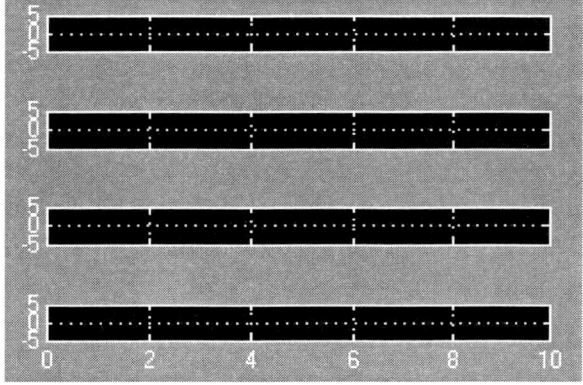

Figure 14.10. The Floating Scope of Figure 14.9 with 4 axes

1. To specify the display of the sine waveform on the first (top) axis, we click on that axis. Simulink draws a blue border around that axis as shown in Figure 14.11.

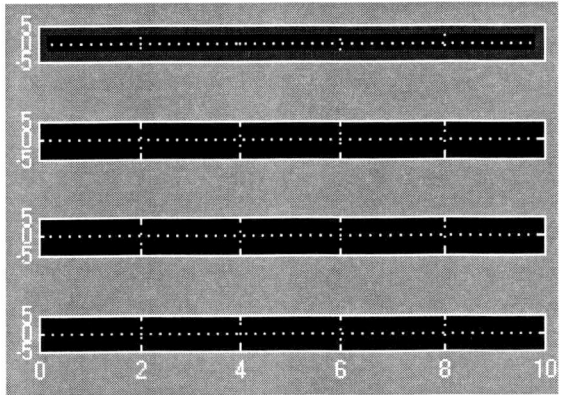

Figure 14.11. Specifying display of a signal on the Floating Scope

2. We return to the model of Figure 14.8 and we select one or more signal (broken) line(s). To select multiple lines, we hold down Shift key while clicking another line.

3. To use a floating scope during a simulation, we must disable the signal storage reuse and block reduction optimization options. To disable them, we click **Simulation** on the model of Figure 14.8, we click on the **Configuration Parameters**, we click on the **Optimization** field (left side), and we deselect the **Signal storage reuse** and **Block reduction optimization** parameters.

4. We right-click on the axis with the blue border around it, we click on **Axis properties** we set the y-axis at −1 (min) and +1 (max), we right-click again, and we click on **Signal selection**. On the Signal Selector window shown in Figure 14.12 we choose the Sine Wave Generator.

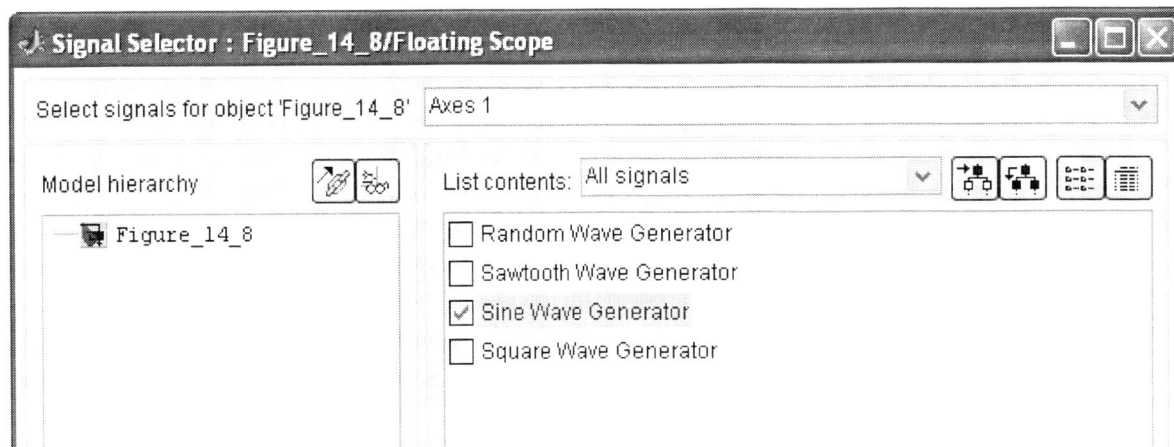

Figure 14.12. The Signal Selector window for the model of Figure 14.8

5. We issue the Simulation command and the displays on the Floating Scope are as shown in Figure 14.13.

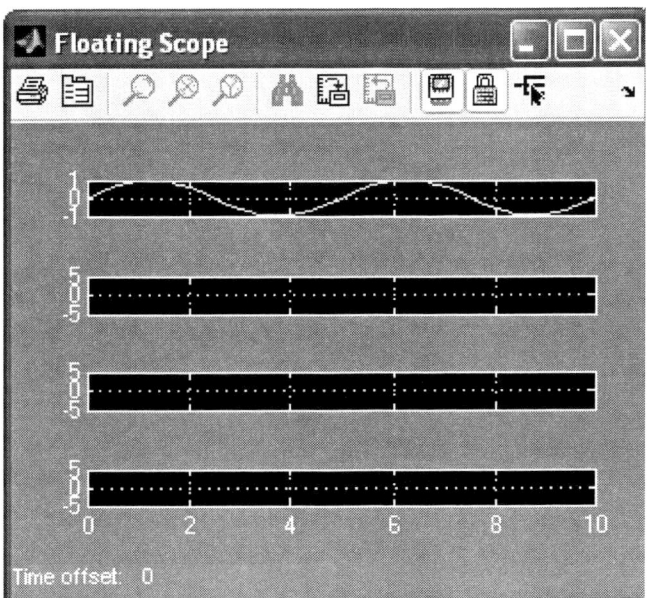

Figure 14.13. The display of the sine waveform on the Floating Scope

We repeat steps 1 through 5 for the remaining axes. The Floating Scope displays are now as shown in Figure 14.14.

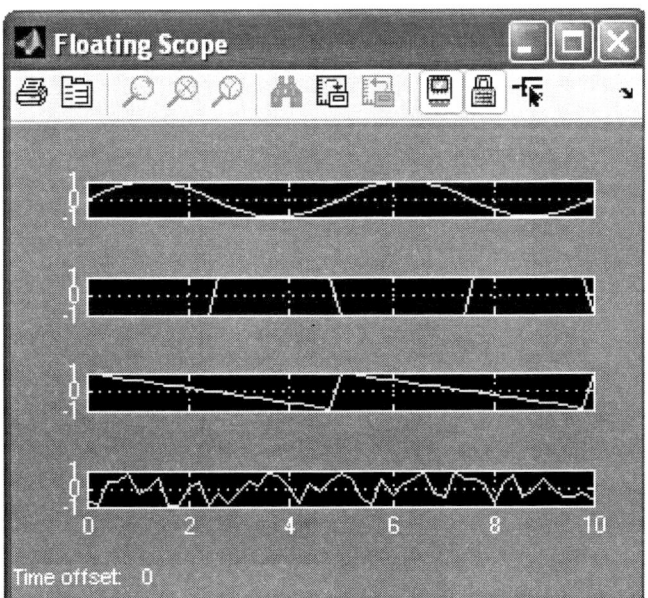

Figure 14.14. Floating Scope for the model of Figure 14.8 with all signals displayed

Chapter 14 The Sinks Library

We can choose to have more than one Floating Scope in a model, but only one set of axes in one scope can be active at a given time. Active floating scopes show the active axes with a blue border.

14.2.3 The XY Graph Block

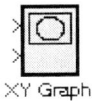

The **XY Graph** block displays an X–Y plot of its inputs in a MATLAB figure window. This block plots data in the first input (the x direction) against data in the second input (the y direction).

Example 14.6

The For Iterator Subsystem in Figure 14.15 is shown in Figure 14.16 where the initial condition for the Memory block is set to $\pi/128$ and for the MATLAB Fcn block we have selected the sine function from the Block Parameters menu. With the values shown, upon execution of the simulation command, the XY Graph block displays the waveform shown in Figure 14.17. This waveform indicates that at the beginning of the simulation cycle the value of y jumps to the value corresponding to 2π and decreases to its minimum value.

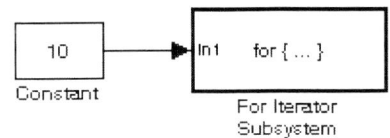

Figure 14.15. Model for Example 14.6

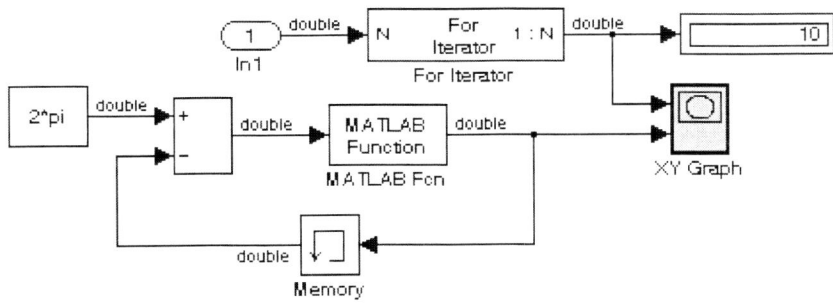

Figure 14.16. The subsystem of Figure 14.15

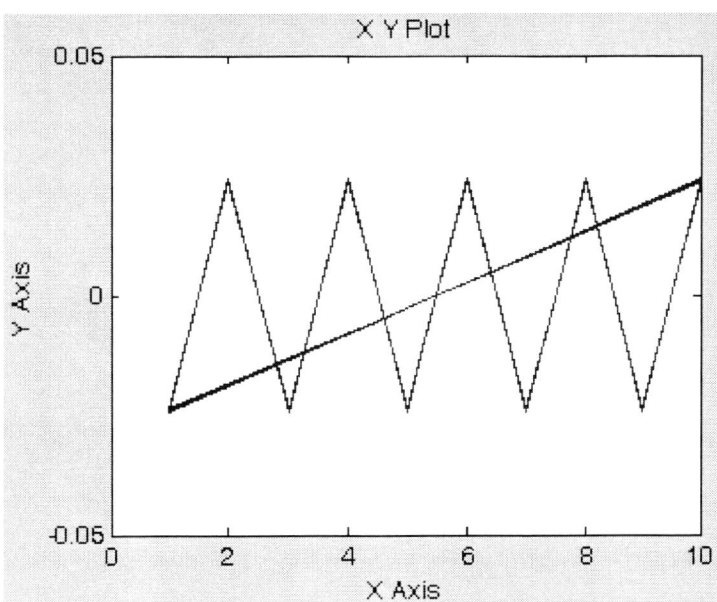

Figure 14.17. The XY Plot displayed by the XY Graph block in Figure 14.16

14.2.4 The Display Block

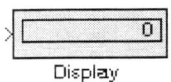

The **Display** block shows the value of its input on its icon. The display formats are the same as those of MATLAB. They are also specified in the Help menu for this block. The Decimation parameter enables us to display data at every *n*th sample, where *n* is the decimation factor. Thus, the default decimation 1 displays data at every time step. We use the Sample time parameter to specify a sampling interval at which to display points. This parameter is useful when we are using a variable–step solver where the interval between time steps might not be the same. The default value of –1 causes the block to ignore the sampling interval when determining the points to display.

If the block input is an array, we must resize the block to see more than just the first element. The Display block can be resized vertically or horizontally. The presence of a small black triangle indicates that the block is not displaying all input array elements.

Example 14.7

The model of Figure 14.18 displays the trigonometric functions $\sin x$, $\cos x$, $\tan x$, $\sinh x$, $\cosh x$, and $\tanh x$ evaluated at $\pi/6$ and $\pi/3$. It was necessary to resize the Display block to display all values.

Chapter 14 The Sinks Library

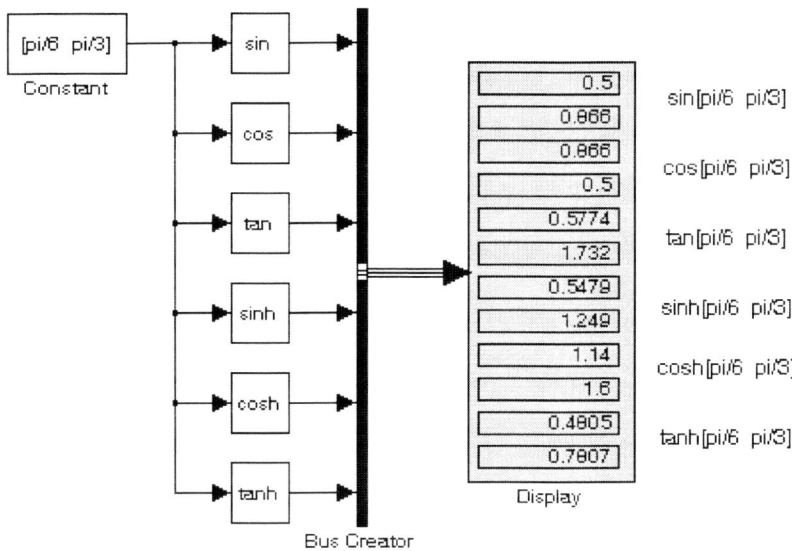

Figure 14.18. Model for Example 14.7

14.3 The Simulation Control Sub-Library

The **Simulation Control Sub-Library** contains only one block, the **Stop Simulation** block described below.

The **Stop Simulation** block stops the simulation when the input is nonzero. A common use of this block is when used in conjunction with a relational operator. The simulation completes the current time step before terminating. If the block input is a vector, any nonzero vector element causes the simulation to stop.

Example 14.8

The model is shown in Figure 14.19 uses a Stop Simulation block and a Relational Operator block to terminate simulation when the first input is equal to the second input. We observe that the simulation stops when the digital clock attains the value 10. The waveforms are shown in Figure 14.20.

The Simulation Control Sub–Library

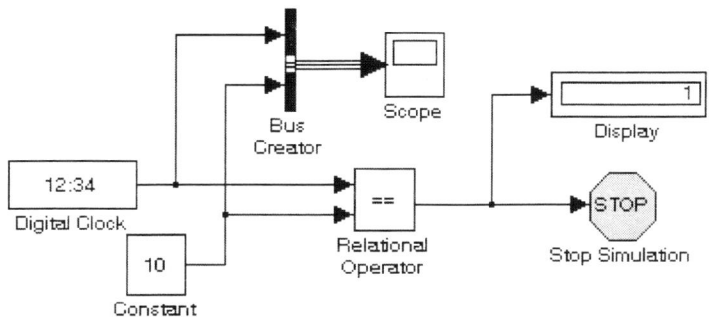

Figure 14.19. Model for Example 14.8

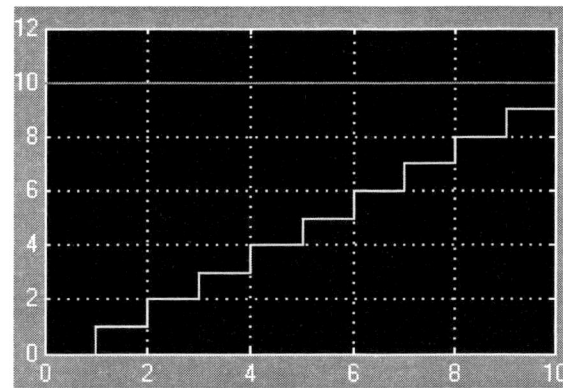

Figure 14.20. Waveforms for the model of Figure 14.19

14.4 Summary

- The **Outport** block creates an external output or an output port for a subsystem.

- The **Terminator** block is used to cap blocks whose output ports are not connected to other blocks. We use Terminator blocks to cap those blocks to avoid warning messages.

- The **To File** block writes its input to a matrix in a MAT-file. The block writes one column for each time step: the first row is the simulation time; the remainder of the column is the input data, one data point for each element in the input vector.

- The **To Workspace** block writes its input to the workspace. The block writes its output to an array or structure that has the name specified by the block's Variable name parameter. The Save format parameter determines the output format.

- The **Scope** block displays its input with respect to simulation time. The Scope block can have multiple axes (one per port); all axes have a common time range with independent y-axes. We can use a Bus Creator block to combine two or more signals to a Scope block with only one input. We can also display the input signals to a Scope block with two or more inputs.

- The **Floating scope** is a Scope block that can display the signals carried on one or more lines.

- The **XY Graph** block displays an X-Y plot of its inputs in a MATLAB figure window. This block plots data in the first input (the x direction) against data in the second input (the y direction).

- The **Display** block shows the value of its input on its icon. The display formats are the same as those of MATLAB. They are also specified in the Help menu for this block. If the block input is an array, we must resize the block to see more than just the first element. The Display block can be resized vertically or horizontally. The presence of a small black triangle indicates that the block is not displaying all input array elements.

- The **Stop Simulation** block stops the simulation when the input is nonzero. A common use of this block is when used in conjunction with a relational operator. The simulation completes the current time step before terminating. If the block input is a vector, any nonzero vector element causes the simulation to stop.

Chapter 15

The Sources Library

This chapter is an introduction to the **Sources** library. This is the fourteenth library in the Simulink group of libraries and consists of two sub-libraries, the **Model & Subsystem Inputs Sub-Library**, and the **Signal Generators Sub-Library** blocks shown below. We will describe the function of each block included in this library and we will perform simulation examples to illustrate their application.

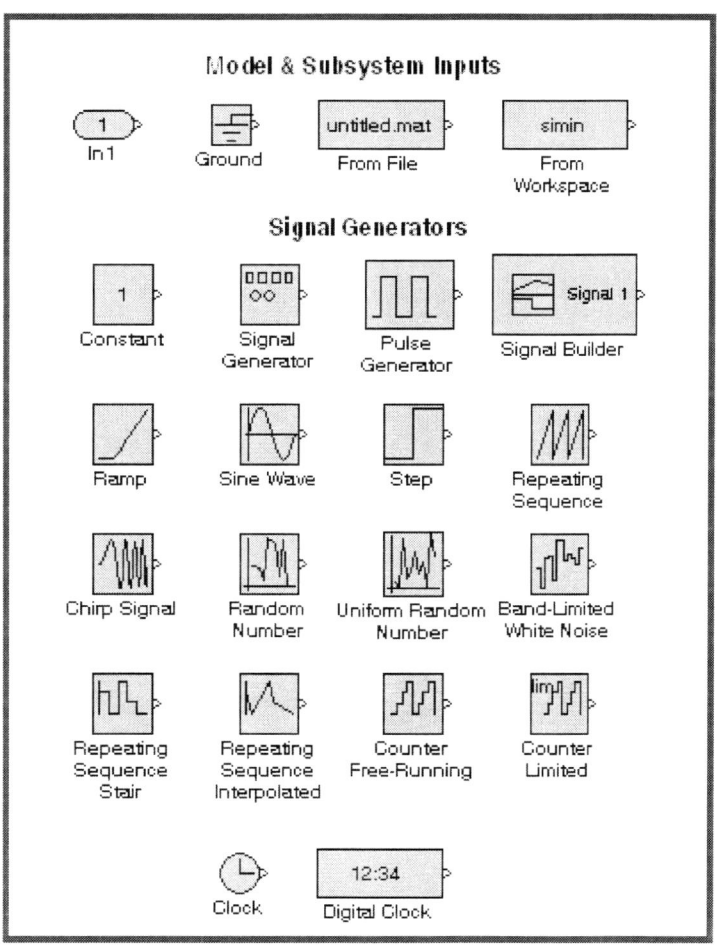

Chapter 15 The Sources Library

15.1 Models and Subsystems Inputs Sub–Library

The **Models and Subsystems Inputs Sub–Library** contains the blocks described in Subsections 15.1.1 through 15.1.4 below.

15.1.1 The Inport Block

The **Inport** block creates an input port for a subsystem or an external input. This block is described in Section 2.1, Chapter 2, Page 2-2.

15.1.2 The Ground Block

The **Ground** block grounds an unconnected input port. This block is described in Section 2.2, Chapter 2, Page 2–4.

15.1.3 The From File Block

The **From File** block outputs data read from a MAT file. The name of the file is displayed inside the block. An example using the From File and the To File blocks was presented in Subsection 14.1.3, Chapter 14, Page 14–2.

15.1.4 The From Workspace Block

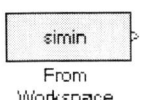

The **From Workspace** block reads data from the MATLAB workspace. The workspace data are specified in the block's Data parameter via a MATLAB expression that evaluates to a 2–D array.

Example 15.1

For the model of Figure 15.1, the MATLAB workspace contains the statement

t=1:10; u=log10(t);

In the Display block, the first 10 values are those specified by t, and the last ten values are those specified by u.

The Signal Generators Sub–Library

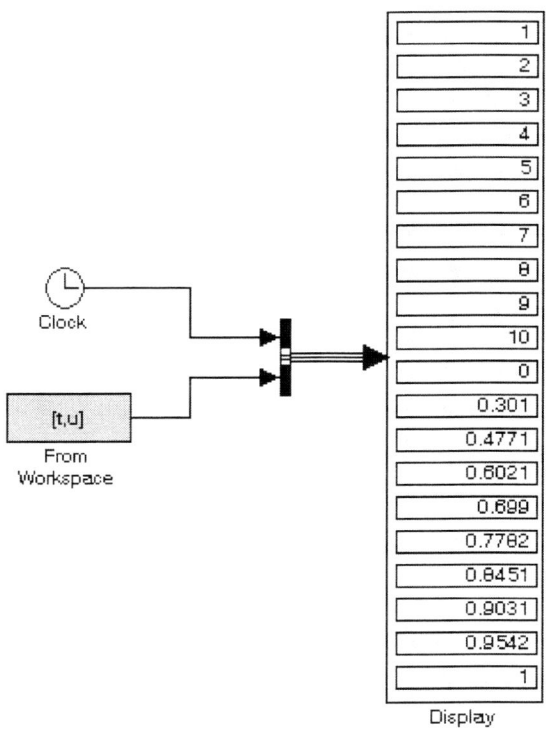

Figure 15.1. Model for Example 15.1

15.2 The Signal Generators Sub–Library

The **Signal Generators Sub–Library** contains the eighteen blocks described in Subsections 15.2.1 through 15.2.18 below.

15.2.1 The Constant Block

The **Constant** block generates a real or complex constant value. This block is described in Section 2.4, Chapter 2, Page 2–6.

Chapter 15 The Sources Library

15.2.2 The Signal Generator Block

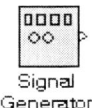
Signal Generator

The **Signal Generator** block can produce one of four different waveforms: sine wave, square wave, sawtooth wave, and random wave. The signal parameters can be expressed in Hertz (the default) or radians per second. We can invert the waveform by specifying a negative amplitude in the block's parameters window.

Example 15.2

The model in Figure 15.2 shows all four possible configurations of the Signal Generator block to produce and display the four different waveforms. Each is specified at 0.2 Hz frequency with the unlisted parameters in their default state. The waveforms are shown in Figure 15.3.

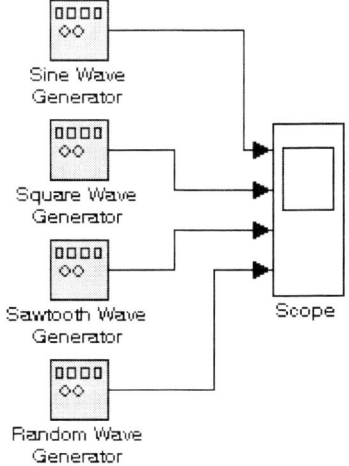

Figure 15.2. Model for Example 15.2

The Signal Generators Sub–Library

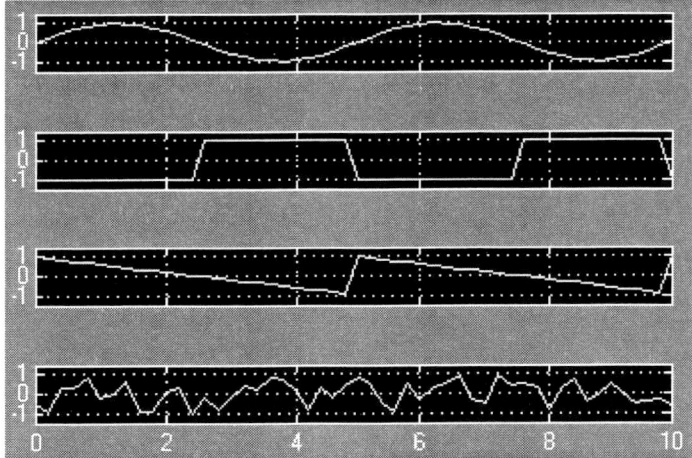

Figure 15.3. Waveforms for sine wave, square wave, sawtooth wave and random wave signal generators

15.2.3 The Pulse Generator Block

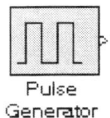

The **Pulse Generator** block generates square wave pulses at regular intervals. The shape of the generated waveform depends on the parameters, Amplitude, Pulse Width, Period, and Phase Delay as shown in Figure 15.4.

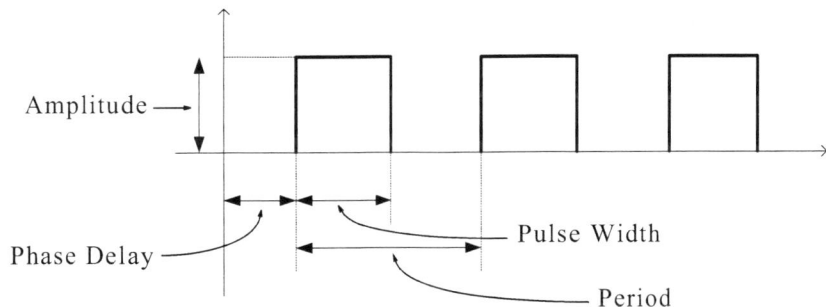

Figure 15.4. Illustration of the Pulse Generator block parameters

Example 15.3

In the model of Figure 15.5, the Pulse Generator block parameters are specified as:

Amplitude: 1, Period: 3, Pulse Width: 50, Phase Delay: 1

Chapter 15 The Sources Library

The unlisted parameters are left in their default states.

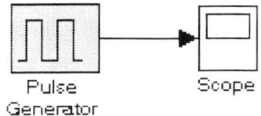

Figure 15.5. Model for Example 15.3

The Scope block displays the waveform shown in Figure 15.6.

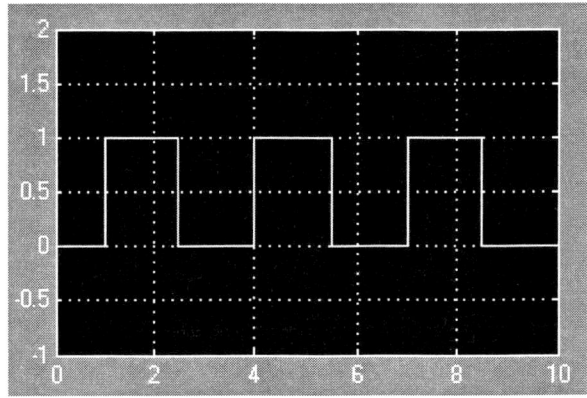

Figure 15.6. Waveform for the model of Figure 15.5

15.2.4 The Signal Builder Block

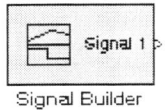

The **Signal Builder** block allows us to create interchangeable groups of piece–wise linear signal sources and use them in a model. The procedure for building a piece–wise linear signal is as follows:

1. We first double-click on the Signal Builder block, a waveform similar to that shown in Figure 15.7 is displayed. The points at the ends of each line segment indicate that this waveform is selected. To deselect it, we press the Esc key.

2. To select a particular point, we position the mouse cursor over that point and we left-click. A circle is drawn around that point to indicate that it is selected.

3. To select a line segment, we left-click on that segment. That line segment is now shown as a thick line indicating that it is selected. To deselect it, we press the Esc key.

The Signal Generators Sub–Library

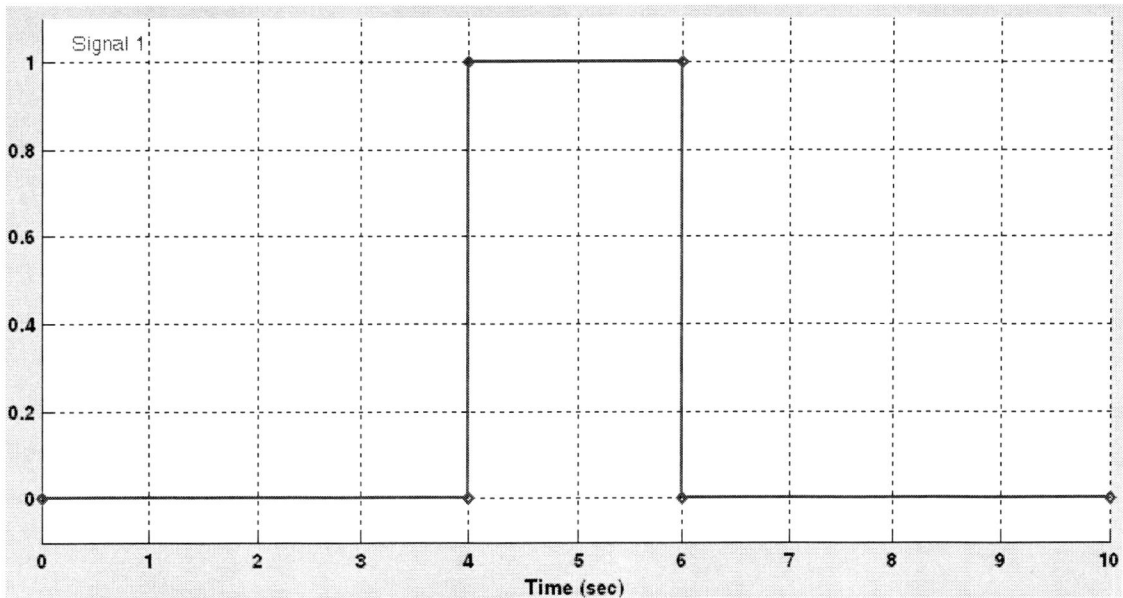

Figure 15.7. Waveform displayed when the Signal Builder block is double-clicked the first time

4. To drag a line segment to a new position, we place the mouse cursor over that line segment and the cursor shape shows the position in which we can drag the segment.

5. To drag a point along the y–axis, we move the mouse cursor over that point, and the cursor changes to a circle indicating that we can drag that point. We can then move that point in a direction parallel to the x–axis.

6. To drag a point along the x–axis, we select that point, and we hold down the Shift key while dragging that point.

7. When we select a line segment on the time axis (x–axis) we observe that at the lower end of the waveform display window the **Left Point** and **Right Point** fields become visible. We can then reshape the given waveform by specifying the Time (**T**) and Amplitude (**Y**) points. For our example we will use the triangular waveform shown in Figure 15.8.

Example 15.4

For the triangular waveform of Figure 15.8 it is specified that the Time (**T**) and Amplitude (**Y**) points are (0,0), (1,1), (2,0), (3,1), (4,0), (5,1), (6,0), (7,1), (8,0), (9,1), and (10,0).

The menu bar at the top contains several icons that we could use to modify our waveform.

After the simulation command is executed, the model of Figure 15.9 displays the triangular waveform and its integrated waveform in Figure 15.10.

Chapter 15 The Sources Library

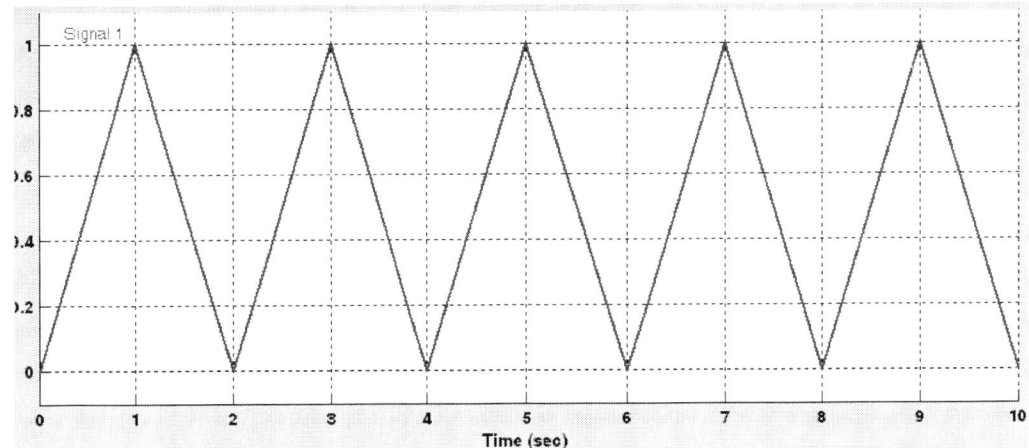

Figure 15.8. Triangular waveform for Example 15.4

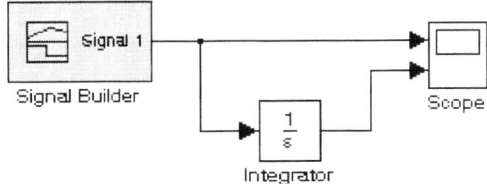

Figure 15.9. Model for Example 15.4

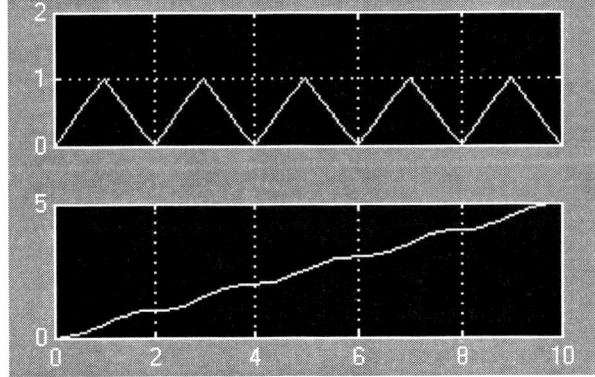

Figure 15.10. Waveforms for the model of Figure 15.9

The Signal Generators Sub–Library

15.2.5 The Ramp Block

The **Ramp** block generates a signal that starts at a specified time and value and changes by a specified rate. The characteristics of the generated signal are determined by the specified Slope, Start time, Duty Cycle, and Initial output parameters.

Example 15.5

With the Ramp block parameters at their default states, the Scope block in Figure 15.11 displays the waveform shown in Figure 15.12.

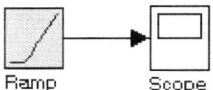

Figure 15.11. Model for Example 15.5

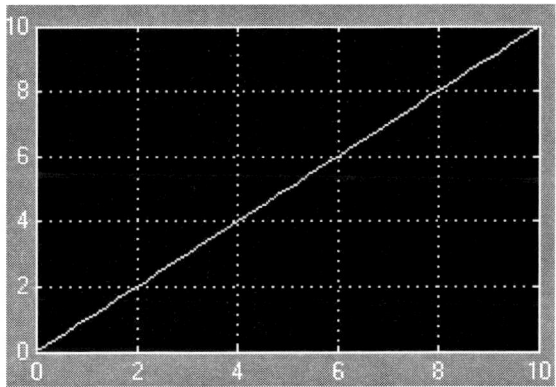

Figure 15.12. Waveform for the model of Figure 15.11

15.2.6 The Sine Wave Block

The **Sine Wave** block generates a sine wave. To generate a cosine wave, we specify the Phase parameter as $\pi/2$. The Sine type can be either **time–based mode** or **sample–based mode** sine wave block.

Introduction to Simulink with Engineering Applications
Copyright © Orchard Publications

Chapter 15 The Sources Library

1. The time–based mode has two submodes: **continuous submode** or **discrete submode**. We use the Sample time parameter to specify that the block will operate in the continuous submode or discrete submode. For the continuous submode we specify the 0 value (the default), and for the discrete submode we specify a value greater than zero.

2. The sample–based mode requires a finite discrete time. A Sample time parameter value greater than zero causes the block to behave as if it were driving a Zero–Order Hold block whose sample time is set to that value. The formulas used are given in the Help menu for this block.

The following parameters appear in the Dialog Box:

Sine type – Type of sine wave generated by this block, either time– or sample–based. Some of the other options presented by the Sine Wave dialog box depend on whether we select time-based or sample-based as the value of Sine type parameter.

Time – Specifies whether to use simulation time as the source of values for the sine wave's time variable or an external source. If we specify an external time source, the block displays an input port for the time source.

Amplitude – The amplitude of the signal. The default is 1.

Bias – Constant (DC) value added to the sine to produce the output of this block.

Frequency – The frequency, in radians/second. The default is 1 rad/s. This parameter appears only if we specify time–based as the Sine type of the block.

Samples per period – Number of samples per period. This parameter appears only if we specify sample-based as the Sine type of the block.

Phase – The phase shift, in radians. The default is 0 radians. This parameter appears only if we specify time–based as the Sine type of the block.

Number of offset samples – The offset (discrete phase shift) in number of sample times. This parameter appears only if we specify sample-based as the Sine type of the block.

Sample time – The sample period. The default is 0. If the sine type is sample-based, the sample time must be greater than 0. We can refer to Specifying Sample Time in the online documentation for more information.

Interpret vector parameters as 1–D – If checked, column or row matrix values for the Sine Wave block's numeric parameters result in a vector output signal; otherwise, the block outputs a signal of the same dimensionality as the parameters. If this option is not selected, the block always outputs a signal of the same dimensionality as the block's numeric parameters.

The Signal Generators Sub–Library

Example 15.6

For the model shown in Figure 15.13 the parameters for the Sine Wave blocks are specified as follows:

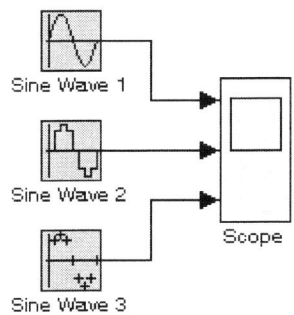

Figure 15.13. Model for Example 15.6

Sine Wave 1 block – All parameters in their default state.

Sine Wave 2 block – Sample time: 0.25. All other parameters in default state.

Sine Wave 3 block – Sine type: Sample based, Sample time: 0.25. All other parameters in default state.

The waveform for each is shown in Figure 15.14.

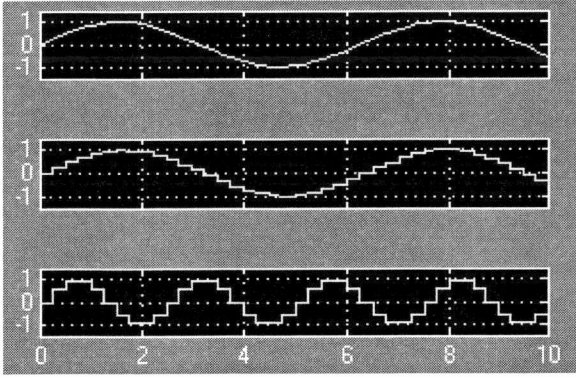

Figure 15.14. Waveforms for the model of Figure 15.13

15.2.7 The Step Block

Chapter 15 The Sources Library

The **Step** block generates a step between two defined levels at some specified time. If the simulation time is less than the Step time parameter value, the block's output is the Initial value parameter value. For simulation time greater than or equal to the Step time, the output is the Final value parameter value.

Example 15.7

For the model shown in Figure 15.15 the parameters for the Step blocks were specified as follows:

Step 1 block – Step time: 1. All other parameters are in their default state.

Step 2 block – Step time: 5. All other parameters are in their default state.

Step 3 block – Step time: 10. All other parameters are in their default state.

The waveforms are shown in Figure 15.16.

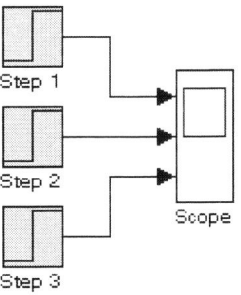

Figure 15.15. Model for Example 15.7

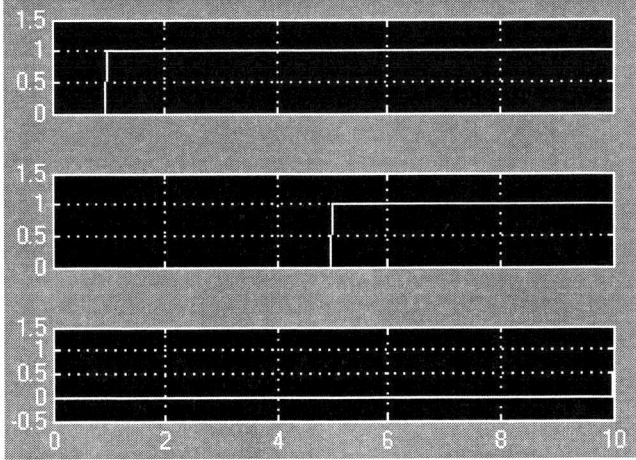

Figure 15.16. Waveforms for the model of Figure 15.15

The Signal Generators Sub–Library

15.2.8 The Repeating Sequence Block

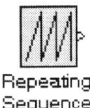

The **Repeating Sequence** block outputs a periodic waveform that we specify using the block dialog's Time values and Output values parameters. The default of the Time values and Output values parameters are both set to [0 2]. This setting specifies a sawtooth waveform that repeats every 2 seconds from the start of the simulation with a maximum amplitude of 2. This block uses linear interpolation to compute the value of the waveform between the specified sample points.

Example 15.8

For the model shown in Figure 15.17, the parameters for the Repeating Sequence blocks are as follows:

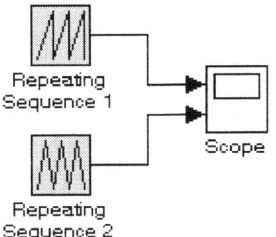

Figure 15.17. Model for Example 15.8

Repeating Sequence 1 block – Time values: [0 2], Output values: [0 2]

Repeating Sequence 2 block – Time values: [0 1 2], Output values: [0 2 0]

With these parameter specifications, the waveforms are as shown in Figure 15.18.

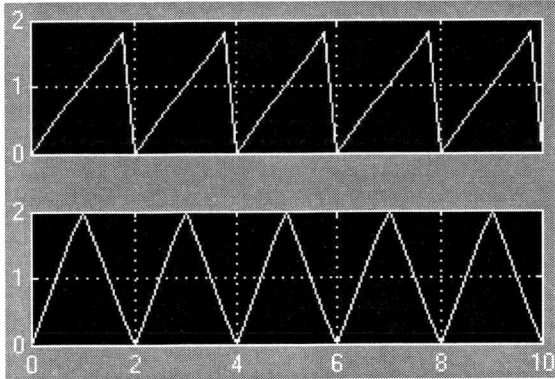

Figure 15.18. Waveforms for the model of Figure 15.17

15.2.9 The Chirp Signal Block

The **Chirp Signal** block generates a sine wave whose frequency increases at a linear rate with time. The model of Figure 15.19 displays the waveform shown in Figure 15.20.

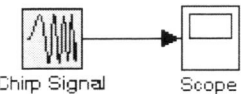

Figure 15.19. Model for displaying the output of the Chirp Signal block

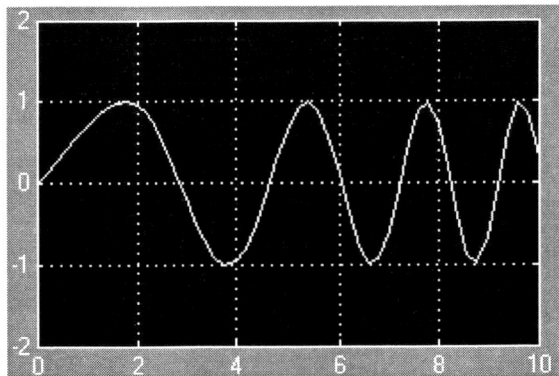

Figure 15.20. Output waveform of the Chirp Signal block

Chirp signals[*] can be used for analyzing the spectral components of a variety of nonlinear systems. They offer practical solutions to problems arising in radar and sonar systems design.

15.2.10 The Random Number Block

The **Random Number** block generates normally distributed random numbers. The seed[†] is reset to the specified value each time a simulation starts. By default, the sequence produced has a mean of 0 and a variance of 1, but we can specify other values for these parameters. The sequence of

---

[*] Another Chirp block is included in the Signal Processing Sources library of the Signal Processing Blockset. This block outputs a swept-frequency cosine (chirp) signal with unity amplitude and continuous phase. We can see an example by typing doc_chirp_ref at the MATLAB command line.
[†] The seed is defined in Appendix C.

The Signal Generators Sub–Library

numbers is repeatable and can be produced by any Random Number block with the same seed and parameters. To generate a vector of random numbers with the same mean and variance, we specify the Initial seed parameter as a vector. To generate uniformly distributed random numbers, we use the Uniform Random Number block which is described in Section 15.2.11, this chapter, Page 15–16.

For a discussion and an example of generating a sequence for a random number generator, please refer to Appendix C.

Example 15.9

With the Random Number block Sample time parameter specified as 0.25 and the remaining at their default states, the Scope block in Figure 15.21 displays the waveform shown in Figure 15.22.

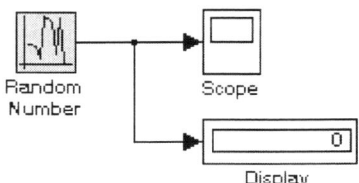

Figure 15.21. Model for Example 15.9

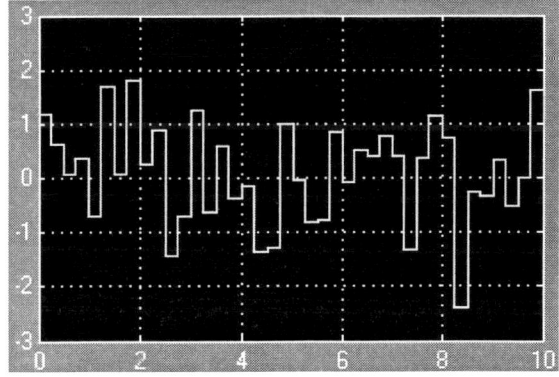

Figure 15.22. Waveform for the model of figure 15.21

15.2.11 The Uniform Random Number Block

Chapter 15 The Sources Library

The **Uniform Random Number** block generates uniformly distributed[*] random numbers over a specified interval with a specified starting seed. The seed is reset each time a simulation starts. The generated sequence is repeated and can be produced by any Uniform Random Number block with the same seed and parameters. To generate normally distributed random numbers, we use the Random Number block which is described in Subsection 15.2.10, this chapter, Page 15–14.

Example 15.10

For comparison, the model of Figure 15.23 contains the Random Number (normally distributed) block and the Uniform Random Number block. With the Sample time parameter at 0.25 for both blocks and the remaining at their default states, the Scope block in Figure 15.23 displays the waveforms shown in Figure 15.24.

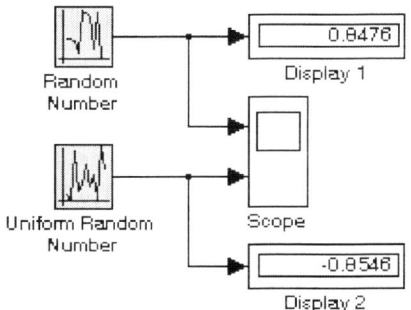

Figure 15.23. Model for Example 15.10

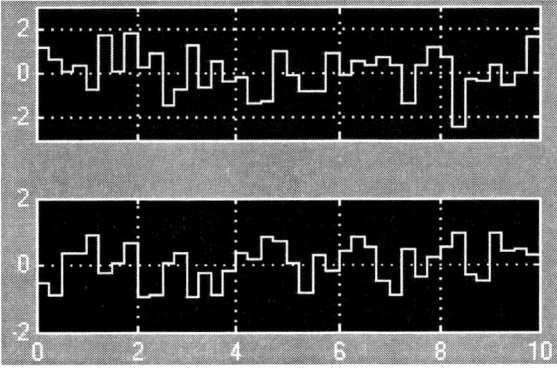

Figure 15.24. Waveforms for the model of Figure 15.23

---

[*] *For a detailed discussion on uniform and normal distributions, please refer to Mathematics for Business, Science, and Technology, ISBN 0-970951108.*

The Signal Generators Sub–Library

15.2.12 The Band Limited White Noise Block

White noise[*] has a constant power, usually denoted as P_0, over a bandwidth that theoretically extends from $-\infty$ to $+\infty$ as shown in Figure 15.25.

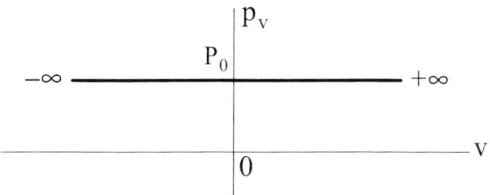

Figure 15.25. White noise in a theoretical sense

In a practical sense, white noise is limited is some way. For instance, the **thermal noise**[†] in a resistor is contained in a certain finite bandwidth extended from $-B$ to $+B$ as shown in Figure 15.26, and thus it is referred to as **band-limited white noise**.

In Simulink, the **Band–Limited White Noise** block is an implementation of white noise into Zero–Order Hold block. As described in Subsection 5.2.3, Chapter 5, Page 5-23, the Zero–Order Hold block samples and holds its input for the specified sample period. The block accepts one input and generates one output, both of which can be scalar or vector.

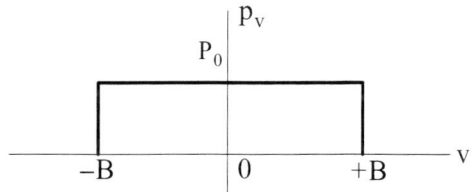

Figure 15.26. Band-limited white noise

---

[*] *The adjective "white" is used to describe this type of noise in analogy with the white light. White light is a blend of all the colors in the visual spectrum, resulting in the color white that is made up of all of the different colors (frequencies) of light combined together. As we know from physics, a prism separates white light back into its component colors.*

[†] *Thermal noise is the result of random fluctuations of the charge carriers in any conductive medium and is dependent on the temperature.*

Chapter 15 The Sources Library

In Simulink, we can simulate the effect of white noise by using a random sequence[*] with a correlation time[†] much smaller than the shortest time constant of the system. The Band–Limited White Noise block produces such a sequence. For good results, the Simulink documentation recommends that we use the relation

$$t_C = \frac{1}{100} \cdot \frac{2\pi}{\omega_{max}} \qquad (15.1)$$

where t_C is the correlation time and ω_{max} is the bandwidth of the system in rad/sec.

Example 15.11

Consider an RC low–pass filter whose input is random noise denoted as $n_{in}(t)$ and the filtered output is denoted as $n_{out}(t)$. The constants are $R = 1\ M\Omega$ and $C = 1\ \mu F$. This network is referred to as **first order low–pass filter**. For this filter we will:

a. Derive the transfer function for this filter and create a model to display the output when the input is a Band-Limited White Noise block.

b. Use the bilinear transformation[‡] to derive the equivalent discrete time transfer function and create a model to display the output when the input is a Band-Limited White Noise block. For simplicity, we will neglect the effect of warping.[**]

The s–domain transformed filter is shown in Figure 15.27.

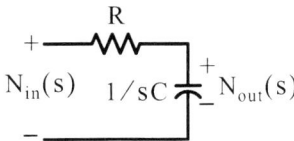

Figure 15.27. The transformed first order RC low–pass filter

1. By the voltage division expression,

---

[*] The Random Number block, described in Subsection 15.2.10, this chapter, Page15–14, produces random sequences also. The primary difference is that the Band–Limited White Noise block produces an output at a specific sample rate, which is related to the correlation time of the noise.
[†] The correlation time of the noise is the sample rate of the Band-Limited White Noise block.
[‡] For a detailed discussion on the bilinear transformation, please refer to Signals and Systems with MATLAB Computing and Simulink Modeling, ISBN 0–9744239–9–8.
[**] The continuous–time frequency to discrete-time frequency transformation results in a non–linear mapping and this condition is known as warping. A detailed discussion appears in the Signals and Systems text cited above.

The Signal Generators Sub–Library

$$N_{out}(s) = \frac{1/sC}{R + 1/sC} N_{in}(s) \qquad (15.2)$$

Rearranging, substituting the given values, and simplifying we get the continuous–time transfer function

$$G(s) = \frac{N_{out}(s)}{N_{in}(s)} = \frac{1}{s+1} \qquad (15.3)$$

The Simulink block for this transfer function is found in the Continuous Library, Chapter 3, and thus we create the model shown in Figure 15.28.

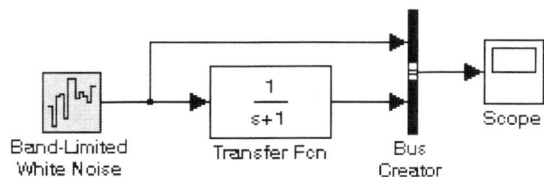

Figure 15.28. Model for Example 15.11 with continuous–time transfer function

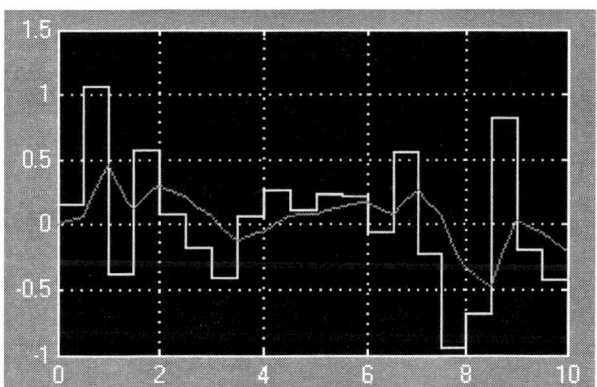

Figure 15.29. Input and output waveforms for the model of Figure 15.28

The parameters for the Band–Limited White Noise block in Figure 15.28 are specified as follows:

Noise power: [0.1] (default)

Sample time: 0.5

Seed: [23341] (default)

2. The bilinear transformation uses the relation

$$H(z) = H(s)\Big|_{s = \frac{2}{T_s} \cdot \frac{z-1}{z+1}} \qquad (15.4)$$

Chapter 15 The Sources Library

For convenience, we will use MATLAB's **bilinear(Z,P,K,Fs)** function where column vectors **Z** and **P** specify the zeros and poles respectively, scalar **K** specifies the gain, and **Fs** is the sample frequency in Hz. In Part (1), the sample time is specified as $T_s = 0.5$ s, therefore, we specify $F_s = 2$ Hz for part (2). Denoting the numerator and denominator of (15.3) as numa = 1 and dena = [1 1], we type and execute the statement

numa=1; dena=[1 1]; Fs=2; [numd,dend]=bilinear(numa,dena,Fs)

and MATLAB displays the discrete-time coefficients as

```
numd =
    0.2000    0.2000
dend =
    1.0000   -0.6000
```

Our model with the discrete-time transfer function is as shown in Figure 15.30 where the Discrete Transfer Fcn block was dragged from the Discrete library and we substituted the values above into that block. The input and output waveforms are shown in Figure 15.31.

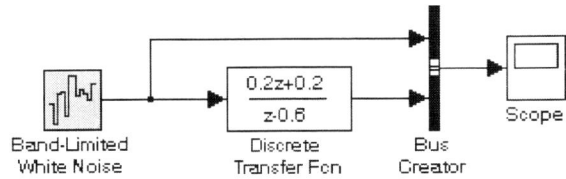

Figure 15.30. Model for Example 15.11 with discrete-time transfer function

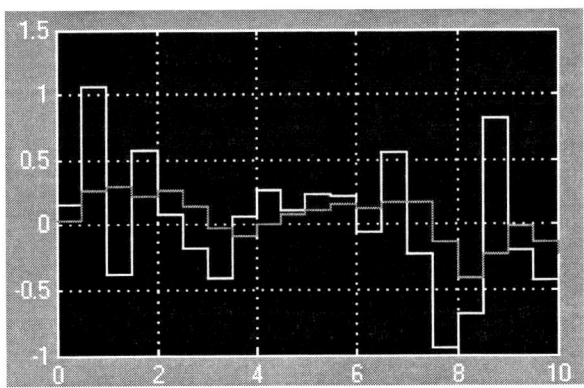

Figure 15.31. Input and output waveforms for the model of Figure 15.30

The Signal Generators Sub–Library

15.2.13 The Repeating Sequence Stair Block

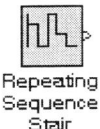

The **Repeating Sequence Stair** block outputs and repeats a discrete time sequence. We specify the stair sequence with the Vector of output values parameter.

Example 15.12

For the model shown in Figure 15.32, the Vector of output values parameter is specified as [-4 -2 0 2 4 2 0 -2 -4 -2] and the Sample time as 0.5. The waveform produced is shown in Figure 15.33.

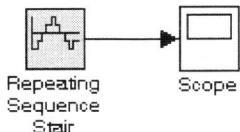

Figure 15.32. Model for Example 15.12

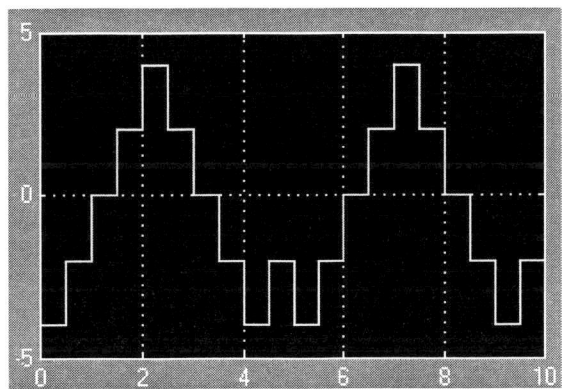

Figure 15.33. Waveform for the model of Figure 15.32

15.2.14 The Repeating Sequence Interpolated Block

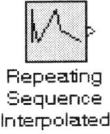

The **Repeating Sequence Interpolated** block generates a repeating discrete–time sequence. This block uses any of the methods specified by the Lookup Method parameter.

Chapter 15 The Sources Library

Example 15.13

For the model shown in Figure 15.34, the parameters for the Repeating Sequence blocks are as annotated inside the model.

The waveforms generated by each of the Repeating Sequence Interpolated blocks are shown in Figure 15.35.

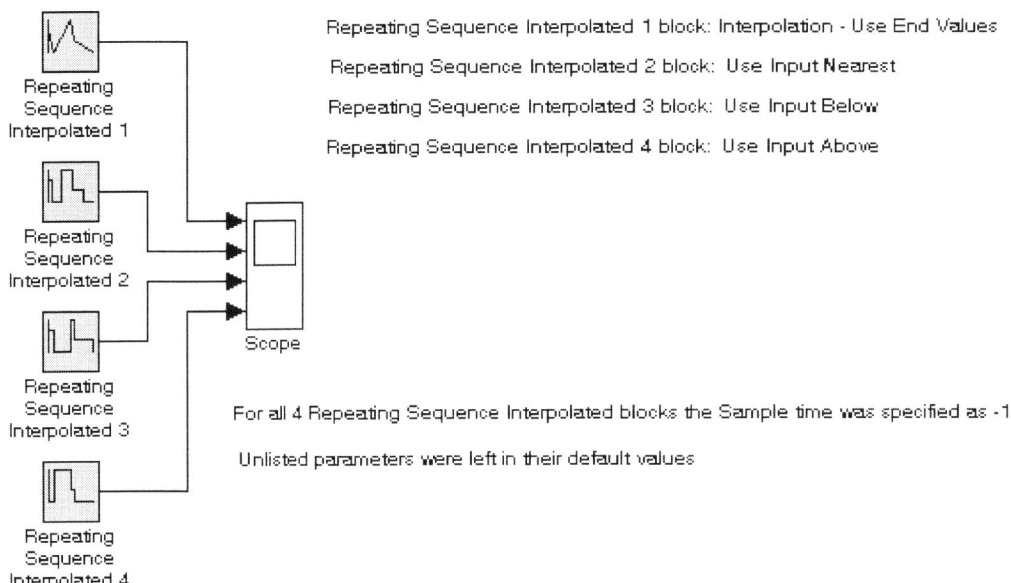

Figure 15.34. Model for Example 15.13

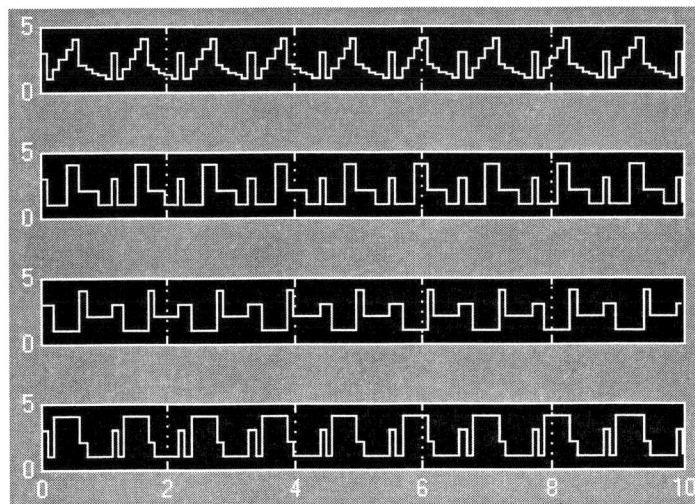

Figure 15.35. Waveforms for the model of Figure 15.34

The Signal Generators Sub–Library

15.2.15 The Counter Free–Running Block

The **Counter Free–Running** block counts up until the maximum possible value, $2^N - 1$, is reached, where N bits is the number of bits. The counter then returns to zero, and restarts counting up. It is always initialized to zero.

Example 15.14

For the model of Figure 15.36, in the Counter Free–Running block the Number of bits was specified as 5, that is, $N = 5$, and thus $2^N - 1 = 2^5 - 1 = 31$. We observe on the Scope block of Figure 15.37 that the counter reaches the value of 31, resets to zero at approximately 6.5 seconds, and restarts counting up. At the end of the simulation time, the counter has reached the value of 18 and this is also indicated in the Display block.

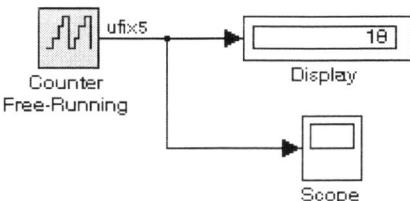

Figure 15.36. Model for Example 15.14

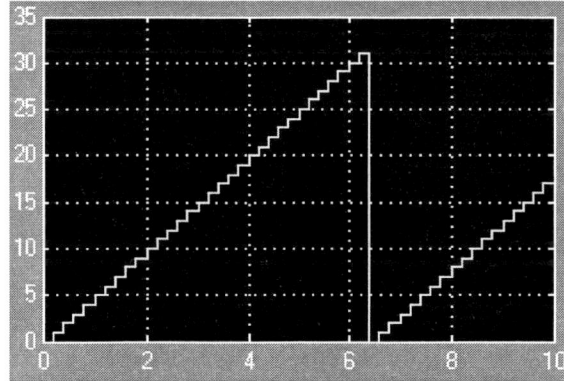

Figure 15.37. Waveform for the model of Figure 15.36

Introduction to Simulink with Engineering Applications
Copyright © Orchard Publications

Chapter 15 The Sources Library

15.2.16 The Counter Limited Block

The **Counter Limited** block counts up until the specified upper limit is reached. Then the counter wraps back to zero, and restarts counting up. The counter is always initialized to zero.

Example 15.15

For the model of Figure 15.38, in the Counter Limited block the Upper limit is specified as 32, and as we observe on the Scope block of Figure 15.39 that the counter reaches the value of 32, resets to zero at approximately 6.6 seconds, and restarts counting up. At the end of the simulation time, that is, 10 sec, the counter has reached the value of 17 and this is also indicated in the Display block.

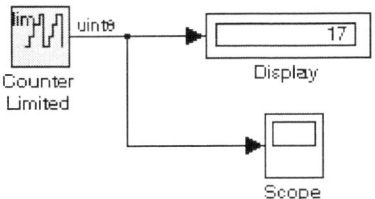

Figure 15.38. Model for Example 15.15

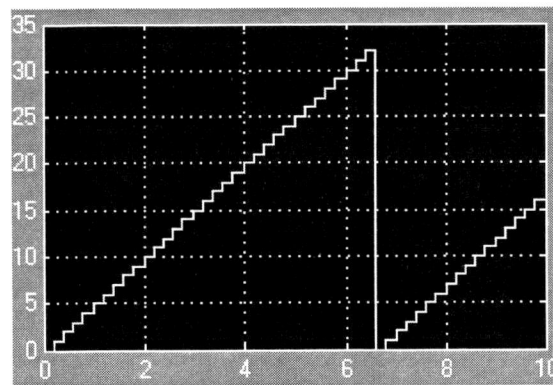

Figure 15.39. Waveform for the model of Figure 15.38

The Signal Generators Sub–Library

15.2.17 The Clock Block

The **Clock** block outputs the current simulation time at each simulation step. This block is useful for other blocks that need the simulation time. For discrete–time systems we use the Digital Clock block which is described in Subsection 15.2.18, this chapter, Page 15–26. We use the Display time check box to display the current simulation time inside the Clock icon. The Decimation parameter value is the increment at which the clock is updated and it can be any positive integer.

Example 15.16

In the model of Figure 15.40, the Display time check box is checked to display the simulation time. The Decimation parameter in Clock 1 is specified as 10, and this is the increment at which the clock is updated. Thus, for a fixed integration step of 1 second, the clock updates at 1 second, 2 seconds, and so on. The Decimation parameter in Clock 2 is specified as 100 and this is the increment at which the clock is updated. Thus, for a fixed integration step of 1/100 second, the clock updates at 1/100 second, 2/100 second, and so on. The Decimation parameter in Clock 3 has been set to 1000 and this is the increment at which the clock is updated. Thus, for a fixed integration step of 1/1000 second, the clock updates at 1/1000 second, 2/1000 second, and so on. The waveforms are shown in Figure 15.41.

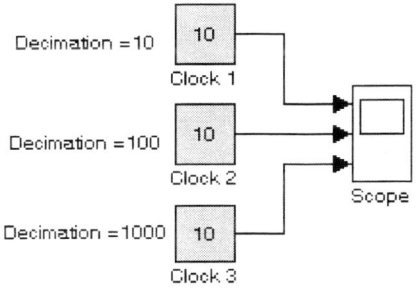

Figure 15.40. Model for Example 15.16

Chapter 15 The Sources Library

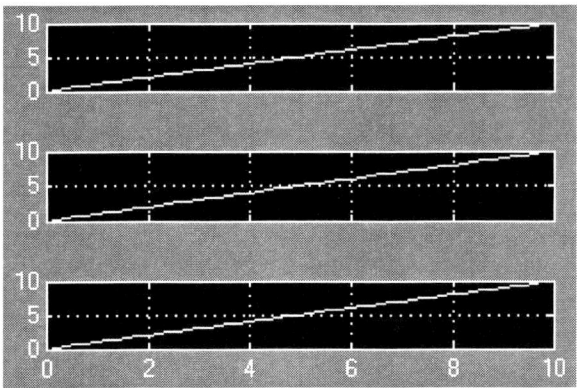

Figure 15.41. Waveforms for the model of Figure 15.40

15.2.18 The Digital Clock Block

The **Digital Clock** block displays the simulation time at a specified sampling interval. At all other times, the output is held at the previous value. This block is useful when we desire to know the current time within a discrete system.

Example 15.17

For the model of Figure 15.42, in the Digital Clock block Sample time was specified as 0.25, and its output is displayed on the Scope block of Figure 15.43.

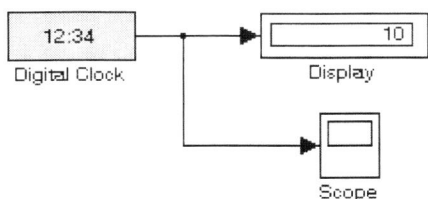

Figure 15.42. Model for Example 15.17

The Signal Generators Sub–Library

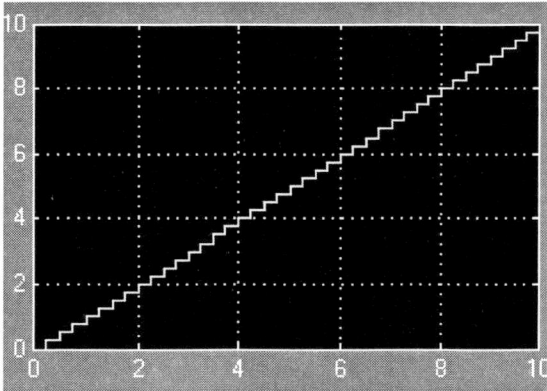

Figure 15.43. Waveform for the model of Figure 15.42

15.3 Summary

- The **Inport** block creates an input port for a subsystem or an external input.

- The **Ground** block grounds an unconnected input port.

- The **From File** block outputs data read from a MAT file. The name of the file is displayed inside the block.

- The **From Workspace** block reads data from the MATLAB workspace. The workspace data are specified in the block's Data parameter via a MATLAB expression that evaluates to a 2–D array.

- The **Constant** block generates a real or complex constant value.

- The **Signal Generator** block can produce one of four different waveforms: sine wave, square wave, sawtooth wave, and random wave.

- The **Pulse Generator** block generates square wave pulses at regular intervals. The shape of the generated waveform depends on the parameters, Amplitude, Pulse Width, Period, and Phase Delay.

- The **Signal Builder** block allows us to create interchangeable groups of piece wise linear signal sources and use them in a model.

- The **Ramp** block generates a signal that starts at a specified time and value and changes by a specified rate. The characteristics of the generated signal are determined by the specified Slope, Start time, Duty Cycle, and Initial output parameters.

- The **Sine Wave** block generates a sine wave. The Sine type can be either time–based or sample–based mode.

- The **Step** block provides a step between two definable levels at a specified time.

- The **Repeating Sequence** block outputs a periodic waveform that we specify using the block dialog's Time values and Output values parameters.

- The **Chirp Signal** block generates a sine wave whose frequency increases at a linear rate with time.

- The **Random Number** block generates normally distributed random numbers. The seed is reset to the specified value each time a simulation starts. By default, the sequence produced has a mean of 0 and a variance of 1, but we can specify other values for these parameters. The sequence of numbers is repeatable and can be produced by any Random Number block with the same seed and parameters.

- The **Uniform Random Number** block generates uniformly distributed random numbers over a specifiable interval with a specifiable starting seed. The seed is reset each time a simulation starts. The generated sequence is repeatable and can be produced by any Uniform Random

Number block with the same seed and parameters. To generate normally distributed random numbers, we use the Random Number block.

- The **Band-Limited White Noise** block is an implementation of white noise into Zero-Order Hold block.

- The **Repeating Sequence Stair** block outputs and repeats a discrete time sequence.

- The **Repeating Sequence Interpolated** block outputs a discrete-time sequence and then repeats it.

- The **Counter Free-Running** block counts up until the maximum possible value, $2^N - 1$, is reached, where N bits is the number of bits. Then the counter overflows to zero, and restarts counting up. The counter is always initialized to zero.

- The **Counter Limited** block counts up until the specified upper limit is reached. Then the counter wraps back to zero, and restarts counting up. The counter is always initialized to zero.

- The **Clock** block outputs the current simulation time at each simulation step. For discrete-time systems we use the Digital Clock block.

- The **Digital Clock** block displays the simulation time at a specified sampling interval. At all other times, the output is held at the previous value.

NOTES:

Chapter 16

The User−Defined Functions Library

This chapter is an introduction to the **User−Defined Functions** Library. This is the fifteenth library in the Simulink group of libraries and contains the blocks shown below. We will describe the function of each block included in this library and we will perform simulation examples to illustrate their application.

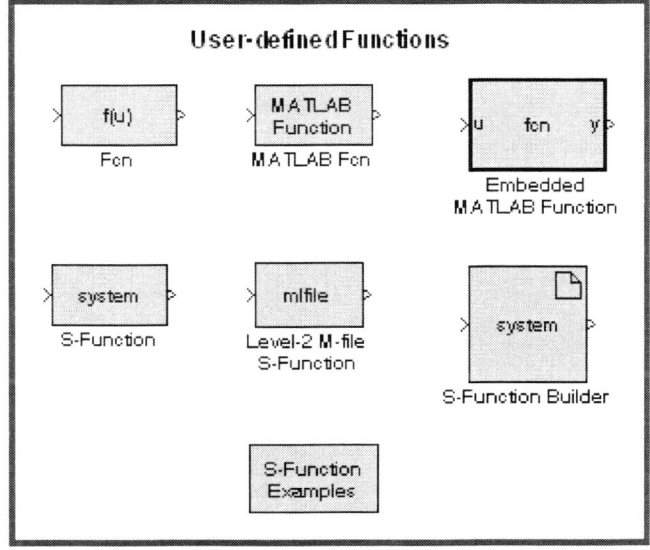

Chapter 16 The User–Defined Functions Library

16.1 The Fcn Block

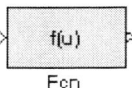

The **Fcn** block applies a specified expression to its input denoted as u. If u is a vector, u(i) represents the ith element of the vector; u(1) or u alone represents the first element. The specified expression can consist of numeric constants, arithmetic operators, relational operators, logical operators, and the math functions abs, acos, asin, atan, atan2, ceil, cos, cosh, exp, fabs, floor, hypot, ln, log, log10, pow, power, rem, sgn, sin, sinh, sqrt, tan, and tanh.

Example 16.1

It can be shown that the solution of the differential equation

$$\frac{d^2 y}{dt^2} + 4y = \tan 2t \qquad (16.1)$$

is

$$y = -(1/4)\cos 2t \cdot \ln(\sec 2t + \tan 2t) + k_1 \cos 2t + k_2 \sin 2t \qquad (16.2)$$

where the constants k_1 and k_2 can be evaluated from the initial conditions. Then we can compute and display any value of y by specifying t, k_1, and k_2, using the model shown in Figure 16.1.

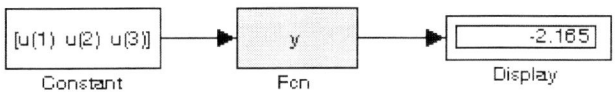

Figure 16.1. Model for Example 16.1

For the model of Figure 16.1 we specified $u(1) = t = \pi/6$, $u(2) = k_1 = -1$, $u(3) = k_2 = -3$, and in MATLAB's Command window we entered:

u(1)=pi/6; u(2)=-1; u(3)=-3;
y=-(1/4)*cos(2*u(1))*log(sec(2*u(1))+tan(2*u(1)))+υ(2)*cos(2*u(1))+υ(3)*cos(2*u(1));

16.2 The MATLAB Fcn Block

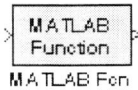

The **MATLAB Fcn** block applies the specified MATLAB function or expression to the input. This block is slower than the Fcn block because it calls the MATLAB parser during each integra-

The Embedded MATLAB Function Block

tion step. As an alternative, we can use built-in blocks such as the Fcn block or the Math Function block, or writing the function as an M–file S–function, then accessing it using the S–Function block.

Example 16.2

In the model of Figure 16.2, the function in the MATLAB Fcn block is specified as **eig** and outputs the eigenvalues of Matrix A.

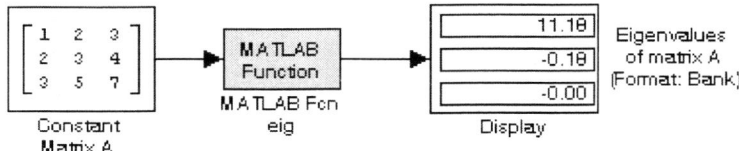

Figure 16.2. Model for Example 16.2

16.3 The Embedded MATLAB Function Block

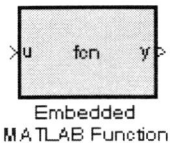

The **Embedded MATLAB Function** block contains a MATLAB language function in a Simulink model. This block accepts multiple input signals and produces multiple output signals. For more information and an example, please refer to the Simulink User's Manual.

Example 16.3

In this example we will create a model using an Embedded MATLAB Function block to accept a 3×3 matrix and output the value of its determinant and its inverse matrix.

We begin with a model that contains a Constant block, an Embedded MATLAB Function block, and two Display blocks as shown in Figure 16.3. We save this model as **matrix_det_inv.mdl**

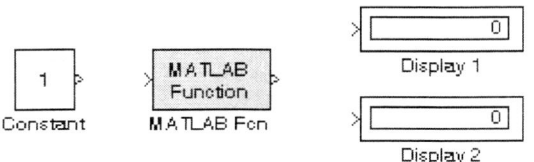

Figure 16.3. Blocks for the model for Example 16.3

Chapter 16 The User–Defined Functions Library

We double-click the Embedded MATLAB Function block to open it for editing, and the Embedded MATLAB Editor appears as shown in Figure 16.4.

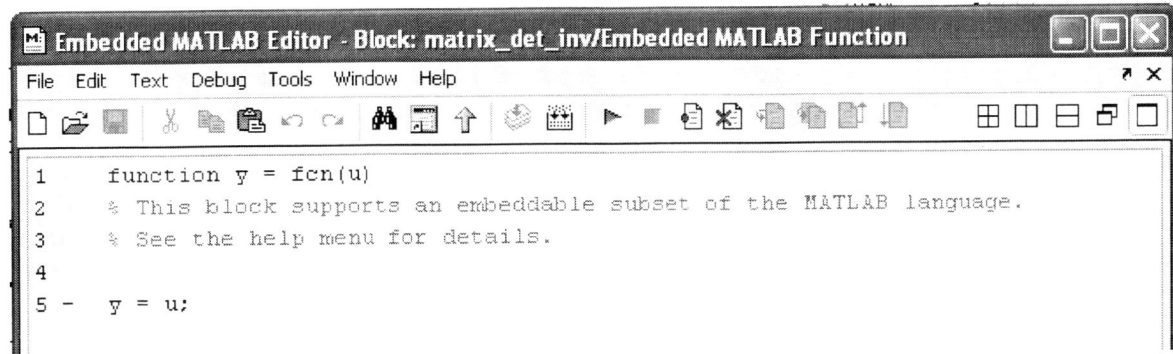

Figure 16.4. The Embedded MATLAB Editor window

Using MATLAB's Editor, we define a new function file as

function [det, inv] = matrix(A)

The contents of this function file as follows:*

```
function [det, inv] = matrix(A)
% This function computes the determinant and the inverse of a 3x3
% matrix A which must be defined in MATLAB's Command Window.
%
det=A(1,1)*A(2,2)*A(3,3)+A(1,2)*A(2,3)*A(3,1)+A(1,3)*A(2,1)*A(3,2)...
    -A(3,1)*A(2,2)*A(1,3)-A(3,2)*A(2,3)*A(1,1)-A(3,3)*A(2,1)*A(1,2);
%
% For a 3x3 matrix where A=[a11 a12 a13; a21 a22 a23; a31 a32 a33],
% the inverse of A is obtained as invA = (1/detA)*adjA where adjA
% represents the adjoint of A. Ref: Numerical Analysis, ISBN 0-9709511-1-6
% The cofactors are defined below.
%
b11=A(2,2)*A(3,3)-A(2,3)*A(3,2);
b12=-(A(2,1)*A(3,3)-A(2,3)*A(3,1));
b13=A(2,1)*A(3,2)-A(2,2)*A(3,1);
b21=-(A(1,2)*A(3,3)-A(1,3)*A(3,2));
b22=A(1,1)*A(3,3)-A(1,3)*A(3,1);
b23=-(A(1,1)*A(3,2)-A(1,2)*A(3,1));
b31=A(1,2)*A(2,3)-A(1,3)*A(2,2);
b32=-(A(1,1)*A(2,3)-A(1,3)*A(2,1));
b33=A(1,1)*A(2,2)-A(1,2)*A(2,1);
%
% We must remember that the cofactors of the elemements of the ith
% row (column) of A are the elements of the ith column (row) of AdjA.
```

---

* *The script for the user defined function used in this example is not the best choice. For the computation of the determinant of a square matrix of any size, we could use for loops such as **for i=1:n**, and for the computation of the inverse of a square matrix of any size, we can use the LU decomposition method.*

The Embedded MATLAB Function Block

```
% Accordingly, for the next statement below,we use the single quotation
% character (') to transpose the elements of the resulting matrix.
%
adjA=[b11  b12  b13;  b21  b22  b23;  b31  b32  b33]';
%
inv=(1/det)*adjA
```

We delete the contents shown in Figure 16.4, we copy the above script into the Embedded MATLAB Editor, from the **File** menu we select **Save as Model,** and we save it as **matrix_det_inv01.mdl**. The content of the modified Embedded MATLAB Editor is now as shown in Figure 16.5.

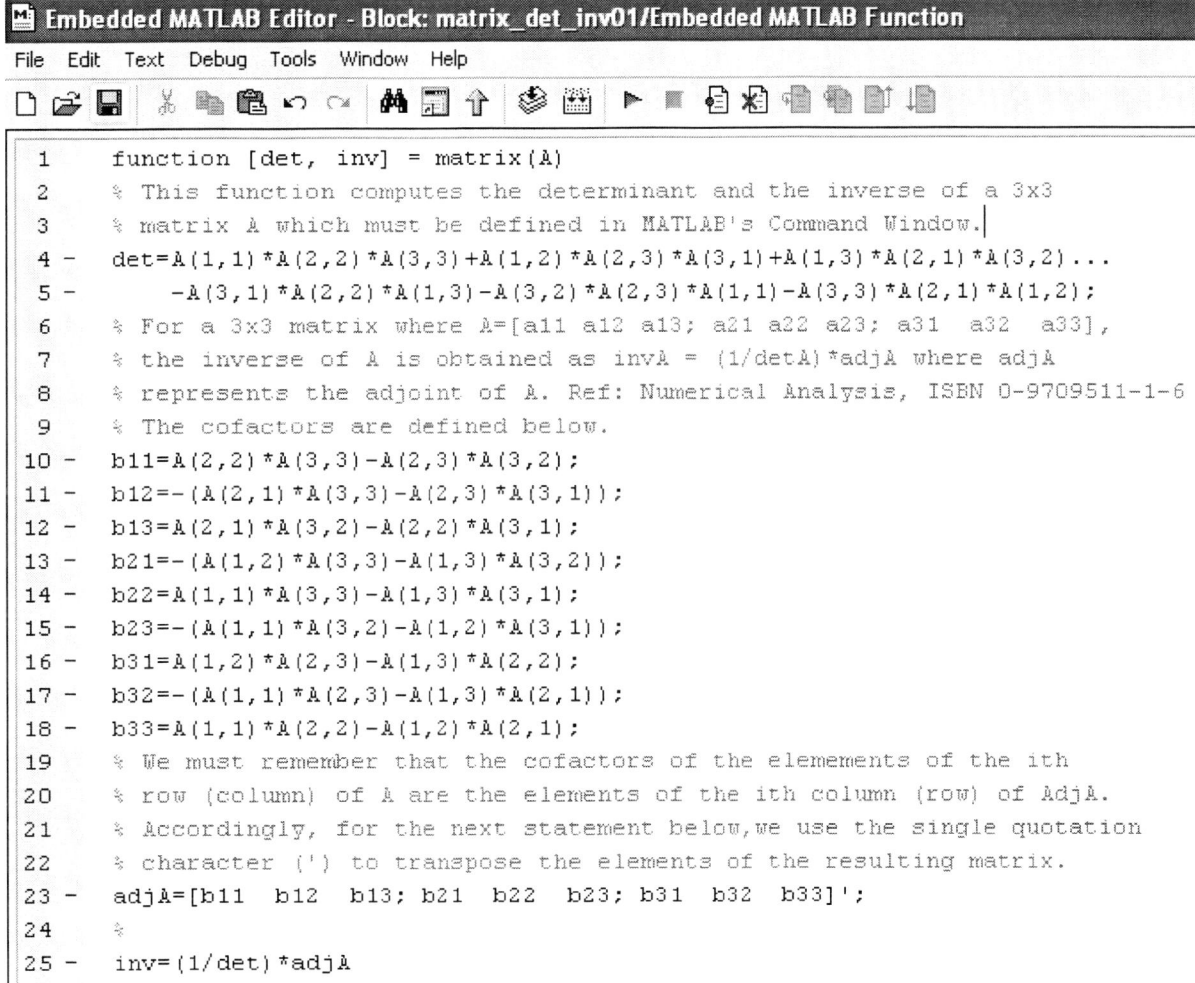

Figure 16.5. Function definition for the computation of the determinant and inverse of a 3x3 matrix

Next, we return to the model of Figure 16.3, and we observe that the Embedded MATLAB Function block appears as shown in Figure 16.6.

Chapter 16 The User–Defined Functions Library

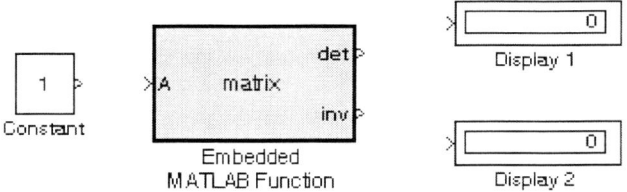

Figure 16.6. Modified model for Example 16.3

Now, we connect the blocks shown in Figure 16.6 as shown in Figure 16.7 where in the Constant block we have assigned matrix A defined in MATLAB's Command window as

A=[1 2 3; 1 3 4; 1 4 3];

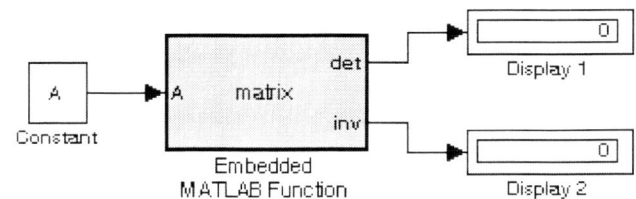

Figure 16.7. The connected blocks for the model of Example 16.3

Finally, in MATLAB's Command Window we type and execute the command

matrix_det_inv01

After execution of the simulation command in Figure 16.7, the model appears as shown in Figure 16.8.

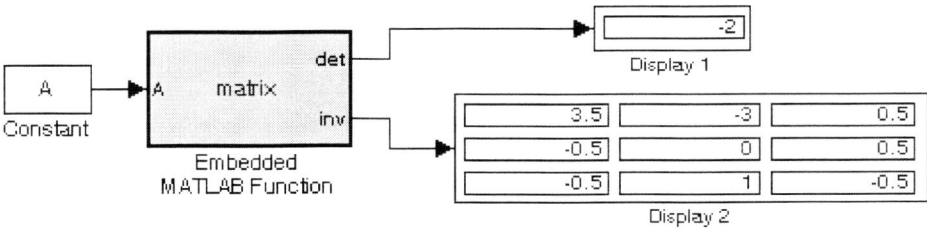

Figure 16.8. The model for Example 16.3 in its final form

The functions det(A) and inv(A) are defined in MATLAB but are not included in the Embedded MATLAB Run–Time Function Library List. This list includes common functions as **sqrt**, **sin**, **cos**, and others. Thus, had we issued the simulation command without defining the function [det, inv] = matrix(A), Simulink would have issued the following warnings:

```
Output det must be assigned before returning from the function
Output inv must be assigned before returning from the function
```

16.4 The S–Function Block

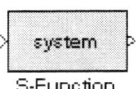

The **S–Function** block provides access to S–functions. The S–function named as the S–function name parameter can be a Level–1 M–file or a Level–1 or Level–2 C MEX–file S–function. We should use the M–File S–Function block to include a Level–2 M–file S–function in a block diagram. This block is described in Section 11.18, Chapter 11, Page 11–43.

16.5 The Level–2 M-file S–Function Block

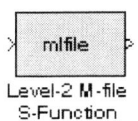

We introduced the S–Function blocks in Section 11.18, Chapter 11, Page 11-43. We will now describe some additional blocks.

A Level–2 M–file S–function is an M–file that defines the properties and behavior of an instance of a Level–2 M–File S–Function block that references the M–file in a Simulink model.

The **Level–2 M–file S–Function** block allows us to use a Level–2 M–file S–function in a model. We do this by creating an instance of this block in the model. Then, we enter the name of the Level–2 M–File S–function in the M–file name field of the block's parameter dialog box.

For a Level–1 M–file S–function we use the S–Function block.

To become familiar with this block, let us review the demos as we did in Section 11.17, Chapter 11, Page 11-41. In MATLAB's Command Window we type

sfundemos

and MATLAB will display the S–Function directory blocks shown in Figure 16.9. In this text we will be concerned with the M–file S–Functions only.

Next, we double-click on the M–file S–Functions block of Figure 16.9 and MATLAB displays the Level–1 and Level–2 M–file S–Functions shown in Figure 16.10.

Chapter 16 The User–Defined Functions Library

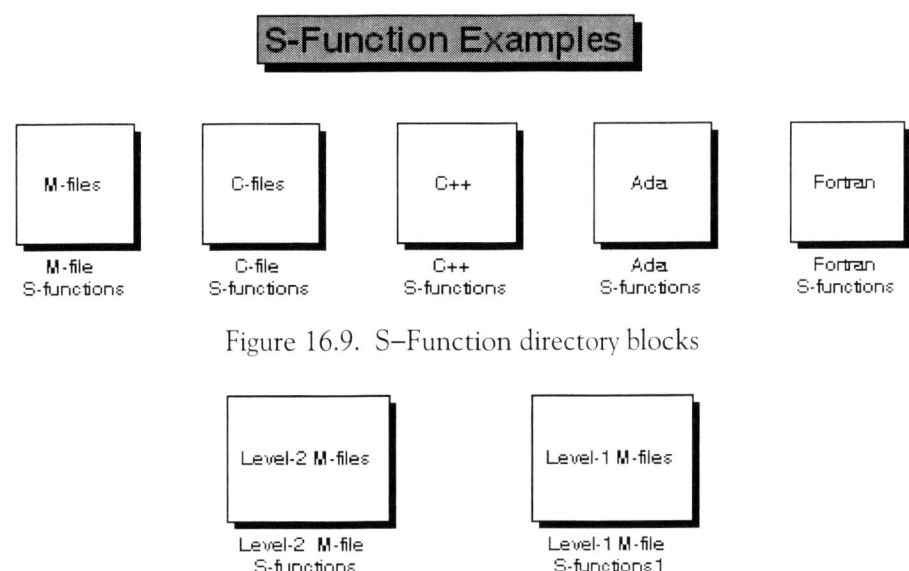

Figure 16.9. S–Function directory blocks

Figure 16.10. Levels of M–file S–Functions

The Level–1 M–file S–Functions are shown in Figure 16.11 and the Level–2 M–file S–Functions are shown in Figure 16.12. We observe that the first 5 models of the Level–2 M–file S–Functions and the same as those of the Level–1 M–file S–Functions but of course are implemented differently in each case.

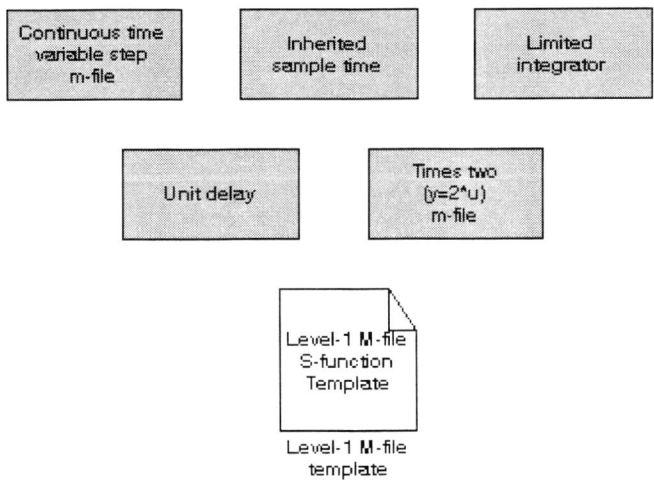

Figure 16.11. List of Level–1 M–file S–Functions

The Level-2 M-file S-Function Block

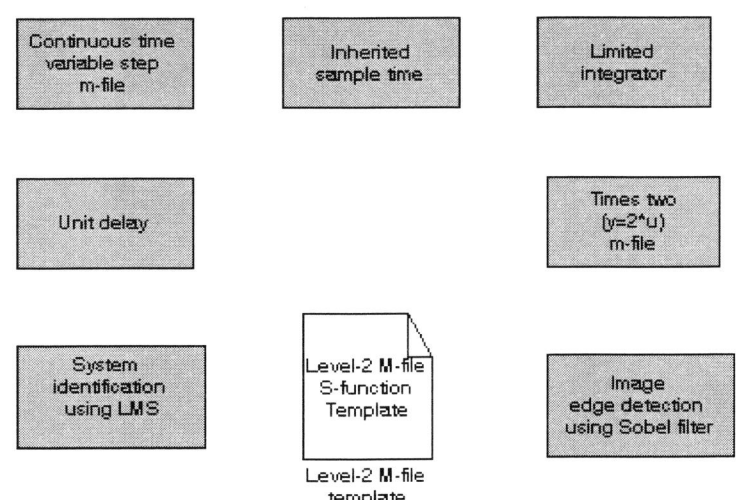

Figure 16.12. List of Level-2 M-file S-Functions

The Level-2 M-file S-function Application Programming Interface (API) allows us to use the MATLAB language to create custom blocks with multiple inputs and outputs and capable of handling any type of signal produced by a Simulink model, including matrix and frame signals of any data type. The Level-2 M-file S-Functions resemble those defined by the C MEX-file S-functions and consist of a set of callback methods that Simulink invokes when updating or simulating the model. The **callback methods** perform the actual work of initializing and computing the outputs of the block defined by the S-function. Thus, the Level-2 M-file S-function API specifies a set of callback methods that an M-file S-function must implement and others that it may choose to omit, depending on the requirements of the block that the S-function defines.

To create an Level-2 M-file S-function, we can begin by making a copy of the template that Simulink provides and edit the copy as necessary to reflect the desired behavior of the S-function you are creating. The comments in the template explain how it is done. To access this template, we double-click on the Level-2 M-file template block shown in Figure 16.11.

To access the Level-1 M-file S-function template, we double-click on the Level-1 M-file template block shown in Figure 16.10.

Table 16.1 lists the Level-2 M-file S-function callback methods and their C MEX-file equivalents.

Chapter 16 The User–Defined Functions Library

TABLE 16.1 Level-2 M-file S-Function and corresponding C MEX-file callback methods

Level-2 M-file callback method	C MEX-file callback method
setup method (see Setup Method)	mdlInitializeSizes
CheckParameters	mdlCheckParameters
Derivatives	mdlDerivatives
Disable	mdlDisable
Enable	mdlEnable
InitializeCondition	mdlInitializeConditions
Outputs	mdlOutputs
ProcessParameters	mdlProcessParameters
SetInputPortComplexSignal	mdlSetInputPortComplexSignal
SetInputPortDataType	mdlSetInputPortDataType
SetInputPortDimensions	mdlSetInputPortDimensionInfo
SetInputPortSampleTime	mdlSetInputPortSampleTime
SetInputPortSamplingMode	mdlSetInputPortFrameData
SetOutputPortComplexSignal	mdlSetOutputPortComplexSignal
SetOutputPortDataType	mdlSetOutputPortDataType
SetOutputPortDimensions	mdlSetOutputPortDimensionInfo
SetOutputPortSampleTime	mdlSetOutputPortSampleTime
Start	mdlStart
Update	mdlUpdate
WriteRTW	mdlRTW
ZeroCrossings	mdlZeroCrossings

Example 16.4

Let us review the Level–1 M-file S–function file script for the Times two m–file shown in Figure 16.11 above, and the Level–2 M-file S–function file script for the Times two m–file shown in Figure 16.12 above. To view the script for these files denoted as **sfundemo_timestwo**, and **msfcn_times_two.m** respectively, we double–click on the Times two blocks and on the annotated blocks shown in green.

The Level–1 M-file S–function file script for the Times two m–file is as shown below where we have disabled the executable mex file. We observe that the script for this file has the same syntax as Example 11.14, Section 11.18, Chapter 11, Page 11-44.

```
function [sys,x0,str,ts] = timestwo(t,x,u,flag)
%TIMESTWO S-function whose output is two times its input.
%   This M-file illustrates how to construct an M-file S-function that
%   computes an output value based upon its input.  The output of this
```

The Level–2 M–file S–Function Block

```
%    S-function is two times the input value:
%
%       y = 2 * u;
%
%    See sfuntmpl.m for a general S-function template.
%
%    See also SFUNTMPL.
%
%    Copyright 1990-2002 The MathWorks, Inc.
%    $Revision: 1.7 $
%
% Dispatch the flag. The switch function controls the calls to
% S-function routines at each simulation stage of the S-function.
%
switch flag,
  %%%%%%%%%%%%%%%%%%%%
  % Initialization %
  %%%%%%%%%%%%%%%%%%%%
  % Initialize the states, sample times, and state ordering strings.
  case 0
    [sys,x0,str,ts]=mdlInitializeSizes;

  %%%%%%%%%%%%
  % Outputs %
  %%%%%%%%%%%%
  % Return the outputs of the S-function block.
  case 3
    sys=mdlOutputs(t,x,u);

  %%%%%%%%%%%%%%%%%%%%
  % Unhandled flags %
  %%%%%%%%%%%%%%%%%%%%
  % There are no termination tasks (flag=9) to be handled.
  % Also, there are no continuous or discrete states,
  % so flags 1,2, and 4 are not used, so return an emptyu
  % matrix
  case { 1, 2, 4, 9 }
    sys=[];

  %%%%%%%%%%%%%%%%%%%%%%%%%%%%%%%%%%%%%%
  % Unexpected flags (error handling)%
  %%%%%%%%%%%%%%%%%%%%%%%%%%%%%%%%%%%%%%
  % Return an error message for unhandled flag values.
  otherwise
    error(['Unhandled flag = ',num2str(flag)]);

end

% end timestwo
```

The Level–2 M–file S–function file script for the Times two m–file is as shown below where we observe that only the required Level-2 N-file callback methods appearing in Table 16.1 are used.

```
function msfcn_times_two(block)
% Level-2 M file S-Function for times two demo.
%   Copyright 1990-2004 The MathWorks, Inc.
%   $Revision: 1.1.6.1 $
```

Chapter 16 The User–Defined Functions Library

```
  setup(block);

%endfunction

function setup(block)

  %% Register number of input and output ports
  block.NumInputPorts  = 1;
  block.NumOutputPorts = 1;

  %% Setup functional port properties to dynamically
  %% inherited.
  block.SetPreCompInpPortInfoToDynamic;
  block.SetPreCompOutPortInfoToDynamic;

  block.InputPort(1).DirectFeedthrough = true;

  %% Set block sample time to inherited
  block.SampleTimes = [-1 0];

  %% Run accelerator on TLC
  block.SetAccelRunOnTLC(true);

  %% Register methods
  block.RegBlockMethod('Outputs',                  @Output);

%endfunction

function Output(block)

  block.OutputPort(1).Data = 2*block.InputPort(1).Data;

%endfunction
```

16.6 The S–Function Builder Block

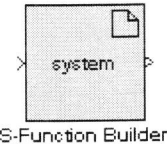

The **S–Function Builder** block creates a C MEX–file S–function from specifications and C source code that we provide. As stated earlier, we will not discuss C MEX–files in this text. To view some examples we type

sfundemos

at the MATLAB Command window, and we choose the appropriate block from those shown in Figure 16.13 below.

The S–Function Examples Block

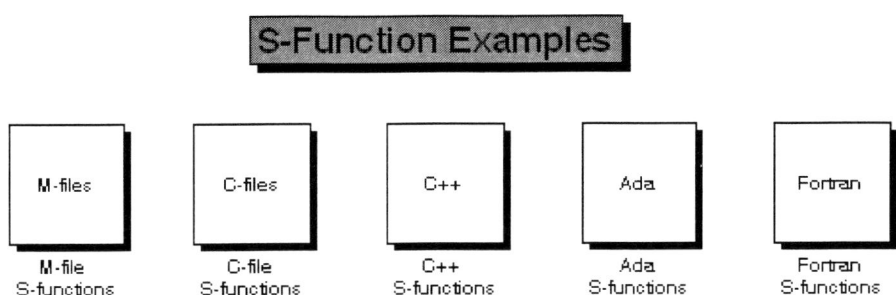

Figure 16.13. Examples of S–Functions

16.7 The S–Function Examples Block

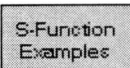

The **S–Function Examples** block displays M–file S–Function, C–file S–Function, C++ S–Function, Ada S–Function, and Fortran S–Function examples shown in Figure 16.13 above.

16.8 Summary

- The **Fcn** block applies a specified expression to its input denoted as u.

- The **MATLAB Fcn** block applies the specified MATLAB function or expression to the input.

- The **Embedded MATLAB Function** block contains a MATLAB language function in a Simulink model. This block accepts multiple input signals and produces multiple output signals.

- The **S-Function** block provides access to S-functions. The S-function named as the S-function name parameter can be a Level–1 M–file or a Level–1 or Level–2 C MEX–file S–function.

- The **Level–2 M-file S-Function** block allows us to use a Level–2 M–file S–function in a model.

- The **S-Function Builder** block creates a C MEX–file S–function from specifications and C source code that we provide.

- The **S-Function Examples** block displays M-file S-Function, C-file S-Function, C++ S-Function, Ada S-Function, and Fortran S-Function examples.

Chapter 17

The Additional Discrete Library

This chapter is an introduction to the **Additional Discrete** Library. This is the sixteenth library in the Simulink group of libraries and contains the blocks shown below. We will describe the function of each block included in this library and we will perform simulation examples to illustrate their application.

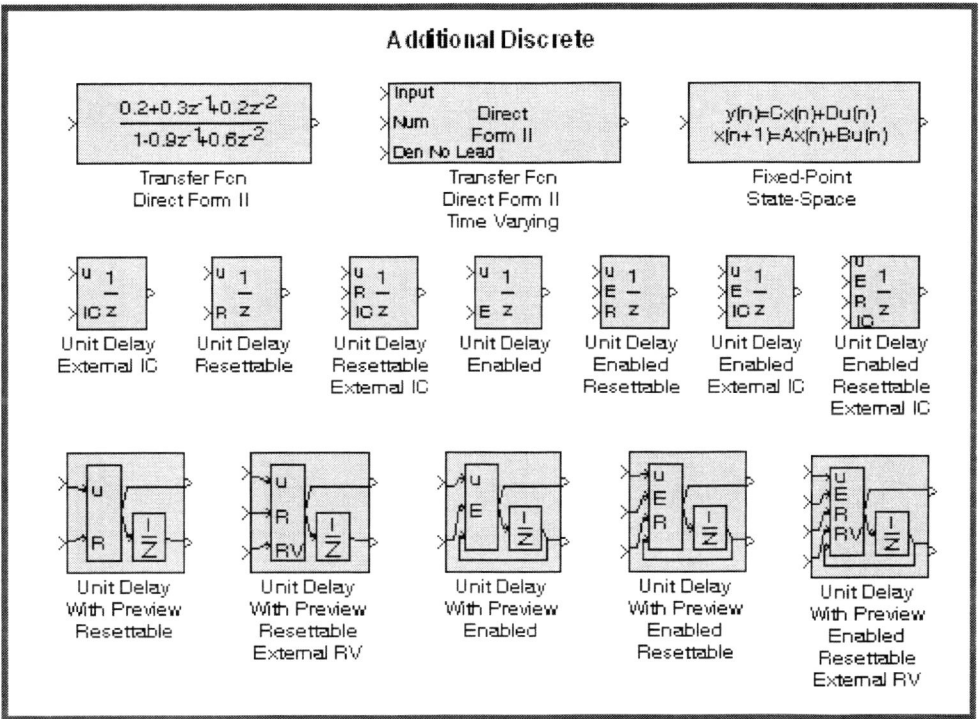

Chapter 17 The Additional Discrete Library

17.1 The Transfer Fcn Direct Form II Block

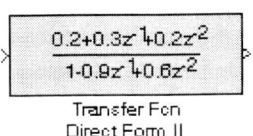

The **Transfer Fcn Direct Form II** block implements a Direct Form II realization of the transfer function specified by the Numerator coefficients and the Denominator coefficients without the leading[*] coefficient in the Denominator.

Example 17.1

The model of Figure 17.1 implements the discrete-time function

$$H(z) = \frac{0.5276 - 1.5828z^{-1} + 1.5828z^{-2}}{1 - 1.7600z^{-1} + 1.1829z^{-2}} \qquad (17.1)$$

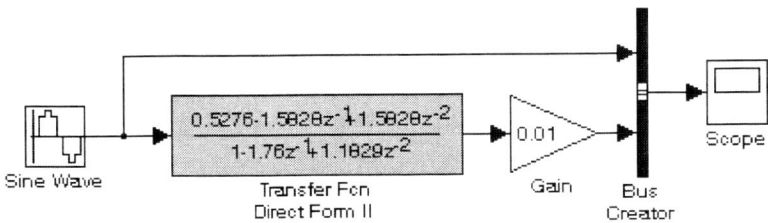

Figure 17.1. Direct Form–II of a second-order digital filter

In Figure 17.1, the Sample time for the Sine Wave block is specified as 0.1. The num(z) for the Transfer Fcn Direct Form II block is specified as [0.5276 −1.5828 1.5828], and the den(z) is specified as [−1.7600 1.1829]. The leading coefficient 1 in the denominator is excluded. The input and output waveforms are shown in Figure 17.2.

---

[*] *By lead we mean that the leading coefficient 1 in the denominator which has the form* $1 + z^{-1} + z^{-2}$.

The Transfer Fcn Direct Form II Time Varying Block

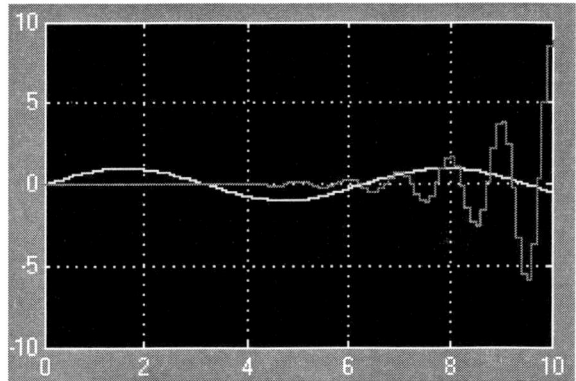

Figure 17.2. Input and output waveforms for the model of Figure 17.1

17.2 The Transfer Fcn Direct Form II Time Varying Block

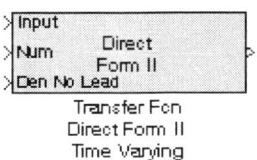

The **Transfer Fcn Direct Form II Time Varying** block implements a Direct Form II realization of a specified transfer function. Essentially, this block performs the same function as that of the Transfer Fcn Direct Form II block which is described in the previous section, except that the numerator and denominator coefficients of the discrete–time transfer function are specified externally by two inputs Num and Den.

Example 17.2

The model of Figure 17.3 is essentially the same as that of Figure 17.1 and thus the input and output waveforms of Figure 17.4 are the same as those of Figure 17.2.

Chapter 17 The Additional Discrete Library

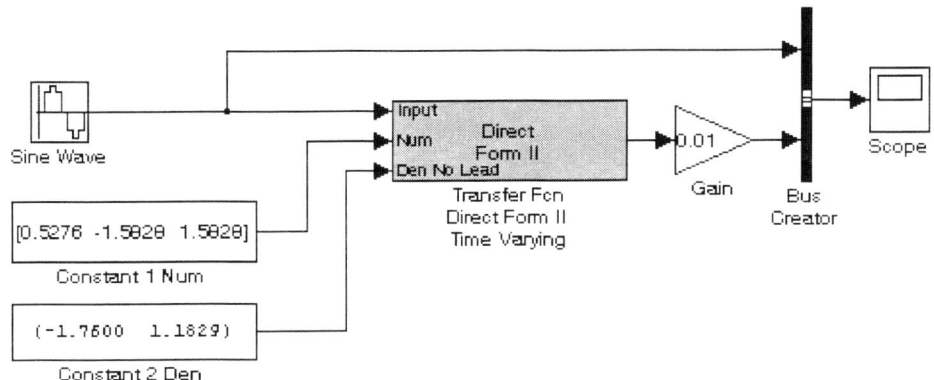

Figure 17.3. Model for Example 17.3

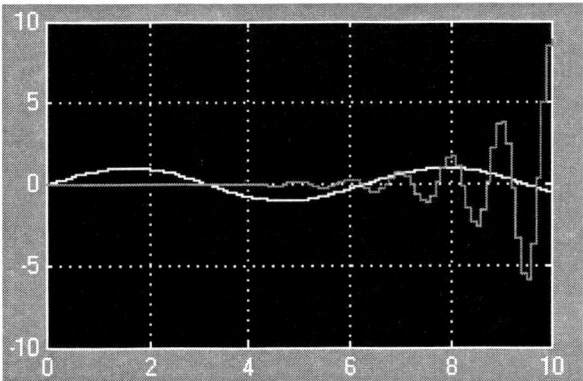

Figure 17.4. Input and output waveforms for the model of Figure 17.3

17.3 The Fixed–Point State–Space Block

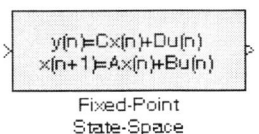

The **Fixed–Point State–Space** block implements the system described by

$$x[n+1] = Ax[n] + Bu[n]$$
$$y[n] = Cx[n] + Du[n] \tag{17.2}$$

where:

A is a matrix with dimensions $n \times n$, n = number of states, B is a matrix with dimensions $n \times m$, m = number of inputs, C is a matrix with dimensions $r \times n$, r = number of outputs, D

The Fixed–Point State–Space Block

is a matrix with dimensions $r \times m$, x = state, an $n \times 1$ vector, u = input, an $m \times 1$ vector, and y = output, an $r \times 1$ vector.

Example 17.3

The matrix form of a 3–input 2–output 3–state discrete–time system is specified as

$$\begin{bmatrix} x_1[n+1] \\ x_2[n+1] \\ x_3[n+1] \end{bmatrix} = \underbrace{\begin{bmatrix} 0.25 & 0 & 0 \\ 0 & 0.5 & 0 \\ 0 & -0.25 & -0.75 \end{bmatrix}}_{A} \cdot \begin{bmatrix} x_1[n] \\ x_2[n] \\ x_3[n] \end{bmatrix} + \underbrace{\begin{bmatrix} 0 & 1 & 0 \\ 0 & 0 & 1 \\ 1 & 0 & 1 \end{bmatrix}}_{B} \cdot \begin{bmatrix} u_1[n] \\ u_2[n] \\ u_3[n] \end{bmatrix}$$

$$\begin{bmatrix} y_1[n] \\ y_2[n] \end{bmatrix} = \underbrace{\begin{bmatrix} 1 & 0 & 1 \\ 0 & 1 & 0 \end{bmatrix}}_{C} \cdot \begin{bmatrix} x_1[n] \\ x_2[n] \\ x_3[n] \end{bmatrix} + \underbrace{\begin{bmatrix} 0 & 1 & 0 \\ 0 & 0 & 1 \end{bmatrix}}_{D} \cdot \begin{bmatrix} u_1[n] \\ u_2[n] \\ u_3[n] \end{bmatrix}$$

(17.3)

In the model of Figure 17.5 we enter the values of matrices A, B, C, and D in the Fixed–Point State–Space block parameters dialog box, and we specify initial condition 0. The input vector is as shown and when the simulation command is given the input and output waveforms are as shown in Figure 17.6.

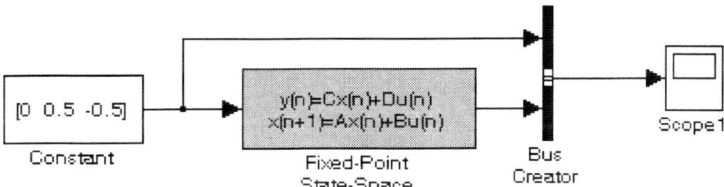

Figure 17.5. Model for Example 17.3

Chapter 17 The Additional Discrete Library

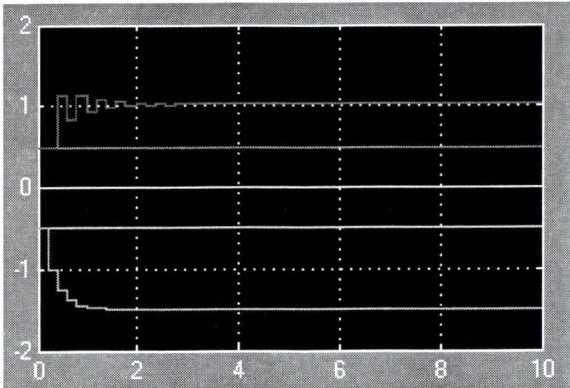

Figure 17.6. Input and output waveforms for the model of Figure 17.5

17.4 The Unit Delay External IC Block

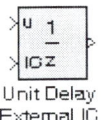

The **Unit Delay External IC** (Initial Condition) block delays its input by one sample period. This block is equivalent to the z^{-1} discrete–time operator. The block accepts one input and generates one output, both of which can be scalar or vector. If the input is a vector, all elements of the vector are delayed by the same sample period. The block's output for the first sample period is equal to the signal IC. The input u and initial condition IC data types must be the same.

Example 17.4

In the model of Figure 17.7, the Pulse Generator block is specified for a period 2 sec. All other parameters are in their default state. The input and output waveforms are shown in Figure 17.8.

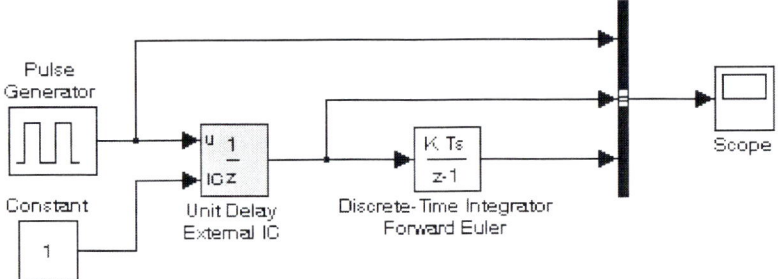

Figure 17.7. Model for Example 17.4

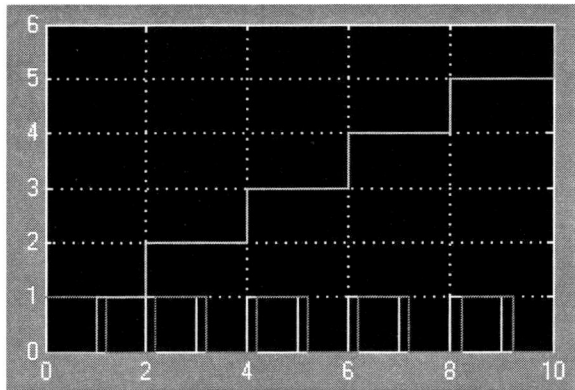

Figure 17.8. Input and output waveforms for the model of Figure 17.7

17.5 The Unit Delay Resettable Block

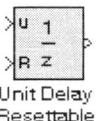

The **Unit Delay Resettable** block delays a signal one sample period. If the reset input signal is false, the block outputs the input signal delayed by one time step. If the reset signal is true, the block resets the current state to the initial condition, specified by the Initial condition parameter, and outputs that state delayed by one time step.

Example 17.5

In the model of Figure 17.9, the Pulse Generator 1 block is specified for a period 2 sec. and the Pulse Generator 2 block is set for a period 4 sec. All other parameters are in their default state. The input and output waveforms are shown in Figure 17.10.

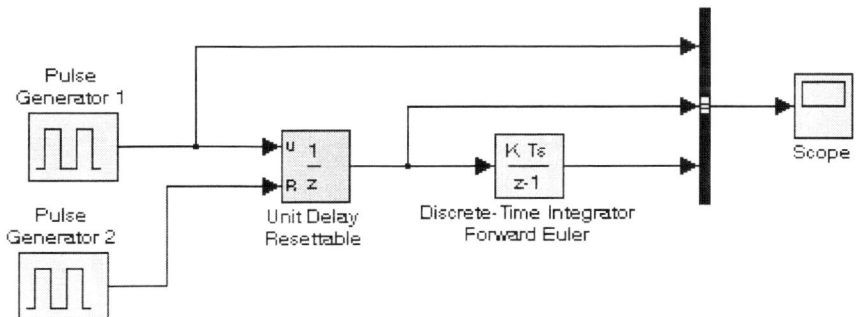

Figure 17.9. Model for Example 17.5

Chapter 17 The Additional Discrete Library

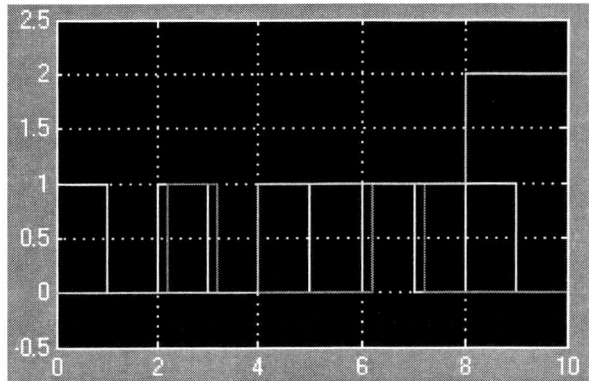

Figure 17.10. Input and output waveforms for the model of Figure 17.9

17.6 The Unit Delay Resettable External IC Block

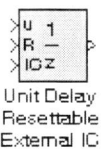

Unit Delay
Resettable
External IC

The **Unit Delay Resettable External IC** block delays a signal one sample period. The block can be reset by the external reset signal R. The block has two input ports, one for the input signal u and the other for the reset signal R. When the reset signal is false, the block outputs the input signal delayed by one time step. When the reset signal is true, the block resets the current state to the initial condition given by the signal IC and outputs that state delayed by one time step.

Example 17.6

In the model of Figure 17.11, the Pulse Generator 1 block is set for a period 2 sec. and the Pulse Generator 2 block is set for a period 4 sec. All other parameters are in their default state. The input and output waveforms are shown in Figure 17.12.

The Unit Delay Enabled Block

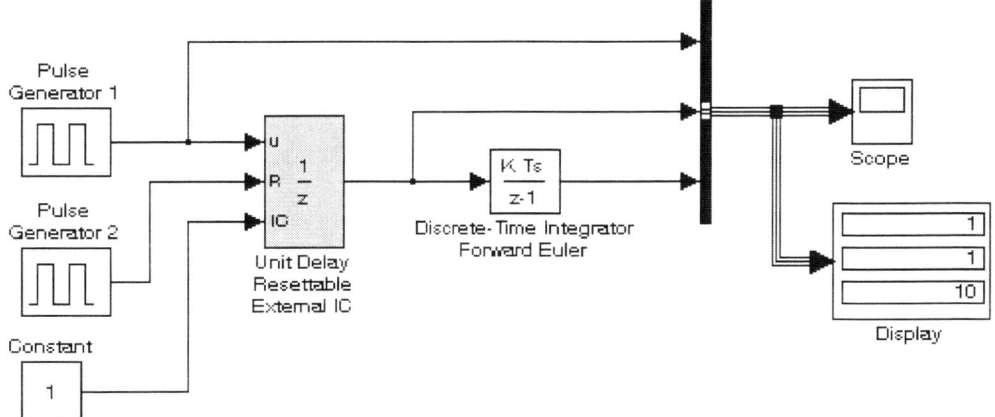

Figure 17.11. Model for Example 17.6

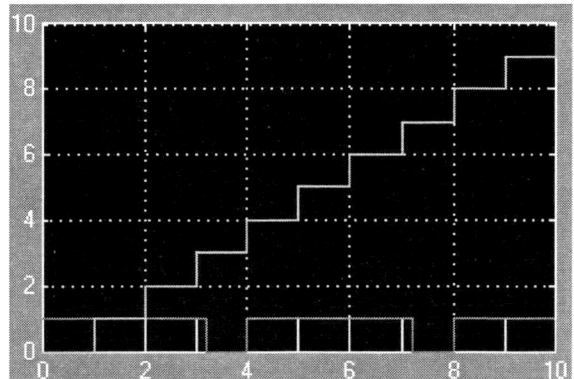

Figure 17.12. Input and output waveforms for the model of Figure 17.11

17.7 The Unit Delay Enabled Block

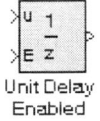

The **Unit Delay Enabled** block delays a signal by one sample period when the external enable signal **E** is on. When the enable signal **E** is off, the block is disabled. The block holds the current state at the same value and outputs that value. The enable signal is on when **E** is not 0, and is off when **E** is 0.

Example 17.7

Figure 17.13 contains two models where in the upper model the Unit Delay Enabled 1 block is disabled and thus its output is zero. In the lower model the Unit Delay Enabled 2 block is enabled and causes a delay in the input signal before being propagated to the Discrete Time Integrator Forward Euler 2 block. The inputs and outputs are shown in Figure 17.14.

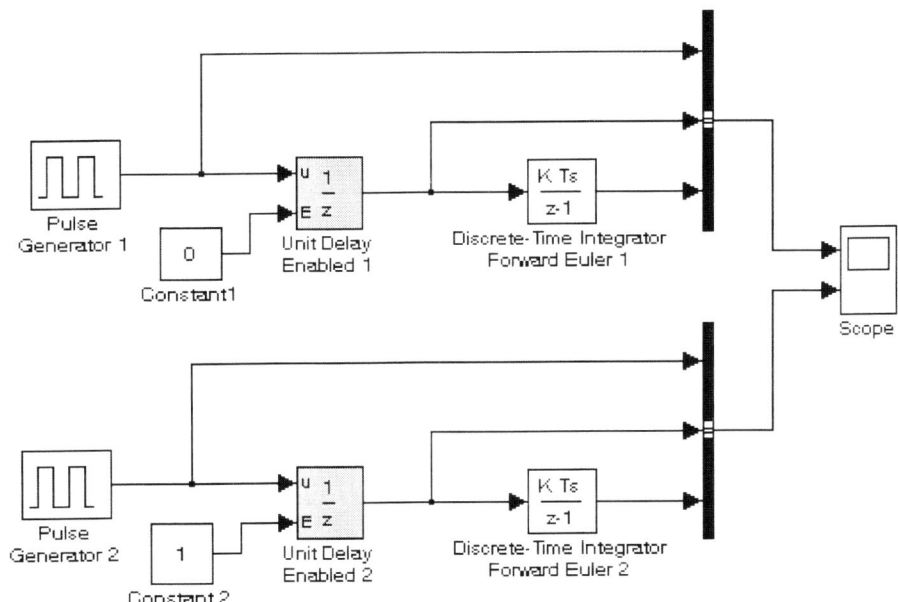

Figure 17.13. Models for Example 17.7

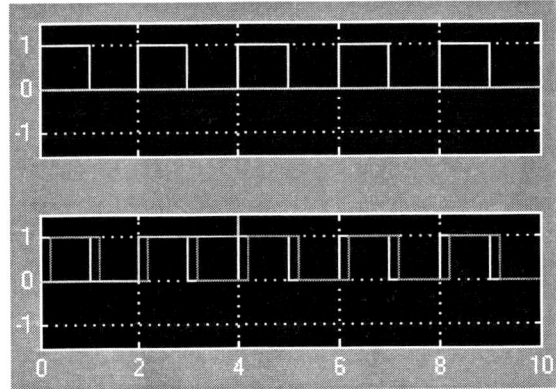

Figure 17.14. Input and Output waveforms for the models of Figure 17.13

17.8 The Unit Delay Enabled Resettable Block

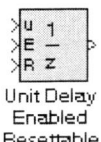

The **Unit Delay Enabled Resettable** block delays a signal one sample period, if the external enable signal is on. This block combines the features of the Unit Delay Enabled and Unit Delay Resettable blocks. When the enable signal **E** is on and the reset signal **R** is false, the block outputs the input signal delayed by one sample period. When the enable signal **E** is on and the reset signal **R** is true, the block resets the current state to the initial condition, specified by the Initial condition parameter, and outputs that state delayed by one sample period. When the enable signal is off, the block is disabled, and the state and output do not change except for resets. The enable signal is on when **E** is not 0, and off when **E** is 0.

Example 17.8

In the model of Figure 17.15, the Pulse Generator 1 block is specified for a period 2 sec., the Pulse Generator 2 block is specified for a period 3 sec., and the Pulse Generator 3 block is specified for a period 4 sec. All other parameters are in their default state. The input and output waveforms are shown in Figure 17.16.

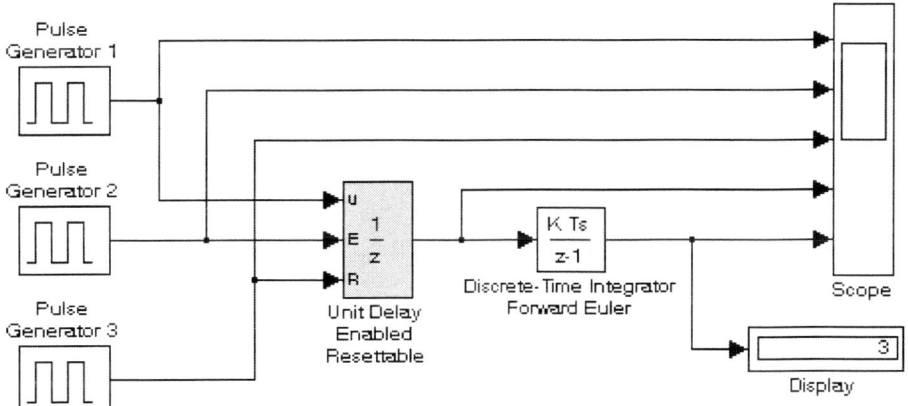

Figure 17.15. Model for Example 17.8

Chapter 17 The Additional Discrete Library

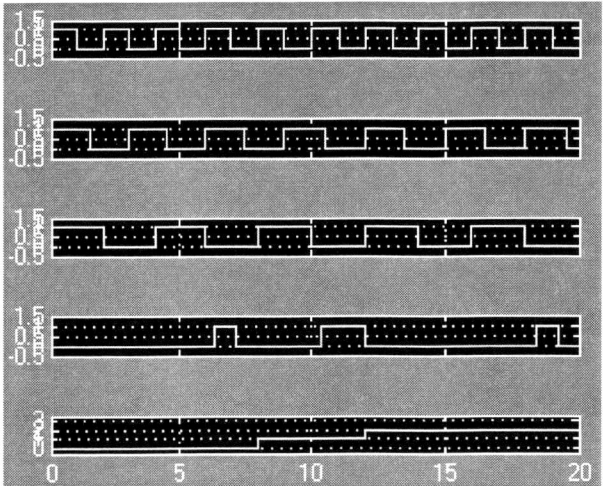

Figure 17.16. Input and output waveforms for the model of Figure 17.15

17.9 The Unit Delay Enabled External IC Block

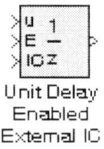

Unit Delay
Enabled
External IC

The **Unit Delay Enabled External IC** block delays a signal by one sample period when the enable signal E is on. When the enable is off, the block holds the current state at the same value and outputs that value. The enable E is on when E is not 0, and off when E is 0. The initial condition of this block is specified by the input signal IC. Essentially, this block is the same as the Unit Delay Enabled block which we described in the previous section of this chapter except that the initial condition is specified by an external block.

Example 17.9

In the model of Figure 17.17, the Constant 1 block enables the Unit Delay Enabled External IC block while the Constant 2 block is set to 1 to specify the initial condition. The input and output waveforms are shown in Figure 17.18.

The Unit Delay Enabled Resettable External IC Block

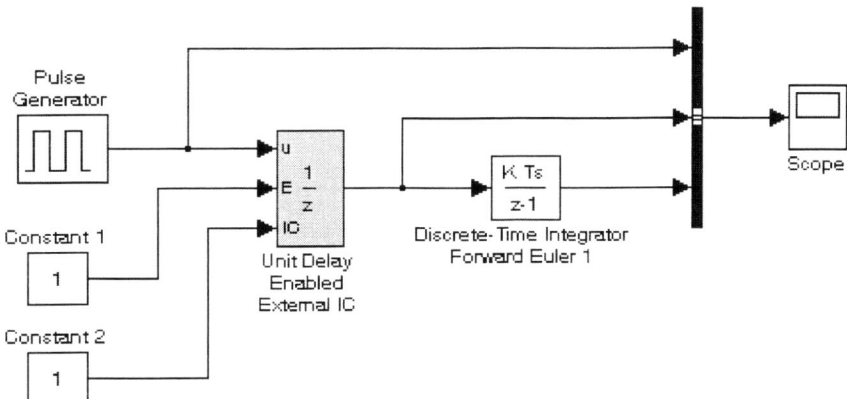

Figure 17.17. Model for Example 17.9

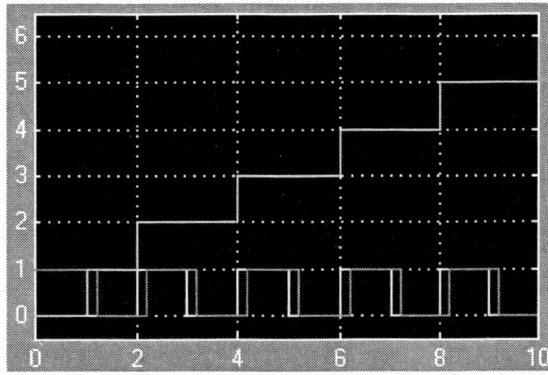

Figure 17.18. Input and output waveforms for the model of Figure 17.17

17.10 The Unit Delay Enabled Resettable External IC Block

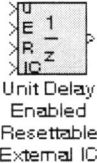

The **Unit Delay Enabled Resettable External IC** block is a combination of the functions performed by the Unit Delay Enabled, Unit Delay External IC, and Unit Delay Resettable blocks. The block can reset its state based on an external reset signal R. When the enable signal E is on and the reset signal R is false, the block outputs the input signal delayed by one sample period. When the enable signal E is on and the reset signal R is true, the block resets the current state to the initial condition given by the signal IC, and outputs that state delayed by one sample period. When the enable signal is off, the block is disabled, and the state and output do not change except for resets. The enable signal is on when E is not 0, and off when E is 0.

Chapter 17 The Additional Discrete Library

Example 17.10

In the model of Figure 17.19, the Pulse Generator 1 block is specified for a period 2 sec., the Pulse Generator 2 block is specified for a period 3 sec., and the Pulse Generator 3 block is specified for a period 4 sec. All other parameters are in their default state. The input and output waveforms are shown in Figure 17.20.

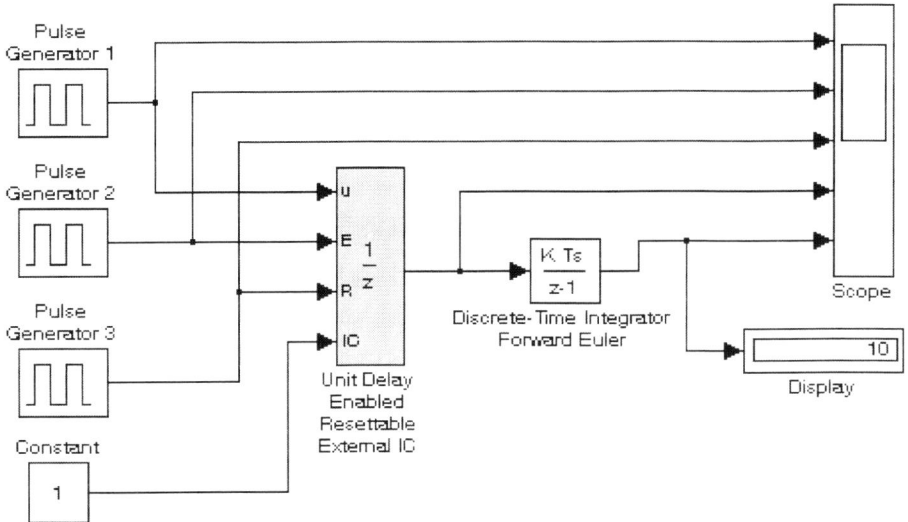

Figure 17.19. Model for Example 17.10

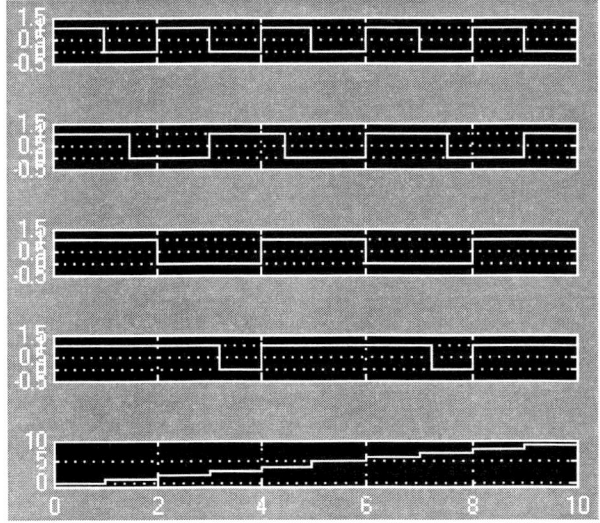

Figure 17.20. Input and output waveforms for the model of Figure 17.19

17.11 The Unit Delay With Preview Resettable Block

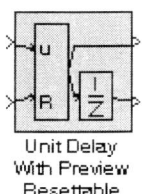

The **Unit Delay With Preview Resettable** block can reset its state based on an external reset signal R. The block has two output ports. When the reset R is false, the upper port outputs the signal and the lower port outputs the signal delayed by one sample period. When the reset R is true, the block resets the current state to the initial condition given by the Initial condition parameter. The block outputs that state delayed by one sample time through the lower output port, and outputs the state without a delay through the upper output port.

Example 17.11

In the model of Figure 17.21, the Pulse Generator 1 block is specified for a period 2 sec. and the Pulse Generator 2 block is specified for a period 4 sec. All other parameters are in their default state. The input and output waveforms are shown in Figure 17.22.

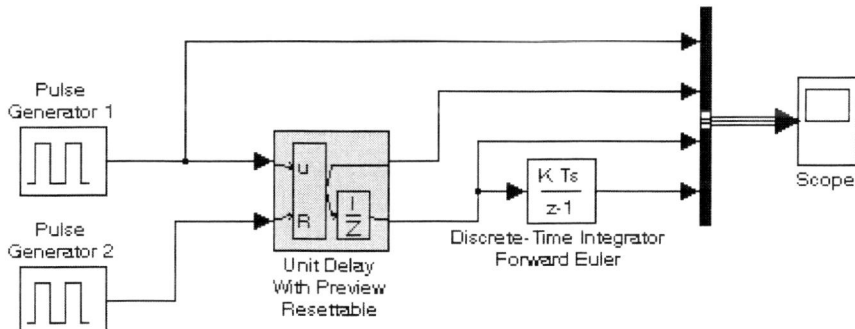

Figure 17.21. Model for Example 17.11

Chapter 17 The Additional Discrete Library

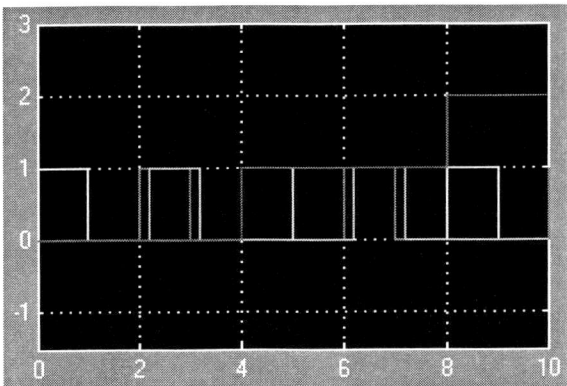

Figure 17.22. Waveforms for the model of Figure 17.21

17.12 The Unit Delay With Preview Resettable External RV Block

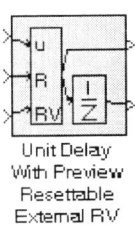

The **Unit Delay With Preview Resettable External RV** block has three input and two output ports. This block can reset its state based on the state of the an external input reset signal R. When the external reset R is false, the upper port outputs the signal and the lower port outputs the signal delayed by one sample period. When the external reset R is true, the upper output signal is forced to equal the external input reset signal RV. The lower output signal is not affected until one time step later, at which time it is equal to the external reset signal RV at the previous time step. The block uses the internal Initial condition only when the model starts or when a parent enabled subsystem is used. The internal Initial condition only affects the lower output signal.

Example 17.12

In the model of Figure 17.23, the Pulse Generator 1, 2, and 3 blocks are specified for the periods shown on the model. All other parameters are in their default state. The input and output waveforms are shown in Figure 17.24.

The Unit Delay With Preview Enabled Block

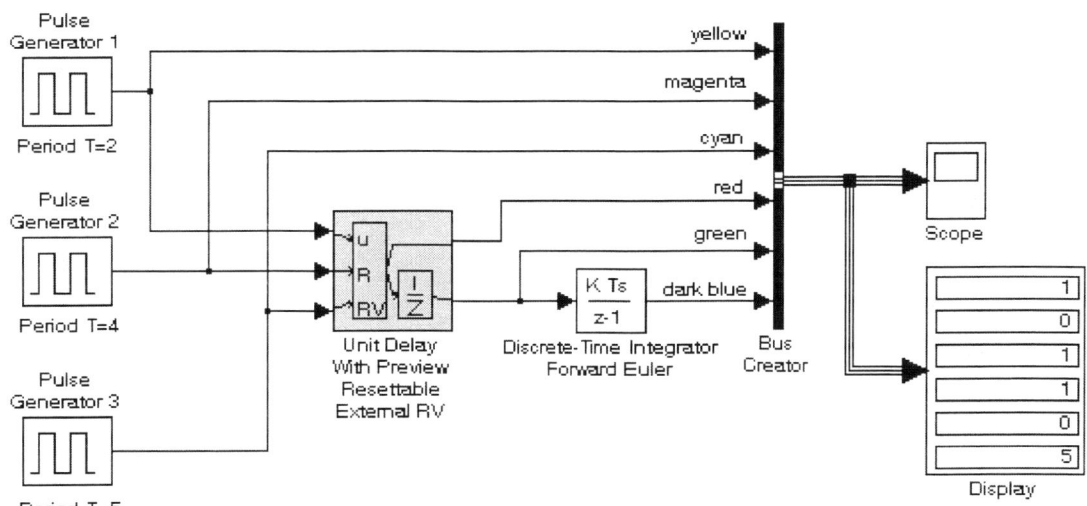

Figure 17.23. Model for Example 17.12

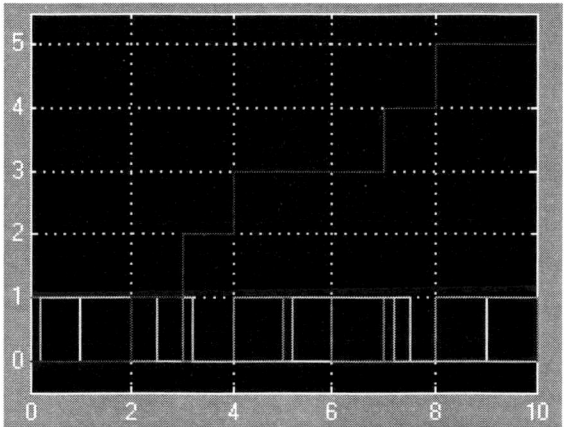

Figure 17.24. Waveforms for the model of Figure 17.23

17.13 The Unit Delay With Preview Enabled Block

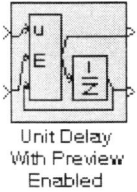

The **Unit Delay With Preview Enabled** block has two input and two output ports. When the external input enable signal **E** is on, the upper port outputs the signal and the lower port outputs

Chapter 17 The Additional Discrete Library

the signal delayed by one sample period. When the enable signal E is off, the block is disabled, and the state and output values do not change. The enable signal is on when E is not 0, and off when E is 0.

Example 17.13

In the model of Figure 17.25, the Pulse Generator block is set for a period 2 sec. All other parameters are in their default state. The input and output waveforms are shown in Figure 17.26.

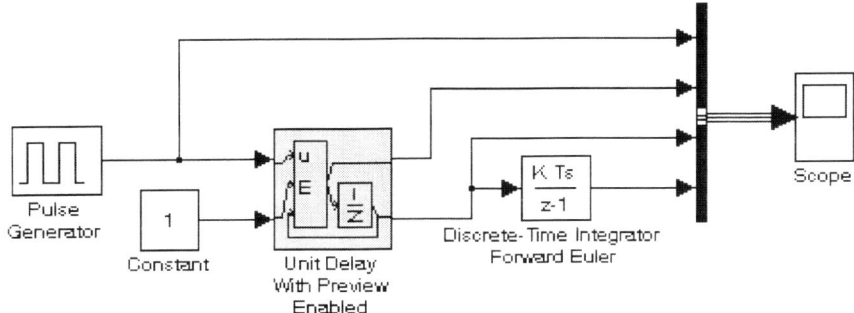

Figure 17.25. Model for Example 17.13

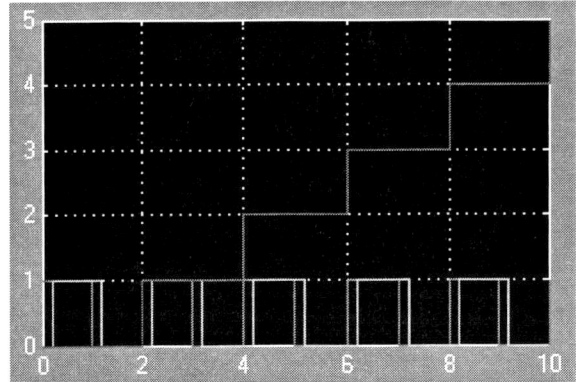

Figure 17.26. Waveforms for the model of Figure 17.25

17.14 The Unit Delay With Preview Enabled Resettable Block

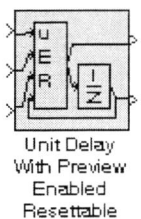
Unit Delay With Preview Enabled Resettable

The **Unit Delay With Preview Enabled Resettable** block has three inputs and two outputs. This block can reset its state based on an external input reset signal **R**. When the external enable signal **E** is on and the reset **R** is false, the upper port outputs the signal and the lower port outputs the signal delayed by one sample period. When the enable input signal **E** is on and the reset **R** is true, the block resets the current state to the initial condition given by the Initial condition parameter. The block outputs that state delayed by one sample time through the lower output port, and outputs the state without a delay through the upper output port. When the Enable signal is off, the block is disabled, and the state and output values do not change, except for resets. The enable signal is on when **E** is not 0, and off when **E** is 0.

Example 17.14

In the model of Figure 17.27, the Pulse Generator 1, 2, and 3 blocks are specified for the period shown on the model. All other parameters are in their default state. The input and output waveforms are shown in Figure 17.28.

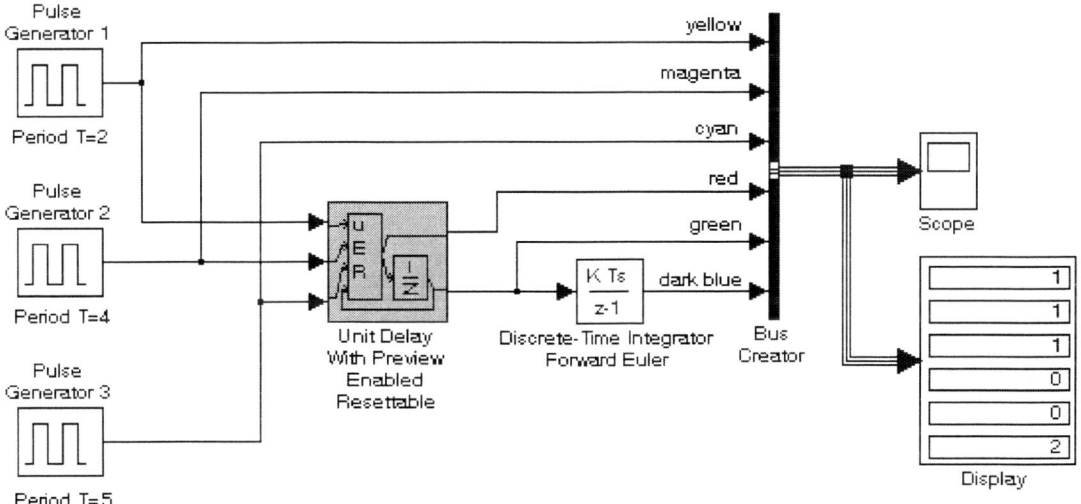

Figure 17.27. Model for Example 17.14

Chapter 17 The Additional Discrete Library

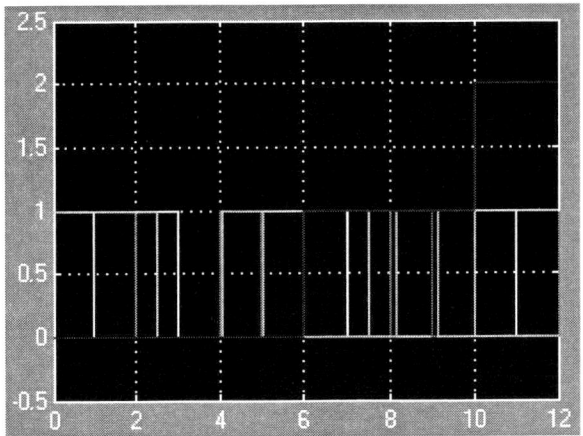

Figure 17.28. Waveforms for the model of Figure 17.27

17.15 The Unit Delay With Preview Enabled Resettable External RV Block

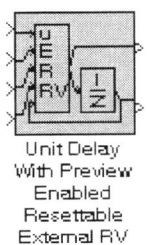

The **Unit Delay With Preview Enabled Resettable External RV** block has four inputs and two outputs. This block can reset its state based on an external reset signal **R**. When the external enable signal **E** is on and the reset **R** is false, the upper port outputs the signal and the lower port outputs the signal delayed by one sample period.

When the enable signal **E** is on and the reset **R** is true, the upper output signal is forced to equal the external input reset signal **RV**. The lower output signal is not affected until one time step later, at which time it is equal to the external reset signal **RV** at the previous time step. The block uses the internal Initial condition only when the model starts or when a parent enabled subsystem is used. The internal Initial condition only affects the lower output signal. When the Enable signal is off, the block is disabled, and the state and output values do not change, except for resets. The enable signal is on when **E** is not 0, and off when **E** is 0.

The Unit Delay With Preview Enabled Resettable External RV Block

Example 17.15

In the model of Figure 17.29, the Pulse Generator 1, 2, and 3 blocks are set for the periods shown on the model. All other parameters are in their default state. The input and output waveforms are shown in Figure 17.30.

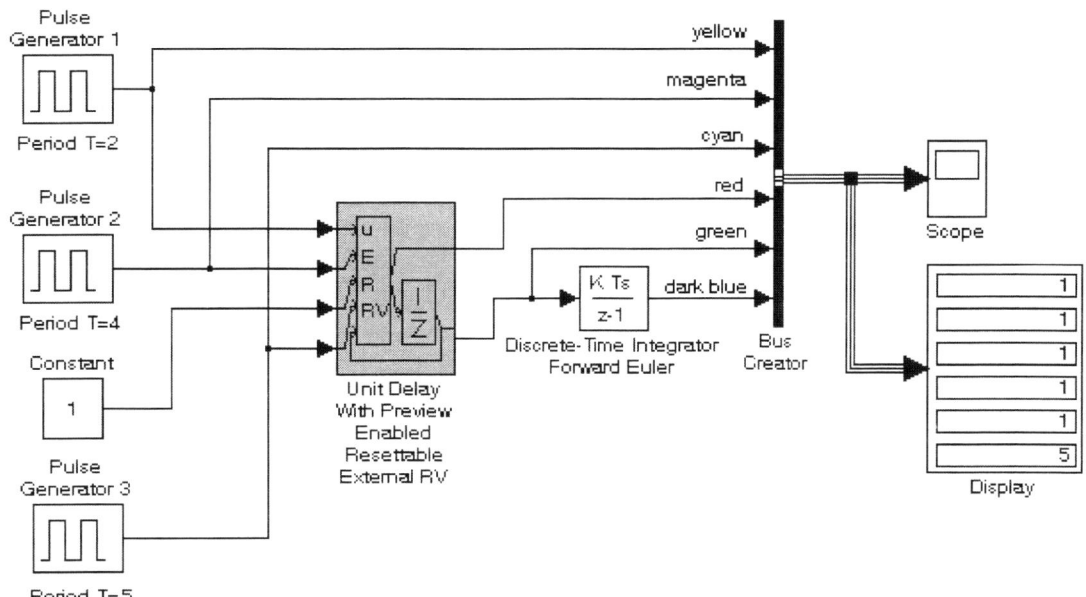

Figure 17.29. Model for Example 17.15

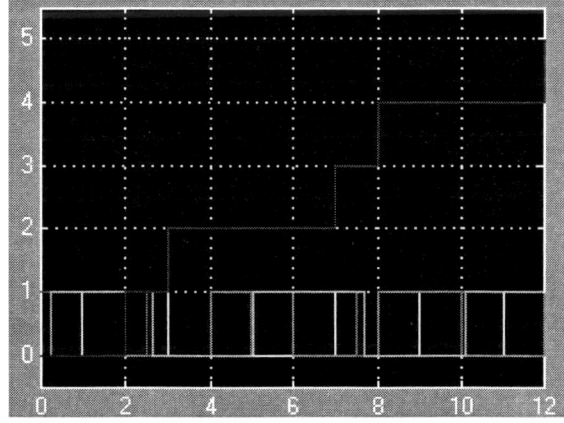

Figure 17.30. Waveforms for the model of Figure 17.29

17.16 Summary

- The **Transfer Fcn Direct Form II** block implements a Direct Form II realization of the transfer function specified by the Numerator coefficients and the Denominator coefficients without the leading coefficient in the Denominator.

- The **Transfer Fcn Direct Form II Time Varying** block implements a Direct Form II realization of a specified transfer function. Essentially, this block performs the same function as that of the Transfer Fcn Direct Form II block.

- The **Fixed–Point State–Space** block implements the system described by

$$x[n+1] = Ax[n] + Bu[n]$$
$$y[n] = Cx[n] + Du[n]$$

- The **Unit Delay External IC** (Initial Condition) block delays its input by one sample period. This block is equivalent to the z^{-1} discrete-time operator. The block accepts one input and generates one output, both of which can be scalar or vector. If the input is a vector, all elements of the vector are delayed by the same sample period. The block's output for the first sample period is equal to the signal IC. The input u and initial condition IC data types must be the same.

- The **Unit Delay Resettable** block delays a signal one sample period. If the reset input signal is false, the block outputs the input signal delayed by one time step. If the reset signal is true, the block resets the current state to the initial condition, specified by the Initial condition parameter, and outputs that state delayed by one time step.

- The **Unit Delay Resettable External IC** block delays a signal one sample period. The block can be reset by the external reset signal R. The block has two input ports, one for the input signal u and the other for the reset signal R. When the reset signal is false, the block outputs the input signal delayed by one time step. When the reset signal is true, the block resets the current state to the initial condition given by the signal IC and outputs that state delayed by one time step.

- The **Unit Delay Enabled** block delays a signal by one sample period when the external enable signal E is on. When the enable signal E is off, the block is disabled. The block holds the current state at the same value and outputs that value. The enable signal is on when E is not 0, and is off when E is 0.

- The **Unit Delay Enabled Resettable** block delays a signal one sample period, if the external enable signal is on. This block combines the features of the Unit Delay Enabled and Unit Delay Resettable blocks.

- The **Unit Delay Enabled External IC** block delays a signal by one sample period when the enable signal E is on. When the enable is off, the block holds the current state at the same

Summary

value and outputs that value. The enable E is on when E is not 0, and off when E is 0. The initial condition of this block is specified by the input signal IC.

- The **Unit Delay Enabled Resettable External IC** block is a combination of the functions performed by the Unit Delay Enabled, Unit Delay External IC, and Unit Delay Resettable blocks.

- The **Unit Delay With Preview Resettable** block has two input and two output ports. This block can reset its state based on the state of the external input reset signal R. When the reset R is false, the upper port outputs the signal and the lower port outputs the signal delayed by one sample period. When the reset R is true, the block resets the current state to the initial condition given by the Initial condition parameter. The block outputs that state delayed by one sample time through the lower output port, and outputs the state without a delay through the upper output port.

- The **Unit Delay With Preview Resettable External RV** block has three input and two output ports. This block can reset its state based on the state of the an external input reset signal R. When the external reset R is false, the upper port outputs the signal and the lower port outputs the signal delayed by one sample period. When the external reset R is true, the upper output signal is forced to equal the external input reset signal RV. The lower output signal is not affected until one time step later, at which time it is equal to the external reset signal RV at the previous time step. The block uses the internal Initial condition only when the model starts or when a parent enabled subsystem is used. The internal Initial condition only affects the lower output signal.

- The **Unit Delay With Preview Enabled** block has two input and two output ports. When the external input enable signal E is on, the upper port outputs the signal and the lower port outputs the signal delayed by one sample period. When the enable signal E is off, the block is disabled, and the state and output values do not change. The enable signal is on when E is not 0, and off when E is 0.

- The **Unit Delay With Preview Enabled Resettable** block has three inputs and two outputs. This block can reset its state based on an external input reset signal R. When the external enable signal E is on and the reset R is false, the upper port outputs the signal and the lower port outputs the signal delayed by one sample period. When the enable input signal E is on and the reset R is true, the block resets the current state to the initial condition given by the Initial condition parameter. The block outputs that state delayed by one sample time through the lower output port, and outputs the state without a delay through the upper output port. When the Enable signal is off, the block is disabled, and the state and output values do not change, except for resets. The enable signal is on when E is not 0, and off when E is 0.

- The **Unit Delay With Preview Enabled Resettable External RV** block has four inputs and two outputs. This block can reset its state based on an external reset signal R. When the external enable signal E is on and the reset R is false, the upper port outputs the signal and the lower port outputs the signal delayed by one sample period. When the enable signal E is on and the reset **R** is true, the upper output signal is forced to equal the external input reset signal **RV**. The lower output signal is not affected until one time step later.

Chapter 18

The Additional Math – Increment / Decrement Library

This chapter is an introduction to the **Additional Math – Increment / Decrement** Library. This is the seventeenth and last library in the Simulink group of libraries and contains the blocks shown below. We will describe the function of each block included in this library and we will perform simulation examples to illustrate their applications.

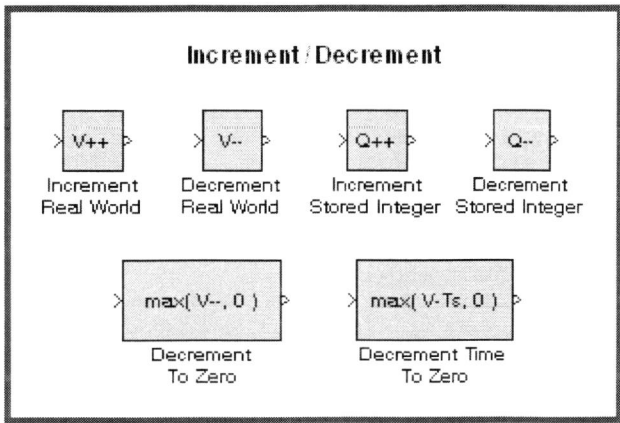

Chapter 18 The Additional Math − Increment / Decrement Library

18.1 The Increment Real World Block

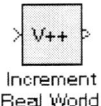

The **Increment Real World** block increases the real-world value of the signal by one.

Example 18.1

The model of Figure 18.1 implements the function $y = 3x + 5$ as indicated by the XY Graph in Figure 18.2.

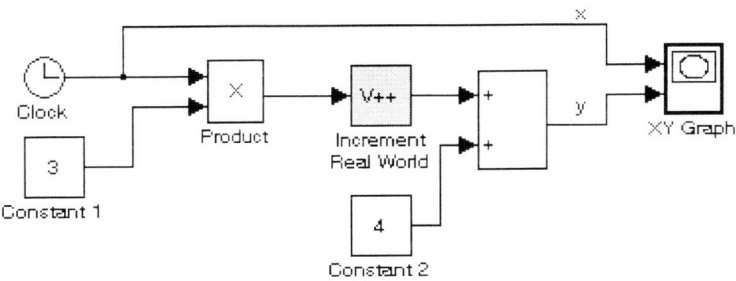

Figure 18.1. Model for Example 18.1

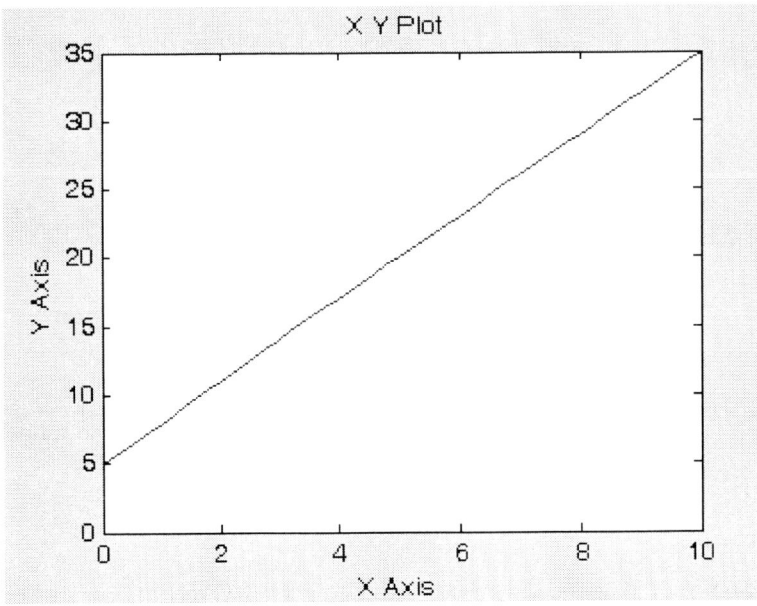

Figure 18.2. The XY graph for the model of Figure 18.1

18.2 The Decrement Real World Block

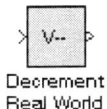

The **Decrement Real World** block decreases the real–world value of the signal by one.

Example 18.2

The model of Figure 18.3 implements the function y = −3(x + 1) as indicated by the XY Graph in Figure 18.4.

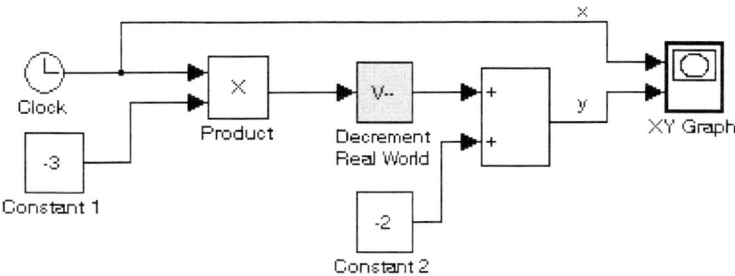

Figure 18.3. Model for Example 18.2

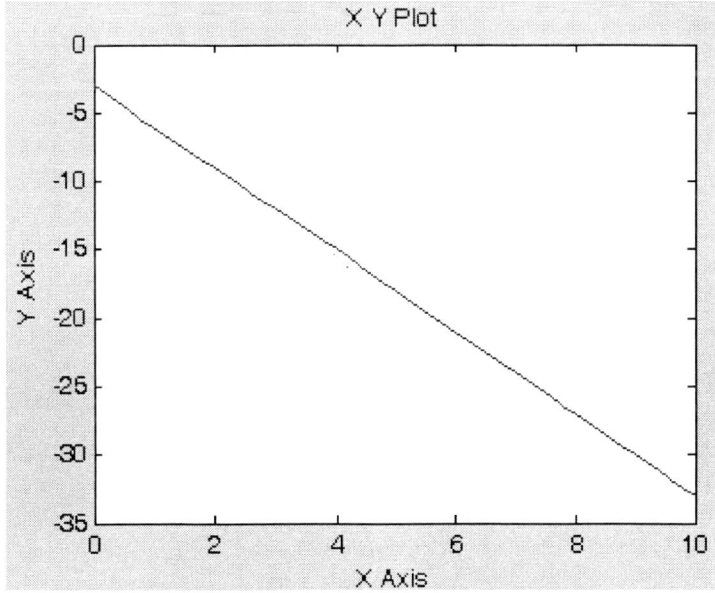

Figure 18.4. XY graph for the model of Figure 18.3

18.3 The Increment Stored Integer Block

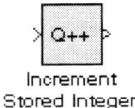

The **Increment Stored Integer** block increases the stored integer value of a signal by one.

Example 18.3

The model of Figure 18.5 implements the function $y = (2 + x)\sin x - 1$. The XY Graph for this model is shown in Figure 18.6.

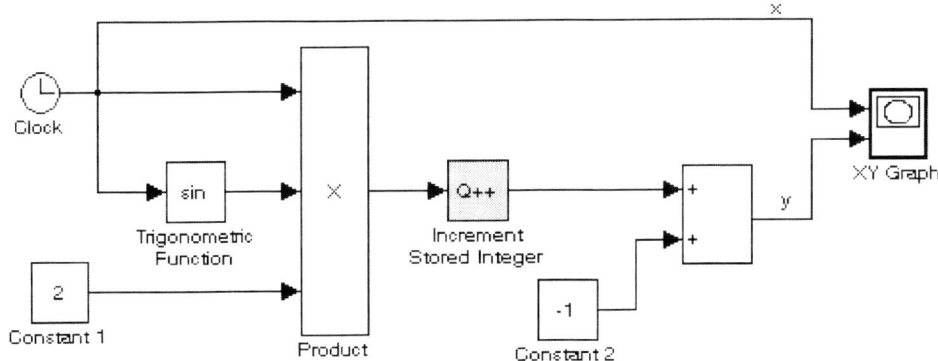

Figure 18.5. Model for Example 18.3

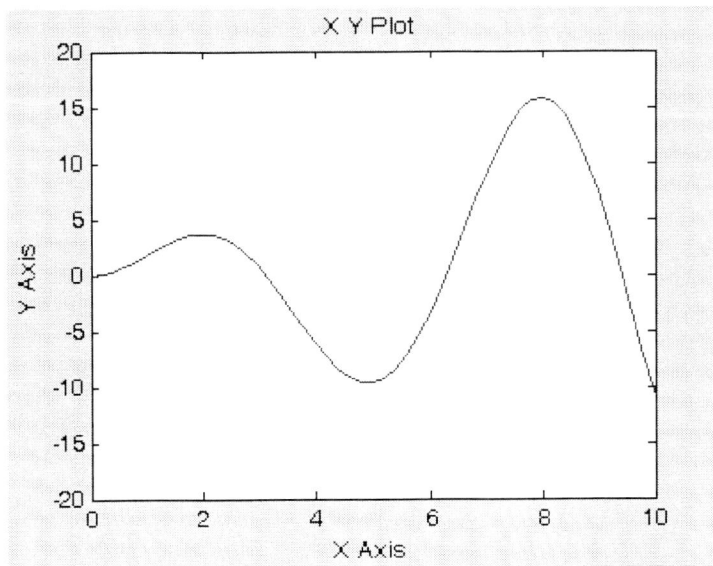

Figure 18.6. XY graph for the model of Figure 18.5

18.4 The Decrement Stored Integer Block

The **Decrement Stored Integer** block decreases the stored integer value of a signal by one.

Example 18.4

The model of Figure 18.7 implements the function $y = 2x^4 + 1$. The XY Graph for this model is shown in Figure 18.8.

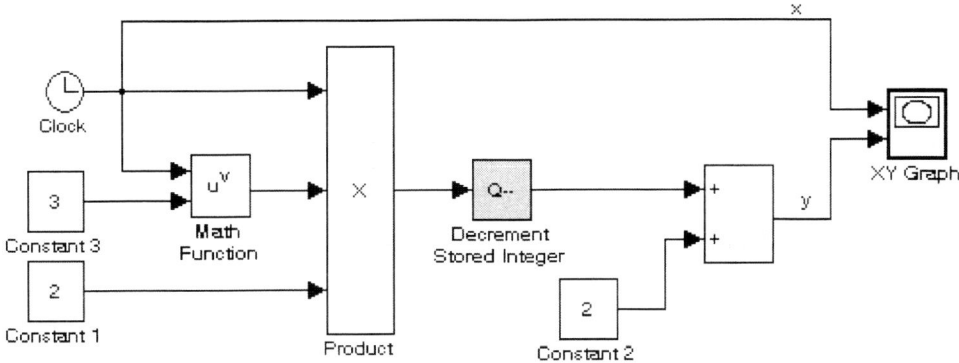

Figure 18.7. Model for Example 18.4

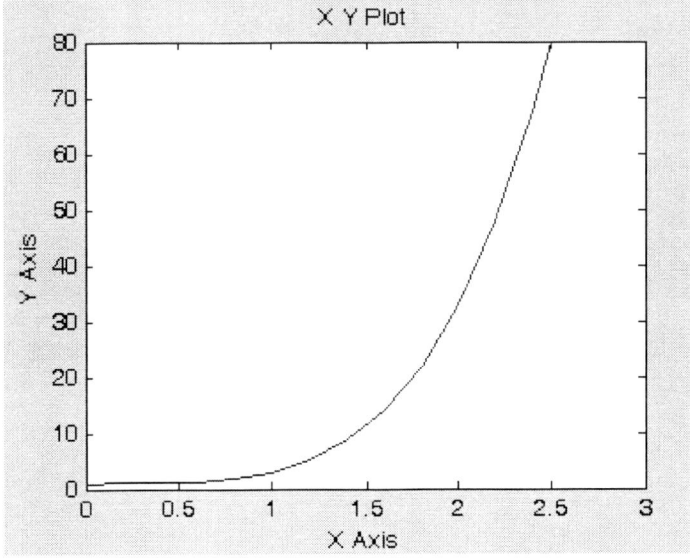

Figure 18.8. XY graph for the model of Figure 18.7

18.5 The Decrement to Zero Block

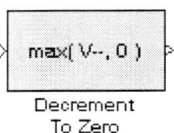

The **Decrement To Zero** block decreases the real-world value of the signal by one. The output never goes below zero.

Example 18.5

For the model of Figure 18.9, the output value never goes below zero as shown in Figure 18.10.

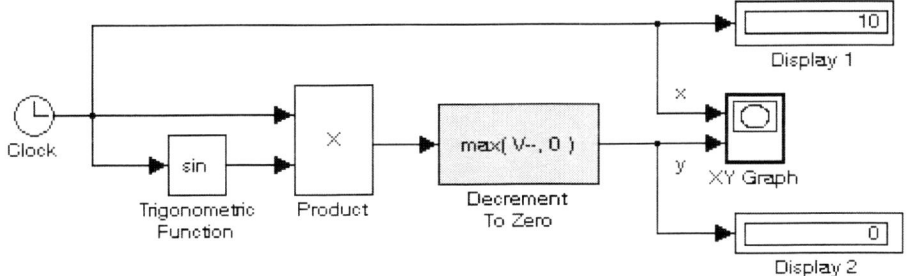

Figure 18.9. Model for Example 18.5

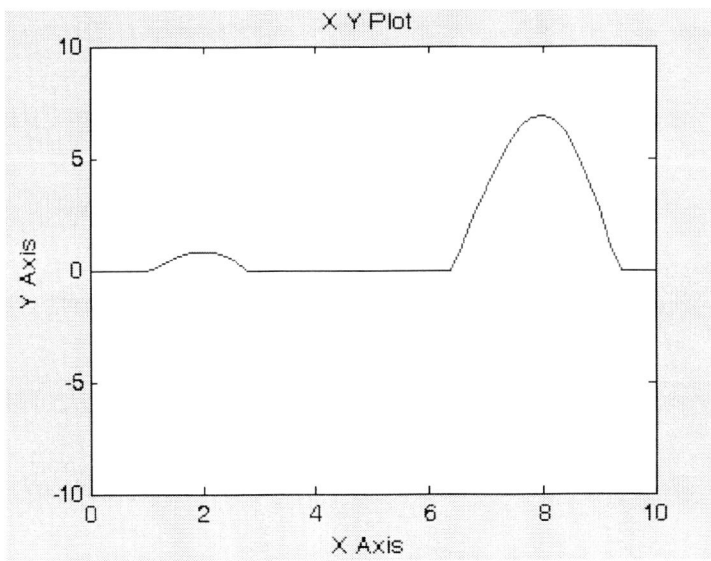

Figure 18.10. XY graph for the model of Figure 18.9

18.6 The Decrement Time To Zero Block

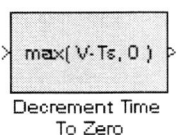
Decrement Time
To Zero

The **Decrement Time To Zero** block decreases the real–world value of the signal by the sample time, Ts. This block works only with fixed sample rates and the output never goes below zero.

Example 18.6

The model of Figure 18.11 implements the waveform shown in Figure 18.12.

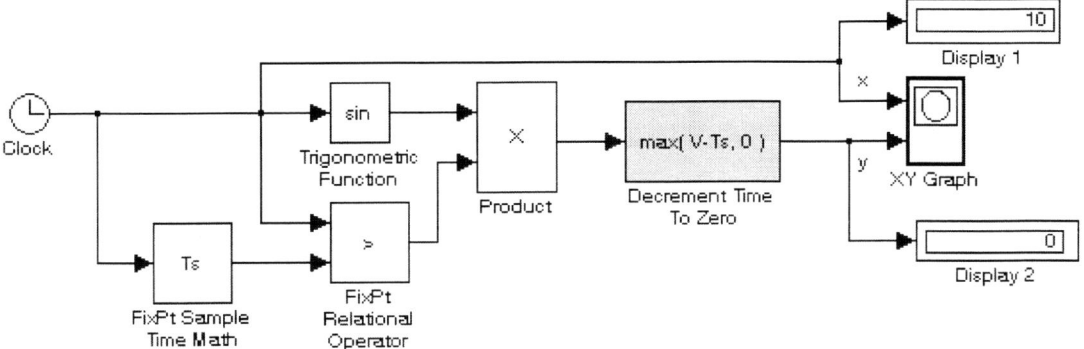

Figure 18.11. Model for Example 18.6

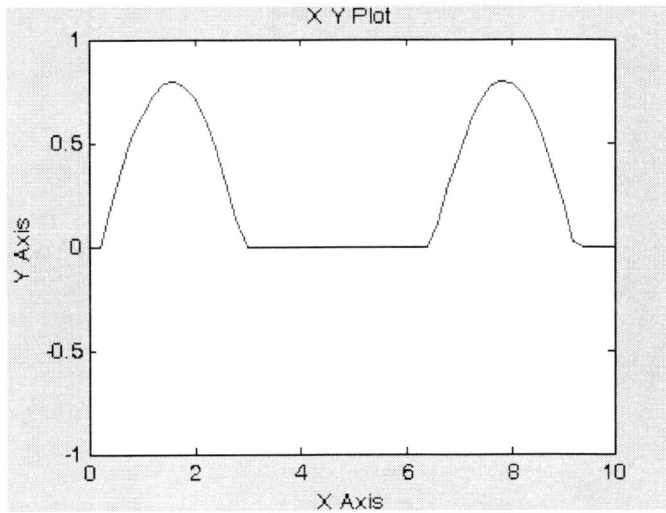

Figure 18.12. XY graph for the model of Figure 18.11

18.7 Summary

- The **Increment Real World** block increases the real-world value of the signal by one.

- The **Decrement Real World** block decreases the real-world value of the signal by one.

- The **Increment Stored Integer** block increases the stored integer value of a signal by one.

- The **Decrement Stored Integer** block decreases the stored integer value of a signal by one.

- The **Decrement To Zero** block decreases the real-world value of the signal by one. The output never goes below zero.

- The **Decrement Time To Zero** block decreases the real-world value of the signal by the sample time, Ts. This block works only with fixed sample rates and the output never goes below zero.

Chapter 19

Engineering Applications

This chapter is devoted to engineering applications using appropriate Simulink blocks to illustrate the application of the blocks in the libraries which we described in Chapters 2 through 18. Most of these applications may be considered components or subsystems of large systems such as the demos provided by Simulink. Some of these applications describe some of the new blocks added to the latest Simulink revision.

19.1 Analog-to-Digital Conversion

One of the recently added Simulink blocks is the **Idealized ADC Quantizer**. Figure 19.1 shows how this block can be used to discretize a continuous-time signal such as a clock. The Function Block Parameters dialog box provides a detailed description for this block.

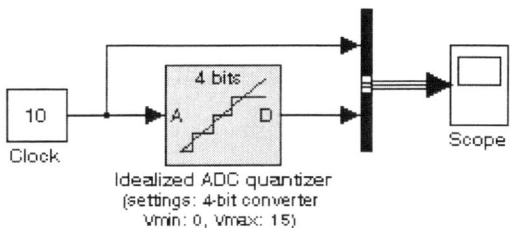

Figure 19.1. Model for Analog-to-Digital conversion

The settings specified for the Idealized ADC Quantizer are noted in Figure 19.1. The output data types for the Clock and the Idealized ADC Quantizer blocks are specified as **double**. The input and output waveforms are shown in Figure 19.2.

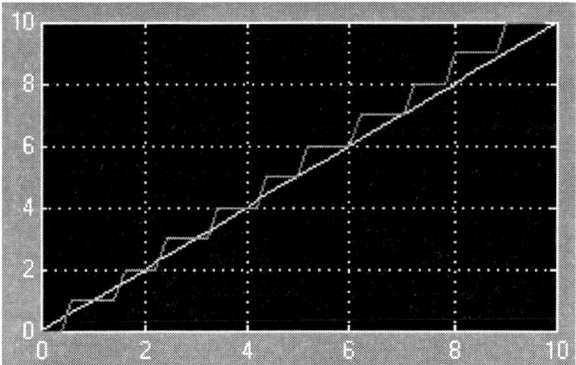

Figure 19.2. Input and output waveforms for the model of Figure 19.1

19.2 The Zero–Order Hold and First–Order Hold as Reconstructors

Suppose that a continuous–time signal x(t) is bandlimited with bandwidth B, and its Fourier transform |X(ω)| is zero for ω > B. The Sampling Theorem states that if the sampling frequency ω_S is equal or greater than 2B, the signal x(t) can be recover entirely from the sampled signal $x_S(t)$ by applying $x_S(t)$ to an ideal lowpass filter with bandwidth B. Another method for recovering the continuous–time signal x(t) from the sampled signal $x_S(t)$ is to use a holding circuit that holds the value of the sampled signal at time nT until it receives the next value at time nT + T. A Zero–Order Hold circuit behaves like a low-pass filter and thus can be used as a holding circuit to recover the continuous–time signal x(t) from the sampled signal $x_S(t)$.

The model of Figure 19.3 shows the output of a Zero–Order Hold block specified at a low sampling frequency, and Figure 19.4 shows the input and output waveforms.

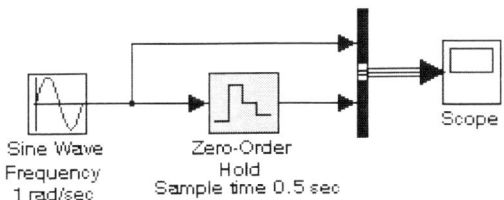

Figure 19.3. Model producing a piecewise constant waveform when the sampling frequency is low

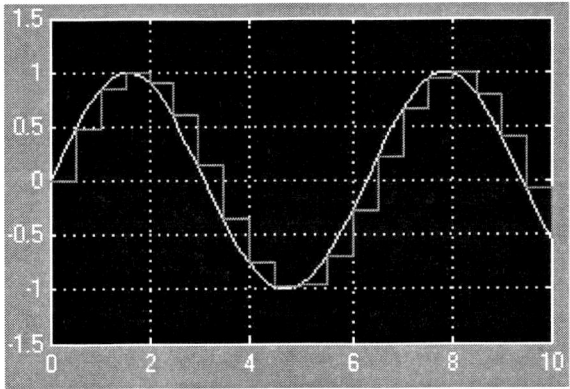

Figure 19.4. Input and output waveforms for the model of Figure 19.3

Whereas the Zero–Order Hold circuit generates a continuous input signal u(t) by holding each sample value u[k] constant over one sample period, a First–Order Hold circuit uses linear interpolation between samples as shown by the model of Figure 19.5 and the waveforms in Figure 19.6.

The Zero–Order Hold and First–Order Hold as Reconstructors

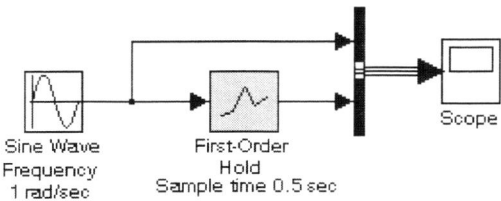

Figure 19.5. The model of Figure 19.3 with a First–Order Hold block

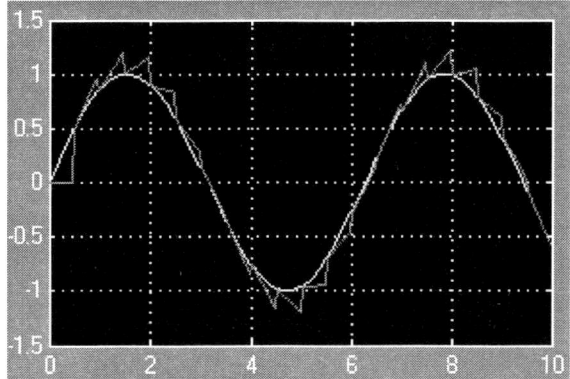

Figure 19.6. Input and output waveforms for the model of Figure 19.5

A comparison of the outputs produced by a Zero-Order Hold block and a First-Order Hold block with the same input, is shown in the model of Figure 19.7. The outputs are shown in Figure 19.8.

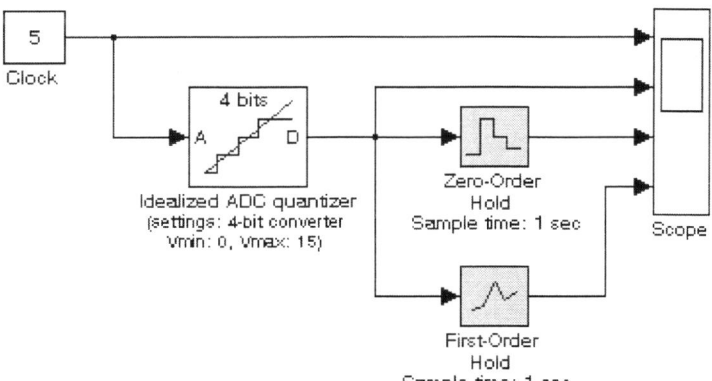

Figure 19.7. Model for comparison of a Zero-Order Hold and a First-Order Hold blocks with same input

Chapter 19 Engineering Applications

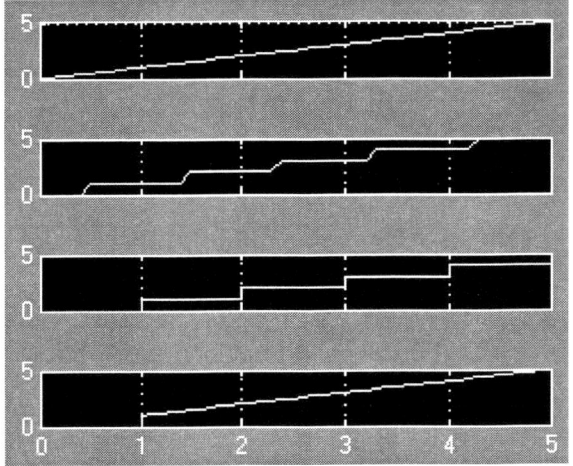

Figure 19.8. Waveforms for the model of Figure 19.7

19.3 Digital Filter Realization Forms

A given transfer function H(z) of a digital filter can be realized in several forms, the most common being the **Direct Form I**, **Direct Form II**, **Cascade (Series)**, and **Parallel**. These are described in Subsections 19.3.1 through 19.3.4 below. Similar demo models can be displayed as indicated in these subsections.

19.3.1 The Direct Form I Realization of a Digital Filter

The **Direct Form I Realization** of a second-order digital filter is shown in Figure 19.9.

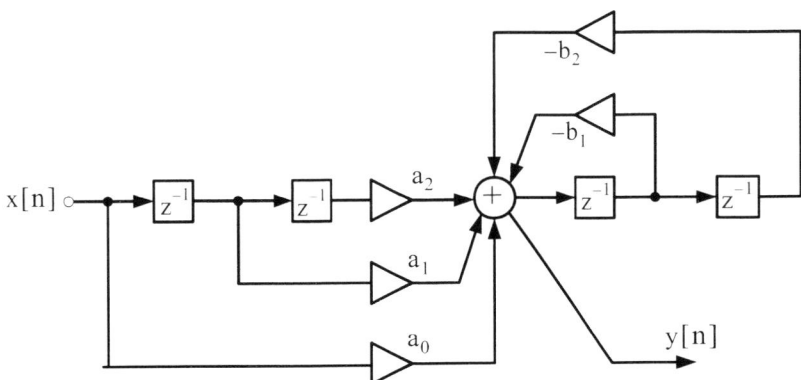

Figure 19.9. Direct Form I Realization of a second-order digital filter

At the summing junction of Figure 19.9 we obtain

$$a_0 X(z) + a_1 z^{-1} X(z) + a_2 z^{-2} X(z) + (-b_1) z^{-1} Y(z) + (-b_2) z^{-1} Y(z) = Y(z)$$

Digital Filter Realization Forms

$$X(z)(a_0 + a_1z^{-1} + a_2z^{-2}) = Y(z)(1 + b_1z^{-1} + b_2z^{-2})$$

and thus the transfer function of the Direct Form I Realization of the second-order digital filter of Figure 19.9 is

$$H(z) = \frac{Y(z)}{X(z)} = \frac{a_0 + a_1z^{-1} + a_2z^{-2}}{1 + b_1z^{-1} + b_2z^{-2}} \qquad (19.1)$$

A disadvantage of a Direct Form I Realization digital filter is that it requires $2k$ registers where k represents the order of the filter. We observe that the second-order ($k = 2$) digital filter of Figure 11.9 requires 4 delay (register) elements denoted as z^{-1}. However, this form of realization has the advantage that there is no possibility of internal filter overflow.[*]

19.3.2 The Direct Form II Realization of a Digital Filter

Figure 19.10 shows the **Direct Form-II**[†] **Realization** of a second-order digital filter. The Simulink **Transfer Fcn Direct Form II** block implements the transfer function of this filter.

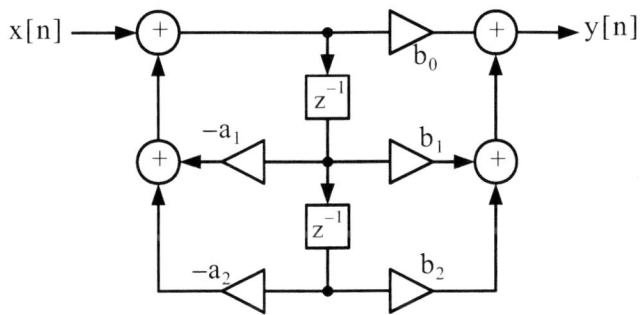

Figure 19.10. Direct Form-II Realization of a second-order digital filter

The transfer function for the Direct Form-II second-order digital filter of Figure 19.10 is the same as for a Direct Form-I second-order digital filter of Figure 19.9, that is,

$$H(z) = \frac{a_0 + a_1z^{-1} + a_2z^{-2}}{1 + b_1z^{-1} + b_2z^{-2}} \qquad (19.2)$$

A comparison of Figures 19.9 and 19.10 shows that whereas a Direct Form-I second-order digital filter is requires $2k$ registers, where k represents the order of the filter, a Direct Form-II second-order digital filter requires only k register elements denoted as z^{-1}. This is because the register

---

[*] For a detailed discussion on overflow conditions please refer to Digital Circuit Analysis and Design with an Introduction to CPLDs and FPGAs, ISBN 0-9744239-6-3, Section 10.5, Chapter 10, Page 10-6.
[†] The Direct Form-II is also known as the **Canonical** Form.

Chapter 19 Engineering Applications

(z^{-1}) elements in a Direct Form–II realization are shared between the zero section and the pole section.

Example 19.1

Figure 19.11 shows a Direct Form–II second–order digital filter whose transfer function is

$$H(z) = \frac{1 + 1.5z^{-1} + 1.02z^{-2}}{1 - 0.25z^{-1} + 0.75z^{-2}} \tag{19.3}$$

The input and output waveforms are shown in Figure 19.12.

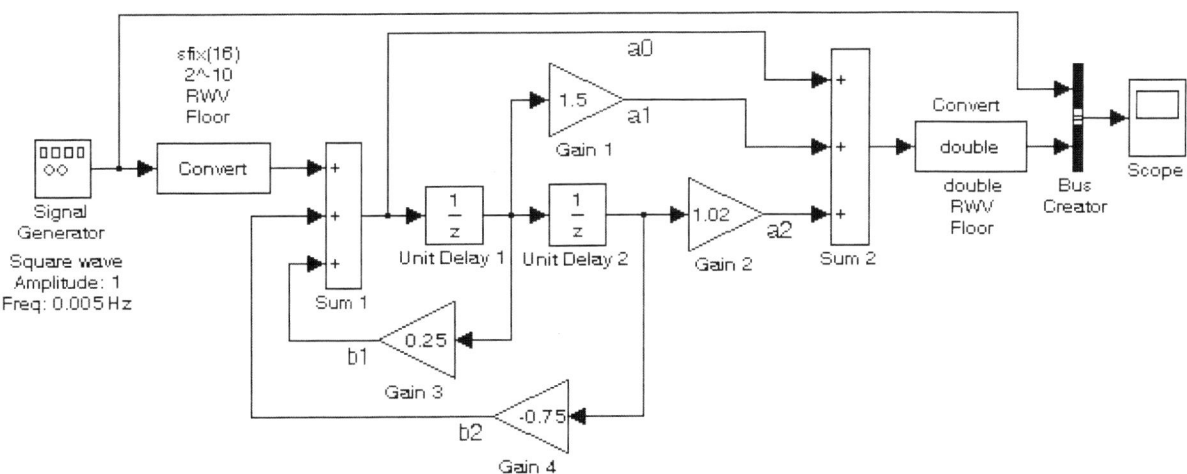

Figure 19.11. Model for Example 19.1

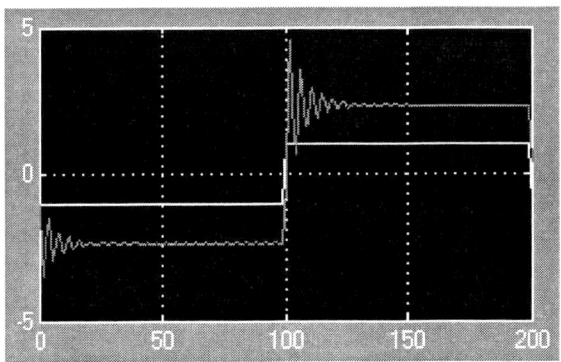

Figure 19.12. Input and output waveforms for the model of Figure 19.11

Digital Filter Realization Forms

A demo model using fixed–point Simulink blocks can be displayed by typing

fxpdemo_direct_form2

in MATLAB's Command Window. This demo is an implementation of the third–order transfer function

$$H(z) = \frac{1 + 2.2z^{-1} + 1.85z^{-2} + 0.5z^{-3}}{1 - 0.5z^{-1} + 0.84z^{-2} + 0.09z^{-3}}$$

19.3.3 The Series Form Realization of a Digital Filter

For the Series* Form Realization, the transfer function is expressed as a product of first–order and second-order transfer functions as shown in relation (19.4) below.

$$H(z) = H_1(z) \cdot H_2((z) \ldots H_R(z)) \tag{19.4}$$

Relation (19.4) is implemented as the cascaded blocks shown in Figure 19.13.

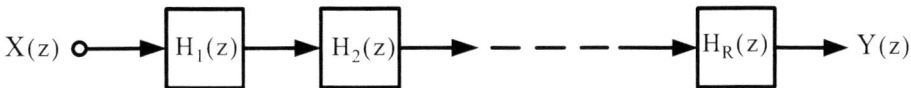

Figure 19.13. Series Form Realization

Figure 19.14 shows the Series–Form Realization of a second–order digital filter.

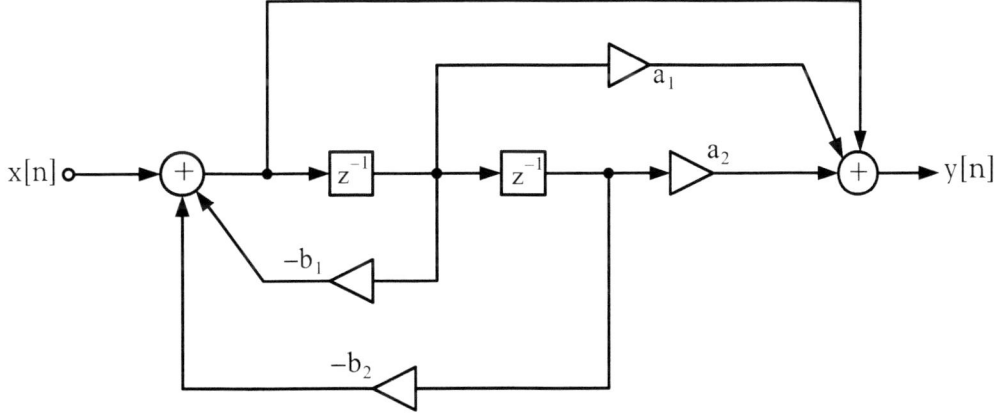

Figure 19.14. Series Form Realization of a second-order digital filter

The transfer function for the Series Form second–order digital filter of Figure 19.14 is

$$H(z) = \frac{1 + a_1 z^{-1} + a_2 z^{-2}}{1 + b_1 z^{-1} + b_2 z^{-2}} \tag{19.5}$$

---

* *The Series Form Realization is also known as the Cascade Form Realization*

Chapter 19 Engineering Applications

Example 19.2

The transfer function of the Series Form Realization of a certain second-order digital filter is

$$H(z) = \frac{0.5(1-0.36z^{-2})}{1+0.1z^{-1}-0.72z^{-2}}$$

To implement this filter, we factor the numerator and denominator polynomials as

$$H(z) = \frac{0.5(1+0.6z^{-1})(1-0.6z^{-1})}{(1+0.9z^{-1})(1-0.8z^{-1})} * \qquad (19.6)$$

The model is shown in Figure 19.15, and the input and output waveforms are shown in Figure 19.16.

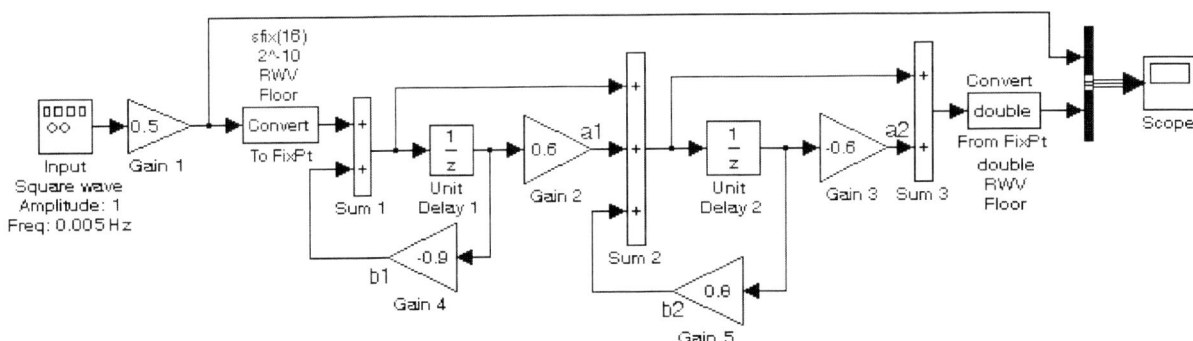

Figure 19.15. Model for Example 19.2

---

* The combination of the of factors in parentheses is immaterial. For instance, we can group the factors as
$\frac{(1+0.6z^{-1})}{(1+0.9z^{-1})}$ and $\frac{(1-0.6z^{-1})}{(1-0.8z^{-1})}$ or as $\frac{(1+0.6z^{-1})}{(1-0.8z^{-1})}$ and $\frac{(1-0.6z^{-1})}{(1+0.9z^{-1})}$

Digital Filter Realization Forms

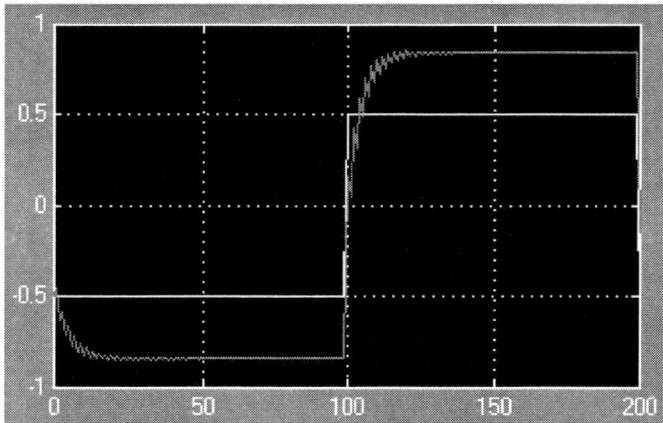

Figure 19.16. Input and output waveforms for the model of Figure 19.15

A demo model using fixed-point Simulink blocks can be displayed by typing

fxpdemo_series_cascade_form

in MATLAB's Command Window. This demo is an implementation of the third-order transfer function

$$H(z) = \frac{(1 + 0.5z^{-1})(1 + 1.7z^{-1} + z^{-2})}{(1 + 0.1z^{-1})(1 - 0.6z^{-1} + 0.9z^{-2})}$$

19.3.4 The Parallel Form Realization of a Digital Filter

The general form of the transfer function of a Parallel Form Realization is

$$H(z) = K + H_1(z) + H_2(z) + \ldots + H_R(z) \tag{19.7}$$

Relation (19.7) is implemented as the parallel blocks shown in Figure 19.17.

Chapter 19 Engineering Applications

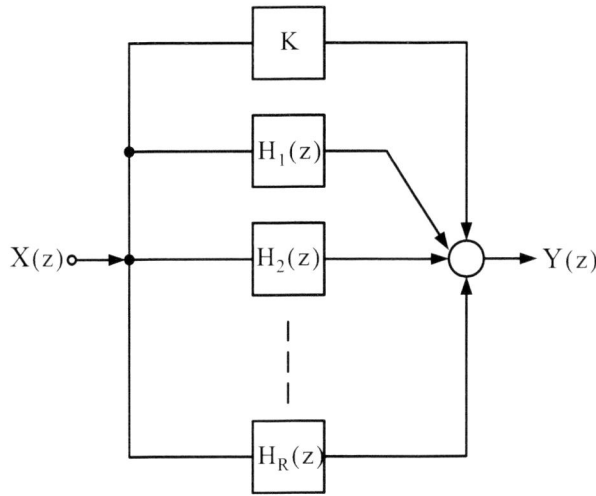

Figure 19.17. Parallel Form Realization

As with the Series Form Realization, the ordering of the individual filters in Figure 19.17 is immaterial. But because of the presence of the constant K, we can simplify the transfer function expression by performing partial fraction expansion after we express the transfer function in the form $H(z)/z$.

Figure 19.18 shows the Parallel Form Realization of a second-order digital filter. The transfer function for the Parallel Form second-order digital filter of Figure 19.18 is

$$H(z) = \frac{a_1 + a_2 z^{-2}}{1 + b_1 z^{-1} + b_2 z^{-2}} \tag{19.8}$$

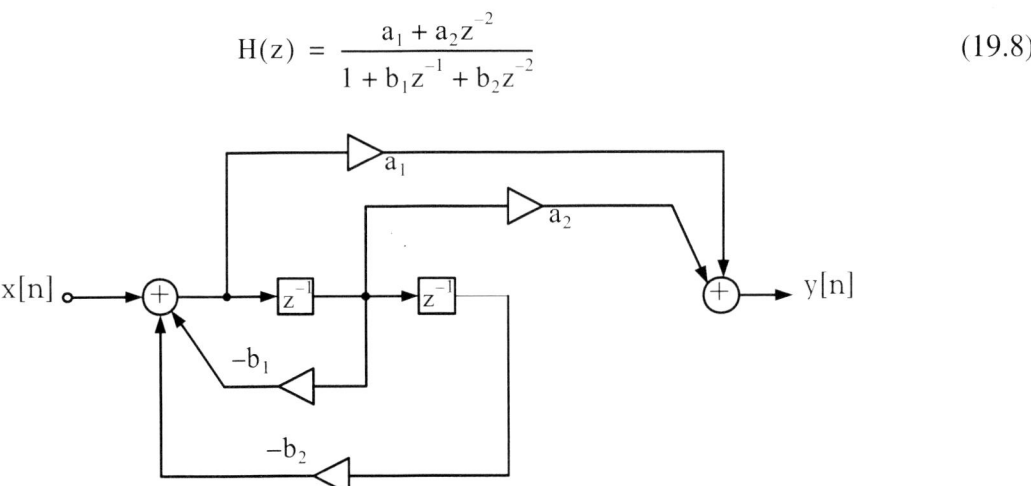

Figure 19.18. Parallel Form Realization of a second-order digital filter

Digital Filter Realization Forms

Example 19.3

The transfer function of the Parallel Form Realization of a certain second–order digital filter is

$$H(z) = \frac{0.5(1-0.36z^{-2})}{1+0.1z^{-1}-0.72z^{-2}}$$

To implement this filter, we first express the transfer function as

$$\frac{H(z)}{z} = \frac{0.5(z+0.6)(z-0.6)}{z(z+0.9)(z-0.8)}$$

Next, we perform partial fraction expansion.

$$\frac{0.5(z+0.6)(z-0.6)}{z(z+0.9)(z-0.8)} = \frac{r_1}{z} + \frac{r_2}{(z+0.9)} + \frac{r_3}{(z-0.8)}$$

$$r_1 = \left.\frac{0.5(z+0.6)(z-0.6)}{(z+0.9)(z-0.8)}\right|_{z=0} = 0.25$$

$$r_2 = \left.\frac{0.5(z+0.6)(z-0.6)}{z(z-0.8)}\right|_{z=-0.9} = 0.147$$

$$r_3 = \left.\frac{0.5(z+0.6)(z-0.6)}{z(z+0.9)}\right|_{z=0.8} = 0.103$$

Therefore,

$$\frac{H(z)}{z} = \frac{0.25}{z} + \frac{0.147}{z+0.9} + \frac{0.103}{z-0.8}$$

$$H(z) = 0.25 + \frac{0.147z}{z+0.9} + \frac{0.103z}{z-0.8}$$

$$H(z) = 0.25 + \frac{0.147}{1+0.9z^{-1}} + \frac{0.103}{z-0.8z^{-1}} \tag{19.9}$$

The model is shown in Figure 19.19, and the input and output waveforms are shown in Figure 19.20.

Chapter 19 Engineering Applications

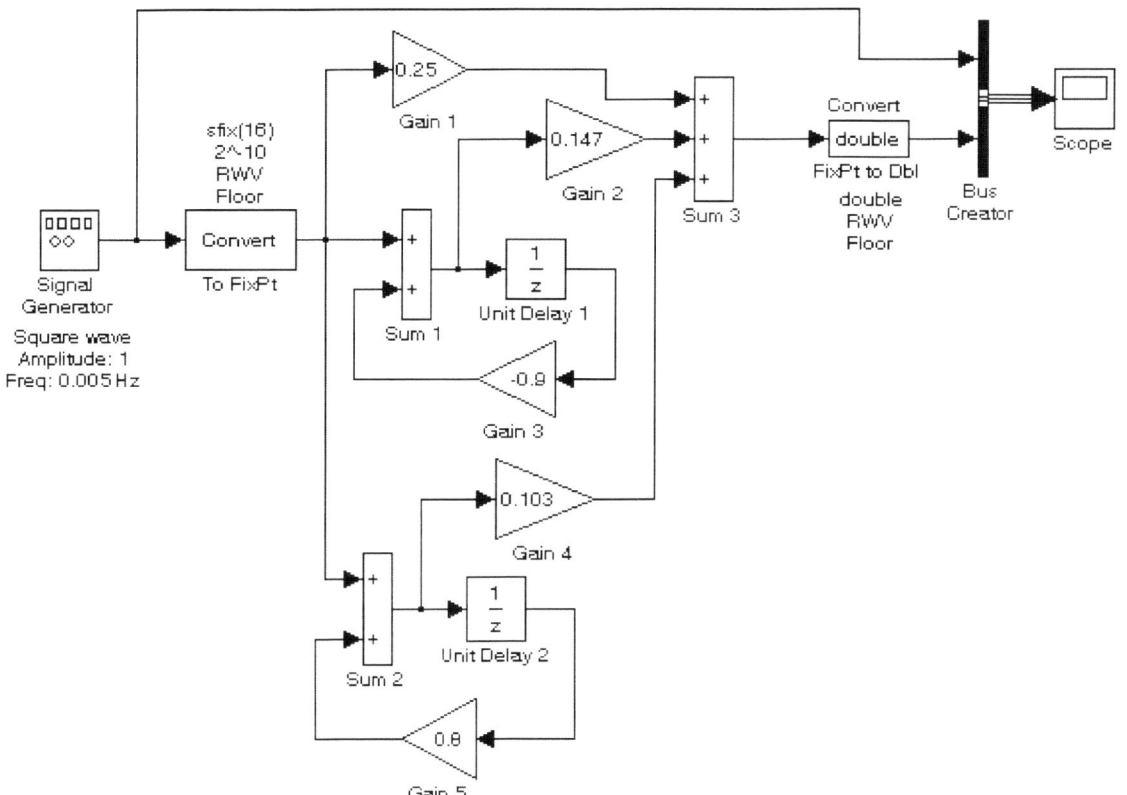

Figure 19.19. Model for Example 19.3

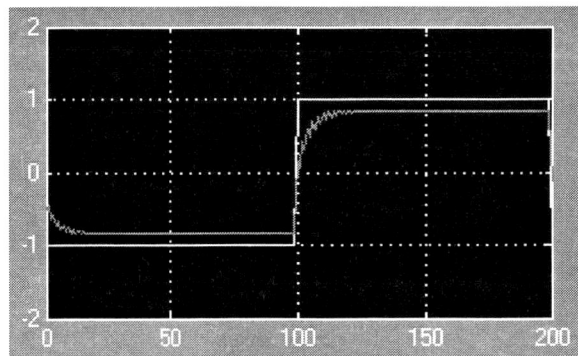

Figure 19.20. Input and output waveforms for the model of Figure 19.19

A demo model using fixed-point Simulink blocks can be displayed by typing

fxpdemo_parallel_form

in MATLAB's Command Window. This demo is an implementation of the third-order transfer function

Models for Binary Counters

$$H(z) = 5.5556 - \frac{3.4639}{(1 + 0.1z^{-1})} + \frac{-1.0916 + 3.0086z^{-1}}{1 - 0.6z^{-1} + 0.9z^{-2}}$$

19.4 Models for Binary Counters

In this section we will draw two models for binary counters.[*] Subsection 19.4.1 presents a 3-bit up / down counter, and Subsection 19.4.2 presents a 4-bit Johnson counter.

19.4.1 Model for a 3-bit Up / Down Counter

A model for the operation of a 3-bit counter with three D Flip-Flop blocks, six NAND gate blocks, a NOT gate (Inverter) block, and a Clock block is shown in Figure 19.21. The D Flip-Flop and Clock blocks are in the **Simulink Extras Toolbox**, Flip-Flops library, and the NAND and NOT gates are in the **Logic and Bit Operations Library**. The D Flip-Flop CLK (clock) inputs are Negative Edge Triggered. The Clock waveform and the D Flip-Flops output waveforms when the Manual Switch block is the Count up position, are shown in Figure 19.22.

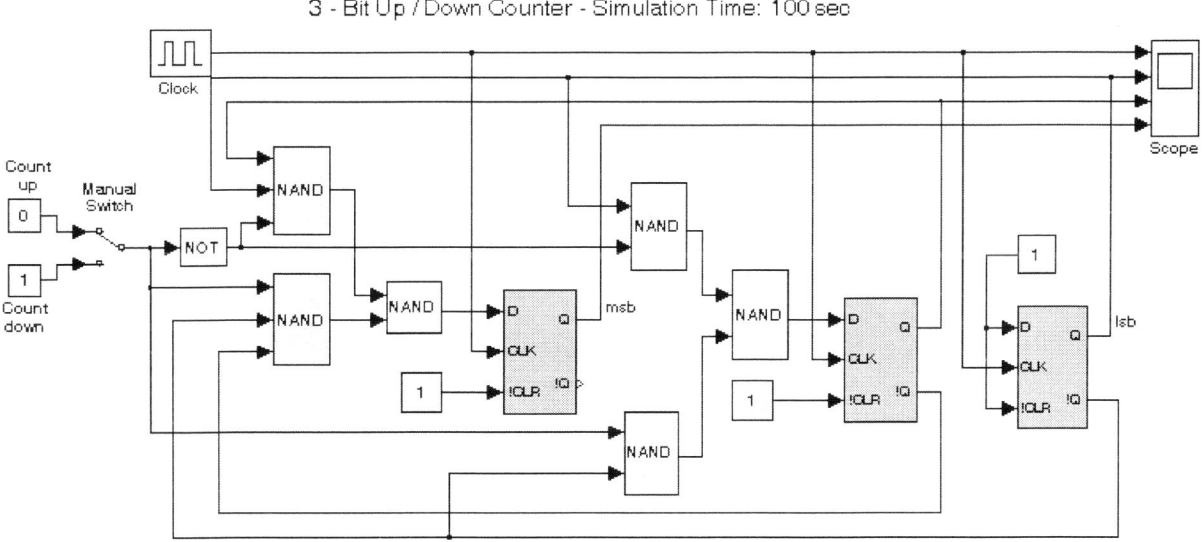

Figure 19.21. Model for a 3-bit Up / Down binary counter

---

[*] *For a detailed discussion on the analysis and design of binary counters, please refer to Digital Circuit Analysis and Design with an Introduction to CPLDs and FPGAs, ISBN 0-9744239-6-3.*

Chapter 19 Engineering Applications

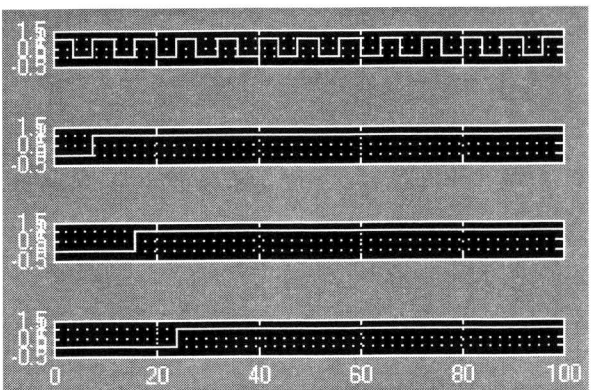

Figure 19.22. Waveforms for the model of Figure 19.21

19.4.2 Model for a 4-bit Ring Counter

The model of Figure 19.23 implements a 4–bit binary counter known as **Johnson counter**. The D Flip–Flop and Clock blocks are in the **Simulink Extras Toolbox**, Flip–Flops library. The waveforms for this model are shown in Figure 19.24.

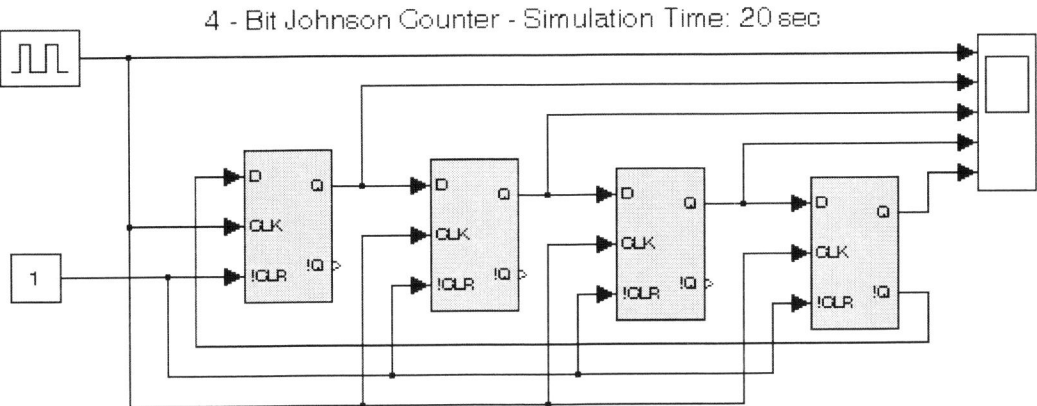

Figure 19.23. Model for a 4–bit Johnson counter

Models for Mechanical Systems

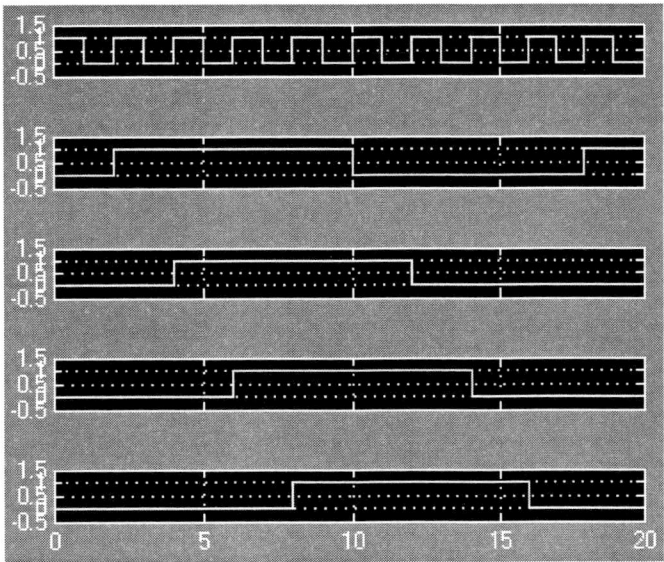

Figure 19.24. Waveforms for the model of Figure 19.23

19.5 Models for Mechanical Systems

In this section we will draw three models for mechanical systems. Subsection 19.5.1 presents a Block–Spring–Dashpot system, Subsection 19.5.2 presents a system with two mass blocks and two springs, and Subsection 19.5.3 is a simple mechanical accelerometer system

19.5.1 Model for a Mass–Spring–Dashpot

Figure 19.25 shows a system consisting of a block, a dashpot, and a spring. It is shown in feedback and control systems textbooks that this system is described by the second-order differential equation

$$m\frac{d^2}{dt^2}x(t) + p\frac{d}{dt}x(t) + kx(t) = F(t) \tag{19.10}$$

where *m* represents the mass of the block, *p* is a positive constant of proportionality of the force that the dashpot exerts on the block, and *k* is also a positive constant of proportionality of the force that the spring exerts on the block, known as **Hooke's law**.

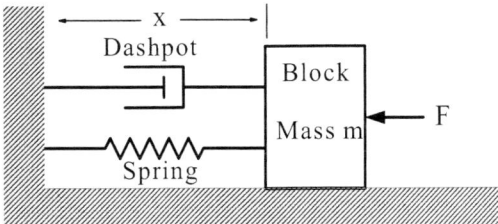

Figure 19.25. Mechanical system with a block, spring and dashpot

Chapter 19 Engineering Applications

The mass of the dashpot and the mass of the spring are small and are neglected. Friction is also neglected. For the system of Figure 19.25, the input is the applied force F and the output is the change in distance x.

Let us express the differential equation of (19.10) with numerical coefficients as

$$\frac{d^2}{dt^2}x(t) + 2\frac{d}{dt}x(t) + 3x(t) = (20\sin t)u_0(t) \tag{19.11}$$

where $u_0(t)$ is the unit step function, and the initial conditions are $x(0) = 4$, and $dx/dt = 0$. For convenience, we denote these are denoted as $x10$ and $x20$ respectively.

For the solution of (19.11) we will use the State–Space block found in the Continuous Library, and thus our model is as shown in Figure 19.26.

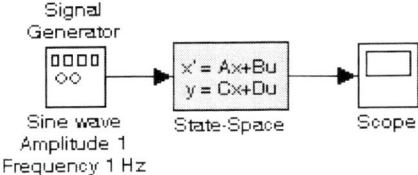

Figure 19.26. Model for Figure 19.25

The state equations are defined as

$$x_1(t) = x(t) \tag{19.12}$$

and

$$x_2(t) = \frac{d}{dt}x_1(t) \tag{19.13}$$

Then,

$$\frac{d}{dt}x_2(t) = \frac{d^2}{dt^2}x_1(t) = \frac{d^2}{dt^2}x(t) \tag{19.14}$$

From (19.11), (19.13), and (19.14) we obtain the system of state equations

$$\begin{aligned}\frac{d}{dt}x_1(t) &= x_2(t) \\ \frac{d}{dt}x_2(t) &= -3x_1(t) - 2x_2(t) + (20\sin t)u_0(t)\end{aligned} \tag{19.15}$$

and in matrix form,

$$\begin{bmatrix}\frac{d}{dt}x_1(t) \\ \frac{d}{dt}x_2(t)\end{bmatrix} = \begin{bmatrix}0 & 1 \\ -3 & -2\end{bmatrix}\begin{bmatrix}x_1(t) \\ x_2(t)\end{bmatrix} + \begin{bmatrix}0 \\ 20\sin t\end{bmatrix}u_0(t) \tag{19.16}$$

Models for Mechanical Systems

The output state equation is

$$y = Cx + Du$$

or

$$y(t) = \begin{bmatrix} 1 & 0 \end{bmatrix} \begin{bmatrix} x_1(t) \\ x_2(t) \end{bmatrix}$$

Therefore, for the model of Figure 19.26, the coefficients A, B, C, and D are

$$A = \begin{bmatrix} 0 & 1 \\ -3 & -2 \end{bmatrix} \quad B = \begin{bmatrix} 0 \\ 5 \end{bmatrix} \quad C = \begin{bmatrix} 1 & 0 \end{bmatrix} \quad D = 0 \qquad (19.17)$$

The initial conditions $x10$ and $x20$ are denoted by the matrix

$$\begin{bmatrix} x10 \\ x20 \end{bmatrix} = \begin{bmatrix} 4 \\ 0 \end{bmatrix} \qquad (19.18)$$

The values in (19.17) and (19.18) are entered in the Block parameters dialog box for the State-Space block, and after the simulation command is issued, the Scope block displays the waveform of Figure 19.27.

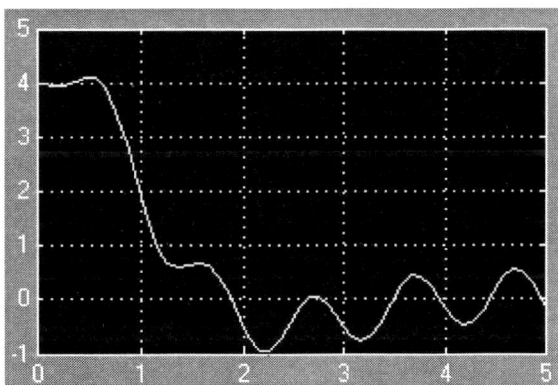

Figure 19.27. Waveform for the model of Figure 19.26

19.5.2 Model for a Cascaded Mass-Spring System

Figure 19.28 shows a a cascaded mass-spring system where F is the applied force, M is the mass, k is the spring constant, f is the friction, and X is the displacement. It is shown in feedback and control systems textbooks that the transfer function $G(s) = X_1/F$ is

$$G(s) = \frac{k_1}{(M_1 s^2 + f_1 s + k_1)(M_2 s^2 + f_2 s + k_1 + k_2) - k_1^2} \qquad (19.19)$$

Chapter 19 Engineering Applications

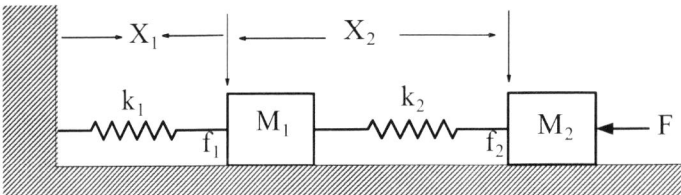

Figure 19.28. Cascaded mass–spring system

For simplicity, let us assume that the constants and conditions are such that after substitution into (19.19), this relation reduces to

$$G(s) = \frac{12}{s^4 + 10s^3 + 36s^2 + 56s + 32} \qquad (19.20)$$

and the force applied at $50\sin t$. The model under those conditions is shown in Figure 19.29, and the input and output waveforms are shown in Figure 19.30.

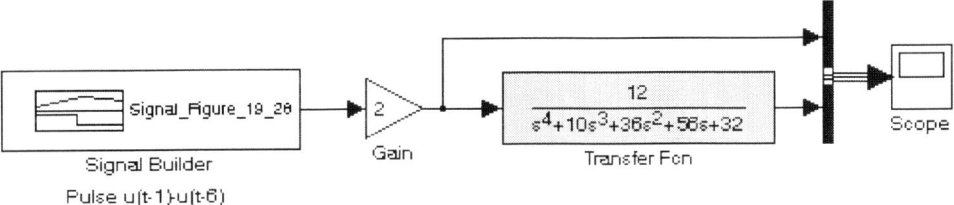

Figure 19.29. Model for the system of Figure 19.28

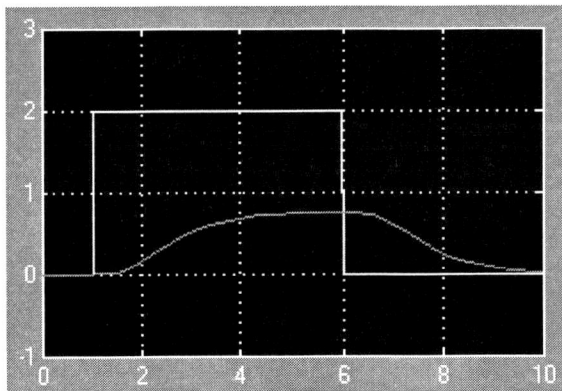

Figure 19.30. Input and output waveforms for the model of Figure 19.29

Models for Mechanical Systems

19.5.3 Model for a Mechanical Accelerometer

A simple mechanical accelerometer system consisting of a block, a dashpot, and a spring is connected as shown in Figure 19.31.

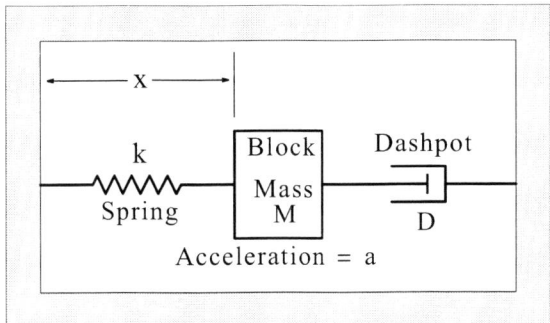

Figure 19.31. A simple mechanical accelerometer

It is shown in feedback and control systems textbooks that the transfer function $G(s) = x/a$ is

$$G(s) = \frac{1}{s^2 + (D/M)s + k/M} \qquad (19.21)$$

For simplicity, let us assume that the constants and conditions are such that after substitution into (19.21), this relation reduces to

$$G(s) = \frac{1}{s^2 + 0.1s + 0.2} \qquad (19.22)$$

and the force applied is $0.8u_0(t)$ where $u_0(t)$ is the unit step function. The model under those conditions is shown in Figure 19.32, and the input and output waveforms are shown in Figure 19.33.

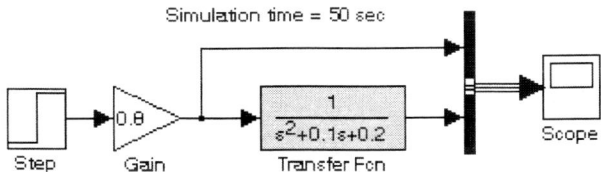

Figure 19.32. Model for the system of Figure 19.31

Chapter 19 Engineering Applications

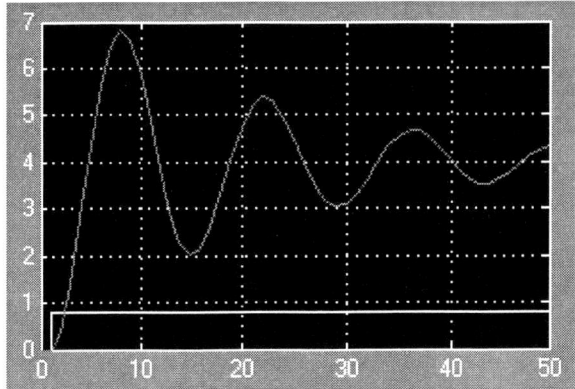

Figure 19.33. Input and output waveforms for the model of Figure 19.32

19.6 Feedback Control Systems

In our previous discussions in this chapter, we have used system components that are interconnected in series. These are referred to as **open–loop control systems**. An example of an open–loop system is a microwave oven which is controlled by a timer. However, most control systems are **closed–loop control systems** where the control action ia affected by the output. An example of a closed–loop system is the autopilot subsystem in an airplane which continuously measures the actual airplane direction and automatically adjusts other subsystems of the airplane to change the airplane heading to the desired direction. Feedback is the characteristic of a closed–loop control system which distinguishes it from open–loop systems. It is beyond the scope of this text to describe feedback control systems in detail. We will only describe some basics to aid the reader in understanding some of the advanced designs of the systems provided by the Simulink demos.

Figure 19.34 shows a simple feedback control system with two elements represented as blocks, the first of which is generally known as the **control element** or **controller**, and the second is known as the **plant**. The feedback (the line connecting the output to the summing point) is the same as the output and for this reason the entire system is referred to as **unity feedback system**. The path E represents the error, that is, the difference $E = X - Y$.

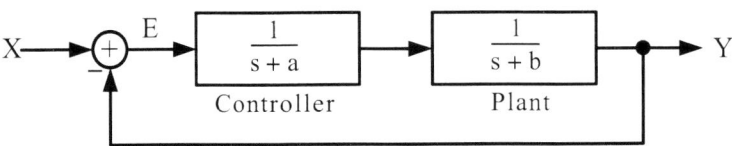

Figure 19.34. A unity feedback system

In Figure 19.34, the Controller and Plant blocks are in series and according to Feedback and Control Systems theory, can be replace by a single block whose transfer function is their product as shown in Figure 19.35.

Feedback Control Systems

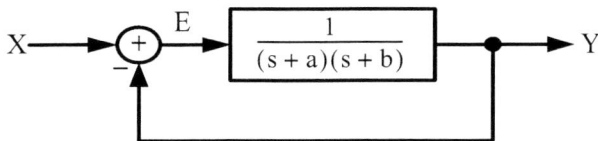

Figure 19.35. Simplified representation for the system of Figure 19.34

To find the overall transfer function $G(s) = Y/X$, observe that

$$Y = \frac{1}{(s+a)(s+b)}E = \frac{1}{(s+a)(s+b)}[X-Y]$$

or

$$Y + \frac{1}{(s+a)(s+b)}Y = \frac{1}{(s+a)(s+b)}X$$

$$Y\frac{(s+a)(s+b)}{(s+a)(s+b)} + \frac{1}{(s+a)(s+b)}Y = \frac{1}{(s+a)(s+b)}X$$

Dividing both sides by $(s+a)(s+b)$ we obtain

$$(s+a)(s+b)Y + Y = X$$

$$[(s+a)(s+b)+1]Y = X$$

and thus

$$G(s) = \frac{Y}{X} = \frac{1}{(s+a)(s+b)+1}$$

Therefore, the block diagram of Figure 19.35 can be replaced with only one block in an open–loop form as shown in Figure 19.36.

$$X \longrightarrow \boxed{\frac{1}{(s+a)(s+b)+1}} \longrightarrow Y$$

Figure 19.36. The system of Figure 19.35 in an open–loop form

A feedback control system in the form of the feedback path shown as in Figure 19.37 is referred to as a feedback control system in **canonical form**. For the system of Figure 19.37, the ratio Y/X is

$$\frac{Y}{X} = \frac{G}{1 \pm GH} \qquad (19.23)$$

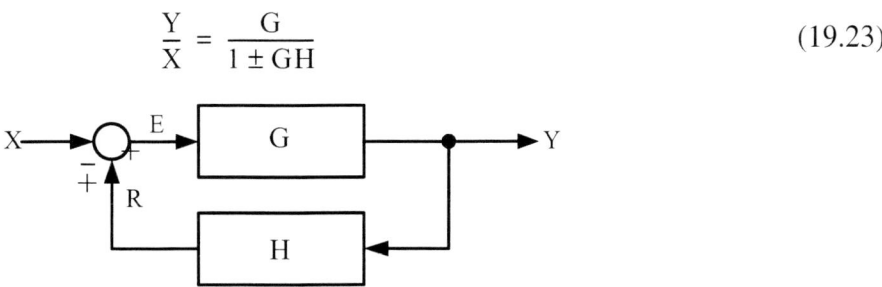

Figure 19.37. Canonical form of a feedback control system

Chapter 19 Engineering Applications

More complicated block diagrams can be reduced by methods described in Feedback and Control Systems textbooks. For instance, the block diagram of Figure 19.38 below,

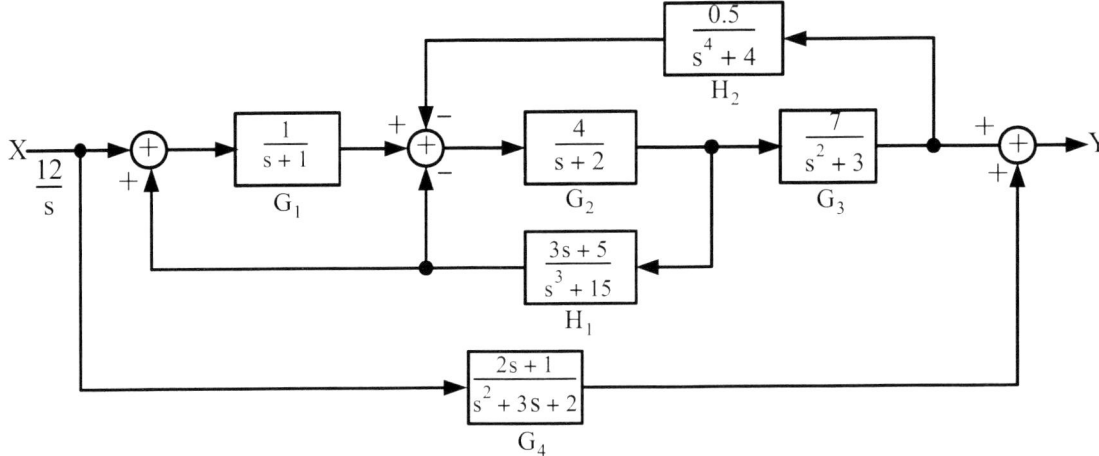

Figure 19.38. Feedback control system to be simplified to an open–loop system

can be replaced with the open-loop system of Figure 19.39.

$$X \longrightarrow \boxed{\frac{G_1G_2G_3 + G_4 - G_1G_2G_4H_1 + G_2G_4H_1 + G_2G_3G_4H_2}{1 - G_1G_2H_1 + G_2H_1 + G_2G_3H_2}} \longrightarrow Y$$

Figure 19.39. Open-loop equivalent control system for the closed–loop system of Figure 19.38

We can prove that the systems of Figures 19.38 and 19.39 are equivalent with Simulink blocks. The system of Figure 19.38 is represented by the model in Figure 19.40 and there is no need to represent it as an open–loop equivalent. Instead, we can represent it as the subsystem shown in Figure 19.41.

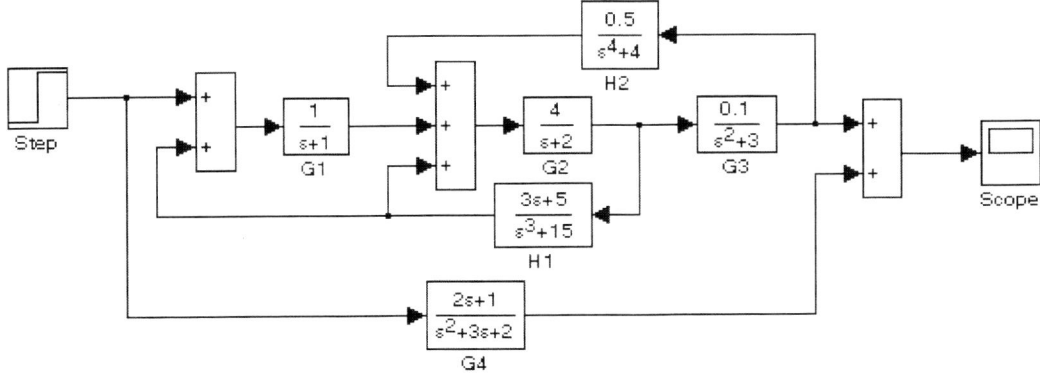

Figure 19.40. Model for the feedback control system of Figure 19.38

Models for Electrical Systems

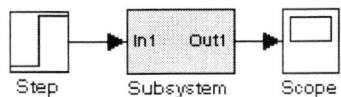

Figure 19.41. The model of Figure 19.40 replaced by a Subsystem block

19.7 Models for Electrical Systems

In this section we will draw two models for mechanical systems. Subsection 19.7.1 presents an electric circuit whose output voltage is determined by application of Thevenin's theorem, and Subsection 19.7.2 presents an electric circuit to be analyzed by application of the Superposition Principle.

19.7.1 Model for an Electric Circuit in Phasor[*] Form

By application of Thevenin's theorem, the electric circuit of Figure 19.42 can be simplified[†] to that shown in Figure 19.43.

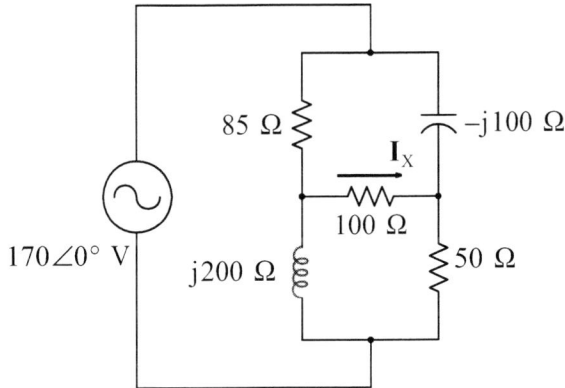

Figure 19.42. Electric circuit to be replaced by its Thevenin equivalent

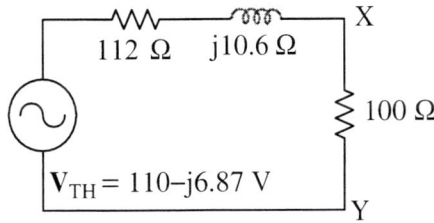

Figure 19.43. The circuit of Figure 19.42 replaced by its Thevenin equivalent

---

[*] A phasor is a rotating vector. Phasors are used extensively in the analysis of AC electric circuits. For a thorough discussion on phasors, please refer to *Circuit Analysis I with MATLAB Applications*, ISBN 0-9709511-2-4.
[†] For a step-by-step procedure, please see same reference.

Introduction to Simulink with Engineering Applications
Copyright © Orchard Publications

Chapter 19 Engineering Applications

Next, we let $V_{IN} = V_{TH}$, $V_{OUT} = V_{XY}$, $Z_1 = 112 + j10$, and $Z_2 = 100$. Application of the voltage division expression yields

$$V_{OUT} = \frac{Z_2}{Z_1 + Z_2} V_{IN} \tag{19.24}$$

Now, we use the model of Figure 19.44 to convert all quantities from the rectangular to the polar form, perform the addition and multiplication operations, display the output voltage in both polar and rectangular forms, and show the output voltage on a Scope block in Figure 19.45. The Simulink blocks used for the conversions are in the Math Operations library.

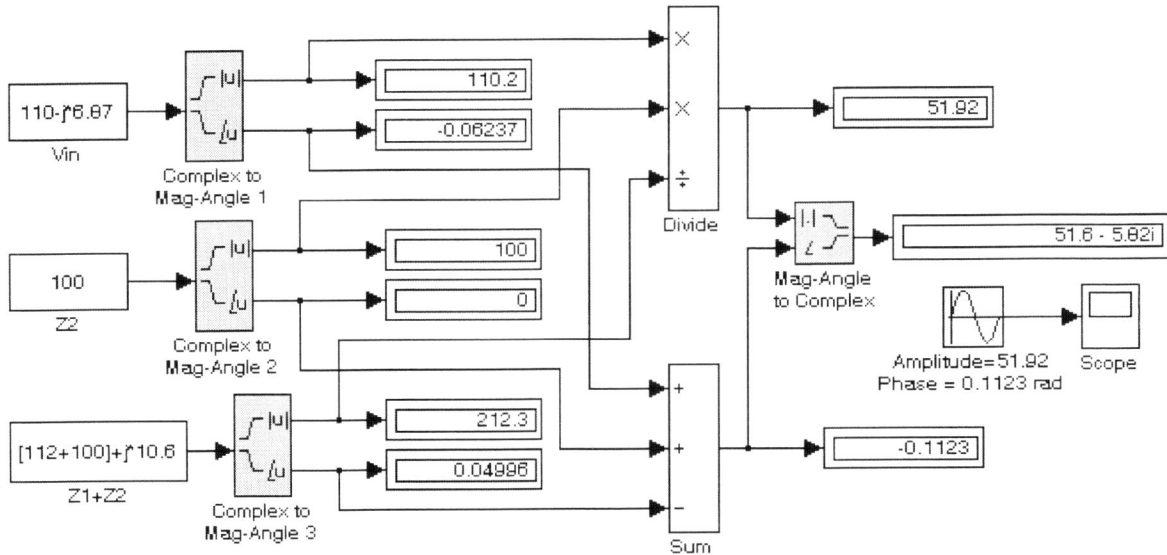

Figure 19.44. Model for the computation and display of the output voltage for the circuit of Figure 19.43

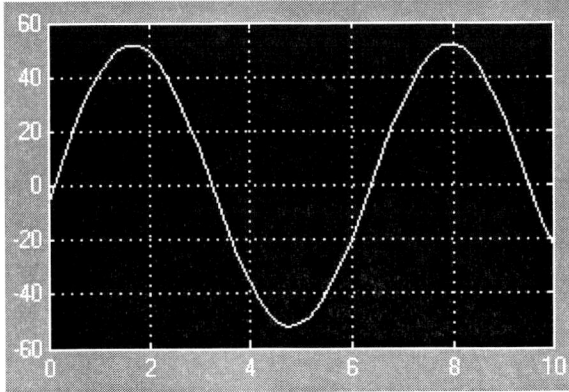

Figure 19.45. Waveform for the output voltage of model of Figure 19.44

19.7.2 Model for the Application of the Superposition Principle

We will create a model to illustrate the superposition principle by computing the phasor voltage across capacitor C_2 in the circuit of Figure 19.46.

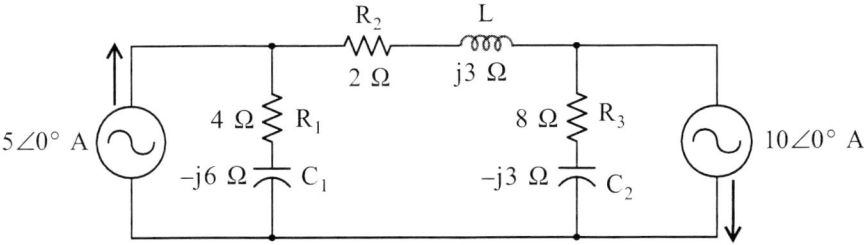

Figure 19.46. Electric circuit to illustrate the superposition principle

Let the phasor voltage across C_2 due to the $5\angle 0°$ A current source acting alone be denoted as $\mathbf{V'}_{C2}$, and that due to the $10\angle 0°$ A current source as $\mathbf{V''}_{C2}$. Then, by the superposition principle,

$$\mathbf{V}_{C2} = \mathbf{V'}_{C2} + \mathbf{V''}_{C2}$$

With the $5\angle 0°$ A current source acting alone, the circuit reduces to that shown in Figure 19.47.

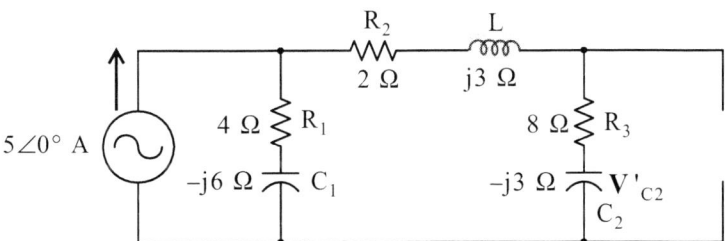

Figure 19.47. Circuit of Figure 7.45 with the $5\angle 0°$ A current source acting alone

By application of the current division expression, the current $\mathbf{I'}_{C2}$ through C_2 is

$$\mathbf{I'}_{C2} = \frac{4-j6}{4-j6+2+j3+8-j3}5\angle 0° = \frac{7.211\angle -56.3°}{15.232\angle -23.2°}5\angle 0° = 2.367\angle -33.1°$$

The voltage across C_2 with the $5\angle 0°$ current source acting alone is

$$\begin{aligned}\mathbf{V'}_{C2} &= (-j3)(2.367\angle -33.1°) = (3\angle -90°)(2.367\angle -33.1°) \\ &= 7.102\angle -123.1° = -3.878 - j5.949\end{aligned} \tag{19.25}$$

Next, with the $10\angle 0°$ A current source acting alone, the circuit reduces to that shown in Figure 19.48.

Chapter 19 Engineering Applications

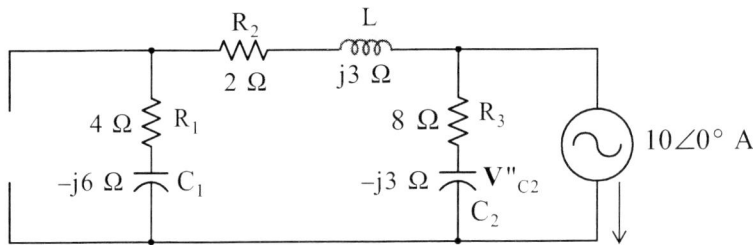

Figure 19.48. Circuit with the $10\angle 0°$ A current source acting alone

and by application of the current division expression, the current $\mathbf{I}''_{C2}$ through C_2 is

$$\mathbf{I}''_{C2} = \frac{4-j6+2+j3}{4-j6+2+j3+8-j3}(-10\angle 0°)$$

$$= \frac{6.708\angle -26.6°}{15.232\angle -23.2°} 10\angle 180° = 4.404\angle 176.6°$$

The voltage across C_2 with the $10\angle 0°$ current source acting alone is

$$\mathbf{V}''_{C2} = (-j3)(4.404\angle 176.6°) = (3\angle -90°)(4.404\angle 176.6°)$$
$$= (13.213\angle 86.6 = 0.784 + j13.189)$$
(19.26)

Addition of (19.25) with (19.26) yields

$$\mathbf{V}_{C2} = \mathbf{V}'_{C2} + \mathbf{V}''_{C2} = -3.878 - j5.949 + 0.784 + j13.189$$

or

$$\mathbf{V}_{C2} = -3.094 + j7.240 = 7.873\angle 113.1°$$

The models for the computation of $\mathbf{V}'_{C2}$ and $\mathbf{V}''_{C2}$ are shown in Figures 19.49 and 19.50 respectively.

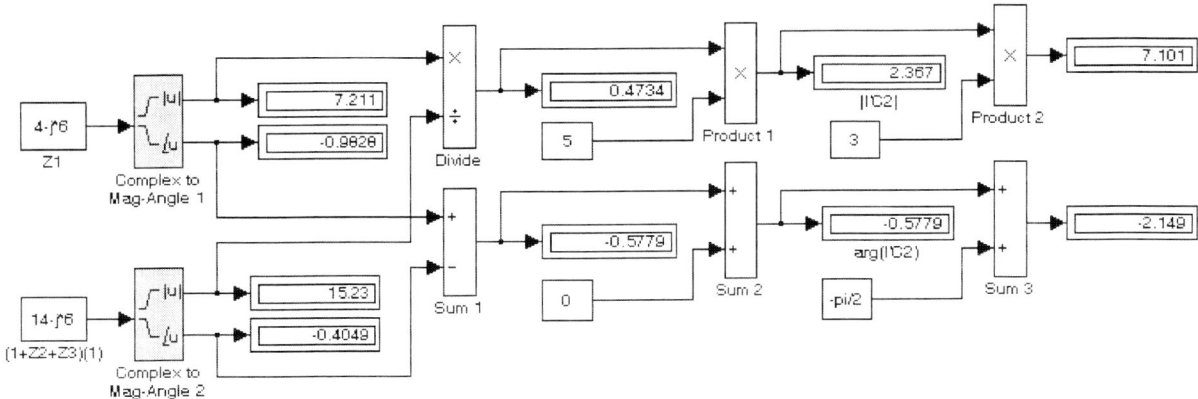

Figure 19.49. Model for the computation of $\mathbf{V}'_{C2}$

Transformations

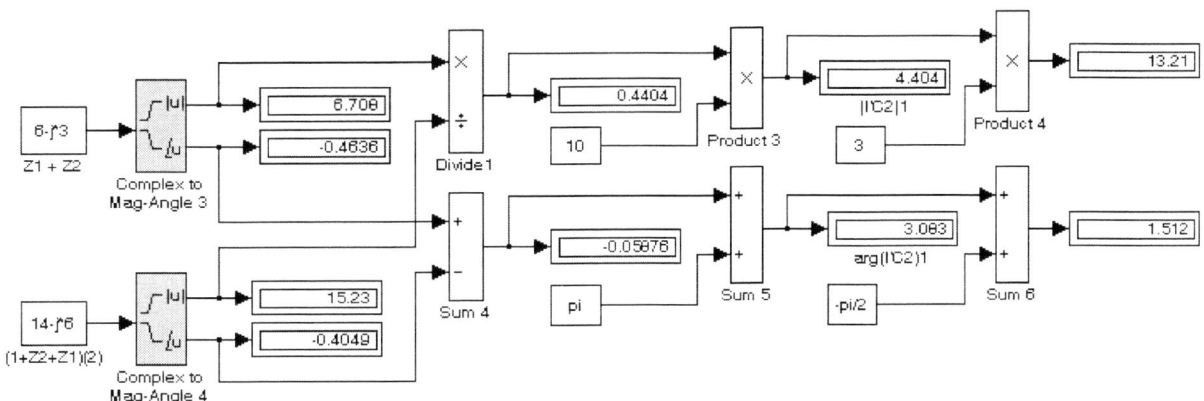

Figure 19.50. Model for the computation of V''_{C2}

The final step is to add V'_{C2} with V''_{C2}. This addition is performed by the model of Figure 19.51 where the models of Figures 19.49 and 19.50 have been converted to Subsystems 1 and 2 respectively.

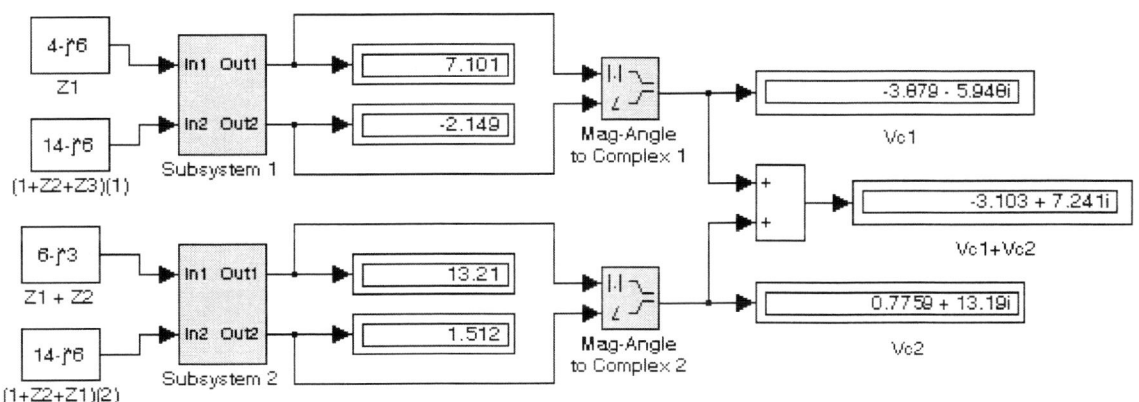

Figure 19.51. Model for the addition of V'_{C2} with V''_{C2}

The model of Figure 19.51 can now be used with the circuit of Figure 19.46 for any values of the impedances Z.

19.8 Transformations

The conversions from complex to magnitude–angle and magnitude–angle to complex used in the previous section, can also be performed with the Cartesian to Polar and Polar to Cartesian blocks. Examples are presented in the model of Figure 19.52 where transformations from Cartesian to Spherical and Spherical to Cartesian are shown. The equations used in these transformations are shown in the Block Parameters dialog box for each block.

Chapter 19 Engineering Applications

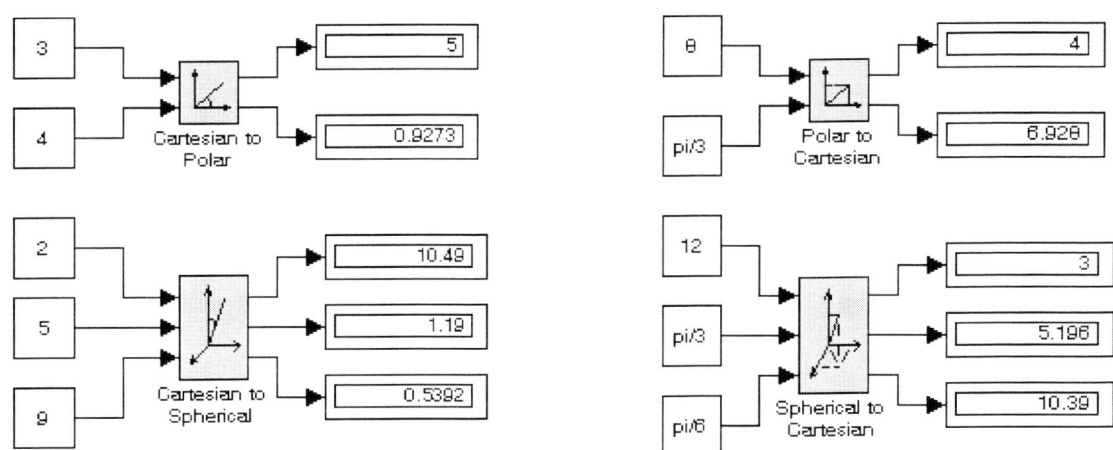

Figure 19.52. Transformation examples

Other transformation blocks include Fahrenheit to Celsius, Celsius to Fahrenheit, Degrees to Radians, and Radians to Degrees.

19.9 Another S–Function Example

An S–Function example is presented in Subsection 11.18, Chapter 11, Page 11–44. In this section, we will present another example.

For semiconductor diodes, the empirical equations describing the temperature coefficient dV_F/dT in mV/°C as a function of forward current I_F in mA are

$$\frac{dV_{F1}}{dT} = 0.6\log 10(I_{ff}) - 1.92 \qquad \text{for gold doped diodes}$$

$$\frac{dV_{F1}}{dT} = 0.33\log 10(I_{ff} - I_{fv}) - 1.66 \qquad \text{for non–gold doped diodes}$$

where, for this example,

I_{ff} = final value of forward current

I_{fv} = variable value of forward current

We begin with the user–defined m–file below which we type in the Editor Window and we save it as **diode.m**

```
function dx=diode(t,x,Ifv)
%
% Model for gold-doped and non-gold-doped diodes
%
Vf1 = x(1);   % Gold-doped diode forward voltage, volts
Vf2 = x(2);   % Non-gold-doped diode forward voltage, volts
```

Another S–Function Example

```
Iff = 100;    % Iff = final value in  of forward current in mA
dVf1 = 0.6*log10(Iff)-1.92;
dVf2 = 0.33*log10(Iff-Ifv)-1.66; % Ifv = variable value of forward current in mA
dx = [dVf1;dVf2];
```

To test this function for correctness, on MATLAB's Command Window we type and execute the command

[t,x,Ifw]=ode45(@diode, [0 10], [1;10],[ ], 50)

where the vector [0 10] specifies the start and the end of the simulation time, the vector [1;10] specifies an initial value column vector, the null vector [ ] can be used for other options, and the input value is set to **50**.

Next, using the Editor Window we write the m–file below and we save it as **diode_sfcn.m**

```
function [sys,x0,str,ts]=...
         diode_sfcn(t,x,u,flag,Vf1init,Vf2init)

switch flag

    case 0                          % Initialize

        str = [];
        ts = [0 0];

        s = simsizes;

            s.NumContStates = 2;
            s.NumDiscStates = 0;
            s.NumOutputs = 2;
            s.NumInputs = 1;
            s.DirFeedthrough = 0;
            s.NumSampleTimes = 1;

        sys =simsizes(s);

        x0 = [Vf1init,Vf2init];

    case 1                          % Derivatives

        Ifw = u

        sys = diode(t,x,Ifw);

    case 3                          % Output

        sys = x;

    case {2 4 9}                    % 2:discrete
                                    % 3:calcTimeHit
                                    % 9:termination
        sys = [];

    otherwise
```

```
            error(['unhandled flag =',num2str(flag)]);
```
end

The syntax for the **diode_sfcn.m** file above is the same as that of Example 11.14, Chapter 11, Page 11–44.

Next, we open a new model window, from the User–Defined Functions Library we drag an S–Function block into it, we double–click this block, in the Function Block Parameters dialog box we name it **diode_sfcn**, and we add and interconnect the other blocks shown in Figure 19.53.

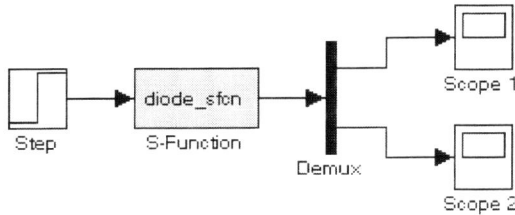

Figure 19.53. Another example illustrating the construction of an S–Function block

The waveforms displayed by the Scope 1 and Scope 2 blocks are shown in Figures 19.54 and 19.55 respectively.

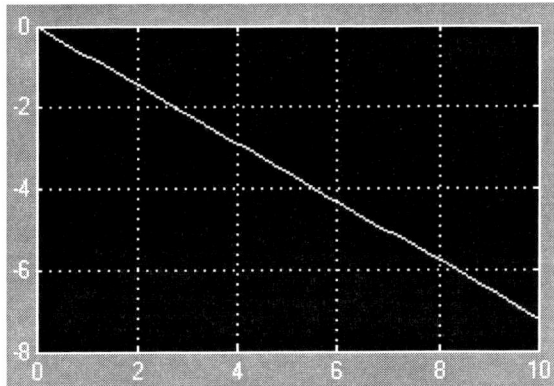

Figure 19.54. Waveform displayed by the Scope 1 block in the model of Figure 19.53

Concluding Remarks

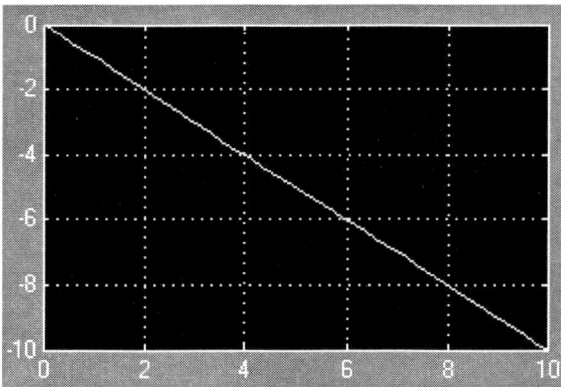

Figure 19.55. Waveform displayed by the Scope 2 block in the model of Figure 19.53

19.10 Concluding Remarks

This text, as its title indicates, is an introduction to Simulink. In Chapters 2 through 18 we have described all blocks of all Simulink Libraries and provided examples to illustrate their application. Chapter 1 and this chapter provided additional examples. This text is not a substitute for the Simulink User's Manual which provides much more information on MATLAB and Simulink, and should be treated as a supplement. Moreover, the **demos** provided with Simulink are real–world examples and should be studied in thoroughly after reading this text. Undoubtedly, new MATLAB and Simulink releases will include new functions and new blocks.

Chapter 19 Engineering Applications

19.11 Summary

- An analog–to–digital conversion (ADC) application with an Idealized ADC Quantizer block was presented in Section 19.1.

- Examples of using Zero–Order Hold and First–Order Hold blocks as reconstructors for digital-to-analog conversion were presented in Section 19.2.

- The four forms of digital filter realization forms were presented in Section 19.3.

- Models for binary counters were presented in Section 19.4.

- Three models for mechanical systems were presented in Section 19.5.

- A brief review of feedback control systems was provided in Section 19.6.

- Two models for AC electric circuit analysis were presented in Section 19.7.

- Four transformations blocks were introduced in Section 19.8.

- An S–Function example was presented in Section 11.18, Chapter 11. Another example was given in Section 19.9, this chapter.

Appendix A

Introduction to MATLAB®

This appendix serves as an introduction to the basic MATLAB commands and functions, procedures for naming and saving the user generated files, comment lines, access to MATLAB's Editor / Debugger, finding the roots of a polynomial, and making plots. Several examples are provided with detailed explanations.

A.1 MATLAB® and Simulink®

MATLAB and Simulink are products of The MathWorks,™ Inc. These are two outstanding software packages for scientific and engineering computations and are used in educational institutions and in industries including automotive, aerospace, electronics, telecommunications, and environmental applications. MATLAB enables us to solve many advanced numerical problems rapidly and efficiently.

A.2 Command Window

To distinguish the screen displays from the user commands, important terms, and MATLAB functions, we will use the following conventions:

Click: Click the left button of the mouse
`Courier Font`: Screen displays
Helvetica Font: User inputs at MATLAB's command window prompt >> or EDU>>[*]
Helvetica Bold: MATLAB functions
Normal Font Bold Italic: Important terms and facts, notes and file names

When we first start MATLAB, we see various help topics and other information. Initially, we are interested in the *command screen* which can be selected from the Window drop menu. When the command screen, we see the prompt >> or EDU>>. This prompt is displayed also after execution of a command; MATLAB now waits for a new command from the user. It is highly recommended that we use the *Editor/Debugger* to write our program, save it, and return to the command screen to execute the program as explained below.

To use the Editor/Debugger:

1. From the *File* menu on the toolbar, we choose *New* and click on *M–File*. This takes us to the *Editor Window* where we can type our *script* (list of statements) for a new file, or open a previ-

---

[*] EDU>> *is the MATLAB prompt in the Student Version*

Introduction to Simulink with Engineering Applications
Copyright © Orchard Publications

Appendix A Introduction to MATLAB®

ously saved file. We must save our program with a file name which starts with a letter. **Important!** MATLAB is *case sensitive*, that is, it distinguishes between upper– and lower–case letters. Thus, *t* and *T* are two different letters in MATLAB language. The files that we create are saved with the file name we use and the extension *.m*; for example, *myfile01.m*. It is a good practice to save the script in a file name that is descriptive of our script content. For instance, if the script performs some matrix operations, we ought to name and save that file as *matrices01.m* or any other similar name. We should also use a floppy disk or an external drive to backup our files.

2. Once the script is written and saved as an *m–file*, we may exit the *Editor/Debugger* window by clicking on *Exit Editor/Debugger* of the *File* menu. MATLAB then returns to the command window.

3. To execute a program, we type the file name ***without*** the *.m* extension at the >> prompt; then, we press <enter> and observe the execution and the values obtained from it. If we have saved our file in drive *a* or any other drive, we must make sure that it is added it to the desired directory in MATLAB's search path. The MATLAB User's Guide provides more information on this topic.

Henceforth, it will be understood that each input command is typed after the >> prompt and followed by the <enter> key.

The command **help matlab\iofun** will display input/output information. To get help with other MATLAB topics, we can type **help** followed by any topic from the displayed menu. For example, to get information on graphics, we type **help matlab\graphics**. The MATLAB User's Guide contains numerous help topics.

To appreciate MATLAB's capabilities, we type `demo` and we see the `MATLAB Demos` menu. We can do this periodically to become familiar with them. Whenever we want to return to the command window, we click on the `Close` button.

When we are done and want to leave MATLAB, we type **quit** or **exit**. But if we want to clear all previous values, variables, and equations without exiting, we should use the command **clear**. This command erases everything; it is like exiting MATLAB and starting it again. The command **clc** clears the screen but MATLAB still remembers all values, variables and equations that we have already used. In other words, if we want to clear all previously entered commands, leaving only the >> prompt on the upper left of the screen, we use the **clc** command.

All text after the **%** (percent) symbol is interpreted as a *comment line* by MATLAB, and thus it is ignored during the execution of a program. A comment can be typed on the same line as the function or command or as a separate line. For instance,

conv(p,q)   % performs multiplication of polynomials p and q
% The next statement performs partial fraction expansion of p(x) / q(x)

are both correct.

One of the most powerful features of MATLAB is the ability to do computations involving *complex numbers*. We can use either i, or j to denote the imaginary part of a complex number, such as 3-4i or 3-4j. For example, the statement

z=3−4j

displays

z = 3.0000-4.0000i

In the above example, a multiplication (*) sign between 4 and j was not necessary because the complex number consists of numerical constants. However, if the imaginary part is a function, or variable such as cos(x), we must use the multiplication sign, that is, we must type cos(x)*j or j*cos(x) for the imaginary part of the complex number.

A.3 Roots of Polynomials

In MATLAB, a polynomial is expressed as a *row vector* of the form $[a_n \ a_{n-1} \ \ldots \ a_2 \ a_1 \ a_0]$. These are the coefficients of the polynomial in descending order. **We must include terms whose coefficients are zero.**

We find the roots of any polynomial with the **roots(p)** function; **p** is a row vector containing the polynomial coefficients in descending order.

Example A.1

Find the roots of the polynomial

$$p_1(x) = x^4 - 10x^3 + 35x^2 - 50x + 24$$

Solution:

The roots are found with the following two statements where we have denoted the polynomial as p1, and the roots as **roots_p1**.

p1=[1 −10 35 −50 24]   % Specify and display the coefficients of p1(x)

p1 =
     1   -10   35   -50   24

roots_p1=roots(p1)   % Find the roots of p1(x)

roots_p1 =
    4.0000
    3.0000
    2.0000

```
    1.0000
```
We observe that MATLAB displays the polynomial coefficients as a row vector, and the roots as a column vector.

Example A.2

Find the roots of the polynomial

$$p_2(x) = x^5 - 7x^4 + 16x^2 + 25x + 52$$

Solution:

There is no cube term; therefore, we must enter zero as its coefficient. The roots are found with the statements below, where we have defined the polynomial as **p2**, and the roots of this polynomial as **roots_ p2**. The result indicates that this polynomial has three real roots, and two complex roots. Of course, complex roots always occur in *complex conjugate*[*] pairs.

p2=[1 -7 0 16 25 52]

```
p2 =
     1    -7     0    16    25    52
```

roots_ p2=roots(p2)

```
roots_p2 =
   6.5014
   2.7428
  -1.5711
  -0.3366 + 1.3202i
  -0.3366 - 1.3202i
```

A.4 Polynomial Construction from Known Roots

We can compute the coefficients of a polynomial, from a given set of roots, with the **poly(r)** function where **r** is a row vector containing the roots.

Example A.3

It is known that the roots of a polynomial are 1, 2, 3, and 4. Compute the coefficients of this polynomial.

---

[*] By definition, the conjugate of a complex number $A = a + jb$ is $A^* = a - jb$

Polynomial Construction from Known Roots

Solution:

We first define a row vector, say r3, with the given roots as elements of this vector; then, we find the coefficients with the **poly(r)** function as shown below.

```
r3=[1 2 3 4]        % Specify the roots of the polynomial
r3 =
     1     2     3     4
poly_r3=poly(r3)    % Find the polynomial coefficients
poly_r3 =
     1   -10    35   -50    24
```

We observe that these are the coefficients of the polynomial $p_1(x)$ of Example A.1.

Example A.4

It is known that the roots of a polynomial are -1, -2, -3, $4+j5$, and $4-j5$. Find the coefficients of this polynomial.

Solution:

We form a row vector, say r4, with the given roots, and we find the polynomial coefficients with the **poly(r)** function as shown below.

```
r4=[ -1  -2  -3  4+5j  4-5j ]
r4 =
  Columns 1 through 4
   -1.0000   -2.0000   -3.0000   -4.0000+ 5.0000i
  Column 5
   -4.0000- 5.0000i
poly_r4=poly(r4)
poly_r4 =
     1    14   100   340   499   246
```

Therefore, the polynomial is

$$p_4(x) = x^5 + 14x^4 + 100x^3 + 340x^2 + 499x + 246$$

Appendix A Introduction to MATLAB®

A.5 Evaluation of a Polynomial at Specified Values

The **polyval(p,x)** function evaluates a polynomial p(x) at some specified value of the independent variable x.

Example A.5

Evaluate the polynomial

$$p_5(x) = x^6 - 3x^5 + 5x^3 - 4x^2 + 3x + 2 \quad (A.1)$$

at $x = -3$.

Solution:

```
p5=[1 -3 0 5 -4 3 2];   % These are the coefficients of the given polynomial
                        % The semicolon (;) after the right bracket suppresses the
                        % display of the row vector that contains the coefficients of p5.
%
val_minus3=polyval(p5, -3)   % Evaluate p5 at x=-3; no semicolon is used here
                             % because we want the answer to be displayed

val_minus3 =
       1280
```

Other MATLAB functions used with polynomials are the following:

conv(a,b) – multiplies two polynomials **a** and **b**

[q,r]=deconv(c,d) –divides polynomial **c** by polynomial **d** and displays the quotient **q** and remainder **r**.

polyder(p) – produces the coefficients of the derivative of a polynomial **p**.

Example A.6

Let

$$p_1 = x^5 - 3x^4 + 5x^2 + 7x + 9$$

and

$$p_2 = 2x^6 - 8x^4 + 4x^2 + 10x + 12$$

Compute the product $p_1 \cdot p_2$ using the **conv(a,b)** function.

Evaluation of a Polynomial at Specified Values

Solution:

```
p1=[1 -3 0 5 7 9];        % The coefficients of p1
p2=[2 0 -8 0 4 10 12];    % The coefficients of p2
p1p2=conv(p1,p2)          % Multiply p1 by p2 to compute coefficients of the product p1p2

p1p2 =
   2  -6  -8  34  18  -24  -74  -88  78  166  174  108
```

Therefore,

$$p_1 \cdot p_2 = 2x^{11} - 6x^{10} - 8x^9 + 34x^8 + 18x^7 - 24x^6$$
$$-74x^5 - 88x^4 + 78x^3 + 166x^2 + 174x + 108$$

Example A.7

Let

$$p_3 = x^7 - 3x^5 + 5x^3 + 7x + 9$$

and

$$p_4 = 2x^6 - 8x^5 + 4x^2 + 10x + 12$$

Compute the quotient p_3/p_4 using the **[q,r]=deconv(c,d)** function.

Solution:

```
% It is permissible to write two or more statements in one line separated by semicolons
p3=[1 0 -3 0 5 7 9]; p4=[2 -8 0 0 4 10 12]; [q,r]=deconv(p3,p4)

q =
    0.5000
r =
    0   4   -3   0   3   2   3
```

Therefore,

$$q = 0.5 \qquad r = 4x^5 - 3x^4 + 3x^2 + 2x + 3$$

Example A.8

Let

$$p_5 = 2x^6 - 8x^4 + 4x^2 + 10x + 12$$

Compute the derivative $\frac{d}{dx}p_5$ using the **polyder(p)** function.

Appendix A Introduction to MATLAB®

Solution:

```
p5=[2  0  -8  0  4  10  12];    % The coefficients of p5
der_p5=polyder(p5)              % Compute the coefficients of the derivative of p5

der_p5 =
    12    0   -32    0    8   10
```

Therefore,

$$\frac{d}{dx}p_5 = 12x^5 - 32x^3 + 4x^2 + 8x + 10$$

A.6 Rational Polynomials

Rational Polynomials are those which can be expressed in ratio form, that is, as

$$R(x) = \frac{\text{Num}(x)}{\text{Den}(x)} = \frac{b_n x^n + b_{n-1} x^{n-1} + b_{n-2} x^{n-2} + \ldots + b_1 x + b_0}{a_m x^m + a_{m-1} x^{m-1} + a_{m-2} x^{m-2} + \ldots + a_1 x + a_0} \tag{A.2}$$

where some of the terms in the numerator and/or denominator may be zero. We can find the roots of the numerator and denominator with the **roots(p)** function as before.

As noted in the comment line of Example A.7, we can write MATLAB statements in one line, if we separate them by commas or semicolons. **Commas will display the results whereas semicolons will suppress the display.**

Example A.9

Let

$$R(x) = \frac{p_{num}}{p_{den}} = \frac{x^5 - 3x^4 + 5x^2 + 7x + 9}{x^6 - 4x^4 + 2x^2 + 5x + 6}$$

Express the numerator and denominator in factored form, using the **roots(p)** function.

Solution:

```
num=[1 -3 0 5 7 9]; den=[1 0 -4 0 2 5 6];    % Do not display num and den coefficients
roots_num=roots(num), roots_den=roots(den)    % Display num and den roots

roots_num =
    2.4186 + 1.0712i    2.4186 - 1.0712i    -1.1633
   -0.3370 + 0.9961i   -0.3370 - 0.9961i
```

Rational Polynomials

```
roots_den =
   1.6760 + 0.4922i      1.6760 - 0.4922i    -1.9304
  -0.2108 + 0.9870i     -0.2108 - 0.9870i    -1.0000
```

As expected, the complex roots occur in complex conjugate pairs.

For the numerator, we have the factored form

$$p_{num} = (x-2.4186-j1.0712)(x-2.4186+j1.0712)(x+1.1633)$$
$$(x+0.3370-j0.9961)(x+0.3370+j0.9961)$$

and for the denominator, we have

$$p_{den} = (x-1.6760-j0.4922)(x-1.6760+j0.4922)(x+1.9304)$$
$$(x+0.2108-j0.9870)(x+0.2108+j0.9870)(x+1.0000)$$

We can also express the numerator and denominator of this rational function as a combination of *linear* and *quadratic* factors. We recall that, in a quadratic equation of the form $x^2 + bx + c = 0$ whose roots are x_1 and x_2, the negative sum of the roots is equal to the coefficient b of the x term, that is, $-(x_1 + x_2) = b$, while the product of the roots is equal to the constant term c, that is, $x_1 \cdot x_2 = c$. Accordingly, we form the coefficient b by addition of the complex conjugate roots and this is done by inspection; then we multiply the complex conjugate roots to obtain the constant term c using MATLAB as follows:

(2.4186 + 1.0712i)*(2.4186 −1.0712i)

```
ans = 6.9971
```

(−0.3370+ 0.9961i)*(−0.3370−0.9961i)

```
ans = 1.1058
```

(1.6760+ 0.4922i)*(1.6760−0.4922i)

```
ans = 3.0512
```

(−0.2108+ 0.9870i)*(−0.2108−0.9870i)

```
ans = 1.0186
```

Thus,

$$R(x) = \frac{p_{num}}{p_{den}} = \frac{(x^2 - 4.8372x + 6.9971)(x^2 + 0.6740x + 1.1058)(x + 1.1633)}{(x^2 - 3.3520x + 3.0512)(x^2 + 0.4216x + 1.0186)(x + 1.0000)(x + 1.9304)}$$

Appendix A Introduction to MATLAB®

We can check this result of Example A.9 above with MATLAB's *Symbolic Math Toolbox* which is a collection of tools (functions) used in solving symbolic expressions. They are discussed in detail in MATLAB's Users Manual. For the present, our interest is in using the **collect(s)** function that is used to multiply two or more symbolic expressions to obtain the result in polynomial form. We must remember that the **conv(p,q)** function is used with numeric expressions only, that is, polynomial coefficients.

Before using a symbolic expression, we must create one or more symbolic variables such as x, y, t, and so on. For our example, we use the following script:

syms x % Define a symbolic variable and use collect(s) to express numerator in polynomial form
collect((x^2–4.8372*x+6.9971)*(x^2+0.6740*x+1.1058)*(x+1.1633))

```
ans =
  x^5-29999/10000*x^4-1323/3125000*x^3+7813277909/
  1562500000*x^2+1750276323053/250000000000*x+4500454743147/
  500000000000
```

and if we simplify this, we find that is the same as the numerator of the given rational expression in polynomial form. We can use the same procedure to verify the denominator.

A.7 Using MATLAB to Make Plots

Quite often, we want to plot a set of ordered pairs. This is a very easy task with the MATLAB **plot(x,y)** command that plots *y* versus *x*, where *x* is the horizontal axis (abscissa) and *y* is the vertical axis (ordinate).

Example A.10

Consider the electric circuit of Figure A.1, where the radian frequency ω (radians/second) of the applied voltage was varied from 300 to 3000 in steps of 100 radians/second, while the amplitude was held constant.

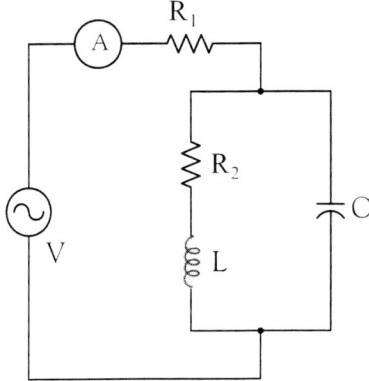

Figure A.1. Electric circuit for Example A.10

Using MATLAB to Make Plots

The ammeter readings were then recorded for each frequency. The magnitude of the impedance $|Z|$ was computed as $|Z| = |V/A|$ and the data were tabulated on Table A.1.

TABLE A.1 Table for Example A.10

ω (rads/s)	|Z| Ohms	ω (rads/s)	|Z| Ohms
300	39.339	1700	90.603
400	52.589	1800	81.088
500	71.184	1900	73.588
600	97.665	2000	67.513
700	140.437	2100	62.481
800	222.182	2200	58.240
900	436.056	2300	54.611
1000	1014.938	2400	51.428
1100	469.83	2500	48.717
1200	266.032	2600	46.286
1300	187.052	2700	44.122
1400	145.751	2800	42.182
1500	120.353	2900	40.432
1600	103.111	3000	38.845

Plot the magnitude of the impedance, that is, $|Z|$ versus radian frequency ω.

Solution:

We cannot type ω (omega) in the MATLAB Command prompt, so we will use the English letter **w** instead.

If a statement, or a row vector is too long to fit in one line, it can be continued to the next line by typing three or more periods, then pressing *<enter>* to start a new line, and continue to enter data. This is illustrated below for the data of **w** and **z**. Also, as mentioned before, we use the semicolon (;) to suppress the display of numbers that we do not care to see on the screen.

The data are entered as follows:

w=[300 400 500 600 700 800 900 1000 1100 1200 1300 1400 1500 1600 1700 1800 1900....
2000 2100 2200 2300 2400 2500 2600 2700 2800 2900 3000];
%
z=[39.339 52.789 71.104 97.665 140.437 222.182 436.056....
1014.938 469.830 266.032 187.052 145.751 120.353 103.111....
90.603 81.088 73.588 67.513 62.481 58.240 54.611 51.468....
48.717 46.286 44.122 42.182 40.432 38.845];

Of course, if we want to see the values of *w* or *z* or both, we simply type w or z, and we press

Appendix A Introduction to MATLAB®

<enter>. To plot z (y−axis) versus w (x−axis), we use the **plot(x,y)** command. For this example, we use **plot(w,z)**. When this command is executed, MATLAB displays the plot on MATLAB's *graph screen* and MATLAB denotes this plot as Figure 1. This plot is shown in Figure A.2.

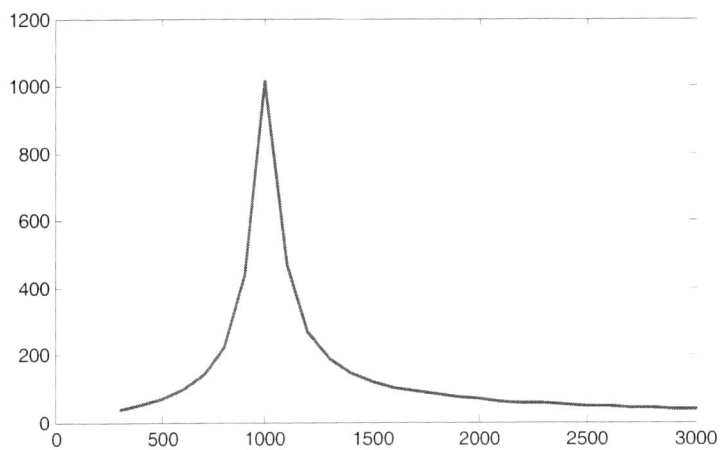

Figure A.2. Plot of impedance |z| versus frequency ω for Example A.10

This plot is referred to as the *magnitude frequency response* of the circuit.

To return to the command window, we press any key, or from the *Window* pull−down menu, we select *MATLAB Command Window*. To see the graph again, we click on the Window pull−down menu, and we choose *Figure 1*.

We can make the above, or any plot, more presentable with the following commands:

grid on: This command adds grid lines to the plot. The **grid off** command removes the grid. The command **grid** toggles them, that is, changes from off to on or vice versa. The default[*] is off.

box off: This command removes the box (the solid lines which enclose the plot), and **box on** restores the box. The command **box** toggles them. The default is on.

title('string'): This command adds a line of the text **string** (label) at the top of the plot.

xlabel('string') and **ylabel('string')** are used to label the x− and y−axis respectively.

The magnitude frequency response is usually represented with the x−axis in a logarithmic scale. We can use the **semilogx(x,y)** command which is similar to the **plot(x,y)** command, except that the x−axis is represented as a log scale, and the y−axis as a linear scale. Likewise, the **semilogy(x,y)** command is similar to the **plot(x,y)** command, except that the y−axis is represented as a

---

[*] *A default is a particular value for a variable that is assigned automatically by an operating system and remains in effect unless canceled or overridden by the operator.*

Using MATLAB to Make Plots

log scale, and the x–axis as a linear scale. The **loglog(x,y)** command uses logarithmic scales for both axes.

Throughout this text it will be understood that *log* is the common (base 10) logarithm, and *ln* is the natural (base e) logarithm. We must remember, however, the function **log(x)** in MATLAB is the natural logarithm, whereas the common logarithm is expressed as **log10(x)**, and the logarithm to the base 2 as **log2(x).**

Let us now redraw the plot with the above options by adding the following statements:

```
semilogx(w,z); grid;          % Replaces the plot(w,z) command
title('Magnitude of Impedance vs. Radian Frequency');
xlabel('w in rads/sec'); ylabel('|Z| in Ohms')
```

After execution of these commands, the plot is as shown in Figure A.3.

If the y–axis represents power, voltage or current, the x–axis of the frequency response is more often shown in a logarithmic scale, and the y–axis in dB (decibels).

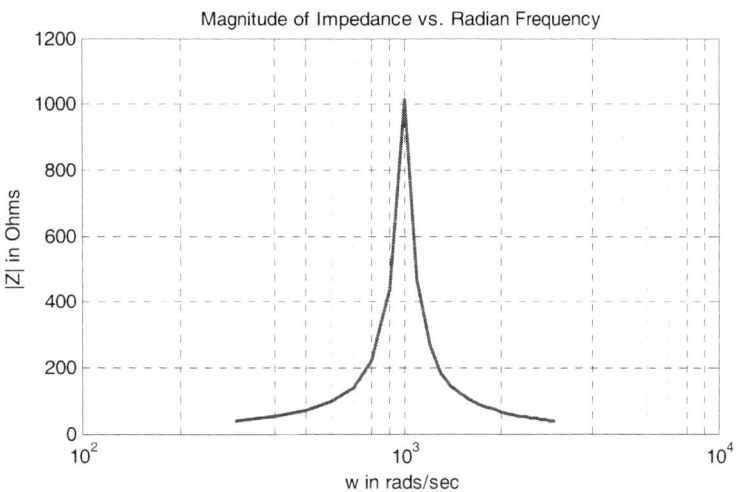

Figure A.3. Modified frequency response plot of Figure A.2.

To display the voltage v in a dB scale on the y–axis, we add the relation **dB=20*log10(v)**, and we replace the **semilogx(w,z)** command with semilogx(w,dB).

The command **gtext('string')**[*] switches to the current *Figure Window*, and displays a cross–hair that can be moved around with the mouse. For instance, we can use the command gtext('Impedance |Z| versus Frequency'), and this will place a cross–hair in the *Figure* window. Then, using

---

[*] With the latest MATLAB Versions 6 and 7 (Student Editions 13 and 14), we can add text, lines and arrows directly into the graph using the tools provided on the Figure Window. For advanced MATLAB graphics, please refer to The MathWorks **Using MATLAB Graphics** documentation.

the mouse, we can move the cross–hair to the position where we want our label to begin, and we press <enter>.

The command **text(x,y,'string')** is similar to **gtext('string')**. It places a label on a plot in some specific location specified by **x** and **y**, and **string** is the label which we want to place at that location. We will illustrate its use with the following example which plots a *3–phase* sinusoidal waveform.

The first line of the script below has the form

linspace(first_value, last_value, number_of_values)

This function specifies *the number of data points* but not the increments between data points. An alternate function is

x=first: increment: last

and this specifies *the increments between points* but not the number of data points.

The script for the 3–phase plot is as follows:

```
x=linspace(0, 2*pi, 60);       %  pi is a built-in function in MATLAB;
%  we could have used x=0:0.02*pi:2*pi or x = (0: 0.02: 2)*pi instead;
y=sin(x); u=sin(x+2*pi/3); v=sin(x+4*pi/3);
plot(x,y,x,u,x,v);              %  The x-axis must be specified for each function
grid on, box on,                %  turn grid and axes box on
text(0.75, 0.65, 'sin(x)');  text(2.85, 0.65, 'sin(x+2*pi/3)');  text(4.95, 0.65, 'sin(x+4*pi/3)')
```

These three waveforms are shown on the same plot of Figure A.4.

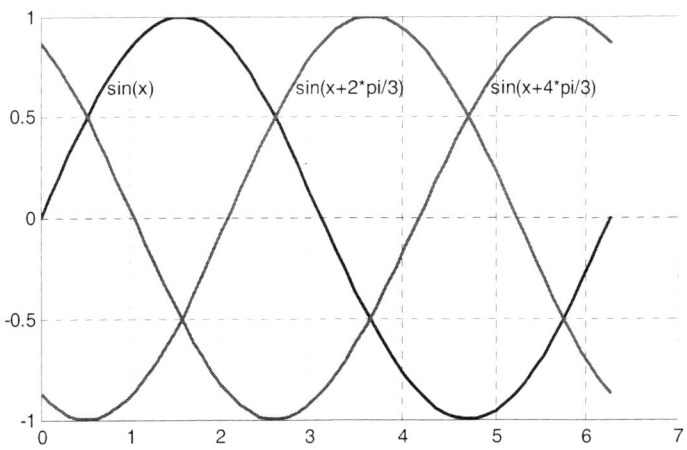

Figure A.4. Three–phase waveforms

Using MATLAB to Make Plots

In our previous examples, we did not specify line styles, markers, and colors for our plots. However, MATLAB allows us to specify various line types, plot symbols, and colors. These, or a combination of these, can be added with the **plot(x,y,s)** command, where **s** is a character string containing one or more characters shown on the three columns of Table A.2. MATLAB has no default color; it starts with blue and cycles through the first seven colors listed in Table A.2 for each additional line in the plot. Also, there is no default marker; no markers are drawn unless they are selected. The default line is the solid line. But with the latest MATLAB versions, we can select the line color, line width, and other options directly from the *Figure Window*.

TABLE A.2 Styles, colors, and markets used in MATLAB

Symbol	Color	Symbol	Marker	Symbol	Line Style
b	blue	.	point	–	solid line
g	green	o	circle	:	dotted line
r	red	x	x–mark	–.	dash–dot line
c	cyan	+	plus	––	dashed line
m	magenta	*	star		
y	yellow	s	square		
k	black	d	diamond		
w	white	∨	triangle down		
		∧	triangle up		
		<	triangle left		
		>	triangle right		
		p	pentagram		
		h	hexagram		

For example, **plot(x,y,'m*:')** plots a magenta dotted line with a star at each data point, and **plot(x,y,'rs')** plots a red square at each data point, but does not draw any line because no line was selected. If we want to connect the data points with a solid line, we must type **plot(x,y,'rs–')**. For additional information we can type **help plot** in MATLAB's command screen.

The plots we have discussed thus far are two–dimensional, that is, they are drawn on two axes. MATLAB has also a three–dimensional (three–axes) capability and this is discussed next.

The **plot3(x,y,z)** command plots a line in *3-space* through the points whose coordinates are the elements of *x*, *y* and *z*, where *x*, *y* and *z* are three vectors of the same length.

The general format is **plot3($x_1,y_1,z_1,s_1,x_2,y_2,z_2,s_2,x_3,y_3,z_3,s_3$,...)** where **$x_n$**, **$y_n$** and **$z_n$** are vectors or matrices, and **s_n** are strings specifying color, marker symbol, or line style. These strings are the same as those of the two–dimensional plots.

Appendix A Introduction to MATLAB®

Example A.11

Plot the function

$$z = -2x^3 + x + 3y^2 - 1 \tag{A.3}$$

Solution:

We arbitrarily choose the interval (length) shown on the script below.

```
x= -10: 0.5: 10;           %  Length of vector x
y= x;                      %  Length of vector y must be same as x
z= -2.*x.^3+x+3.*y.^2-1;   %  Vector z is function of both x and y*
plot3(x,y,z); grid
```

The three–dimensional plot is shown in Figure A.5.

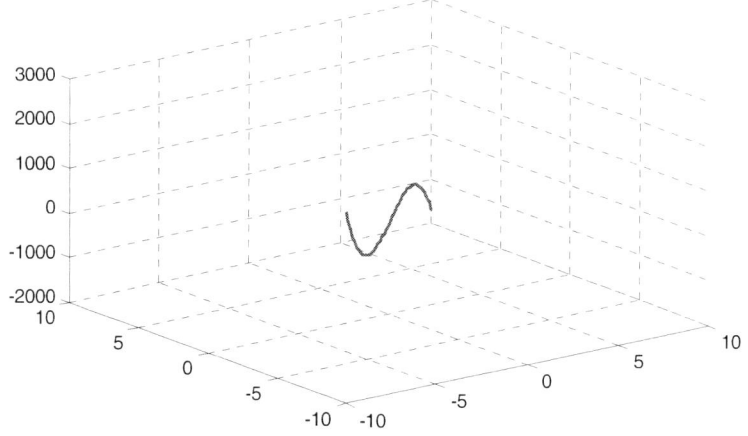

Figure A.5. Three dimensional plot for Example A.11

In a two–dimensional plot, we can set the limits of the *x–* and *y–axes* with the **axis([xmin xmax ymin ymax])** command. Likewise, in a three–dimensional plot we can set the limits of all three axes with the **axis([xmin xmax ymin ymax zmin zmax])** command. It must be placed after the **plot(x,y)** or **plot3(x,y,z)** commands, or on the same line without first executing the **plot** command. This must be done for each plot. The three–dimensional **text(x,y,z,'string')** command will place **string** beginning at the co–ordinate (x,y,z) on the plot.

For three–dimensional plots, **grid on** and **box off** are the default states.

We can also use the **mesh(x,y,z)** command with two vector arguments. These must be defined as

---

* This statement uses the so called dot multiplication, dot division, and dot exponentiation where the multiplication, division, and exponential operators are preceded by a dot. These important operations will be explained in Section A.9.

Using MATLAB to Make Plots

length(x) = n and length(y) = m where [m, n] = size(Z). In this case, the vertices of the mesh lines are the triples {x(j), y(i), Z(i, j)}. We observe that **x** corresponds to the columns of Z, and **y** corresponds to the rows.

To produce a mesh plot of a function of two variables, say z = f (x, y), we must first generate the X and Y matrices that consist of repeated rows and columns over the range of the variables *x* and *y*. We can generate the matrices X and Y with the **[X,Y]=meshgrid(x,y)** function that creates the matrix X whose rows are copies of the vector **x**, and the matrix Y whose columns are copies of the vector **y**.

Example A.12

The volume V of a right circular cone of radius r and height h is given by

$$V = \frac{1}{3}\pi r^2 h \qquad (A.4)$$

Plot the volume of the cone as r and h vary on the intervals $0 \le r \le 4$ and $0 \le h \le 6$ meters.

Solution:

The volume of the cone is a function of both the radius *r* and the height *h*, that is,

$$V = f(r, h)$$

The three–dimensional plot is created with the following MATLAB script where, as in the previous example, in the second line we have used the dot multiplication, dot division, and dot exponentiation. This will be explained in Section A.9.

```
[R,H]=meshgrid(0: 4, 0: 6);   % Creates R and H matrices from vectors r and h;...
V=(pi .* R .^ 2 .* H) ./ 3;  mesh(R, H, V);...
xlabel('x–axis, radius r (meters)'); ylabel('y–axis, altitude h (meters)');...
zlabel('z–axis, volume (cubic meters)'); title('Volume of Right Circular Cone'); box on
```

The three–dimensional plot of Figure A.6 shows how the volume of the cone increases as the radius and height are increased.

The plots of Figure A.5 and A.6 are rudimentary; MATLAB can generate very sophisticated three–dimensional plots. The MATLAB User's Manual and the Using MATLAB Graphics Manual contain numerous examples.

Appendix A Introduction to MATLAB®

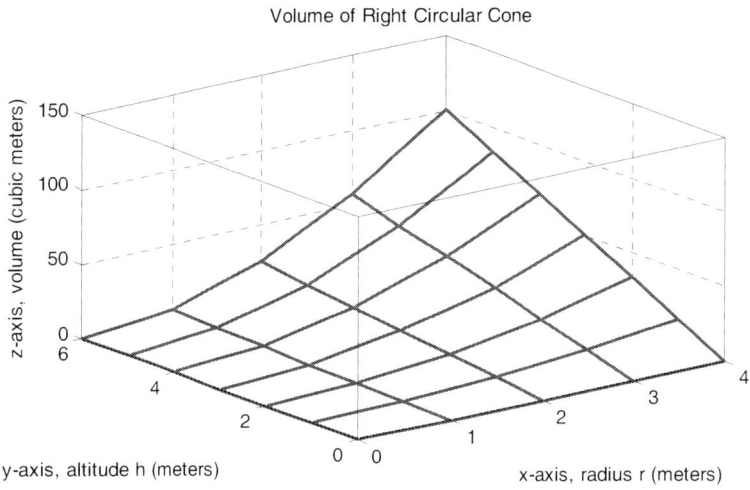

Figure A.6. Volume of a right circular cone.

A.8 Subplots

MATLAB can display up to four windows of different plots on the *Figure* window using the command **subplot(m,n,p)**. This command divides the window into an $m \times n$ matrix of plotting areas and chooses the *pth* area to be active. No spaces or commas are required between the three integers m, n and p. The possible combinations are shown in Figure A.7.

We will illustrate the use of the **subplot(m,n,p)** command following the discussion on multiplication, division and exponentiation that follows.

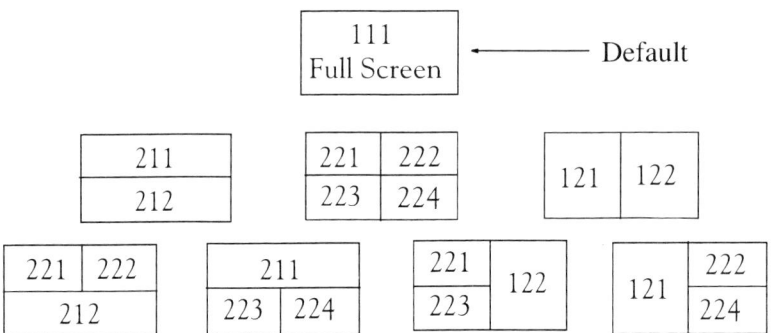

Figure A.7. Possible subplot arrangements in MATLAB

A.9 Multiplication, Division, and Exponentiation

MATLAB recognizes two types of multiplication, division, and exponentiation. These are the **matrix** multiplication, division, and exponentiation, and the **element–by–element** multiplication, division, and exponentiation. They are explained in the following paragraphs.

Multiplication, Division, and Exponentiation

In Section A.2, the arrays [a b c ...], such a those that contained the coefficients of polynomials, consisted of one row and multiple columns, and thus are called *row vectors*. If an array has one column and multiple rows, it is called a *column vector*. We recall that the elements of a row vector are separated by spaces. To distinguish between row and column vectors, the elements of a column vector must be separated by semicolons. An easier way to construct a column vector, is to write it first as a row vector, and then transpose it into a column vector. MATLAB uses the single quotation character (') to transpose a vector. Thus, a column vector can be written either as

b=[−1; 3; 6; 11]

or as

b=[−1 3 6 11]'

As shown below, MATLAB produces the same display with either format.

b=[−1; 3; 6; 11]

```
b =
    -1
     3
     6
    11
```

b=[−1 3 6 11]'   % Observe the single quotation character (')

```
b =
    -1
     3
     6
    11
```

We will now define Matrix Multiplication and Element–by–Element multiplication.

1. **Matrix Multiplication** (multiplication of row by column vectors)

   Let
   $$\mathbf{A} = [a_1 \ a_2 \ a_3 \ ... \ a_n]$$
   and
   $$\mathbf{B} = [b_1 \ b_2 \ b_3 \ ... \ b_n]'$$

   be two vectors. We observe that **A** is defined as a row vector whereas **B** is defined as a column vector, as indicated by the transpose operator ('). Here, multiplication of the row vector **A** by the column vector **B**, is performed with the matrix multiplication operator (*). Then,

   $$\mathbf{A}*\mathbf{B} = [a_1 b_1 + a_2 b_2 + a_3 b_3 + ... + a_n b_n] = \text{single value} \quad (A.5)$$

Appendix A Introduction to MATLAB®

For example, if
$$A = [1 \quad 2 \quad 3 \quad 4 \quad 5]$$
and
$$B = [-2 \quad 6 \quad -3 \quad 8 \quad 7]'$$

the matrix multiplication **A*B** produces the single value 68, that is,

$$A*B = 1 \times (-2) + 2 \times 6 + 3 \times (-3) + 4 \times 8 + 5 \times 7 = 68$$

and this is verified with the MATLAB script

A=[1 2 3 4 5]; B=[-2 6 -3 8 7]'; A*B   % Observe transpose operator (') in B

ans =

 68

Now, let us suppose that both **A** and **B** are row vectors, and we attempt to perform a row–by–row multiplication with the following MATLAB statements.

A=[1 2 3 4 5]; B=[-2 6 -3 8 7]; A*B   % No transpose operator (') here

When these statements are executed, MATLAB displays the following message:

??? Error using ==> *

Inner matrix dimensions must agree.

Here, because we have used the matrix multiplication operator (*) in **A*B**, MATLAB expects vector **B** to be a column vector, not a row vector. It recognizes that **B** is a row vector, and warns us that we cannot perform this multiplication using the matrix multiplication operator (*). Accordingly, we must perform this type of multiplication with a different operator. This operator is defined below.

2. **Element–by–Element Multiplication** (multiplication of a row vector by another row vector)

    Let
    $$C = [c_1 \quad c_2 \quad c_3 \quad \ldots \quad c_n]$$
    and
    $$D = [d_1 \quad d_2 \quad d_3 \quad \ldots \quad d_n]$$

    be two row vectors. Here, multiplication of the row vector **C** by the row vector **D** is performed with the *dot multiplication operator (.*)*. There is no space between the dot and the multiplication symbol. Thus,

    $$C.*D = [c_1 d_1 \quad c_2 d_2 \quad c_3 d_3 \quad \ldots \quad c_n d_n] \qquad (A.6)$$

Multiplication, Division, and Exponentiation

This product is another row vector with the same number of elements, as the elements of **C** and **D**.

As an example, let
$$\mathbf{C} = [1 \quad 2 \quad 3 \quad 4 \quad 5]$$
and
$$\mathbf{D} = [-2 \quad 6 \quad -3 \quad 8 \quad 7]$$

Dot multiplication of these two row vectors produce the following result.

$$\mathbf{C}.*\mathbf{D} = 1 \times (-2) \quad 2 \times 6 \quad 3 \times (-3) \quad 4 \times 8 \quad 5 \times 7 = -2 \quad 12 \quad -9 \quad 32 \quad 35$$

Check with MATLAB:

```
C=[1 2 3 4 5];     %  Vectors C and D must have
D=[-2 6 -3 8 7];   %  same number of elements
C.*D               %  We observe that this is a dot multiplication
ans =
    -2    12    -9    32    35
```

Similarly, the division (/) and exponentiation (^) operators, are used for matrix division and exponentiation, whereas dot division (./) and dot exponentiation (.^) are used for element-by-element division and exponentiation, as illustrated in Examples A.11 and A.12 above.

We must remember that *no space is allowed between the dot (.) and the multiplication, division, and exponentiation operators.*

Note: A dot (.) is never required with the plus (+) and minus (−) operators.

Example A.13

Write the MATLAB script that produces a simple plot for the waveform defined as

$$y = f(t) = 3e^{-4t}\cos 5t - 2e^{-3t}\sin 2t + \frac{t^2}{t+1} \tag{A.7}$$

in the $0 \leq t \leq 5$ seconds interval.

Solution:

The MATLAB script for this example is as follows:

```
t=0: 0.01: 5;        %  Define t-axis in 0.01 increments
y=3 .* exp(-4 .* t) .* cos(5 .* t)-2 .* exp(-3 .* t) .* sin(2 .* t) + t .^2 ./ (t+1);
plot(t,y); grid; xlabel('t'); ylabel('y=f(t)'); title('Plot for Example A.13')
```

The plot for this example is shown in Figure A.8.

Appendix A Introduction to MATLAB®

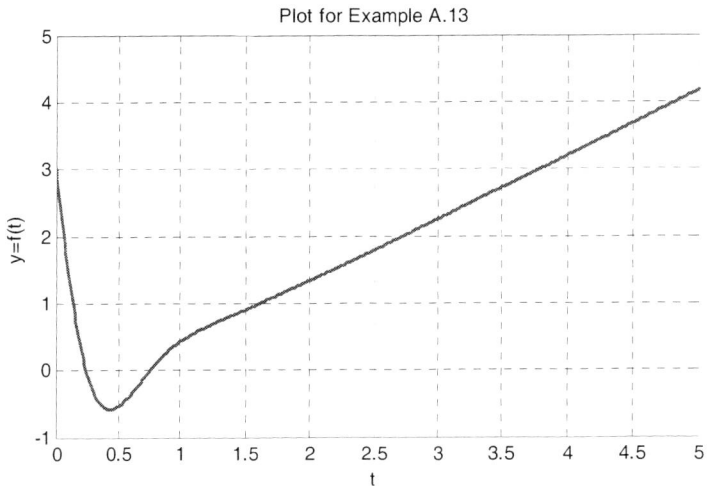

Figure A.8. *Plot for Example A.13*

Had we, in this example, defined the time interval starting with a negative value equal to or less than -1, say as $-3 \leq t \leq 3$, MATLAB would have displayed the following message:

`Warning: Divide by zero.`

This is because the last term (the rational fraction) of the given expression, is divided by zero when $t = -1$. To avoid division by zero, we use the special MATLAB function **eps,** which is a number approximately equal to 2.2×10^{-16}. It will be used with the next example.

The command **axis([xmin xmax ymin ymax])** scales the current plot to the values specified by the arguments **xmin, xmax, ymin and ymax.** There are no commas between these four arguments. This command must be placed *after* the plot command and must be repeated for each plot. The following example illustrates the use of the dot multiplication, division, and exponentiation, the **eps** number, the **axis([xmin xmax ymin ymax])** command, and also MATLAB's capability of displaying up to four windows of different plots.

Example A.14

Plot the functions

$$y = \sin^2 x, \quad z = \cos^2 x, \quad w = \sin^2 x \cdot \cos^2 x, \quad v = \sin^2 x / \cos^2 x$$

in the interval $0 \leq x \leq 2\pi$ using 100 data points. Use the **subplot** command to display these functions on four windows on the same graph.

Multiplication, Division, and Exponentiation

Solution:

The MATLAB script to produce the four subplots is as follows:

```
x=linspace(0,2*pi,100);          % Interval with 100 data points
y=(sin(x).^ 2);  z=(cos(x).^ 2);
w=y.* z;
v=y./ (z+eps);% add eps to avoid division by zero
subplot(221);% upper left of four subplots
plot(x,y); axis([0 2*pi 0 1]);
title('y=(sinx) ^ 2');
subplot(222);                    % upper right of four subplots
plot(x,z); axis([0 2*pi 0 1]);
title('z=(cosx) ^ 2');
subplot(223);                    % lower left of four subplots
plot(x,w); axis([0 2*pi 0 0.3]);
title('w=(sinx) ^ 2*(cosx) ^ 2');
subplot(224);                    % lower right of four subplots
plot(x,v); axis([0 2*pi 0 400]);
title('v=(sinx) ^ 2/(cosx) ^ 2');
```

These subplots are shown in Figure A.9.

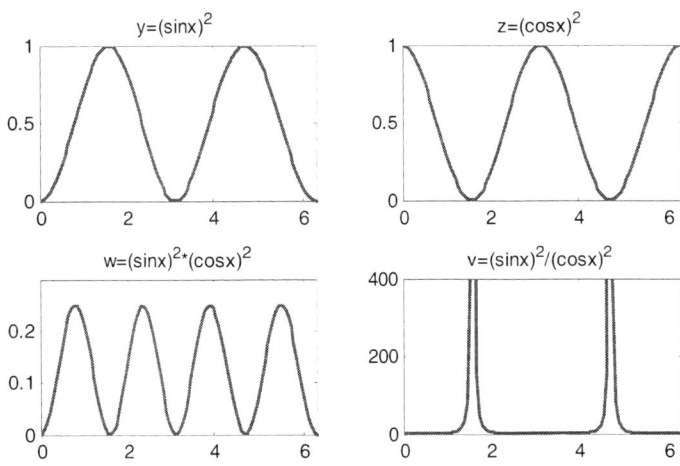

Figure A.9. Subplots for the functions of Example A.14

The next example illustrates MATLAB's capabilities with imaginary numbers. We will introduce the **real(z)** and **imag(z)** functions that display the real and imaginary parts of the complex quantity $z = x + iy$, the **abs(z)**, and the **angle(z)** functions that compute the absolute value (magnitude) and phase angle of the complex quantity $z = x + iy = r\angle\theta$. We will also use the **polar(theta,r)** function that produces a plot in polar coordinates, where **r** is the magnitude, **theta**

Appendix A Introduction to MATLAB®

is the angle in radians, and the **round(n)** function that rounds a number to its nearest integer.

Example A.15

Consider the electric circuit of Figure A.10.

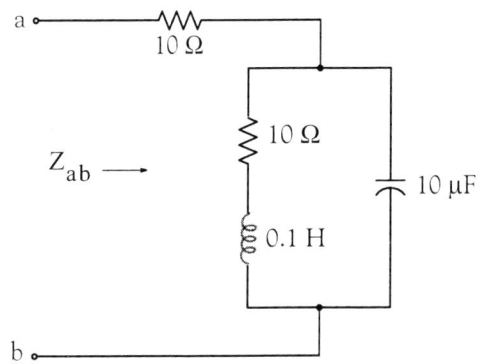

Figure A.10. Electric circuit for Example A.15

With the given values of resistance, inductance, and capacitance, the impedance Z_{ab} as a function of the radian frequency ω can be computed from the following expression:

$$Z_{ab} = Z = 10 + \frac{10^4 - j(10^6/\omega)}{10 + j(0.1\omega - 10^5/\omega)} \tag{A.8}$$

a. Plot Re{Z} (the real part of the impedance Z) versus frequency ω.

b. Plot Im{Z} (the imaginary part of the impedance Z) versus frequency ω.

c. Plot the impedance Z versus frequency ω in polar coordinates.

Solution:

The MATLAB script below computes the real and imaginary parts of Z_{ab} which, for simplicity, are denoted as z, and plots these as two separate graphs (parts a & b). It also produces a polar plot (part c).

```
w=0: 1: 2000;              %  Define interval with one radian interval;...
z=(10+(10 .^ 4 –j .* 10 .^ 6 ./ (w+eps)) ./ (10 + j .* (0.1 .* w –10.^5./ (w+eps))));...
%
%  The first five statements (next two lines) compute and plot Re{z}
real_part=real(z); plot(w,real_part);...
xlabel('radian frequency w');  ylabel('Real part of Z'); grid
```

Multiplication, Division, and Exponentiation

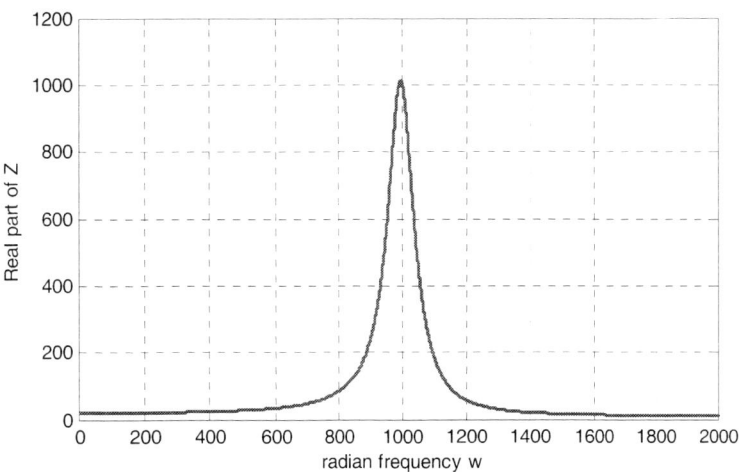

Figure A.11. Plot for the real part of the impedance in Example A.15

```
%  The next five statements (next two lines) compute and plot Im{z}
imag_part=imag(z);  plot(w,imag_part);...
xlabel('radian frequency w');  ylabel('Imaginary part of Z');  grid
```

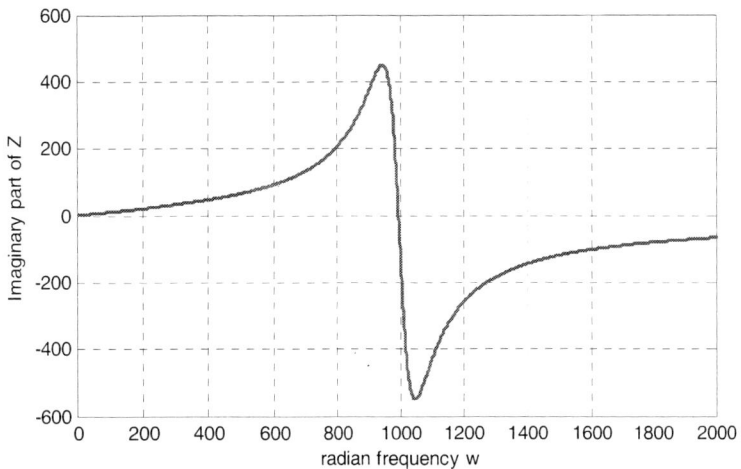

Figure A.12. Plot for the imaginary part of the impedance in Example A.15

```
%  The last six statements (next five lines) below produce the polar plot of z
mag=abs(z);              % Computes |Z|;...
rndz=round(abs(z));      % Rounds |Z| to read polar plot easier;...
theta=angle(z);          % Computes the phase angle of impedance Z;...
polar(theta,rndz);       % Angle is the first argument
ylabel('Polar Plot of Z');  grid
```

Appendix A Introduction to MATLAB®

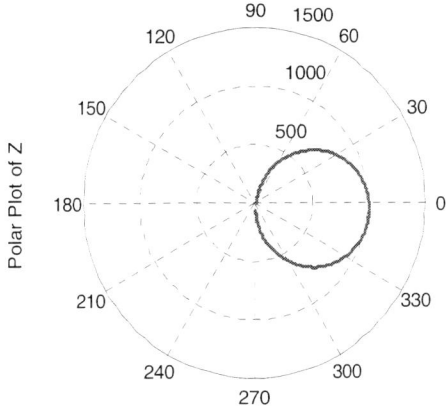

Figure A.13. Polar plot of the impedance in Example A.15

Example A.15 clearly illustrates how powerful, fast, accurate, and flexible MATLAB is.

A.10 Script and Function Files

MATLAB recognizes two types of files: *script files* and *function files*. Both types are referred to as *m–files* since both require the *.m* extension.

A *script file* consists of two or more built–in functions such as those we have discussed thus far. Thus, the script for each of the examples we discussed earlier, make up a script file. Generally, a script file is one which was generated and saved as an m–file with an editor such as the MATLAB's Editor/Debugger.

A *function file* is a user–defined function using MATLAB. We use function files for repetitive tasks. The first line of a function file must contain the word *function*, followed by the output argument, the equal sign (=), and the input argument enclosed in parentheses. The function name and file name must be the same, but the file name must have the extension *.m*. For example, the function file consisting of the two lines below

```
function y = myfunction(x)
y=x.^ 3 + cos(3.* x)
```

is a function file and must be saved as *myfunction.m*

For the next example, we will use the following MATLAB functions:

fzero(f,x) – attempts to find a zero of a function of one variable, where **f** is a string containing the name of a real–valued function of a single real variable. MATLAB searches for a value near a point where the function **f** changes sign, and returns that value, or returns NaN if the search fails.

Script and Function Files

Important: We must remember that we use **roots(p)** to find the roots of polynomials only, such as those in Examples A.1 and A.2.

fplot(fcn,lims) – plots the function specified by the string **fcn** between the x–axis limits specified by **lims = [xmin xmax]**. Using **lims = [xmin xmax ymin ymax]** also controls the y–axis limits. The string **fcn** must be the name of an *m–file* function or a string with variable x.

NaN (Not–a–Number) is not a function; it is MATLAB's response to an undefined expression such as $0/0$, ∞/∞, or inability to produce a result as described on the next paragraph. We can avoid division by zero using the **eps** number, which we mentioned earlier.

Example A.16

Find the zeros, the minimum, and the maximum values of the function

$$f(x) = \frac{1}{(x-0.1)^2 + 0.01} - \frac{1}{(x-1.2)^2 + 0.04} - 10 \qquad (A.9)$$

in the interval $-1.5 \leq x \leq 1.5$

Solution:

We first plot this function to observe the approximate zeros, maxima, and minima using the following script.

```
x=-1.5: 0.01: 1.5;
y=1./ ((x-0.1).^ 2 + 0.01) -1./ ((x-1.2).^ 2 + 0.04) -10;
plot(x,y); grid
```

The plot is shown in Figure A.14.

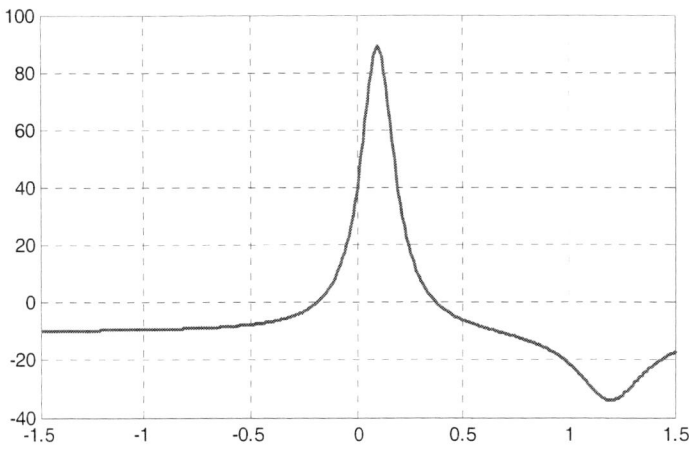

Figure A.14. Plot for Example A.16 using the plot command

Appendix A Introduction to MATLAB®

The roots (zeros) of this function appear to be in the neighborhood of $x = -0.2$ and $x = 0.3$. The maximum occurs at approximately $x = 0.1$ where, approximately, $y_{max} = 90$, and the minimum occurs at approximately $x = 1.2$ where, approximately, $y_{min} = -34$.

Next, we define and save *f(x)* as the **funczero01.m** function m–file with the following script:

```
function y=funczero01(x)
% Finding the zeros of the function shown below
y=1/((x–0.1)^2+0.01)–1/((x–1.2)^2+0.04)–10;
```

To save this file, from the File drop menu on the Command Window, we choose New, and when the Editor Window appears, we type the script above and we save it as **funczero01**. MATLAB appends the extension **.m** to it.

Now, we can use the **fplot(fcn,lims)** command to plot f(x) as follows:

```
fplot('funczero01', [–1.5  1.5]); grid
```

This plot is shown in Figure A.15. As expected, this plot is identical to the plot of Figure A.14 which was obtained with the **plot(x,y)** command as shown in Figure A.14.

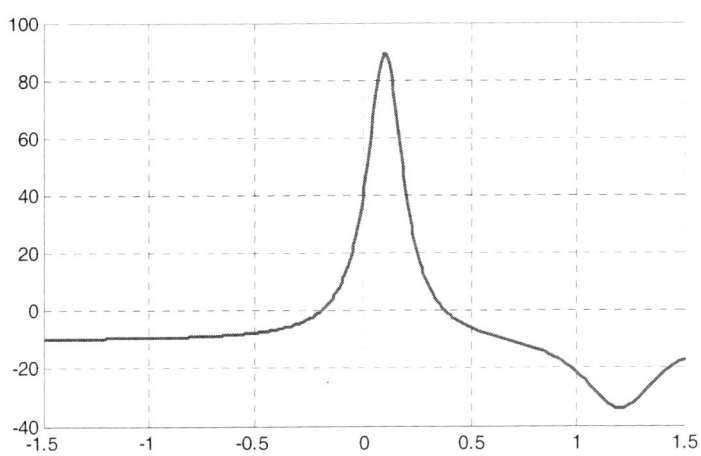

Figure A.15. Plot for Example A.16 using the fplot command

We will use the **fzero(f,x)** function to compute the roots of f(x) in Equation (A.9) more precisely. The MATLAB script below will accomplish this.

```
x1= fzero('funczero01', –0.2);
x2= fzero('funczero01', 0.3);
fprintf('The roots (zeros) of this function are r1= %3.4f', x1);
fprintf(' and r2= %3.4f \n', x2)
```

Script and Function Files

MATLAB displays the following:

```
The roots (zeros) of this function are r1= -0.1919 and r2= 0.3788
```

The earlier MATLAB versions included the function **fmin(f,x1,x2)** and with this function we could compute both a minimum of some function f(x) or a maximum of f(x) since a maximum of f(x) is equal to a minimum of –f(x). This can be visualized by flipping the plot of a function f(x) upside–down. This function is no longer used in MATLAB and thus we will compute the maxima and minima from the derivative of the given function.

From elementary calculus, we recall that the maxima or minima of a function y = f(x) can be found by setting the first derivative of a function equal to zero and solving for the independent variable x. For this example we use the **diff(x)** function which produces the approximate derivative of a function. Thus, we use the following MATLAB script:

syms x ymin zmin; ymin=1/((x–0.1)^2+0.01)–1/((x–1.2)^2+0.04)–10;...
zmin=diff(ymin)

```
zmin =
-1/((x-1/10)^2+1/100)^2*(2*x-1/5)+1/((x-6/5)^2+1/25)^2*(2*x-12/5)
```

When the command

solve(zmin)

is executed, MATLAB displays a very long expression which when copied at the command prompt and executed, produces the following:

```
ans =
   0.6585 + 0.3437i
ans =
   0.6585 - 0.3437i
ans =
    1.2012
```

The real value 1.2012 above is the value of x at which the function y has its minimum value as we observe also in the plot of Figure A.15.

To find the value of y corresponding to this value of x, we substitute it into f(x), that is,

x=1.2012; ymin=1 / ((x–0.1) ^ 2 + 0.01) –1 / ((x–1.2) ^ 2 + 0.04) –10

```
ymin = -34.1812
```

We can find the maximum value from –f(x) whose plot is produced with the script

x=–1.5:0.01:1.5; ymax=–1./((x–0.1).^2+0.01)+1./((x–1.2).^2+0.04)+10; plot(x,ymax); grid

and the plot is shown in Figure A.16.

Appendix A Introduction to MATLAB®

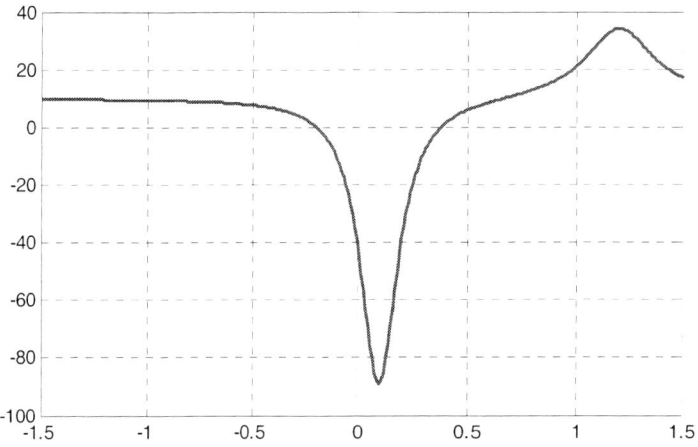

Figure A.16. Plot of $-f(x)$ for Example A.16

Next we compute the first derivative of $-f(x)$ and we solve for x to find the value where the maximum of ymax occurs. This is accomplished with the MATLAB script below.

syms x ymax zmax; ymax=-(1/((x-0.1)^2+0.01)-1/((x-1.2)^2+0.04)-10); zmax=diff(ymax)

```
zmax =
  1/((x-1/10)^2+1/100)^2*(2*x-1/5)-1/((x-6/5)^2+1/25)^2*(2*x-12/5)
```

solve(zmax)

When the command

solve(zmax)

is executed, MATLAB displays a very long expression which when copied at the command prompt and executed, produces the following:

```
ans =
   0.6585 + 0.3437i

ans =
   0.6585 - 0.3437i

ans =
   1.2012
ans =
   0.0999
```

From the values above we choose x = 0.0999 which is consistent with the plots of Figures A.15 and A.16. Accordingly, we execute the following script to obtain the value of ymin.

x=0.0999;   % Using this value find the corresponding value of ymax
ymax=1 / ((x–0.1) ^ 2 + 0.01) –1 / ((x–1.2) ^ 2 + 0.04) –10

```
ymax = 89.2000
```

A.11 Display Formats

MATLAB displays the results on the screen in integer format without decimals if the result is an integer number, or in short floating point format with four decimals if it a fractional number. The format displayed has nothing to do with the accuracy in the computations. MATLAB performs all computations with accuracy up to 16 decimal places.

The output format can changed with the **format** command. The available MATLAB formats can be displayed with the **help format** command as follows:

help format

```
FORMAT Set output format.
All computations in MATLAB are done in double precision.
FORMAT may be used to switch between different output display formats
as follows:

FORMAT   Default. Same as SHORT.
FORMAT SHORT Scaled fixed point format with 5 digits.
FORMAT LONG Scaled fixed point format with 15 digits.
FORMAT SHORT E Floating point format with 5 digits.
FORMAT LONG E  Floating point format with 15 digits.
FORMAT SHORT G Best of fixed or floating point format with 5 digits.
FORMAT LONG G Best of fixed or floating point format with 15 digits.
FORMAT HEX Hexadecimal format.
FORMAT + The symbols +, - and blank are printed for positive, negative,
         and zero elements.Imaginary parts are ignored.
FORMAT BANK Fixed format for dollars and cents.
FORMAT RAT Approximation by ratio of small integers.

Spacing:

FORMAT COMPACT Suppress extra line-feeds.
FORMAT LOOSE  Puts the extra line-feeds back in.

Some examples with different format displays age given below.

format short   33.3335   Four decimal digits (default)
format long   33.33333333333334 16 digits
format short e   3.3333e+01   Four decimal digits plus exponent
format short g    33.333   Better of format short or format short e
format bank   33.33 two decimal digits
format +   only + or - or zero are printed
```

Appendix A Introduction to MATLAB®

```
format rat 100/3 rational approximation
```

The **disp(X)** command displays the array **X** without printing the array name. If **X** is a string, the text is displayed.

The **fprintf(format,array)** command displays and prints both text and arrays. It uses specifiers to indicate where and in which format the values would be displayed and printed. Thus, if **%f** is used, the values will be displayed and printed in fixed decimal format, and if **%e** is used, the values will be displayed and printed in scientific notation format. With this command only the real part of each parameter is processed.

This appendix is just an introduction to MATLAB.[*] This outstanding software package consists of many applications known as *Toolboxes*. The MATLAB Student Version contains just a few of these Toolboxes. Others can be bought directly from The MathWorks,™ Inc., as add–ons.

---

[*] *For more MATLAB applications, please refer to Numerical Analysis Using MATLAB and Spreadsheets,* ISBN 0–9709511–1–6.

Appendix B

Difference Equations

This appendix is a treatment of linear difference equations with constant coefficients and it is confined to first- and second-order difference equations and their solution. Higher-order difference equations of this type and their solution is facilitated with the Z-transform.[*]

B.1 Recursive Method for Solving Difference Equations

In mathematics, a *recursion* is an expression, such as a polynomial, each term of which is determined by application of a formula to preceding terms. The solution of a difference equation is often obtained by recursive methods. An example of a recursive method is Newton's method[†] for solving non-linear equations. While recursive methods yield a desired result, they do not provide a **closed-form** solution. If a closed-form solution is desired, we can solve difference equations using the Method of Undetermined Coefficients, and this method is similar to the classical method of solving linear differential equations with constant coefficients. This method is described in the next section.

B.2 Method of Undetermined Coefficients

A second-order difference equation has the form

$$y(n) + a_1 y(n-1) + a_2(n-2) = f(n) \tag{B.1}$$

where a_1 and a_2 are constants and the right side is some function of n. This difference equation expresses the output $y(n)$ at time n as the linear combination of two previous outputs $y(n-1)$ and $y(n-2)$. The right side of relation (B.1) is referred to as the **forcing function**. The general (closed-form) solution of relation (B.1) is the same as that used for solving second-order differential equations. The three steps are as follows:

1. Obtain the **natural response** (complementary solution) $y_C(n)$ in terms of two arbitrary real constants k_1 and k_2, where a_1 and a_2 are also real constants, that is,

$$y_C(n) = k_1 a_1^n + k_2 a_2^n \tag{B.2}$$

---

[*] For an introduction and applications of the Z-transform please refer to *Signals and Systems with MATLAB Computing and Simulink Modeling, Third Edition*, ISBN 0-9744239-9-8.

[†] For a detailed discussion of Newton's Method, please refer to *Numerical Analysis Using MATLAB and Spreadsheets*, ISBN 0-9709511-1-6.

Appendix B Difference Equations

2. Obtain the forced response (particular solution) $y_P(n)$ in terms of an arbitrary real constant k_3, that is,

$$y_P(n) = k_3 a_3^n \tag{B.3}$$

where the right side of (B.3) is chosen with reference to Table B.1.[*]

TABLE B.1 Forms of the particular solution for different forms of the forcing function

Form of forcing function	Form of particular solution[a]
Constant	k – a constant
an^k – a is a constant	$k_0 + k_1 n + k_2 n^2 + \ldots + k_k n^k$ – k_i is constant
$ab^{\pm n}$ – a and b are constants	Expression proportional to $b^{\pm n}$
$a\cos(n\omega)$ or $a\sin(n\omega)$	$k_1 \cos(n\omega) + k_2 \sin(n\omega)$

    a. As in the case with the solutions of ordinary differential equations with constant coefficients, we must remember that if $f(n)$ is the sum of several terms, the most general form of the particular solution $y_P(n)$ is the linear combination of these terms. Also, if a term in $y_P(n)$ is a duplicate of a term in the complementary solution $y_C(n)$, we must multiply $y_P(n)$ by the lowest power of n that will eliminate the duplication.

3. Add the natural response (complementary solution) $y_C(n)$ and the forced response (particular solution) $y_P(n)$ to obtain the total solution, that is,

$$y(n) = y_C(n) + y_P(n) = k_1 a_1^n + k_2 a_2^n + y_P(n) \tag{B.4}$$

4. Solve for k_1 and k_2 in (B.4) using the given initial conditions. It is important to remember that the constants k_1 and k_2 must be evaluated from the total solution of (B.4), not from the complementary solution $y_C(n)$.

It is best to illustrate the Method of Undetermined Coefficients with examples.

Example B.1

Find the total solution for the second-order difference equation

---

[*] For a complete discussion on the solution of ordinary differential equations with constant coefficients, please refer to *Numerical Analysis Using MATLAB and Spreadsheets*, ISBN 0-9709511-1-6.

Method of Undetermined Coefficients

$$y(n) - \frac{5}{6}y(n-1) + \frac{1}{6}y(n-2) = 5^{-n} \qquad n \geq 0 \tag{B.5}$$

subject to the initial conditions $y(-2) = 25$ and $y(-1) = 6$

Solution:

1. We assume that the complementary solution $y_C(n)$ has the form

$$y_C(n) = k_1 a_1^n + k_2 a_2^n \tag{B.6}$$

The homogeneous equation of (B.5) is

$$y(n) - \frac{5}{6}y(n-1) + \frac{1}{6}y(n-2) = 0 \qquad n \geq 0 \tag{B.7}$$

Substitution of $y(n) = a^n$ into (B.7) yields

$$a^n - \frac{5}{6}a^{n-1} + \frac{1}{6}a^{n-2} = 0 \tag{B.8}$$

Division of (B.8) by a^{n-2} yields

$$a^2 - \frac{5}{6}a + \frac{1}{6} = 0 \tag{B.9}$$

The roots of (B.9) are

$$a_1 = \frac{1}{2} \qquad a_2 = \frac{1}{3} \tag{B.10}$$

and by substitution into (B.6) we get

$$y_C(n) = k_1\left(\frac{1}{2}\right)^n + k_2\left(\frac{1}{3}\right)^n = k_1 2^{-n} + k_2 3^{-n} \tag{B.11}$$

2. Since the forcing function is 5^{-n}, we assume that the particular solution is

$$y_P(n) = k_3 5^{-n} \tag{B.12}$$

and by substitution into (B.5),

$$k_3 5^{-n} - k_3\left(\frac{5}{6}\right)5^{-(n-1)} + k_3\left(\frac{1}{6}\right)5^{-(n-2)} = 5^{-n}$$

Division of both sides by 5^{-n} yields

$$k_3\left[1 - \left(\frac{5}{6}\right)5 + \left(\frac{1}{6}\right)5^2\right] = 1$$

Appendix B Difference Equations

or $k_3 = 1$ and thus

$$y_P(n) = 5^{-n} \tag{B.13}$$

The total solution is the addition of (B.11) and (B.13), that is,

$$y(n) = y_C(n) + y_P(n) = k_1 2^{-n} + k_2 3^{-n} + 5^{-n} \tag{B.14}$$

To evaluate the constants k_1 and k_2 we use the given initial conditions, i.e., s $y(-2) = 25$ and $y(-1) = 6$. For $n = -2$, (B.14) reduces to

$$y(-2) = k_1 2^2 + k_2 3^2 + 5^2 = 25$$

from which

$$4k_1 + 9k_2 = 0 \tag{B.15}$$

For $n = -1$, (B.14) reduces to

$$y(-1) = k_1 2^1 + k_2 3^1 + 5^1 = 6$$

from which

$$2k_1 + 3k_2 = 1 \tag{B.16}$$

Simultaneous solution of (B.15) and (B.16) yields

$$k_1 = \frac{3}{2} \qquad k_2 = -\frac{2}{3} \tag{B.17}$$

and by substitution into (B.14) we obtain the total solution as

$$y(n) = y_C(n) + y_P(n) = \left(\frac{3}{2}\right) 2^{-n} + \left(-\frac{2}{3}\right) 3^{-n} + 5^{-n} \qquad n \geq 0 \tag{B.18}$$

To plot this difference equation for the interval $0 \leq n \leq 10$, we use the following MATLAB script:

n=0:1:10; yn=1.5.*2.^(−n)−(2./3).*3.^(−n)+5.^(−n); stem(n,yn); grid

The plot is shown in Figure B.1.

Method of Undetermined Coefficients

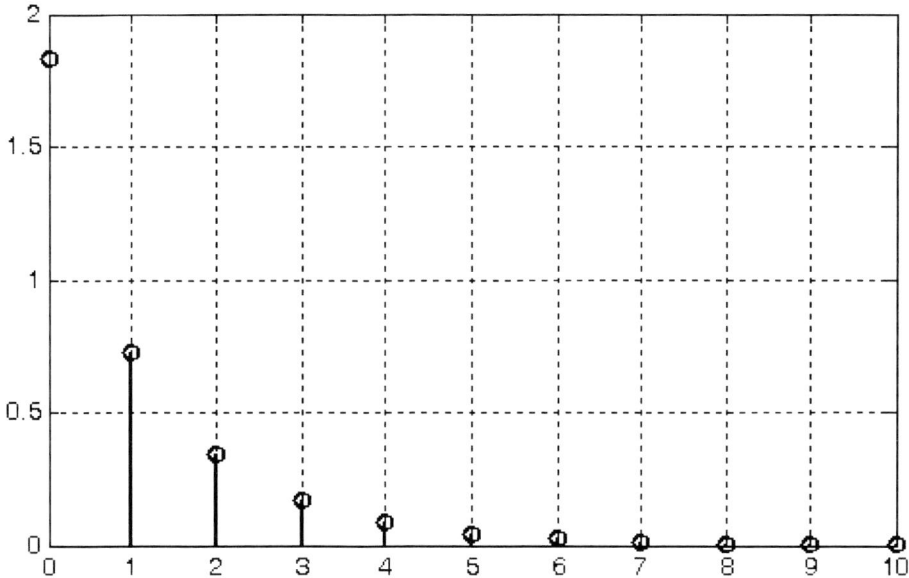

Figure B.1. Plot for the difference equation of Example B.1

Example B.2

Find the total solution for the second-order difference equation

$$y(n) - \frac{3}{2}y(n-1) + \frac{1}{2}y(n-2) = 1 + 3^{-n} \qquad n \geq 0 \qquad (B.19)$$

subject to the initial conditions $y(-2) = 0$ and $y(-1) = 2$

Solution:

1. We assume that the complementary solution $y_C(n)$ has the form

$$y_C(n) = k_1 a_1^n + k_2 a_2^n \qquad (B.20)$$

The homogeneous equation of (B.19) is

$$y(n) - \frac{3}{2}y(n-1) + \frac{1}{2}y(n-2) = 0 \qquad n \geq 0 \qquad (B.21)$$

Substitution of $y(n) = a^n$ into (B.21) yields

$$a^n - \frac{3}{2}a^{n-1} + \frac{1}{2}a^{n-2} = 0 \qquad (B.22)$$

Division of (B.22) by a^{n-2} yields

Appendix B Difference Equations

$$a^2 - \frac{3}{2}a + \frac{1}{2} = 0 \qquad (B.23)$$

The roots of (B.23) are

$$a_1 = \frac{1}{2} \qquad a_2 = 1 \qquad (B.24)$$

and by substitution into (B.20) we get

$$y_C(n) = k_1\left(\frac{1}{2}\right)^n + k_2(1)^n = k_1 2^{-n} + k_2 \qquad (B.25)$$

2. Since the forcing function is $1 + 3^{-n}$, in accordance with the first and third rows of Table B.1, we would assume that the particular solution is

$$y_P(n) = k_3 + k_4 3^{-n} \qquad (B.26)$$

However, we observe that both relations (B.25) and (B.26) contain common terms, that is, the constants k_2 and k_3. To avoid the duplication, we choose the particular solution as

$$y_P(n) = k_3 n + k_4 3^{-n} \qquad (B.27)$$

and by substitution of (B.27) into (B.19) we obtain

$$k_3 n + k_4 3^{-n} - \left(\frac{3}{2}\right)k_3(n-1) - \left(\frac{3}{2}\right)k_4 3^{-(n-1)} + \frac{1}{2}k_3(n-2) + \left(\frac{1}{2}\right)k_4 3^{-(n-2)} = 1 + 3^{-n}$$

$$k_3 n + k_4 3^{-n} - \left(\frac{3}{2}\right)k_3 n + \left(\frac{3}{2}\right)k_3 - \left(\frac{9}{2}\right)k_4 3^{-n} + \frac{1}{2}k_3 n - k_3 + \left(\frac{9}{2}\right)k_4 3^{-n} = 1 + 3^{-n}$$

$$k_4 3^{-n} + \left(\frac{3}{2}\right)k_3 - k_3 = 1 + 3^{-n}$$

Equating like terms, we get

$$\left(\frac{3}{2}\right)k_3 - k_3 = 1$$

$$k_4 3^{-n} = 3^{-n}$$

and after simplification,

$$k_3 = 2 \qquad k_4 = 1$$

By substitution into (B.27),

$$y_P(n) = 2n + 3^{-n} \qquad (B.28)$$

Method of Undetermined Coefficients

The total solution is the addition of (B.25) and (B.28), that is,

$$y(n) = y_C(n) + y_P(n) = k_1 2^{-n} + k_2 + 2n + 3^{-n} \tag{B.29}$$

To evaluate the constants k_1 and k_2 we use the given initial conditions, i.e., s $y(-2) = 0$ and $y(-1) = 2$. For $n = -2$, (B.29) reduces to

$$y(-2) = k_1 2^2 + k_2 - 4 + 9 = 0$$

from which

$$4k_1 + k_2 = -5 \tag{B.30}$$

For $n = -1$, (B.29) reduces to

$$y(-1) = k_1 2^1 + k_2 - 2 + 3^1 = 2$$

from which

$$2k_1 + k_2 = 1 \tag{B.31}$$

Simultaneous solution of (B.30) and (B.31) yields

$$k_1 = -3 \qquad k_2 = 7 \tag{B.32}$$

and by substitution into (B.29) we obtain the total solution as

$$y(n) = y_C(n) + y_P(n) = (-3)2^{-n} + 7 + 2n + 3^{-n} \qquad n \geq 0 \tag{B.33}$$

To plot this difference equation for the interval $0 \leq n \leq 10$, we use the following MATLAB script:

n=0:1:10; yn=(-3).*2.^(-n)+7+2.*n+3.^(-n); stem(n,yn); grid

Appendix B Difference Equations

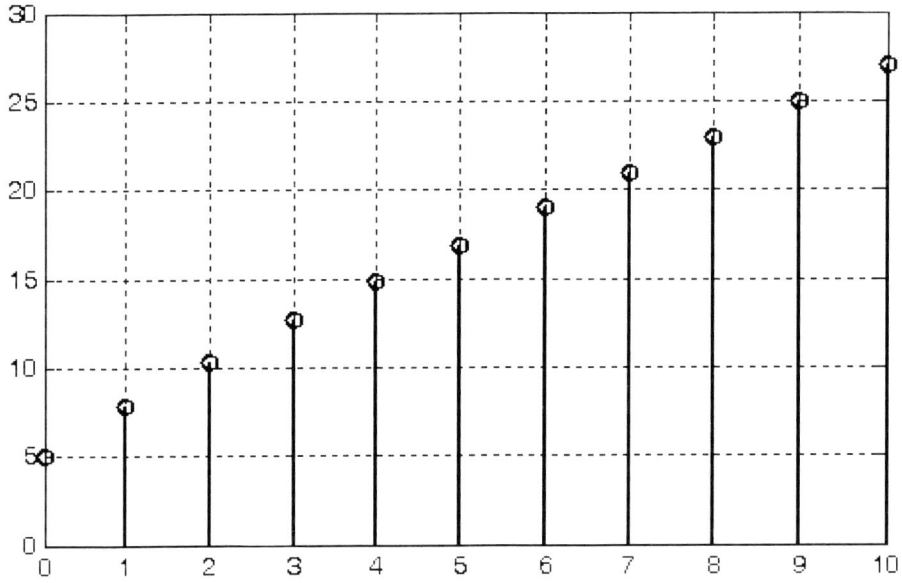

Figure B.2. *Plot for the difference equation of Example B.2*

Example B.3

Find the total solution for the first-order difference equation

$$y(n) - 0.9y(n-1) = 0.5 + (0.9)^{n-1} \qquad n \geq 0 \tag{B.34}$$

subject to the initial condition $y(-1) = 5$

Solution:

1. We assume that the complementary solution $y_C(n)$ has the form

$$y_C(n) = k_1 a^n \tag{B.35}$$

The homogeneous equation of (B.34) is

$$y(n) - 0.9y(n-1) = 0 \qquad n \geq 0 \tag{B.36}$$

Substitution of $y(n) = a^n$ into (B.35) yields

$$a^n - 0.9a^{n-1} = 0 \tag{B.37}$$

Division of (B.22) by a^{n-1} yields

$$a - 0.9 = 0$$

Method of Undetermined Coefficients

$$a = 0.9 \tag{B.38}$$

and by substitution into (B.35) we get

$$y_C(n) = k_1(0.9)^n \tag{B.39}$$

2. Since the forcing function is $0.5 + (0.9)^{n-1}$, in accordance with the first and third rows of Table B.1, we would assume that the particular solution is

$$y_P(n) = k_2 + k_3(0.9)^n \tag{B.40}$$

However, we observe that both relations (B.39) and (B.40) contain common terms, that is, the constants $k_1(0.9)^n$ and $k_3(0.9)^n$. To avoid the duplication, we choose the particular solution as

$$y_P(n) = k_2 + k_3 n(0.9)^n \tag{B.41}$$

and by substitution of (B.41) into (B.34) we obtain

$$k_2 + k_3 n(0.9)^n - 0.9 k_2 - 0.9 k_3 (n-1)(0.9)^{(n-1)} = 0.5 + (0.9)^{n-1}$$

$$0.1 k_2 + k_3 n(0.9)^n - 0.9 k_3 n(0.9)^{(n-1)} + 0.9 k_3 (0.9)^{(n-1)} = 0.5 + (0.9)^{n-1}$$

$$0.1 k_2 + k_3 n(0.9)^n - 0.9 k_3 n(0.9)^n 0.9^{-1} + 0.9 k_3 (0.9)^n 0.9^{-1} = 0.5 + (0.9)^{n-1}$$

$$0.1 k_2 + k_3 n(0.9)^n - k_3 n(0.9)^n + k_3(0.9)^n = 0.5 + (0.9)^{n-1} = 0.5 + (0.9)^{-1}(0.9)^n$$

Equating like terms, we get

$$0.1 k_2 = 0.5$$

$$k_3 (0.9)^n = (0.9)^{-1}(0.9)^n$$

and after simplification,

$$k_2 = 5 \qquad k_3 = \frac{10}{9}$$

By substitution into (B.41),

$$y_P(n) = 5 + \frac{10}{9} n(0.9)^n \tag{B.42}$$

The total solution is the addition of (B.39) and (B.42), that is,

$$y(n) = y_C(n) + y_P(n) = k_1(0.9)^n + \frac{10}{9} n(0.9)^n + 5 \tag{B.43}$$

To evaluate the constant k_1 we use the given initial condition, i.e., $y(-1) = 5$. For $n = -1$, (B.43) reduces to

Appendix B Difference Equations

$$y(-1) = k_1(0.9)^{-1} + \frac{10}{9}(-1)(0.9)^{-1} + 5 = 5$$

$$\frac{10}{9}k_1 - \frac{100}{81} = 0$$

from which

$$k_1 = \frac{10}{9} \tag{B.44}$$

and by substitution into (B.43) we obtain the total solution as

$$y(n) = (0.9)^{n-1} + n(0.9)^{n-1} + 5$$

$$y(n) = (n+1)(0.9)^{n-1} + 5 \qquad n \geq 0 \tag{B.45}$$

To plot this difference equation for the interval $0 \leq n \leq 10$, we use the following MATLAB script:

n=0:1:10; yn=(n+1).*(0.9).^(n–1)+5; stem(n,yn); grid

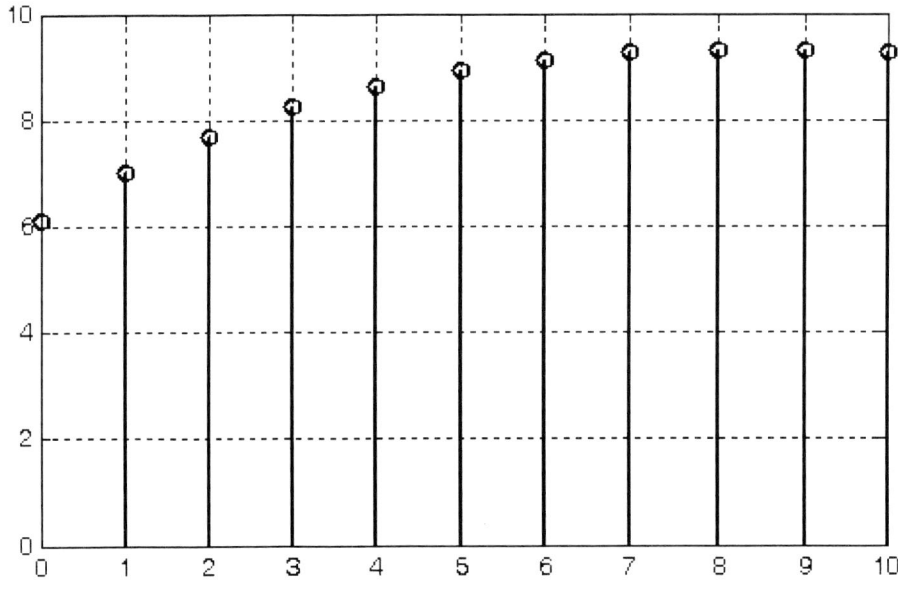

Figure B.3. Plot for the difference equation of Example B.3

Example B.4

Find the total solution for the second–order difference equation

Method of Undetermined Coefficients

$$y(n) - 1.8y(n-1) + 0.81y(n-2) = 2^{-n} \qquad n \geq 0 \qquad (B.46)$$

subject to the initial conditions $y(-2) = 25$ and $y(-1) = 6$

Solution:

No initial conditions are given and thus we will express the solution in terms of the unknown constants.

1. We assume that the complementary solution $y_C(n)$ has the form

$$y_C(n) = k_1 a_1^n + k_2 a_2^n \qquad (B.47)$$

The homogeneous equation of (B.46) is

$$y(n) - 1.8y(n-1) + 0.81y(n-2) = 0 \qquad n \geq 0 \qquad (B.48)$$

Substitution of $y(n) = a^n$ into (B.48) yields

$$a^n - 1.8a^{n-1} + 0.81a^{n-2} = 0 \qquad (B.49)$$

Division of (B.49) by a^{n-2} yields

$$a^2 - 1.8a + 0.81 = 0 \qquad (B.50)$$

The roots of (B.50) are repeated roots, that is,

$$a_1 = a_2 = 0.9 \qquad (B.51)$$

and as in the case of ordinary differential equations, we accept the complementary solution to be of the form

$$y_C(n) = k_1 (0.9)^n + k_2 n (0.9)^n \qquad (B.52)$$

2. Since the forcing function is 2^{-n}, we assume that the particular solution is

$$y_P(n) = k_3 2^{-n} \qquad (B.53)$$

and by substitution into (B.46),

$$k_3 2^{-n} - k_3 (1.8) 2^{-(n-1)} + k_3 (0.81) 2^{-(n-2)} = 2^{-n}$$

Division of both sides by 2^{-n} yields

$$k_3 [1 - (1.8)2 + (0.81)2^2] = 1$$

$$k_3 [1 - 3.6 + 3.24] = 1$$

$$k_3 = \frac{1}{0.64} = \frac{25}{16}$$

Appendix B Difference Equations

and thus

$$y_P(n) = \left(\frac{25}{16}\right)2^{-n} \qquad (B.54)$$

The total solution is the addition of (B.52) and (B.54), that is,

$$y(n) = y_C(n) + y_P(n) = k_1(0.9)^n + k_2n(0.9)^n + \left(\frac{25}{16}\right)2^{-n} \qquad (B.55)$$

Example B.5

For the second–order difference equation

$$y(n) - 1.8y(n-1) + 0.81y(n-2) = (0.9)^n \qquad n \geq 0 \qquad (B.56)$$

what would be the appropriate choice for the particular solution?

Solution:

This is the same difference equation as that of Example B.4 where the forcing function is $(0.9)^n$ instead of 2^{-n} where we found that the complementary solution is

$$y_C(n) = k_1(0.9)^n + k_2n(0.9)^n \qquad (B.57)$$

Row 3 in Table B.1 indicates that a good choice for the particular solution would be $k_3(0.9)^n$. But this is of the same form as the first term on the right side of (B.57). The next choice would be a term of the form $k_3n(0.9)^n$ but this is of the same form as the second term on the right side of (B.57). Therefore, the proper choice would be

$$y_P(n) = k_3n^2(0.9)^n \qquad (B.58)$$

Example B.6

Find the particular solution for the first–order difference equation

$$y(n) - 0.5y(n-1) = \sin\left(\frac{n\pi}{2}\right) \qquad n \geq 0 \qquad (B.59)$$

Solution:

From Row 4 in Table B.1 we see that for a sinusoidal forcing function, the particular solution has the form

Method of Undetermined Coefficients

$$y_P(n) = k_1 \sin\left(\frac{n\pi}{2}\right) + k_2 \cos\left(\frac{n\pi}{2}\right) \tag{B.60}$$

and by substitution of (B.60) into (B.59)

$$k_1 \sin\left(\frac{n\pi}{2}\right) + k_2 \cos\left(\frac{n\pi}{2}\right) - 0.5 k_1 \sin\left[\frac{(n-1)\pi}{2}\right] - 0.5 k_2 \cos\left[\frac{(n-1)\pi}{2}\right] = \sin\left(\frac{n\pi}{2}\right)$$

$$k_1 \sin\left(\frac{n\pi}{2}\right) + k_2 \cos\left(\frac{n\pi}{2}\right) - 0.5 k_1 \sin\left[\frac{n\pi}{2} - \frac{\pi}{2}\right] - 0.5 k_2 \cos\left[\frac{n\pi}{2} - \frac{\pi}{2}\right] = \sin\left(\frac{n\pi}{2}\right) \tag{B.61}$$

From trigonometry,

$$\sin\left(\theta - \frac{\pi}{2}\right) = -\cos\theta$$

$$\cos\left(\theta - \frac{\pi}{2}\right) = \sin\theta$$

Then,

$$\sin\left[\frac{n\pi}{2} - \frac{\pi}{2}\right] = -\cos\left(\frac{n\pi}{2}\right)$$

$$\cos\left[\frac{n\pi}{2} - \frac{\pi}{2}\right] = \sin\left(\frac{n\pi}{2}\right)$$

and by substitution into (B.61)

$$k_1 \sin\left(\frac{n\pi}{2}\right) + k_2 \cos\left(\frac{n\pi}{2}\right) + 0.5 k_1 \cos\left(\frac{n\pi}{2}\right) - 0.5 k_2 \sin\left(\frac{n\pi}{2}\right) = \sin\left(\frac{n\pi}{2}\right) \tag{B.62}$$

Equating like terms, we get

$$k_1 - 0.5 k_2 = 1 \tag{B.63}$$

$$0.5 k_1 + k_2 = 0 \tag{B.64}$$

and simultaneous solution of (B.63) and (B.64) yields

$$k_1 = \frac{4}{5} \qquad k_2 = -\frac{2}{5}$$

Therefore, the particular solution of (B.59) is

$$y_P(n) = \frac{4}{5}\sin\left(\frac{n\pi}{2}\right) - \frac{2}{5}\cos\left(\frac{n\pi}{2}\right) \tag{B.65}$$

Appendix B Difference Equations

NOTES:

Appendix C

Random Number Generation

This appendix is a short tutorial on Random Number Generation. An example is presented to illustrate the sequence which most random generators use.

C.1 Random Numbers

Random numbers are used in many applications. Random number generation is the production of an unpredictable sequence of numbers in which no number is any more likely to occur at a given time or place in the sequence than any other. Truly random number generation is generally viewed as impossible. The process used in computers would be more properly called **pseudorandom number generation.**

C.2 An Example

A typical random number generator creates a sequence in accordance with the following recurrence:

$$x_{n+1} = P_1 x_n + P_2 \pmod{N} \quad n=0,1,2,\ldots \quad x_0 = \text{seed} \tag{C.1}$$

where mod N is used to indicate that the sum $P_1 x_n + P_2$ is divided by N and then is replaced by the remainder of that division. The values of x_0 (seed), P_1, P_2, and N must be specified. As an example, let

$$x_0 = 1 \quad P_1 = 281 \quad P_2 = 123 \quad N = 75$$

then, in MATLAB notation

```
x0=1, P1=281, P2=123, N=75
x1=P1*x0+P2, y1=mod(x1,N)
x2=P1*y1+P2, y2=mod(x2,N)
............
xn=P1*y(n-1)+P2, yn=mod(xn,N)
```

To find the sequence of numbers for the random number generator, we use the following MATLAB script:

```
P1=281; P2=123; N=75; x=1:100; y=zeros(100,2);
y(:,1)=x'; y(:,2)=mod((P1.*x+P2),N)'; fprintf('   x    y \n'); disp('  ------');
fprintf('%3.0f\t %3.0f\n',y')
```

Appendix C Random Number Generation

MATLAB outputs the following table:

```
   x    y
  ------
   1   29
   2   10
   3   66
   4   47
   5   28
   6    9
   7   65
   8   46
   9   27
  10    8
  11   64
  12   45
  13   26
  14    7
  15   63
  16   44
  17   25
  18    6
  19   62
  20   43
  21   24
  22    5
  23   61
  24   42
  25   23
  26    4
  27   60
  28   41
  29   22
  30    3
  31   59
  32   40
  33   21
  34    2
  35   58
  36   39
  37   20
  38    1
```

39	57
40	38
41	19
42	0
43	56
44	37
45	18
46	74
47	55
48	36
49	17
50	73
51	54
52	35
53	16
54	72
55	53
56	34
57	15
58	71
59	52
60	33
61	14
62	70
63	51
64	32
65	13
66	69
67	50
68	31
69	12
70	68
71	49
72	30
73	11
74	67
75	48
76	29
77	10
78	66
79	47
80	28
81	9

Appendix C Random Number Generation

```
 82   65
 83   46
 84   27
 85    8
 86   64
 87   45
 88   26
 89    7
 90   63
 91   44
 92   25
 93    6
 94   62
 95   43
 96   24
 97    5
 98   61
 99   42
100   23
```

We observe that for $x = 1$, $y = 39$, and for $x = 76$, $y = 39$ also. This indicates that the sequence repeats. For this reason, this generator is referred to as a pseudo-random generator. For a true random number generator[*] all numbers from 0 to 99 should be included in the sequence, of course, in a random manner.

If we wanted to transform the above sequence in the interval 0 to 1, we would divide the original sequence of numbers again by N.

---

[*] *Truly random number generation is considered as impossible.*

References and Suggestions for Further Study

A. The following publications by The MathWorks, are highly recommended for further study. They are available from The MathWorks, 3 Apple Hill Drive, Natick, MA, 01760, www.mathworks.com.

1. *Getting Started with MATLAB*
2. *Using MATLAB*
3. *Using MATLAB Graphics*
4. *Using Simulink*
5. *Sim Power Systems*
6. *Fixed–Point Toolbox*
7. *Simulink Fixed–Point*
8. *Real–Time Workshop*
9. *Signal Processing Toolbox*
10. *Getting Started with Signal Processing Blockset*
10. *Signal Processing Blockset*
11. *Control System Toolbox*
12. *Stateflow*

For the complete list of all of The MathWorks products and MATLAB / Simulink based books, please refer to:

http://www.mathworks.com/index.html?ref=pt

B. Other references indicated in footnotes throughout this text, are listed below.

1. *Signals and Systems with MATLAB Computing and Simulink Modeling, Third Edition*, ISBN 0–9744239–9–8
2. *Digital Circuit Analysis and Design with an Introduction to CPLDs and FPGAs*, ISBN 0–9744239–6–3
3. *Electronic Devices and Amplifier Circuits with MATLAB Applications*, ISBN 0–9709511–7–5
4. *Circuit Analysis I with MATLAB Applications*, ISBN 0–9709511–2–4
5. *Circuit Analysis II with MATLAB Applications*, ISBN 0–9709511–5–9

6. *Mathematics for Business, Science, and Technology*, ISBN 0-9709511-0-8
7. *Numerical Analysis Using MATLAB and Spreadsheets*, ISBN 0-9709511-1-6

Index

Symbols

% (percent) symbol in MATLAB A-2

A

Abs block 8-10
abs(z) MATLAB function A-23
Accuracy defined 9-14
acos in Trigonometric Function block 8-16
acosh in Trigonometric Function block 8-16
Add block 8-2
Additional Discrete library 17-1
Additional Math
 Increment / Decrement library 18-1
Algebraic Constrain blocks 1-18, 8-18
algebraic loop 2-22
Analog-to-Digital Conversion 19-1
angle(z) MATLAB function A-23
annotations in Simulink models 2-10
asin in Trigonometric Function block 8-16
asinh in Trigonometric Function block 8-16
Assertion block 9-12
Assignment block 8-20
atan in Trigonometric Function block 8-16
atan2 in Trigonometric Function block 8-16
atanh in Trigonometric Function block 8-16
Atomic Subsystem block 11-4
autoscale icon 1-12
axis in MATLAB A-16

B

Backlash block 4-10
Band-Limited White Noise Block 15-17
Bias block 8-4
bilinear transformation 5-6, 15-18
bilinear MATLAB function 15-20
Bit Clear block 6-13
Bit Operations Group Sub-Library 6-11
Bit Set block 6-12
Bitwise Operator block 6-14
Block reduction optimization 14-10
Block Support Table block 10-9
box in MATLAB A-12
Breakpoint data parameter 7-7
Bus Assignment block 13-2
Bus copy 12-7
Bus Creator block 2-8
Bus Editor 2-10
Bus Selector block 2-8

C

C MEX-file S-function 16-12
c2d MATLAB function 5-12
callback methods 16-9
canonical form 19-21
Cartesian to Polar transformation 19-27
Cartesian to Spherical
 transformation 19-26
Cascade Form Realization 19-7
characteristic table 6-7
Check Discrete Gradient block 9-13
Check Dynamic Gap block 9-10
Check Dynamic Lower Bound block 9-7
Check Dynamic Range block 9-9
Check Dynamic Upper Bound block 9-8
Check Input Resolution block 9-14
Check Static Gap block 9-5
Check Static Lower Bound block 9-2
Check Static Range block 9-4
Check Static Upper Bound block 9-3
Chirp Signal block 15-14
clc MATLAB command A-2
clear MATLAB command A-2
Clock block 15-25
closed-form B-1
closed-loop control systems 19-20
Code Reuse Subsystem block 11-9
column vector in MATLAB A-19
Combinatorial Logic block 6-4
command screen in MATLAB A-1
Command Window in MATLAB A-1
commas in MATLAB A-8
comment line in MATLAB A-2
Commonly Used Blocks Library 2-1
Compare To Constant block 6-10
Compare To Zero block 6-9
complementary solution B-1
complex conjugate in MATLAB A-4
complex numbers in MATLAB A-3
Complex to Magnitude-Angle block 8-24
Complex to Real-Imag block 8-25
Complex Vector Conversions Group
 Sub-Library 8-24
Configurable Subsystem block 11-19
Configuration Parameters 1-12, 2-9
conj (complex conjugate) in
 Math Function block 8-11
Constant block 2-6
Contents Pane 1-7
Contiguous copy 12-7
Continuous Blocks Library 3-1
continuous mode
 Sine Wave Function block 8-17
control element 19-20
control input 13-10
control signal 11-2
controller 19-20
conv MATLAB command A-6
correlation time 15-18
cosh in Trigonometric Function block 8-16
Cosine block 7-16
cosine in Trigonometric
 Function block 8-16
Coulomb and Viscous Friction 4-14
Coulomb Friction 4-14
Counter Free-Running block 15-23
Counter Limited block 15-24

D

data inputs 13-10
data points in MATLAB A-14
Data Store Memory block 13-15
Data Store Read block 13-14
Data Store Write block 13-15
Data Type Conversion block 2-30
Data Type Conversion Inherited block 12-5
Data Type Duplicate block 12-2
Data Type Propagation block 12-4
Data Type Propagation
 Examples block 12-12
Data Type Scaling Strip block 12-5
data types 2-29
Data Viewers 14-1
Data Viewers Sub-Library 14-5
Dead Zone block 4-4
Dead Zone Dynamic block 4-5
deadband 4-10
decibels A-14
decimal-to-BCD encoder 11-9
deconv MATLAB command A-6
Decrement Real World block 18-3
Decrement Stored Integer block 18-5
Decrement Time To Zero block 18-7
Decrement To Zero block 18-6
default values in MATLAB A-12
default color in MATLAB A-15
default line in MATLAB A-15
default marker in MATLAB A-16
demo in MATLAB A-2
Demux block 2-12
Derivative block 3-2
Derivative for linearization 3-5
Detect Change block 6-21
Detect Decrease block 6-20
Detect Fall Negative block 6-24
Detect Fall Nonpositive 6-25
Detect Fall Nonpositive block 6-25
Detect Increase block 16-9
Detect Rise Nonnegative block 6-23
Detect Rise Positive block 6-22
Difference block 5-9
difference equations B-1
Digital Clock block 15-26
Digital Filter Realization Forms 19-4
digital multiplexer 11-4
Direct Form I Realization 19-4
Direct Form-II Realization 19-5
Direct Lookup Table (n-D) block 7-9
Discontinuities Blocks library 4-1
Discrete Derivative block 5-10

Discrete Filter block 5-5
Discrete Blocks Library 5-1
discrete mode in
    Sine Wave Function block 8-17
Discrete State-Space block 15-1
discrete time system
    transfer function 2-25
Discrete Transfer Fcn block 5-4
Discrete Zero-Pole block 5-8
Discrete-Time Integrator block 2-26
Display block 1-37, 14-13
display formats in MATLAB A-31
Divide block 8-7
dlimod MATLAB function 10-2
Doc Text block 10-8
DocBlock 10-8
Documentation Sub-Library 10-6
dot multiplication operator
    in MATLAB A-20
Dot Product block 8-8

E

Edge Detection Group Sub-Library 6-18
Editor Window in MATLAB A-1
Editor/Debugger in MATLAB A-1
element-by-element division and
    exponentiation in MATLAB A-21
element-by-element multiplication
    in MATLAB A-20
Embedded MATLAB Function 16-3
Enable Subsystem block 11-27
Enabled and Triggered
    Subsystem block 11-30
Engineering Applications 19-1
Environmental Controller block 13-9
eps in MATLAB A-22
execution context bars 11-33
execution context indicators 11-33
exit MATLAB command A-2
exp in Math Function block 8-11
Exponential Moving Average 5-19
Extract Bits block 6-17

F

Fcn block 16-2
Feedback Control Systems 19-20
Figure Window in MATLAB A-13
Finite Impulse Response (FIR)
    digital filter 5-6
first harmonic 7-16
First-Order Hold block 5-22
First-Order Hold Reconstructor 19-2
first-order low-pass filter 15-18
Fixed-Point State-Space block 17-4
Flip Block command 1-11
Floating Scope block 14-8
fmax MATLAB command - invalid
fmin MATLAB command A-29
For Iterator Subsystem block 36

forcing function B-1
format MATLAB command A-31
fplot in MATLAB command A-27
frequency response plot A-12
From block 13-11
From File block 15-2
From Workspace block 15-2
Function Block Parameters 1-10
function files in MATLAB A-28
Function-Call Generator block 3
function-call initiator 34
Function-Call Subsystem block 34
fundamental frequency 7-16
fzero MATLAB command A-26

G

Gain block 2-16
Goto block 13-13
Goto Tag Visibility block 13-12
grid MATLAB command A-12
Ground block 15-11
Ground block 2-4
gtext MATLAB command A-13

H

half-wave symmetry 7-17
help in MATLAB A-2
hermitian in Math Function block 8-12
Hide Name 2-3
Hit Crossing 4-13
Hit Crossing block 4-13
hypot in Math Function block 18-1

I

IC (Initial Condition) block 12-6
Idealized ADC Quantizer 19-1
If Action Subsystem block 11-40
If block 11-40
IIR digital filter 5-6
imag(z) MATLAB command A-23
Impulse Response Duration 5-6
Increment Real World block 18-2
Increment Stored Integer block 18-4
increments between points
    in MATLAB A-14
Index Vector block 13-7
Infinite Impulse Response (IIR)
    digital filter 5-6
Inherit via back propagation 2-31
Inport block 2-2
Integer Delay block 5-2
Integrator block 2-20
Integrator block 3-2
Interpolation (n-D) Using
    PreLookup block 7-8
Interval Test block 6-2
Interval Test Dynamic block 6-3
Introduction to MATLAB A-1

L

lag compensator 5-15
lead compensator 5-15
lead-lag compensator 5-15
Level-1 M-file S-Functions 11-41, 16-8
Level-2 M-file S-Function block 16-7
Level-2 M-file S-Functions 11-41, 16-8
limod MATLAB function 10-2
lims= in MATLAB A-27
linear factor - expressed as A-9
linearization 3-3
Linearization of Running
    Models Sub-Library 10-2
Link Library Display 11-23
linmod MATLAB command 3-3
linspace in MATLAB A-14
ln (natural log) A-14
log in Math Function block 8-11
log in MATLAB A-14
log(x) MATLAB function A-13
log10 in Math Function block 8-11
log10(x) MATLAB function A-13
log2(x) MATLAB functionA-13
Logic and Bit Operations Library 6-1
Logic Operations Group Sub-Library 6-2
Logical Operator block 2-18
loglog MATLAB command A-13
Lookup Table (2-D) block 7-3
Lookup Table (n-D) block 7-5
Lookup Table block 7-2
Lookup Table Dynamic block 7-15
Lookup Tables Library 7-1

M

magic sinewaves 7-17
magnitude^2 in Math Function block 8-11
Magnitude-Angle to Complex block 8-24
Manual Switch block 13-9
Math Function block 8-11
Math Operations Group Sub-Library 8-2
Math Operations Library 8-1
MATLAB Demos A-2
MATLAB Fcn block 16-2
MATLAB's Editor/Debugger A-1
Matrix Concatenation block 8-21
matrix multiplication in MATLAB A-19
Memory block 5-21
Merge block 13-8
mesh(x,y,z) MATLAB command A-17
meshgrid(x,y) MATLAB command A-19
method of undetermined coefficients B-1
m-file in MATLAB A-2, A-28
M-file S-Functions 11-41
MinMax block 8-14
MinMax Running Resettable block 8-15
mod in Math Function block 12
Model & Subsystem Outputs 14-1
Model block 11-17
Model for 3-bit Up / Down Counter 19-13

Model for 4-bit Ring Counter 19-14
Model for Cascaded
    Mass-Spring System 19-17
Model for a Mass-Spring-Dashpot 19-15
Model for Mechanical
    Accelerometer 19-19
Model for Electric Circuit
    in Phasor Form 19-23
Model for Application of the
    Superposition Principle 19-25
Model Info block 10-6
Model Verification Library 9-1
Modeling Guides Sub-Library 10-9
Models and Subsystems
    Outputs Sub-Library 14-2
Model-Wide Utilities Library 10-1
moving average defined 5-19
Multiport Switch block 13-10
Mux block 2-12

N

NaN in MATLAB A-29
natural response B-1
Non-Recursive Realization digital filter 5-6
Nonvirtual bus 12-8
Nonvirtual subsystems 11-43

O

open-loop control systems 19-20
Outport block 2-2

P

Parallel Form Realization 19-9
Paste Duplicate Inport 2-3
plant 19-20
plot MATLAB command A-10
polar plot in MATLAB A-24
Polar to Cartesian transformation 19-27
polar(theta,r) MATLAB function A-23
poly MATLAB function A-4
polyder MATLAB function A-7
Polynomial block 8-14
polynomial construction from
    known roots in MATLAB A-4
polyval MATLAB function A-6
Port Data Types 2-31
Ports & Subsystems library 11-1
pow (power) in Math Function block 8-11
precedence in Boolean expressions 2-18
PreLookup Index Search block 7-7
Probe block 12-14
Product block 2-6
Product of Elements block 8-8
pseudocode 11-40
pseudorandom number generation. C-1
Pulse Generator Block 2-28, 15-5

Q

quadratic factor - expressed as A-9

Quantizer block 4-12
quarter wave symmetry 7-17
quit MATLAB command A-2

R

Ramp block 15-9
Random Number block 15-14
random number generation C-1
random number generation example C-1
random numbers 1
Rate Limiter block 4-7
Rate Limiter Dynamic block 4-8
Rate Transition block 12-8
Rational Polynomials defined A-8
Real World Value 2-30
real(z) MATLAB function A-26
Real-Imag to Complex block 8-26
Real-Time Workshop 11-43
reciprocal in Math Function block 8-11
recursion B-1
recursive method B-1
Recursive Realization digital filter 5-6
Refresh button 13-2
Relational Operator block 2-17
Relational Operator block 6-2
Relay block 4-11
rem in Math Function block 8-12
Repeating Sequence block 15-13
Repeating Sequence
    Interpolated block 15-21
Repeating Sequence Stair block 15-21
Reshape block 8-21
resolution 9-14
roots MATLAB function A-3
roots of polynomials in MATLAB A-3
roots(p) MATLAB function A-3
round(n) MATLAB function A-24
Rounding Function block 8-13
row vector in MATLAB A-3
Running Simulink 1-7
RWV (Real World Value) 2-30

S

Saturate on integer overflow 8-10
Saturation block 2-19
Saturation Dynamic block 4-3
Scope block 14-6
script file in MATLAB A-26
script in MATLAB A-2
second harmonic 7-16
seed C-1
Selector block 13-6
semicolons in MATLAB A-8
semilogx MATLAB command A-12
semilogy MATLAB command A-12
Series Form Realization 19-7
Set-Reset (SR) flip-flop 6-7
S-Function block 11-43, 16-7
S-Function Builder block 16-13
S-Function Examples 11-44, 19-27
S-Function Examples block 16-13

S-Functions 11-41
Shift Arithmetic block 6-16
Sign block 8-9
Signal Attribute
    Detection Sub-Library 12-13
Signal Attribute
    Manipulation Sub-Library 12-2
Signal Attributes library 12-1
Signal Builder block 15-6
Signal Conversion block 12-7
Signal Displays 2-31
Signal Generator block 15-4
Signal Routing Group Sub-Library 13-2
Signal Routing library 13-1
Signal selection 14-10
Signal Specification block 12-11
Signal Storage and Access Group 13-14
Signal Storage and Access
    Group Sub-Library 13-14
Signal storage reuse 14-10
Signals in the bus 13-2
Signals that are being assigned 13-3
Simout block 2-9
simout To Workspace block 1-12
Simulation Control 14-1
Simulation Control Sub-Library 14-14
Simulation drop menu 1-12
simulation start icon 1-12
Simulink Extras 3-5
Simulink icon 1-7
Simulink Library Browser 1-8
Sine block 7-16
sine in Trigonometric Function block 8-16
Sine Wave block 15-9
Sine Wave Function block 8-17
sinh in Trigonometric Function block 8-16
Sinks library 14-1
slew rate 4-7
Slider Gain block 8-6
Source Block Parameters window 1-32
Sources library 15-1
Specify via dialog 2-31
Spherical to Cartesian
    transformation 19-27
sqrt in Math Function block 8-11
square in Math Function block 8-11
SR flip-flop 6-7
ssCallSystemWithTid 11-34
ssEnableSystemWithTid 11-34
Start simulation 1-11, 2-6
Stateflow 11-3
State-Space block 3-6
Step block 15-12
Stop Simulation block 14-14
Stored Integer 2-30
string in MATLAB A-16
subplots in MATLAB A-18
Subsystem block 2-2, 11-2
Subsystem Examples block 11-41
Subsystem Semantics 11-43
Subtract block 8-3
Sum block 2-15, 8-2
Sum of Elements block 8-4

swept-frequency
    cosine (chirp) signal 15-14
Switch block 2-14
Switch Case Action
    Subsystem block 11-41
Switch Case block 11-41

T

tangent in Trigonometric
    Function block 8-16
tanh in Trigonometric Function block 8-16
Tapped Delay block 5-3
Taylor polynomial 3-3
Taylor series 3-3
Terminator block 2-5
text MATLAB command A-14
thermal noise 15-17
third harmonic 7-16
Time-Based Linearization block 10-4
title('string') MATLAB command A-12
To File block 14-2
To Workspace block 14-4
Transfer Fcn block 3-7
Transfer Fcn Direct
    Form II block 17-2, 19-5
Transfer Fcn Direct Form II
    Time Varying block 17-3
Transfer Fcn First Order block 5-14
Transfer Fcn Lead or Lag block 5-15
Transfer Fcn Real Zero block 5-18
Transformations 19-27
Transport Delay block 3-10
transpose in Math Function block 8-12
Tree Pane 1-7
Trigger block 11-2
Trigger-Based Linearization block 10-2
Triggered Subsystem block 11-25
Trigonometric Function block 8-16

U

Unary Minus block 8-11
Uniform Random Number block 15-16
Unit Delay block 2-24
Unit Delay Enabled block 17-9
Unit Delay Enabled
    External IC block 17-12
Unit Delay Enabled Resettable block 17-11
Unit Delay Enabled Resettable
    External IC block 17-13
Unit Delay External IC block 17-6
Unit Delay Resettable block 17-7
Unit Delay Resettable
    External IC block 17-8
Unit Delay With Preview
    Enabled block 17-17
Unit Delay With Preview Enabled
    Resettable block 17-19
Unit Delay With Preview Enabled
    Resettable External RV block 17-20
Unit Delay With Preview
    Resettable block 17-15
Unit Delay With Preview Resettable
    External RV block 17-16
unity feedback system 19-20
Update Diagram 2-3
User-Defined Functions 16-1

V

Variable Time Delay 3-11
Variable Transport Delay 3-11
Vector / Matrix Operations
    Group Sub-Library 8-19
Vector Concatenate block 8-23
Virtual bus 12-8
Virtual subsystems 11-43
Viscous Friction 4-14

W

warping 15-18
Weighted Moving Average block 5-19
Weighted Sample Time block 12-15
Weighted Sample Time Math block 8-5
While Iterator Subsystem block 11-38
white light 15-17
white noise 15-17
Width block 12-16
Workspace blocks 2-9
Wrap To Zero block 4-16

X

xlabel MATLAB command A-12
XY Graph block 14-12

Y

ylabel MATLAB command A-12

Z

Zero-Order Hold block 5-23
Zero-Order Hold Reconstructor 19-2
Zero-Pole block 3-8